The Chattel Principle

Since its founding in 1998, Yale's Gilder Lehrman Center for the Study of Slavery, Resistance and Abolition has sponsored an annual international conference on some major aspect of the Atlantic slave system and its destruction. Topics have varied from a comparison of the often neglected internal or domestic slave trades in the U.S., Brazil, and the British West Indies to the controversial but widespread arming of slaves from antiquity to the American Civil War. Because the research and discoveries presented in these conferences do so much to enrich our knowledge of humanity's most dehumanizing institution and its place in the founding of the modern world, as well as the first historical movements for civil rights, we are immensely grateful to Yale University Press for publishing the edited papers of our conferences. These conference volumes are designed not only for the scholarly community but for the wider public which, after years of being misled and kept in the dark concerning the centrality of racial slavery on the global scale, has expressed a growing interest in this grim subject. The Gilder Lehrman Center, which is part of the Yale Center for International and Area Studies, is supported by Richard Gilder and Lewis Lehrman through the Gilder Lehrman Institute for American History in New York City. We are especially dedicated to the translation of scholarly information into public knowledge through publications, educational outreach, and other programs and events.

David Brion Davis, *Director*

Edited by
WALTER JOHNSON

The Chattel Principle

INTERNAL SLAVE TRADES IN THE AMERICAS

Yale University Press
New Haven &
London

Set in Sabon Roman type by Keystone Typesetting, Inc., Orwigsburg, Penn.
Printed in the United States of America by Sheridan Books, Ann Arbor, Michigan.

Library of Congress Cataloging-in-Publication Data

The chattel principle : internal slave trades in the Americas / edited by Walter
Johnson.
      p.   cm.
Papers from the first Gilder Lehrman Center international conference held at Yale
University in Oct. 1999.
Includes bibliographical references and index.
ISBN 0-300-10355-7 (pbk. : alk. paper)

1. Slavery — United States — History — 19th century — Congresses. 2. Slavery —
West Indies, British — History — 19th century — Congresses. 3. Slavery — Brazil —
History — 19th century — Congresses. 4. Slave trade — United States — History —
19th century — Congresses. 5. Slave trade — West Indies, British — History — 19th
century — Congresses. 6. Slave trade — Brazil — History — 19th century —
Congresses. I. Johnson, Walter, 1967– II. Gilder Lehrman Center for the Study of
Slavery, Resistance, and Abolition.
E449.C48 2004
306.3'62'091812 — dc22

                                                                    2004057608

A catalogue record for this book is available from the British Library.

The paper in this book meets the guidelines for permanence and durability of the
Committee on Production Guidelines for Book Longevity of the Council on
Library Resources.

10 9 8 7 6 5 4 3 2 1

To my mother and the memory of my father

Contents

Foreword

DAVID BRION DAVIS

When America's black slaves suddenly learned that they were about to be sold and transported to some unknown region to the west or the south, few of them were literate or "free" enough to convey their sense of horror and despair to spouses or other family members on different plantations. Yet in 1852 a slave named Maria Perkins of Charlottesville, Virginia, wrote a profoundly depressing letter to her husband: "Dear Husband I write you a letter to let you know my distress my master has sold albert [her son] to a trader on Monday court day and myself and other child is for sale also and I want you to let [me] hear from you very soon before next cort if you can. . . . I don't want a trader to get me they asked me if I had got any person to buy me and I told them no they took me to the court house too they never put me up a man buy the name of brady bought albert and is gone I don't know where. . . . I don't expect to meet with the luck to get that way till I am quite heartsick nothing more I am and ever will be your kind wife Maria Perkins."[1]

The mention of "a trader" refers to the large number of professional domestic slave traders who transported hundreds of thousands of slaves from states such as Virginia to the lower Mississippi valley and Texas, where by the late 1850s they could be sold at prices equivalent to those of today's new cars. Maria Perkins's only hope was that her husband could persuade one "Doctor Hamelton" or his master to purchase her before she was taken to another auction at the courthouse, but it is almost certain that she was swept into the enormous tidal wave that moved a total of a million or more slaves from their original places of residence to the Old Southwest. As it happened, the 1850s also saw the beginning of a similar massive internal slave trade in Brazil, which had stopped the further importation of slaves from Africa despite the soaring demand for such labor in the coffee-producing regions far to the southwest of localities such as Bahia, where the majority of slaves were still concentrated.

When Harriet Beecher Stowe and earlier antislavery writers sought to expose the worst evils of American slavery, they concentrated on the agonizing breakup of slave families—the separation of spouses such as Maria Perkins and her husband, the wrenching sale of parents away from their children, and the severe suffering and mortality of long coffles of chained slaves as they were marched hundreds of miles overland or crammed into ships that sailed from southeastern harbors southward and then around the Florida Keys to New Orleans or other distant ports. Nevertheless, in recent times historians have tended to highlight the horrors of the transatlantic slave trade, a subject worthy of such attention, but then to portray a relatively static institution in which movement was peripheral at best. That is the way southern slaveholders, who tended to despise slave traders, wished to think of their labor system. The ideal of planter "paternalism" could be maintained only if the monetary negotiations with traders were kept in the dark. But of course, as time went on and as the demand for and price of slaves kept soaring in the Old Southwest, planters became more open about such transactions.

This was the background for the choice of domestic passages as the subject of the first Gilder Lehrman Center international conference at Yale University in October 1999. Remembering that British abolitionists succeeded in limiting the flow of slaves from the older Caribbean colonies to new frontier zones such as Trinidad and Guiana and that some American abolitionists contended that the Constitution allowed Congress to regulate or stop the interstate trade in slaves, the participants concluded that a comparison of internal slave trades in the United States, the British West Indies, and Brazil would perfectly suit their mission to explore and clarify transnational histories of slavery, resistance, and abolition.

Note

1. David Brion Davis, ed., *Antebellum American Culture: An Interpretative Anthology* (London: D. C. Heath, 1979), pp. 324–25.

Introduction
The Future Store

WALTER JOHNSON

When, in 1849, the fugitive slave James W. C. Pennington wrote that "the being of slavery" lay in "the chattel principle," he meant to trouble the boundary between "the slave trade" and the "rest of slavery." He did so by arguing that even slaves who seemed for the moment to live good lives would inevitably be drawn into the worst abuses of the system by the price that was on their heads and the trade it represented. Sale from "the mildest form of slavery" to "the worst of which the system is possible" and from "the comparatively favorable circumstances" of slavery in the Upper South to the desperate abuses of slavery in the Lower South was, he asserted, "the legitimate working of the great chattel principle."[1] Pennington, that is, figured the relation of the slave trade to the rest of slavery in a way that was both spatial and temporal: the trade was a means of spreading slavery over space and (adversely) transforming it over time. The trade, he argued, was a passageway from slavery's present to its future.

The idea that slavery's future ran through the slave market was commonplace among nineteenth-century opponents of slavery in Great Britain and the United States. They saw regulating or entirely closing the internal trade as a way to cut off the flow of slaves between declining and emerging regions of slavery in the British West Indies and the United States, thus throwing the expansion of slavery into reverse and the system of slavery into decline. By controlling slavery spatially, they hoped to control it temporally as well. The trade, of course, had its defenders, too, and their estimation of its importance to the future of slavery was similar to that of its opponents, but their hopes rested on the continuation rather than the contraction of the trade. As Robert Slenes suggests, prices offered for slaves in the Brazilian market reflected slave-holders' expectations for the value of slave property over time — they were, that is, speculations on the future of slavery in Brazil. Many of the futures imagined in the slave market, of course, were of a more quotidian sort. As Daina Ramey Berry suggests, many buyers hoped to secure their own future by buying women, who would bear more slaves. Others, sugar planters in par-ticular, bought many more men than they did women, relying on the con-tinued availability of slaves in the market to replace, in essence, the foregone children of the women they widowed by refusing to buy them along with their husbands. In its capacity to sell both the hope of a self-reproducing slave force and its replacement — its capacity, that is, to reformulate (or negate) over time the gendered meanings and reproductive capacities of the bodies of enslaved men and women — to produce a slaveholding legacy from the broken pieces of a slave family and to broaden slavery's hold over space and extend its history through time, the trade was, most of its opponents and many of its defenders would have agreed, the market of slavery's future.[2]

But if it might have been easy for defenders and opponents of slavery to agree that its future was, one way or another, going to be shaped in the slave market, it might have been harder to get them to agree on exactly where "the slave trade" began and where it ended. In the United States, at least, slave-holders often argued that their participation in the trade was limited to the time they spent within the physical premises of the slave market or to those who adopted a posture of "speculation" in the way they thought about their property. They applied, as Adam Rothman argues, a sometimes evanescent distinction between slave trading and slaveholding to their daily practice. As several of the essays suggest, slaves often had a very different definition of the parameters of the slave trade — where it began and ended, when they were in it and out of it, who was responsible for it and who was not — than did their owners. As the fugitive slave Lewis Hayden put it, "The trader was all around, the slave pens at hand, and we did not know what time any of us might be in it."[3] These opposed perspectives, rooted in the property and power relations of a system in which an action that took a slaveholder a matter of minutes to conclude would have a lifetime's consequences for a slave, were reflected in debates between opponents, defenders, and reformers of slavery, all of whom defined the relation of the slave trade to the rest of slavery in a way that reflected their moral universes and suited their political goals.

Indeed, as several of the essays suggest, the categories that framed those (mostly nineteenth-century) debates about the boundaries of "the slave trade" are sedimented in the way we define the topic today, making it hard to say with any precision where to draw the boundary around the internal slave trades that are the topic of this collection. All of the authors agree that there were institutions in Brazil, the Caribbean, and the southern United States that made up a slave trade that was internal to each region, and yet in their own ways almost every essay questions how the boundary around the topic should be drawn: What should be left in and what should be left out? Were imported Africans who were resold after having been purchased by an American slaveholder part of an internal trade or an Atlantic one? What about slaves who were sold at estate sales and state-ordered auctions rather than by professional traders or slaves who were sold between neighbors who never would have identified themselves as slave traders and may never have set foot within the physical perimeter of a place called a slave market? What about slaves who were never actually sold but nevertheless had a price attached to them that enabled their owners to estimate their wealth, secure their debts, and settle their estates? Were they part of the internal slave trade?

The answers to these questions are political ones. One reason is that they boil down to issues of interpretation rather than of economics or demographics. Another is that they are, in fact, framed by the nineteenth-century political boundaries along which so many of the debates about the trade were contested: jurisdictional boundaries between nations, between colonies, between states, and between provinces. Defining an "internal slave trade," after all, invokes and gives credence to the national or colonial boundaries that supposedly contain it. Seen in that context, the closing of the transatlantic slave trade (acceded to more or less willingly by many slaveholders in the United States and unwillingly by most in the British Caribbean in 1808 and only after years' worth of British diplomatic pressure in Brazil and Cuba, in 1850 and 1866, respectively) becomes visible as a part of the process by which transnational processes — in particular, British imperial policy, which attempted to outlaw the slave trade not only for British subjects but for everyone else in the world — were shaped into the national and colonial histories that succeeded them. The closing of the transatlantic slave trade gave the boundaries of the southern United States, the British West Indies, and, eventually, Cuba and Brazil a novel and important sort of solidity: prices of slaves in Virginia, for example, fluctuated in relation to the prices being offered in Louisiana but not in relation to prices in Havana, Kingston, or Rio de Janeiro. As the repeated references to Atlantic finance and commodity markets, slave smuggling, and international networks of communication and resistance among enslaved people in the pages that follow suggest, these boundaries remained permeable (and in important ways wholly fictive) long after the closing of the transatlantic trade. And yet they made it possible to identify for the first time and attempt to control something that had not previously been a subject of knowledge or regulation: the internal slave trade.

There had certainly been sales of slaves within various territorially defined jurisdictions as long as there had been slavery in the Americas. As Richard Graham points out, there was a trade in Indians in seventeenth-century Brazil (as well as throughout the rest of the Americas), and as Phillip Troutman suggests, the portability of slave property inhered in the definition of slaves as "chattel" property. The essays in this collection suggest, however, that after the closing of the transatlantic trade such sales became a matter of national and colonial public interest, first in the United States, then in the British Caribbean, and finally in Brazil.

In each case, regulating (or resisting the regulation of) the newly discovered internal slave trade came to be seen as an important way of managing both the future of slavery and the future of the state. In the early nineteenth-century United States, positions in the debate about the future of slavery varied from enthusiastic support for slave trading by expansion- and development-minded slaveholders to outright opposition from humanitarian and political quarters. Perhaps most often overlooked is the vast middle ground, which included qualified support for slave trading from ambivalent slaveholders (such as Thomas Jefferson) who thought that the diffusion of slaves over space would make them less likely to rebel in the short term and easier to get rid of in the long run. As several of the essays point out, slaveholders' ambivalence about the trade was reflected in the fact that each of the Deep South states (the states most actively engaged in the practice) banned the importation of slaves for some of the time between 1787 and 1840. Although they were generally ineffective, these laws signaled deep anxieties among slaveholders about the inflow of slaves to areas where they increasingly outnumbered whites by large margins and the outflow of specie from an economy overextended by speculation. In the South, these laws soon gave way to buyer-protecting warranty laws, and the argument against the trade, by the end of the 1830s, passed wholly into the hands of abolitionists who saw the closing of the trade as the easiest way to loosen slavery's grip on the South.

The debates about regulating the trade fell out differently in the West Indies, where, after the closing of the transatlantic trade, proponents of regulation saw curtailing the internal trade as a way to ensure that the potentially productive frontier areas of the British Caribbean would not provide a new foothold for slavery by providing an outlet for surplus slaves shipped from the empire's declining islands. In Brazil, according to Robert Slenes, it was the defenders rather than the opponents of slavery who wanted to close the internal trade: by the beginning of the 1880s they had come to fear that slaveholders in declining regions would dump their slaves onto the market, bank their profits, and head directly to the polls to vote for abolition.

In addition to illustrating the variety of ways in which the arguments of opponents and defenders of slavery twisted together the destinies of slave trade and state, these political histories of the trade highlight the importance of jurisdictional boundaries in defining the problem of the internal slave trade. As Seymour Drescher suggests, it was when sold slaves in transit crossed a political threshold that their condition seemed to become most susceptible of regulation and thus of controversy. Nineteenth-century opponents of the trade had very little to say about slave sales that occurred between neighbors or within regions as large as Caribbean islands, Brazilian provinces, or American states, although these were as disruptive of slave life and emblematic of chattel slavery as intercolony, interprovincial, or interstate trades. Similarly, although the auction block was the metonym that abolitionists such as William Lloyd Garrison used to highlight the commercial element of their critique of slavery, they most often used it as a symbol of the interstate trade (where, in fact, most sales were sealed in private bargaining) rather than, say, debt or estate sales (both of which were generally effected by the public crying of an auction sale). The spatial dimensions of interregional trades, however, put them at the center of the debate over the future of slavery: it was only by long-distance trade that slaveholders could continue to colonize territory that lay within the boundaries of their polities but, for the moment, outside the grasp of their slave-based political economy. In their focus on long-distance trades made by "professional" slave traders, then, many of the essays in this collection build on a definition of the problem of the internal slave trade that was itself shaped by the horizons of political possibility that framed nineteenth-century discussions: subnational jurisdictional boundaries were the frontiers in debates about regulation, debates that produced most of the contemporary images — statistical, literary, and visual — on which historians of the internal slave trade necessarily rely.

There were, of course, many in the nineteenth century who resisted the reductive redefinition of the quicksilver capacity of cash value to disrupt the lives of enslaved people into a set of debates about the rights of traders to move slaves across jurisdictional boundaries, most notably enslaved people themselves. Slaves in Mississippi, for example, feared being sold across the Mississippi River much more than being sold down the river: the physical features of the landscape were of much more immediate concern to them than the abstract lines of jurisdiction laid on top of it. As several of the essays suggest, fear of being sold (whether into the slave trade as usually defined or not) suffused the lives of enslaved people in the antebellum United States and in Brazil after the closing of the transatlantic trade. (The much smaller volume of intercolonial transfers and the comparatively dire conditions in the exporting areas of the West Indies seem to have made this somewhat less of an issue in the British Caribbean.) Indeed, as several of the essays show, slaves often used whatever means they could to resist or at least ameliorate the threat of sale. They begged and lied and hid and ran away and killed themselves and conspired and revolted. But, by at least one common measure, perhaps the most important one, they failed: they remained enslaved. And they were sold by the hundreds of thousands. Their bodies were pieced out, priced, and sold, transformed from vessels of their own feelings and hopes into vehicles of their owners' plans and receptacles of their masters' fantasies. Their loved ones were stolen, their children disappeared or went unborn, and their fractured lineages were scattered across the landscape. Taken together, the essays in this collection outline a history of subjection that in demographic scale, cultural impact, and sheer psychological terror ranks as one of the most obscene in human history. Perhaps only amidst the bloody chronicle of wrongs perpetrated against people of African descent in the New World could the internal slave trades of the Americas have slipped out of historians' sight for so long.

In addition to documenting the devastating impact of the chattel principle on the lives of enslaved people throughout the Americas (and in particular in the United States and Brazil), the contributors suggest new ways to think about "slave resistance." It has become conventional among historians of slavery (especially of slavery in the United States) to distinguish day-to-day resistance (such as running away to avoid the threat of sale or misrepresenting one's abilities in the slave market) from revolutionary forms of resistance (such as slave revolts theorized as attacks on the system of slavery itself).[4] These essays, however, map a series of connections between these two supposedly distinct types of resistant practice. A simple and very direct set of connections emerges from the material culture of the slave trade. Historians have often accepted that the jails and whips and chains that defined the disciplinary parameters of the trade were what the traders said they were—symbols of power. And yet they might just as well be seen as artifacts of uncertainty and fear, of the traders' knowledge that slaves did not go to market willingly and that they sometimes ran away from and revolted against the traders who were trying to sell them. Although it might be argued that those revolts often failed, remained isolated from one another, or failed to pose a real challenge to the system of slavery itself, it must also be recognized that the imagery of domination that figured so prominently in attacks on the slave trade was, in fact, the result not of slaveholders' certainty of their own power but of their sense of their own vulnerability. The information necessary to sustain the revolutionary abolitionist attack on slavery was created by the action of resistant slaves in the South.[5]

Another set of connections, as the essays by Daina Ramey Berry and Robert Gudmestad suggest, might be observed in its beginnings in southern fields and slave quarters where slaves talked to one another about the trade, sharing their terror of being sold. In so doing and, especially, in publicly remembering those whom it had carried away, enslaved people converted their own lonely fears into a common account of what it meant to be enslaved. That account (what Pennington called "the chattel principle") was carried along the pathways that escaped slaves (many of them fleeing a threatened sale) took to the North, where its clandestine history might be further traced through the black self-defense organizations that aided fugitive slaves in northern cities before it finally burst into the broad light of white awareness on the abolitionist speakers' circuit. Still another set of connections between "day-to-day" and "revolutionary" forms of resistance might be seen in the feedback loop between slave politics and state politics in a place such as Demerara, where, Hilary Beckles argues, the system of slave registration put in place by the British government in an effort to control the extent of the intercolonial trade (and thus in response to enslaved people's demonstrated resistance to the trade) was interpreted by slaves as a prelude to their own emancipation, which they rose by the thousands to seize for themselves in 1823. Or it might be seen in the series of cane field burnings and mass flights of the 1870s and 1880s that Richard Graham and Robert Slenes, in separate essays, cite as reactions to the devastating effect of the internal slave trade on Brazilian slaves and crucial determinants of the pace of the debate about abolition. One after another, the essays in this collection suggest the historical importance of what Phillip Troutman calls "alternative geographies" of slavery and the trade: both individual and collective in character and varying from straightforward responses to a moment of danger to fully theorized attacks on the system, slaves' everyday actions had intended as well as unimagined consequences in the epochal struggle against slavery. As Robert Gudmestad's essay suggests, even an anonymous slave's suicide attempt could spark a national discussion about the slave trade.

The other perennial topic of the slavery scholarship taken up in this collection is the question of capitalism. Traditionally, this question has been posed according to some variant of the following formula: What can Adam Smith or Karl Marx tell us about slavery? The answers that have emerged have been shaped by the fact that Smith and Marx, in very different ways, treated slavery as a sort of historical backdrop to what they saw as the main tendency of history (here conceived in terms of the secular eschatologies of their respective versions of political economy): the development of wage (or "free") labor relations. Both framed the discussion of slavery as a story of temporal supersession: in Smith's case, the inevitable decline of slavery in the face of the superior efficiency of workers motivated to work in their own interest, in Marx's case as part of a larger history of expropriative "primitive accumulation" by means of which the capitalist class made proletarians out of peasants and gained control of the means of production—the backstory to the history of capitalism proper.[6]

Turning the question around—asking what slavery tells us about Smith or Marx—reveals that the institution of slavery in general and the histories and perspectives of enslaved people in particular remain unthought in the foundational texts of Western political economy. In them the peculiar plight of people of African descent in the market economies of the West exists in a state of erasure, acknowledged only to be superseded by capitalism (here understood to be uniquely characterized by wage labor and generally, though not exclusively or explicitly, European-descended workers). What would have happened to the orthodox definition of "capitalism," if, rather than adducing a timeless truth about the relation of human motivation to self-interest from the history of wage labor he saw around him in Britain, Adam Smith had addressed himself to the historical etiology of the so-called undermotivation of enslaved workers—to what you or I might call the resistance of enslaved people? Likewise, what would have happened if Karl Marx had begun his magnificent critique of the commodity form with a detailed consideration not of a bolt of finished linen but of a bale of cotton? What would a theory of political economy that treated the labor, products, and experiences of people of African descent as central to (rather than prior to) the history of Western capitalism look like?[7]

By putting the words "slavery" and "market" together, the essays in this collection begin the project of rethinking the relation of the history of slavery to the philosophy and practice of Western political economy. If this was not "capitalism," they suggest, then in some important way the descriptive power of that term as a tool of historical analysis has been diminished. For slaves, Daina Ramey Berry suggests, were pieced out and priced on a grid that applied abstract notions of physical ability and potential to their very real, very saleable, and very moveable bodies. They were, Edward Baptist argues, distanced from any real notion of themselves in the slave market, their own histories and identities overwritten by their status as commodities. Their capital value, Steven Deyle shows, was, in 1860, greater than the capital value of almost any other type of property held in the United States. Their rate of exchange, Robert Slenes argues, was the best index of the belief of Brazilian slaveholders in the future of slavery. And so on. In this light, Adam Rothman's observation that American slavery was not fully capitalist because it was labor itself rather than abstracted labor power (the capacity of a human body to work for an hour) that was being bought and sold comes to seem less a comment on the character of American slavery than a comment on the orthodox definition of the term "capitalism."

Such evidence of the commercial character of slavery in the Americas, how-ever, must be reconciled with slaveholders' repeated statements that their rela-tions with their slaves were nothing of the kind. Although the contributors take various approaches to this question, they all seem to agree that reform-minded talk about the benevolence of slavery coexisted uneasily with its ap-parent negation—the sale of those very slaves—and must somehow be ex-plained.[8] In addition to the explanations provided here, which generally treat the relation between slaveholders' statements and their actions as contradic-tory, it might be worth thinking about the slave trade not as the negation of the "paternalist" project of proslavery reformers but as that project's historical predicate—the material condition that made it possible to imagine reforming slavery without legislating it out of existence. The problem facing proslavery reformers was finding a way to convince slaveholders that they could get their slaves to work hard without relying on the pornographic tortures that charac-terized much of seventeenth- and eighteenth-century slavery. Perhaps it is true that the benevolent side of the solution to that problem was an implicit bar-gain in which slaveholders exchanged good treatment for hard work. But as the by-now massive literature on day-to-day resistance to slavery suggests, slaves, at least, did not always hold up their side of the implicit bargain. Slaveholders, even reforming slaveholders, still had the problem of disciplin-ing their slaves, and, as several of these essays suggest, in the developing interstate slave trade they found a solution. "I govern them . . . without the whip," one Southern slaveholder proudly wrote in 1838, "by stating to them that I should sell them if they do not conduct themselves as I wish."[9] It requires little imagination to understand the character of the bargain he proposed, nor to understand the dependence of his posture of ostensible moderation on a ready market for his "well-treated" slaves. It may be that the emergence of an internal slave trade allowed for a transformation in the character of the ter-ror by means of which slaveholders governed their slaves from the individual sort registered directly on their bodies to a more displaced, systemic sort of violence that was registered in the (forcible) redistribution of those bodies over space.

In their effort to discharge their debt to the existing historiography of slavery, many of the essays seem to rub up against the limits of the terms in which that historiography has been handed down to us. It is perhaps less important at this point, the essays seem to suggest, to keep asking whether slavery was "capitalist" (or not) according to a set of terms that were created in self-conscious opposition to the condition of slavery than to try to diagram the connections between the slave market and the broader political economy of slavery and to analyze the way that economy was insinuated into the most intimate aspects of the lives of enslaving and enslaved people. So, too, perhaps, is it less important to try to come to a final conclusion about whether the character of the slaveholding regime was capitalist, paternalist, Christian, corrupt, or otherwise than it is to trace the various nineteenth-century accounts of the relations between masters and slaves — paternal, commercial, racial, metaphysical, and so on — back to the circumstances of their production (who thought these things up, where did they do it, and why?). Focusing on this aspect of the intellectual history of slavery would illuminate the connections between the everyday life of slavery (how slaveholders and slaves used ideas about the nature of slavery to solve the quotidian problems they faced in the households, the fields, the shops, and the slave markets of the antebellum South) and the historical process by which the material circumstances of everyday use conditioned and redefined the meaning of those terms even as they were passed on for the use of other generations of slaveholders and slaves.

One such history might concern the role of racial categories in the slave market, or, more particularly, the relations among the law, slavery, and race — the interrelated histories, that is, of national sovereignty, economic exploitation, and racial domination. The question of whether racism led to slavery or whether slavery needed race has, even in its most brilliant and influential applications, been characterized by a level of analytical abstraction that might, as Thomas Holt has pointed out, be sharpened by closer attention to the everyday processes by which ideas of race were employed and reproduced.[10] Focusing on the situated employment (in the slave market) of ideas about difference provides a thickening of the notion of the social that subtends the by-now almost rote invocation of the idea of "the social construction of race."[11] For, in addition to closing off the supply of slaves to the Americas, the closing of the Atlantic slave trade closed off slaveholders' access to the theory of difference they had commonly used to compare imported slaves to one another: national stereotyping. In the years that followed, slaveholders' "knowledge" that Coramantee slaves were likely to revolt or Igbo slaves were likely to commit suicide or Angolan slaves were especially suited to the cultivation of rice became increasingly useless as they attempted to differentiate among the people they bought and sold. And so they turned instead to race: a set of explicitly biological ideas that related productive and reproductive capacity to skin color.

The slave market became, in the era of the internal trade, a major site for the employment (as a price-setting standard of comparison) and reproduction (by repetition before an ever-changing audience of white observers) of the sort of biological racism that increasingly underwrote the defense of the system as a whole.[12] Or, put another way, in the slave market, slaveholders turned from a theory of difference that had embedded within it a history of the politics of slavery, and specifically the history of African traditions of knowledge and noncompliance, to one that used a natural history of race as a vehicle for reducing slaves to a spectrum of color based on varying proportions of black blood and white blood. The commodity categories that governed the internal trade produced the abstractions Negro, griffe, and mulatto, which were themselves suggestive of subjects with no history beyond natural history and what Edward Baptist describes as a half-remembered, half-forgotten history of their mothers' and grandmothers' sexual violation at the hands of other — always other — white slaveholders.

The transformation of the terms of the business done every day in the slave market from nation to race were in turn, it could be argued, reflected in the terms of its regulation, at least in the United States. The early proposals to ban the trade, Adam Rothman asserts, reflected fears that a hostile nation of Africans might take root in the Mississippi Valley. When those bans (and their successors) were finally repealed they were replaced by laws that employed the racial terms increasingly employed in the slave market: warranty laws concerning health and character that treated slaves as knowable biological and psychological subjects rather than as unfathomable outsiders. These were laws that telegraphed an image of slaves as individual and governable rather than serial and disposable. The transformation of the slave trade from external to internal and the terms of its business from national to racial, then, must be seen as partial determinants of the process by which an image of slaves as subjects that were susceptible of "paternalist" governance was produced and passed on.[13]

The idea that the transition from the external to the internal slave trade in the United States played an important role in the transformation of enslavement based on categories of national otherness to those based on racial otherness might be productively counterposed to the histories of slavery and race in Cuba and Brazil. These histories stand out among those of other New World slave societies for (at least) three reasons: first, these were the nations that had the longest histories of importing African slaves (Brazil closed the trade in 1850, Cuba not until 1866); second, they held out the longest before finally abolishing slavery (Cuba in 1886, Brazil in 1888); and, third, among the former slave societies of the Americas, they produced the most obvious and influential articulations of a political ideology of multiracial democracy — the clear and continuing divergence of the social and political experience of people of African descent from those stated ideals notwithstanding. A tentative explanation of the seeming riddle of how nations distinguished by the depth of their commitment to slavery were so quickly transformed into nations distinguished by their commitment to racial inclusion might be found in the fact that the persistence of the African trade in Cuba and Brazil kept alive categories of difference that were based on national origin — the dominant axis of differentiation being, as Robert Slenes suggests, that between creole (native-born) and African slaves. These categories, which rendered the formerly enslaved populations susceptible of transformation into indigenous inhabitants of the nation — into citizens — persisted alongside the emerging racial categories that would so powerfully define the limitations of the achievement of citizenship over time.[14]

Set side by side, the essays in this collection suggest a number of other illuminating comparisons between the internal slave trades in the British Caribbean, Brazil, and the United States. First, as I suggested above, the internal slave trades of the Americas only became visible as such in the serial aftermath of the closing of the Atlantic trade in these regions. Second, the categories produced by nineteenth-century debates about the relation of the internal trade to the rest of slavery persist in the way the topic has been defined down to the present day. Related to that is the extent to which contending visions of the future of slavery invoked terms that brought questions of the movement of slaves across space, and thus of slave trading, to the center of the question. Whether it was proslavery Mississippians in the last decade of the eighteenth century arguing that their land would be "of no more value than an equivalent quantity of waste" without the capacity to move slaves onto it at will, or William Wilberforce hoping that slavery had reached its "natural limit" in the Caribbean at the beginning of the nineteenth century, or the last true believers in Brazil in the 1880s hoping to close the trade to their region in order to keep the rest of the nation as implicated in the future of slavery as they were, the ability to trade slaves across space was seen by contemporaries as a crucial determinant of slavery's unfolding timeline. Finally, in the cases of Brazil and the United States especially, there is the scale of the human devastation concealed within the phrase "the internal slave trade": hundreds of thousands of people driven from their homes and their families, a concentrated and repeated pattern of sales that charged every attachment among slaves with the proximate threat of its dissolution.

Important differences, too, emerge from comparison. That the slave population in the United States, alone among those in the Americas, was self-reproducing shaped both the relative ease with which U.S. slaveholders could accept the closing of the transatlantic trade and the fact that the substantial redistribution of the enslaved population by the internal trade could cement the regions of the South in an economy of mutual benefit rather than — as was the case in the Caribbean and Brazil — attenuating the commitment of the exporting regions to the institution of slavery even as it intensified that of the importing regions. Similarly, slaveholders in the United States seem to have been a good deal more concerned with incorporating the distinction between slaveholding and (internal) slave trading into their political defense of slavery than were those in Brazil or the Caribbean. The relation of slavery's defenders to the defense of the trade also varied widely over time and space. In the end, a fundamentalist defense of the internal slave trade seems to have emerged only in the United States, where by the late 1850s proslavery hotheads were arguing that even the African trade should be reopened.[15] In Brazil, we have seen, the most reactionary defenders of slavery eventually came to the conclusion that too much trading would sap the country's overall commitment to slavery. And in the British Caribbean, when already embattled slaveholders were faced with a battle about the regulation of the intercolonial trade in the 1820s, they simply decided to sit it out (or to quietly smuggle their slaves out of the islands). Finally, there is the comparatively smaller scale of the internal trade in the British Caribbean, although its effects on traded Caribbean slaves (and the families and communities they left behind) were not reduced by the fact that the trade that destroyed their lives was, in aggregate terms, a good deal smaller than that practiced elsewhere.

As interesting as the comparisons are the moments when these histories seem to spill out of their national containers (containers that were themselves historically shaped and made meaningful by the transformation from external to internal slave markets) and into the others around them. Because of the fulcrum effect of diminished supply in the Atlantic sugar market, the revolution in Haiti spurred the trading of slaves to Louisiana and the frontier regions of the British Caribbean. The regulation of the slave trade in the British Caribbean in the 1820s and early 1830s was a spur to the illegal trading of slaves to Cuba. The effect of the American Civil War on the cotton trade was an important factor in repatterning the slave trade in Brazil. In 1841, rebellious slaves on a ship from Virginia, guarded by British soldiers from Africa (who had themselves been rescued from slave ships traveling to Brazil or Cuba), made common cause with free people in Nassau even as slaves illegally exported from the same port years earlier struggled for their freedom in Cuba.[16] These images point to what lies just behind the essays in this collection: a narrative in which the history of nationally bounded slave trades in the Americas had critical determinants in the transnational process of European political and economic imperialism and in the experience and actions of slaves whose presence outlines an alternative to the nation-state-and-colony map of the Americas — a black Atlantic. The insistent presence of European cotton, sugar, and coffee prices as determinants of the history of the internal slave trades of the Americas seems to press in on the spatial boundaries of these essays, even as the diverse histories of African peoples in the New World — improvisationally forged into collective politics in the *Creole* revolt, the multi-ethnic revolt that followed the registration of slaves in Demerara, and the slavery-ending mass actions in Brazil — explodes them outwards.

Adam Rothman's essay explores the history of the idea that there was a hard-and-fast distinction between slave trading and other sorts of slaveholding. That distinction, Rothman argues, emerged from the efforts of proslavery reformers, especially in the Upper South, to withdraw from the Atlantic slave trade (which they believed was daily infusing their new nation with shiploads of potential enemies and keeping them dependent on their imperial masters in Britain) even as they tried to support slavery (on which they were realistic enough to realize the development of their new nation was critically dependent), and it became a central element of early proslavery thought in the United States. It was, however, a defense that was increasingly at odds with the institution's daily practice as slavery began to expand westward through a growing interstate trade.

The domestic slave trade was never simply that — Rothman is careful to trace the international economic and diplomatic conditions that made cotton production in the southwest both possible and profitable — but its regulation was a domestic affair, and Rothman traces the series of regulations and bans by means of which the defenders of the distinction between slaveholding and slave trading attempted to bring reality into closer alignment with their philosophy. After it went into effect in 1808, the ban on the Atlantic trade was generally supported by slaveholders, but applying the distinction between slave trading and slaveholding to the internal trade was a less popular proposition. Early efforts to limit slave importation to the Mississippi Valley to bona fide owners (slaveholders rather than slave traders, in Rothman's terms) disappeared into the evanescence of the distinction on which they relied. Indeed, Rothman points out that the very fear of slave revolt that informed the opposition to the international trade could be used to justify the internal trade: by spreading slaves as widely as possible over available territory, the argument went, the threat they represented would be reduced. As it turned out, the lasting result of the closing of the international and the expansion of the domestic trade was not the diffusion of slavery but the consolidation of a slaveholding region that stretched from Virginia to Texas by the time of the Civil War.

Although they recognized their dependence on slavery and on the slave trade, many slaveholding reformers continued to worry about the effects of the trade. They were concerned about the moral implications of wholesaling human beings and destroying their families and the practical implications of moving large numbers of slaves of "bad character" to the vulnerable frontier of white settlement. Again and again, Rothman argues, various states attempted to regulate the trade by applying the distinction between slave trading and slaveholding to importations, and again and again their laws were overruled by the courts, not enforced by local authorities, evaded by savvy speculators, or, most often, simply ignored. The major effect of these laws, asserts Rothman, was not to limit the spread of slavery but to reproduce a set of terms — the distinction between slave trading and slaveholding — that defenders of slavery were able to use to argue for the benevolence of their institution even as they bought and sold slaves by the thousands.

Daina Ramey Berry's essay opens with a scene from a sale held by one of those "ordinary" slaveholders: an enslaved man on a Georgia auction block nudging his wife forward to be examined by a slave buyer. Using a combination of statistical and literary analysis, Ramey Berry gradually unpacks that disturbing scene to reveal a world in which enslaved people and their owners each attempted to use the dollar values assigned in the slave market to suit their own purposes. For slaveholders this meant comparing the incommensurable — no matter their age, sex, temperament, or skill, enslaved people could be run together on a single scale of comparative value — and the author carefully parses the characteristics of slave pricing schemes. Indeed, Ramey Berry argues, in pricing slaves, planters relied more on the assignment of an abstract "rate" (full hand, half hand, quarter hand) than they did on the most obvious physical characteristics of the human bodies they bought and sold: age and sex. Part of the work that planters required of their females slaves, of course, was reproductive, and Ramey Berry further argues that although sex was not a statistically significant component of slave prices when taken on its own, women's prices began to rise earlier in their lives than did those of men. For slaves, the question of value was less economic than it was existential, and drawing on journalistic and autobiographical accounts of slaves' experience in the market, Ramey Berry outlines both the family-destroying capacity of the regime of rate and the efforts that many slaves made to keep their families together by advertising themselves and their loved ones in the terms of the market.

Similarly, Robert Gudmestad's essay begins with the story of a slave in trade — in this case, one who jumped from the roof of the Washington, D.C., tavern where she had to been sent to await sale to the South. Picked up by Congressman John Randolph of Virginia, the story of her suicide attempt framed the earliest effort to ban the trade within the District of Columbia (1816). In contrast to those who followed him in seeking the abolition of the trade in the nation's capitol, Randolph was a defender rather than an opponent of slavery. For him, however, the abuses of the trade seemed to compromise rather than emblematize what he thought to be the rightful claims of those who owned slave property. Although Randolph's proposal never made it to the floor of the House, Gudmestad sees it as an important window into the politics of slavery in the early Republic. It was, he points out, the work of a slaveholder from the Upper South rather than an abolitionist from the North. And more important, perhaps, it died quietly with little of the debate or publicity that would attend subsequent efforts to abolish the trade.

In Gudmestad's telling, however, an issue that the nation's leaders were content to let die was continually brought back to life by the resistant actions of the nation's slaves. Although slaves' terror of the trade provided slaveholders with an extraordinary means of preserving order under regular circumstances (and one that left no evident scars), it also ensured that when the moment of sale finally came it was often messy. The memory of each escape, each suicide, each murder, and each mutiny was sedimented into the brutal material culture of the trade — the barred jails, cuffed chains, and brandished weapons — where it could be readily decoded by those who witnessed a public auction or saw a coffle passing along a southern road as evidence of that system's brutality. The interstate slave trade, Gudmestad argues, was not only extremely disruptive of slave life and extremely brutal, it was extremely obvious.

The abolitionist attack on the trade that coalesced around images of slave resistance, the overall growth of the trade, and the sectional politics of surrounding the expansion of slavery in the western territories came together to produce, in 1820, a critique of the admission of a slaveholding Missouri to the union that focused on the "speculation" in slaves that would attend it. Whereas those who defended the admission of Missouri as a slave state continued to argue that migration rather than speculation was the dominant form of slavery's westward expansion, Gudmestad argues that the debates about Missouri showed that enslaved peoples' resistance had flushed the character of the trade out into the open. In the years that followed, critics of slavery again and again returned to the spectacle of the trade — to the scenes of slaves' anguish and resistance — as they framed their attack on the whole of slavery.

Steven Deyle's essay likewise focuses on the debate between opponents and defenders of slavery about the relation of the interstate slave trade to the rest of slavery in the antebellum South. Deyle begins by charting the importance of the domestic slave trade to the regional political economy of slavery, and he goes on to illustrate the capital value of the enslaved population (a value supported by the interstate trade). The three billion dollars' worth of capital invested in slaves in 1860, Deyle writes, was three times greater than the amount of capital invested in the manufacturing sector nationwide, seven times the value of all the currency in circulation in the national economy, and forty-eight time the federal government's annual budget. The slave trade was big business.

It was also a big target. From the first issue of William Lloyd Garrison's *Liberator,* Deyle argues, the slave pen, the auction block, and the southbound coffle were essential elements of the abolitionist case against slavery. That case took various forms: some abolitionists argued that by turning people into property, the slave trade stole them from God; some emphasized the devastating effect of the trade on enslaved families as well as its corrupting effect on the families of their owners; some emphasized the corrosive effect of the trade on republican institutions; some hoped to divide the interests of the Upper South from those of the Lower by getting Congress to abolish the interstate trade; in particular, many urged that the thriving slave trade operating in the shadow of the Capitol and the direct authority of Congress should be abolished forthwith. Deyle argues that as the Free Soil and Republican Parties sought to broaden their support in the 1840s and 1850s, the opponents of slavery focused less of their attention on the slave trade per se than they did on the future of slavery in the west. Southern Democrats and defenders of slavery, on the other hand, continued to argue that Republican rule would mean the immediate end of the slave trade if not of slavery itself.

Since the Missouri Compromise (1820), those defenders had been arguing that the responsibility to regulate the slave trade lay not with Congress but with the states — many of which, they pointed out, had already regulated and even periodically banned the trade. The interstate commerce clause, they argued, was designed to keep interests in one section of the country from making laws that interfered with the interests in another. Although the defenders of the trade managed to hold their position through the fitful series of fragile compromises leading up to the Civil War, Deyle argues, they could never hide the trade and found themselves instead forced to dismiss or explain it: it was the slave traders' fault for being avaricious, or the slaves' fault for behaving badly, or the abolitionists' fault for making slaveholders fear that their lawful property would be stolen from them, or, perhaps, it simply did not exist at all.

Michael Tadman's essay takes on the question of the relation between the slave trade and the rest of slavery from the other side of the emerging sectional divide, asking how a society in which so many so frequently proclaimed their benevolent intentions toward their slaves could have supported a thriving trade in those very slaves. What was the relation of the slave trade to the system of slavery and the ideology that supported it? Tadman begins by outlining the contrasting accounts that defenders and opponents of slavery gave of this relation. The proslavery argument was that the trade was simply the pastime of a few marginal men who were forced to make up their lots of runaways and criminal because few planters worthy of the name would separate the families of their slaves by selling them to the traders. For defenders of slavery, criticizing the traders was a good way to defend the rest of slavery. The abolitionist account of the trade focused instead on the links between the trade and the rest of slavery. According to this account, the planters of the Upper South gained much of their income by "breeding" slaves destined to replace the slaves who were being worked to death in the Lower South. For opponents of slavery, attacking the slave trade was a good way to attack the rest of slavery.

The reality of the situation, Tadman contends, lies in the numbers, and the central portion of the essay is devoted to a statistical reconstruction of the scope and scale of the interstate slave trade using a study of the age structure of the westward-moving slave population (a full run of ages being associated with the "intact" migration of plantations and a highly age-selective sample indicating a commercial process of selection) and intensive study of the daily business of the trade in South Carolina. Altogether, Tadman estimates, more than a million slaves were traded across the United States between 1790 and 1860. Of these, most were sold not in the urban auctions that figure so prominently in abolitionist and subsequent historical accounts of the trade but in private bargains made between an itinerant speculator and a slaveholder who was often standing in his own front yard. Most of those who sold slaves to the traders, Tadman argues, did so by choice rather than from necessity: most slaves were sold from regions of the Upper South, where staple crop production was still highly profitable and the traders' preference for dealing in cash (as opposed to credit) offered a substantial incentive for selling to them.

The final sections of Tadman's essay contrast the scale of family destruction wrought by the trade to the prevalence of slaveholders' statements about the degree to which they cared for and about their slaves. Estimating that one-third of slave marriages in the Upper South were destroyed by the trade, Tadman argues that there is little chance that enslaved people adopted their masters' benevolent view of the institution that bound them together. By focusing their attention on certain "key slaves," slaveholders were able both to pursue their own (financial and disciplinary) interests when it came to selling slaves and point to an object of their paternalism when it came to wanting to feel good about themselves. Thus, Tadman concludes, could slaveholders demonize the traders as hard-hearted speculators even as they continued to do business with them; thus could those who already had slaves promote self-interested bans on the trade and blame the traders for importing large numbers of diseased and malign slaves while exporting vast quantities of specie; and thus could the plantation legend of the sunny South coexist down to the present day with the hard facts and material remains of the slave trade.

Lacy Ford's essay places debates about the role of the antebellum slave trade in the context of the historiographical discussion of slaveholders' "paternalism." Ford's essay begins by contrasting Eugene D. Genovese's characterization of the slaveholders' regime as one structured by the back-and-forth play of accommodation and resistance (which always stopped short of threatening the system itself) expressed in the idea that there was a familial (hence "paternalism") rather than a commercial relation between masters and slaves with recent critiques of that notion. These critiques, Ford argues, emphasize the commercial and coercive character of the relations between masters and slaves at the expense of a nuanced understanding of the capacity of the (hegemonic) ideology of paternalism to reframe individual acts of resistance in terms that were not threatening to the institution itself. Ford nevertheless argues that the more recent scholarship makes a substantial (though, he believes, unwitting) contribution by hitching the historiography of the South to that of the "market revolution." Seen in that light, Ford argues, recent work on the internal slave trade bound the regions of the South together in a system of capital transfer and labor allocation.

Ford emphasizes that behind slave traders' unsavory reputation for being speculators lay the fact that they were the economic actors in the South who were willing to take the risk of transporting slaves between the low-profit Upper South sector of the slave economy to its high-profit Lower South sector, thus promoting the long-term growth of the southern economy. Noting his debt to the work of Gavin Wright, Ford argues that the interstate slave trade linked slave values in these regions (as opposed to the value of land, which fluctuated widely across space) and thus promoted the solidification of (planter) class interests in protecting slave values across the South.

To this broad accounting of the importance of the trade to the regional coherence of the southern political economy Ford adds an account of the tensions generated by the trade as evidenced by southern efforts to tax, regulate, and abolish the trade. This discussion, as several of the essays point out, pitted Upper South slaveholders hoping to "whiten" their polities against Lower South slaveholders wary of importing a potentially insurrectionary mass of slaves into theirs even as they exported specie via the traders to the Upper South. In the Lower South, doubts about the trade, particularly in the aftermath of the 1831 insurrection led by Nat Turner in Southampton County, Virginia, resulted in periodic bans on the trade in slave-importing states from South Carolina to Louisiana. Although such bans were always controversial (pitting as they did the portion of the white population interested in preserving the status quo against that interested in bettering its own position by buying slaves) and often honored in the breach (occurring as they did at different times in states that shared long borders and developed transportation and financial networks), they demonstrate the diversity of interests in and opinions about slavery in a region that is too often treated as if its support of slavery was uniform across time, space, and class position. In the arguments about the trade Ford sees the "counterfactual" possibility that, in the absence of the interstate slave trade, a genuine paternalism might have emerged in at least the Upper South, where slaveholders would have had to reform themselves in order to stave off both the threat of insurrection they associated with having so many slaves and the colonizationist and emancipationist sentiments that were emergent though, in the event, dampened by the existence of the trade. By thus isolating the trade's effect in shaping the whole of southern slavery, Ford posits, it becomes possible to imagine writing a history in which events in the slave South are integrated into an account of broader regional, national, and international trends.

Edward Baptist's paper adds a sexual dimension to the interpretation of the slave trade. The essay begins with a bonhommic exchange of letters between slave traders about the rape—their rape—of women owned by their firm, Franklin and Armfield. Employing both Marxian and Freudian theory, Baptist uses the notion of enslaved women as fetishes—as objectifications of the desires of white men—as a way into the tangled history of sexual and economic exploitation in antebellum slavery. In these men's leering expression of their supposedly forbidden desire for their slaves, Baptist argues, was encoded a process of "half-forgetting and half-remembering" that characterized antebellum slaveholding culture as a whole.

The forgetting was in the fetishism of the commodity: the capacity (as identified by Marx) of capitalists and consumers to view the objects they bought and sold as having an existence independent of the social relations that, in fact, produced them. In this case, Baptist uses commodity fetishism to high-light the way in which slaveholders regularly and unabashedly treated individual slaves as serial manifestations of "Cuffy," the perfect (and perfectly price-able) slave—the process, that is, by which they took parents and children, lovers and friends and repeatedly made them into dollars and cents. The process of commodification, Baptist argues, was one in which enslaved people had very few avenues of resistance and very little effect on the intentions and actions of their owners, so few that slave traders sometimes half forgot that the market in human beings posed different challenges than did the markets for other retail goods.

It was, however, not in the forgetting that underwrote their economy but in the remembering that presaged its reproduction that slave traders massaged their pleasure out of their work. In repeatedly referring to one another as "one-eyed men" as they discussed their business, the traders of Franklin and Armfield, Baptist argues, invoked a well-known phallic metaphor that invested their forays into the slave market with the sadistic thrill of rapine. It was a thrill through which enslaving men generally, like the traders in these letters, repeatedly replayed a fantasy of their own independence: that they could take what they wanted from women and from blacks. And it was one through which they commingled their society's history of sexual exploitation, their own desires, and the social reproduction of the slaveholding regime in general in a matrix of past, present, and future exploitation grafted onto (and in some ways definitive of) the bodies of light-skinned women. For by fetishizing light-skinned women, they focused their desire on those who embodied both the centuries of sexual assault that tracked the history of their class and the con-temporary control over enslaved women's sexuality on which its future rested. The rough trade made manifest in these women's bodies, Baptist concludes, suffused the whole of the business of slavery with "the promise and pleasure of rape."

While Baptist's essay seemingly calls into question the standard empirical methods—especially demographic statistics and cliometrics—that historians have used to fashion their interpretations of the slave trade, Phillip Troutman's implicitly contrasts the geographic pattern of the slave traders' business (the parameters of which have bounded most historians' accounts of the internal slave trade) with the slaves' geography of the trade. In Troutman's formulation the successful 1841 revolt aboard the slave ship *Creole* was not simply an event that took place at some point along a fixed way southward: it was an "inversion of the slave traders' network of communication and transporta-tion," a forcible superimposition of the slaves' geography on that of their erstwhile masters. Troutman notes that the rebels' success in taking over the ship that was to carry them to New Orleans and having it steered instead for the Bahamas, where they knew they would stand a chance — a good chance, as it turned out — of being freed by the British colonial authorities is a testament to a slave "grapevine" that stretched filaments of information and hope throughout the United States and the Americas generally. Troutman terms this information "geopolitical literacy," knowledge of the abstract boundaries that divided slavery from freedom in the Americas.

Troutman is careful to spell out the limitations as well as the possibilities of access to the information transmitted over the grapevine. Much of the information was carried by (and limited to) men, for they were the visiting spouses in abroad marriages (those in which spouses lived on different plantations) and the sailors, boatmen, herdsmen, teamsters, and slave trade stewards whose movements traced a negative image of the commercial connections that tied American slaveholders to one another and to those in the Caribbean. And in addition to helping build a community across space (and time), the grapevine could undermine trust between those who had information they were afraid to share and those who wanted that information for their own purposes.

The slaves aboard the *Creole*, Troutman argues, may well have heard of prior shipboard slave revolts along the Atlantic coast, and, as testimony that followed the revolt shows, they had definitely heard of the emancipation of the cargo of a slave ship that had been grounded in the Bahamas the year before. Troutman suggests several passageways (most of them leading through the slave pen of Richmond trader Robert Lumpkin, who had housed many of the slaves aboard the *Creole* before their shipment) by which the slaves could have gained the geopolitical literacy evident in the revolt. And though their knowledge of cartography and Caribbean geography was limited, they were able to piece together enough information and among them had enough skill to make sure that the ship's white crew steered the course to freedom. Slaves' ability to reverse the current that flowed through the slave-selling, staple-cropping network of American and Atlantic trade, Troutman argues, was limited by slaveholders' efforts to keep them in "geographic ignorance" and by the traders' daily practice of tearing them away from the places and people they already knew. In the back-and-forth violence and resistance of the slave trade and the grapevine, he concludes, we can see the outline of an interpretation of slavery that takes space and motion seriously as dimensions of contested power.

Seymour Drescher's essay tells the story of how the islands for which the *Creole* rebels steered their ship ended slavery with particular attention to debates about the internal slave trade. He begins by noting that throughout its history, the Atlantic slave trade transcended politics: no matter who controlled the trade to any given place at any given moment, no matter the winners and losers in imperial wars, the slave trade persisted. And yet, he concludes, it was jurisdictional boundaries — between countries, between colonies, and between states — that offered abolitionists their best opportunity to chip away at the margin of the system they ultimately hoped to abolish: the transfer of slaves across political boundaries increased both the visibility of their subjection and the potential for its public regulation. And in the years between the closing of the Atlantic trade and emancipation, Drescher argues, the struggle over the future of slavery in the British Caribbean occurred along the jurisdictional boundaries that divided the island colonies of the Caribbean from those along the empire's South American frontier. This was, however, a struggle accompanied by little of the public clatter of the debates about the abolition of the Atlantic trade and, later, the abolition of slavery itself. Having lost the first of these battles and apparently girding themselves for the second, the West Indian interests in Parliament seemed to have taken the restrictions on intercolonial trading as a fait accompli.

Comparing the British intercolonial trade to the U.S. interstate trade, Drescher notes the relative prevalence of state regulations concerning the condition of slaves transported in the West Indian trade and argues that in the last decade of British slavery these amounted to a "virtual abolition" of the intercolonial trade. Although he argues that any economic effects of such regulation were clearly secondary to the effect of closing that Atlantic trade — slaveholders forced to trade within the political boundaries of the British Empire had no pool of ready exports (as did Virginia, for example) on which to draw — Drescher emphasizes that the restrictions on the intercolonial trade had significant effects on the daily life of slaves in the British Caribbean. The primary effects of these restrictions were to intensify planters' commitments to use their (aging and shrinking) labor forces to produce sugar rather than less profitable crops such as coffee and to reduce planters' ability to control their slaves using the threat of sale. Indeed, the ameliorative restrictions on the trade often forced slaveholders planning the transfer of their slaves to obtain approval from the slaves in question in order to receive an export license from the government. In the progression of trade-limiting laws Drescher sees a fairly successful "gradualist" evolution from slavery to pseudoserfdom to full emancipation.

Like Drescher's essay, that of Hilary Beckles places the interregional movement of slaves within the British Caribbean in the context of shifts within that region's economy, particularly the opportunity provided British sugar planters by the success of the slave revolt in Haiti and the decline of the sugar economy in the smaller islands (Barbados and the Leeward and the Windward Islands). This occurred at the same time that planters in the larger islands and frontier colonies (Jamaica, Trinidad, Demerara, and Essequibo) were expanding their sugar production and, in the aftermath of the closing of the Atlantic trade, looking for a ready source of slaves to supply their murderous labor regime (which Beckles delicately terms "systemic natural decline"). His account of the pattern of intercolonial trade emphasizes the "uneven" situation of the various colonies at the moment the slave trade was closed: the closing accelerated the transfer of slaves from the islands (with the notable exception of Jamaica) to the frontier colonies along the northern coast of South America.

Current estimates suggest that the intercolonial trade in the Caribbean was a good deal smaller in relative terms than that in the United States or Brazil — twenty-two thousand slaves were legally traded in the years between 1808 and 1830 (a figure comparable to a single year's interstate trading in the United States during the 1830s) — and Beckles concludes that it was, taken as a whole, too small to significantly alter the demographic profile of either the exporting or the importing colonies. More important, he argues, were the political effects of the trade: a series of fights between metropolitan opponents of slavery and its colonial defenders over where to draw the line between legal and illegal trading. The rising power of antislavery forces in the British Parliament, he argues, can be tracked by the laws that regulated the intercolonial trade. As they gradually gained power they managed to move from a system of licenses and duties designed to regulate the pattern of intercolonial transfers, to a slave-registering census to track the degree of smuggling, to a law that required exporters to prove that transfer was in the best interest of their slaves (generally to keep families together), to, finally, a law that limited intercolonial transfers to "domestic" slaves. Colonial slaveholders (and authorities) combined to evade and subvert most of these regulations using a combination of fraud and outright smuggling, but the laws' import was not lost on colonial slaves. Slave revolts in Barbados (1816) and Demerara (1823), Beckles argues, were partially spurred by the slaves' belief that "registration procedures were a prelude to emancipation."

Manuel Barcia Paz's paper tells the fascinating story of a family of Bahamian slaves carried illegally into Cuba in the 1820s, not to reemerge until the 1840s. As the Bahamian planter Mary Elizabeth Kelsall foresaw the abolition of colonial slavery, Barcia Paz argues, she took steps to try to preserve her property from history, duping her slaves into signing their own emancipation papers (so that they would be allowed to depart from the Bahamas) before shipping them to Cuba and continuing to hold them as slaves. The Kelsalls were among the estimated thousands of Bahamian blacks being held in Cuba as slaves. Whereas Barcia Paz's narrative focuses on the diplomacy that eventually freed a few of the Kelsalls (though it left many more behind) and the complexity of the position of antislavery British officials in a Cuba overcome with the fear of slave revolt, it also provides a tantalizing glimpse of a slave society in the middle of Cuba that was populated by English speakers and Africans — the living evidence of the shadowy networks of smuggling and illegal trade that haunt the edges of so many of the essays in this collection.

Richard Graham seeks to outline the macroeconomic profile of the internal trade in Brazil and to explore the stories of some of the slaves whose experience that statistical profile claims to represent. After a survey of the deep history of internal trading in Brazil, which included both an early seventeenth-century trade in Indian slaves and an interregional trade in imported Africans in the later seventeenth and eighteenth centuries, Graham turns his attention to the internal trade that expanded after the Brazilians (under pressure from the British) closed their Atlantic trade in the early 1850s. The internal trade in Brazil, Graham argues, extended generally from the Northeast and the extreme South to Rio de Janeiro and São Paulo, from relatively minor sectors of the slave economy (mining, castor beans, salted beef, and, before and after but not during the American Civil War, cotton) to the coffee sector, from northeastern sugar plantations to southern sugar plantations, and from urban areas to rural ones. Following the estimates of Robert Slenes, Graham suggests that more than two hundred thousand people, perhaps as many as two-thirds of them men and the vast majority of them between the ages of ten and forty, were relocated in the four decades between the effective closing of the African trade to Brazil and the abolition of slavery in 1888. Although the numbers of people traded were, in the aggregate, smaller than they were in the United States, the trade in Brazil in the 1870s and 1880s was, much like that in the United States in the 1830s, associated with the threat of slave rebellion, and one province after another moved to shut down slave importations in the years leading up to 1888.

Graham uses several case studies to outline the biographical diversity of those whose lives were forcibly channeled into the slave trade but also identifies some commonalities that bound them together: the ease with which poor people who were legally free could be sucked into the trade, the desire of traded slaves to return home and see their families again, the disorientation caused by geographical relocation and the imposition of new, violently enforced labor regimes, and the prevalence of resistance ranging from shamming sickness and committing suicide to flight and open revolt. Graham's conclusion powerfully brings together many of the themes of the collection by revisiting the epochal history of the trade in the light of its everyday functions. The deracinating experience of being traded away from families and communities, Graham argues, created a set of enslaved people (mostly male, mostly young) with nothing left to lose, which slaveholders in importing regions increasingly saw as a threat to the order and even the continued existence of their communities. Indeed, the "revolutionary" mass flights and field firings that immediately preceded and spurred Brazilian abolition occurred in regions that had been among the country's greatest importers.

Robert Slenes's essay on the internal trade in Brazil both deepens the economic and demographic overview of that trade provided by Graham and adds an argument about its political history. In Brazil after about 1850, Slenes argues, there were actually two semiautonomous regional slave trading complexes: one serving the coffee planters of the Center-South region and one serving the sugar planters of the Northeast. Especially in the years after 1870, when coffee was exported in increasing quantities, the number of people traded into the Center-South was quite large, and Slenes puts the number of those traded from 1850 to the effective closing of the trade (by high provincial excise taxes) in 1881 at almost a quarter of a million. Considered as an aggregate number and as a proportion of the total slave population, Slenes argues, the internal trade in Brazil was comparable in magnitude to that in the United States. Indeed, because the bulk of sales were concentrated in the period between 1870 and 1880 and because slaves in Brazil were often traded over much longer distances than they were in the United States, the Brazilian trade may have, at least during the 1870s, been even more brutal than that which had functioned in the antebellum South.

Although the coffee-producing regions of the country received the greatest number of slaves traded from other regions, Slenes notes that the fact that the price of slaves in the Northeast did not track that in the Center-South suggests the existence of a fairly autonomous slave market. He compares the records tracking the interregional movement of slaves to censuses of the slave populations on sugar plantations and suggests that even when sugar prices were low and slaves were being exported from the Northeast, they were rarely being sold by sugar planters. Rather, they were being sold interregionally by smallholders, urban slaveowners, and cotton planters suffering from the resumption of exports from the United States after 1865, all of whom would have found a market in the Northeast for their slaves if sugar prices had remained high. These exported slaves, Slenes argues, were increasingly traded to the Center-South, where they became a large component of a market that had, before the 1870s, been largely intraregional (drawing its slaves largely from the urban sector of the economy, where they could be easily replaced by free workers who refused to work in the sugar fields).

Slenes argues that the expansion of the internal trade after 1850 put to an end a period of relative stability in the family life of creole slaves, an effect that was magnified by the large proportion of young men among the traded slaves and was especially acute on the smaller plantations that accounted for the bulk of the exports. He suggests that the expansion of the trade and its focus on the young undermined an "implicit paternalist agreement" between those slaves and their masters. Whereas they expected that their families would be protected in exchange for their good behavior, slaves born in Brazil found that their owners were coming to care less about their origins than about their age and their salability. These shattered expectations, Slenes (along with Graham) suggests, contributed to increasing unrest among creole slaves in the decades before emancipation.

Finally, Slenes notes that the expansion of the internal slave trade occurred at a time when the future of slavery in Brazil was increasingly being called into question. Thus demand in that market represented speculation regarding the political future: the belief that slavery would not be abolished too quickly for buyers to make their money back. Between 1881 and 1883 belief in that future faded. Slave prices crashed, hire rates expanded, and banks stopped accepting human collateral to secure long-term loans. Slenes locates the proximate cause of this crash in the fears of planters and politicians in the South-Center that those in the Northeast would seek to dump their (soon-to-be-freed) slaves onto the market, sell them southward, and then vote for abolition. Rather than continuing to import slaves who would soon be transformed into impoverished free people, the South-Central provinces placed high taxes on the interregional slave trade in the early 1880s, effectively taxing it out of existence.

It was William Wells Brown, the once enslaved steward of a Mississippi River slave trader, who wrote that "slavery has never been represented, slavery never can be represented."[17] Brown's point, first and foremost, was that the true story of slavery could only have been told by those who lived their whole lives and died without ever having the chance to tell it. But his fear of losing contact with a history buried beneath the backfill of its own destructive consequences seems likewise to illuminate the dilemma facing the scholars whose work is collected here: how to represent the enormity of the history of slave trading in the Americas. Taken together, their work surveys the genres of historical writing — comparative, demographic, biographical, political, social, cultural, theoretical — as each seeks to grasp and convey what it meant to live through a history that was being made in the slave market. It is a measure of their success that, by the end of the collection, some of the most persistent of historians' settled categories have been roiled. They make clear, for example, why some slave-trading practices became historically visible as "internal" slave trades while others did not and suggest the ways in which the history of slave trading was implicated in helping create and maintain the distinction between a national "inside" and a transnational "outside," a distinction that subtends the very definition of some slave trading practices as internal. They provide new ways to think about the interplay of domination, dependence, race, and resistance, rework longstanding debates about the interrelation of capitalism, sovereignty, and slavery, and reconnect the history of the politics and resistance of enslaved people to the politics practiced in the legislative chambers and courtrooms of the Americas.

Most important perhaps, they call into question the distinction between the human side and the economic side of the slave trade that has defined the parameters of so many of our histories of the trade. By labeling the history of enslaved people the human side, historians have long underestimated the salience of economics to the condition of enslaved humanity. At the same time, by treating the history of the slave traders as "economic history" they have defined away the very humanity of the nevertheless objectionable avarice and savagery of the slave business. Relegating the history of the perpetrators of the slave trade to the category of the merely (or inevitably) economic invites us to misunderstand our human condition as being both beyond economics and morally blameless. Perhaps, living as we do in the long historical shadow of the chattel principle, it is time to start thinking otherwise.

Notes

My thanks to Thomas Bender, Ira Berlin, David Brion Davis, Alejandro de la Fuente, Ada Ferrer, Robert Forbes, Adam Green, Maria Grazia Lolla, Alison Mackeen, James Oakes, Daniel Rodgers, and Stephanie Smallwood for help with this essay.

1. James W. C. Pennington, *The Fugitive Blacksmith: Or Events in the Life of James W. C. Pennington* (London: n.p., 1849), iv–vii. For overviews of the internal trade in the United States see Frederic Bancroft, *Slave Trading in the Old South* (Baltimore: J. H. Furst, 1931); Laurence J. Kotlikoff, "The Structure of Slave Prices in New Orleans, 1804–1862," *Economic Inquiry* 17 (1979): 496–517; Michael Tadman, *Speculators and Slaves: Masters, Traders, and Slaves in the Old South* (Madison: University of Wisconsin Press, 1989); H. Freudenberger and J. B. Pritchett, "The Domestic United States Slave Trade: New Evidence," *Journal of Interdisciplinary History* 21 (1991): 447–477; Jonathan B. Pritchett and Herman Freudenberger, "A Peculiar Sample: The Selection of Slaves for the New Orleans Market," *Journal of Economic History* 52 (1992): 109–128; Thomas D. Russell, "South Carolina's Largest Slave Auctioneering Firm," *Chicago-Kent Law Review* 68 (1993): 1241–1282; Walter Johnson, *Soul by Soul: Life Inside the Antebellum Slave Market* (Cambridge: Harvard University Press, 1999); Adam Rothman, "The Expansion of Slavery in the Deep South, 1790–1820," Ph.D. diss. (Columbia University, 2000); Robert Gudmestad, "A Troublesome Commerce: The Transformation of the Interstate Slave Trade," Ph.D. diss. (Louisiana State University, 2000); Ira Berlin,

Generations of Captivity: A History of African American Slaves (Cambridge: Harvard University Press, 2003), 159–244; and Steven Deyle, *Carry Me Back: The Domestic Slave Trade in American Life* (New York: Oxford University Press, forthcoming). For overviews of the internal trade in the British West Indies see David Eltis, "The Traffic in Slaves Between the British West Indian Colonies, 1807–1833," *Economic History Review* 25 (1972): 55–46; and Barry Higman, *Slave Populations of the British Caribbean, 1807–1834* (Baltimore: Johns Hopkins University Press, 1984). For Brazil see Herbert S. Klein, "The Internal Slave Trade in Nineteenth-Century Brazil: A Study of Slave Importations into Rio de Janeiro," *Hispanic American Historical Review* 51 (1971): 567–585; Robert W. Slenes, "The Demography and Economics of Brazilian Slavery, 1850–1888, Ph.D. diss. (Stanford University, 1975).

2. For a fuller account of the slaveholding futures available for purchase in the slave markets of the antebellum South see Johnson, *Soul by Soul,* 78–116.

3. Lewis Hayden, quoted in Harriet Beecher Stowe, *A Key to "Uncle Tom's Cabin," Presenting the Original Facts and Documents upon Which the Story Is Founded* (Boston: J. P. Jewett, 1853), 154.

4. The classic formulation of this distinction in the slavery literature is Eugene D. Genovese, *Roll, Jordan, Roll: The World the Slaves Made* (New York: Vintage, 1976), esp. 598–599.

5. See Walter Johnson, "A Nettlesome Classic Turns Twenty-Five," *Common-Place* 1:4 (July 2001), www.common-place.org/vol-01/no-04/reviews/johnson.html; and Walter Johnson, "On Agency," *Journal of Social History* (Fall 2003): 113–124.

6. For Smith see James Oakes, "The Bourgeois Critique of Slavery," in *Slavery and the American South: Essays and Commentaries,* ed. Winthrop Jordan (Oxford: University of Mississippi Press, 2003); for slavery as "primitive accumulation" see Karl Marx, *Capital* (New York: International Publishers, 1967), 1:710–712, and Cedric Robinson, *Black Marxism: The Making of the Black Radical Tradition,* 2nd ed. (Chapel Hill: University of North Carolina Press, 2000), 81–82, 110–116.

7. See Walter Johnson, "The Pedestal and the Veil: Rethinking the Capitalism/Slavery Question," *Journal of the Early Republic* 24 (Summer 2004): 301–310. Marx, at least, seems to have wrestled with the question of converting the images of temporal succession which frame the idea of slavery-as-primitive-accumulation (and which have characterized much of the subsequent discussion of slavery and capitalism into a set of spatial images of "unevenness"). To wit: "Whilst the cotton industry introduced child-slavery in England, it gave in the United States a stimulus to the transformation of the earlier, more or less patriarchal slavery into a system of commercial exploitation. In fact the veiled slavery of the wage-workers in Europe needed, for its pedestal, slavery pure and simple in the new world." The image of new world slavery as a pedestal is remarkable for its precision in evoking the idea of something that is, at once, functionally distinct from and structurally integral to the edifice it supports (Marx, *Capital,* 1:711). The figure of "commercial slavery" appears several other times in the first volume of *Capital,* most notably for the project at hand when Marx exemplifies a point about the merciless expansion of the working day to the point that laborers perish and have to be replaced by those imported from other nations by quoting from a pamphlet about the internal slave trade in the United States. Marx's own description of the relevance of the internal slave trade to

the condition of European wage workers interestingly refers to slaves as both labor and capital, and thus apparently transcending conventional "Marxist" usage: "The slave-owner buys his laborer as he buys his horse. If he loses his slave, he loses capital that can only be restored by new outlay in the slave-mart. . . . *Mutato nominee de te fabula narrator* [with the name changed the story applies to you]. For slave-trade read labour-market, for Kentucky and Virginia, Ireland, etc." (Marx, *Capital,* 1:253–254).

8. One might push this question a step further by questioning the assumption (generally accepted in the literature on the internal trade in the United States, at least) that uprooting people and forcing them to move hundreds of miles, even with their families intact, was an action that somehow indicated slaveholders' benevolence or paternalism or anything else of the kind. This would involve prying the history of the migration of enslaved people out of the familial terms in which nineteenth-century supporters of slavery tried to situate it, a set of terms in which slaves and slaveholders alike were simply families moving westward. As the proslavery theorist George Fitzhugh described it in 1857, the migratory pattern of slaveholders ensured that "the breaking up of families of whites and blacks keeps equal pace" (George Fitzhugh, *Cannibals All! Or, Slaves Without Masters,* ed. C. Vann Woodward, [Cambridge: Harvard University Press, 1960], 158). Future scholars might do well to resituate these claims of slaveholders' paternalism in the history of forced migration, the appalling frequency of which in our own time is scarcely palliated by the fact that most of its victims have been driven from their homes with their families "intact."

9. Thomas Maskell to Samuel Plaisted, August 8, 1838. Samuel Plaisted Collection, Lower Mississippi Valley Collection, Hill Memorial Library, Louisiana State University.

10. Thomas C. Holt, "Marking Race: Race-Making and the Writing of History," *American Historical Review* 50 (1995): 1–20.

11. The slave market, according to this view, would be only one, though perhaps the most important, of a host of institutional settings — churches, medical schools, court-rooms, census tallies, minstrel shows, antislavery societies, and, it should be remembered, slave quarters and secret meetings — that produced and reproduced an ever more tangled set of interrelated but nonidentical notions of "race" throughout the Americas.

12. For the general point about the transformation of the categories of bondage from national to racial ones see Colette Guillaumin, *Racism, Sexism, Power, and Ideology* (London: Routledge, 1995); for the specific argument about the reproduction of racial "knowledge" in the slave market see Johnson, *Soul by Soul,* 135–161.

13. Indeed, one of the arguments made by slaveholders who opposed the proslavery radicals' calls to reopen the African slave trade in the late 1850s was that if the trade were reopened "the slaveholder would become — instead of the patriarchal friend and master of his slave — a bloody, brutal, and trembling tyrant." Quoted in Ronald T. Takaki, *A Proslavery Crusade: The Agitation to Reopen the African Slave Trade* (New York: Free Press, 1971), 128.

14. For the general problem see Frank Tannenbaum, *Slave and Citizen: The Negro in the Americas* (New York: Knopf, 1946), and Frederick Cooper, Thomas C. Holt, and Rebecca J. Scott, *Beyond Slavery: Explorations of Race, Labor, and Citizenship in Post-emancipation Societies* (Chapel Hill: University of North Carolina Press, 2000); for an interesting recent rereading of Tannenbaum that spurred my own thinking on the topic

see Alejandro de la Fuente, "Slave Law, Claims-Making, and Citizenship in Cuba: The Tannenbaum Debate Revisited," paper delivered at the American Society of Legal Historians meeting, San Diego, California, November 7, 2002; for the (incomplete) conversion of slaves into citizens of a multiracial democracy in Cuba see Rebecca J. Scott, *Slave Emancipation in Cuba: The Transition to Free Labor, 1860–1899* (Princeton: Princeton University Press, 1985); Aline Helg, *Our Rightful Share: The Afro-Cuban Struggle for Equality, 1886–1912* (Chapel Hill: University of North Carolina Press, 1995), and Ada Ferrer, *Insurgent Cuba: Race, Nation, and Revolution in Cuba, 1868–1898* (Chapel Hill: University of North Carolina Press, 1999). For Brazil see Thomas Skidmore, *Black into White: Race and Nationality in Brazilian Thought* (New York: Oxford University Press, 1974); George Reid Andrews, *Blacks and Whites in São Paulo, Brazil, 1888–1988* (Madison: University of Wisconsin Press, 1991); and the essays in Richard Graham, ed., *The Idea of Race in Latin America, 1870–1940* (Austin: University of Texas Press, 1990).

15. See Takaki, *Proslavery Crusade*, esp. 23–85.

16. Later, some Cuban slaveholders would favor annexation to the United States on the ground that if the British ever succeeded in closing the Atlantic slave trade, by then officially illegal even in Cuba, they would be able to replenish their labor forces through an "internal" trade with the Upper South. Some Upper South slaveholders opposed annexation for exactly the same reason: they feared that, in the absence of a reopened African trade (an idea that was being broached in the South of the late 1850s), an "internal" trade to an annexed Cuba would drain slaves from their faltering economies and leave them vulnerable to abolition. See Robert E. May, *The Southern Dream of Caribbean Empire, 1854–1861* (Baton Rouge: Louisiana State University Press, 1973), 25, 202–203.

17. William Wells Brown, "Lecture," reprinted in *Four Fugitive Slave Narratives*, ed. Robin Winks (Reading, MA: Addison-Wesley, 1969), 82.

2

The Domestication of the Slave Trade in the United States

ADAM ROTHMAN

I

In the half-century from 1770 to 1820, slaveowners in the United States withdrew from the international slave trade. During the same period, they pioneered a substantial movement of slaves within the United States, uprooting slaves from the Atlantic seaboard and transplanting them to the south and west. This combination of isolation and expansion constituted the domestication of the slave trade in the United States, one of the most important transformations of slavery in North America from the American Revolution to the Civil War. It was one of American slaveowners' primary responses to the revolutionary changes in the world around them, changes that brought both new economic opportunities and unprecedented political challenges.[1]

By withdrawing from the international slave trade, southern reformers pursued a dangerous strategy. The same principles of humanity, security, and political economy that informed the Anglo-American movement against the international trade might be turned against slavery itself. In order to prevent the movement against the international trade from doubling back against domestic slavery, reformers in the southern United States elaborated a pro-slavery worldview that distinguished between slave trading and slaveholding. Slave trading, they argued, represented European commercialism and mercantilism; it sapped the country's economic resources and undermined their political security. Slaveholding, in contrast, had become part of the fabric of republican society, adding to the wealth of the nation and the independence of its citizens. As a political doctrine, the proslavery argument rested in part on southern reformers' efforts to withdraw from the international slave trade and simultaneously justify domestic slavery.

But at the same time, the territorial and economic expansion of the slave regime in the southern United States presented slaveowners with a dilemma. The emerging domestic trade clashed with the emerging proslavery argument and could not be ignored. Before 1820, legislators in every southern state enacted statutory or constitutional restrictions on the interstate slave trade. In these measures, proslavery reformers generally distinguished between slaveholding and slave trading, reinforcing the logic of the proslavery argument. But precisely because the distinction between the two evaded a basic reality of chattel slavery — that slaveholding required slave trading — legislative restrictions failed to regulate or curtail the internal trade, which became a standing rebuke to the professed benevolence of North American slaveowners and an ever-present terror for American slaves.

II

Between the American Revolution and the Missouri Compromise, transatlantic revolutionary forces reinvigorated the economic foundation of American slavery, but these same forces presented southern slaveowners with a prolonged crisis that challenged the moral and political legitimacy of slavery. In response, they acceded to the withdrawal of the United States from the international trade, "domesticating" slavery in the double sense of confining it within the country's borders while reining in its more dangerous potentialities.

The Atlantic revolutions of the last quarter of the eighteenth century and first quarter of the nineteenth opened up new opportunities for profit from slave labor.[2] An industrial revolution in Great Britain created a seemingly insatiable demand for American cotton. Slaveowners in the new United States, suffering from dislocations in the tobacco, indigo, and rice economies, eagerly shifted their cultivation to the new staple. Lured by exceptionally high prices for cotton in the 1790s, slaveowners in the Lower South set their slaves to the production of long-staple cotton and, after the widespread dissemination of the cotton gin, to short-staple cotton as well.[3]

Political revolution in France and the colonial upheaval that followed also created new opportunities for slaveowners in North America.[4] Revolutionary wars in Europe weakened demand for tobacco, forcing many slaveowners in the Upper South who had been committed to tobacco in the 1770s and 1780s to diversify their agricultural practices. The complex changes that attended the shift to mixed farms enabled many slaveowners in the Upper South to decrease their reliance on slave labor by freeing, hiring out, or selling their slaves. Not all slaveowners in the region abandoned slavery, however. Some planters prospered even in hard times, and others migrated with their slaves for more promising fields in the west. The transformation of agricultural production in the region positioned it to serve as a major source of slave labor for the expanding plantation system to the south and southwest.[5]

The slave rebellion in St. Domingue opened up the way for the expansion of sugar production in the lower Mississippi valley and the Gulf Coast of North America. The collapse of sugar production in the French West Indies created a vacuum soon filled by rival producers. Sugar planters in Jamaica, Cuba, and Brazil stepped into the breach created by the collapse of sugar production in St. Domingue, but the extraordinary prices earned by sugar exports in the latter half of the 1790s and the early 1800s also opened up the possibility of profitable sugar production in marginal areas such as Louisiana.[6] Free and slave refugees from St. Domingue brought knowledge of sugar-making (as well as necessary labor) to the lower Mississippi valley, where they were welcomed by local planters seeking an alternative to tobacco and indigo.[7]

Transatlantic revolutionary war also provided the United States with the opportunity for an unprecedented territorial expansion at the expense of Spain, France, and the indigenous nations of North America. In the Treaty of San Lorenzo in 1795 and the Louisiana Purchase in 1803, the United States gained from turmoil in Europe. Spain and France recognized that they could not forestall the westward expansion of the United States forever, so, confronted with a hostile Great Britain, they traded land in North America for peace with the United States. British power, ironically, fostered the very expansion that the anglophobic Jeffersonians cherished and the anglophilic Federalists feared.[8] By acquiring the Mississippi Territory and Louisiana from rival European powers, the United States undermined the southern Indians' capacity to resist the spread of plantation agriculture, opened up to eastern slaveowners a substantial regional market capable of absorbing their "surplus" slaves, and rendered the transplantation of slaves from the eastern United States to the Deep South a domestic rather than an international concern.

Slaveowners in the new United States capitalized on changes in the global market for agricultural commodities and manipulated their opportunities in the realm of international diplomacy. They were also creative, innovative, and adaptive in securing a slave labor force adequate to their needs. Many large slaveowners responded to the need for labor by encouraging (if that is the proper word) biological reproduction among their slaves. Some prominent slaveowners believed that biological reproduction cost less than purchasing slaves and that slaves organized into families became more tractable and productive. Slaveowners' interest in slave families for purposes of reproduction and social control coincided with American slaves' own desire to establish and maintain stable families.[9]

Biological reproduction was a strategy for the *longue dureé*. It could not satisfy planters who wished to build their labor force quickly or those who had to start from nothing. Where the demand for slaves was most acute, slaveowners and would-be slaveowners eagerly tapped into available local, regional, national, and international markets for slaves. Drawing from substantial archival research and informed statistical analysis, the historian James McMillin has recently estimated that approximately 170,000 slaves were introduced into North America between 1783 and 1810, with more than 100,000 of these arriving in the first decade of the nineteenth century.[10] Moreover, the geographic expansion of the plantation system within North America began to pull large numbers of slaves from the eastern seaboard into the southwestern interior, Gulf Coast and lower Mississippi valley. In short, demand for slave labor in the expanding American South was growing, not declining, when the national government prohibited the importation of slaves once and for all in 1808, and it was not at all clear that the biological reproduction of the slave population would keep pace with the demand for slaves.

So why did slaveowners in the United States concede to their country's withdrawal from the international slave trade at the very moment when demand for slave labor was increasing? The nationalist impetus of the American Revolution was crucial.[11] The revolution infused southern slaveowners with a powerful Anglophobia that reinforced southern opposition to the international slave trade, especially in the Upper South. After the revolution, southern slaveowners in Virginia and Maryland not only indicted England for having refused to prohibit the slave trade to its North American colonies, but they condemned England's continued domination of the international slave trade.[12] Slaveowners and their northern allies believed that the abolition of the African slave trade would emancipate America from British slave traders and was therefore consistent with the principles of the revolution.[13] At the same time, most southern slaveowners also believed that the revolutionary tradition protected the property rights of slaveowners, that emancipation would release a hostile nation of Africans into their midst, and (though this was more controversial) that the Bible sanctioned slaveowning.[14]

By the end of the eighteenth century, most slaveowners in the Upper South had come to believe that further importation of slaves into the United States was uneconomical, dangerous, and disgraceful. At the same time, they became even more strident defenders of their rights as slaveowners. In Virginia, this consensus formed by 1788, when George Mason and James Madison debated the ratification of the proposed federal Constitution. Mason, the leading Anti-federalist, criticized the proposed Constitution on the grounds that it neither prohibited the importation of slaves nor provided sufficient protection for the property rights of slaveowners. Madison easily defended the Federalist position by demonstrating how the proposed Constitution improved the prospects for an eventual prohibition on the importation of slaves and also provided added security for the rights of slaveowners through the fugitive slave clause.[15] Mason and Madison disagreed on the proposed Constitution, but they agreed on the political requirements of slavery. Throughout the Upper South, slave-owners absorbed the distinction between domestic slavery and the international slave trade, forging a consensus in favor of the domestication of the slave trade.

This consensus took longer to coalesce in the Lower South, where slave-owners depended more on the international trade and were therefore less eager to abandon it. At the Constitutional Convention, delegates from South Carolina and Georgia strongly defended slave importation on grounds of principle and utility, winning a clause that prevented the federal government from prohibiting the importation of slaves until 1808.[16] During the debates about ratification, Federalists in South Carolina tried to ease fears that the Constitution would doom South Carolina to a shortage of slaves. Presaging the domestication of the slave trade, David Ramsay argued that the slave trade clause should not worry Carolinians. He predicted that northern shipping interests would support the slaveowners' interests in due time, and if they did not, southern slaveowners could fall back on their own devices. "Besides, we have other sources of supply," Ramsay predicted; "the importation of the ensuing 20 years, added to the natural increase of those we already have, and the influx from our northern neighbours, who are desirous of getting rid of their slaves, will afford a sufficient number for cultivating all the lands in this state."[17]

Even though representatives from the Deep South vigorously defended their constituents' right to import slaves, many of those same constituents had already begun to turn against slave importation. In 1786, petitioners from the lower district of Camden complained to the South Carolina House of Representatives that "a sufficient check has not been put to the Importation of Negro Slaves, altho it appears evident that has allways thrown the ballance of Trade against, has drained us of our cash, and prevented the increase of Population, and growth of Manufactures." The Camden petitioners warned, "This is a grievance which we conceive ought to be speedily remedied least a total loss of the Ballance of Power should at no distant period subject us to all that wretchedness which is the usual attendant upon Political Weakness & Luxury."[18] In 1787 the South Carolina General Assembly imposed a temporary prohibition on the importation of slaves as part of a series of measures designed to relieve the burdens of debt that were crippling farmers and planters throughout the state. The state legislature maintained the prohibition on slave importation for fifteen years before reopening the trade at the end of 1803.[19]

In the Deep South, where plantation agriculture began to take off in the 1790s, many slaveowners favored the continued importation of African slaves, whom they generally considered less expensive and more productive than creole slaves from the eastern United States. In 1797, the Permanent Committee of the Natchez District asserted in a petition to Congress that without slaves, "the farms in this District would be but of little more value to the present occupiers than equal quantity of waste land."[20] After Congress outlawed the importation of African slaves to the Orleans Territory, the leading citizens of New Orleans sent a memorial to Congress declaring that without African slaves, "cultivation must cease, the improvements of a century be destroyed, and the great river resume its empire over our ruined fields and demolished habitations."[21] Sympathetic eastern politicians supported the southwestern slaveowners' plea for continued importation. During the debates about the status of slavery in the Orleans Territory, James Jackson of Georgia and Jonathan Dayton of New Jersey argued that the southwest could not be cultivated without slaves and warned that the southwest would be "abandoned" unless Congress permitted slavery there.[22]

Slaveowners in the southeastern United States might have encouraged the importation of slaves as the plantation economy took off, but world-historical events in Europe and the Caribbean infused them with a deep sense of dread. The slave rebellion in St. Domingue, inspired and enabled by the French Revolution, transformed the political consciousness of Afro-Caribbean and Afro-American men and women. In the United States, people of African descent heard of the slave rebellion in St. Domingue and considered their own prospects for self-emancipation. Moreover, the Anglo-French wars for the Caribbean uprooted countless thousands of men and women of African descent and transplanted them in new places. Perhaps ten thousand slaves and free people of color from the Caribbean, and probably more, landed in the United States from the Caribbean between 1790 and 1810. These immigrants included sailors, soldiers, refugees, and slaves imported for sale. Slaveowners cracked down on the influx of Afro-Caribbean and African people into the United

States, prepared against a possible invasion by Afro-Caribbean soldiers, and generally tried to defend themselves against the Jacobinism that was hurtling their world towards disaster.[23]

Impressed by the slave rebellion in St. Domingue, North American slave-owners stiffened their opposition to the importation of slaves. All the states that still permitted the importation of foreign slaves in 1789 closed the trade in the 1790s. North Carolina prohibited importation in 1794 and the following year prohibited immigrants from the West Indies or from French, Dutch, and Spanish America from bringing their own slaves into the state. The Georgia legislature prohibited the importation of slaves from the West Indies in 1793 and slaves from Africa early in 1798.[24] Throughout the 1790s in South Carolina, low country planters defeated efforts to reopen the importation of foreign slaves. Even when the South Carolina legislature revived slave importation in 1803, it maintained the ban on slaves coming from the West Indies.[25] South Carolina's restoration of the African slave trade in 1803 was deeply unpopular in the rest of the South and disturbing to some planters in South Carolina as well. In 1805, as thousands of African slaves landed in Charleston, South Carolina governor Paul Hamilton warned that slave importation "increases our weakness, not our strength."[26]

Fear of slave rebellion not only intensified southern slaveowners' opposition to slave importation. Paradoxically, this fear also helped slaveowners justify the expansion of slavery into new territory in the southwestern United States. During the congressional debates about the status of slavery in the Mississippi and Orleans territories, some advocates of its expansion argued that the combination of prohibition and expansion would lessen the proportion of slaves in the total population, improve the slaves' circumstances, and diminish the potential for a slave rebellion. This argument, known as "diffusionism," is associated most closely with Thomas Jefferson, who hoped the process would set the stage for gradual emancipation.[27] But even Jefferson seems to have recognized that the most immediate and predictable consequence of diffusion was to strengthen the security of the slave regime. In a letter to John Dickinson in 1807, Jefferson recommended that the planters of Louisiana be permitted to import slaves from the eastern states, "which, by dividing the evil, would lessen its danger."[28] John Breckenridge, the Kentucky senator who managed the bill to organize the Louisiana cession through Congress, put the case succinctly: "I think it is good policy to permit slaves to be sent there from the United States. This will disperse and weaken the race — and free the southern states from a part of its black population, and of its danger."[29] The discovery of Gabriel's conspiracy, a well-organized plot to overthrow slavery in Richmond, Virginia, in 1800 and other indications of African American discontent within the United States gave the diffusionist position force and immediacy notwithstanding the natural growth of the slave population.

Arguing for a prohibition on the importation of foreign slaves and for the transplantation of eastern slaves into the west, diffusionists won the debate about the status of slavery in the Mississippi and Orleans Territories. In 1798, the United States Congress outlawed the importation of foreign slaves into the Mississippi Territory but allowed slaves from the United States to enter the Mississippi Territory without restriction. In 1804, Congress outlawed the importation of foreign slaves into the Orleans Territory, the introduction into the territory of slaves that had been brought into the United States after May 1, 1798, and the introduction of any slaves into the Orleans Territory from the United States "except by a citizen of the United States, removing into said territory for actual settlement, and being at the time of such removal the bona fide owner of such slave or slaves."[30] By so restricting the flow of slaves into the Orleans Territory, Congress hoped to discourage the development of a systematic interstate slave trade while respecting the rights of slaveowners and promoting American settlement in the lower Mississippi valley. Congress thus applied the distinction between slaveholding and slave trading to the system of slavery within the United States.

Despite these restrictions, thousands of slaves were brought into the Orleans Territory from the United States, including many slaves recently imported from Africa. After the Orleans Territory passed into the second stage of territorial government in 1805, local authorities in the territory effectively nullified the restrictions on the importation of slaves from the eastern United States, and African slaves recently imported into South Carolina were transshipped to New Orleans by the hundreds.[31] In June 1806, the New Orleans mercantile firm of Kenner & Henderson advertised the sale of seventy-four "Prime Slaves" of the Fantee nation, brought to the Orleans Territory from Charleston on board the schooner *William*, and in October, Kenner & Henderson advertised the sale of another sixty-six "prime young slaves of the Congo nation," brought to New Orleans from Charleston on board the *Carolina*.[32] Later in the same year, two agents for the Rhode Island firm of Gardner and Dean discovered that African slaves were selling for more than three hundred dollars in Charleston, the prices inflated because "the demand from the back country and New Orleans is very considerable."[33] The efflorescence of the slave trade between Charleston and New Orleans in the first decade of the nineteenth century prefigured the difficulty that proslavery reformers would have in policing the domestic slave trade for years to come.

The United States outlawed the importation of slaves in 1807; the prohibition went into effect on January 1, 1808, the earliest moment permitted by the

Constitution.[34] After 1808, the leading southern politicians and intellectuals became even more united in their opposition to the international slave trade. They condemned it, supported military efforts to crack down on slave smuggling through Amelia Island and Galveston, and endorsed the movement to revise and strengthen the laws punishing illegal slave trading as piracy in 1819. When Andrew Jackson referred to the illegal importation of slaves through Florida as a "dreaded evil" in 1821, nobody questioned his sincerity.[35] At the same time, slaveowners insisted that the national and international campaign to suppress the international trade should not endanger slavery in the United States. They fended off proposals to emancipate Africans captured from illegal slavers, prevented the United States from joining international conventions to prohibit the slave trade, and rejected any attempt to extend the ban on the international slave trade to the domestic trade. Southern slaveowners wanted to police their own borders in their own way and for their own reasons.[36]

III

Despite weak enforcement and persistent smuggling, the prohibition on slave importation nevertheless prevented hundreds of thousands of Africans from being transported to the United States and sold as slaves. Compared with Cuba or Brazil, the success of the prohibition on slave importation in the United States is remarkable.[37] It also, however, required slaveowners in the United States who might otherwise have purchased African slaves to purchase American slaves instead. The simultaneous closing of the African slave trade to the United States and expansion of slavery in North America fueled the growth of the domestic slave trade.[38]

The domestic slave trade brought economic, social, and political benefits to southern slaveowners. By selling slaves to the south and west, eastern slaveowners financed improvements to their farms, rid themselves of difficult slaves, and held the threat of sale over the heads of the rest of their slaves. By purchasing eastern slaves, southwestern slaveowners not only secured and augmented their slave labor force, but they also won the political support of eastern slaveowners who might otherwise have blocked western aspirations for the rapid settlement and development of public lands. By ripping apart settled communities of slaves and scattering the fragments across half a continent, slaveowners throughout the South immeasurably weakened American slaves' capacity for collective resistance, which is exactly what the diffusionists had hoped would happen. In short, the emergence of the domestic slave trade, which was made possible by the prohibition on slave importation, helped consolidate a southern regional bloc committed to the preservation and expansion of slavery.[39]

Despite all these advantages, the development of a systematic interstate slave trade was hard for some southern politicians and intellectuals to swallow. Having articulated the distinction between slaveholding and slave trading during the campaign against the importation of foreign slaves, proslavery reformers could not completely ignore the repercussions of their doctrine at home. Although they recognized the importance of geographic expansion to the vitality of plantation slavery, many slaveowners were suspicious of the internal trade. Between 1790 and 1820, every southern state adopted measures of one sort or another to regulate or curtail the interstate trade, but a substantial interstate slave trade developed anyway. Like the campaign to prohibit the importation of foreign slaves, southern reformers' efforts reflected the distinction between slaveholding and slave trading at the foundation of proslavery doctrine in the United States. In contrast to the successful campaign to prohibit the importation of foreign slaves, however, the efforts to regulate and curtail the interstate trade failed. The development of a substantial interstate trade in the early nineteenth century exposed the contradiction between proslavery doctrine and the commercial nature of the slave regime in the antebellum United States. The utter failure to contain the domestic slave trade revealed the limits of proslavery reform.[40]

John Randolph understood the ethical dilemma facing his class. Randolph was deeply committed to the property rights of slaveowners, but he opposed the slave trade, foreign and domestic.[41] In 1816, Randolph declared to the House of Representatives that he "had never directly or indirectly acquiesced in the weak and wailing plans of those who, by way of relieving the unfortunate African, would throw the States into danger; he would never weaken the form of the contract between the owner and his slave, and he would never deny that the citizens of other States coming into the slaveholding States might exercise the right of ownership over the slaves they might purchase," but he bitterly attacked the slave trade taking place in the District of Columbia. Randolph asserted, "As to the right of passing through the place, as ordinary occasions might require, it was unquestionable; but there was a great difference between that and making the District a depot for a systematic slave market — an assemblage of prisons where the unfortunate beings, reluctant, no doubt, to be torn from their connexions, and the affections of their lives, were incarcerated and chained down, and thence driven in fetters like beasts, to be paid for like cattle."[42]

Randolph was not alone in his concerns about the interstate slave trade.

White southerners disliked the internal trade for various reasons.[43] The men and women who regarded themselves as benevolent and humane, like John Randolph, regarded the trade as a moral outrage because it separated families and brutalized its victims. This concern infused a Quaker petition in 1802, which requested that the Virginia legislature pass a law "to prevent the forcible separation of Husbands & Wives; and prohibiting the traffic in Slaves from, or through this, to other States."[44] Others, especially in the Deep South, contended that the interstate trade introduced slaves of bad character into their midst. Hence, shortly after the 1811 slave rebellion in the Orleans Territory, Governor William C. C. Claiborne implored the territorial legislature to prohibit the "indiscriminate importation of slaves."[45] The common denominator of these complaints was a concern that the commercial incentives of the slave market violated important paternal obligations, whether of humanity or security. With this concern in mind, southern reformers tried to domesticate the domestic slave trade by means of legal restrictions on slave traders' moving slaves between states "as merchandise for sale" and on the interstate movement of slaves who had been convicted of serious crimes.[46]

All the statutory and constitutional restrictions that southern states placed on the interstate trade reflected the distinction between slaveholding and slave trading. In 1792, the Virginia state legislature required immigrants from other states to swear that they had not brought any slaves with them into Virginia "with an intention of selling them."[47] The South Carolina General Assembly augmented its ban on African slaves with a ban on the importation of slaves from other states, but it permitted settlers to bring their slaves with them.[48] In 1798, Georgia prohibited the importation of slaves for sale from other states but adopted a constitutional provision guaranteeing the right of emigrants from other states to bring their slaves with them into Georgia.[49] After a protracted debate about slavery, Kentucky adopted a constitution that allowed the state legislature to prohibit the importation of slaves as merchandise for sale but prevented it from prohibiting immigrants from other states from bringing their slaves with them into Kentucky.[50] Constitution-makers in Mississippi and Alabama adopted similar provisions in their initial state constitutions, empowering their legislatures to prohibit the introduction of slaves as merchandise for sale but prohibiting them from preventing migrants from bringing their slaves into the state or from preventing bona fide residents from importing slaves for their own use.[51] Tennessee's first state constitution was silent on the subject of slavery, but the Tennessee legislature prohibited the introduction of slaves into the state as merchandise for sale in 1812 and added a prohibition on the introduction of convict slaves into the state in 1826.[52]

But southern states' efforts to regulate the interstate slave trade did not have much impact on the movement of slaves. Not only were restrictive laws rarely enforced, but even when public officials tried to enforce them, they ran into deeper obstacles that effectively nullified the entire effort. Mississippi's experience demonstrates the impossibility of restricting the domestic slave trade given the assumptions underlying the restrictionist laws. Armed with a state constitution that enabled them to regulate the introduction of slaves "as merchandise for sale," legislators in Mississippi quickly grappled with the domestic slave trade. Governor David Holmes informed the state legislature in 1817 that "great numbers [of slaves] will be brought to this State, and principally those of the most vicious character, unless by some means we can render the trade at least precarious to those who engage in it."[53] In 1819, the Mississippi legislature took Holmes's advice and passed a comprehensive law regulating the introduction of slaves into the state. The Mississippi law upheld both the legislature's constitutional right to regulate the introduction of slaves as merchandise for sale and its constitutional obligation not to interfere with the rights of resident slaveowners or the rights of migrants settling in Mississippi with their own slaves.

The Mississippi law required all persons bringing a slave into Mississippi to register the slave with local authorities and to swear that the slave had not been guilty of murder, burglary, arson, rape, or grand larceny, according to the knowledge or belief of the owner. Any person bringing or importing a slave without registering the slave was subject to forfeiture and a fine of $500, one-half for the use of the informer and one-half for the use of the state. Any person purchasing an unregistered slave would be subject to the same penalties as the importer. Any slave brought into the state for sale as merchandise would be subject to a $20 tax. If the tax was not paid, the assessor and collector for the county was obligated to seize the slave or slaves and sell them at public auction to the highest bidder, the proceeds going to pay tax and expenses, with the balance going to the owner of the slave or slaves. None of the provisions of the act applied to "any person residing in this state, who shall bring or import any slave or slaves from any of the United States or territories therefor, for their own use, except from the state of Louisiana, or the Alabama Territory," this last exception likely designed to prevent smuggling.[54] The Mississippi law was quickly put to the test, and it failed.[55]

Shortly after the law passed, a group of planters brought a gang of slaves into Mississippi, some for the purpose of sale and some for their own use. When the slaves were brought to Woodville in Wilkinson County, the assessor and collector for the county demanded that the men pay the $20 head tax on slaves introduced as merchandise for sale. After the men refused to pay the taxes, the collector seized five of the slaves and committed them to jail until they could be sold by the county to pay the tax. The slaves' owners appealed to Judge John Taylor, chief justice of the Mississippi High Court, whereupon Taylor issued a writ of habeas corpus forcing the sheriff of Wilkinson County to produce the slaves and defend their incarceration. Lawyers for the State of Mississippi argued that the United States Constitution granted to the states exclusive police and taxing power over slaves and that the tax on slave merchandise amounted to an "indirect prohibition" on the importation of slaves for sale. Taylor rejected these arguments on the grounds that the slaves were articles of commerce, and the United States Constitution did not permit states to raise revenue from interstate trade. Taylor "would not say, because it was not before him, how far the state might go in prohibiting the importation or introduction of slaves from other states in the regulations of its intercourse with them, but that we had no power to *permit* the introduction and raise a *revenue* from it he was clear."[56]

The decision invalidated the laws regulating the introduction of slaves, much to Governor Holmes's chagrin. He pleaded with the Mississippi legislature to remedy the law by enacting a total prohibition on the importation of slaves as merchandise for sale. Holmes warned, "The evils arising from this odious practice are constantly tho' imperceptibly increasing and must ultimately result in consequences of a most serious nature unless the traffic is wholly prohibited."[57] The legislature did not heed Holmes's advice, nor did it move to limit the importation of slaves for another decade, but even if it had enacted a new law totally prohibiting the introduction of slaves as merchandise for sale, Mississippi planters could have continued to import slaves for their own use, and slaveowning migrants could have continued to bring their slaves with them into Mississippi, as was their right according to the state constitution.[58]

The failure of Mississippi's 1819 slave trade regulation demonstrates that even sincere efforts to regulate or curtail the interstate trade confronted crippling legal and constitutional obstacles as long as these efforts remained constrained by southern slaveowners' greater commitment to the rights of slaveholders. In order to curtail this trade, southern reformers would have had to block migrants from carrying their slaves from state to state, and they would have had to prevent resident slaveowners from importing slaves for their own use. Such measures would have fundamentally altered the structure of the southern slave regime, so it should come as no surprise that the reformers backed off from the most radical sort of reform.[59] For the most part, the domestic slave trade in the antebellum United States was regulated by means of the enforcement of legal conventions that protected slaveowners when they unwittingly purchased unhealthy or intractable slaves. These conventions were far more attuned to the commercial complexities of American slavery than blanket restrictions on the interstate slave trade.[60]

Even in failure, the reformers contributed to the development of proslavery doctrine. By their efforts to domesticate the interstate slave trade by legal and constitutional means at the level of state government, they reinforced the ethical content of the slaveowners' worldview. Many slaveowners (though certainly not all, or even most) continued to adhere to the distinction between slave trading and slaveholding. During the era in which the slave trade was domesticated, leading southern slaveowners insisted that though they owned slaves, and even sold slaves now and then for various reasons, they were not traders. Sometimes such declarations were designed to meet (or evade) legal restrictions, as in 1801, when Thomas Satur Jerman swore to the South Carolina General Assembly that the slaves he wished to carry from Georgia to South Carolina were intended for the cultivation of cotton and not for sale.[61] But this was not always the case. Why, for instance, did William Dunbar of Natchez consider it necessary to inform the Charleston firm of Tunno and Price that "I am not a merchant but a Cotton Planter of this place" when he submitted a request for £3,000 worth of African slaves in 1807? Perhaps he merely wanted a better price, but perhaps the honor-conscious Dunbar genuinely thought his reputation was at stake.[62]

In reality, slaveholding and slave trading were not discrete elements of the slave regime. The experiences of David Rees, a Louisiana planter, reveal the contradiction between southern doctrine and practice. In the spring of 1820, Rees traveled to Maryland in search of slaves. He carried a letter of introduction from a fellow planter from Attakapas that declared, "I introduce Col. Rees to you as a gentleman in whom *you may place every confidence* and worthy of your friendship in every respect — He is one of our most respectable Planters and goes to Maryland to purchase some negroes for his own use — He is no *speculator* or *trader*."[63] When he arrived in Maryland, however, Rees gave in to temptation. He wrote back to a friend in Louisiana, explaining that "prime fellows" could be purchased for $350, women and boys aged twelve to sixteen could be purchased for $250, and girls for $200. At these prices, Rees suggested, investors could reap 100 percent net profits by reselling the slaves in Louisiana. The ever-generous Rees suggested to his correspondent, "I have thought you might perhaps wish to purchase some more Negroes yourself for your plantations or that perhaps some of your friends might be willing to adventure in a speculation of that kind."[64] When Rees returned to Louisiana in November, he advertised the sale of sixteen "likely young negroes of both sexes, among which are two young women, one with four & the other with three fine children, a young creole girl &c."[65] As Rees's junket demonstrates, a man could be a respectable planter one day and a slave trader the next.[66]

The distinction between slaveholding and slave trading tried to exorcise the commercial spirit from the master-slave relation, which was a principal concern of proslavery reform. The whole project was an impossible one, because southern slavery was at its core a commercial system producing agricultural commodities for the world market, with slaves functioning as both the principal source of labor and the principal source of capital available to slaveowners in the American South.[67] Slaveowning households were not capitalist units of production, because they were not organized on the basis of free labor, but neither were they havens from market pressure. The sticky webs of credit spun by merchant capitalists and slaveowners to finance their system caught up southern slaves, who were often sold so that their masters could meet obligations to creditors.[68] Many slaveowners found themselves in the same position as John Palfrey, who wrote to his factors in 1812, "In addition to my crop I have no other resources but the disposal of some of the negroes which however ruinous that may be to my future prospects, I must submit to rather than expose myself to the certain expense & sacrifice that must attend a prosecution."[69] Other slaveowners sold slaves in order to raise money for improvements to their farms and plantations, for migration to new and more productive lands, or for any other endeavors for which they needed cash on hand. In 1808, Robert Butler planned to use the sale of slaves to finance his move from Nashville to the Mississippi Territory. He explained to Thomas Butler, "I have in contemplation to move to the Mississippi Territory as soon as I can realize my property in this country, and for the purpose I wish to commune with you, as I fell anxious to settle near you and have our Sister with us as long as she remains single; my plan will be to invest my funds in Negroes, and as I am informed that land can be purchased very low on the west side of the river, and Negroes bearing a high price then I can make sale of some for that purpose."[70] In a social system where slaves were the principal source of labor and capital, the proslavery reformers' effort to regulate or curtail the interstate slave trade could not succeed.

Slaveowners in the United States found themselves in a quandary by the time of the Missouri crisis. In the course of their prolonged effort to preserve their way of life in the face of revolutionary pressures against them, the leading politicians, clergymen, and secular intellectuals committed southern slaveowners to an ethical worldview that distinguished between slaveholding and slave trading. The more proslavery reformers urged masters to look after the welfare of their slaves, the more the domestic slave trade appeared as a standing rebuke to their principles. Yet a sincere and thorough attempt to bring their plantation system into conformity with this ethical worldview would have destroyed the commercial mechanisms on which plantation slavery ultimately depended. Most slaveowners chose to live with this contradiction as best they could, comforting themselves in the dismal conviction that the hypocrisies of their own system paled before the growing evils of free society.[71]

Notes

I thank Betsy Blackmar, David Eltis, Eric Foner, Walter Johnson, and Philip Morgan for their comments on earlier drafts of this essay. I am grateful to the University of Houston Black History Workshop of March 1999 and the Domestic Passages conference hosted by the Gilder Lehrman Institute for the Study of Slavery, Resistance, and Abolition in October 1999 for giving me an opportunity to present and refine some of the ideas that have finally settled in this essay.

1. For two valuable essays on the closing of the international slave trade and the development of an internal slave trade, see Allan Kulikoff, "Uprooted Peoples: Black Migrants in the Age of the American Revolution 1790–1820," in *Slavery and Freedom in the Age of the American Revolution*, ed. Ira Berlin and Ronald Hoffman (Charlottesville: University Press of Virginia, 1983), 143–171, and Steven Deyle, "The Irony of Liberty: The Origins of the Domestic Slave Trade," *Journal of the Early Republic* 12 (Spring 1992): 37–62. The importance of the closing of the African slave trade to the development of proslavery ideology in the United States was also suggested by Eugene Genovese in *The World the Slaveholders Made: Two Essays in Interpretation* (Hanover, NH: Wesleyan University Press, 1988), 97–99. I have adapted the idea of "domestication" from Willie Lee Rose, "The Domestication of Domestic Slavery," in *Slavery and Freedom*, ed. William Freehling (New York: Oxford University Press, 1982), 18–36. For a recent extension of Rose's thesis, see Jeffrey Young, *Domesticating Slavery: The Master Class in Georgia and South Carolina, 1670–1837* (Chapel Hill: University of North Carolina Press, 1999).

2. On the "dual revolution," see Eric Hobsbawm, *The Age of Revolution, 1789–1848* (London: Abacus, 1962).

3. Lewis Cecil Gray (assisted by Esther Katherine Thompson), *History of Agriculture in the Southern United States to 1860* (New York: Peter Smith, 1941), 1:673–690; Rachel Klein, *Unification of a Slave State: The Rise of the Planter Class in the South Carolina Backcountry, 1760–1808* (Chapel Hill: University of North Carolina Press, 1990), 246–257; Joyce Chaplin, "Creating a Cotton South in Georgia and South Carolina, 1760–1815," *Journal of Southern History* 57, no. 2 (May 1991): 171–200.

4. Robin Blackburn, *The Overthrow of Colonial Slavery, 1776–1848* (London: Verso, 1988), 24–25.

5. Ira Berlin, *Many Thousands Gone: The First Two Centuries of Slavery in North America* (Cambridge: Belknap Press of Harvard University Press, 1998), 266–267; Richard S. Dunn, "Black Society in the Chesapeake, 1776–1810," in *Slavery and Freedom in the Age of the American Revolution*, 49–82; Jean B. Russo, "A Model Planter: Edward

Lloyd IV of Maryland, 1770–1796," *William and Mary Quarterly*, 3d. ser., 49, no 1 (January 1992): 62–88..

6. Dale W. Tomich, *Slavery in the Circuit of Sugar: Martinique and the World Economy, 1830–1848* (Baltimore: Johns Hopkins University Press, 1990), 15, 21–31.

7. Robert Paquette, "Revolutionary Saint Domingue in the Making of Territorial Louisiana," in *A Turbulent Time: The French Revolution and the Greater Caribbean*, ed. David Barry Gaspar and David Patrick Geggus (Bloomington: University of Indiana Press, 1997), 204–225. On the development of the sugar economy in Louisiana, see Richard J. Follett, "The Sugar Masters: Slavery, Economic Development, and Modernization on Louisiana Sugar Plantations, 1820–1860" (Ph.D. diss., Louisiana State University, 1997), 43–117.

8. On the Treaty of San Lorenzo, see Arthur P. Whitaker, *The Spanish-American Frontier: 1783–1795* (Boston: Houghton Mifflin, 1927); Samuel Flagg Bemis, *Pinckney's Treaty: America's Advantage from Europe's Distress, 1783–1800* (New Haven: Yale University Press, 1960). On the Louisiana Purchase, see Arthur Preston Whitaker, *The Mississippi Question, 1795–1803: A Study in Trade, Politics, and Diplomacy* (New York: Appleton-Century, 1934); Marshall Sprague, *So Vast, So Beautiful a Land* (Boston: Little, Brown, 1974); James E. Lewis Jr., *The American Union and the Problem of Neighborhood: The United States and the Collapse of the Spanish Empire, 1783–1829* (Chapel Hill: University of North Carolina Press, 1998), 24–32.

9. Phillip Hamilton, "Revolutionary Principles and Family Loyalties: Slavery's Transformation in the St. George Tucker Household of Early National Virginia," *William and Mary Quarterly*, 3d ser., 55, no 4 (October 1998), 545–551; Philip D. Morgan, *Slave Counterpoint: Black Culture in the Eighteenth-Century Chesapeake and Lowcountry* (Chapel Hill: Published for the Omohundro Institute of Early American History and Culture, Williamsburg, Virginia, by the University of North Carolina Press, 1998), 79–95; Mary Beth Norton, Herbert G. Gutman, and Ira Berlin, "The Afro-American Family in the Age of Revolution," in *Slavery and Freedom in the Age of the American Revolution*, 175–191. For a debate about the conditions of slave life in the Chesapeake during the eighteenth century, see Allan Kulikoff, "The Origins of Afro-American Society in Tidewater Maryland and Virginia, 1700 to 1790," *William and Mary Quarterly*, 3d ser., 35, no. 2 (April 1978): 226–259, and Jean Butenhoff Lee, "The Problem of Slave Community in the Eighteenth-Century Chesapeake," *William and Mary Quarterly*, 3d ser., 43, no 3 (July 1986): 333–361. On the congruence of interests between slaves and slaveowners, see Christopher Morris, "The Articulation of Two Worlds: The Master-Slave Relationship Reconsidered," *Journal of American History* 85 (December 1998): 988–994.

10. James McMillin, "The Final Victims: The Demography, Atlantic Origins, Merchants, and Nature of the Post-Revolutionary Foreign Slave Trade to North America, 1783–1810" (Ph.D. diss., Duke University, 1999), 40–98. McMillin's estimate is much lower than Robert Fogel's estimate of 291,000 slaves arriving between 1781 and 1810 but much higher than Allan Kulikoff's estimate of fewer than 100,000 African and West Indian slaves arriving between 1790 and 1810. Compare Robert W. Fogel, "Revised Estimates of the U.S. Slave Trade and of the Native-Born Share of the Black Population," in *Without Consent or Contract: The Rise and Fall of American Negro Slavery: Evidence*

and Methods, ed. Robert W. Fogel and Stanley L. Engerman (New York: W. W. Norton, 1992), 56; Kulikoff, "Uprooted Peoples," 149, 168–171. McMillin's estimate seems to me to be the best available one, since it is based on the most thorough archival research, though even his estimate (as he readily acknowledges in the dissertation) depends to no small degree on debatable assumptions about rates of slave population growth, the prevalence of smuggling, and deficiencies in the archival record.

11. Deyle, "Irony of Liberty," 47; Duncan J. MacLeod, *Slavery, Race, and the American Revolution* (New York: Cambridge University Press, 1974), 32–34.

12. Southern slaveholders were not wrong to identify England as the great slave trading nation. Between 1780 and 1810, British slavers carried almost 45 percent of all slaves transported from Africa to the Americas, more than any other country. See David Eltis, *Economic Growth and the Ending of the Transatlantic Slave Trade* (New York: Oxford University Press, 1987), 248. For the Virginia gentry's opposition to the importation of slaves before the American Revolution, see Bruce A. Ragsdale, *A Planters' Republic: The Search for Economic Independence in Revolutionary Virginia* (Madison, WI: Madison House, 1996), 111–136; Woody Holton, *Forced Founders: Indians, Debtors, Slaves, and the Making of the American Revolution in Virginia* (Chapel Hill: University of North Carolina Press, 1999), 66–73.

13. When Great Britain became the center of Atlantic abolitionism, southern Anglophobia was once again yoked to the proslavery argument. On Anglophobia in proslavery thought, see Robert Pierce Forbes, "Slavery and the Meaning of America, 1819–1837" (Ph.D. diss., Yale University, 1994), 120–121; Kenneth S. Greenberg, "Revolutionary Ideology and the Proslavery Argument: The Abolition of Slavery in Antebellum South Carolina," *Journal of Southern History* 42 (August 1976): 365–384; Larry Tise, *Proslavery: A History of the Defense of Slavery in America, 1701–1840* (Athens: University of Georgia Press, 1987), 43–52.

14. For early antiabolitionist, proslavery statements, see Fredrika Teute Schmidt and Barbara Ripel Wilhelm, "Early Proslavery Petitions in Virginia," *William and Mary Quarterly,* 3rd ser., 30 (January 1973), 133–146; David W. Robson, "'An Important Question Answered': William Graham's Defense of Slavery in Post-Revolutionary Virginia," *William and Mary Quarterly,* 3rd ser., 37 (October 1980): 644–652. See also Peter Onuf, "'To Declare Them a Free and Independant People': Race, Slavery, and National Identity in Jefferson's Thought," *Journal of the Early Republic* 18 (Spring 1998): 1–46.

15. Bernard Bailyn, ed., *The Debate on the Constitution* (New York: Library of America, 1993), 2:706–708.

16. On the debate about the slave trade at the Constitutional Convention, see Donald Robinson, *Slavery in the Structure of American Politics, 1765–1820* (New York: Harcourt Brace Jovanovich, 1971), 224–234; Jack N. Rakove, *Original Meanings: Politics and Ideas in the Making of the Constitution* (New York: Alfred A. Knopf, 1997), 87–88.

17. Bailyn, *Debate on the Constitution,* 2:152. During debate in the South Carolina legislature in 1785, Ramsay had argued in favor of prohibiting the importation of slaves. In the course of his remarks, he noted that if the British ceased carrying slaves "the African trade could be carried on by the New England states, he meant as merchants, not as Christians, with as much advantage, as by any country under the sun." Ramsay, like

many other slaveholders, held slave traders in contempt but relied on them anyway. Elizabeth Donnan, *Documents Illustrative of the History of the Slave Trade to America* (New York: Octagon Books, 1969), 4:488–489.

18. Lark Emerson Adams and Rosa Stoney Lupkin, eds., *Journals of the House of Representatives, 1785–1786* (Columbia: University of South Carolina Press, 1979), 372.

19. Patrick S. Brady, "The Slave Trade and Sectionalism in South Carolina, 1787–1808," *Journal of Southern History* 38 (November 1972): 603–605; Klein, *Unification of a Slave State*, 123–125. For a defense of the African slave trade, see the argument of South Carolina Antifederalist Rawlins Lowndes in Bailyn, *Debate on the Constitution,* 2:20. For a taste of the argument about slave importation in the South Carolina legislature, see Donnan, *Documents Illustrative of the History of the Slave Trade to America,* 4:480–489, 494.

20. Clarence Carter, ed., *Territorial Papers of the United States* (Washington, DC: Government Printing Office, 1937), 5:10–11.

21. *Annals of Congress*, Eighth Cong., 2d sess., 1606.

22. Everett S. Brown, ed., "The Senate Debate on the Breckenridge Bill for the Government of Louisiana, 1804," *American Historical Review* 22 (January 1917): 349.

23. Alfred N. Hunt, *Haiti's Influence on Antebellum America: Slumbering Volcano in the Caribbean* (Baton Rouge: Louisiana State University, 1988), 107–115; Paul Lachance, "The Politics of Fear: French Louisianians and the Slave Trade, 1786–1809," *Plantation Society* 1, no. 2 (June 1979): 162–197; Howard Albert Ohline, "Politics and Slavery: The Issue of Slavery in National Politics, 1787–1815" (Ph.D. diss., University of Missouri, 1969), 287–297; Paquette, "Revolutionary Saint Domingue"; Julius Sherrard Scott III, "The Common Wind: Currents of Afro-American Communication in the Era of the Haitian Revolution" (Ph.D. diss., Duke University, 1986), 274–294; James Sidbury, "Saint Domingue in Virginia: Ideology, Local Meanings, and Resistance to Slavery, 1790–1800," *Journal of Southern History* 63 (August 1997): 531–552.

24. Stephen J. Goldfarb, "An Inquiry into the Politics of the Prohibition of the International Slave Trade," *Agricultural History* 68, no. 2 (Spring 1994): 27. For the prohibition on the slave trade in Georgia, see Ruth Scarborough, *The Opposition to Slavery in Georgia Prior to 1860* (New York: Negro Universities Press, 1968), 108–110.

25. Brady, "Slave Trade and Sectionalism," 612.

26. Quoted in ibid., 617.

27. On diffusionism, see Deyle, "Irony of Liberty," 48; MacLeod, *Slavery, Race, and the American Revolution,* 47–61; Robert McColley, *Slavery in Jeffersonian Virginia* (Chicago: University of Illinois Press, 1973), 171–181; Drew McCoy, *The Last of the Fathers: James Madison and the Republican Legacy* (New York: Cambridge University Press, 1989), 265–276. For the congressional debates on the expansion of slavery into the Mississippi and Orleans Territories, see Robinson, *Slavery in the Structure of American Politics,* 386–400; Ohline, "Politics and Slavery," 298–303, 354–380. For a record of the congressional debate on slavery in the Mississippi Territory, see *Annals of Congress*, vol. 8, 1306–1312, and for the debate on slavery in the Orleans Territory, see Brown, "Senate Debate on the Breckenridge Bill."

28. Thomas Jefferson to John Dickinson, January 13, 1807, in *Thomas Jefferson, Writings,* ed. Merrill D. Peterson (New York: Library Classics of the United States, 1984), 1169–1170.

29. Brown, "Senate Debate on the Breckenridge Bill," 354.

30. For the enabling act for the Mississippi Territory, see Carter, *Territorial Papers of the United States*, 5:18–22. For the enabling act for the Orleans Territory, see ibid., 9:209.

31. W. E. B. Du Bois, *The Suppression of the African Slave Trade to the United States of America, 1638–1870* (New York: Schocken Books, 1969), 89–90; Lachance, "Politics of Fear," 180–181; Donnan, *Documents Illustrative of the History of the Slave Trade to America*, 4:513, 665.

32. *Louisiana Gazette*, June 27, 1806, October 31, 1806.

33. Quoted in Ronald William Bailey, "The Slave Trade and the Development of Capitalism in the United States: A Critical Reappraisal of Theory and Method in Afro-American Studies" (Ph.D. diss., Stanford University, 1979), 240.

34. For the legislative history of the bill to prohibit the importation of slaves in 1807, see Du Bois, *Suppression of the African Slave Trade*, 94–108; Robinson, *Slavery in the Structure of American Politics*, 324–338.

35. Judd Scott Harmon, "Suppress and Protect: The United States Navy, the African Slave Trade, and Maritime Commerce, 1794–1862" (Ph.D. diss., The College of William and Mary, 1977), 63–72, 118–125; Frank Lawrence Owsley Jr. and Gene A. Smith, *Filibusters and Expansionists: Jeffersonian Manifest Destiny, 1800–1821* (Tuscaloosa: University of Alabama Press, 1997), 118–140; Frances J. Stafford, "Illegal Importations: Enforcement of the Slave Trade Laws Along the Florida Coast, 1810–1828," *Florida Historical Quarterly* 46, no. 2 (October 1967): 124–133. For Jackson's comment, see Stafford, 128. I believe that Du Bois underestimated southern slaveholders' commitment to ending the illegal importation of slaves. For Du Bois's position, see *Suppression of the African Slave Trade*, 94–130.

36. Du Bois, *Suppression of the African Slave Trade*, 136–150; Robinson, *Slavery in the Structure of American Politics*, 338–346. For a good expression of this sentiment, see Robert Hayne's speech in Congress in 1826 on the issue of the Panama Congress. *Abridgment of the Debates in Congress from 1789 to 1856* (New York: D. Appleton, 1860), vol. 8, 8:426 (19th Cong., 1st sess., March 14, 1826). Hayne declared, "The question of slavery . . . must be considered and treated as entirely a DOMESTIC QUESTION. With respect to foreign nations, the language of the United States ought to be, that it concerns the peace of our own political family, and therefore we cannot permit it to be touched; and in respect to the slaveholding States, the only safe and constitutional ground on which they can stand, is, that they will not permit it to be brought into question, either by their sister States, or by the Federal Government. It is a matter, Mr. President, for ourselves."

37. For different evaluations of the effectiveness and significance of the federal prohibition on slave importation, compare W. E. B. Du Bois, "The Enforcement of the Slave-Trade Laws," *Annual Report of the American Historical Association* (1891): 163–174; William Freehling, "The Founding Fathers and Slavery," *American Historical Review* 77 (February 1972): 81–93; Goldfarb, "Inquiry into the Politics of the Prohibition of the International Slave Trade."

38. Kulikoff, "Uprooted Peoples," 151.

39. In the long run, as Eugene Genovese has argued, the flow of slaves from the Upper South to the Deep South threatened the southern regional bloc by eroding the

commitment to slavery in slave-exporting regions. This effect did not become manifest until the late antebellum period, however. Eugene Genovese, *The Political Economy of Slavery: Studies in the Economy and Society of the Slave South* (New York: Vintage Books, 1967), 136–141.

40. Robert Gudmestad, "A Troublesome Commerce: The Interstate Slave Trade, 1808–1840" (Ph.D. diss., Louisiana State University, 1999). For an extended treatment of the contradiction between proslavery doctrine and the domestic slave trade in the late antebellum era, see Michael Tadman, *Speculators and Slaves: Masters, Traders, and Slaves in the Old South* (Madison: University of Wisconsin Press, 1989).

41. Gudmestad, "Troublesome Commerce," 133–140. For Randolph's proslavery career, see Russell Kirk, *John Randolph of Roanoke* (Indianapolis: Liberty Press, 1978), 155–189.

42. *Annals of Congress*, 29:1115–1117.

43. Gudmestad, "Troublesome Commerce," 106–116.

44. Accession #11680207. December 1802. In Loren Schweninger, ed., *Race, Slavery, and Free Blacks: Series 1, Petitions to Southern Legislatures, 1777–1867* (University Publications of America, 1999), Reel 16.

45. Dunbar Rowland, ed., *Official Letter Books of W.C.C. Claiborne, 1801–1816* (Jackson, MS: State Department of Archives and History, 1917), 5:123.

46. On southern states' efforts to regulate domestic slave trade, see Gudmestad, "Troublesome Commerce," 160–216; Andrew Fede, "Legal Protection for Slave Buyers in the U.S. South: A Caveat Concerning Caveat Emptor," *American Journal of Legal History* 31, no. 4 (October 1987): 350–353; Tadman, *Speculators and Slaves*, 13–21, 83–93.

47. Du Bois, *Suppression of the African Slave Trade*, 235.

48. Ibid., 236; Klein, Unification of a Slave State, 254–255.

49. Du Bois, *Suppression of the African Slave Trade*, 238, 239; Scarborough, *Opposition to Slavery in Georgia*, 108–110.

50. Oscar B. Chamberlain, "The Evolution of State Constitutions in the Antebellum United States: Michigan, Kentucky and Mississippi" (Ph.D. diss., University of South Carolina, 1996), 45–50, 56–59; Ivan E. McDougle, *Slavery in Kentucky, 1792–1865* (Westport, CT: Negro Universities Press, 1970), 43–45.

51. For Mississippi, see Chamberlain, "Evolution of State Constitutions," 79–87; Winbourne Magruder Drake, "Mississippi's First Constitutional Convention," *Journal of Mississippi History* 18, no. 2 (April 1956): 79–110. For Alabama, see Malcolm Cook McMillan, "The Alabama Constitution of 1819: A Study of Constitution-Making on the Frontier," *Alabama Review* 3, no. 4 (October 1950): 263–285.

52. Caleb Perry Patterson, *The Negro in Tennessee, 1790–1865* (New York: Negro Universities Press, 1968), 43–44.

53. For Holmes's speech, see *Journal of the Mississippi Senate*, 1818, 16.

54. "An Act to amend the act entitled, 'An act regulating the importation of slaves, and for other purposes,'" *Acts Passed at the First Session of the Second General Assembly of the State of Mississippi* (Natchez: Marschalk and Evans — State Printer, 1819), 4–8.

55. The details of the case come from an article in the *Mississippi Republican*, July 27, 1819.

56. Ibid. (italics in original).

57. Governor Holmes's Address, January 4, 1820, Official Archives, Governors' Rec-

ords (RG27), Administration of David Holmes, Dec. 10, 1817–Jan. 5, 1820. Correspondence and Documents, October 7, 1817–January 29, 1820. Mississippi Department of Archives and History, Jackson.

58. For the equally frustrated efforts to stop the importation of slaves for sale after the adoption of Mississippi's second constitution in 1832, see Meredith Lang, *Defender of the Faith: The High Court of Mississippi, 1817–1875* (Jackson: University Press of Mississippi, 1977), 48–68.

59. On the challenge and the failure of proslavery reform in the late antebellum period and during the Civil War, see Eugene Genovese, *A Consuming Fire: The Fall of the Confederacy in the Mind of the White Christian South* (Athens: University of Georgia Press, 1998), 99–121. It should be remembered that the southern slave codes were notoriously ineffective in general. Laws prohibiting slaves from owning property, assembling in groups, learning to read, carrying firearms, buying liquor without the permission of their owners, and numerous others were routinely ignored except in moments of crisis, yet historians have taken such laws as indicators of the slaveholders' worldview.

60. On private suits regarding the sale of slaves, see Fede, "Legal Protection for Slave Buyers"; Thomas Morris, *Southern Slavery and the Law* (Chapel Hill: University of North Carolina Press, 1996), 102–120; Judith Kelleher Schafer, " 'Guaranteed Against the Vices and Maladies Proscribed by Law': Consumer Protection, the Law of Slave Sales, and the Supreme Court in Antebellum Louisiana," *American Journal of Legal History* 31, no. 4 (October 1987), 306–321. This is not to say that southern state legislatures did not continue to pass (and repeal) laws regulating the interstate slave trade. Indeed, they continued to do so throughout the Jacksonian era, but these laws invariably failed to stanch the trade. See Lacy K. Ford, "Making the 'White Man's Country' White: Race, Slavery, and State-Building in the Jacksonian South," *Journal of the Early Republic* 19 (Winter 1999), 727–730.

61. Joyce Chaplin, *An Anxious Pursuit: Agricultural Innovation and Modernity in the Lower South, 1730–1815* (Chapel Hill: University of North Carolina Press, 1993), 321fn72.

62. William Dunbar to Tunno and Price, February 1, 1807, quoted in Eron Rowland, *Life, Letters, and Papers of William Dunbar of Elgin, Morayshire, Scotland, and Natchez, Mississippi, Pioneer Scientist of the United States* (Jackson: Press of the Mississippi Historical Society, 1930), 351. On southern slaveowners' (legendary) disdain for slave traders, see Frederic Bancroft, *Slave-Trading in the Old South* (Baltimore: J. H. Furst, 1931), 365–381; Tadman, *Speculators and Slaves,* 179–210.

63. [William?] Brent to George Brent, May 3, 1820, in David Rees Papers, 1804–1835, St. Martin's Parish, Louisiana. Collection #165, Howard-Tilton Library, Tulane University. Records of Ante-Bellum Southern Plantations from the Revolution through the Civil War. Series H, Reel 29. Emphasis in original.

64. Rees to unidentified correspondent, July 16, 1820, David Rees Papers.

65. Advertisement, November 4, 1820, David Rees Papers.

66. For other examples of the porous boundary between slaveholding and slave trading, see Michael Tadman, "The Hidden History of Slave Trading in Antebellum South Carolina: John Springs III and Other 'Gentlemen Dealing in Slaves,' " *South Carolina Historical Magazine* 97 (January 1996): 6–29.

67. For variations on this theme, see Douglas Egerton, "Markets Without a Market

Revolution: Southern Planters and Capitalism," *Journal of the Early Republic* 16 (Summer 1996): 207–221; Eugene Genovese and Elizabeth Fox-Genovese, *Fruits of Merchant Capital: Slavery and Bourgeois Property in the Rise and Expansion of Capitalism* (New York: Oxford University Press, 1983); Philip McMichael, "Bringing Circulation Back into Agricultural Political Economy: Analyzing the Antebellum Plantation in Its World Market Context," *Rural Sociology* 52, no 2 (Summer 1987): 242–261. In his work on the Angolan slave trade, Joseph Miller has demonstrated the myriad ways that international merchant capital can penetrate and transform local relations of production and exchange without necessarily introducing capitalist social relations. Joseph Miller, *Way of Death: Merchant Capitalism and the Angolan Slave Trade, 1730–1830* (Madison: University of Wisconsin Press, 1988).

68. On credit relations and the sale of slaves, see Richard Holcombe Kilbourne Jr., *Debt, Investment, Slaves: Credit Relations in East Feliciana Parish, Louisiana 1825–1885* (Tuscaloosa: University of Alabama Press, 1995), 49–74; Thomas Morris, " 'Society Is Not Marked by Punctuality in the Payment of Debts': The Chattel Mortgage of Slaves," in *Ambivalent Legacy: A Legal History of the South*, ed. David J. Bodenhamer and James W. Ely (Jackson: University of Mississippi Press, 1984), 147–170; Thomas D. Russell, "Sale Day in Antebellum South Carolina: Slavery, Law, Economy, and Court-Supervised Sales" (Ph.D. diss., Stanford University, 1993).

69. John Palfrey to Messrs. Chew and Relf, Atakapas, April 15, 1812, in Palfrey Family Papers (William T. Palfrey), 1776–1918, St. Mary and St. Martin Parishes, Louisiana. Selections from Louisiana State University. Records of Ante-Bellum Southern Plantations from the Revolution through the Civil War. Series I, pt. 1, reel 1.

70. Robert Butler to Thomas Butler, November 12, 1808. Folder 4, box 2, Butler Family Papers, Mss 1026, Hill Memorial Library, Louisiana State University.

71. Eugene Genovese, " 'Our Family, Black and White': Family and Household in the Southern Slaveholders' World View," in *In Joy and in Sorrow: Women, Family, and Marriage in the Victorian South, 1830–1900*, ed. Carol Bleser (New York: Oxford University Press, 1991), 69–87.

3

"We'm Fus' Rate Bargain"

Value, Labor, and Price in a Georgia Slave Community

DAINA RAMEY BERRY

In 1859, while standing on the auction block, a slave named Elisha pleaded with potential buyers to purchase his family as one unit. Each time prospective buyers approached, he encouraged them to buy his wife Molly, son Israel, and three-year-old daughter Sevanda ("Vardy"). "Look at me, Mas'r," he claimed, "am prime rice planter; sho' you won't find a better man den me; no better on de whole plantation." Elisha continued promoting himself, assuring potential buyers that he was "not a bit old yet" and that he could "do carpenter work, too." In the same breath, he spoke for his wife, Molly, claiming that she was a "fus' rate rice hand; mos as good as me." Then he instructed her to step forward so that they could inspect her. "Stan' out yer, Molly," he requested, "and let the gen'lm'n see. . . . Show mas'r yer arm . . . she do a heap of work mo' with dat arm yet. . . . Let good Mas'r see yer teeth, Molly . . . teeth all reg'lar, all good—she'm young gal yet." After Elisha presented his children, he gave one final plea: "Better buy us, Mas'r, we'm fus' rate bargain."[1]

Slaves such as Elisha developed a keen understanding of their value, going to great lengths to negotiate their sale in such a way as to maintain family ties. They understood the importance of the monetary value assigned to them and used this knowledge to persuade buyers to purchase their entire families. Some boasted about their muscular physique, while others assured interested parties that a long-term investment in them would bring quality offspring in the future. Yet beneath the bargaining and sometimes begging, a slave's primary objective was to maintain familial ties. This family went to the auction block on March 2 and 3, 1859, in Savannah, Georgia, when their owner, Major Pierce Butler, had to sell all 429 slaves to settle his debts. According to several accounts, this auction represented the "largest sale of human chattels" in American history.[2] Although Elisha's testimony is unusual, the details of this sale provide compelling information regarding the role of price, gender, and skill among U.S. slaves.[3]

Scholars agree that slavery was an economic institution that utilized human chattels as property. This system placed values on nearly everything from plantation tools, silverware, furniture, linen, and livestock to slaves. In addition to purely economic aspects of slavery, the system had important social implications as well. It is difficult to examine slave sales without acknowledging that a human being was being poked, fondled, bartered, traded, or sold to the highest bidder. Herein lies the social aspect of slave prices, auctions, and ultimately sales. Studying slave prices from the perspectives of both slave and master makes it possible to personalize the story behind the numbers. Although planters and traders considered age, sex, health, temperament, and skill, among other factors, in determining slave prices, it is clear that the priority of those being sold was to keep their family units intact. Slaves such as Elisha, who actively participated in their sale, sought to avoid physical separation from loved ones because family represented the primary source of emotional, material, and physical stability.

This study explores slave prices on eight plantations in Glynn County, Georgia, during the years 1830, 1841, and 1859. The primary purpose is to create an economic and social perspective on slave prices. In order to accomplish this, a wide variety of primary documents — estate inventories, bills of sale, census records, newspaper advertisements, slave narratives, and letters — have been examined. This research is unique because of its original data set and its strategy of encompassing economic, social, and gendered aspects of slavery. The goal of this study is twofold: to determine how planters priced their slaves and to explore slaves' interpretation of their own values and sales. More specifically, it attempts to answer the following questions: What factors did planters consider when pricing their slaves? Were slaves aware of their monetary value? Did age, gender, and plantation have an impact on a slave's value? Or did planters consider strength, skill, and sickness the primary determinants? By analyzing a handful of plantations in one community, this study uses statistical tests on quantitative data to determine the "peculiar" monetary value of slaves within the plantation economy of low country Georgia. It also reinforces the traditional analysis of more narrative texts.

Historical Context: The Emergence of Slave Prices

The questions regarding a slave's value and the profitability of the institution are not new ones. Scholars expressed an interest in slave prices as early as the first decade of the twentieth century and continue to study this subject today. A careful review of the literature indicates that most discussions of slave prices and value appeared in the context of three larger issues: the slave trade including international, domestic, regional, and local markets; the economic profitability or rationality of slaveholding; and the expansion of slavery into new territories. Some studies explored all three issues, whereas others focused on one in great detail. In the first instance, the literature on the slave trade often addressed the value of slaves. This literature suggests that price fluctuations occurred when the markets shifted owing to legal restrictions, to increases in the supply of or demand for additional workers, or to labor specialization.[4] The recent work of Edward Baptist, however, brilliantly moves this discussion to explore issues of rape and commodification in the domestic trade, a direction that will certainly change the way scholars think about slave trading in the United States.[5] Those interested in the economic profitability and rationality of slaveholding often compare slave prices to the amount invested to care for each slave or, as Robert Fogel and Stanley Engerman term it, "the rate of return on an investment in slaves."[6] Studies of the expansion of slavery into new territories draw comparisons between buying and selling states, slave breeding, and whether territorial expansion was a solution for planters.[7] The historian Walter Johnson adds to this discussion in his recent study of Louisiana slave markets by claiming that the trade represented the institution of slavery as a whole.[8]

The fact that discussions of slave prices are embedded in historical literature focused on larger contexts and themes suggests that internal and external factors affected planters' decisions about the value of their laborers. Several studies focus solely on prime males and skilled artisans between the ages of eighteen and thirty, and many altogether overlook price patterns for females (with the exception of Baptist's and Johnson's work). Gender bias is not the only shortcoming in the literature, because age distinctions were not always clear, either. Part of this problem rests largely on planters because many did not specify the age of their workers; thus historians are not solely at fault for this omission. Some inventories and bills of sale do identify slaves as "man," "woman," "boy," or "girl," making it difficult to discern the importance of age. Finally, with the exception of Baptist and Johnson, few scholars have explored the impact of slave sales on the slaves themselves, in particular, females.[9] The present study seeks to address the shortcomings in the literature by adding slave testimonies to a statistical analysis of data concerning slaves who were appraised and sold in Georgia during the thirty years prior to the Civil War.

Anatomy of a Sale: Evidence of Slave Prices

Evidence of slave prices appears in a variety of extant documents. Some of the more complete sources include bills of sale, estate inventories, newspaper advertisements, wills, diaries, and personal letters. Bills of sale represent the actual price of an individual slave or group. They were not always formal. Some bills of sale contained a short handwritten note between a buyer and seller that confirmed the transaction.[10] Others administered in court proceedings were much more formal transactions.[11] Estate inventories, on the other hand, contain lists with data about the human workforce ranging from birth and death dates to physical characteristics. Some planters kept meticulous records of their slaves, listing their names, ages, sexes, skills, and appraised values. Others listed them in family groupings with an overall price for the family unit. The appraised price of slaves, however, did not always reflect the amount an owner received for his or her slave.[12]

Although bills of sale and estate inventories serve as excellent sources for an examination of slave prices, newspaper advertisements, letters, and wills provide useful documentation as well. Local newspapers in cities with large slave markets, such as Savannah, New Orleans, and Charleston, were rich with notices of upcoming sales. In a Savannah newspaper, J. Bryan, a prominent auctioneer, announced the sale of "138 Negroes, Accustomed to the Culture of Rice," which took place from 15 to 20 January 1860.[13] This descriptive list contained the names, ages, and field rates for each slave as well as remarks about them. Field rates represented appraised values or classifications of work ranging from quarter hands to full hands (rate 1). Rate increments increased by quarters and created four different categories of workers (quarter, half, three-quarter, and full). Remarks included information about health, skill, and temperament. Bryan also indicated familial relationships by listing slaves in family groupings. One family included Jimmy the slave driver, whom he described as a full hand, "strong, prime and tall, ploughman." Jimmy's wife, Fatima, also rated as a full hand, was described as a "hearty prime woman." Jimmy and Fatima had two "fine" children, Tira and Cain. According to handwritten notes, it is inferred that this family sold for $2,340.[14]

Other slave families on this list had specific skills worth noting in the "remarks" column. Janvier, a fifty-seven-year-old male half hand, was described as a "Fair Carpenter — House builder — Hearty old man," while his wife, Hannah, aged forty-eight and also a half hand, appeared as "Delicate, but well disposed—good for light work." They had six children. Handwritten notes suggest that the entire family cost $5,175.[15] Although the fate of these two families and the other slaves described in this advertisement is unknown, their ages, health, family ties, and skills are clearly depicted. The prices handwritten in the margins, however, do not necessarily reflect the amount each family cost.[16] These figures could be the notes of a potential buyer computing what he or she would pay for the described slaves or it could be the appraised value of these families. Without confirmation it is difficult to determine whether these figures were representative of actual slave prices. The records of planters in Glynn County, Georgia, offer more complete evidence of appraised slave prices.

Data: An Economic Perspective

Slave prices occupy a central place in the estate records of planters and their correspondence with relatives and friends in Glynn County. This coastal community was approximately fifty-eight miles south of Savannah and contained a harbor in the city of Brunswick. Although trade took place here during the antebellum era, most slave owners went to Savannah, Augusta, or Charleston to trade their human property. Glynn County also contains St. Simons and Jekyll Island, the former the home of several prominent slaveholders. The data set used in the current study relies on the estate inventories of eight plantations: six from 1830, one from 1841, and one from 1859. The name, age, estate, and price of 1,046 slaves were examined to determine how planters placed values on human property (see table 3.1). Using a stepwise regression model, with price as the dependant variable and sex, age, estate, and rate as independent variables, this study first generated the statistical significance of these variables. Other variables in the sample include the field rates of 437 slaves listed on four of the eight plantations, sex, determined by the author based on nineteenth-century slave naming patterns, and occasional references to a slave's physical condition. Of the 1,046 slaves in the sample, 526 (50.3 percent) were female, 477 (45.6 percent) were male, and 43 (4.1 percent) were of indeterminate sex.[17]

Results: Slave Price Patterns in Glynn County

Statistical tests demonstrate that these variables (rate, age, estate, and price) were statistically significant at the .001-level and that together they determined 52 percent of a slave's price (see tables 3.2 and 3.3). Rate, which

Table 3.1. Data Set for Glynn County Slave Plantations

Estate	Estate Name	Owner	Year	Slaves	Rate System Used	Age[a]	Price[a]
1	Cabbage Bluff	James Hamilton	1830	101	Yes	27.4	$312.23
2	Hamilton	James Hamilton Couper	1830	125	Yes	24.35	$305.28
3	Harrington Hall	Raymond Demere	1830	85	No	27.65	$275.00
4	Hopeton	James Hamilton	1830	390	Yes	26.24	$307.38
5	Kelvin Grove	Benjamin F. Cater	1841	90	No	23.54	$352.00
6	Mulberry Grove	John, Lewis, & Paul Demere	1830	89	No	24.50	$280.90
7	Noddings Point	James Hamilton	1830	37	Yes	33.68	$253.65
8	Retreat	Anna Matilda Page King, wife of Thomas Butler King	1859	129	No	20.60	$612.80

[a]Based on an average of all slaves on the estate.

slave owners calculated using an external judgment of the amount of work an individual could perform, accounted for the greatest amount of variance (26.5 percent). The best workers received a rate of 1, which indicated a "full-hand" or "A-1 prime slave." Sex accounted for the least amount of variance according to this sample, suggesting that planters made little or no distinction between males and females in terms of their appraised values and work assignments. A bivariate regression on sex with price as the dependent variable, however, demonstrates that sex is statistically significant ($p = .004$) but only accounts for a variance of 1 percent.

Looking at a stepwise regression for estates 5 and 8 using age, estate, and sex as the independent variables demonstrates that sex was not a statistically significant predictor of price ($p = .993$) for the estates with data from the years 1841 and 1859. The age and estate, however, determined 23 percent of a slave's price according to this test (see tables 3.4 and 3.5). The fact that sex accounted for a minimal amount of variance in the first analysis and was not a statistically significant predictor in the second speaks volumes to the discussion of gender and slavery in this county. Sex was not a predictor of price unless rate was omitted from the regression. But whether slaves were male or female only represented a small percentage of planters' decisions about the value of their workforce. Apparently, Glynn County planters were more concerned with the amount of work a slave performed than with maintaining the nineteenth-century gender conventions operating in the dominant society. Such observations encourage further studies on the role of gender in slave

Table 3.2. Regression for 1830 Estates

Mode l	R	R^2	Adjusted R^2	Std. Error of the Estimate
1	0.514[a]	0.265	0.263	82.6559
2	0.667[b]	0.445	0.442	71.9028
3	0.704[c]	0.496	0.493	68.5804
4	0.722[d]	0.521	0.517	66.9444

[a]Predictors: (Constant), rate; [b]Predictors: (Constant), rate, age; [c]Predictors: (Constant), rate, age, estate; [d]Predictors: (Constant), rate, age, estate, sex.

Table 3.3. Analysis of Variance — 1830 Estates

Mode l		Sum of Squares	df	Mean Square	F	Sig.
1	Regression	1072319	1	1072318.833	156.955	0.000[a]
	Residual	2978751	436	6831.997		
	Total	4051069	437			
2	Regression	1802116	2	901058.200	174.286	0.000[b]
	Residual	2248953	435	5170.007		
	Total	4051069	437			
3	Regression	2009847	3	669949.046	142.443	0.000[c]
	Residual	2041222	434	4703.277		
	Total	4051069	437			
4	Regression	2110556	4	527639.106	117.736	0.000[d]
	Residual	1940513	433	4481.554		
	Total	4051069	437			

Note: Price-dependent variable.

[a]Predictors: (Constant), rate; [b]Predictors: (Constant), rate, age; [c]Predictors: (Constant), rate, age, estate; [d]Predictors: (Constant), rate, age, estate, sex.

communities, research that would focus on various contributions to the plantation regime.[18]

Although an economic analysis of slave prices indicates that sex did not matter, an examination of individual plantations tells a different story. General findings for slave prices based on age categories in increments of ten years illustrate that enslaved females carried higher prices than did males on some estates until the age of thirty. Four of the estates — Kelvin Grove, Mulberry

Table 3.4. Regression for Kelvin Grove (1841) and Retreat (1859)

Model	R	R^2	Adjusted R^2	Std. Error of the Estimate
1	0.418[a]	0.174	0.171	277.9328
2	0.479[b]	0.230	0.222	269.1344

[a]Predictors: (Constant), estate; [b]Predictors: (Constant), estate, age.

Grove, Noddings Point, and Retreat — show age groups in which females carried higher prices than did males in the same age group. Data from these four plantations confirm this finding for those aged twenty and under. Perhaps women received higher values because of their unique skills or because of their capacity to give birth. Regardless of the reason, these trends had an impact on those in bondage. Awareness of this would have given females leverage or power within the hierarchy on their respective plantations. On Mulberry Grove Plantation, Sally, age four, received the value of $400, whereas most other slaves under ten (male or female) rarely exceeded $250.[19] Why did Sally have a high value at such a young age? It could not have been because of her reproductive capacity, but perhaps she was the offspring of two prime workers and the owner justified this value based on the productivity and strength of her parents. Likewise, Sally may have displayed special skills or strength compared to others in her age group. Whatever the case, one thing is certain: Sally received an exceptionally high value for her cohort. Similar patterns occurred on the Noddings Point and Retreat Plantations. Fansey, a twenty-six-year-old woman at Noddings Point, carried a higher price than did males in her cohort.[20] Enslaved women on Retreat also claimed higher values during childbearing years (defined as ages sixteen to thirty), but because these are such small samples further investigation in the records of other plantation regions is required to confirm these patterns.[21]

Since rate, age, estate, and sex in this sample account for only 52 percent of the variance in slave pricing, it is clear that planters had other concerns beyond these variables. It is safe to assume that health, temperament, and physical attributes such as those Elisha described on the auction block represent important variables. Planters did not provide data about these factors in their records, however, so this requires some speculation and additional research. The data, particularly for the estates with rate information, reveal obvious trends relating to slave prices.

Rates were given to slaves beginning at age twelve and ending around age sixty with the exception of a few cases. Jeffrey of Hopeton Plantation was only

Table 3.5. Analysis of Variance—Kelvin Grove and Retreat Plantations

Mode I		Sum of Squares	df	Mean Square	F	Sig.
1	Regression	3459551	1	3459550.986	44.786	.000[a]
	Residual	1.6E + 07	212	77246.663		
	Total	2.0E + 07	213			
2	Regression	4552413	2	2276206.590	31.425	.000[b]
	Residual	1.5E + 07	211	72433.319		
	Total	2.0E + 07	213			

Note: Price-dependent variable.

[a]Predictors: (Constant), estate; [b]Predictors: (Constant), estate, age.

ten years old, rated as a three-quarter hand, and valued at $350. No other slaves under age twelve, male or female, received rates. Ironically, the oldest slave with a rate, Martin, also resided at Hopeton. At age sixty-seven he appeared on the list as a three-quarter hand worth $350, the same price as Jeffrey.[22] Rates were not assigned to other slaves in their sixties with the exceptions of Jack and Lewis of Noddings Point, who were sixty-five and sixty-two, respectively. Jack was rated a three-quarter hand worth $200, and Lewis a quarter hand, was valued at $100.[23] That these slaves had rates whether they were age ten or in their late sixties indicates that the planters' focus was on the physical capabilities of their slaves rather than their ages. One cannot make a direct correlation between the value of slaves and their ages, because physical strength and skill clearly played a role in determining their value.

Yet some planters questioned and commented on the physical ability or inability of slaves relative to their rates. Diana, advertised in a Savannah newspaper, was a forty-six-year-old three-quarter hand. The remarks next to her name indicate that she may have been feigning an illness to avoid being sold: "Complaining, *but looks* well."[24] Molly, a female slave auctioned from the Butler estate in 1859, caused quite a stir among potential buyers. When it was her turn to step up on the auction block, the auctioneer announced that "Molly insisted that she was lame in her left foot." The auctioneer was not convinced that this was the case, however, and had a physician examine her. "Molly was put though her paces, and compelled to trot up and down along the stage," the report stated, but her "left foot *would* be lame." The report does not indicate why Molly was "complaining" about her left foot or why she resisted her sale. But one can easily imagine a myriad of reasons she feigned her injury, assuming that she was indeed in good health, as the witnesses suggested. Perhaps Molly had a loved one already sold to another owner and she sought to discourage all other potential masters from purchasing her. Or maybe Molly knew that she could remain with the Butler family if the sale were unsuccessful. She may have feared moving to an unfamiliar plantation community and tried to do all she could to stay in the physical environment to which she had grown accustomed. Many bystanders thought she was "shamming" her injury; Molly sold for $695 that day.[25]

Estates represented in this sample also contain data about health and skill. For example, sixty-year-old John of Mulberry Grove Plantation was listed as having no value, but next to his name the owner wrote "blind," indicating the reason John had no value.[26] Others, such as Cudjo, a forty-five-year-old male slave driver on Cabbage Bluff Plantation, and Sam, a twenty-five-year-old carpenter listed in the Hamilton estate, received higher prices than did other slaves in their age cohort because they had unique skills.[27] Men were not the only ones with special skills. Among the women at Kelvin Grove, Mary had nursing skills, Chloe served as the estate cook, Peggy had the ability to sew, and Pender served as the plantation housemaid.[28] Again, gender alone was not a significant factor in determining a slave's value.

Social Impact: The Slave's Perspective

Although statistical tests help explain economic trends in planters' decisions about slave values, bondmen and bondwomen had different thoughts about their worth. Many former slaves recalled their experiences on the auction block and commented on their separation from family members. They did whatever they could to discourage potential buyers from dividing their families. To them, family represented the ultimate survival mechanism because relatives helped each other cope with the hardships of slavery. The term "family" is used here to describe persons related by conjugal, consanguine, fictive, abroad (off-plantation), extended, or polygamous connections. By examining the social impact of slave prices and sales on family unity, this study moves beyond prices to identify the effects of placing a monetary value on a human life.

Slave testimonies are replete with commentary about auctions, sales, and prices.[29] Esther Brown, for example, recalled the day she and her six siblings went to "de block": "All of us wuz sold," she explained, and sadly she remembered that "dey wuz all sold off to diffunt parts of de country, and us never heared from 'em no more." Furthermore, Brown could not forget that she was young at the time: "I wuz so little dat when dey bid me off, dey had to hold me up so folkses could see me."[30] Clearly planters sold slaves of all ages and ruined what little emotional, physical, and material stability slaves had by destroying their family ties. Mary Ferguson, another Georgia slave, said she was only thirteen when her master separated her from her family. It was "a day I'll never forget," she avowed. After dinner with her entire family, Ferguson remembered that she felt "lak sumpin was gwineter hapin'. . . . O, I never has forgot dat last dinner wit my folks" she recalled, and when the speculators came to take her away she "c'menced [to] cryin' an' beggin'," but that did not prevent the sale and separation. Sadly, she stated, "I ain't never seed nor heared tell o' my Ma an' Paw, an' bruthers, an' susters from dat day to dis."[31] Ferguson may have found other slave adults at a new plantation who provided some of the affection and support she once received from her biological mother and father; however, "none would be the parents or relatives from whom market transactions had separated" her.[32]

Slave sales such as those described by Brown and Ferguson were quite common during the antebellum era. Their experiences of separation differed only in that Brown went to the auction block and Ferguson was literally taken from her family's cabin. The 1859 Butler Plantation sale provides probably the best description of a slave auction in U.S. history. A reporter from the *New York Tribune* who attended the auction wrote about the event in great detail and, although some historians question the accuracy of his report, it serves as a good portrait of slave sales because of its detail.[33] It took days to transport the 429 slaves to Savannah from McIntosh and Glynn Counties, and when they arrived the auctioneer placed them in horse stables at the Ten Broeck racecourse.[34] Prospective buyers had the opportunity to view the slaves for several days prior to the sale. The *Tribune* writer described the scene: "The Negroes were examined with as little consideration as if they had been brutes indeed; the buyers pulling their mouths open to see their teeth, pinching their limbs to find how muscular they were, walking them up and down to detect any signs of lameness, making them stoop and bend in different ways that they might be certain there was no concealed rupture or wound; and in addition to all this treatment, asking them scores of questions relative to their qualifications and accomplishments."[35]

One woman named Sally caught the attention of a few bystanders. A man interested in her noted that she was the wife of "shoemaker Bill." As he examined her and noticed that she was a "big strapping gal and can do a heap o'work," he decided to pass and move on to the next slave because Major Butler said, "It's been five years since she had any children."[36] This suggests that some planters valued female slaves for their reproductive ability. Yet the capacity to bear children added to the constraints of female slavery in ways unknown to males.

The story of Daphney exemplifies one of the challenges faced by enslaved women. Along with her husband, Primus, and their three-year-old daughter Dido, Daphney stepped up to the auction block amidst a small controversy. Apparently Daphney had wrapped herself in a blanket, which prevented potential buyers from administering a thorough examination of her limbs. "What's the matter with that gal? Has she got a headache?" one person asked. "Who is going to bid on that nigger, if you keep her covered up?" another added. But when they took the blanket off, the bidders were surprised to find a three-week-old infant concealed in her bosom. Writing about this incident, the *Tribune* reporter made an appeal to female readers. "Since her confinement," he noted, "Daphney had traveled from the plantation to Savannah, where she had been kept in a shed for six days. On the sixth or seventh day after her sickness, she had left her bed, taken a railroad journey across the country to the shambles, was there exposed for six days to the questionings and insults of the Negro speculators, and then on the fifteenth day after her confinement was put up on the block, with her husband and her other child, and with her newborn baby in her arms, sold to the highest bidder."[37] This family sold for $625 each, a total of $2,500.[38]

Although some slaves, like Daphney, tried to conceal their offspring, other slaves employed different methods to stay together. Several sources reported that slave families involved in this sale were to remain together, but it is difficult to ascertain whether the motivation behind this claim was political. One might argue that the goal to keep families intact at this sale represented a political strategy to minimize the appearance of inhumanity at such auctions. Although others might appreciate this historical interpretation because it encourages scholars to focus on the "good" in planters and traders rather than the "evil," this study, along with the work of Baptist, acknowledges that more slave families were separated by sale than historians have generally admitted. In other words, the pleading, begging, and crying by slaves to be allowed to stay together rarely resulted in intact families.[39]

Consider the case of Jeffrey and Dorcas, slave partners separated by this sale. Because they were not married, there was no chance that they would be sold as a family. Thus, Jeffrey begged and pleaded with his prospective buyer to purchase them as a unit. "I loves Dorcas, young mas'r; I loves her well an' true," he began, hoping that his new master would sympathize with him. Jeffrey then assured him that the two would marry and "be good sarvants." Jeffrey thought about long-term family stability and spoke of his future offspring with Dorcas, claiming, "de chillum will be healthy and strong mas'r and dey'll be good sarvants, too." Like Elisha, Jeffrey began showing off his love's physical strength in one final attempt to encourage his owner to buy her. "Young mas'r, Dorcas prime woman — A 1 woman, sa. Tall gal, sir; long arms, strong, healthy, and can do a heap of work in a day." He even went so far as to place a monetary value on his loved one: "She is one of de best rice hands on de whole plantation; worth $1,200 easy, mas'r, an' fus' rate bargain at that."[40] Playing on the financial interests of potential buyers, Jeffrey did all he could to speak their language by using descriptive words that planters understood so that the two of them could have the same master. Although the prospective buyer seemed touched by his remarks, Jeffrey and Dorcas were sold to different owners the following day. When the two learned of their fate, Jeffrey had "tears streaming down his honest face," while Dorcas sat "motionless as a statue, with her head covered with a shawl."[41]

Conclusions

The findings presented in this study are important for several reasons. They offer an economic portrait of an antebellum slave community from the perspective of the slave. This research also provides a clear view of the value of slaves by analyzing pricing patterns on several plantations in one community. Moreover, it shows that the skill and health of slaves were directly related to price. Addressing this relation clarifies the social and work hierarchy in the slave quarters. Finally, the most significant contribution of this work is that it humanizes the economic study of slavery, particularly by showing that, in addition to planters and traders, slaves (as was the case of Jeffrey and Dorcas) attempted to use their monetary value to persuade prospective buyers to purchase them with their loved ones. Nevertheless, the testimony of Jeffery and Dorcas reinforces what scholars already know — but some are afraid to acknowledge — that slavery was an economic institution and that the laborers were reduced to commodities.

Analyzing prices from plantation records on a micro level for Glynn County, Georgia, from 1830 to 1859 shows clearly the impact prices had on those in bondage. Glynn County planters determined slave prices by considering a slave's age, rate, health, sex, and skill. Statistical tests demonstrate that gender was not as important as some believe. The skill, age, and estate of the slave received more consideration than gender in determining prices. Slave prices were well understood by slaves as well as by plantation owners and traders. Planters' itemization of slaves in records such as estate inventories provide an excellent source for data. From the planters' perspective, the decision to purchase a slave was based on economic interest. But from the slaves' perspective the auction block was approached not only with trepidation and fear but also with overt manipulation and covert strategies to maintain family ties. Slaves knew their value, and they used their knowledge to try to keep relatives and loved ones together. After all, according to Elisha and Jeffrey, purchasing them with their loved ones was indeed a "fus' rate bargain."

Notes

The author thanks Peter Lindert, Gavin Wright, Slynovie and John P. Merchant, Randy Fotiu, Dave Witherspoon, Kimberly Ellis, Jessica Millward, Merrilee Burr, and John Wess Grant for their assistance with data collection, analysis, technical support, and comments. The author also extends heartfelt thanks to the members of the Michigan State University Women's Resource Center Writing Group, Alfiee M. Breland, Sheila M. Contereas, and Karen D. King, and Michigan State University History Department colleagues Anne Meyering, Peter and Erika Beattie, Robert Bonner, Leslie Butler, Kirsten Fermaglich, and Tom Summerhill for their close reading of this study.

1. Philander Doesticks, "Great Auction Sale of Slaves at Savannah, Georgia, March 2nd and 3rd, 1859" (New York, 1859), 10–11.

2. Ibid. See also Frederic Bancroft, *Slave Trading in the Old South* (1931; reprint, Columbia: University of South Carolina Press, 1996), 222–236, and U. B. Phillips, *American Negro Slavery* (1918; reprint, Baton Rouge: Louisiana State University Press, 1994), 374–375.

3. The terms "gender" and "sex" are used throughout this study with different meanings. "Gender" addresses broad social and cultural distinctions between the male and female slave experience, and "sex" refers to biological definitions of male and female used during statistical discussions.

4. See, e.g., Paul E. Lovejoy and David Richardson, "British Abolition and Its Impact on Slave Prices Along the Atlantic Coast of Africa, 1793–1850," *Journal of Economic History* 55, no. 1 (1995): 98–119; Herman Freudenberger and Jonathan B. Pritchett, "The Domestic United States Slave Trade: New Evidence," *Journal of Interdisciplinary History* 21, no. 3(1991): 447–477; Bancroft, *Slave Trading in the Old South;* Lewis Cecil Gray, *History of Agriculture in the Southern United States to 1800,* 2 vols. (Washington, DC: Carnegie Institute, 1933), 663–667; Michael Tadman, *Speculators and Slaves: Masters, Traders, and Slaves in the Old South* (Madison: University of Wisconsin Press, 1989); Peter C. Mancall, Joshua L. Rosenbloom, and Thomas Joseph Weiss, "Slave Prices in the Lower South, 1722–1815," National Bureau of Economic Research Working Paper 120 (Cambridge, Massachusetts, 2000); and Walter Johnson, *Soul by Soul: Life Inside the Antebellum Slave Market* (Cambridge: Harvard University Press, 1999).

5. Edward E. Baptist, "Cuffy," "Fancy Maids," and "One-Eyed Men": Rape, Commodification, and the Domestic Slave Trade in the United States," *American Historical Review* 106, no. 5 (2001): 1619–1650.

6. Robert W. Fogel and Stanley L. Engerman, *Time on the Cross: The Economics of American Negro Slavery* (Boston: Little, Brown, 1974), 67. For other studies on slave profitability, see Alfred H. Conrad and John R. Meyer, *The Economics of Slavery and Other Studies in Econometric History* (Chicago: Aldine Publishing 1964); U. B. Phillips, "The Economic Cost of Slaveholding in the Cotton Belt," *Political Science Quarterly* 20 (June 1905): 257–275; Phillips, *American Negro Slavery;* and Laurence J. Kotlikoff,

"The Structure of Slave Prices in New Orleans, 1804–1862," *Economic Inquiry* 17 (1979): 496–518.

7. See Peter Passell and Gavin Wright, "The Effects of Pre–Civil War Territorial Expansion on the Price of Slaves," *Journal of Political Economy* 80, no. 6 (1972): 1188–1202; Laurence J. Kotlikoff and Sebastian Pinera, "The Old South's Stake in the Inter-Regional Movement of Slaves, 1850–1860," *Journal of Economic History* 37, no. 2 (1977): 434–450; and Richard Sutch, "The Breeding of Slaves for Sale and the Westward Expansion of Slavery, 1850–1860," Southern Economic History Project Working Paper 10 (Berkeley: University of California, 1972).

8. Johnson, *Soul by Soul*.

9. Baptist, "Cuffy." Although Walter Johnson examines slave sales and the impact on the enslaved, Baptist cautions him for placing "emancipatory hopes on a process of marketing" more than "the evidence will bear." Ibid., 1634n41. Agreeing with Baptist, this study seeks to uncover evidence that supports the notion that slaves had little bargaining power, despite their desperate attempts to maintain family ties.

10. The African-American History Association compiled a list of transactions relating to slave sales that is available at the Georgia Archives in Morrow, Georgia, formerly the Georgia Department of Archives and History (GDAH). These documents contain not only descriptive information about the slaves, but they have the names of the buyer and the seller, the price of the slave(s) or slaves, and the location of the transaction. See *Slave Bills of Sale Project* (Atlanta: African-American History Association, 1986).

11. Jane Catterall, *Judicial Cases Concerning American Slavery and the Negro*, 4 vols. (Washington, DC: Carnegie Institution of Washington, 1932).

12. The author wishes to credit Dale Couch of the GDAH for conversations regarding this distinction. See also Malcom Bell Jr., *Major Butler's Legacy: Five Generations of a Slaveholding Family* (Athens: University of Georgia Press, 1987), 325–340.

13. "Descriptive list of 138 NEGROES," J. K. Williams Collection, Coastal Georgia Historical Society, St. Simons Island, Georgia.

14. Ibid. Typically, slaves aged ten and younger did not have rates.

15. Ibid.

16. For the purpose of this study, "price" refers to the appraised value according to the planters' judgment. "Cost" represents that amount a person paid to purchase the slave or slaves.

17. A total of forty-three names in the sample were either illegible or unisex and therefore coded as "unknown." Thus, 96 percent of the names are gender-specific, which leaves a 4 percent margin of error. See Cheryl Cody, "There Was No 'Absalom' on the Ball Plantations: Slave Naming Practices in the South Carolina Low Country, 1720–1865," *American Historical Review* 92, no. 2 (1987): 563–596.

18. For a discussion of historical biases among historians and an examination of female slaves' contributions in one community, see Daina L. Ramey, " 'She Do a Heap of Work': Female Slave Labor on Glynn County Rice and Cotton Plantations," *Georgia Historical Quarterly* 82, no 4 (1998): 707–734.

19. "Lewis, John, & Paul Demere Division of Estate of Raymond Demere," Glynn County Court of Ordinary, Estate Records, Wills, Inventories, and Appraisements, book D, 1810–1843, GDAH.

20. These estimations are based on average male price versus average female price, and in this case, Fansey was the only female in her cohort. The number of males totaled three. "Noddings Point Plantation," Glynn County Court of Ordinary, Estate Records, Wills, Inventories, and Appraisements, book D, 1810–1843, GDAH.

21. "Anna Matilda Page King Will, 7 March 1859," Glynn County Court of Ordinary, Estate Records, Wills, Inventories, and Appraisements, book E, GDAH; "Anna Matilda Page King Estate Inventory," 18 January 1860, William Audley Couper Papers, Southern Historical Collection, University of North Carolina. For further discussion of these trends, see Daina L. Ramey, "'A Place of Our Own': Labor Family and Community among Female Slaves in Piedmont and Tidewater Georgia, 1820–1860" (Ph.D. diss., University of California, 1998).

22. "An Inventory of the Goods & Chattels of James Hamilton at Hopeton Plantation, 1830," Glynn County Court of Ordinary, Estate Records, Wills, Inventories, and Appraisements, book D, 1810–1843, GDAH.

23. "An Inventory of the Goods & Chattels of James Hamilton at Noddings Point Plantation, 1830," Glynn County Court of Ordinary, Estate Records, Wills, Inventories, and Appraisements, book D, 1810–1843, GDAH.

24. "Descriptive List of 138 NEGROES," emphasis added.

25. "Great Auction Sale of Slaves," 26, emphasis in original. See the average price for Retreat slaves in 1859 in table 3.1 for comparison.

26. "Lewis, John, & Paul Demere Division of Estate of Raymond Demere," Glynn County Court of Ordinary, Estate Records, Wills, Inventories, and Appraisements, book D, 1810–1843, GDAH.

27. "An Inventory of the Goods & Chattels of James Hamilton at Cabbage Bluff and Hamilton Plantation, 1830," Glynn County Court of Ordinary, Estate Records, Wills, Inventories, and Appraisements, book D, 1810–1843, GDAH.

28. "Kelvin Grove Plantation Book, January 1, 1853," Margaret Davis Cate Collection, University of Georgia (microfilm).

29. In the 1930s the Works Progress Administration sent a team of interviewers, predominately whites, to various southern regions to interview the last generation of former slaves. These interviews represent one of the few extant sources for slaves' perspectives. Caution must be exercised in using these testimonies, however, because of racial bias evidenced by the questions asked as well as by the dialect and tone of these edited narratives. For a discussion of the strengths and weaknesses of these sources, see John W. Blassingame, ed., *Slave Testimony: Two Centuries of Letters, Speeches, Interviews, and Autobiographies* (Baton Rouge: Louisiana State University Press, 1977), especially the introduction. See also Johnson, *Soul by Soul*, 9–11.

30. George P. Rawick, ed., *The American Slave: A Composite Autobiography*, 26 vols. (1941; reprint, Westport: Greenwood Publishing, 1972), 12:136.

31. Ibid., 12:327.

32. Baptist, "Cuffy," 1636.

33. Bell, *Major Butler's Legacy*, 329–340.

34. Ibid., 329.

35. Doesticks, "Great Auction Sale of Slaves," 10.

36. Ibid., 12.

37. Ibid., 20.

38. Such numbers are similar to those found on the list of 138 slaves advertised in the Savannah newspaper one year later. See "Descriptive List of 138 NEGROES."

39. Baptist, "Cuffy," 1630–1631, especially n. 34.

40. Doesticks, "Great Auction Sale of Slaves," 22–23.

41. Ibid., 24.

4

Slave Resistance, Coffles, and the Debates over Slavery in the Nation's Capital

ROBERT H. GUDMESTAD

She did not know that she would ignite a national debate when she tried to leap to her death from the third floor of George Miller's tavern. Miller's seedy establishment had gained a reputation as the most notorious slave depot in Washington. The woman, known only as Anna, jumped because a slave trader purchased her and two of her children but declined to take their siblings and father. The price she paid for her impulsive action was a broken back and two shattered arms. Her crumpled body, moreover, bore strong testimony to the destructive impact of the interstate slave trade. When asked about the reason for her attempted suicide, Anna explained her deed by simply saying, "I did not want to go." When John Randolph learned of the incident, he rose to his feet in the House of Representatives and blasted the inhuman sale of slaves carried on in the district. In so doing, he cast doubt on the efficacy of the interstate slave trade by closely linking it to abhorrent activities and results. It was the first direct denunciation of the interstate slave trade in Congress. Randolph pointed a finger of scorn toward an issue that most others, southerners as well as northerners, would rather avoid or ignore.[1]

The Virginia representative began by pointing to events that were happening under the very noses of his colleagues. Not even on the rivers of Africa, he contended, was such a sin committed before God and man. At least the African trade plucked "savages" from their native wilds, rather than "tearing the civilized, informed negro, habituated to cultivated life" from his family.

Lest slaveowners become concerned that Randolph was going to propose drastic measures, he clearly distinguished between the movement of slaves as a natural consequence of ownership and a systematic slave market. The former was not offensive to Randolph, and he thought the government had no business meddling with it; the latter, though, was indeed offensive, and Randolph thought something should be done to rectify the situation. That Washington had become a depot for the nefarious traffic was regrettable. He was mortified when a high-ranking foreigner told him that even though America called itself the land of the free, the workings of the slave trade caused Europeans to be "horrorstruck and disgusted."[2]

Randolph sounded almost like an abolitionist when he described "hard-hearted masters" who sold slaves for pecuniary gain. Employing a technique that would eventually become standard fare with antislavery advocates, he used an emotional plea depicting the struggles of a few heroic slaves as a way to appeal to the finer senses of his listeners. Randolph told the story of a slave who had saved enough money to purchase the freedom of his wife and child. When the man died, his master sold the family anyway, contrary to the standards of decent society. This and other stories put a human face on a trade that treated its subjects as commodities. By ignoring abstract arguments and dwelling on concrete examples, Randolph hoped to prod the House into taking some type of action to prevent the worst abuses of slavery within Washington. At the end of his long diatribe, he moved that the Committee for the District of Columbia devise a speedy means to stop the lawful trading of slaves in the district. If the House declined to act, Randolph, with his characteristic bluster, threatened to undertake the business himself "and ferret out of their holes and corners the villains who carried it on."

Randolph's speech, the subsequent congressional investigation, and further debates on Capitol Hill demonstrate how the slave trade was working its way into the national consciousness. As speculation progressed from its inchoate nature into something more complex, it posed numerous problems for many southerners. They began to struggle with how to reconcile the negative consequences of slave trading with the necessity of its existence. Speculation posed difficult questions concerning property rights in slaves, caused debate about whether there was any legitimate distinction between an owner migrating with slaves or a speculator transporting them, and even raised issues about the nature of slavery itself. Politicians and other thoughtful southerners grappled with these issues. The end result was frustration, confusion, and no solid answers.

Northerners, too, were becoming aware of the interstate slave trade's importance to the young nation. Public officials from free states who came to Washington often encountered slavery for the first time. Such contact might be relatively benign: servants, waiters, or footmen. It might also be harsh: ragged clothing, bare feet, or coffles. The grim sight of bondspeople and the heroic acts of resistance by individual slaves helped some northern congressmen break free from the tight grip of racism. They could envision slaves not as property to be exploited but as people to be free.[3]

The debate that began on the street below Miller's tavern indicates the intellectual and ideological distances that many Americans had traveled between the closure of the international slave trade and rise of the internal one. Almost a decade earlier, Randolph had fought desperately to increase the tonnage requirement for the ships that carried slaves in the coastwise trade. His argument was based on a keen desire to prevent the federal government from limiting the authority of masters over their slaves. He wanted no controls placed on slavery or the slaveholder. Randolph's ravings helped win him the reputation as one of the South's foremost defenders of slavery. Now, in 1816, he was asking Congress to end the slave trade in the District of Columbia, a far more drastic step than limiting the tonnage of ships engaged in the coastwise trade. Randolph was doing the very thing he earlier had opposed: asking for controls on the activities and behavior of masters. He was acutely aware that he might be opening a Pandora's box of federal legislation and hastened to explain his about-face. This new policy did not interfere in "the contract between the owner and his slave," he intoned, and he pointed out his previous efforts to preserve that relationship. The irascible Virginian went on to explain that the unique status of the district justified an exception to his usual pleas for federal noninterference.

Randolph's new line of reasoning makes sense only in light of previous federal policy regarding the ownership and sale of slaves in Washington. The district was under direct control of the federal government, and in 1794 Congress asserted its authority over the sale of slaves in Washington. The resulting statute prevented the exchange of bondservants from Virginia and Maryland within the city limits. Eighteen years later Congress amended this law and allowed Alexandria residents to take slaves into the district. Residents of Washington still could not enter Alexandria to buy slaves in order to bring them back to the district to sell or reside. The intended effect of the amendment was to prevent the sale of slaves in the capital. As a consequence, most of the transactions for the purchase or sale of slaves took place in Alexandria, usually in private jails. Some traders, however, temporarily housed slaves in Washington's taverns or small hotels on the outskirts of town. The nation's capital became a depot for the exhibition of slaves rather than a market, with the large speculators of the 1820s operating out of Alexandria or Baltimore. The perception, however, was that the District of Columbia had a thriving slave trade because of the coffles that marched through the city and because of taverns like George Miller's.[4]

The oversight of commerce within federal territory was, in Randolph's mind, a different matter from regulation of trade between the states. The federal nature of the district set it apart, and Randolph did not ask for regulation of the trade outside of Washington. He shrank from full interference with the trade but wanted to find a moderate solution for a public eyesore. His rhetoric, however, does much to reveal his frame of mind. Randolph referred to a "crying sin before God and man" that separated slave families and drove them through the streets like "beasts." The increased visibility of the interstate slave trade, its obvious brutality, and the vehement reactions of bondservants gave Randolph reason to pause. He had no desire to abolish slavery or impair the rights of masters, but he did see the worst side of slavery and wanted to remove the most odious aspects of the peculiar institution. Randolph was no abolitionist and was not intending to create a groundswell for the institution's destruction. Instead, he wanted to strengthen slavery. The best way to preserve the institution, he felt, was to reform it so that its opponents would have no room for criticism. Randolph was sensitive to the South's reputation, as is obvious from his reference to the foreigner's stinging remark. He also had a regard for the treatment of the slaves themselves, seeing them not as brutes but as humans who needed the protection of the federal government. Randolph's proposal, according to his line of thought, was good for the master and the slave. He sought to domesticate domestic slavery.[5]

Randolph's colleagues met his proposal with blank stares and a general sense of apathy. The interstate slave trade was simply an issue that most Americans did not want to confront. Northerners remained mute on the issue, and southerners had little more to say. If northerners wanted to pounce on slavery, now was their chance. If southerners felt compelled to defend the peculiar institution, they had an excuse. Robert Wright of Maryland broke the silence and weakly protested that the laws concerning the trade were sufficient. Referring to the War of 1812, he said that Europeans practiced a worse type of slavery when they impressed sailors, so there was no reason to draw attention to the interstate slave trade. He tried to bury the issue by diverting attention to a noncontroversial topic. Fellow Maryland representative Charles Goldsborough agreed with Randolph's assessment and noted that he, too, had seen coffles in Washington's streets. Goldsborough did not want to limit the trade, though, and observed that laws would be of no value in arresting the trade because they would not be enforced. He advocated doing nothing. When Henry St. George Tucker of Virginia suggested that a select committee would be the best method for addressing the situation, the House readily complied.[6]

After spending two months gathering information, the committee turned over its evidence to the House. Southerners filled four of the five positions on the committee, and they were able to dictate the results to their liking. The report detailed numerous abuses associated with the interstate slave trade. It described the typical slave pen in the area as a "dungeon" in which slaves were "confined in their filth." The report also singled out the "atrocious" kidnapping of free persons. Such strong descriptions, however, had virtually no effect. Committee members rejected federal action to deal with the situation. The final report recommended that state authorities deal with the problem, thus precluding any changes in the District. That was a convenient way to dodge the situation, since neither Virginia nor Maryland had direct jurisdiction over Washington. It was also a suggestion that fit well with the traditional southern preference for state authority instead of federal control. The final copy even struck out the word "commerce" in describing the trade and substituted "traffic" in its place. Although this may have been an attempt to portray the trade negatively, it is more likely that it was meant to circumvent the wording in the Constitution that allowed Congress to regulate interstate commerce. The report, however, was not shared with the entire House; it was ordered to lie on the table just before Congress adjourned. The House did not want to take on the seemingly unimportant issue of the interstate slave trade, and most members were content to let the matter die. Although there was a vague sentiment against the trade and a slight impulse to reform it, there was not enough of a commitment to actually do anything. Despite its recent growth, the interstate trade was more of a minor irritant to the congressmen than anything else.[7]

Even though Randolph's tirade led to no specific action, this incident reveals how southerners were grappling with the implications of a growing interstate slave in the early republic. It is significant that the first direct attack on speculation in the Capitol had come not from a northerner but from a southerner, and one who had a solid reputation as a defender of slavery. Another southerner supported his opinion. This examination of the slave trade also stemmed from the Upper South, while the Lower South remained silent on the issue. Southern members did not defend the trade, justify it, or shift the blame onto the back of the slave trader, as they would do later. Just as important, northern members refused to attack the trade as emblematic of the harsh state of slavery in the South or call for an immediate end to slave trading and the abolition of slavery in the District of Columbia. In a few short years, northerners would use the slave trade as the "door to the slave Bastille" because of its effectiveness in illustrating slavery's evil consequences. In 1816 discussions about the slave trade generated no light and no heat. It was not yet a part of the national debate on slavery and hardly entered into most people's consciousness. The trade was still growing in strength and had not reached the point where it caused trouble for southerners.[8]

Despite this slowness to recognize the immense importance of the interstate slave trade, southerners were beginning to realize that it posed a problem when considering the property rights of slaveholders. Randolph wanted the federal government to regulate the movement and sale of slaves in Washington in order to render slavery more benign. He desired an end to abuses associated with bondage. In doing so, however, he had to acknowledge that the interstate slave trade treated slaves as commodities by means of speculation. This assumption presented two major problems for southerners. It turned the traditional southern presumption about slaveholding on its head by denying that an organic relationship existed between master and slave. An effective way to explain away the exploitative nature of slavery was to assume blithely that masters cared for slaves and looked out for their best interest. Masters could rest easy with slavery if they could convince themselves that their slaves received food, clothing, and shelter in return for their labor. A public and thriving interstate slave trade contradicted this assumption. If slave traders were increasing in number, then many slaveholders must be resorting to speculation and were thus not acting in a way that preserved the master-slave relationship. Such owners had then denied the fundamental premise that allowed them to support and maintain the peculiar institution. Instead of being kind and generous they were cruel and exploitative. Another problem involved the debate about whether the slave trade was a form of commerce. Randolph did not specifically assert that it was, but the implications of his thinking were clear and held out the specter of federal intervention. Article I, section 8 of the Constitution gives Congress the power to regulate interstate commerce. Should the interstate slave trade become widely known as such, it would create an easy argument for federal oversight. Slaveholders, always concerned to maintain as absolute power as possible over their slaves, would hardly consent to such a scenario. Their most common rebuttal of this idea was to minimize the volume of the interstate slave trade. Since it was minimal, they asserted, there was no need to monitor speculation. Southerners emphasized the migration of slaves, rather than the forced speculation. That mind-set fit comfortably with the concomitant emphasis on the benevolent aspects of slavery. If the interstate slave trade was minimal, then there was no apparent reason to examine the philosophical underpinnings of the peculiar institution.[9]

It was the jarring actions of some determined slaves and the growth of the interstate slave trade that continually brought the subject to the surface. In the fifteen years or so after the War of 1812 bondspeople shaped the nature of the public debate about slavery. Their bravery in the face of crushing dehumanization injected a new element into the scene — the idea that they were not merely property and deserved a better life. Slaves, of course, had always resisted their situation in one form or another. Speculation, however, created conditions under which slaves were more likely to resist servitude because it generated intense emotional reactions in the bondservants. Slave traders, with an eye for profit, used highly selective purchasing practices and tended to buy younger slaves. Such practices may have been necessary for profitability, but they were destructive of marriages and families. It is estimated that in the nineteenth century more than half of all the slaves in the Upper South were separated from a parent or child because of forced migration. The slave John Brown, for instance, remembered how his mother begged the speculator to let her kiss her son one last time. Charles Ball's last memory of his mother was her sobbing and beating the shoulders of the speculator who had just purchased him. The sundering of child from parent was just the start. Forcible separation also destroyed approximately one-third of all slave marriages in the Upper South. For Moses Grandy, the slave trade ruined his life. He tried to speak to his wife while a speculator carried her away, but the trader used a pistol to keep Grandy at a distance. Grandy later confided that he could have said very little anyway because his heart was broken. "I have never seen or heard from her from that day to this," he lamented. "I loved her as I love my life."[10]

The interstate slave trade had a shattering impact on bondspeople. It also influenced whites because it was also a very public form of slave degradation. Beatings and escapes, for instance, were usually confined to a plantation or a locality. Few outsiders would view them. Revolt scares were fairly common, but rarely could they be construed as being exploitative of slaves. Auctions were another matter and had been closely associated with slavery since its beginning in North America. Speculation, though, could seem more menacing. Should a slave become the property of a trader, he was definitely going to be torn from everything he knew. That process would normally involve marching in a coffle, something more commonplace by about 1820. Slaves not sold to traders might stay in the area or move away with their new owners. In the latter case, they did not have the automatic assumption of coffles and brutality. This combination, the unique visibility of the interstate slave trade and the emotional reactions of the slaves, helped force a reappraisal of slavery.

Slaves in the Upper South dreaded the prospect of having to abandon everything they knew. Maryland slaves of the 1820s viewed their removal to Georgia or New Orleans as a virtual death sentence. James Williams, a slave who lived in Powhatan County, Virginia, before escaping, knew that slaves feared the power of their masters to sell them. He wrote that it was an awful threat for Virginia slaves to be sold to the Deep South. Slaves' aversion to the inter-state trade was so great that some masters used the threat of sale to Georgia as a means of changing a slave's behavior. Rumors of harsh conditions in distant states swirled through the quarters. Frederick Douglass remembered how his friends were scared of being sold to a trader who would carry them to Georgia. Some slaves whispered stories of having family members who marched bare-foot for hundreds of miles with a minimum of food and clothing. The words of one song testify to speculation's threat:

> Mammy, is Ol' Massa gwin'er sell us tomorrow?
> Yes, my chile.
> Whar he gwin'er sell us?
> Way down South in Georgia.

It was too much for many slaves to bear; they wept bitterly but found no solace. Henry Box Brown remembered the "frantic screams" and "scalding tears" associated with auctions and coffles. For Brown it was as simple as the declaration that slaves have feelings and knew too well the permanence of family separations.[11] Twenty-first century observers tend to think of the whip as emblematic of slavery's harshness, but the lash "was not the ultimate sanc-tion of the master's authority." Sale or simply the threat of sale "may have been the keystone of coercive slave control" because it relied on terror rather than torture. A master's ability to separate slaves irrevocably from their families and loved ones was a type of punishment that inflicted mental and spiritual anguish far in excess of the physical pain produced by the whip. The sale of disobedient slaves was the most powerful long-term technique of discipline because bondservants feared it more than anything else. This threat seems to contradict owners' impulses to reform slavery by promoting strong families. The concepts, however, could be used to accomplish the same end: control. An owner who encouraged family development could suddenly revoke that "priv-ilege" and use it as leverage to extract the maximum amount of labor from his slaves. In this way, manipulation of the slave family became one of the owner's most effective tools in maintaining control of his people. It became the "fre-quent custom" in the Chesapeake area for owners to intimidate their slaves with the threat of sale to distant lands. According to one abolitionist, slave traders became a type of "boogey man" who could be trotted out to keep slaves in line. When a sale took place, it was a decisive way to jettison difficult slaves. The selling of one slave would often be powerful enough to influence the behavior of other slaves in the community. Owners understood very well the dramatic impact that sales had upon their workforce. John Haywood wrote that one of his slave women was becoming discontented and unwilling to work. He could not tolerate her poor example because it encouraged other slaves to avoid their chores. Haywood, who had purchased the woman at a court sale, quickly sold her in order to be rid of the headache and to ward off further idleness. If nothing else, using speculators as part of a scare tactic to intimidate slaves also reduced them to a caricature in the white mind. After all, if masters were to be successful in scaring their slaves they had to exaggerate the traders' evil qualities. Such efforts to cow their slaves contained the seed that eventually ripened into the stereotype of the evil slave trader.[12]

Once speculators became the personification of evil for slaves, it became clear that bondservants would react unpredictably to such a great threat. Speculators, probably more than most, realized that they dealt with a potentially volatile slave population and took steps to prevent opposition. That traders tried to keep a lid on slave resistance obviously stemmed from motives of personal preservation. Another reason, however, dealt with the way southerners perceived the interstate slave trade. If they assumed that traders mainly dealt with unruly slaves, an increasingly common assumption in the Lower South, then the business of slave trading would be threatened. Potential buyers would be loathe to purchase slaves if they suspected them to be violent or uncontrollable. The hostile actions of bondservants then, could be a powerful, if unintended, way to shape white attitudes. Speculators countered such unpredictable behavior by asserting control over their commodities. They marched their coffles through cities at night, kept their slaves confined in private jails, and used other methods to exert their authority. The South, in many ways, used slavery as a means of economic and racial control, with traders being one mechanism of power. Should traders be capable of controlling their slaves with a minimum of disruption, then they would mesh smoothly in the system. Speculators proved themselves necessary for the maintenance of slavery — removing any slaves who proved nettlesome and inspiring dread in those left behind.

Speculators used a variety of tactics to prevent or minimize slave resistance. A common method was surprise. Traders and masters often worked together to make sure that slaves had no time to consider how to thwart a sale. An Alabama planter told his agent to use secrecy lest the slave he had just sold try to run away. Reuben Madison was sold so suddenly that he had no chance to say good-bye to his wife. Once traders took possession of slaves, they used numerous measures to reduce the chance of outright revolt and force compliance. The most obvious was physical punishment. Traders who were dissatisfied with their slaves could flog them, trying to beat them into "looking bright." In the coastwise trade, speculators segregated slaves by sex, prohibited males from seeing the females at night, and confined all slaves in the ship's hold at night. During the day bondservants normally roamed the deck, lest they become too resentful of being confined in close quarters. Should they prove to be unmanageable, they could be bolted to the deck.[13]

Some traders tried to lift the spirits of slaves forced to march in coffles, and thus reduce the risk of resistance, by forcing them to sing, dance, or listen to an instrument. Music was not usually sufficient, so traders frequently used chains to keep male slaves from fleeing the coffle, fighting one another, or killing the trader. These slaves, especially those who had just been forcibly separated from their families, were more likely to feel that they had nothing to lose in an escape attempt. The threat of a beating or even death had no hold over them. Traders knew from experience the necessity of leg irons and handcuffs as means of control. Similarly, traders normally did not permit slaves to speak to one another unless heard by one of the white escorts. They did not want slaves encouraging one another to resort to desperate measures. Others used bribes to cajole their slaves into cooperating. The speculator Obadiah Fields used small presents as incentives for good behavior in the slaves he purchased.[14]

Slaves resisted traders often enough that the threat of rebellion was omnipresent in coffles. Some bondservants only wanted to escape and did not contemplate further violence. Slaves encamped near Raleigh, for instance, fled when one member of the coffle bashed the speculator in the head with a stone. Similarly, traders named Whitfield and Tompkins traveled through North Carolina with a coffle of seventeen bondservants. Near the Chowan River, six armed runaway slaves attacked the group and drove off the speculators. Two of the slaves in the coffle joined the band while the others fled.[15]

More serious were slaves' efforts to kill speculators. In 1826 Austin Woolfolk put twenty-nine Maryland slaves on board the *Decatur*, a ship scheduled to sail from Baltimore to New Orleans. Somewhere off the coast of Georgia the slaves mutinied, threw the captain and the mate overboard, and steered the ship toward Haiti. The *Constitution* overtook the *Decatur* and took seventeen slaves from it, as many as could be safely transferred. Three days later the *Rooke* found the *Decatur* and escorted it to New York. One slave, William Bowser, stood trial in that city for mutiny and murder. After his conviction, Bowser made a farewell speech from the gallows on Ellis Island where he reputedly addressed Woolfolk. Bowser forgave the speculator and said he hoped to see him in heaven. Woolfolk supposedly answered with an angry profanity and muttered that Bowser "was now going to get what he deserved, and he was glad of it." Whether or not Bowser knew it, he was influencing thought about slavery and the slave trade. If the story is true, his actions showed him to be a better man than Woolfolk. He acted nobly while Woolfolk seemed petty. Even if the details of the story are apocryphal, they show that it was possible to imagine that slaves possessed dignity. The murderer instead of the speculator received sympathetic treatment, at least in the North.[16]

The homicide of speculators was one extreme form of resistance; slaves used other methods to undermine the trade as well. Some refused to submit to a sale and killed or maimed themselves or their family members. In Baltimore, for instance, a slave cut his throat in public view on a wharf as he was boarding a ship for New Orleans, and a woman in nearby Snow Hill killed her child and then herself when learning of her sale. Suicide to prevent speculation was frequent enough that it drew the attention of a visitor to Virginia. Such activities worried slaveowners. Slaves who killed themselves illustrated dramatically one of the fundamental problems of speculation, namely, that it was exploitation. Such suicides spoke volumes as to how the trade ruined slaves' lives and were powerful reminders that bondservants were possessors of free wills. The fact that slaves exerted power in such extreme ways also challenged white perceptions of slaves and the slave trade. When southerners read or heard stories of bondservants who attacked speculators or of slaves who committed suicide, they had to face the fact that slaves were human and not beasts. The irony is that a business that labored mightily to reduce slaves to just another commodity accidentally promoted the fact of their humanity. Speculation, moreover, did so in a public way that observers could not ignore. A young woman bound for New Orleans gave powerful testimony to this fact. She carried a young child who had not been sold with her. "When they reached the wharf, she sat down, unconscious of everything but the presence of her infant, upon whose face she continued to gaze, in apparent agony, while affording it nourishment for the last time from her breast." When it came time to depart, her former master took the infant while the mother poured forth "the most agonizing cries." The bystanders were deeply moved but could do nothing. John Randolph had a similar experience. He said the greatest orator he ever heard was a woman. "She was a slave. She was a mother, and her rostrum was the auction block." Sale, then, is best understood less as a master's prerogative and more as a complex system of negotiation within an exploitative system. It also called into question some of the foundational principles of slavery.[17]

It has been suggested that southerners often created reality and insisted that it be honored, even though it was false. Masters also tried to fashion reality for their slaves. These two ideas merged in the interstate slave trade. Owners wanted to make an artificial world where slaves hardly felt the effects of speculation. Reality could not be more different, and slaves "gave the lie" to masters when they angrily chopped off their hands or sobbed uncontrollably. When bondservants would not accept slaveowners' reality, they called into question what was known and believed about slavery. Slaves' reactions to the trade revealed the disparity between what owners wanted the master-slave relationship to be and what actually existed.[18]

These and other issues would surface during the debates surrounding the admission of the state of Missouri to the United States. An examination of the rhetoric involved in the dispute reveals that northerners and southerners were giving more thought to the consequences of a growing interstate slave trade. For their part, northerners raised the issue as a way to seize the moral high ground and argue that slavery should be prohibited in Missouri. James Tallmadge triggered the discussion when he moved that slaves be prohibited from entering Missouri and slave children born after statehood be free at age twenty-five. His intention was to provide a plan of gradual emancipation for the state. The northern representatives who allied themselves with Tallmadge used their observation of the slave coffles and slavery in the Washington area to bludgeon the South. They depicted the trade as emblematic of slavery and drew the conclusion that such an evil institution must not be allowed to expand. Their experience with the District of Columbia's slave trade became the basis for their remarks about how bondspeople would be treated in Missouri. In the face of this outside attack on slavery and the trade, southerners relied on apologetics to deflect the accusations. They refused to discuss the moral implications of speculation but concentrated instead on the constitutional right of southern migrants to carry bondservants into new territory. Southerners carefully differentiated between speculation and migration in the hopes of keeping the slave trade out of the debates. They had no coherent explanation for the commerce in slaves and were not willing to defend it. The best strategy, they thought, was to deny it.

It was Arthur Livermore of New Hampshire who fired the first salvo when he used the slave trade to denounce the South. In dramatic fashion, he described how the separation of mothers and children led to agonies of grief among the slaves. Opening Missouri to slavery would only magnify the pain. Tallmadge then kept up the pressure by refusing to listen to any excuses for the trade. He noted that a slave trader carrying a whip had just driven a coffle past the Capitol. Tallmadge hinted that a providential hand placed the coffle there to provide a dramatic illustration for his argument. He portrayed the slaves positively to his colleagues, observing that the men were prevented from protecting their families from destruction. Tallmadge could not believe that such scenes took place in "Republican America." These vivid descriptions formed a powerful indictment of slavery's dark side. Livermore and Tallmadge used scenes with which most of their fellow representatives were familiar in order to connect slavery's expansion to speculation. In doing so, they tried to mobilize opposition to the spread of slavery by arguing that the admission of Missouri as a slave state would increase slaves' suffering. The two men hoped to tap into the emotions of their colleagues by describing slavery in the most dismal way possible.[19]

If northern representatives intended to use these condemnations of the trade to aggravate their southern colleagues, they failed. The indictment of slavery via the interstate slave trade drew no heated response from the southern delegates. Only Louis McLane of Delaware directly addressed the issue, and he coolly argued that slavery's expansion had beneficial effects. Dispersing slaves into lands west of the Mississippi River, McLane maintained, would make them less restless. He also tried to convince his colleagues that such bondservants would live better lives because they would be on superior land. McLane apologetically noted that, on a personal level, he would not permit slaves to be sold by traders or become the objects of profit. As for the microscopic interstate slave trade that did exist, it fell under the purview of the states. His home state, he explained, prohibited the introduction or exportation of slaves for sale. McLane's bland appeal failed to rouse his colleagues to action. No other southern representative referred to the interstate slave trade during the Missouri debates. Even South Carolina senator William Smith, who defended the institution without reservation, did not mention the trade. Southerners' virtual silence suggests that they were quickly learning the lessons their slaves were teaching them. It was becoming all too apparent that speculation exposed slavery for what it was — an ugly stain on humanity. Although they may have had private doubts, there was no room for their expression in the halls of Congress. Southerners would not allow speculation to become an object lesson that illustrated slavery's immorality.[20]

Northern representatives changed tactics once it became apparent that their criticism would not draw out southerners. They alleged that the spread of slavery into Missouri would increase the smuggling of Africans into the United States. On this account, they tried to tar the legal interstate trade with the brush of the illegal African trade. John W. Taylor argued that an expansion of slave territory would make the whole country west of the Mississippi River a "market overt for human flesh." The natural consequence of allowing slaves into Missouri, his argument ran, would be to encourage smuggling. On the shores of Africa there would be an increase of unscrupulous men who bought slaves with "a few gewgaws or a bottle of whiskey" and then sold them in New Orleans. Like the earlier attack on slave coffles, this denunciation of the international trade drew a muted response from southerners, who merely asserted that the foreign trade was illegal and they did not wish to revive it.[21]

Although using the interstate trade as a moral indictment of slavery and dredging up the African trade did not cause southerners to rise to the bait, another tactic did draw a heated response. When northern senators linked the interstate trade with the migration of bondservants across state lines, southerners responded quickly. This method relied on a creative interpretation of the ninth section of the Constitution's first article to argue that Congress could prevent the importation and migration of slaves into new territories or states. This passage was obviously intended for the African slave trade, but, as we have seen, northerners were willing to do almost anything to link the two types of commerce. Timothy Fuller of Massachusetts was the first to try this approach. He injected a moral indictment into his argument by saying that he feared that the opening of an extensive slave market in Missouri would "tempt the cupidity" of southerners who might otherwise emancipate their slaves. Philip P. Barbour of Virginia brushed past the allegations of a vast slave market and defended the right of southerners to carry their slaves into Missouri. Prohibiting such movement would effectively prevent slaveholders from settling in the new state. He pointed out that slave labor was necessary to establish farms, and since few slaves would be available for purchase (because, of course, southerners would not stoop to dealing with speculators) there would be no incentive for migration. Barbour tried to avoid the topic of the slave trade, merely noting that only financial necessity or slave criminality induced masters to sell their slaves. Barbour was one of the first southerners to make the connection between the interstate slave trade and southern expansion. The desire for more territory was often foremost in southern thinking, but speculation added a new dimension. Only dimly did slaveholders grasp the true significance of defending speculation as well as migration. The Fifteenth Congress adjourned having accomplished nothing except to show that southerners were reluctant to face the moral criticisms of slavery and eager to steer the debate to a strict interpretation of the Constitution that defended property rights.[22]

The Missouri debates continued into the next session, but when discussing the movement of slaves, the congressmen continued to talk past one another. Northern representatives continually mentioned the movement of slaves by traders, while their southern counterparts constantly spoke of migration. In the Senate, Jonathan Roberts of Pennsylvania referred to a Louisiana law that outlawed the carrying of slaves into that state unless done by a United States citizen who intended to settle there. Southern senators produced an argument similar to that of their counterparts in the House. John Elliot of Georgia responded by noting that slaves were not subject to federal restrictions on migration because they had no volition or self-determination. They might be carried, but they did not migrate. The Constitution, he explained, did not allow Congress to inhibit transfer or removal of slaves from one state to

another. Such a right lay exclusively in the states, and they would never surrender it. He went on to admit that slavery was an "evil," but sound policy
dictated migration because the slave population was safer when it was dispersed instead of being cooped up in a few slave states. Senators from Mississippi, South Carolina, Virginia, and Kentucky all concurred that Congress
could lawfully outlaw the importation of slaves from areas outside the United
States but could not "regulate the internal distribution" of slaves. They seemed
to be caught unawares. They advanced a welter of ideas: slaves were treated
well, they were property, they were rarely sold, they were not commerce, they
were dangerous. It seems they had not given much thought to speculation.[23]

Northern congressmen were ahead of their southern counterparts in understanding the importance of the interstate slave trade. They had observed how
slaves had fought speculation, either in a blind fury or with quiet dignity. It
was becoming clear to them that the interstate trade was the Achilles' heel of
the South. Benjamin Lundy, William Lloyd Garrison, and other abolitionist
leaders would also instinctively seize upon the trade to heap shame upon the
South. Southern congressmen, on the other hand, would not acknowledge the
presence of an interstate trade that destroyed slave families and caused untold
hardship. Their way of dealing with the situation was to carefully separate
speculation from migration. The references to the inhumanity or barbarity of
the slave trade were moot, they argued, because most bondservants moved
with owners rather than speculators. They also asserted that Congress had no
power to regulate the migration of bondservants. The use of the word "migration" was intentional, because it did not paint as harsh a picture of the slaves'
conditions and bypassed constitutional questions. Southerners were also beginning to realize that the slave trade was vital to slavery's continued existence. They were not, however, willing to admit publicly that slave owners
participated in the trade or in activities similar to speculation. Southerners
were struggling with how to reconcile their defense of slavery with their mis-
givings surrounding speculation, especially in the face of outside pressure to
control slavery.

In the end, of course, Missouri retained slavery, and the interstate slave trade
remained unregulated on the national level. What the debates revealed is that
the trade was a convenient tool with which to attack the South. Vivid rhetoric
describing the markets of human flesh and the cries of bondservants separated
from their families would eventually become standard fare in abolitionist
denunciations of slavery. Those who opposed the peculiar institution tried to
cut through some of the abstractions and make the discussion personal. They
hoped to sidestep the theoretical issues of law and policy by stirring up the
emotions of their listeners. Although the Missouri debates may have identified
"the doctrine of states' rights with the defense of slavery," the nature of the

discussion reveals that the interstate slave trade was excluded from the defense perimeter. More often than not, southerners ignored the issue in the hope that it would go away. The embryonic nature of the trade in 1820, specifically the fact that it was just developing into a major source of labor for the Deep South, meant that southerners were not yet in a position to defend it or had not fully considered its implications for the defense of slavery. Although they began to recognize the importance of the slave trade — if not because of the resistance of slaves or the presence of coffles in the South, then because of the persistent attacks of northern representatives — it remained to be seen how southerners could reconcile the trade's brutality with their optimistic assumptions concerning slavery. The legalistic tactic of ignoring the slave trade by hiding slave movement under the guise of state sovereignty had a hollow ring to it, especially in the face of the heated and emotional indictments. They needed to draw a sharper distinction between migration and the slave trade, because the former was widely regarded as legitimate whereas the latter was suspect because selfish motives could be imputed to it. The slave trade, furthermore, seemed to contradict one of the main reasons for accepting slavery — that the institution improved bondservants' lives. Eventually most southerners, especially those in the Upper South, would construct more elaborate ways to explain away the existence of the interstate slave trade. For now, as speculation slowly gained force in the South, the issue seemed inconsequential.[24]

What is especially surprising is that thoughtful southerners seriously considered placing limits on bondage. They emphasized the relational aspects of slavery rather than unfettered property rights. Speculation challenged the concept of implied responsibilities of masters toward slaves, particularly protection from adversity. A reliance on the organic nature of the master-slave relationship was more comfortable for most masters. The slave trade, and its tilt toward exploitation, intruded into this tidy dream. Those who recognized the problem wanted limits that would redress the issues raised by a growing interstate slave trade. Carefully excising speculation from slavery was the logical cure. Snuffing out the interstate trade would give slaves less cause for resistance, mute outside criticism, and restore the relational emphasis of masters. Such reforms, unfortunately, would be scattered and ineffective in the following decade. The interstate trade thrived and became an essential part of the southern culture.

Slaves, however, would not surrender, and their actions were noticed and celebrated, at first in the Upper South and then throughout the North. Although unsuccessful in their individual acts of resistance against the interstate slave trade, bondservants were able to provide powerful ammunition for the critics of slavery in their attacks on the peculiar institution. Anna, who tried to kill herself rather than walk in a coffle, became the central figure in an

Alexander Rider etching. The image later became prominent in the American Anti-Slavery Society's broadsides and was a poignant example of one slave's humanity in the face of sheer brutality. The simple dignity of Anna and countless slaves like her was the most effective way to raise doubts about the consequences of the interstate trade. Their actions, particularly in Washington, led the way to making the capital a symbol of freedom for all Americans.

Notes

1. Jesse Torrey to John Randolph, April 29, 1816 (quotation), Deposition of Francis Scott Key, April 22, 1816, and Sworn Statement of Samuel Booker, March 7, 1816, all in Papers of the Select Committee to Inquire into the Existence of an Inhuman and Illegal Traffic in Slaves in the District of Columbia, HR 14A-C.17.4, National Archives, Washington, D.C.; Jesse Torrey, *A Portraiture of Domestic Slavery in the United States* (1817; reprint, St. Clair Shores, Mich., 1970), 42–44; Debates and Proceedings in the Congress of the United States (Washington, 1854), 14th Cong., 1st sess., March 1, 1816, 1115; *Washington National Intelligencer,* September 28, 1815, and May 7, 1816.

2. Debates and Proceedings, 14th Cong., 1st sess., March 1, 1816, 1115–17 (these and the following quotations are from this speech); *Washington National Intelligencer,* March 2, 1816; *Niles' Weekly Register,* March 9, 1816, 30; Russell Kirk, *John Randolph of Roanoke: A Study in American Politics* (Chicago, 1964), 131–39.

3. James L. Huston, "The Experiential Basis of the Northern Antislavery Impulse," *Journal of Southern History* 56 (1990): 609–40, describes northern revulsion at seeing slave auctions and coffles, albeit for a later time period. He convincingly argues that northerners who had first-hand experience with slavery were likely to be shocked by what they saw and actively oppose the institution.

4. Francis Hall, *Travels in Canada, and the United States, in 1816 and 1817* (London, 1818), 425; *Mobile Commercial Register,* September 12, 1822; Frederic Bancroft, *Slave Trading in the Old South* (1931; reprint, Columbia, S.C., 1966), 49–53; Mary Tremain, *Slavery in the District of Columbia* (1892; reprint, New York, 1969), 31–33; Walter C. Clephane, "The Local Aspect of Slavery in the District of Columbia," *Records of the Columbia Historical Association* (1900): 224–28, 235; William T. Laprade, "The Domestic Slave Trade in the District of Columbia," *Journal of Negro History* (1926): 19–21, 27–30; Richard S. Newman, *The Transformation of American Abolitionism: Fighting Slavery in the Early Republic* (Chapel Hill, 2002), 49–59; Michael Ridgeway, "A Peculiar Business: Slave Trading in Alexandria, Virginia, 1825–1861" (master's thesis, Georgetown University, 1976), 1–95.

5. Kirk, *John Randolph of Roanoke,* 131–33; Willie Lee Rose, "The Domestication of Domestic Slavery," in *Slavery and Freedom,* ed. William W. Freehling (New York, 1982), 18–36.

6. Debates and Proceedings, 14th Cong., 1st sess., March 1, 1816, 1117. That northerners were mute is an assumption based on the lack of any statements in the public records of the day. The other committee members were Joseph Hopkinson (Pennsylvania), Charles Goldsborough (Maryland), William Mayrant (South Carolina), and John Kerr (Virginia).

7. Papers of the Select Committee to Inquire into the Existence of an Inhuman and Illegal Traffic in Slaves . . . in the District of Columbia, HR 14A-C.17.4, National Archives, Washington, D.C. (quotations); Debates and Proceedings, 14th Cong., 1st sess., April 30, 1816, 1465; *Washington Daily National Intelligencer,* May 1, 1816; *Niles' Weekly Register,* May 4, 1816, 165.

8. David L. Lightner, "The Door to the Slave Bastille: The Abolitionist Assault upon the Interstate Slave Trade, 1833–1839," *Civil War History* 34 (1988): 235–52; David L. Lightner, "The Interstate Slave Trade in Antislavery Politics," *Civil War History* 36 (1990): 119–36.

9. David L. Lightner, "The Founders and the Interstate Slave Trade," *Journal of the Early Republic* 22 (2002): 46–48. The Constitution reads: "Congress shall have Power . . . To regulate Commerce with foreign Nations, and among the several States, and with the Indian Tribes." The Constitution of the United States (Washington, D.C.: U.S. Government Printing Office, 1989), 6.

10. F. Nash Boney, ed., *Slave Life in Georgia: A Narrative of the Life, Sufferings, and Escape of John Brown, a Fugitive Slave* (Savannah, 1972), 15; Charles Ball, *Slavery in the United States: A Narrative of the Life and Adventures of Charles Ball, a Black Man* (1837; reprint, New York, 1969), 11 (quotations); Moses Grandy, *Narrative of the Life of Moses Grandy, Late a Slave in the United States of America* (Boston, 1844), 11; Michael Tadman, *Speculators and Slaves: Masters, Traders, and Slaves in the Old South* (Madison, 1989), 146–54, 169–77.

11. Quoted in Lawrence Levine, *Black Culture and Black Consciousness: Afro-American Folk Thought from Slavery to Freedom* (New York, 1977); see also James Williams, *Narrative of James Williams, an American Slave* (New York, 1838), 32; T. Stephen Whitman, *The Price of Freedom: Slavery and Manumission in Baltimore and Early National Maryland* (Lexington, Ky., 1997), 75; Torrey, *Portraiture of Domestic Slavery,* 61; Dickson J. Preston, *Young Frederick Douglass: The Maryland Years* (Baltimore, 1980), 76; Henry Box Brown, *Narrative of Henry Box Brown* (Boston, 1849), 31.

12. George M. Fredrickson, "Masters and Mudsills: The Role of Race in the Planter Ideology of South Carolina," *South Atlantic Urban Studies* 2 (1978): 40 (first and second quotations); Emily West, "Surviving Separation: Cross-Plantation Marriages and the Slave Trade in Antebellum South Carolina," *Journal of Family History* 24 (1999): 212–31; Norrece T. Jones Jr., *Born a Child of Freedom Yet a Slave: Mechanisms of Control and Strategies of Resistance in Antebellum South Carolina* (Hanover, N.H.: 1990), 3, 37–38; William Dusinberre, *Them Dark Days: Slavery in the American Rice Swamps* (New York, 1996), 126; John Haywood to Mrs. Brickell, April 25, 1815, Ernest Haywood Papers, Southern Historical Collection, University of North Carolina, Chapel Hill; Torrey, *Portraiture of Domestic Slavery,* 61 (remaining quotations).

13. Steven H. Deyle, "The Domestic Slave Trade in America" (Ph.D. diss., Columbia University, 1995), 219; Boney, *Slave Life in Georgia,* 98, 115–16 (quotation); *Niles' National Register,* January 22, 1842, 323–26; John W. Blassingame, ed., *Slave Testimony: Two Centuries of Speeches, Interviews, and Autobiographies* (Baton Rouge, 1977), 175, 180, 185.

14. *Southern Agriculturist* 9 (1836): 70–75; List of Slave Sales, February 11, 1828, Obadiah Fields Papers, Duke University, Durham, North Carolina; Deyle, "Domestic Slave Trade," 102.

15. Unidentified Raleigh newspaper, as quoted in *Western Luminary,* November 9, 1825, 279; *Lexington Virginia Intelligencer,* May 29, 1824. Other examples of slave resistance may be found in the *Washington National Gazette,* August 6, 1825, as quoted in *Western Luminary,* August 24, 1825, 110; William H. Blane, *An Excursion Through the United States and Canada During the Years 1822–23* (New York, 1969), 226–27.

16. Undated *New York Christian Inquirer* as quoted in *Genius of Universal Emancipation,* January 2, 1827, 109–10 (quotation); *Niles' Weekly Register,* May 20, 1826, 262, September 5, 1829, 18–19, December 26, 1829, 277, September 9, 1830, 328; Merton L. Dillon, *Benjamin Lundy and the Struggle for Negro Freedom* (Urbana, 1966); *Genius of Universal Emancipation,* January 1, 1830, 131; *Lexington Kentucky Reporter,* September 9, 1829, as quoted in J. Winston Coleman Papers, King Library, University of Kentucky, Lexington; Edward D. Jervey and C. Harold Huber, "The *Creole* Affair," *Journal of Negro History* 65 (1980): 196–211.

17. William Wells Brown, *Narrative of William Wells Brown: A Fugitive Slave* (Boston, 1847), 40; E. S. Abdy, *Journal of a Residence and Tour in the United States of America,* 3 vols. (London, 1835), 3:350 (first and second quotations); Kirk, *John Randolph,* 147 (final quotation); Benjamin Brand to Martin Dawson, March 17, 1819, Benjamin Brand Papers, Virginia Historical Society, Richmond, Virginia; Jordan M. Saunders to David Burford, October 29, 1829, David Burford Papers, University of Tennessee, Knoxville; Whitman, *Price of Freedom,* 77; Christopher Phillips, *Freedom's Port: The African American Community of Baltimore* (Urbana, 1997), 45–54; Walter Johnson, *Soul by Soul: Life Inside the Antebellum Slave Market* (Cambridge, Mass., 2000), 176–87.

18. Kenneth S. Greenberg, *Honor and Slavery: Lies, Duels, Noses, Masks, Dressing as a Woman, Gifts, Strangers, Humanitarianism, Death, Slave Rebellions, the Proslavery Argument, Hunting, and Gambling in the Old South* (Princeton, 1996), 32–42.

19. Debates and Proceedings, 15th Cong., 2d sess., February 16, 1819, 1:1191–92, 1210 (quotation); Glover Moore, *The Missouri Controversy, 1819–1821* (Lexington, Ky., 1953), 33–51; Leonard L. Richards, *The Slave Power: The Free North and Southern Domination, 1780–1860* (Baton Rouge, 2000), 52–82.

20. Debates and Proceedings, 15th Cong., 2d sess., February 17, 1819, 2:1233–34; Don Fehrenbacher, *The South and the Three Sectional Crises* (Baton Rouge, 1980), 9–23.

21. Debates and Proceedings, 15th Cong., 2nd sess., February 15, 1819, 1:1175.

22. Ibid., February 15, 1819, 1:1183–84, 1188 (quotations); Lightner, "Founders and the Interstate Slave Trade," 47–48. The wording of the Constitution is clear: "The Migration or Importation of such Persons as any of the States now existing shall think proper to admit, shall not be prohibited by the Congress prior to the Year one thousand eight hundred and eight, but a Tax or duty may be imposed on such Importation, not exceeding ten dollars for each Person." *Constitution,* 7.

23. Debates and Proceedings, 16th Cong., 1st sess., January 17, 1820, 2:125–26, 129–35 (quotations on 134), January 18, 1820, 1:1010–12, and January 26, 1820, 2:259–64.

24. Norman K. Risjord, *The Old Republicans: Southern Conservatism in the Age of Jefferson* (New York, 1965), 220.

5

The Domestic Slave Trade in America
The Lifeblood of the Southern Slave System

STEVEN DEYLE

In one of his first public appearances, at the second annual meeting of the American Anti-Slavery Society in 1835, James G. Birney told his audience that contrary to popular opinion, slavery was not any milder in the Upper South than in the Lower South, nor less harsh than in the past. According to Birney, however, slavery was changing. The number of "coffles of slaves traversing the country to a market" was increasing daily, and "the system now growing into practice is for the farming states to supply those farther south with slaves, just as regularly and systematically the slave coast of Africa used to supply the colonists of Brazil or St. Domingo." In fact, a few months later, Birney claimed that slavery in the Upper South "would, long since, have been relinquished, had it not been for the establishment of the American Slave trade, intoxicating the holders of the marketable commodity, everywhere, and by its great profits, blinding them to the inhumanity of the traffic."[1]

Birney became one of the most popular and effective abolitionist speakers of the 1830s, in large part because of his firsthand knowledge of the American slave system. He had lived in Kentucky and Alabama and had bought and sold slaves. Birney's experience made him an expert on the relation between the slave-selling and slave-buying states, and he often discussed this in his speeches and writings. But, most important, he also spoke of the domestic slave trade and the crucial economic role it played in sustaining the slave system.[2]

As Birney noted, southern slavery had changed by the nineteenth century, and the main reason for this transformation was the development of a traffic in American-born slaves. Especially important was the emergence of an inter-regional trade that carried slaves from the parts of the South that had an excess of such property to areas where it was more in demand. This trade linked the two major subregions of the South into a common economic concern and led to an increase in the monetary value of human property for everyone who owned it. In fact, over time it made slave property the most valuable form of investment in the South, surpassing even land. Therefore, not only did this new domestic trade help solidify the commitment of most white southerners to their region's "peculiar" institution, but its very success likewise made it impossible for them to ever give it up.

Unfortunately for the white South, the economic activity that brought them so many financial rewards also proved to be the one aspect of their slave system that most people outside of the region found difficult to accept. Not surprisingly, then, when an organized antislavery movement emerged in the North, it made the domestic slave trade a fundamental component of its attack. This traffic was central in the development of antislavery theory and tactics, and it remained a prominent feature throughout the life of the movement. Even after the American Anti-Slavery Society split into two groups in 1840 — with some abolitionists following William Lloyd Garrison's moral suasionist approach to eliminating slavery and others, like Birney, believing that the best way of achieving this goal was by using the political process — the domestic trade continued to play a pivotal role for both groups. For those who tried to persuade the nation that slavery was morally wrong, few aspects of the system better exemplified the horrors of southern slavery than the domestic slave trade. And the political abolitionists understood that as interstate commerce, this traffic was subject to governmental regulation and even prohibition. Together, both groups were able to turn the domestic slave trade into a powerful symbol of the evil inherent in the slaveholding world and use this trade to threaten the very existence of the institution of slavery.

Therefore, by the 1830s white southerners increasingly found themselves in a bind. On one hand, they needed to employ whatever political or legal arguments were necessary to protect the lifeblood of their institution or face economic and social collapse. But they also had to do this in such a way as to fend off the abolitionists' moralistic attacks. This would not be easy, and southerners found this essential aspect of their slave system one of the most difficult to defend. Yet by denying its impact and horrors as best they could, for the most part, they were successful, at least until outside pressures eventually gave them little choice but to leave the Union. Although this action ultimately brought their system to an end, it ironically only added to the nation's acceptance of the white South's defense of their region's most important form of commerce. And, unfortunately, more than anything else, it has been the dominance and persistence of this apologist view of the domestic trade that has left most people today completely unaware of the prominent role that this essential feature of the southern slave system played in antebellum American life.

I

The buying and selling of human beings had always been a part of American society, yet the nature of this traffic had changed over time. In the colonial period most slaves sold in British North America were individuals imported from Africa or the West Indies, although by the mid-eighteenth century a small locally based domestic trade had also developed. Following the American Revolution this changed, especially after the closing of the African trade in 1808. By the early nineteenth century, the slave trade had become an indigenous operation, transporting thousands of enslaved men and women from the Upper South to the Lower South each year and transferring an even greater number locally from one owner to another.[3]

It is hard to overemphasize the impact that this new traffic in human commodities had on the southern states and the role that it played in the southern economy. Between 1790 and 1860 Americans transported more than one million African American slaves from the Upper South to the Lower South; approximately two-thirds of these slaves arrived there as a result of sale. Moreover, twice as many individuals were sold locally. During this period, slave sales occurred in every southern city and village, and coffles of slaves could be found on every southern highway, waterway, and railroad. The domestic trade, in all its components, was the lifeblood of the southern slave system, and without it, the institution would have ceased to exist.[4]

The interregional slave trade also performed an important function by transferring slaves from places that had more than were needed to areas where they were more in demand. Changes in agricultural production during the mid-eighteenth century meant that most southern slave owners, especially those in the Chesapeake region, found themselves with a surplus of human slaves. Not only did this lead to a drop in prices, but following the revolution, it also made many in the Upper South question the future of the institution itself. This all changed with the invention of the cotton gin in 1792 and the explosion of King Cotton in the early nineteenth century. As more and more land was opened up or turned over to the production of cotton, an almost insatiable demand for slaves developed in the new cotton states of the South-west. And because the nation had closed off all outside sources of supply in 1808, this demand could only be met by means of a redistribution of the existing slave population. Recognizing that planters in the new cotton states were willing to pay hundreds of dollars more per slave than were owners in the older states, thousands of speculators transported hundreds of thousands of bondspeople from the Upper South and seaboard states to the markets of the Southwest.[5]

The result was the creation of a regionwide slave market that tied together all of the various slaveowning interests into a common economic concern and helped put to rest whatever doubts slave owners in the Upper South may have had about the future of the institution. One of the defining characteristics of this new domestic slave market was the emergence of separate slave-exporting and slave-importing subregions within the South. Differences between the Upper South and Lower South had existed since before the revolution, but by the early nineteenth century, those distinctions turned increasingly on whether a state was a net exporter or a net importer of slaves. By serving as the eco-nomic conduit between the exporting and importing states, the interregional slave trade not only linked together the two main subregions, but it also provided numerous benefits for both. The demand for slave labor in the South-west supplied owners in the Upper South with an outlet for their surplus or "troublesome" slaves and furnished the region with much-needed revenue. The Lower South benefited from the domestic trade as well because planters no longer had to depend on foreign sources for their slaves and were guar-anteed a steady supply of native-born, acculturated bondspeople for their plantations.

Most significant, the creation of a regionwide slave market resulted in an escalation of property values across the South. Prices continued to vary from state to state, and slaves were still often sold for several hundred dollars less in the Upper South than the Lower South, but the high prices in the cotton states influenced the rates offered throughout the region. Or, to put it another way, the price paid for a slave in New Orleans generally affected the amount ob-tained for a similar individual in Richmond, Charleston, or St. Louis, which in turn determined property values in the remotest southern village or hamlet. Not everyone in the Upper South welcomed the consequences of the inter-regional trade for their local slave market. As one Virginia writer noted when complaining of the thousands of slaves that traders had carried from his state: "We cannot even enter into competition with them for their purchase. . . . Their price here is not regulated by our profits, but by the profits of their labor in other states."[6] This rise in slave prices, though it sometimes made it difficult for individuals who wished to purchase, nevertheless proved beneficial for the region as a whole. Most important, it increased the monetary value of human property for everyone who owned it. Over the course of the nineteenth century, southern slave prices more than tripled. The rate for a prime male field hand in New Orleans began at around $500 in 1800 and rose to as high as $1,800 by the time of the Civil War.[7]

This rise in slave prices made human property one of the most costly, and valuable, forms of investment in the country. Although $1,800 is a lot of money in any case, that amount in 1860 dollars would be equal to more than $30,000 today.[8] By anyone's definition, a prime male hand was a major purchase. Even more significant is the aggregate value of all slave property. According to economic historians, the total value of slave property in 1860 was at least $3 billion. This figure assumes an average price of only $750 per slave, which most recent studies have indicated is probably too low.[9] Even with this conservative an estimate, the value of the southern slave population was still enormous when placed in a comparative perspective. It was roughly three times greater than the total amount of all capital invested in manufacturing in the North and the South combined, three times the amount invested in railroads, and seven times the amount invested in banks. It was also equal to about seven times the total value of all currency in circulation in the country, three times the value of the entire livestock population, twelve times the value of all American farm implements and machinery, twelve times the value of the entire U.S. cotton crop, and forty-eight times the total expenditures of the federal government that year. The domestic slave trade had made human property one of the most prominent forms of investment in the country, second only to land. In fact, by 1860, in the slaveholding states alone, slave property had surpassed the assessed value of real estate (see table 5.1).[10]

Therefore, it is impossible to comprehend the Old South and its subsequent history without understanding the crucial role that the domestic slave trade played in its development. By linking the South's two major subregions into a common economic concern and making the entire slaveholding class wealthier as a result, the creation of a regionwide slave market solidified the entire South's commitment to the institution of chattel slavery. For that reason, it is probably no coincidence that the emergence of this market, which began to take full effect in the 1820s, occurred at exactly the same time that the defense of slavery was shifting from that of a necessary evil to one of a positive good. There is no denying that for most slave owners, the rise in their property values was becoming more and more of a positive good for them personally. Of course, there was also another important reason for this transformation. By the 1830s a growing number of outsiders had escalated their attack on the

Table 5.1. Estimated Value of U.S. Assets and Expenditures in 1860

Asset or Expenditure	Value
Southern slave population	$3,000,000,000
Capital invested in manufacturing	$1,050,000,000
Capital invested in railroads	$1,166,422,729
Capital invested in banks	$421,890,095
Currency in circulation	$442,102,000
Livestock	$1,107,490,216
Farm implements and machinery	$247,027,496
Cotton crop	$250,291,000
Expenditures of federal government	$63,131,000
Assessed value of real estate	
Free states	$4,562,104,152
Slaveholding states	$2,411,001,897
Total real estate	$6,973,106,049

Source: Joseph C. G. Kennedy, *Preliminary Report on the Eighth Census, 1860* (Washington, 1862), 190, 193–94, 197, 199, 231; U.S. Bureau of the Census, *Historical Statistics of the United States: Colonial Times to 1957* (Washington, 1960), 647, 711; Stuart Bruchey, *Cotton and the Growth of the American Economy: 1790–1860* (New York, 1967), table 3-A.

region's predominant form of investment, and most disturbingly, they threatened to cut off the lifeblood of the system and destroy the white South's cherished way of life.

II

The first issue of the *Liberator* is justly famous for William Lloyd Garrison's bold opening manifesto. Virtually every history textbook or monograph on the abolitionist movement quote some part of the well-known passage: "I *will be* as harsh as truth, . . . AND I WILL BE HEARD." But little mention is ever made of the other two articles that also appeared on the front page of that famed publication. In "District of Columbia" Garrison described how in the nation's capital "the worst features of slavery are exhibited; and as a mart for slave-traders, it is unequalled." Also included was a petition to Congress asking for the abolition of slavery in the District of Columbia and "for the preventing of bringing slaves into that District for purposes of traffic." If that article left anyone unmoved, the next piece was intended to startle the reader's apathy, "unless he be morally dead—dead—dead." In "The Slave Trade in the Capital," Garrison presented examples of the hardships caused by the domestic trade and concluded with sentiments reminiscent of those in his statement of purpose: "Such are the scenes enacting in the heart of the American nation. Oh, patriotism! where is thy indignation? Oh, philanthropy! where is thy grief? OH SHAME, WHERE IS THY BLUSH!"[11]

The prominent coverage that the domestic slave trade received in the opening issue of the *Liberator* foreshadowed the important role that this feature of slavery would play throughout the entire thirty-five-year history of that publication. Literally hundreds of pieces appeared touching on some aspect of the business. Lengthy in-depth articles described how the slave trade worked, and firsthand accounts provided authentic testimony. Perhaps the best example of how important the domestic trade was for the *Liberator*'s message can be found in its masthead. Originally the masthead contained only the words "THE LIBERATOR." But beginning with the seventeenth issue, a large woodcut illustration appeared together with the title. This drawing was of a horse market where a distraught family of black slaves was being sold at auction. Posted on the auctioneer's stand was the announcement "SLAVES HORSES & OTHER CATTLE TO BE SOLD AT 12 OC."[12] During the long run of the *Liberator* two more mastheads would replace this one, but in all of them an auction represented slavery. Not everyone agreed with Garrison's decision to include a picture of a slave auction on his masthead. His friends initially cautioned him against it, and southerners found it especially disturbing. In describing the reaction of slaveholders who had seen the paper, one Georgia resident reported that the "engraving in the title is galling to them, and often elicits a deep and bitter curse." Garrison, however, realized the powerful effect that images of the slave trade had on his audience, and for all but the first sixteen issues the *Liberator* prominently featured an illustration of a slave auction in its masthead.[13]

One reason why Garrison and the other abolitionists focused so heavily on the domestic trade was the larger social and economic changes that had taken place in America during the first half of the nineteenth century. Not only had slavery been abolished in the northern states in the aftermath of the American Revolution, but another revolution in market activities resulted in an increased commitment in those states to a social system based on a diversified economy and free labor. This was in stark contrast to the South, where these same market forces and the emergence of the interregional slave trade led to the development of the Cotton Kingdom, with its heightened reliance on chattel slavery. Consequently, many northerners began to view the South and its way of life as not only backward and old-fashioned but at times downright cruel. This proved especially true by the 1830s as more and more young northerners came of age with no personal recollection of slavery or of having seen an enslaved person, for that matter. This made all the horrors associated with the institution seem that much more pronounced and brutal. And few features of the system had a bigger impact on a northern audience than the dramatic accounts of humans being sold on an auction block or the tearing of husbands away from their wives or screaming children from their mothers' arms. Therefore, what had become commonplace in the South came to be seen far differently by those outside the region.[14]

The growing isolation of northerners from the domestic trade also helps explain why seeing it firsthand had such a dramatic impact on so many people and why they frequently cited an encounter with a coffle or an auction sale as a major turning point in their understanding that slavery was wrong. Many of the leaders of the abolitionist movement, including Garrison, had such encounters, as well as countless other northerners who traveled into the slave-holding states. This was also why the Upper South unwittingly played such a crucial role in converting so many people to the antislavery cause. Being closest to the North and most accessible to visitors from that region, it was here, in the states of Maryland, Virginia, and Kentucky, where the majority of outsiders saw the workings of slavery for themselves. And much to the white South's dismay, it was also in these states that many of the worst features of the slave system were exhibited. These states had come to rely on the sales of thousands of enslaved persons to the Deep South each year, and it was impossible to hide all of the wrenching scenes that this produced. For that reason, in many respects, the Upper South came to be an important and influential middle ground where people from outside of the region formed their impressions of slavery and the South. And, unfortunately for the white South, many of these visitors went home transformed by what they had seen.[15]

Therefore, given their keen understanding of the effect that this aspect of the slave system had on their audience, it was only natural that Garrison and the other abolitionists featured the domestic trade in the *Liberator* and that from the very beginning they made it a fundamental component of organized antislavery activity. At the first American Anti-Slavery Society meeting in December 1833, delegates approved a Declaration of Sentiments expressing the association's goals and intentions. This document praised the nation's revolutionary ancestors but noted that "*their* grievances, great as they were, were trifling in comparison with the wrongs and sufferings of those for whom we plead. Our fathers were never slaves—never bought and sold like cattle" or "recognized by the laws, and treated by their fellow beings, as marketable commodities—as goods and chattels—as brute beasts." One of the organization's objectives as stated in its constitution was "to influence Congress to put an end to the domestic slave trade," and in its first annual report the association called on all members to persevere "in the face of all opposition, till the seat of our nation's power and honor is no longer a slave-mart — till the coffle of the domestic traffic no longer stains with blood its weary track from the Potomac to the Mississippi."[16]

The domestic trade was also central to the formation of antislavery theory and tactics, and it remained a prominent feature throughout the life of the movement. Most important was the role the slave trade played in abolitionist ideology. The Garrisonian abolitionists based their call for the immediate abolition of slavery on their belief that it was a sin. And for them, slavery *was* a sin because it was a crime against nature and a rebellion against God. By transforming humans into property, by making them into articles that could be bought and sold, slavery essentially turned people into "things." This not only contradicted God's intentions, but it also interfered with man's relation to God. Slavery destroyed the moral accountability of mankind by making slaves answerable to their human masters and not God. In effect, slavery had reversed the order of creation by putting man above God, and slaveholders and God were competing for control over mankind. This is what the abolitionists meant when they continually referred to slave owners as "manstealers." Slaveholders had stolen the humanity from their slaves and mankind from God. Therefore, as one antislavery tract explained it, turning *"men into merchandise"* was a principle "openly at war with all the relations which God has established between His creatures, and between Himself and them," and any attempt to justify it was "sin."[17]

In addition to playing a fundamental role in abolitionist ideology, the domestic trade became an important symbol of the inherent cruelty of American slavery. By constantly presenting heartrending examples of slaves' being sold, the abolitionists proved that such events were not isolated incidents but common occurrences in the South. The sale of human beings as property violated most outsiders' perceptions of civilized behavior, and the abolitionists understood the effect that this distasteful feature of the system had on their audience, especially individuals who may not have previously supported their cause. As one abolitionist put it: "I wish every pro-slavery man and woman in the North could witness one slave auction." The slave trade epitomized American slavery at its worst, and tales of families being divided, children torn from their mothers, and humans on an auction block simply could not be defended. No explanation was needed to show that such action was wrong. As Garrison put it: "I know that their bodies and spirits (which are God's) are daily sold under the hammer of the Auctioneer as articles of merchandize; I need no nice adjustment of abstractions, no metaphysical reasonings, to convince me, that such scenes are dreadful, and such practices impious." As a result, most antislavery publications included either sale notices or some mention of the devastating scenes that the domestic trade produced.[18]

Finally, the abolitionists emphasized the destructive effect that slavery, and especially the slave trade, had on southern families. Despite the paternalistic arguments used by many white southerners to defend their way of life, abolitionists continually reminded their audience of the "strange misnomer" of referring to slavery as the "domestic institution." In their eyes, nothing could have been further from the truth, because they saw the disruption of southern families, particularly black families, as central to the institution of slavery. Consequently, they filled their publications with tales of children torn from their mothers and husbands from their wives and of the depredations of licentious planters who then callously sold their own offspring.[19]

Although the abolitionists directed this aspect of their argument to both male and female audiences, it played an especially prominent role in their appeals to northern women. Virtually all of the special tracts written for female readers focused on the destructive effect that slavery had on southern families. In one article appearing in the *Anti-Slavery Record,* women were asked: "Do the mothers of our land know that American slavery, both in theory and practice, is nothing but a system of *tearing asunder the family ties?*" And in the pamphlet *Slavery Illustrated in Its Effects upon Woman and Domestic Society* (1837), female readers were told that it was "the duty and privilege of women" to correct this.[20]

One reason for this emphasis was the abolitionists' belief that issues concerning the domestic sphere were of special importance to women and that this was an area in which women had both a right and a moral responsibility to act. Female abolitionists also used this argument when justifying their presence in the public sphere. In their opening address, the members of the New York Female Anti-Slavery Society argued that "whatever else it may be, slaveholding must be eminently *a domestic evil*. It works its mischiefs among the sweet charities which naturally flourish in the family circle. . . . Can it be pretended that here is ground in which *woman* has no interest?" Because of its harmful effect on families, for most women the slave trade was the harshest of all the evils of slavery, and even those who disagreed with the abolitionists could concur that this was an aspect of the institution that women had a responsibility to oppose. In her essay attacking the antislavery movement as being too extreme and outside the proper sphere of women, Catharine Beecher conceded that the domestic trade was a wrong that Christian women, by means of their gentle persuasion, could do much to bring to an end.[21]

After the 1830s, when the Garrisonian wing of the abolitionist movement became increasingly eclipsed by its political arm, the domestic trade continued to play an important role in the moral argument against slavery. This can be best seen in that most influential of all antislavery works, Harriet Beecher Stowe's *Uncle Tom's Cabin* (1852). From the opening scene, when the slave trader Haley convinces the paternalistic planter Shelby to part with his two favorite slaves, to her concluding remarks about how the internal trade was "at this very moment, riving thousands of hearts, shattering thousands of families, and driving a helpless and sensitive race to frenzy and despair," Stowe continually made the point that the buying and selling of humans was not an isolated occurrence but a fundamental and frequent requirement of American slavery.[22]

III

The Garrisonian abolitionists successfully used the domestic trade to shape northern opinion about the evils of southern slavery, but even more threatening to white southerners was the role this traffic played in the political abolitionists' attack on the institution. Their perceptive understanding of the regional differences within the South and the fundamental economic role that the slave trade played in maintaining the slave system bolstered their argument. The political abolitionists realized that it was this interregional trade that had revitalized slavery in the Upper South and fueled the institution's expansion into the Deep South. Note that many abolitionists often overstated the magnitude of this trade, and they frequently made the claim that slave owners in the Upper South deliberately "bred" their slaves for sale like livestock. Despite these slight exaggerations, the political abolitionists still understood how the interstate trade made both sections of the South dependent on one another while strengthening the institution across the region.

Given this economic understanding of the South, with separate slave-exporting and slave-importing regions held together by the interstate trade, it is not surprising that James G. Birney and several other political abolitionists saw the domestic slave trade as the key to the destruction of slavery. In an 1838 tract Birney argued that if the slave-selling states "could be restrained from the *commerce* in slaves, slavery could not be supported by them for any length of time, or to any considerable extent."[23] Others pushed this line of reasoning even further, asserting that the interregional slave trade was the linchpin that held the entire system together, and as such, it was here that they needed to focus their attack. In a speech before the 1839 meeting of the American Anti-Slavery Society, Henry B. Stanton called the internal trade "the great jugular vein of slavery" and argued that if they could "cut this vein, slavery would die of starvation in the southern, and of apoplexy in the northern slave states." The abolitionist who most thoroughly developed this argument, however, was Alvan Stewart of New York. Stewart made the interstate trade a major topic in his speeches, referring to it as "the great door to the slave Bastille." In an 1836 speech, Stewart claimed that if the internal trade could be abolished, "slavery would come to an end by its own weight, in Virginia, Maryland, Kentucky, Tennessee, and the western parts of North and South Carolina" and that within ten years, two-thirds of the slaves in the United States would be freed.[24]

Stewart and most other abolitionists believed that banning the domestic slave trade was not only desirable but legally possible. Although the majority of abolitionists did not think that Congress had the right to interfere with slavery in the states, from the beginning of the movement, the American Anti-Slavery Society and virtually every other antislavery group argued that Congress had the right to regulate the interstate trade. They based this opinion on constitutional interpretation and historical precedent. They believed that the nation's founders had wanted to eliminate slavery and had given Congress the power to do so in the Constitution.[25]

Much of their argument was based on the nation's previous actions against the African slave trade. Political abolitionists such as Birney and Stewart noted that earlier in the century the country had declared the African trade a great moral crime and treated it as piracy, made punishable by death. In their eyes the domestic trade was no different, and in fact, they often argued that it was worse because it dealt in American-born slaves. These abolitionists also used the opposition to the African trade as the basis for arguing that Congress had the power to abolish the interstate trade. As Alvan Stewart put it: "The same words, clauses and sections of the Constitution, which gave Congress the power to abolish the African slave trade, give Congress the ability to pass a law to abolish the internal slave trade now carried on between the slave States, in defiance of the loudest cries of humanity."[26]

The main clause of the Constitution to which Stewart referred was article 1, section 8, which granted Congress the power "to regulate commerce with foreign nations, and among the several states." The abolitionists believed that this clause gave Congress the power to regulate all forms of commerce, including the traffic in human property, and it was primarily on this point that they based their argument. One of the most prominent abolitionist writers on this subject was William Jay, a New York judge and son of the first chief justice, John Jay. In *A View of the Action of the Federal Government, on Behalf of Slavery* (1839), Jay argued that the commerce clause was the sole authority for

Congress's power to abolish the African trade, and he noted that when it did so, few people questioned its right. Jay then made a similar claim for the domestic trade, asking, "By what logic then will it be shown that the power to regulate the commerce among the several States, does not include the power to interdict a traffic in men, women, and children? Is it more wicked, more base, more cruel, to traffic in African savages than in native born Americans?"[27]

Also important for their argument was article 1, section 9, which stated that "the migration or importation of such persons as any of the states now existing shall think proper to admit, shall not be prohibited by the Congress prior to the year one thousand eight hundred and eight." According to the abolitionists, this clause was added because at the time of the Constitution's framing it was so well understood that Congress had the power to abolish the African trade that another clause was felt necessary to protect the slaveowning interests in the Deep South for a limited number of years. In other words, denying Congress the power to prohibit the African trade for twenty years proved that Congress did indeed have the power to prohibit it. Otherwise, there would have been no need to temporarily restrict Congress's right to do so. As Gerrit Smith phrased it in a public letter to Henry Clay, "The implication in this clause of the existence of the power in question, is as conclusive, as would be the express and positive grant of it." Smith also noted that this clause made the founders' intentions clear as to what this power entailed: "The power of Congress over 'migration or importation,' which this clause implies, is a power not merely to 'regulate,' as you define the word, but to 'prohibit.'" Therefore, according to the abolitionists, article 1, section 9, proved that Congress had the power to prohibit as well as regulate the slave trade, and, in addition, by using the words "migration" and "importation," this clause had granted to Congress, after 1808, the power to prohibit not only the importation of slaves from Africa but also the migration of slaves across state lines.[28]

In addition to constitutional arguments, there were several historical precedents for congressional regulation of the interstate slave trade. In the Louisiana Ordinance Bill of 1804, Congress had prohibited the importation of slaves into the territory for sale. Also, when the African trade was banned, Congress set limitations on the coastal trade, making it illegal to transport slaves in ships of less than forty tons. After citing this earlier regulation of the coastal trade, William Jay noted that Congress clearly had the power to destroy the entire coastal trade, if for no other reason than that "it would not be easy to show that the Constitution forbids its prohibition in vessels *over* forty tons." Moreover, if Congress could regulate the coastal trade, the same power should apply to the overland trade as well.[29]

The most influential precedent, however, came from the Missouri debates of

1819–1820, when congressmen argued about the question of Congress's ability to prevent the spread of slavery and the slave trade into the new states and territories. Although much of this debate focused on the migration and importation clause and on the question of planters' migrating with their slaves, numerous speeches were made concerning the regulation of the interstate slave trade, and practically all of the arguments that the abolitionists were later to use appeared at that time. Representative John Sergeant of Pennsylvania was one of many northerners who maintained that "slaves are every where articles of trade, the subject of traffic and commerce" and that "the general power to regulate commerce, includes in it, of course, a power to regulate this kind of commerce." Among the well-known politicians of the time who endorsed this opinion were John Jay, Daniel Webster, and John Quincy Adams.[30]

The abolitionists hoped to achieve their goal by petitioning governments at the state and federal levels for action. Petitions against slavery and the slave trade had appeared as early as the Washington administration, but during the 1830s their numbers soared, especially after the passage of the infamous "gag rule" that prohibited their reading and discussion in Congress in 1836.[31] The topics represented in the petition drive covered a range of subjects, but as a circular to antislavery women noted, the most important object was "obtaining petitions for the abolition of slavery in the District of Columbia and the Territory of Florida, and the cessation of the internal slave-trade; all of which are generally conceded to be perfectly within the power of Congress." Although the issues often overlapped and multiple petitions were common, the largest number concerned banning slavery in the nation's capital. Few people questioned Congress's jurisdiction over the district, and they naturally felt more comfortable supporting this measure than the far more radical proposal to prohibit the interstate slave trade. Some political abolitionists, however, such as Alvan Stewart, protested, arguing that "slavery never can be abolished in the District of Columbia or the Territories, with any expectation of advantage, until the internal slave trade is abolished between the States."[32]

Although Stewart was, of course, correct, the abolitionists' petition drive still proved to be a limited success, and the slave trade played a major role in accomplishing this. Most important, the dismissal of their petitions by Congress helped increase the sense among northerners that there was a threatening Slave Power that was out to deprive them of their constitutional rights. In addition, the petition drive helped heighten awareness in the North that the domestic trade was, as one New Hampshire group put it, "an enormous abuse which calls loudly for redress" and that the people had a duty to speak out against it. Between December 1838 and March 1839, 54,547 people signed their names to 1,496 petitions to the House calling for a ban on the interstate slave trade, a figure second only to the 80,755 signatures for the abolition of slavery in the District of Columbia.[33]

The response to the petition drive stimulated many abolitionists to pursue political action elsewhere, and the domestic trade remained an integral part of their campaign. When the Liberty Party was formed in 1840, all of the original founders thought that Congress had the right to abolish the interstate slave trade and advocated that it do so. The program they developed was a continuation of the ideas and tactics they had formed during the previous decade. They called for congressional action against slavery in all areas under federal control; this included abolishing slavery in the District of Columbia and the territories as well as prohibiting the interstate trade. In addition, the political abolitionists gave the slave trade a prominent place in their speeches and writings, and for many, it was seen as the key to the destruction of the institution. According to one of their tracts, once the slave trade was removed, slavery would die of *"surfeit"* in the Upper South and of *"starvation"* in the Lower South, and "thus by *your vote,* and the votes of Northern men, can slavery be struck lifeless at both extremes."[34]

Despite the importance that members of the Liberty Party gave to abolishing the domestic trade, by the late 1840s this issue began to receive less attention, even as the political and economic critique of slavery took on greater prominence in the North. The main reason for this change can be found in the decision the political abolitionists made in the late 1840s to broaden their base of support. To attract as many voters as possible, new issues were added, and the more radical ideas, such as abolishing the interstate trade, were given less attention. The best example of this was in the alterations that occurred in the party platforms. Beginning with the Free Soil platform of 1848 and continuing through the Republican platforms of 1856 and 1860, the abolition of the interstate slave trade was no longer explicitly called for but was only implied in the demand that the federal government "relieve itself from all responsibility for the existence or continuance of slavery."[35]

Despite its decreased prominence, the domestic trade continued to play an important role in antislavery politics. Although it was touted less and less as the key to the removal of slavery and advocated by only a minority of Free Soil and Republican politicians, many individuals still believed that the interstate trade was an essential component of the political attack against slavery. This was especially true for the radicals, who interpreted their parties' platforms as calling for the slave trade's prohibition. And although by the 1850s fewer and fewer northern politicians were talking about the interstate trade and no major party had called for its prohibition, many southerners continued to believe that it was part of the Republican program and that it would be among the antislavery measures that the party would enact if it ever took power in Washington. As one 1860 editorial in a Kentucky newspaper warned: "The prohibition of the inter-State slave trade" was among "the avowed purposes of the republican party," and "its history leaves no doubt that it will undertake to carry out these purposes."[36] Of course, southerners also understood the implications of this action. In one of the many articles on this subject in the influential southern journal *DeBow's Review*, Edmund Ruffin predicted that after gaining power, a northern administration would quickly outlaw the interstate slave trade, "as long threatened," and "the institution of slavery would be hastened toward its doomed extinction."[37]

Although it is perhaps easy to dismiss such claims as being part of the heightened sense of anxiety that could be found in the South by this time, it is important to remember the consequences that such a threat posed for slaveholders in that region. No other issue of the day, including the expansion of slavery into the territories, was more crucial for the survival of the southern slave system than protecting the interstate trade. Simply put, it was this trade that was responsible for making human property the largest form of investment in the South, and there was absolutely no way that southern slave owners could have given that up. It is, of course, impossible to know what would have happened had northern politicians actually attempted to prohibit the interstate trade, although it does seem almost certain that slaveholding southerners would have had little choice but to leave the Union. What is important, however, is that many in the South did think that this was something that a Republican administration was going to do.

IV

Therefore, in many ways, the domestic trade always posed a problem for white southerners. On one hand, it was essential for the smooth running of the slave system, as well as the foundation for the region's primary source of wealth. Yet the very nature of the business was offensive to many people and difficult to hide. Moreover, it was interstate commerce, and, according to the U.S. Constitution, subject to congressional regulation. For that reason, slaveholders needed to protect this traffic from the political abolitionists' constitutional assault, while somehow defending the institution from the Garrisonian abolitionists' moralistic attacks.

Of the two, guaranteeing the right of slaveholders to transport their human property across state lines as articles of commerce always remained of greater importance, simply because without it their system would have collapsed. As with northern critics of this trade, southern defenders developed most of their legal arguments during the tumultuous Missouri debates of 1819–1820. Central to their defense was the fifth paragraph in article 1, section 9, of the Constitution, which states that "no preference shall be given by any regulation of commerce or revenue to the ports of one state over those of another." They used this clause to argue that any regulation of commerce must apply to all of the states equally and that Congress did not have the power to regulate the commerce of a limited number of states. In fact, according to southerners, that was the reason why the founders had given Congress the right to regulate commerce in the first place: to prevent individual states from abusing one another by means of state-issued regulations. As Representative Louis McLane of Delaware noted, "Partial regulations of commerce was [*sic*] precisely the evil which the power vested in the Congress was intended to guard against." Southerners also expanded on this argument by claiming that only the states had the right to regulate the internal slave trade, and many of them had already done so. Representative James Pindall of Virginia added an interesting twist to this defense when he pointed out that if only Congress had the right to regulate the interstate movement of slaves, then all state laws on this subject would be void, including those outlawing slavery in the northern states. Finally, southerners argued that the power to regulate commerce did not equal the power to destroy commerce. And many noted that northerners did not want to simply ban the commerce in slaves; they were ultimately seeking the destruction of the entire institution of southern slavery.[38]

The Missouri Compromise, of course, never settled this constitutional question, and it would continue to be an issue of concern to white southerners until the forming of the Confederacy. When the question next arose, during the great petition campaign of the mid-1830s, southerners were able to get a northern Democrat, Representative Charles Atherton of New Hampshire, to help them out. In a series of resolutions renewing the gag rule in 1838, Atherton noted that "petitions for the abolition of slavery in the District of Columbia and the Territories of the United States, and against the removal of slaves from one State to another, are a part of a plan of operations set on foot to affect the institution of slavery in the several States, and thus indirectly to destroy the institution within their limits." Arguing that Congress had no right to do indirectly what it cannot do directly, he included a resolution stating that "all attempts on the part of Congress to abolish slavery in the District of Columbia or the Territories, or to prohibit the removal of slaves from State to State, . . . are in violation of the Constitution, destructive of the fundamental principle on which the Union of these States rests, and beyond the jurisdiction of Congress."[39]

Although passage of the Atherton resolutions temporarily eased southern concerns, the matter was troubling enough by 1850 for Henry Clay to include it in his famous compromise. In the initial proposal, one resolution called for a declaration that "Congress has no power to prohibit or obstruct the trade in slaves between the slaveholding states." This resolution, however, was quickly dropped owing to pressure from northerners who refused to make such an admission, and in fact, another resolution was approved that did grant Congress the power to prohibit the slave trade within the District of Columbia, much to southerners' dismay.[40]

Finally, the interstate trade played a role in the various proposed compromises that emerged after the election of Abraham Lincoln in the winter of 1860. Senator Andrew Johnson of Tennessee proposed an amendment that, among other things, would prohibit Congress from touching "the inter-State trade, coastwise or inland." And, as a lesser-known part of his more well-known compromise, Senator John Crittenden of Kentucky proposed a constitutional amendment stating that "Congress shall have no power to prohibit or hinder the transportation of slaves from one State to another, or to a Territory in which slaves are by law permitted to be held, whether that transportation be by land, navigable rivers, or by the sea." The importance of protecting this form of commerce can ultimately be seen in the constitution that southerners adopted after forming a confederacy. They granted their Congress the power "to regulate commerce with foreign nations, and among the several States"; however, they also included two separate provisions guaranteeing their citizens the right to carry their slave property from state to state and into whatever territories the new nation may acquire in the future.[41]

Southerners were able to successfully prevent outsiders from destroying the lifeblood of their slave system, but they also faced a dilemma in defending their institution from the charge that it routinely tore families apart and turned humans into things. On this front, the task proved more difficult and the defense more diverse. Part of the problem was the very public nature of the slave trade. Auction sales needed to be advertised and were open to anyone who chose to attend. Traders likewise advertised their business, and they carried their merchandise, often shackled and chained, along public roads and waterways. Such activity was necessary for the smooth running of the system, but it was also distasteful and seemingly at odds with the way that southerners liked to depict their institution as a supposedly loving one based on paternalistic relationships.

Yet by offering an array of explanations, the white South did attempt to deflect these charges. One common strategy was to argue that outsiders did not understand the reality behind such events. In a series of sketches of southern life, the Virginia journalist Edward Pollard wrote: "I can assure you that the inhuman horrors of the slave auction-block exist only in imagination. Many instances of humanity may be observed there." Pollard and others claimed that instead of tearing families apart, slave auctions were frequently occasions when humane owners, often at great expense to themselves, stepped in to purchase individuals for the purpose of reuniting families or keeping them together. In addition, enslaved men and women of good character were almost always purchased by local owners who would keep them in the neighborhood. They added that when individual slaves needed to be sold, they usually were given the opportunity to choose their new owners. Of course, the system's defenders could not deny that some slave families were destroyed by the domestic trade; however, once again they argued that outsiders did not really understand such events and overestimated the impact of these partings. They claimed that owing to innate differences between the races, blacks did not feel the pain of separation as deeply as whites would and quickly got over whatever sorrow they may have initially felt.[42]

Southerners also liked to compare the treatment their slaves received to the conditions of the laboring poor in other parts of the world, especially in the North and in England. They noted that family breakups occurred in those areas as well and argued that families in slavery were more stable than the families of any other laboring group. Furthermore, they noted that there were individuals who abused any system. That some men battered and even murdered their wives did not mean that the institution of marriage should be abolished. Finally, even in cases where slaves were sold, defenders argued that only their labor was sold and that unlike northern laborers who lost their jobs, slaves were taken care of and did not have to seek further employment or starve. As William Harper of South Carolina explained it: "The slave is certainly liable to be sold. But, perhaps, it may be questioned, whether this is a greater evil than the liability of the laborer, in fully peopled countries, to be dismissed by his employer, with the uncertainty of being able to obtain employment, or the means of subsistence elsewhere. With us, the employer cannot dismiss his laborer without providing him with another employer. His means of subsistence are secure, and this is a compensation for much."[43]

The most effective argument, however, that southerners used to counter the charge that the horrors of the domestic trade were a fundamental component in their slave system was to simply deny that such events took place, or at least that they did not take place on as pervasive a scale as the abolitionists liked to claim. They argued that most owners were reluctant to sell their slaves and almost never did so purely for economic gain. Southerners insisted that owners loved their "people," as they liked to call them, and would just as soon part with a member of their family than with one of their slaves. Even in the Upper South, where the sale of surplus slaves could not be denied, southerners claimed that such sales supposedly brought greater anxiety and suffering to the owner than to the person being sold. As Henry Clay phrased it, an owner "takes care of his slaves; he fosters them, and treats them often with the tenderness of his own children. They multiply on his hands; he can not find employment for them, and he is ultimately, but most reluctantly and painfully, compelled to part with some of them because of the increase of numbers and the want of occupation."[44]

Of course, everyone knew that a certain number of sales did take place, so an important corollary to this argument was to shift the blame for these sales to someone else. More often than not, it was the person being sold who was saddled with the responsibility for his or her sale. Owners frequently sold slaves as a form of punishment and argued that the fault for such sales did not lie with them or with their system but with the individual being sold. Another popular tactic was to denounce the slave trader, or more accurately, use him as a scapegoat for the system. Southerners argued that most owners loved their slaves and would never part with them, but a few bad apples were responsible for all the evils that the slave trade produced. In addition to taking part in all the public aspects of this business, these "monsters in human form" took advantage of decent owners during times of economic hardship, enticing them to let go of individuals whom they would never sell under normal circumstances. Finally, one of the more interesting arguments was offered by a clergyman, Nathan L. Rice, who blamed the abolitionists for the increased evils of the interstate trade. According to Rice, these outsiders "have sought to make the slaves discontented in their condition; they have succeeded in decoying many from their masters, and running them to Canada. Consequently masters, for fear of losing their slaves, sell them to the hard-hearted trader; and they are marched to the South. . . . Such is human nature, that men provoked by such a course of conduct as that of the abolitionists, will, in many instances, resort to greater severity."[45]

It is impossible to know for certain how effective the system's defenders were in their attempt to deflect criticisms against the evils that the slave trade produced. Those sympathetic to the South and looking for an excuse probably found these arguments persuasive. But it seems more likely that a majority of northerners were not convinced, at least not in the short term. If they were, the Garrisonian abolitionists would not have continued to emphasize what they obviously considered a weak link in the proslavery defense. Or to put it another way, they talked about the slave trade because they knew that it forced Americans to confront the morality of southern slavery, and if it did not,

Garrison would have switched to another symbol of slavery in his masthead. The horrors of the slave trade were also what made *Uncle Tom's Cabin* so powerful, and they were a regular feature in virtually all of the fugitive slave narratives that increasingly appeared in the 1840s and 1850s and that northern readers found so irresistible.

In the long term, however, southerners may have proved more successful. In the effort to reunite the country after the Civil War, white Americans chose to forget the earlier abolitionist critiques of the Old South and allowed former slaveholding southerners to define what life had been like under their peculiar institution. In books and in plays, popular culture romanticized the Old South, and tales of the auction block and slave coffles disappeared from public memory. The same was true for more scholarly accounts, despite all the evidence to the contrary, as the work of Ulrich B. Phillips dominated the treatment of slavery in American universities for decades. And even today, after more than forty years of excellent scholarship on southern slavery and northern abolition, the domestic trade has not received the treatment or emphasis that it rightfully deserves. Despite all of our increased knowledge of the profitability of slavery, the slave community, and the motives and membership of the abolitionist movement, little mention is made of the domestic slave trade and the fundamental role it played in American society in the first half of the nineteenth century.

In part, this absence of historical scholarship is a result of the ambiguous place that slavery itself has held in American society, beginning with emancipation and continuing to the present. As the historian George Frederickson recently noted, "slavery is still the skeleton in the American closet." Whatever the reason, most Americans, black and white, continue to be uncomfortable talking about the subject of southern slavery and are divided over how it should be publicly remembered. Although some believe that its victims should be commemorated, others would just as soon have this troubling part of their history forgotten. If most people today are uncomfortable discussing the institution as a whole, it is doubly true that they do not want to be reminded that earlier generations of Americans bought and sold their ancestors like cattle or that some of their family fortunes were built upon this trade.[46]

Yet, although the domestic slave trade is certainly a painful part of the American past, it is also one that needs to be examined before we can truly understand the early history of the United States. It was a major factor in the rise of the Cotton Kingdom, and it helps explain why so many white southerners believed that they had no choice but to secede. In addition, it makes clear why so many Americans outside of the South increasingly believed that there was something wrong with the institution of slavery and why they thought that it had no place in the young republic. Ultimately, of course, these conflicting views could only be resolved by war.

As with so many other things, the long-term consequences of the domestic slave trade were made most clear by that insightful abolitionist, James Birney. In an address he wrote in 1833 for the Kentucky Society for the Gradual Relief of the State from Slavery, Birney predicted: "We think it very probable, that the general movement, which is now going on, of the slaves, from the middle to the southern states, will be noted by the future historian as one of the prominent causes, which *hastened* the termination of slavery in the United States." Although Birney was correct in his observation that the domestic trade did exactly that, unfortunately, the rest of his prediction has yet to come true. It is time that we return this unpleasant business to its proper place in our histories, and with it, gain a fuller understanding of southern slavery and antebellum American life.[47]

Notes

1. *Liberator* (Boston), May 23, 1835; James Birney to Charles Hammond, Nov. 14, 1835, in Dwight L. Dumond, ed., *Letters of James Gillespie Birney, 1831–1857,* 2 vols. (New York, 1938), 1:268.

2. Betty Fladeland, *James Gillespie Birney: Slaveholder to Abolitionist* (Ithaca, NY, 1955).

3. Steven Deyle, "The Irony of Liberty: The Origins of the Domestic Slave Trade," *Journal of the Early Republic* 12 (Spring 1992): 37–62.

4. For the best account of the magnitude of the domestic slave trade, see Michael Tadman, *Speculators and Slaves: Masters, Traders, and Slaves in the Old South* (Madison, 1989), esp. chap. 2. For a full discussion of the total slave migration to the Lower South and the percentage attributable to the interregional slave trade, as well as a discussion of the estimated number of local slave sales and the total number of southern slave sales, see Steven Deyle, "The Domestic Slave Trade in America" (Ph.D. diss., Columbia University, 1995), appendices A and B. For the best account of the cultural implications of turning humans into property, see Walter Johnson, *Soul by Soul: Life Inside the Antebellum Slave Market* (Cambridge, MA, 1999).

5. Tadman, *Speculators and Slaves,* chap. 2; Deyle, "Domestic Slave Trade in America," chap. 2.

6. *Farmers' Register* (Petersburg, VA), May 1835.

7. This was not the average price given for a southern slave; in the slave market, the term "prime" only referred to the best male and female workers, those who were young, healthy, and strong. The average bondsperson sold for roughly half the price of a prime male hand (and prime women sold for slightly less than prime men). Moreover, prime hands often sold in New Orleans for as much as $300 more than in other parts of the South. Nevertheless, the price paid for a prime hand is still the most useful for understanding the dimensions of the trade, especially when assessing long-term trends in the

market. Ulrich B. Phillips, *American Negro Slavery* (1918; reprint, Baton Rouge, 1966), 368–71; Robert J. Evans, "Some Economic Aspects of the Domestic Slave Trade, 1830–1860," *Southern Economic Journal* 27 (Apr. 1961): 330; Laurence J. Kotlikoff, "The Structure of Slave Prices in New Orleans, 1804 to 1862," *Economic Inquiry* 17 (Oct. 1979): 496–518; Roger Ransom and Richard Sutch, "Capitalists Without Capital: The Burden of Slavery and the Impact of Emancipation," *Agricultural History* 62 (Fall 1988): 133–60; Herman Freudenberger and Jonathan B. Pritchett, "The Domestic United States Slave Trade: New Evidence," *Journal of Interdisciplinary History* 21 (Winter 1991): 447–77.

8. John J. McCusker, *How Much Is That in Real Money? A Historical Price Index for Use as a Deflator of Money Values in the Economy of the United States* (Worcester, MA, 1992), 328–32.

9. In 1860 the total slave population was approximately four million. Claudia D. Goldin, "The Economics of Emancipation," *Journal of Economic History* 33 (Mar. 1973): 66–85; Jeremy Atack and Peter Passell, *A New Economic View of American History: From Colonial Times to 1940*, 2nd ed. (New York, 1979), 356; Ransom and Sutch, "Capitalists Without Capital," 149–52.

10. The assessed value of real estate is the amount at which real estate was assessed for purposes of taxation. Therefore, the true value of the property may, and most likely was, actually somewhat higher. Still, it seems unlikely that in 1860 the true value of southern real estate was greater than the value of the slave population. The slaveholding states included Alabama, Arkansas, Delaware, Florida, Georgia, Kentucky, Louisiana, Maryland, Mississippi, Missouri, North Carolina, South Carolina, Tennessee, Texas, Virginia, and the District of Columbia.

11. *Liberator,* Jan. 1, 1831 (emphasis in original).

12. *Liberator,* Apr. 23, 1831.

13. The masthead was changed to represent scenes of both contemporary slavery and emancipation in the future on March 2, 1838, and May 31, 1850. The quotation is from *Liberator,* Nov. 5, 1831; see also Wendell P. Garrison and Francis J. Garrison, *William Lloyd Garrison, 1805–1879: The Story of His Life Told by His Children,* 4 vols. (New York, 1885–89), 1:232.

14. For a good account of the shocking effect that slavery had on northern audiences, especially by the 1830s, see James L. Huston, "The Experiential Basis of the Northern Antislavery Impulse," *Journal of Southern History* 56 (Nov. 1990): 609–40.

15. Garrison witnessed the slave trade while working for Benjamin Lundy in Baltimore. The concept of a middle ground has taken on a number of meanings in recent years, but it is most often associated with encounters along the American frontier; see especially Richard White, *The Middle Ground: Indians, Empires, and Republics in the Great Lakes Region, 1650–1815* (New York, 1991). Yet the idea has also been effectively used in describing parts of the Upper South and its unique version of slavery, most notably by Barbara J. Fields in her study *Slavery and Freedom on the Middle Ground: Maryland During the Nineteenth Century* (New Haven, 1985). For another account that looks at the Upper South as a borderland that the abolitionists used to their advantage, see Stanley Harrold, "On the Borders of Slavery and Race: Charles T. Torrey and the Underground Railroad," *Journal of the Early Republic* 20 (Summer 2000): 273–92.

I thank James B. Stewart for pointing out the possibilities of viewing the Upper South as a middle ground that shaped northern impressions of slavery.

16. *Declaration of Sentiments and Constitution of the American Anti-Slavery Society* (New York, 1835), emphasis in original; *First Annual Report of the American Anti-Slavery Society* (New York, 1834), 59.

17. "Are Slaveholders Man-Stealers?" *Anti-Slavery Record*, Sept. 1837 (emphasis in original); see also Lewis Perry, *Radical Abolitionism: Anarchy and the Government of God in Antislavery Thought* (Ithaca, NY, 1973), 48–53.

18. "The Gentlemen Farmers of Virginia Attending Their Cattle-Market," Leeds Anti-slavery Series, No. 48, *Five Hundred Thousand Strokes for Freedom: A Series of Anti-Slavery Tracts, of Which Half a Million Are Now First Issued by the Friends of the Negro* (London, 1853), 1; William Lloyd Garrison to Edward M. Davis, Jan. 8, 1838, in Walter M. Merrill and Louis Ruchames, eds., *The Letters of William Lloyd Garrison*, 6 vols. (Cambridge, MA, 1971–81), 2:334.

19. A Former Resident of the Slave States, *Influence of Slavery upon the White Population*, Anti-Slavery Tracts, No. 9 (New York, [1855]), 6; Ronald G. Walters, *The Antislavery Appeal: American Abolitionism after 1830* (Baltimore, 1976), chap 6.

20. *Anti-Slavery Record*, Mar. 1836 (emphasis in original); Isaac Knapp, *Slavery Illustrated in Its Effects upon Woman and Domestic Society* (Boston, 1837), vii. For a later argument that northern women were responsible for the continuation of slavery because they had not exerted their influence to abolish it, see Mrs. E. L. Follen, *To Mothers in the Free States*, Anti-Slavery Tracts, No. 8 (New York, [1855]).

21. *Constitution and Address of the Female Anti-Slavery Society of Chatham-Street Chapel* (New York, 1834), 8 (emphasis in original); Catharine E. Beecher, *An Essay on Slavery and Abolitionism, with Reference to the Duty of American Females* (Philadelphia, 1837), 109. For good accounts of the female abolitionists, see Alma Lutz, *Crusade for Freedom: Women of the Antislavery Movement* (Boston, 1968); Jean F. Yellin, *Women and Sisters: The Antislavery Feminists in American Culture* (New Haven, 1989); Lori D. Ginzberg, *Women and the Work of Benevolence: Morality, Politics, and Class in the Nineteenth-Century United States* (New Haven, 1990); and Julie R. Jeffrey, *The Great Silent Army of Abolitionism: Ordinary Women in the Antislavery Movement* (Chapel Hill, 1998).

22. Harriet Beecher Stowe, *Uncle Tom's Cabin; or, Life Among the Lowly* (1851; repr., Boston, 1888), 494. This novel first appeared in serial form in 1851 and was not published as a book until the following year.

23. *Correspondence, between the Hon. F. H. Elmore, One of the South Carolina Delegation in Congress, and James G. Birney, One of the Secretaries of the American Anti-Slavery Society* (New York, 1838), 29–30 (hereafter *Elmore-Birney Correspondence*).

24. For a good account of the role the domestic trade played in developing a political argument against slavery, see David L. Lightner, "The Door to the Slave Bastille: The Abolitionist Assault upon the Interstate Slave Trade, 1833–1839," *Civil War History* 34 (Sept. 1988): 235–52. The Stanton speech [May 7, 1839] is quoted in ibid., 244; Alvan Stewart, "Report of a Speech Delivered Before a Joint Committee of the Legislature of Vermont [Oct. 25–27, 1838]" and "Address to the Abolitionists of the State of New York [Oct. 1836]," in Luther R. Marsh, ed., *Writings and Speeches of Alvan Stewart, on Slavery* (New York, 1860), 175–79, 98–107.

25. William M. Wiecek, *The Sources of Antislavery Constitutionalism in America, 1760–1848* (Ithaca, NY, 1977), esp. chaps. 7–8.

26. Stewart, "Address to the Abolitionists," 99.

27. William Jay, *A View of the Action of the Federal Government, on Behalf of Slavery* (New York, 1839), 88–89.

28. *Letter of Gerrit Smith to Hon. Henry Clay* [Mar. 21, 1839] (New York, 1839), 4–6.

29. Jay, *View of the Federal Government,* 185–86.

30. *Annals of Congress,* 16th Cong., 1st sess., 1820, 1199–1200. According to Harriet Martineau, an elderly James Madison also "believed that Congress has power to prohibit the internal slave trade," *Retrospect of Western Travel,* 2 vols. (London, 1838), 1:193. See Lightner, "Door to the Slave Bastille," 236–37. For a good account of the founders' original intentions concerning Congress's ability to regulate the interstate trade and the conflicting interpretations that had developed by the time of the Missouri debates, see Walter Berns, "The Constitution and the Migration of Slaves," *Yale Law Journal* 78 (Dec. 1968): 198–228.

31. It is impossible to know how many petitions were sent or how many people signed them. James Birney estimated that between January 1837 and March 1838 more than half a million people signed antislavery petitions; the number of signatures was probably much higher and increased over the next few years. Henry B. Stanton put the figure at more than two million signatures in 1838 and 1839. *Elmore-Birney Correspondence,* 46, 65. For a discussion of these petitions, see Dwight L. Dumond, *Antislavery: The Crusade for Freedom in America* (Ann Arbor, 1961), 245–48; William L. Miller, *Arguing About Slavery: The Great Battle in the United States Congress* (New York, 1995), 305–11.

32. Anti-Slavery Convention of American Women, *Circular to the Societies of Anti-Slavery Women in the United States* (n.d., n.p.), Boston Public Library; Stewart, "Address to the Abolitionists," 103.

33. *Proceedings of the N. H. Anti-Slavery Convention, Held in Concord, on the 11th & 12th of November, 1834* (Concord, NH, 1834), 37; Dumond, *Antislavery,* 246. Note that although these were the two most common petition topics in the third session of the Twenty-fifth Congress (Dec. 1838–Mar. 1839), by the Twenty-sixth Congress, the anti-Texas petitions numbered more than all other subjects combined.

34. *The Influence of the Slave Power,* Emancipator Extra, Tract No. 3 (Boston, 1843), 2 (emphasis in original). The best account of the role the slave trade played in antislavery politics is David L. Lightner, "The Interstate Slave Trade in Antislavery Politics," *Civil War History* 36 (June 1990): 119–36. For a good account of the development of the Liberty Party and later antislavery politics, see Richard H. Sewell, *Ballots for Freedom: Antislavery Politics in the United States, 1837–1860* (New York, 1976).

35. The Free Soil Party platform of 1848 and 1852 is quoted in Sewell, *Ballots for Freedom,* 198.

36. *Kentucky Statesman* (Lexington), Jan. 6, 1860. The best account of the ideology of the Republican Party can be found in Eric Foner, *Free Soil, Free Labor, Free Men: The Ideology of the Republican Party Before the Civil War* (New York, 1970).

37. Edmund Ruffin, "Consequences of Abolition Agitation," *DeBow's Review* (New Orleans), June 1857, 588. For other articles in *DeBow's Review* that argued that one of the first actions of a Republican administration would be the prohibition of the interstate

slave trade, see A. Roane, "The South, in the Union or Out of It," Oct. 1860, 453; Speech of Henry A. Wise, Jan. 1861, 117; and B. M. Parker, "Why We Resist, and What We Resist," Feb. 1861, 246.

38. *Annals of Congress,* 16th Cong., 1st sess., 1820, 1162, 1274. For a sampling of southern speeches on this topic, see the remarks of Senator John Elliott (Georgia) and Representatives Alexander Smyth (Virginia), Benjamin Hardin (Kentucky), Philip Barbour (Virginia), Charles Pinckney (South Carolina), and Christopher Rankin (Mississippi), ibid., 131, 996–97, 1079–80, 1239, 1317–18, 1343–44.

39. *Congressional Globe,* 25th Cong., 3rd sess., 1838, 22–23.

40. *Remarks of Mr. Clay, of Kentucky, on Introducing His Propositions to Compromise, on the Slavery Question* (Washington, 1850), 10.

41. *Congressional Globe,* 36th Cong., 2nd sess., 1860, 83, 114. The clauses in the Confederate constitution concerning commerce and slaves are art. 1, sec. 8; art. 4, sec. 2; and art. 4, sec. 3. Emory M. Thomas, *The Confederate Nation, 1861–1865* (New York, 1979), 311, 319–20.

42. Edward A. Pollard, *Black Diamonds Gathered in the Darkey Homes of the South* [1859], in *Slavery Defended: The Views of the Old South,* ed. Eric L. McKitrick (Englewood Cliffs, NJ, 1963), 166–67.

43. William Harper, *Memoir on Slavery* [1837], in *The Ideology of Slavery: Proslavery Thought in the Antebellum South, 1830–1860,* ed. Drew G. Faust (Baton Rouge, 1981), 110.

44. Henry Clay, Senate speech of July 22, 1850, in *The Works of Henry Clay: Comprising His Life, Correspondence and Speeches,* ed. Calvin Cotton, 10 vols. (New York, 1904), 9:547.

45. J. Blanchard and N. L. Rice, *A Debate on Slavery: Held in the City of Cincinnati, on the First, Second, Third, and Sixth Days of October, 1845, upon the Question: Is Slave-Holding in Itself Sinful, and the Relation between Master and Slave, a Sinful Relation?* (Cincinnati, 1846), 28–29. For a good account of using the slave trader as a scapegoat, see Tadman, *Speculators and Slaves,* chap. 7.

46. George M. Frederickson, "The Skeleton in the Closet," *New York Review of Books,* Nov. 2, 2000, 61–66 (quotation on p. 61).

47. Dumond, *Letters of James Gillespie Birney,* 1:108.

6

The Interregional Slave Trade in the History and Myth-Making of the U.S. South

MICHAEL TADMAN

The domestic slave trade has had a curious place in southern history and has always posed problems for those seeking to portray slavery as a benign and paternal institution. In antebellum polemics about the slavery controversy, white southern propagandists pretended that the trade was of only marginal importance and that slave traders were social outcasts: in the post-slavery years the hiding of the slave trader became a compulsory ingredient in the promotion of the plantation legend. This essay looks beyond these rationalizations and tries to discover how it was possible for the slaveholding society of the South to maintain its benevolent self-image and at the same time take part in a massive slave traffic that terrified slaves and destroyed many of their families. The essay looks first at contemporary antebellum debates about the significance of the trade and then turns to the fundamental question of establishing how extensive this business really was. Evidence of scale (and grass-roots organization) then makes it possible to consider how deeply the trade impacted the lives of the enslaved. Later sections of the essay reflect on how slaveholders and their inheritors rationalized the omnipresent slaving business.

Antebellum Debates About the Trade: Abolitionists and the Defenders of Slavery

The domestic trade had deep roots in the later colonial period and was not simply a by-product of America's 1807 prohibition of foreign slave importation. Indeed, the domestic traffic overlapped with at least the last several decades of the African trade.[1] Essential for the development of the internal trade was, first, the fact that by the eighteenth century North America's slave population grew by natural increase, thereby producing a reservoir of slaves for sale. The second essential factor was demand for slaves — the booming demand that came with the opening up of new slave territories from the late eighteenth century onward. As new land was opened, the southern frontier and the range of the trade rapidly advanced southward and westward. With natural increase and rising slave populations, a succession of states went through the transition from net importer to net exporter. In the 1790s, the core areas of slave exportation within the United States were Maryland, Delaware, and substantial parts of Virginia (and there was also a well-established pattern of quite significant exportation from more northerly states). By the 1820s, the Carolinas and Kentucky had been added to the ranks of the exporters, and by the 1850s Tennessee and parts of Missouri, Georgia, and Alabama had been added. For broad indications of these importing and exporting patterns, see the maps in figure 6.1, and for some indications of numbers, see table 6.1.

Although the trade had deep late-colonial roots, it was in the great abolitionist years from 1830 onward that it became the focus of huge sectional debate. The trade raised matters that were difficult for proslavery propagandists to defend, and as a result the slaveholder strategy, in the public press at least, was denial. Essentially, the proslavery thesis presented the master as the patriarch and protector of his "family white and black," and the trader appeared as a distasteful outcast who threatened families but whose efforts could muster only a handful of unfortunate slaves. As James Stirling, a Scottish visitor, observed in the 1850s, "the slave traffic was a sore subject with the defenders of slavery. . . . They fain would . . . load all the iniquities of the [slavery] system on . . . [the trader's] unlucky back."[2] Since propagandists maintained that the slaveholders' mission was not to make profits but to "civilize" slaves, they were willing to suggest that many owners fell into debt and that in such cases some might be obliged to sell slaves. Propagandists, though, were well-rehearsed in dealing with the embarrassments of the "peculiar institution," and J. T. Randolph's proslavery novel *The Cabin and the Parlor* (1852) gives us a characteristic glimpse of what supposedly happened when owners fell on hard times: "The slaves . . . were all purchased to remain

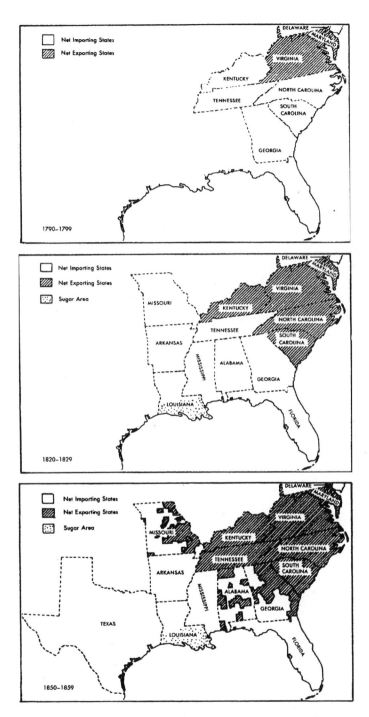

Figure 6.1. Principal Slave-Exporting and Slave-Importing States, 1790s, 1820s, and 1850s. *Source:* Michael Tadman, *Speculators and Slaves: Masters, Traders, and Slaves in the Old South* (Madison: University of Wisconsin Press, 1989), pp. 6–7.

Table 6.1. Estimates of Net Importations and Exportations of Slaves

	1790–1799	1800–1809	1810–1819	1820–1829	1830–1839	1840–1849	1850–1859
Alabama			+35,500	+54,156	+96,520	+16,532	+10,752
Arkansas			+1,000	+2,123	+12,752	+18,984	+47,443
Delaware	−4,523	−3,204	−817	−2,270	−1,314	−912	−920
D.C.		−1,123	−576	−1,944	−2,575	−2,030	−1,222
Florida			+1,000	+2,627	+5,833	+5,657	+11,850
Georgia	+6,095	+11,231	+10,713	+18,324	+10,403	+19,873	−7,876
Kentucky	+21,636	+25,837	+18,742	−916	−19,907	−19,266	−31,215
Louisiana*		+2,642	+47,148	+37,426	+66,795	+68,227	+60,484
Maryland	−22,221	−19,960	−33,070	−32,795	−33,753	−21,348	−21,777
Mississippi		+2,152	+9,123	+19,556	+101,810	+53,028	+48,560
Missouri			+5,460	+10,104	+24,287	+11,406	+6,314
N. Carolina	+3,671	−407	−13,361	−20,113	−52,044	−22,481	−22,390
S. Carolina	+4,435	+6,474	+1,925	−20,517	−56,683	−28,947	−65,053
Tennessee	+6,645	+21,788	+19,079	+31,577	+6,930	+4,837	−17,702
Texas						+28,622	+99,190
Virginia	−22,767	−41,097	−75,562	−76,157	−118,474	−88,918	−82,573

Source: Adapted from Michael Tadman, *Speculators and Slaves; Masters, Traders, and Slaves in the Old South* (Madison: University of Wisconsin Press, 1989), p. 12. *Notes:* Basic evidence is derived from federal censuses. The method used is the comparison of decennial growth rates of the slave population. For an explanation of the procedures involved and for adjustments made to cancel out importations from the African trade, see ibid., pp. 225–27. At least 60 to 70 percent of *state* totals are attributable to trading and the rest to planter migrations. The *net* total for a given state will significantly undercount actual totals of slave movements and of slaves traded. This is because net-exporting states often contained subregions of net importation (and net importers often had sub-regions of net exportation). * Totals for Louisiana are scaled up to allow for the exceptionally high mortality and exceptionally low birth rates of the sugar parishes. See Tadman, "The Demographic Cost of Sugar: Debates on Slave Societies and Natural Increase in the Americas," *American Historical Review* 105 (December 2000), pp. 1534–75.

in the district. Even among those planters who showed little concern for the ruined Courtneys, there was a sentiment of honor on this point. . . . A trader who had made his appearance was hustled away rather rudely by one or two present, so that, after making a few ineffectual bids, he thought it prudent to retire."[3] Sometimes, it was conceded, traders did manage to buy slaves in such circumstances. Supposedly, however, they usually made up most of their meager collections with runaway and "criminal" slaves, that is, with individuals who supposedly stood to benefit from the shock and "discipline" of being sold.[4]

The abolitionists' case, of course, was fundamentally different, and the trade was seen as vital to the survival of the slave system. Slaves, they argued, lacked *positive* incentives to work well, plantation monocultures supposedly led to soil exhaustion, and so slave-based agriculture was seen as hopelessly unprofitable in the Upper South. From this, abolitionists went on to argue that what kept the slave system alive in the Upper South were the supplementary incomes gained from selling surplus slaves to professional "Negro specula-tors." And, they claimed, associated with this was the deliberate "rearing" and "breeding" of slaves for sale.

The abolitionist Alvan Stewart believed that if the internal trade could be outlawed "the great door to the slave Bastille" would be broken. He argued that without the interstate market "the slaves of Maryland and Virginia would eat up their masters, and the masters must emancipate in self-defence, to save themselves from destruction." In Alabama, Louisiana, and Mississippi, he continued, "there is such havoc annually by death among the slaves of the great planters . . . that in less than seven years, if no slave could be imported into those southern regions, one half of the plantations would lie uncultivated for want of slaves."[5] But, abolitionists argued, with the domestic trade un-checked, the cash inducements of the speculator meant that owners routinely resorted to the callous separation of thousands of families.[6]

The proslavery position was self-serving and fundamentally misleading, but it formed the basis of a plantation legend that still commands some influence. The abolitionists' stance was essentially correct about the scale of the trade and about the scapegoating of the trader, but their thesis also led to certain misrepresentations. They exaggerated planter debt and vastly exaggerated the slaveowners' resort to systematic slave breeding. Their debt thesis, as we shall see, led to an underestimate of the voluntary participation of slaveowners in the business of slave selling. At the same time, their accusation of slave breed-ing greatly overstated some aspects of dislocation within the slave community. Often too, abolitionists assumed that natural *decrease* dominated slave com-munities in the importing states; in fact, such decrease was confined to the small number of Lower South slaves who worked on sugar plantations.[7]

The Scale of the Trade

In order to have any real sense of the significance of the trade, numbers are highly important—numbers of slaves bought and sold, numbers of fami-lies separated, numbers of dollars gained when slaves were turned into cash. Without such numbers, we lack context and can only guess at the significance of the trade for black lives and for white lives. Numbers allow us to see the everyday presence of the trader in southern communities. This presence, and statistics suggesting motives for selling to the trader, form a basis for inferring the trader's status in white society. And numbers allow us to judge what the great mass of slaves thought of a slaveholding society that showed so little respect for black families and emotions.

The full extent of the trade is at first hidden by the nature of the historical records that have survived. Antismuggling legislation connected with the closure of the African slave trade in 1808 required that coastwise shipments of slaves be officially recorded; this means that, for the coastal branch of the trade, we have a store of ships' manifests that, though incomplete, is still massive. The problem, however, as we shall see below, is that coastwise shipments represented only a small part of the trade. The vast bulk of trading was not coastal but instead operated in the countryside and in villages and small towns scattered across the whole of the South. In the dominant land-based trade there was rarely any legal requirement to record trading activity, and this means that considerable effort is needed to reconstruct this traffic.

Some help in identifying traders is provided by occupational descriptions in the federal censuses of 1850 and 1860, but, as we shall see, traders were often men of considerable wealth, with interests including not only trading but planting and perhaps a general store. On a great many occasions, therefore, individuals known to have been active slave traders appear simply as "merchant" or "planter" rather than "Negro trader." Furthermore, the census often abbreviated "Negro trader" or "Negro speculator" to "trader" or "speculator." Problems arise, too, when we turn for help to the numerous county histories that were written in the fifty or so years after slavery ended. After the Civil War, local histories advanced the plantation legend of the "Sunny South," and their authors were not keen to document the trade. As a result, traders appear as men of property and standing, but their "Negro speculation" tends not to be mentioned.

Frederic Bancroft's pioneering 1931 study *Slave Trading in the Old South* made a great contribution to establishing the scale of the trade, and in so doing, Bancroft, as he had intended, launched a powerful assault on U. B. Phillips's benign view of slavery.[8] The essential foundation of Bancroft's work was the compilation, after many years of research in newspaper files, of vast numbers of slave traders' advertisements. To these he added the results of interviews that, in about 1902, he had conducted with black and white southerners who remembered the trade. The result was a still-unrivaled set of profiles and lists of slave traders in towns and cities across the South. Bancroft had achieved a major breakthrough, but the great limitation of his work was that it related almost exclusively to the urban trade. There could no longer be any doubt that long-distance slave trading was intensely active in the towns of the South, but the overall volume of the trade and the level of its impact across the rural South still remained unclear.

In 1974, Robert W. Fogel and Stanley L. Engerman's *Time on the Cross* made important claims about the domestic slave trade, arguing that it accounted at most for about 16 percent of slave movements between the states (the rest being made up by planters who moved west with their slaves).[9] Fogel and Engerman's reading of the trade contributed significantly to their overall interpretation of slavery as a system based on willing workers and high slave morale, but it turns out that their estimate of the trade rested on an unrepresentative sample. They took as their sample the coastal traffic between the Chesapeake ports and New Orleans, and their key (but unreliable) assumption was that the composition of that trade to New Orleans (60 percent male) was typical of the internal trade as a whole. Since they correctly calculated that there was virtually no surplus of male slaves in the overall westward movement of slaves (combining planter migrations and the trade), their assumption concerning the sex ratio of the trade led them to suggest that trading had little influence on this total slave exodus. For Fogel and Engerman, planter migration was far more important than the trade, and as a result family separations were few. I show below, however, that, with the single exception of the New Orleans market, the domestic trade carried more or less equal numbers of males and females, and this means that calculations using male-female ratios are not helpful in establishing the importance of the trade.

My own quantitative estimate, in *Speculators and Slaves*, used two parallel methods, both of which indicate that trading accounted for at least 60 to 70 percent of interregional slave movements — vastly more than the maximum of 16 percent suggested by Fogel and Engerman. One method was basically demographic, but it focused on the highly *age-selective* nature of the trade, not on sex ratios. I found that the structure of the total movement of slaves between the states fitted very closely with the age-selective nature of the trade (on age selectivity see below) and did not fit with the basically nonselective character of planter migrations. This demographic analysis covered all of the slave states and suggests the dominance of the trade across the whole South. My second method was a case study taking the example of traders exporting slaves from South Carolina in the 1850s. This investigation went beyond the urban focus of Bancroft and found intensive export trading in all districts of the state.[10]

There is not the space in this short essay to reproduce the detailed evidence developed in *Speculators and Slaves*, but some of the essentials can be outlined. The estimate which I based on age structures used the survival-rate technique. This method assumes that, in the different states, slaves of the same age and sex would have shared a similar mortality rate over a given decade. In other words, they should have had similar survival rates (that is, similar percentages should have survived from the start to the end of the decade). Where major state or regional differences in age-specific (or sex-specific) survival rates are found, the contrasts are attributed to interstate or interregional movement.[11]

What happens in practice when we look at slave survival rates is that exporting states such as Maryland show (for, say, males aged ten to nineteen at the 1850 census and therefore aged twenty to twenty-nine in 1860) a survival rate as low as 60 percent, whereas in an importing state such as Texas the survival rate might be a massive 250 percent. These sharp regional contrasts in age-specific survival rates indicate that massive and highly age-selective slave movement must have taken place. In addition, we know that planter migrations would have been essentially nonselective (typically involving the western movement of whole slaveholdings made up of mixed ages). The age-selective nature of the slave exodus means, therefore, that trading must have played the dominant role in slave movements. Detailed calculations suggest, in fact, that trading represented at least 60 to 70 percent of the interregional movement of slaves. And they suggest, too, that the total number of slaves traded in the period from 1790 to 1860 would have been well over one million.[12]

My second method developed a case study of a particular state (South Carolina) and undertook a direct count of slave-trading firms which exported from that state in a sample decade (the 1850s). Auction firms were not included, nor were dealers of any kind who were involved merely in intrastate sales. Basic county-level evidence of trading firms was found by checking occupational categories in the census and by searching newspapers for traders' advertisements. Using leads from these sources, court and other records were then investigated. These sources brought a significant but far-from-complete count of trading firms. (The incomplete nature of the results arose partly because of the problems of census categorization that have already been mentioned, partly because traders, being migratory, very often did not use newspaper advertisements, and it arose also because for several districts virtually all antebellum newspaper and court files have been destroyed.) Although incomplete, this stage of my count of traders nevertheless identified ninety-seven fully documented trading firms (spread very widely across the state) and identified a further sixteen probable or very probable trading firms and forty-four possible firms.

The chance survival of several hundred letters of one firm, that of Ziba Oakes, allowed me to take the count of South Carolina traders a significant stage further, and this began to reveal the true number of active firms.[13] One of the most important sets of evidence in the Oakes collection comes from a substantial series of letters written to Oakes by A. J. McElveen, a buying agent based near Sumterville, a South Carolina town that was a little more than a hundred miles northwest of Charleston. In the first stage of my study, a complete surviving set of Sumter District's newspaper files had documented only three trading firms active in that district during the 1850s, and the census failed to give conclusive evidence regarding any firms. But for the few years for which they survive (late August 1853 to October 1857), the McElveen-Oakes letters directly document eleven firms that were active locally. Sumter District exported an annual average of 288 slaves in the 1850s (an average of 26 slaves per fully documented firm), and the Oakes letters suggest that traders must have accounted for a very high percentage of these slave movements.[14]

As one of Oakes's many district agents, McElveen bought slaves and sent them on to Charleston, where Oakes sold them to long-distance buyers. It is clear that McElveen's competition in Sumter District came not from suppliers of the Charleston resale market but from "traders west," who carried their slaves directly to the western markets.[15] In December 1856 McElveen wrote that "the prices of negroes are such that [buying for a quick turnover at Charleston] I don't see any chance to buy to make a dollar and what I am to do I can't say. The traders West are here buying everything." The previous month, after many months of active trading, he reported: "I reckon that will be the last of the traders flying round. We had 8 or 10 in Sumter." Two weeks later, however, he wrote: "Our country are [*sic*] never clear of buyers. I am certain if I could keep a lot of negroes in Sumter I could sell them [to traders]. We have not been clear of one or more buyers since last July." In the following February McElveen reported that he had just attended a Sumter-area sale and that there were "some ten western traders here. A good many bought and paid cash." By June 1857 he was advising: "I think it would do very well to commence to buy soon as the traders flood through the market in the summer." And in August he reported that traders were "floating through the country." He mentioned several, including one Mr. Owens from Hamburg, South Carolina, one Mr. Witherspoon, from Tennessee, and one Mr. Willey from Mississippi, and he added that numerous traders had agents in the area.[16]

Evidence from Sumter suggests that traders must have accounted for a large majority of the slaves who left that area in the 1850s, and it seems reasonable to extend a similar conclusion to South Carolina as a whole. The Sumter location was not unusually favorable, and in any case traders would have followed market forces, seeking the cheapest slaves rather than giving excessive attention to one district. The traders who appear in the McElveen letters almost certainly bought heavily in that district, even though some, probably most, would also have bought in neighboring districts.[17] Indeed, had they not bought extensively on his patch, McElveen would surely have shown only passing interest in them. There is also no reason why the years covered by the McElveen letters should have been exceptionally active ones for 1850s South Carolina. The dominance of the trade in the western movement of slaves is therefore shown both by the broad-based survival-rate data for the South as a whole and by the South Carolina and Sumter case study.

The Grassroots and the Special Case of New Orleans

Historical and popular literature has tended to focus on the urban centers of the trade, especially New Orleans, but it would be wrong to assume either that New Orleans was a typical market or that traders and clients usually met at urban markets. New Orleans was of special importance, and in supplying the specialist demands of that city and its hinterland, Chesapeake ports such as Richmond, Virginia, were of great significance. Still, most traders acquired their slaves by touring the farming districts of their buying area and also by meeting clients at small market towns and hamlets. In selling, too, the major towns and cities were far from being dominant: most traders, after marching their slaves southward in coffles, sold them by touring the plantations and small settlements. The scattered, intensely rural nature of the South meant that most of the trader's buying and selling was rural, and it meant, too, that the great majority of transactions were private sales, rather than being public auctions.

New Orleans did have a special place in the trade. Of more than a quarter of a million slaves imported into the Lower South in the 1850s, that city accounted for about 20 percent, but, in the importing states, all other major urban centers put together probably accounted for no more than another 10 percent. The New Orleans market gained notoriety for several reasons. First, it was the preeminent urban market for handling slaves. Second, it was a spectacular city that attracted travel writers whose books seldom failed to comment on slave-selling. Third, the trade to this renowned center of pleasure and indulgence included a sensational subspecialty—the "fancy" trade, a traffic in light-skinned slave women sold for the sexual pleasure of their buyers. Traders' records suggest that New Orleans was unrivaled in the trade in "fancy maids," and every year, hundreds of such girls and women brought huge prices in the Crescent City. Finally, the city's reputation was special because slaves knew, and the threatening tales of masters frequently reminded them, that this was the great entry point for sale to the dreaded sugar plantations of Louisiana.[18]

Traders' bills of sale and correspondence show an almost universal practice of buying roughly equal numbers of male and female slaves, the only significant exception being when traders bought for the New Orleans market and for the sugar plantations of its southern Louisiana hinterland.[19] The extreme labor regime that sugar planters demanded meant an insistence on a workforce with a permanent excess of sturdy adult males, and this in turn led to specialist importation. Proximity to the sugar parishes meant, therefore, that the composition of the New Orleans slave market was highly exceptional. Importations to that city were about 58 percent male, and when we look at the slaves actually selected by sugar planters, we find that about two-thirds were male.[20] Significantly, the debilitating labor regime and the shortage of potentially childbearing women that resulted from male-dominated importation meant that the Louisiana sugar area, uniquely for North America, suffered from very marked excess of deaths over births.[21]

Much of the supply to New Orleans and the sugar parishes came by the traditional overland routes, but sea communication was convenient between the Chesapeake and the Crescent City, so a well-organized coastal shipping trade flourished, and specialized slave ships operated during the season (about October to February) from Richmond and some other ports. As we have seen, this coastal traffic is relatively well documented in ships' manifests, travelers' accounts, and elsewhere. Apart from the New Orleans route, however, the coastal trade was of only slight importance, probably accounting for no more than 5 percent of the entire interstate trade.[22]

The essentially rural foundations of the domestic trade as a whole showed up in the South Carolina case study. My 1850s sample revealed slave-exporting firms based in all parts of the state, but the great majority had no connection with Charleston or Columbia. Doctor Thomas C. Weatherly, although his title was more dignified than most, was typical of the 1850s South Carolina traders in his methods. A fellow speculator met him at Hayneville, Alabama, and reported: "Dr. Weatherly is here. He lives in his tents. He told me he sold ten negroes last week at fair prices. [As a means of meeting customers] he is following the counties round attending the courts." In 1846, the North Carolina trader T. W. Burton wrote from Lowndes County, Mississippi, and again illustrated typical trading patterns. He reported, "There is a vast quantity of negroes in the Market [in Lowndes County] and traders are holding them high," and in neighboring Monroe County he found that traders were offering slaves "at every village in the county" and that the area was "full of Negroes." Having moved to Alabama, he found that "there is negroes [offered by traders] all through the state." Charles Ball, part of a coffle of slaves taken from Virginia to Georgia, recalled: "At last we stopped at one Ben Tarver's place in Jones County, Georgia. . . . During the time I stayed there, which was two weeks, Finney [the speculator] used to take out his slaves every day, to try to sell them, bringing those back whom he failed to dispose of."[23]

Trading Practices

The auction block often appears in published descriptions of slave dealing, but it would be wrong to assume that public auctions were the principal means that traders employed in buying and selling. Especially at Richmond there were firms made up of professional auctioneers that acted as links between locally based and long-distance traders, but in most of the trade, even in the towns and cities, private transactions with clients were much more important than public auctions. Auctions were used when sheriffs sold slaves for debt, and they were often used at the probate (or "estate") sales that sometimes followed the death of an owner. Such auctions were highly visible, often being held in public squares and in other prominent locations, and they were therefore the sales most likely to be witnessed and written about by travelers to the South. Traders did buy some of their slaves at estate and sheriff's sales, but the main importance of such sales for traders usually lay in the fact that they were significant local events where contacts could be made and where potential clients could be found.

The trader's limited involvement in probate and sheriff's sales stemmed from practical considerations. First, at probate sales especially, it was usual for all of the deceased's slaves to be offered, no matter what their age, health, or ability. For this purpose the slaves would be divided into mixed-age lots that approximated to families or parts of families. Traders, however, had special requirements, and such mixed lots, with too many hard-to-sell slaves, were therefore of little interest. Demand in the Lower South was for "young and likely Negroes" (strong, healthy teenagers and young adults), and traders bought selectively to satisfy this demand.

The second major problem with probate and with many sheriff's sales concerned the terms of sale. The South was essentially a credit-based society, and southerners could not normally command large sums in cash, and, in keeping with this, estate sales were usually conducted on the basis of payments over three (sometimes two) years. Traders, however, had a very strong preference for buying and selling for cash. In a society where credit transactions dominated, the traders' offers of cash would have brought great temptations.[24] The cash system also seems to have developed because slave trading represented capital investment on a scale that, for the antebellum period, was huge. Selling for cash meant that the banks and other financial backers from whom traders borrowed could be fairly confident about a safe return on their loans. Moreover, traders needed to sell for cash partly because collecting credit payments over several years and from a geographically dispersed set of customers would have been impossibly risky and labor-intensive.[25]

Slaveholder Motivations

The trading practices just outlined have a significance that is wider than simply informing us about technical business arrangements: they suggest something about the motivations of traders' customers. First, we should note that work by econometricians seems to have established the generally profitable nature of antebellum slavery, and this suggests that debt sales would have been far less common than many contemporary propagandists assumed. The specific patterns discussed above help directly to establish that—contrary to the claims of both proslavery and abolitionist commentators—those selling to traders were not usually forced to do so by pressure of debt. In particular, it looks as though traders bought no more than 5 percent of their slaves from debt, probate, and other court sales, and it appears furthermore that, even when court proceedings were not involved, sellers were not usually staving off imminent financial trouble when they sold to the trader.[26] Runaway slaves and those termed "criminal" by their owners do not seem to have made up more than a small proportion of the trade. Evidence for this comes from the fact that although runaways were nearly always male, the trade was made up of roughly equal numbers of males and females. In addition, we might expect that "criminal" slaves would often have been marked by whipping, and we know that traders regarded slaves with such scars as risky buys.[27]

A closer investigation of the profitability of agriculture in the selling states allows us to say more about slaveholder motivations in those states. According to abolitionists, the lands of the selling states had become exhausted by plantation monocultures, and if they wanted to avoid bankruptcy, slaveholders there had no choice but to sell off slaves. In reality the situation was not so dramatic, and selling was optional. First, the slave population of the United States grew rapidly by natural increase (as censuses show, at a rate of about 25 percent per decade), so Upper South owners had the choice of whether to sell some of that increase. Second, agricultural activities did make healthy profits, and for most, revenue from slave exportation seems to have supplemented income, rather than making the difference between survival and bankruptcy. Trading revenues seem, in fact, to have been equivalent to about 15 to 20 percent of the value of that agricultural output.[28]

A case study of South Carolina shows significant agricultural and demographic patterns. From as early as the 1820s, South Carolina was a persistent net exporter of slaves, and yet by 1860 it sustained a population of 402,000 slaves, which was 150,000 more slaves than in 1820. During the 1850s, despite heavy exportation, the state's slave population rose from 385,000 to 402,000 — and its land was clearly far from exhausted. In the same decade, its total area of improved land rose from 4 to 4.5 million acres, and cotton production increased from 300,901 to 353,412 bales. The agricultural economy of this major slave-exporting state expanded vigorously: its lands were far from exhausted, and it sustained an increasing slave population.[29]

Overall, the pattern in the selling states seems to have been that natural increase and the western demand for slaves created options. Slaveowners would routinely weigh the relative advantages of working slaves at home and of selling some slaves for ready cash. At the macro level, slave trading was vital for the growth of the slave economy, but at a micro level most of the individual sales were voluntary. Slaveholders had choices, and their choices hurt slaves.

Family Separations and the Values of Slaves and Owners

From both the nineteenth-century autobiographies of slaves and the 1930s interviews with aged ex-slaves, the inescapable message is the dread of being sold South, the awful fear that your owner would sell you or your loved ones to the trader.[30] Because of the way in which traders bought their slaves, the greatest shocks of immediate separation would have come in the exporting states. Most separations would have taken place in private transactions on farms and plantations, but the shock of family destruction would, of course, have reverberated in the slave community just as widely as if it had taken place in the most public of auctions.

We can begin to gauge the nature and extent of this family dislocation by analyzing the bills of sale of traders in the exporting region and by noting the units in which slaves were bought from owners.[31] About 50 percent of those traded were young adults, but, my sample suggests, there were almost no cases where husband and wife (with or without children) could have been bought together. Women sold with young children (but without husband) made up about 7 percent of the sample (the children in these sales making up another 14 percent). Significantly, there were no equivalent cases of men sold with children but without wives. Nineteen percent of the sample was made up of men aged twenty and older and sold without any family, and another 19 percent was made up of women aged fifteen and older and sold without any family. Two percent of the sample consisted of children under eight years old and sold without any parent; 8 percent were children aged eight to eleven and sold alone, and 15 percent were children aged twelve or thirteen and sold alone.

The units of sale suited the convenience of sellers, who often wanted to cash in a limited portion of their stock of slaves, and they fitted the demands of the trader's Lower South buyers, who usually bought in small numbers to fit immediate priorities. After weighting my statistics to allow for likely percentages who might typically have been married by certain ages, and allowing for voluntary separation and separation by death, I was able to estimate the level of wreckage brought by the interregional trade. My conclusion was that, for slaves born in the exporting states, one in five marriages would have been destroyed by the trade and one in three children aged under fourteen years would have been separated from one or both parents.

Families would also have been dislocated by local sales, by divisions of estates at the death of owners, and by the giving of slaves as presents, but slave narratives and interviews suggest that such separations were feared much less than those at the hands of the trader. To an important extent slaves could probably adjust not only to local cross-plantation marriages but also to what we might call local cross-plantation families — that is, to situations in which adult and child members of a family might be spread among several local owners. But the long-distance trade was a different matter.

The specific pattern of long-distance separation was not only hugely significant in an overall moral sense for the level of suffering that it inflicted on slaves but also for the nature of its impact on master-slave relationships. It is significant that although almost all slaves would have lived in dread of separation and would have known slaves who had been separated, my statistics suggest that the majority of marriages and of parent-child bonds were not broken by long-distance sale. This situation meant that the slave's sense of family could remain strong, but it also meant that, across the slave communities of the antebellum South, there would have been deep distrust of owners as a group.[32] With slaves, family life was the norm and was the great source of comfort for most. Still, however, owners constantly threatened the closest of family ties — and slaves judged owners on the basis of their behavior toward them.

At first sight, separations on the scale just described and slave resentments as deep and as far-reaching would seem to rule out, for the great mass of owners, any self-image of benevolence. In practice, however, as work by Eugene Genovese has shown, a self-image of benevolent paternalism dominates slaveholders' records. We find even in letters written for no special public propaganda purpose a strong slaveowner tradition of referring, apparently benevolently, to "my people" and to "my family white and black."[33] How could owners actively sustain a culture that was so permissive of the breaking up of slave families and still, probably in a majority of cases, see themselves as benevolent paternalists? The answer to the paradox seems to be given by what might be called the "key slave" phenomenon.[34]

For psychological and ideological reasons, most owners needed to see themselves as benevolent—and a process of distinguishing between the "coarse mass of slaves" and those they saw as "worthy" or as more sophisticated allowed them to maintain a benevolent self-image no matter what they did to family ties. Owners could see themselves as being close to certain worthy slaves (those I call "key slaves"), and these would usually be the driver (who supervised the field work of other slaves), the caretaker, and perhaps the head butler. By affording key slaves special privileges, including considerable protection of family ties, owners could see themselves as benevolent heads of the "family white and black," but this also meant that they could treat the family ties of the coarse mass of slaves with indifference. A romantic racism toward key slaves allowed the crudest attitudes and treatment toward the mass of slaves.

Almost every published reminiscence by a slaveowner centers on the key slaves, and romantic myths connected with these elite slaves were central to the plantation legend, both during slavery times and for generations afterward. The mass of slaves, who "had little sense of family," could therefore be traded at will, and still the plantation legend could remain intact. It was possible, then, for the trade to be the backbone of slavery, for family separations to threaten almost every slave, and yet for slaveowners sincerely to believe, and in good faith to tell later generations, that theirs had been the "Sunny South." Evidence concerning slave trading and family separations, and regarding key slaves, leads me to conclude, in contrast to Genovese, that the typical owner's concept of paternalism was shallow and highly selective and leads me to suggest that the great mass of slaves did not see themselves as being linked to their masters by an intimate web of paternalistic relationships. Since owners could rationalize their selling of slaves to traders, they could in practice, as we shall see, accept the great mass of traders into their world.

Slaveholders' Attitudes Toward the Trade: Evidence from Trading Restrictions

According to white southern tradition, the trader was supposed to have been an outcast, and legislation that restricted "Negro speculation" might seem at first to support the notion of the disreputable trader. Closer examination shows, however, that the restrictions that were from time to time imposed were designed to protect particular interest groups and were not aimed against the trade in principle. Whites were not concerned with the morality of the trade or with the protection of slave families. Instead their concerns were to protect white lives and white families—against excessive financial speculation, against economic competition, and against possible threats from supposedly vicious and unruly slaves. At the same time, the restrictions on the trade show that slaveholding society would, in particular circumstances, opportunistically recruit the trader as a convenient scapegoat.

The period from 1780 to about 1818 saw several southern states, probably very ineffectively, prohibiting importation by means of the interstate trade.[35] In the cases of Delaware, Maryland, and Virginia the prohibitions would have been uncontroversial, since those states were already net exporters of slaves. There would have been little demand to import, and prohibition would have served local slaveholders' interests both by helping to keep prices up and also by easing fears about a possible influx of subversive slaves from more northerly states. Other states that introduced bans were net importers of slaves, and the loosely enforced prohibitions reflected fears about the building up of excessive debt, alarm about the introduction of "dangerous" northern slaves, and intrastate struggles over vested economic interests. Conservative sections within the importing states favored prohibition, but other expanding sections demanded new slaves—and successfully imported them. In 1795, for example, the governor of South Carolina reported that "slaves brought in [illegally over the last six months] by land I have not been able to procure any accounting of, although I have reason to believe there have been many."[36]

A series of petitions and grand jury presentments to the South Carolina General Assembly exemplifies both the security fears connected with the introduction of northern slaves and intrastate clashes of interest. Generally, whereas the lowcountry had plenty of slaves, feared any great increase in the black population, and was keen to protect its slave prices from the competition of imported slaves, the upcountry sought to expand its slave labor force and petitioned for the import ban to be lifted.[37] Presentments from upcountry Abbeville District (1802), Spartanburg (1817), and Chester (1818) all spelled out their grievances as would-be importers, the Chester Presentment complaining that "the law[s] existing at present prohibiting the Introduction of slave[s] from the sister states . . . have been proven by experience to be unjust in their operation and particularly detrimental to the substantial interests of the Upper Country."[38] In contrast, presentments opposing importation placed much emphasis on security issues. For example, in 1792 citizens from Beaufort complained of the "notorious" practice of northerners who "have for a number of years past been in the habit of shipping to these Southern States, slaves, who are scandalously infamous and incorrigible." And a York District Presentment of 1816 complained: "Having taken into consideration the policy of several of the northern states in the emancipation of their slaves and the consequent unparalleled ingress of them into our state, [we] consider it a grievance of no inconsiderable magnitude, considered in a moral point of view, and as a political evil fraught with dangerous consequences as it respects ourselves and as it respects posterity." In such fears were some of the roots of the trader-as-outcast image.[39]

At the state level, Alabama (1827–29 and 1832), Mississippi (1837–46), and Louisiana (1826–28 and 1831–34) operated fairly short-lived bans that were clearly triggered by concerns about excessive financial speculation. In the cases of Alabama's 1832 ban and Louisiana's 1831–34 ban, Nat Turner's slave revolt of 1831 was also a significant factor, creating fears about importing unruly slaves.[40] More interesting is the explanation for the very long-running bans by Georgia (for much of the period between 1817 and 1855) and Tennessee (1825–1853). These were both mixed states, that is to say, they included both net-importing and net-exporting sections, and the clash of sectional interests (as in the earlier South Carolina case) does much to explain attitudes toward the ban. Net-exporting sections might favor a ban, but net-importing sections made sure that it was routinely flouted.[41] In 1821, the *Milledgeville Journal,* a newspaper reflecting the interests of the net-exporting section of Georgia, urged that the prohibition be continued: "Everyone knows that [otherwise] the speculators would constantly introduce into the state the dregs of the colored population of the states to the north of us . . . and the jails of North and South Carolina, Maryland, and Virginia would be disgorged upon this deluded state."[42] In 1855, Judge H. L. Benning of the Georgia Supreme Court drew together his thoughts about the mix of motivations behind Georgia's prohibition. Benning wrote:

> The main reason for the enactment was, I think, a fear that the traffic, if permitted, would in the end, empty the more northerly of the slave states of their slaves, and thus convert those states from friends and allies into enemies and assailants. The chief reason was, I think, not at all the promotion of abolition in this state, but to prevent abolition in other states. Another reason was, no doubt, a disposition to keep the proportion of the free population to the slave from being materially changed. And avarice probably had some degree of influence — the avarice of slaveholders already in the state, the value of whose slaves would be diminished as the supply from abroad should be increased.[43]

Georgia's policy was to ban the professional trade, but individuals could move to the state with their own slaves, and Georgians were legally permitted to make private out-of-state buying trips. The hoped-for result was that migrants and those buying for their own use would bring only safe and reliable slaves. The law did not in fact effectively curb traders, but, significantly, its aims had nothing to do with moral disapproval of buying and selling slaves or with the breaking up of families: instead it was concerned with vested interests and the safety of whites.

Regulations at the local level also, from time to time, made reference to the trade, but again the concern was white self-interest, not the welfare of slaves. An 1856 meeting of the Charleston City Council is particularly interesting in this respect. At this time South Carolina was a major net exporter of slaves, and no objections were raised to the selling south of its own slaves. But a concern did arise in connection with the transit trade from the Upper South, through South Carolina, and on to Georgia. Because Georgia officially operated a ban on importations by traders, some speculators brought slaves from Virginia and other states and used Charleston as a place for selling to Georgia clients. The council thought that the Georgia transit trade brought many inconveniences but few benefits to the city: "The committee apprehended that this community entertains no morbid or fanatical sentiment on the subject of slavery. The discussions over the last twenty years have led it to clear and decided opinions as to its complete consistency with moral principle and with the highest order of civilization. It regards the removal of slaves from place to place, and their transfer from master to master, by gift, purchase or otherwise, as incidents necessarily connected with the institution." But the council was concerned that "it was thought a common spectacle to see troops of slaves, of all ages and both sexes, uniformly dressed, paraded for air, exercise and exhibition, through the streets and thoroughfares. This spectacle of a large number of negroes, for the most part single, brought together from all quarters, without regard to family ties, for purposes purely of speculation and cupidity, entailed on this community by strangers, citizens of other states, was repugnant to the moral tone and sense of our people." The council continued that it did not wish that "the interest of agriculture [should] suffer" but added that "capital which seeks investment in slaves for agricultural purposes within the state [Georgia] need not be defeated in its object." There were no objections in principle to the transit trade through South Carolina (but it should bypass Charleston); neither were there objections to traders involved in the export of slaves from South Carolina. The council was mainly concerned with threats to public order. In addition, the people were probably troubled by the fact that, without bringing any great benefit to the city, out-of-state speculators were (in a sense, gratuitously) making a spectacle of the least domesticated side of slavery.[44]

As the Charleston City Council indicated, objections to the principle of slave trading were impossible in a slaveholding society. It was one thing to ban the importation of new African slaves (as America did from 1807), but it would have been something very different to impose major restrictions on an American owner's right to sell his or her slaves. Any general trading restrictions based on notions of suffering by slaves would have suggested acceptance of the notion that owners could not be trusted to judge what was best for their slaves.[45] Even more fundamentally, such restrictions would have changed the nature of property rights in slaves, would have transferred significant rights to the enslaved, and would have tended to set up a movement toward serf or peasant status. Proposals to restrict the right to sell and dispose of slaves unhindered never gathered significant support. Slaveholders could always comfort themselves, if necessary, with the self-serving notion that the disruption of slave families was not a problem — such disruptions being seen as exceptional and in any case as not deeply felt by blacks.

The Reputation of the Trader in the Antebellum South

The prohibitions against the trade give significant clues to the status of the trader. As we have seen, within the South there was a debate about the trade, and that debate turned almost exclusively on conceptions of white self-interest. Some, strongly influenced by sectional interest, saw the trade as a cause for concern and worried that it brought violent, alienated, and possibly disease-ridden slaves into their midst — and here lay important roots for the tradition of the trader as outcast. From the days of the "Georgiamen" who brought slaves southward to Georgia in the eighteenth century, there was the notion of the disreputable trader.[46] This could flourish as a concept, but, in practice, few had any problems in dealing with and, as we shall see, respecting the trader. Those who sold to the trader had no problems. They could tell themselves that they acted honorably because, unless it was absolutely unavoidable, they did not sell worthy slaves. Moreover, sellers were likely to be seen in their locality as acting respectably, since by selling they eased the pressure on the local black population and they disciplined troublesome elements. Similarly, those who bought from traders had no cause for self-doubt since they served the needs of agriculture and since they would domesticate incoming slaves.

Such slaveholder anxiety as there was about the business of slave trading almost always sprang from particular moments or locations of vested interest. For example, lowcountry South Carolinians, who no longer needed to buy new slaves, feared that buying by upcountry farmers might flood their state with "the dregs" from further north. The image of the trader as disreputable had connections with deep-seated fears and might be passionately felt among some, but still it coexisted with the reality of the trader's high social standing.

This paradoxical situation was possible because sectional, and sometimes personal, anxieties about social stability existed, but at the same time most whites with sufficient resources were keenly interested in buying or selling slaves.

A further element of the reputation of the trader in the antebellum South was that, even among those who were keen to deal with him, there might be wariness about the sort of bargain they might strike. Slaveowners needed traders, but a slave represented a very large investment and might turn out to have health problems or might prove to be insubordinate or a poor worker. Where substantial financial risks were involved, there was always scope for stories of sharp practices. A letter referring to the South Carolina speculator Colonel E. S. Irvine points to this element. Elizabeth F. Perry sold slaves to various traders, and in November 1850 she wrote to tell her husband that Irvine had just sold their Jim for $900 and had passed him off as a "first rate carpenter." Clearly, when selling him, he had made a good profit and had "forgotten some of the faults" that had troubled him earlier when buying Jim from Mrs. Perry. The latter wrote, with an amused sigh: "How drovers do deceive. They live by cheating." Irvine might have been a deceiver, but it turns out that she approved of him! She and Irvine's wife were great friends and often met for tea. Elizabeth Perry's letters repeatedly referred to the colonel as buying "a drove of Negroes" or as having "gone to the west to sell a drove of Negroes." She entertained his wife when the latter was left in lonely isolation during her husband's expeditions to the west. Irvine's wife, furthermore, was not one to mix with the disreputable: she was very well connected, and her husband was a member of the South Carolina legislature. Moreover, Irvine, according to 1850s observers who assessed his character and creditworthiness for R. G. Dunn and Co., was "honorable and worthy," a "highly respected gentleman," and "a man of property."[47]

Evidence presented in *Speculators and Slaves* and elsewhere establishes the social profiles of a large sample of mainly South Carolina traders and shows that Irvine was not an unusual case.[48] Across the districts of South Carolina, traders were among the wealthiest and most influential in their communities; indeed, in terms of wealth they were part of a tiny group at the top of American society. They also served in city, state, and national politics. Moreover, it was not usually a case of slave-trading wealth buying a way into the planting elite: rather, it was a matter of those who were already wealthy and respected taking the opportunity to add to their wealth by practicing speculation. In the antebellum period, then, traders were no outcasts from southern society.

All of this did not mean, however, that the trader could be acknowledged in the South's propaganda initiatives: a debate about the morality of slavery would have been hard to win if one gave speculation the place that in reality it occupied. In proslavery novels and polemics, then, the trader was an outcast and a scapegoat. The aspects of the trade that some worried about—unruly slaves and threats to public order—could be added to common notions about sharp practice, and with this the convenient composite of the evil trader was ready for use as propaganda in any debate. This self-serving proslavery construction would be handed on for many generations when whites turned their thoughts to slavery times.

Slave Trading and Southern Myths

In his 1904 book, the thoroughly southern historian Winfield H. Collins maintained that the ill repute of traders was such that "they were accounted the abhorrence of everyone." And, he added, "their descendants, when known, had a blot upon them and the property acquired in the traffic as well."[49] His reference to a universal stigma in the antebellum period was clearly wrong; his comment on the descendants of traders was interesting but equally wrong. What does seem to have happened after slavery ended, though, is that, because of the urge to invent and promote a history of the benevolent Southland, former traders, while continuing as "honorable citizens," now found their trading past being played down in the public press. In the 1897 history of his county, T. C. Weatherly, who in the 1850s had been both a prominent slave trader and a member of the South Carolina House of Representatives, was simply referred to as having had a "business career" and as having been "a man of quick mind, ready action, public spirit and generous impulse . . . [who] exercised a large influence."[50] Similarly, the death of Charles Logan in 1903 merited considerable attention from the *State* newspaper in South Carolina, but no mention was made of his career as a highly successful slave trader. The notice of 30 November 1903 simply recorded that his wealth had been accumulated "through speculative deals of various sorts." Logan was praised for his generous bequests to a school, a hospital, a Catholic church, and to officials charged with preventing cruelty to animals. He had apparently led a good life, and the *State* concluded its praise by remarking that "next to the care of children, kindness to animals is the mark of a good heart."[51]

The southern reaction to the 1931 publication of Frederic Bancroft's *Slave Trading in the Old South* gives a later indication of the mythical career of the trader: southern white reviewers were uncomfortable with the "almost abolitionist ardor" with which Bancroft pointed "his long moral finger at the Sinful South," and such reviewers showed no inclination to recognize the true reputation and importance of the trader.[52] Today, academic opinions are considerably changed, but still the major vehicles of public history in the South advance the plantation legend and push the trader to the shadows. A plaque placed by the Preservation Society of Charleston at a house on State Street, Charleston, is typical. The plaque marks the Eleanor Cook Tenement and notes that the building was erected between 1810 and 1812. It adds: "The interior woodwork and unusual façade with tripartite windows centered on the upper floors are in the Regency style which was current in Charleston after 1815. For several decades the building was used in conjunction with various coffee houses and inns (the Bank Coffee House, the Carolina Coffee House and the Alhambra), and after 1844 housed auctioneers, brokers, and other businesses." No mention is made of the fact that this was a slave dealer's office or that slaves awaiting sale would have looked out of the Regency-style windows across to the Slave Mart. They would have looked, too, at the neighboring buildings and seen there the offices of traders such as John S. Riggs, A. J. Salinas, Robert Austin, Ziba Oakes, John E. Bowers, and G. V. Anker. Most of these were aldermen of Charleston, and, in addition to being citizens of the first rank, were major players in the interstate trade. The Cook Tenement was owned by Thomas Ryan, another alderman, and was the office of William B. Ryan, who, together with Thomas, was "doing a negro trading business and making money."[53] Individual plaques hide the slave trade, but the preserved antebellum plantations of the South do this on a far grander and a truly alarming scale. Every year, tens of thousands, perhaps hundreds of thousands, tour the plantations of South Carolina and of other states and, with hardly an exception, find that the planter family concerned never broke up slave families. They hear of loyal slaves who hid the planter's silver from invading Yankees, they view an elite slave cabin, and they see perhaps a graveyard where key slaves were buried with the white owners. The plantation legend lives on, the trade is once more hidden, and a dangerously unrealistic history is renewed.

Notes

1. For some indications of the early trade, see Michael Tadman, *Speculators and Slaves: Masters, Traders, and Slaves in the Old South* (Madison: University of Wisconsin Press, 1989), pp. 11–21, and Steven Deyle, "The Irony of Liberty: Origins of the Domestic Slave Trade," *Journal of the Early Republic* 12 (1992): 37–62.

2. James Stirling, *Letters from the Slave States* (London: Parker, 1857), pp. 292–93.

3. J. T. Randolph, *The Cabin and the Parlor; or, Slaves and Masters* (Philadelphia: T. B. Petersen, 1852), pp. 31, 42.

4. On the essentials of the abolitionist and proslavery positions, see Tadman, *Speculators and Slaves,* pp. 3–5, 180–84, 212–16.

5. Stewart, cited in David L. Lightner, "The Door to the Slave Bastille: The Abolitionist Assault upon the Interstate Slave Trade, 1833–1839," *Civil War History* 34 (1988): 245.

6. On these abolitionist arguments, see, e.g., Executive Committee of the American Anti-Slavery Society, eds., *Slavery and the Internal Slave Trade . . . Being Replies to Questions Transmitted by the British and Foreign Anti-Slavery Society* (London: T. Ward and Co., 1841).

7. For excellent discussions of abolitionists and the question of abolishing the domestic slave trade (and thereby undermining slavery in general), see David L. Lightner, "The Interstate Slave Trade in Antislavery Politics," *Civil War History* 36 (1990): 119–36; and Lightner, "Door to the Slave Bastille," pp. 235–52. On slave demography, see below.

8. Frederic Bancroft, *Slave Trading in the Old South* (New York: Frederick Unger, 1931).

9. Robert William Fogel and Stanley L. Engerman, *Time on the Cross: The Economics of American Negro Slavery* (Boston: Little, Brown, 1974).

10. Tadman, *Speculators and Slaves,* pp. 11–46.

11. The survival rate method assumes that within a given population (in this case the southern slave population) there were no significant variations resulting from international immigration or emigration. Within the slave population as a whole, some fairly small-scale local variations in mortality would be expected, as would some variations in the accuracy of the census information. Results at the state level, and even more so at the broad regional level, are, however, assumed to have canceled out these local mortality and recording fluctuations. For justification of my assumption and on my method generally, see *Speculators and Slaves*, pp. 225–47, 2–31.

12. Table 6.1 underestimates slave movements because it shows only interstate and not interregional movements. This means that where a state combined sections of net importation and net exportation, many of these movements would have been canceled out since the state-level calculations used reflect only net movement. The 1850–59 map in figure 6.1 was based in part on county-level, not state-level, evidence, and it gives some idea of the extent of canceling out that occurred with state-by-state calculations shown in table 6.1.

13. The Oakes Papers have survived because an antislavery supporter who witnessed the fall of Charleston to the northern army retrieved the manuscripts from the slave dealer's office, and this led to their eventual preservation in archives in Boston.

14. The figure of 288 slaves is based on survival-rate calculations.

15. My study identified more than thirty Charleston-based slave-exporting firms.

16. McElveen to Oakes, 2 Dec. 1856, 4 and 19 Nov. 1856, and 2 Feb. 1857, Ziba Oakes Papers (Boston Public Library); McElveen to Oakes, 15 June 1857, 14 Aug. 1857, Slave Sales Letterbook (New England Historic Genealogical Society), Boston.

17. For a typical fairly small firm, annual slave purchases would have been between thirty and forty slaves, and for a major firm the number would have been many times larger.

18. On the scale of the New Orleans trade, see Michael Tadman, "The Demographic Cost of Sugar: Debates on Slave Societies and Natural Increase in the Americas," *American Historical Review* 105 (Dec. 2000): 94–97 and appendix 4. On "fancies," see Tad-

man, *Speculators and Slaves,* pp. 125–27, and Edward E. Baptist, "'Cuffy,' 'Fancy Maids,' and 'One-Eyed Men': Rape, Commodification, and the Domestic Slave Trade in the United States," *American Historical Review* 106 (2001): 1619–50. On the New Orleans trade in general, see Walter Johnson, *Soul by Soul: Life Inside the Antebellum Slave Market* (Cambridge: Harvard University Press, 1999), and on "fancies," see ibid., pp. 113–15, 154, 155.

19. See Tadman, *Speculators and Slaves,* esp. pp. 23–25.

20. Ibid., pp. 64–71.

21. For the link between the sugar plantations of the Americas and natural decrease, see Tadman, "Demographic Cost."

22. On the coastal route, see Tadman, *Speculators and Slaves,* pp. 79–82.

23. McElveen to Oakes, 21 Oct. 1856, Oakes Papers (Boston Public Library); Burton to his partner Long, 16 and 24 Jan. 1846, 9 Mar. 1846, Long Papers (North Carolina State Archives, Raleigh); Charles Ball, *Fifty Years in Chains; or, The Life of an American Slave* (New York: H. Dayton, 1858), pp. 141–42.

24. On these buying patterns, see Tadman, *Speculators and Slaves,* esp. pp. 47–110.

25. Individual clients usually bought only one or two slaves at a time from traders, and if necessary could get credit locally. See ibid., pp. 102–5.

26. See ibid., pp. 113–21.

27. See ibid., pp. 184–90.

28. Ibid., pp. 113–21, 129–32.

29. For evidence, see United States Bureau of the Census, *The Seventh Census of the United States: 1850* (Washington, D.C., 1853), pp. 346–47; United States Bureau of the Census, *Agriculture in the United States in 1860* (Washington, D.C., 1862), pp. 128–29.

30. For the 1930s interviews see the many volumes edited by George P. Rawick in *The American Slave: A Composite Autobiography* (Westport: Greenwood, 1972). To a much lesser extent than the trade, plantation migrations also caused interregional splits of families. See Tadman, *Speculators and Slaves,* pp. 154–59.

31. For detailed evidence of sampling and calculations, see ibid., pp. 132–78, 296–302.

32. Had abolitionist claims of stud farms and of systematic slave breeding been accurate, vast pressures on slave morale and on the sense of family would have obtained, but in practice the natural increase of U.S. slaves came about without a system of heavily manipulated breeding. See Tadman, "Demographic Cost."

33. See Eugene D. Genovese, *Roll, Jordan, Roll: The World the Slaves Made* (New York: Pantheon Books, 1974), and numerous other publications by Genovese over the past thirty years.

34. For fuller development of my concept of the "key slave," see the introduction to the 1996 paperback edition of *Speculators and Slaves;* see also Tadman, "The Persistent Myth of Paternalism: Historians and the Nature of Master-Slave Relationships in the American South," *Sage Race Relations Abstracts* 23 (1998): 7–24. This concept is the organizing device for Tadman, *On the Old Plantation* (forthcoming).

35. On prohibitions against importation, see Tadman, *Speculators and Slaves,* pp. 83–87. On Maryland's and Delaware's attempted restrictions on exports in the 1780s and 1790s, see ibid., p. 13.

36. A. Vander Horst to Senate, Senate Messages from Governor (3 Dec. 1795, No. 15), Eleventh General Assembly, in Miscellaneous Records of Secretary of State for South Carolina (South Carolina Department of Archives, Columbia, S.C.).

37. For a further discussion of intrastate clashes of interest regarding the Atlantic and domestic trades, see Tadman, *Speculators and Slaves,* pp. 13–15.

38. Grand Jury Presentments to the South Carolina General Assembly, South Carolina Department of Archives, Columbia, S.C.

39. Ibid. Kershaw, Lexington, Richland, and Spartanburg Districts also made presentments warning that the importation of northern slaves was "dangerous to the safety of the State."

40. On these prohibitions, see Tadman, *Speculators and Slaves,* pp. 84–87.

41. On the ineffectiveness of the prohibitions, see ibid., pp. 87–97.

42. *Milledgeville Journal,* quoted in J. R. Commons et al., eds., *A Documentary History of Industrial Society* (Cleveland: A. H. Clark, 1910–11), 2:67–70.

43. Benning is cited in Ralph B. Flanders, *Slavery in Georgia* (Chapel Hill: University of North Carolina Press, 1933).

44. Proceedings of the council are reported in the *Charleston Daily Courier,* 10 Jan. 1856.

45. See Eugene D. Genovese, *A Consuming Fire: The Fall of the Confederacy in the Mind of the Christian South* (Athens: University of Georgia Press, 1998) for an excellent discussion of the soul-searching of proslavery clerics concerning slavery and slave families during the crisis of the Civil War.

46. On Georgiamen, see Jesse Torrey, *A Portraiture of Slavery in the United States* (London: J. M. Cobbett, 1822).

47. Elizabeth Perry to Benjamin Perry, 30 Nov. 1850, 6 Dec. 1846, Benjamin F. Perry Papers, South Carolina Library, Columbia, S.C.; Dun & Co. Collection, South Carolina, 2:49, 65, 72F, Baker Library, Harvard University Graduate School of Business Administration, Cambridge, Mass.

48. Tadman, *Speculators and Slaves,* pp. 179–211.

49. Winfield H. Collins, *The Domestic Slave Trade of the Southern States* (New York: Broadway Publishing, 1904), p. 108.

50. J. A. W. Thomas, *A History of Marlboro County, with Traditions and Sketches of Numerous Families* (Atlanta: Foote and Davies, 1897), p. 146.

51. The *State* is quoted in John Hammond Moore, *Columbia and Richland County: A South Carolina Community, 1740–1990* (Columbia: University of South Carolina Press, 1992), p. 120.

52. See Michael Tadman, introduction, in Frederic Bancroft, *Slave Trading in the Old South* (Columbia: University of South Carolina Press, 1996), pp. xix–xxxiii.

53. On State St., see *Census of the City of Charleston, South Carolina, for the Year 1861* (Charleston: Evans and Cogswell, 1861). On the traders concerned, see Tadman, *Speculators and Slaves,* pp. 192–94, 253–60; Dun & Co. Collection, South Carolina, vol. 7, Charleston Ledger 2, p. 296.

7

Reconsidering the Internal Slave Trade
Paternalism, Markets, and the
Character of the Old South

LACY FORD

Doubtless many Americans who are by no means students of the Old South's internal slave trade can readily recall, with just a little prompting, the powerful fictional characterizations of the inhumane domestic slave trade and the mischievous traders rendered in Harriet Beecher Stowe's *Uncle Tom's Cabin*. First there was Haley, the trader who carried Tom south, congratulating himself on "how humane he was" because "other men" chained their slave merchandise "hand and foot both" whereas "he only put fetters on the feet."[1] Later in the novel, two men arguing about the compatibility of Christianity and slavery asked Haley his opinion on the subject as a professional trader. Haley hesitated a moment and replied: "I never thought on it. . . . I took up the trade just to make a living; if it ain't right, I calculated to 'pent on it in time, ye know." As Haley listened a little longer to more pointed discussion of divine disapproval of the traffic in human beings, the seasoned slave trader mused to himself, "If I make pretty handsomely on one or two next gangs, . . . I reckon I'll stop off this year; it's really getting dangerous."[2] More chilling, and more evocative of the horrors of the domestic slave trade, was Topsy's claim to Miss Ophelia that she "never was born, . . . never had no father, nor mother, nor nothin.' I was raised by a speculator, with lots of others."[3] Through voices as different as Haley, the avaricious trader, and Topsy, innocently outspoken slave, Stowe clearly presented her view, a view emphasized again and again in the novel as well as in the broader abolition literature, concerning the centrality of the slave trade and the slave trader to antebellum southern society. The active presence of the internal slave trade, Stowe and other critics of slavery argued, offered a direct refutation of emerging southern claims for the paternalistic nature of their peculiar institution.

Certainly the burgeoning proslavery argument in the antebellum South, that sporadic series of pamphlets, speeches, sermons, letters, and even a smattering of books prompted initially by the Missouri debates and the Denmark Vesey insurrection scare and later driven toward enhanced sophistication, greater volume, and a less apologetic tone by the abolitionist petition and mailing campaigns launched in 1835, increasingly argued that the paternalism practiced by southern slaveholders exonerated the institution of aspersions cast upon it by antislavery advocates. Within a generation after the defeat of the Confederacy, another round of paternalist defenses of the slave system echoed across the national intellectual scene, culminating in the elaborate and carefully nuanced portraits of an allegedly paternalistic Old South sketched by the early twentieth-century scholarship of U. B. Phillips, the historian who presented the first systematic academic treatment of antebellum southern slavery as a "paternalistic institution." Often somewhat misleadingly characterized as the "Moonlight and Magnolias" school of southern history, the work of Phillips and many of his like-minded contemporaries tried to exonerate antebellum slaveholders from abolitionist charges of sinfulness, immorality, and inhumanity while nevertheless indicting slavery, not as a moral abomination, but as an expensive and inefficient labor system that left the American South ill-prepared for industrialization and modern economic development. Phillips's interpretation of the Old South, important as it was to the founding of southern history as an academic field and to segregated America's guarded acceptance of the South as a fully American region during the first half of the twentieth century, has long since been exploded empirically and analytically by civil rights era and post–civil rights era scholarship produced by historians representing virtually all points on the modern political spectrum.[4]

But during this outpouring of scholarship, which blasted once and for all any notion that antebellum southern slavery had been a kind, benevolent, or even necessary institution, another scholarly argument emerged which insisted that slavery in the Old South could be best understood as the functioning of a society defined by paternalism, provided that paternalism was understood as something more than the notion that slaves were treated kindly. This new and intellectually formidable, if politically curious, formulation of the paternalist thesis emanated from the pen of a gifted young Marxist scholar, Eugene Genovese. Though Genovese, to his credit, repeatedly refined his formulation of the paternalist argument over the next thirty years, it remained, as slavery studies entered the new millennium, a formulation that exerts a formidable influence on scholarship concerning slavery even if it no longer enjoys the hegemonic position it once held.[5]

Of course, paternalism, as Genovese presented it, hardly resembled that of either the antebellum proslavery apologists or postbellum scholars from the Phillips school. For both groups, paternalism grew out of the good intentions, and perhaps the good business sense, of masters. For Genovese and other scholars adopting his perspective, paternalism in the Old South emerged directly from the material and psychological circumstances of the master-slave relationship, which, in their view, lay at the heart of southern slave society and defined its essence. Genovese readily characterized antebellum southern slavery as an "enormity" and not as a benevolent institution of any sort, but it was an enormity that rested directly on the nature of the personal relationship, as opposed to a cash, contractual, or market relationship, between masters and slaves and the process of negotiation and coercion that inevitably grew out of that relationship. Genovese maintained that the master-slave relationship, when appropriately viewed as a dialectical one based on accommodation to resistance and resistance to accommodation, generated a broad social ideology of patriarchy and paternalism grounded in personal command and control, not kindness. In Genovese's view, this Gramscian paternalism emerged from the daily give and take between masters and slaves in an arena where masters wielded overweening power but also where slaves sometimes effectively employed "the weapons of the weak" to exercise a modicum of control over their own work routines and create family, community, and religious life and even, ultimately, to generate enough resistance to undermine the institution of slavery. And, according to Genovese, this dialectical paternalism lent its character not only to the master-slave relationship but to the Old South's other social relations as well.[6]

To many scholars, but perhaps most significantly to Herbert Gutman and Ira Berlin, the Achilles' heel of Genovese's argument for paternalism as the dominant ideology of the Old South lay in antebellum southern slaveholders' frequent and usually profitable recourse to the internal slave trade, a trade that separated mothers from children, destroyed slave marriages, and savaged the slave family generally despite slaveholder claims to the contrary.[7] Yet it was not until fifteen years after Genovese's *Roll, Jordan, Roll* appeared that a systematic scholarly reevaluation of the internal trade began. But now, as a result of recent and impressive additions to the scholarly literature, historians know a great deal more than they did a generation ago about the centrality of the Old South's often underemphasized internal slave trade to the functioning of the region's staple economy, its influence on an emerging regional political economy, its impact on the daily lives of masters and slaves, and the trade's dramatic role in shaping an emerging African American culture.

Among recent studies of the internal slave trade, monographs by Michael Tadman and Walter Johnson further developed the objections to Genovese's formulation of paternalism first levied by Gutman and Berlin. Tadman's impressive cliometric work belongs to (and represents the mature best of) the justifiably proud tradition of social science history, the interdisciplinary innovation that promised so much to the profession during the late 1960s and early 1970s. In contrast, Johnson's more recent work fulfills the promise of the recent postmodernist turn among historians by looking at the complex "interiors" of slavery, including messages sent by nuances of language and descriptions of the body. Tadman, the quantifier, finds the slave traders and counts their sales; Johnson, the new cultural historian, describes how slaves viewed their own "commodification." These contrasting approaches complement each other nicely, and together, they present American historians with portraits of both the broader economic dynamics and the interior psychology of the interregional slave trade that they have lacked for decades.[8]

Tadman's book constitutes a calculated attempt to strip away the armor of myth that late nineteenth- and early twentieth-century architects of the "Lost Cause" apologia developed to minimize the importance of the internal slave trade as they worked to make the memory of the vanquished Old South palatable to white Americans from all regions. Seeking to set the record straight, Tadman uses both sound quantitative methods and careful qualitative research to discover that at least 60 percent of the migration of slaves from one state to another came as result of the internal slave trade (and only forty percent as part of a presumably more benign forced migration with slaveholding families). Hence the redistribution of the region's slave population from the upper and seaboard South to the lower and interior South resulted from the functioning of the market rather than the relocation of the extended slaveholding "family" of popular lore. Moreover, the interregional trade broke up at least one in five slave families, and when local trades (trades in which slaves were not sold across state lines) were added to the total, Tadman estimates, nearly half of all antebellum slave families experienced the horror of separation. Nor were most masters "reluctant" participants in the internal slave trade, putting their slaves up for sale only when financial distress of the master or chronic bad behavior on the part of the slave suggested the necessity of sale. Instead, masters sold slaves for profit and convenience even as they used a variety of subterfuges to either justify their actions to and hide their plans from suspicious slaves.[9]

In addition, contrary to popular mythology and some previous scholarship, Tadman maintains that the presence of active slave traders, though not necessarily of the men who supervised the long march of slave coffles overland to the markets of old Southwest, among the antebellum South's planter elite indicated that these traders suffered little or no social ostracism in the slaveholding communities where they resided. The self-deception by which southern slave sellers rationalized their behavior and generated a social portrait of themselves as paternalistic masters loath to break up slave families and eager to avoid participation in the unseemly traffic in human beings, Tadman argues, proved as endless as it was ingenious but could in no way disguise the vigor and frequency with which most antebellum slaveholders resorted to the slave trade to enhance their own interests.[10]

Writing a decade after Tadman, Walter Johnson, in *Soul by Soul*, details a dimension of the trade sketched only in broad outline by Tadman: the psychology of the slaves, masters, and traders who lived and breathed the trade at first hand. *Soul by Soul* reformulates Tadman's cliometric conclusions into a new theoretical understanding of the role the slave trade played in southern society. Viewing the trade less as a process than a series of defining existential moments, Johnson maintains that "the chattel principle," the right to buy and sell human beings as property, must be considered the signature right defended by the antebellum southern social order. By means of the interstate slave trade, slaveholders bound the various southern subregions together in a peculiar political economy characterized by a unified regional market in a single crucial and defining "commodity" (slaves). But Johnson's main contribution lies not in documenting the centrality of the internal trade to the Old South's economy, a point already well established by Tadman and other cliometricians, but in his insistence that "the daily process by which two million people were bought and sold" during the antebellum era had been unintentionally "hidden from historical view by the very aggregations that have been used to represent it." Johnson yearns to understand not so much the market or the macroeconomic function of the regional slave trade as the existential reality of the slave pen, the show room, the auction block, the plantation gate, the backwoods encampments, and others places where slaves were sold or held for sale, places (and moments) where the "broad trends and abstract totalities thickened into human shape." In these places, Johnson contends, "the contingent bargaining of trader, buyer, and slave" made and unmade the "epochal" history of the slave trade writ large.[11]

Johnson's probing of the oft-masked interiors of the antebellum southern slave trade succeeds admirably in restoring a sense of contingency to the individual bargains of the slave trade. In vivid and often moving language,

Johnson explained how slaves, by action and attitude, could on occasion affect the terms, and the likelihood, of their sale, as well as how slaves, even as children, learned that sellers and buyers viewed their bodies as commodities. The idea of the commodification of the body, and what the body told potential buyers not only about the health and strength but also about the history and "character" of the slave, emerges in telling fashion from Johnson's stirring account. This provocative work forcefully reasserts Tadman's insistence that sales separated slave families with shocking frequency, that traders and prospective buyers abused slaves with regularity, and that slaveholders participated in the trade routinely rather than reluctantly. Above all, Johnson succeeds in evoking the sense of personal shame and horror felt by slaves as a result of the trade and the power that the chattel principle gave masters and traders over slaves, whether or not those slaves were actively on the market.[12]

Whether in overt or subtle fashion, both of these historians mount aggressive attacks on the notion that paternalism of any sort characterized antebellum southern society. Led by Tadman's carefully targeted cliometrics and followed ultimately by Johnson's postmodern critique, this assault on the ever-evolving but nonetheless persistent notion that paternalism served as the central organizing principle of that society appears at first glimpse to make its mark. Tadman's attack emerges directly from his important and generally reliable empirical findings. He asserts that the consistent, vigorous, and profit-oriented trading of slaves, a commerce in human beings that accounted for nearly two-thirds of the forced migration of antebellum slaves, one that ended marriages, separated children from parents, and forced the westward movement of at least 10 percent of the southern slave population during the antebellum era, readily belied claims that a genuinely paternalistic slaveholding society flourished in the Old South.[13] Moreover, in proving the centrality of the internal trade to that society, Tadman believes that he has undermined one of the last vestiges of the old "plantation legend," a legend that insisted that despite the overall moral obtuseness of the regime, it nevertheless abhorred the slave trade and engaged it as a necessary evil and only when forced by adverse circumstances to do so.[14]

Like Tadman, Johnson debunks the ongoing use of paternalism as an analytical tool for understanding the society of the Old South and its master-slave relationship. Johnson concedes, and indeed emphasizes, that the processes of accommodation and resistance and professions of paternalism infiltrated the trade, giving slaves a hint of leverage at perhaps their most vulnerable point: the moment at which they were about to be sold. Yet Johnson characterizes paternalism as a form of "nuzzling violence" arising from a strange "mixture of ostensible moderation and outright threat" and argues that the "chattel principle," the existence of property rights in human beings, and the force needed to maintain that relationship, rather than the processes of accommodation and resistance between master and slave, emerged as the defining characteristic of antebellum southern slavery.[15]

In a subsequent review assessing the influence of *Roll, Jordan, Roll* more than a quarter-century after its original publication, Johnson refines his critique of Genovese further, attacking the paternalist argument conceptually as well as on empirical grounds. Johnson's review separates Genovese's conceptualization of paternalism from his idea of hegemony, critiquing each concept in isolation. Johnson sees paternalism as a language developed by slaveholders and their intellectual allies for deployment as a defense against deepening outside criticism of slavery, rather than as a social system rooted in the master-slave relationship. The shallowness and hypocrisy of paternalism as a language of humanitarianism in the world the slaveholders made was both self-evident and easily unmasked empirically, for example, by the frequent breakups of slave families by sale. Genovese's argument that masters eventually gained Gramscian-style hegemony over slaves in the Old South, a domination that may have begun in force but culminated in tacit acceptance, requires intricate refutation, in Johnson's view. But, simply put for our purposes, Johnson believes that although masters sought hegemony they failed to achieve it, largely because slaves resisted and even defied their masters. According to Johnson, the scope of slave resistance went well beyond the type of day-to-day resistance whose existence Genovese emphasized and included dramatic and revolutionary acts of defiance. Thus, according to Johnson, not only was the alleged paternalism of the Old South little more than calculated rhetoric crafted to blunt outside criticism, but the hegemony of the master class, a concept central to Genovese's interpretation, remained elusive, frustrated by the resistance and resolve of slaves despite the heavy odds against them.[16]

Johnson's treatment of paternalism as the language, or idiom, of slaveholding preferred by slaveholders has much to recommend it.[17] Thus paternalism was the language of the proslavery tract, the slave management essay, the monthly sermon, and even the daily lives of some masters, but it was only one language of slavery. And it was rarely the language of the auction block, the slave pen, the brush arbor slave meeting, the plantation "street," or the hearthsides of slave cabins. Yet to say that paternalism was a language, an idiom, or even an ideology used by slaveholders and their allies to defend slavery hardly disproves the existence of a dialectic of resistance and accommodation between masters and slaves that continually redefined their relationship. That dialectic may not be best described as paternalism, but the existence of the dialectic is hard to deny. At the same time, Johnson is surely right to point out that threats, coercion, and violent punishment always remained part of the dialectic of paternalism in the antebellum South, just as Tadman was right to note that slaveholders' readiness to profit from frequent slave sales betrayed the notion that the master's devotion to his slave family extended to the sacrifice of profit. Thus, whether considered individually or taken together, the work of Johnson and Tadman launched a seemingly potent attack on Genovese and his idea of paternalism, an attack hinging largely on the notion that truly paternalistic masters could never have trafficked in slaves as regularly and as acquisitively or conducted themselves in such coercive and lecherous fashion as antebellum southern slaveholders did.

But on closer examination, this assault on paternalism scarcely draws blood, or at least not enough blood to worry anyone of Sicilian heritage. Genovese's interpretation of the Old South as a paternalistic planter regime does not rest on the presumed kindness of masters or the alleged contentment of slaves; hence it does not disintegrate in the face of evidence of cruel punishments, wanton lusts, an active internal slave trade, or even proof that one of every five slave families was likely broken by sale. Instead, paternalism for Genovese grew out of the incontrovertible material and psychological circumstances of slavery, the efforts of masters to control slaves and efforts of slaves to limit or resist that control. These efforts, in Genovese's view, lay at the defining core of southern slave society in the same manner that the free labor market lay at the defining core of bourgeois society. Thus, that paternalism would have its cruel side, that it served as the means by which a cruel system achieved its ends, hardly rendered it any less a part of a system of ongoing resistance and accommodation that could be meaningfully characterized as paternalism. That the slaveholders' rhetoric of paternalism disguised deep malignity or callous indifference toward black bondsmen in their hearts, that proslavery pamphlets overstated the prevalence of paternalism's calculated kindnesses, and that slaveholders indulged in the grossest forms of self-deception to justify their harsh and insensitive actions in respectable paternalist terms all prove that slavery was never the benevolent or benign institution that the slaveholders and their erstwhile post-emancipation apologists claimed. Slavery was certainly never an institution defined by the masters' paternal love or acceptance of that profession of love by slaves; only the most disingenuous neo-Confederate poseurs could now advance that argument. But the fact that paternalism as an ideological construct designed by antebellum southerners to defend the peculiar institution proved a self-serving sham in no way refutes the broader understanding of paternalism as a social system, growing out of the daily management of unfree labor, which Genovese (with Elizabeth Fox-Genovese) has asserted.[18]

Arguably, it may not be possible to refute the paternalist argument as conceptualized by Genovese with empirical evidence, no matter how impressive its quality or quantity. For a committed empiricist such as this writer, the fact that the paternalist interpretation of the Old South seems so impervious to refutation by contrary evidence remains a disconcerting prospect. It is intellectually troubling that the concept of paternalism can retain viability in the face of so much seemingly contradictory evidence. But, as other scholars have noted, the Genovesean thesis absorbs contrary evidence like a historiographical sponge, using it to give even more weight to the underlying notion of a pattern of negotiations between highly unequal parties, negotiations influenced heavily by the context of coercion, violence, and sale as well as a genuine desire (on both sides) to find accommodations that could make life in a slave society bearable, at least for the short term.

The persistent if loosening grip of Genovesean paternalism on the historiography of slavery will likely be broken not by the accumulation of ever more evidence belying the practice of paternalism but rather a paradigm shift that generates a new model of master-slave relations, or a new theory of the functioning of the institution of slavery. But paradigm shifts are hard to conjure. Good history is always a dialogue with other historians, and often the dialogue with a hegemonic interpretation often perpetuates its influence. Still, there are signs in this recent work on the Old South's internal slave trade that current historians are, perhaps, writing in the eye of a paradigm shift, a process already under way but with its full force yet to be felt. The new scholarship on the slave trade suggests, albeit inadvertently in some instances, not simply that the practice of paternalism in the Old South fell short of the ideal but also that at least three salient characteristics of antebellum southern slaveholders (and some nonslaveholders as well) — racism, avarice, and fear — worked effectively to prevent the full and final triumph of paternalism as a social ideology in the region.

This scholarship suggests that the internal slave trade, by means of its regular activity, its economic impact, and the regulations and restrictions adopted by states to manage or control it, revealed a rather unexpected place for the Old South in the voluminous and sometimes disputatious historiography of the market revolution.[19] To put it another way, scholarly study of the domestic slave trade and its regulation not only removed the mask of benevolence from southern masters and exposed a race-based insensitivity to the family life of slaves but also revealed the depths of slaveholders' acquisitive urge to sell slaves for profit and their periodic concern about internal security in the face of slave unrest. Thus, although it was not their focus or chief intent, these accounts offer a view of southern slaveholders as vigorous participants in a market revolution of substantial proportion and great reach, the creation of a functioning regional market in slaves. Largely of the slaveholders' own making, the southern version of the market revolution left southern slaveholders and aspiring slaveholders with a market society, albeit a rather peculiar one, that often proved fundamentally at odds with both the paternalistic social order urged by antebellum pastors and other intellectual defenders of slavery and the version posited for modern historiography by Genovese and other scholars working within his model.[20]

Thus, viewing the antebellum domestic slave trade in light of the burgeoning recent literature on the market revolution as well as part of the debate about paternalism and slave resistance opens new lines of sight for historians of the Old South. Tadman's data, particularly at the macroeconomic level, and Johnson's evidence, especially in the microeconomic sense, indicate that an extraordinarily active and well-articulated internal slave trade not only helped create a regional market for the Old South's primary source of liquid capital, chattel slaves, but in the process enhanced the efficiency and productivity of southern staple agriculture by helping distribute labor to its most profitable use. This well-articulated regional market in slaves, one that by the 1830s connected the Chesapeake with the Red River valley and South Carolina's Edisto basin with the so-called Choctaw lands of northern Mississippi, brought tangible market activity home to antebellum southerners of all social ranks in a highly visible manner. From masters and would-be masters who bought and sold to the nonslaveholding plain folk who merely watched as local traders made their rounds or observed as the long coffles of slaves that occasionally traversed their counties headed for points south and west, and to the slaves themselves, who lived daily knowing that a sale devastating to family and community lay no further away than a death, a debt, a punishment, a profit, or merely an owner's whim, the slave trade was an integral part of life in the Old South.

In addition, Tadman's account presents the slave traders of the Old South as a cohort of speculators possessing a high level of market specialization and sophistication. Ranging from wealthy planters who attended the best society balls and owned pews in Episcopal churches to rough-hewn roving buyers, men who traveled more than Methodist itinerants and attended sheriff's sales as religiously as they chewed tobacco, these traders and speculators helped the antebellum southern economy effectively distribute its peculiar combination of labor and capital according to the signals of a regional market. Indeed, Tadman's pioneering account of slave traders emphasizes the varying market niches that antebellum slave traders supplied so effectively.[21] As neoclassical economists have argued for years, commodity speculators, however unsavory their reputations among their contemporaries or seemingly unproductive their pursuits, actually play a role crucial to the efficiency of market economies. In simple terms, speculators allocate resources (and spread risks) over time and space, across weeks or generations, and over local or global geopolitical boundaries, using their capital to hold resources now that may prove to be of enhanced value (to themselves or their heirs and to society) later. If the future were certain, there would be no economic need for speculation. But with uncertainty, speculators carry the costs of inventory (whether it be land, gold, or slaves), and associated risks, over time. Whoever carries these risks, in this case the slave traders, moves resources away from low returns toward higher ones, promoting, in a significant way, long-term growth of the economy. Slave traders, of course, did exactly that, buying slaves and embarking on a dangerous journey, on which they carried uninsurable risks, from the less productive lands of the old Chesapeake tobacco region and older South Atlantic cotton areas to the fresh cotton lands of the old Southwest and the deadly sugar bowl of southeastern Louisiana, where those slaves would fetch higher prices (reflecting the expectation of higher returns). And, as we know, during the late antebellum era the states of the old Southwest emerged as the high-income region of the Old South, and at least 30 percent of the Old South's impressive economic growth in this era was attributable to the movement of population from the lower-income South Atlantic regions (the older staple areas) to higher income areas further south and west rather than to the qualitative economic development that helped grow per capita income in the antebellum North.[22]

In an impressive series of books and articles, Gavin Wright has argued that this well-functioning regional market in slaves, a market that served a peculiar dual function as the region's primary market for both labor and capital, not only shaped the antebellum southern economy in dramatic ways but also helped define the Old South's political choices.[23] Because the internal slave trade functioned effectively, Wright maintained, the value of slave property, a major portion of southern assets, was determined by the regional market. High slave prices meant capital gains for slaveholders, whether they elected to realize those gains or not. Thus the regionally determined value of slaves, rather than local land and asset values, shaped investment decisions and entrepreneurial style in the Old South, pushing southerners toward decisions and policies designed to maintain and enhance the value of slave property rather than toward promoting intensive local development through infrastructural improvement and town development.[24] Wright also posited that, in the political realm, the regional market in slaves nurtured a unified class interest committed to the protection of slave values among masters across the region.

Because of the regional market, a threat to the value of slaves anywhere was a threat everywhere, producing a singular sensitivity among slaveholders to any such threat, real or imagined. And, ultimately, southern perceptions of such threats, including the fear that a Republican administration might restrict the interstate slave trade, played a key role in the unfolding secession drama.[25]

Yet in order to fully understand the impact of the slave trade on the political economy of the Old South, historians must reexamine another important set of issues raised by the presence of an active internal slave trade: the tension and uncertainty generated within the antebellum white South by public policy questions related to the slave trade, and particularly the efforts to ban, restrict, tax, and otherwise regulate the interregional traffic. Indeed, throughout the early republican and Jacksonian eras, such efforts remained commonplace in the slave-purchasing states of the lower or cotton South.[26] As Tadman points out, few if any of the restrictions and regulations proposed were designed to meliorate the condition of slaves or to grant any special protection to slave families or slave children. Instead, the restrictions and regulations sought to protect and enhance the welfare, security, and wealth of the white population.[27] Yet the Old South's internal debate about regulation of the domestic slave trade nevertheless revealed many of the anxieties that troubled and sometimes divided antebellum southern white society, and, as a result, adds yet another dimension to any effort to assess the full impact of the internal trade on the character of that society.

The states of the lower South worried constantly about becoming the "solution" to the upper South's slavery "problem," and they all periodically considered restriction of the internal slave trade for precisely that reason.[28] After all, in the debates about emancipation held in Virginia in the aftermath of the Turner insurrection, friends and foes of gradual emancipation and colonization identified "whitening" the Old Dominion, the state with the most slaves, by the sale of slaves to the deep South as a desired goal. In Virginia's 1832 legislative debate about slavery, Petersburg lawyer John Thompson Brown, an opponent of state-sponsored emancipation and colonization, recommended reducing the influence of slavery in the Old Dominion by encouraging the "drain of slaves" from Virginia to the lower South via the interstate trade. Brown knew that his remarks evoked concern in some portions of the lower South but nonetheless confidently predicted that the cotton states would ultimately repeal any and all statutes restricting the internal slave trade owing to an overweening desire to procure adequate labor for their burgeoning cotton fields.[29] Thomas Roderick Dew, another critic of legislative emancipation and colonization, also acknowledged that slavery in Virginia appeared headed toward "ultimate extinction" as tobacco declined as a cash crop and entrepreneurs in the cotton states of the lower South eagerly purchased the Old Dominion's surplus slaves.[30] And even Dew's chief critic, the Virginia colonizationist Jesse Burton Harrison, agreed that the end of slavery in Virginia might be hastened by the sale of slaves to the cotton South as well as by a plan for gradual emancipation and removal.[31]

Partially in response to the upper South's efforts to thus "whiten" itself and partially as a result of slave unrest and rumors of unrest closer to home, every lower South state, at some point, considered legislation to restrict or regulate the domestic slave trade. Crafted to prevent the importation of "undesirable" or troublesome slaves and to keep the respective states from growing "too black," these proposed restrictions also protected the value of the slaveholders' existing investment in slave property.[32] Even the fanatically proslavery South Carolina banned the importation of slaves for sale, whether by traders or residents, between 1816 and 1818 at the urging of Governor David Rogerson Williams and several upcountry grand juries in the aftermath of an aborted Camden insurrection plot discovered in 1816. By 1818, however, the new governor, Andrew Pickens, an upcountry native and son of the Revolutionary war hero of the same name, complained that the ban was regularly "violated . . . with impugnity [*sic*]" because it had proved "repugnant to the interests of many of our fellow citizens." Pickens recommended repeal, and the legislature readily concurred, lifting the ban completely during its December 1818 session.[33]

Across the Savannah River in Georgia, state policy concerning the domestic slave trade changed frequently throughout the antebellum era. After softening the laws against importing slaves for sale in 1816, Georgia's 1817 legislature again prohibited the importation of slaves for sale but allowed citizens and immigrants to bring slaves into the state for their own use. In 1824 the ban was again lifted, only to be partially reinstated again in 1829. In 1830, Governor George Gilmer viewed the growth of the trade with such alarm that he recommended a draconian ban that would eliminate the importation of slaves for use as well as sale. Gilmer proclaimed the "danger of having the slave population in this state disproportionately great to the free" and insisted that he saw "no benefit" from a law that "prohibits the introduction of slaves by negro traders, but permits every citizen to bring them into the State for his own use." This distinction, Gilmer reasoned, not only encouraged citizens to become thinly disguised traders but also made any law restricting the activity of traders "extremely difficult" to enforce. Ignoring Gilmer's plea for an absolute prohibition, the 1833 Georgia legislature tightened its restrictions on the slave trade but left residents able to import slaves for their own use. The tougher law remained in effect until repealed in 1849, as Georgia evolved, as did South

Carolina, from a slave-importing state to slave-exporting state as the cotton economy's center of gravity moved steadily to the southwest during the Jacksonian era.[34]

Nowhere did the internal slave trade emerge as a matter of more debate and concern, and more vacillations in public and legislative sentiment, than along the cotton frontier of the old Southwest, where Alabama, Mississippi, and Louisiana remained major slave-importing states in the Jacksonian era. Throughout the 1820s Alabama debated the desirability of limiting or closing the interstate slave trade. State residents and legal immigrants could always import slaves for their own use, but popular pressure to regulate the activity of slave traders produced annual legislative initiatives. Late in 1826 the Alabama legislature passed an outright ban on the importation of slaves for sale or hire and included stiff penalties for violators. Alabama repealed its ban in 1829 but reimposed it in 1832 as a response to the Turner insurrection. Yet public pressure forced an almost immediate legislative about-face, and in early December 1832 the teeth were removed from the earlier ban. Traders were back in business in Alabama, and, despite occasional complaints from heavy slave-holding areas in the state's western black belt during the 1840s and 1850s, the internal slave trade flourished with little governmental interference for the rest of the antebellum era.[35]

In Louisiana, fears of slave insurrection dated back to the failed slave rebellion of 1811 in St. John the Baptist parish and beyond. The heavy slave majorities in the sugar parishes along the lower Mississippi frequently spawned frequent discussion of balancing the racial demographics of the state and regulating the slave trade to avoid the introduction of potentially incendiary slaves. Following the Denmark Vesey scare in South Carolina, renewed concern emerged in Louisiana about the rapid growth of the state's slave population and the outward flow of capital to slave-selling regions. In 1826, after several years of legislative stalemate, the Louisiana legislature passed a two-year ban on the importation of slaves for sale, only to repeal the ban a year later. In 1829, the state established a character test for imported slaves, requiring two affidavits from freeholders in the county of the slave's former residence vouching for the slave's good character in an effort to prevent the state from becoming a dumping ground for troublesome slaves from other states.[36] Still, concern about slave unrest proved no match for the thirst for the labor needed to grow cotton in Louisiana's rich river valleys. The Louisiana planter E. G. W. Butler noted that a "desire to continually purchase land and Negroes appears to be a characteristic of planters." Indeed, Louisiana planters as a whole believed it "impracticable" to ban the importation of slaves, and Alexander Barrow denounced such a ban as both "unconstitutional and impolitic."[37]

In 1831, however, news of the Nat Turner insurrection prompted Louisiana politicians to reconsider. A special session of the legislature approved a bill that allowed new settlers and current citizens to bring slaves for use but banned the activity of traders. The new law required even those who imported slaves for use to appear before parish judges to explain their intentions.[38] The Louisiana planter J. S. Johnston thought the new restrictions might prevent the state from being "drained of our Capital for the purchase of more Negroes." Johnston reasoned that the cessation of the interstate slave trade might prompt Virginians and other upper South slaveholders to move to Louisiana rather than simply selling off slaves to Louisiana buyers and privately gloated that Virginia would "feel the difference between selling slaves for money and having them carried away by her own people," a prospect that he predicted "will be as beneficial to us as it will be injurious to her."[39]

Clearly, at least in times of crisis, the desire of Virginia and other upper South states to rid themselves of the "evil" of slavery, or at least the "threat" presented by troublesome slaves, by means of the sale and migration of slaves to the Southwest raised alarm in these deep South states. But Louisiana's 1831 restriction on the interregional slave trade had minimal lasting impact. It was difficult if not impossible to prevent potential Louisiana buyers from doing business at the active Natchez market just across the river (even though such imports were explicitly prohibited by the 1831 statute). By March 1833 the portions of the law restricting Louisiana freeholders from importing slaves were repealed, and in 1834 the remaining ban on traders was lifted as well, ushering in a new heyday for slave traders in slave-hungry Louisiana.[40] As one observer of the booming cotton economy of the fertile Red River Valley noted during the 1830s, "slaves were introduced into the country by the thousands . . . [as] farms were extended as if by the hand of magic, [and] people were generally so absorbed in making money that they seemed to be infatuated."[41]

In neighboring Mississippi, the original state constitution, approved in 1817, gave the legislature the "full power to prevent slaves from being brought into this State as merchandise" but guaranteed in-migrants the right to bring slaves with them. Yet, despite enjoying the constitutional prerogative to ban slave traders, from 1817 until the state's second constitution of 1832, the Mississippi state legislature chose to regulate and tax the interstate trade rather than prohibit it. In 1822, reviving a lapsed territorial practice, the legislature approved a character test for imported slaves, anticipating Louisiana's similar move a few years later. The character test statute required either the traders or prospective buyers to procure character references for the slaves in question from two freeholders in the slaves' previous area of residence. Designed to slow the work of slave traders, this regulation did not apply to either Mississippi residents or immigrants who intended to settle permanently in Mississippi. In 1825, the legislature attempted to both regulate the slave trade and raise revenue with a tax of 2.5 percent on all slaves purchased at auction, but, in response to public outcry, the legislature lowered the tax to 1 percent the following year. In 1828 Governor Gerard Brandon again recommended closing the internal slave trade because he believed that Mississippi had become a "receptacle for the surplus black population of the Middle States," a trend that rightly "excited uneasiness in the minds of many of our fellow-citizens." Yet despite Brandon's recommendation and other similar concerns expressed by members of the powerful Natchez elite, all legislative initiatives restricting the trade failed until news of the Nat Turner rebellion reached the state.[42]

But in 1832, with slaves pouring into the state and concerns about the Southampton insurrection and related rumors of conspiracy circulating widely, the Mississippi Constitutional Convention of that year adopted a clause prohibiting the introduction of slaves "as Merchandise" after March 1, 1833. Like the statutory prohibitions in Alabama and Louisiana, the new constitutional provision guaranteed Mississippi citizens and immigrants the right to import slaves for their own use until at least 1845. The ban on trading emerged almost entirely from the efforts of an odd coalition of Natchez-area planters and poor whites from the piney woods to block the "dumping" of troublesome and rebellious slaves from the upper South into Mississippi's rapidly expanding cotton economy.[43]

Mississippi's new ban triggered an immediate and powerful popular backlash. The 1833 session of the Mississippi legislature not only refused to adopt statutory penalties for violators of the prohibition but instead approved an amendment to lift the ban and submitted it to voters for a decision in the fall elections. In November 1833, four out of five Mississippi voters who cast ballots on the amendment question favored repealing the ban on the domestic slave trade, but the amendment failed to win approval because it received less than the required majority of all votes cast in that year's legislative elections. Thus, in 1834, the state legislature, still ignoring the constitutional ban, changed its course again and adopted a 2.5 percent tax on the gross sale price of slaves. Four years later, the Mississippi legislature finally approved a system of fines and penalties for those who sold or purchased slaves imported solely for the purpose of sale or hire and left the question of the internal slave trade in Mississippi mired in a bog of contradictory legal claims.[44]

During the Panic of 1837 the financial distress that plagued the Mississippi cotton economy precipitated a minor constitutional crisis over the interstate slave trade. Overextended slaveholders sought temporary relief from heavy debts arising from recent slave purchases by arguing that these debts were invalid because the transactions had been banned by the 1832 constitution. In a series of sometimes inconsistent decisions, state courts in Mississippi tended to void debts that planters owed slave traders who operated on a regional basis but upheld debts that purchasers owed to indigenous Mississippi slaveholders. Eventually slave traders, often citizens of other states who conducted business in several states, sought relief in federal court. The case, centered on the legality of debts incurred in the interstate slave trade between the beginning of the constitutional prohibition in 1833 and the passage of enforcement statutes in 1837, wound its way to the United States Supreme Court as *Groves v. Slaughter*.[45] In a narrowly reasoned decision that avoided the issue of whether a state constitutional provision such as Mississippi's ban on the interstate slave trade violated the federal Constitution's grant of authority over interstate commerce to Congress, the Court ruled the debts legitimate and binding on the ground that Mississippi's constitutional provision took effect only after the state legislature passed the requisite enabling legislation in 1837. This decision gave indirect support to creditors' rights. By 1844, however, as financial distress receded, demand for slaves prompted the Mississippi legislature to again support amending the constitution to remove the ban on the importation of slaves for sale and return the power to regulate the trade to the state legislature. The fall election campaign produced very little discussion of the issue, and the amendment allowing the legislature to reopen the domestic slave trade passed overwhelmingly. The amendment became part of the Mississippi state constitution in 1846, and the 1846 Mississippi legislature promptly repealed the 1837 statute that prohibited the importation of slaves as merchandise. By 1847, the internal slave trade resumed, and Mississippi returned to the unrestricted importation of slaves. [46]

The prolonged controversy regarding the domestic slave trade revealed that even as most lower South whites wanted slaves to cultivate their highly profitable cotton fields, they also grew concerned about the potential dangers of a large black population as well as about the flow of investment capital back to the upper South. Thus they periodically debated methods designed to control the fluctuating racial demographics of the region. By the late 1830s, most whites in the lower South saw slave labor as the key to wealth and upward social mobility. But, despite their confidence in slavery as an economic benefactor, even they agonized over the size and the proportion of the black population in the region. Some wanted to restrict the number of slaves allowed to enter their region as part of an effort to manage its racial demography; others thought slave labor so essential to the flourishing of the staple economy and economic opportunity for white southerners that no state should be legislatively or constitutionally denied the option of importing more slaves. This ongoing disagreement revealed that even within the nominally proslavery lower South very substantial room for maneuver and internal disagreement about issues related to slavery remained; only external challenge to the institution inspired unified denunciation.[47] In the upper South, even the most adamant defenders of slavery recognized the continuation of an active interstate slave trade as crucial to their ability to modulate the size and proportion of their region's slave population and their efforts to prosper despite the region's relatively stagnant staple economy. In addition, upper South advocates of gradual emancipation and colonization also recognized that their efforts to slowly rid the upper South of slavery depended in large part on the continued ability of the region's slaveholders to sell slaves further south.[48]

The tensions within the South concerning the question of the domestic slave trade revealed that the trade had created a "connected" regional political economy more than a truly unified one and that questions related to slavery could still divide white southerners during the Jacksonian era as well as unite them. Moreover, the scholarly enterprise of imagining a counterfactual Jacksonian South, one in which the internal slave trade was either banned entirely or was so carefully regulated that the restrictions effectively limited the buying and selling of slaves from upper South to lower South, permits historians to conjure a counterfactual South where something approaching the "paternalism" Genovese described might have enjoyed more sweeping influence. Without an active internal trade, something more closely approaching paternalism might have prevailed, certainly in the older South Atlantic staple-growing areas, locales with large slave populations that emerged as slave-exporting regions soon after the first cotton boom subsided. Moreover, without the trade as a mechanism for selling unneeded slaves, struggling Chesapeake-area slaveholders would have faced even more internal defections to the emancipation or colonization ranks and the ideology of paternalism might have emerged as a necessity for personal security and economic survival rather than as a rationalization offered to blunt criticism. In this fictive South without a slave trade (or with a severely limited one), the values of the market might have been more readily deflected by slaveholding paternalists and a different, and infinitely more un-American, society created in the region. When surveyed from this perspective, the many ways in which the Old South's active internal trade limited and contradicted the triumph of paternalism as an ideology as well as a practice become more evident.

Hence Stowe's Topsy merely explained in *Uncle Tom's Cabin* what many slaveholders in the upper and lower South had known all along about the centrality of the slave trade to antebellum southern life and thought. In Stowe's novel, Miss Ophelia tried to instruct the troublesome but entertaining Topsy in sound Christian doctrine. She catechized the young slave girl every Sunday. When learning about the fall of Adam, Topsy recited, "Our first parents, being left to the freedom of their own will, fell from the state wherein they were created." But Topsy promptly stopped at that point to quiz Ophelia on the matter. "Please, missus," Topsy implored, "was that state Kintuck?" "What state, Topsy?" Ophelia replied. "Dat state they fell out of. I used to hear mas'r tell how we came down from Kintuck." Observing the scene with amusement, Augustine St. Clare laughed and advised his cousin Ophelia, "You'll have to give her a meaning or she'll make one. There seems to be a theory of emigration suggested there."[49]

Just as St. Clare saw a theory of emigration emerging from Topsy's apparent confusion of geography and theology, the recent studies of various aspects of the Old South's domestic slave trade suggests an interpretation of the evolution of antebellum southern society as a process influenced heavily by the forced migration of enslaved people in an intensely market-oriented, staple-growing economy. This interpretation not only gives prominence to the immorality and exploitation of the auction block and the slave pen but also emphasizes that the internal trade served as a crucial yet controversial connection between the upper and the lower South. This interpretation insists that the slave trade reveals much about the larger internal dynamics and character of an Old South that needed it so desperately. As this emerging interpretation is fleshed out, it must include the process of accommodation and resistance, a process in which both master and slave were agents, albeit of vastly unequal power, as well as the larger political and market pressures afoot in the society, pressures that made European consumers, congressional tariff writers, white southern male voters, and many others part of the agency mix and thus help facilitate, as William Freehling has urged, the development of a reintegrated history of the slaveholding society of the antebellum American South.[50]

Notes

1. Harriet Beecher Stowe, *Uncle Tom's Cabin* (London: G. Routledge, 1853), 155–156.

2. Ibid., 163–165.

3. Ibid., 303–304.

4. For a comprehensive introduction to the various forms and aspects of the proslavery argument, see Larry Tise, *Proslavery: A History of the Defense of Slavery in America, 1701–1840* (Athens: University of Georgia Press, 1987), and William Sumner Jenkins, *Proslavery Thought in the Old South* (Chapel Hill: University of North Carolina Press, 1935). On the emergence of the "Lost Cause" ideology in the postbellum South, see

Gaines M. Foster, *Ghosts of the Confederacy: Defeat, the Lost Cause, and the Emergence of the New South, 1865–1913* (New York: Oxford University Press, 1987); on Phillips, see Daniel Joseph Singal, *The War Within: From Victorian to Modernist Thought in the South, 1919–1945* (Chapel Hill: University of North Carolina Press, 1982), 37–57, and U. B. Phillips, *American Negro Slavery* (New York: D. Appleton, 1918). See also Eugene D. Genovese, *In Red and Black: Marxist Explorations in Southern and African-American History* (New York: Pantheon, 1968), 259–298.

5. The scholarly literature on slavery over the past half-century has indeed been voluminous. For three excellent book-length surveys of this literature, see Mark M. Smith, *Debating Slavery: Economy and Society in the Antebellum South* (Cambridge: Cambridge University Press, 1998); Peter Kolchin, *American Slavery, 1619–1877* (New York: Hill and Wang, 1993); and Peter J. Parish, *Slavery: History and Historians* (New York: Harper and Row, 1989).

6. This paragraph attempts to summarize the views expressed and refined in the large and impressive corpus of work that Genovese has produced over the past forty years. The highlights and evolution of that work can be traced in the titles listed herein. See Eugene D. Genovese, *The Political Economy of Slavery: Studies in the Society and Economy of the Slave South* (New York: Pantheon, 1965); *The World the Slaveholders Made: Two Essays in Interpretation* (New York: Pantheon, 1969); *Roll, Jordan, Roll: The World the Slaves Made* (New York: Pantheon, 1974); *The Slaveholders' Dilemma: Freedom and Progress in Southern Conservative Thought, 1820–1860* (Columbia: University of South Carolina Press, 1991); and with Elizabeth Fox-Genovese, *Fruits of Merchant Capital: Slavery and Bourgeois Property in the Rise and Expansion of Capitalism* (New York: Oxford University Press, 1983). To notice Genovese's shift from Marxism to cultural conservatism, see Genovese, *The Southern Front: History and Politics in the Culture War* (Columbia: University of Missouri Press, 1995).

7. For an introduction to the thinking of Berlin and Gutman, see Ira Berlin and Herbert G. Gutman, *Power and Culture: Essays on the American Working Class* (New York: Pantheon, 1987).

8. Michael Tadman, *Speculators and Slaves: Masters, Traders and Slaves in the Old South* (Madison: University of Wisconsin Press, 1989); Walter Johnson, *Soul by Soul: Life Inside the Antebellum Slave Market* (Cambridge: Harvard University Press, 1999).

9. Tadman, *Speculators and Slaves,* esp. 11–46, 111–178.

10. Ibid., 111–132, 179–210.

11. Johnson, *Soul by Soul,* 14–20.

12. Ibid., esp. 117–161. For a clever and imaginative article supporting Johnson's points about the physical as well as psychological trauma often inflicted on slaves by the slave trade (and slave traders), see Edward E. Baptist, " 'Cuffy,' 'Fancy Maids,' and 'One-Eyed Men': Rape, Commodification, and the Domestic Slave Trade in the United States," *American Historical Review* 106 (December 2001): 1619–1650.

13. Tadman, *Speculators and Slaves,* esp. 211–221; Johnson, *Soul by Soul,* 22–36.

14. Tadman, *Speculators and Slaves,* 179–221.

15. Johnson, *Soul by Soul,* 22–23.

16. See Walter Johnson, "A Nettlesome Classic Turns Twenty-Five," www.common-place.org, 1 July 2001.

17. Johnson's formulation is similar to one offered in Lacy K. Ford Jr., *Origins of Southern Radicalism: The South Carolina Upcountry, 1800–1860* (New York: Oxford University Press, 1988), 352–359.

18. See works cited in note 6 above.

19. For a thorough introduction to the extensive literature on the market revolution, see Paul A. Gilje, ed., *Wages of Independence: Capitalism in the Early Republic* (Madison: University of Wisconsin Press, 1997); Melvyn Stokes and Stephen Conway, eds., *The Market Revolution in America: Social, Political, and Religious Expressions, 1800–1880* (Charlottesville: University of Virginia Press, 1996); and Richard Ellis et al., "A Symposium on Charles Sellers' *The Market Revolution: Jacksonian America, 1815–1846*," *Journal of the Early Republic* 12 (Winter 1992): 445–476.

20. For contrary views, see Douglas R. Egerton, "Markets Without a Market Revolution: Southern Planters and Capitalism," *Journal of the Early Republic* 16 (Summer 1996): 237–256; Paul E. Johnson, "The Market Revolution," in *Encyclopedia of American Social History*, ed. Mary Kupiec Cayton et al. (New York: Scribner, 1993), 1:545–560.

21. Tadman, *Speculators and Slaves*, 47–108.

22. Harold Woodman, "Economic History and Economic Theory: The New Economic History in America," *Journal of Interdisciplinary History* 3 (Autumn 1972): 323–350.

23. For a good sampling of Gavin Wright's work, see his *The Political Economy of the Cotton South: Households, Markets, and Wealth in the Nineteenth Century* (New York: W. W. Norton, 1978), and *Old South, New South: Revolutions in the Southern Economy Since the Civil War* (New York: Basic Books, 1986).

24. Wright, *Old South, New South*, 17–80.

25. Wright, *Political Economy of the Cotton South*, 128–157.

26. The following discussion draws heavily on, but also expands upon, Lacy K. Ford Jr., "Making the 'White Man's Country' White: Race, Slavery, and State-Building in the Jacksonian South," *Journal of the Early Republic* 19 (Winter 1999): 713–737.

27. Tadman, *Speculators and Slaves*, 83–93.

28. Ford, "Making the 'White Man's Country' White," esp. 726–731.

29. *Speech of John Thompson Brown, in the House of Delegates of Virginia, on the Abolition of Slavery. Delivered Wednesday, January 18, 1832* (Richmond: n.p., 1832). For good overviews of these debates, see Alison Goodyear Freehling, *Drift Toward Dissolution: The Virginia Slave Debate of 1831–32* (Baton Rouge: Louisiana State University Press, 1982), 122–195, and William Freehling, *The Road to Disunion: Secessionists at Bay* (New York: Oxford University Press, 1990), 178–196. In the latter work, William Freehling explicitly develops the theme of a sometimes tense dialectic between the upper and the lower South that has influenced my thinking on these issues.

30. Thomas Roderick Dew, "Abolition of Negro Slavery," *American Quarterly Review* 12 (September 1832): 189–265.

31. Jesse Burton Harrison, "Abolition Question," *American Quarterly Review* 12 (December 1832): 1–42.

32. Ford, "Making the 'White Man's Country' White," 716–722.

33. Message of Governor David Rogerson Williams, November 25, 1816, and Message

No. 1 of Governor Andrew Pickens, November 24, 1818, South Carolina Department of Archives and History, Columbia, SC; Howell M. Henry, *The Police Control of the Slave in South Carolina* (1914; reprint, New York: Negro Universities Press, 1968), 105–107.

34. Ruth Scarborough, *Opposition to Slavery in Georgia Prior to 1860* (1933; reprint, New York: Negro Universities Press, 1968), 107–123. Gilmer is quoted on pages 118–119.

35. James B. Sellers, *Slavery in Alabama* (Tuscaloosa: University of Alabama Press, 1950), 140–194; J. Mills Thornton III, *Politics and Power in a Slave Society: Alabama, 1800–1860* (Baton Rouge: Louisiana State University Press, 1978), 319–320.

36. James Dormon, "The Persistent Specter: Slave Rebellion in Territorial Louisiana," *Louisiana History* 18 (Fall 1977): 389–404; Adam Rothman, "The Expansion of Slavery in the Deep South, 1790–1820" (Ph.D. diss., Columbia University, 2000), esp. 97–113; Joe Gray Taylor, *Negro Slavery in Louisiana* (Baton Rouge: Louisiana State University Press, 1963), esp. 21–58.

37. Taylor, *Slavery in Louisiana*, 21–58; Herman E. Sterkx, *The Free Negro in Antebellum Louisiana* (Rutherford, NJ: Fairleigh Dickinson University Press, 1972), 285–315; Alexander Barrow to William S. Hamilton, January 25, 1830, William S. Hamilton Papers, Lower Mississippi Valley and Louisiana Collection, Louisiana State University, Baton Rouge.

38. Taylor, *Negro Slavery in Louisiana*, 41–47.

39. J. S. Johnston to Thomas Butler, March 12, 1832, Butler Family Papers, Louisiana State University, Baton Rouge.

40. Taylor, *Negro Slavery in Louisiana*, 44–46.

41. W. E. Paxton, *A History of the Baptists of Louisiana from the Earliest Times to the Present* (St. Louis: n.p., 1888), 149–150.

42. Winburne McGruder Drake, "The Framing of Mississippi's First State Constitution," *Journal of Mississippi* 29 (April 1956): 79–110; Charles Sydnor, *Slavery in Mississippi* (New York: D. Appleton–Century, 1933), 161–165; Charles Sydnor, "The Free Negro in Mississippi," *American Historical Review* 32 (July 1927): 769–788; Edwin A. Miles, *Jacksonian Democracy in Mississippi* (Chapel Hill: University of North Carolina Press, 1960), 41–42. Brandon is quoted in Sydnor, *Slavery in Mississippi*, 161–162.

43. Winburne McGruder Drake, "The Mississippi Constitution of 1832," *Journal of Southern History* 23 (August 1957): 354–370; *Natchez Courier*, November 9, 1832.

44. Sydnor, *Slavery in Mississippi*, 161–171; *Natchez Courier*, August 23 and November 13, 1833.

45. Oscar B. Chamberlain, "The Evolution of State Constitutions in the Antebellum United States: Michigan, Kentucky, and Mississippi" (Ph.D. diss., University of South Carolina, 1996), 89–123; Sydnor, *Slavery in Mississippi*, 164–170.

46. Sydnor, *Slavery in Mississippi*, 168–170.

47. Ford, "Making the 'White Man's Country' White," 716–724.

48. Alison Goodyear Freehling, *Drift Toward Dissolution*, 122–195, and William Freehling, *Road to Disunion*, 178–196.

49. Stowe, *Uncle Tom's Cabin*, 314–315.

50. William Freehling, *The Reintegration of American History: Slavery and the Civil War* (New York: Oxford University Press, 1994): 253–274.

8

"Cuffy," "Fancy Maids," and "One-Eyed Men"

Rape, Commodification, and the Domestic Slave Trade in the United States

EDWARD E. BAPTIST

In January 1834, the slave trader Isaac Franklin wrote from New Orleans to his Richmond partner and slave buyer, Rice Ballard: "The fancy girl, from Charlattsvilla [Charlottesville], will you send her out or shall I charge you $1100 for her. Say quick, I wanted to see her. . . . I thought that an old Robber might be satisfied with two or three maids." Franklin implied that his partner was holding the young woman, one of many "fancy maids" handled by the firm of Franklin, Armfield, and Ballard, for his own sexual use. Unwilling, the jest implied, to share his enslaved sex objects, Ballard was keeping the desirable Charlottesville maid in Richmond instead of passing her on to his partners so that they might take their turn. The joke, and the desire it did not seek to disguise, was business as usual. In this case, the business was a slave-trading partnership, and systematic rape and sexual abuse of slave women formed part of the normal practice of the men who ran the firm—and the normal practice of many of their planter customers as well. Franklin, Armfield, and Ballard supplied field hands and carpenters to the raw new plantations of Louisiana, Mississippi, and Arkansas in the 1830s, but they also supplied planters with many a fancy maid. In fact, the letter quoted went on to suggest, tongue in cheek, that such women were in such heavy demand that the firm might do better selling coerced sex retail rather than wholesale. Referring to two enslaved women, Franklin mused self-indulgently on the conversion of female labor into slavers' money: "The old Lady and Susan could soon pay for themselves by keeping a whore house." Yet what did Franklin indulge most? Was sexual or monetary greed the trump suit in his own decision-making? Perhaps, he continued, in the vein of aggressive sexual banter that pervades the traders' letters, the partners would rather see the house "located and established at your place, Alexandria, or Baltimore for the Exclusive benefit of the consern & [its] agents."[1]

Franklin and his colleagues passionately wanted mulatto women, and black people generally, as bodies to rape and bodies to sell. If these men were more than mere exceptions in the society in which they lived—and I argue that they illustrate that society's half-denied and half-remembered assumptions about commerce and rape—then the stakes of explaining their desires are high. What sort of society did slaveowning white men create in the antebellum southern United States? What sorts of ideas and psychological forces cemented their devotion to the supposedly pre-modern institution of racial slavery to a deep involvement in the rapid commercial expansion that reached a peak during the 1830s?

The present essay seeks to explain the ideas about slavery, rape, and commerce embedded in and produced by the passionate desires of Franklin and his partners. For years, historians interpreting the institutions and ideology of nineteenth-century southern slavery focused their attentions on explaining slaveholders' paternalist defenses of their planter institution. Like some of their sources, such histories have often explicitly or implicitly portrayed the domestic slave trade as a contradiction within an otherwise stable system.[2] Recent works have returned the issue of that trade to the forefront, arguing that the commerce in human beings was an inescapable and essential feature of the region's pre–Civil War society and culture.[3] In the drop of water that is the correspondence between Franklin, Ballard, and their associates, one might perceive a need to push historians' revisions of the slave South's whole world further still. Indeed, these men reveal themselves as being so devoted to their picture of the slave trade as a fetishized commodification of human beings that we may need to insist on such a mystification as one of the necessary bases of the economic expansion of the antebellum South. They also assert, especially in their frequent discussions of the rape of light-skinned enslaved women, or fancy maids, their own relentlessly sexualized vision of the trade. Finally, the traders insist in accidental testimony that sexual fetishes and commodity fetishism intertwined with such intimacy that coerced sex was the secret meaning of the commerce in human beings, while commodification swelled its actors with the power of rape. Such complexities lead one to wonder whether historians might do well to reinterpret the antebellum South—a society in which the slave trade was a motor of rapid geographical and economic expansion—as a complex of inseparable fetishisms.[4]

Admittedly, the correspondence of the partners and employees of the slave-trading firm of Franklin, Ballard, and Armfield is a single group of sources from one of the several dozen trading firms operating in the southern United States during the boom years of the 1830s. Thus the question of representativeness inevitably arises. Indeed, the firm's records are not typical, in part because they are so extensive. But they are also atypical because they are so candid, so powerfully illustrative. These men, to borrow a phrase, "articulated the language that history had put at [their] disposal" and articulated it with stunning indiscretion.[5] The unrepresentativeness of their apparent honesty exposes representative elements of the world in which they lived. More openly than most, these men described the ways in which the sexual history of slaves and masters fogged their vision of enslaved black women with an erotic haze. And they depicted the enslaved in mystical terms as standardized objects: units of trade, transparent in history, ready for sale and use.

Of course, African and African American opposition to such ideas was constant. Women of color, and black communities in general, waged constant rhetorical and physical battles against the sexual assaults of white men and against whites' demeaning ideas about black people.[6] But such efforts were not always successful, and they were particularly likely to fail when waged from the vulnerable height of the auction block. Resistance by enslaved African Americans also undoubtedly made more impact on the day-to-day lives of black folks than on whites' ideas, popular or erudite, about African American women. Black resistance, of course, does not need to change whites' minds— or even register an impact on white culture—for it to matter, and matter beyond easy measure. Resistance is not the subject of this essay. Instead, I focus on explaining why and how some white men identified rapes and slave sales as conjoined and essential parts of their very selves.

To explain the words left behind by Franklin and Ballard, we must talk about sexual coercion and sexual obsession and also about the desire for commodities. These disturbing phenomena are not merely products of male biology, transhistorical psychological topology, sui generis individual perversion, or quotidian consumer behaviors. Although, like antebellum apologists for slavery, many historians have blamed sexual violence on the allegedly unusually low morals of slave traders, not even the act of rape is a transparent product of an essential male nature.[7] Likewise, the ability to perceive and treat human beings as commodities also grew from and supported social and cultural institutions and ideas that had their own tortured histories. In the case of this group of nineteenth-century slave traders, the concept of the fetish, or "the objectivized form of our desire," can help us understand the way in which they interpreted their roles and experiences. Admittedly, the senses of this term are many and perhaps, within academic language, form a fetish of their own. But the two best-known uses of the word—Karl Marx's definition of the commodity fetish and Sigmund Freud's argument that forms of sexual fetishism are central to male desires—offer terms that can begin an exploration of the passion for slaves shared by traders and buyers.[8]

Describing what he called "commodity fetishism," Marx argued that, in the process of industrial capitalist production, goods appear as abstractions with their own existence and their own value, independent of the social labor of the actual human beings who created them. To the mind of the consumer and the capitalist apologist alike, such goods have no relation to the exploitative process of production. Like the wooden god-images called *fetiço* by early Portuguese voyagers to Africa, commodities, to believers, appear to have their own life and their own powers. Yet the fetishists themselves are the ones who ascribe such powers to the objects. Likewise, capitalists deny their own creation and control of the commodity, explaining it as objective, natural reality. For that very reason, one cannot distinguish in any useful way between "real" and "false" commodities, for each one of these social and cultural "facts," whether an inanimate object or an enslaved human being, is the product of determined and meaningful self-deception and forgetting.[9]

Marx emphasized a process of half-forgetting, but Freud's argument concerning sexual fetishism leaned toward the forms of half-remembering, which he placed at the center of his explanation of male sexuality. Formative castration dramas of infancy and early childhood, he argued, led men to layer meaning onto simultaneously rejected and desired objects such as shoes or parts of women's bodies (the foot, the breast, the hair). In his classic example, Freud depicted the birth of a shoe fetish in a young boy's act of peering up a woman's skirt. The boy's discovery of the absence of the female penis leads to traumatic fears of his own castration and to dread of the woman's genitalia whose discovery occasioned such terrors. The woman's shoes, which the boy also saw, provide a redirected object for the traumatized boy as he becomes a young man. This choice of the conscious mind seems to forget its own cause. Yet the unconscious remembers the discovery of female difference and returns to it compulsively as an object both titillating and fearful, desired and reviled.[10] The specific example used here may suggest that fetishism explains only a few rare perversions. But Freud sought to find not only keys to unlock individual psychologies but also culture-wide issues of male sexuality.[11] Fetishism, Freud argued, normally proceeded without neurosis. This was the typical course of development of male sexuality. In the early nineteenth-century South, history had structured sexuality on differences of "race" or class, as well as on sex and gender. There, skin color and other racialized characteristics (or still more, the social and cultural myths to which racists wired such characteristics) could serve as signs of displaced castration anxiety and sexual discovery.[12]

Neither Marx nor Freud is the final word on fetishism, and neither explains the sexual and economic obsessions that emerge so disturbingly from the letters of these slave traders. Freud's understanding of sexuality is completely masculinist and also reifies the culture of bourgeois fin-de-siècle Vienna as the transhistorical model of psychological formation.[13] Yet what Marx and Freud do tell us is that seeming contradictions might not be examples of intellectual bad faith but keys to the not-so-secret, yet disavowed, relationships that have come to structure ways in which we perceive and act on symbols and things. By looking at sexual and other forms of desire and their self-deceptions, historians might uncover such acts of simultaneous forgetting and remembering, self-deception and aggressive desire — acts or the historical detritus of acts that displace deeply contradictory issues onto objects or other persons. Indeed, historically constructed questions of group and individual identity are often charged with fierce, even erotic passions and surrounded by processes of forgetting and remembering that defy constraint in simplistic paradigms. Having once forgotten his or her creation of the "impassioned object," the fetishist returns compulsively, often renewing relationships of exploitation in the process. By doing so, he or she pleasures the self with the unacknowledged remembrance of a transgression without blame, an ambiguity controlled and fixed, a memory displaced onto and encoded in the fetish object. So even in our own day, we see the fetishization of flags, of skin color, battlefields, historic mansions, presidents' reputations, or black athletes.[14]

The slave traders' own half-hidden thought about impassioned objects emerges first from their letters as commodity fetishism. Only later, as one learns their private language, does the sexual emerge. Even the forgetting and remembering that made human beings into commodities was complicated. In his brilliant *Sweetness and Power*, Sidney Mintz argues that the evolution of slave-made sugar into a commodity with malleable meanings influenced the tandem development of industrialization and imperialism, as well as that of their renounced parent, plantation slavery. Sugar, he argues, even shaped the growth of the modern concept of the commodity itself. Mintz balks, however, at considering the slave as an object of trade subject to the forces and distortions of the Atlantic world. "Slaves," he writes, "were a 'false commodity' because a human being is not an object, even when treated as one." Perhaps we ought to be glad that we respond with aversion to the prospect of analyzing the enslaved human being as an abstracted, fetishized commodity. No doubt

Mintz is morally right. Human beings should not be treated as objects, and social conventions that claim that certain people have no humanity or independent personhood are false and contradictory. But as a description of historical forces, his flat denial is incomplete. Commodification is a process that takes place in the eye of the commodifier, not the commodified. In the case of slavery in the Atlantic world, the fictions of commodification were powerful enough to ensure that some people were treated as objects. Slave traders and owners were in practice far from reluctant to treat, think of, and talk about humans as commodities.[15]

In fact, the domestic slave trade made the social, cultural, and psychological fiction of the slave-as-commodity — and the white man as slavery's fetishist — ubiquitous practice in the antebellum South. Between 1790 and 1860, the trade moved more than half a million enslaved Africans and African Americans from older states to the plantation frontiers of the South.[16] We now tend to imagine slave traders as a group fundamentally different from the planter class. Abolitionists deployed the trade as a rhetorical symbol of the worst aspects of the South's "peculiar institution." Slave traders appeared in critiques as generally despicable, déclassé, and callous destroyers of black families.[17] Opponents of slavery made their own fetish of stories about women stripped nude on the auction block and of young mulatto women sold into sexual servitude to depraved masters. Even defenders of slavery were ready by the 1850s to sacrifice the traders, if only in rhetoric, depicting them as a despised and degraded lot in the paternalistic society of the Old South — an unrepresentative bunch, no doubt entirely poor white or Yankee in origin.[18]

Perhaps, then, the slave traders are not representative of the *mentalité* of most planters, and, by inference, of plantation society in the pre–Civil War South. Perhaps, as early as the 1830s, even slave traders perceived themselves as a group distinct from and disagreeable to planters. After all, Isaac Franklin and his nephew called their partners and employees "old robbers" and "pirates," and Isaac liked to paint himself as the wise elder among a gang of lawless outcasts. "The Old Chief," he wrote in an 1833 letter, referring to himself in the third person, "has felt [distress over the vagaries of the market] . . . but must endeavour to bear up, knowing his friends are all young men and if they Loose everything they can Robb far more."[19]

In fact, the symbolic opposition between planter and trader has its roots in the crocodile tears of paternalism publicly shed by slavery's defenders during the late antebellum period. During the 1830s, the slave trader's symbolic place in southern culture was more ambivalent. This was a period of exuberant growth in regional and national economies, and the slave trade was an important engine of capital formation and economic dynamism. Although Franklin referred to fellow slave traders as "pirates," he also called the planters with whom he dealt "robbers." Bill brokers and merchants were "land pirates" and "shavers." There may have been little difference, after all. Franklin's jaundiced description of the world in which he moved admits that virtually every elite or would-be elite white man in the Southwest in this crucial period bent laws and pushed aside conventions to obtain economic and political power.[20] The ex-slave John Brown once saw a Georgia slave trader named Sterling Finney steal a white woman's slave maid, rape her, and march her south before anyone could realize what had happened. Finney, also a wealthy planter, later won election to the state legislature. The traders' willingness to rob slaves and the individuals with whom they traded — the willingness to put profit above all ethical inhibitions — made them neither too distasteful for polite society nor radically different from planters in the 1830s. Indeed, many traders became planters, and planters became traders. All could, quite literally, represent southern society.[21]

Thus, in this context of a rapidly expanding plantation regime, the partners of the Franklin, Armfield, and Ballard slave trading firm were not very different from most other white masters in their origins, actions, or attitudes.[22] The trajectories of their careers certainly reinforce such a conclusion. The early history of Franklin, the eldest member of the firm, is murky, but by the early 1820s he had teamed up with a man named John Armfield.[23] At the time the two had begun to ship enslaved African Americans from the Chesapeake to the lower Mississippi Valley. There they sold the human cargoes to planters relocating year after year from Virginia, Maryland, and the Carolinas. Small markets that organized to supply such migrants' needs for slave labor sprang up in cities such as Natchez, Mobile, and Tallahassee. But the grandest of all was New Orleans. By 1830, Franklin and Armfield had become perhaps the most prominent slave dealers in the country's biggest and most notorious market for human flesh.[24]

Around 1831, the two dealers added a partner: Rice Carter Ballard, a man who originally made his home in eastern Virginia. Soon the three were shipping as many as a thousand people per annum from Ballard's Richmond depot to New Orleans.[25] Ballard paid operatives to scour the interior counties of the Virginia Piedmont, inquiring at run-down tobacco plantations and sheriff's sales for surplus labor to ship south and west. In June and July 1834, for instance, James G. Blakey traveled through Orange, Culpeper, Madison, and Albemarle Counties. Ballard mailed him multiple bank drafts, each for a thousand dollars, "to be laid out in negroes or returned undiminished." Blakey found some bargains in Orange, happening upon three apprentice coopers for sale — "very likely indeed; three brothers." But two weeks later he wrote, "I have just returned from Charlottesville court, great many buyers and negroes was scarce and high." Whether prices were high or low, Ballard kept Blakey flush with the cash needed to sweep in Virginia's abundant surplus labor. Ballard counted and valued the slaves sent in by Blakey and other operatives. Then he shipped the unfree migrants in vessels owned or hired by the firm.[26] The ships sailed south around the capes of Florida and on to New Orleans, where Isaac Franklin brought his nephew James Franklin on board as the company's agent in Natchez. The younger Franklin became an important cog in the trading concern, especially after a Louisiana law banning the import of slaves for sale within the state took effect in 1832. In response, the company moved most selling operations up the Mississippi River to Natchez. Even after Louisiana's legislature repealed its ban on the slave trade in 1834, proximity to customers made the younger Franklin's location ideal for the task of cashing out more than $400,000 in Mississippi and upper Louisiana accounts receivable accumulated by the firm in 1833 alone.[27]

At New Orleans and Natchez, the Franklins sold enslaved African Americans to purchasers who paid in cash, notes (promises to pay in the near future), or drafts on their own "factors." The latter were merchants who shipped and sold planters' cotton and sugar and provided them with commercial credit and other financial services. Franklin and Ballard, however, dealt directly with the commercial banks of the South and the North, which they used to secure ready access to cash for making slave purchases throughout the distressed plantation counties of Maryland and Virginia. After selling the slaves at New Orleans and Natchez, the firm routed their gains in cash and commercial paper back through New York and Philadelphia banks. Chesapeake banks and merchants then supplied Armfield and Ballard with a steady stream of cash that restarted the cycle. Thus slave traders and bankers cooperated to send bound laborers to the plantation frontier, where they produced cotton, the raw material of industrial textile manufacture. British and northern bankers and merchants also provided the credit necessary for frontier planters to purchase both the slaves sent southwest from Chesapeake plantations, of which enslaved human beings often represented the only economically viable product, and the cloth bought to cover them. Money and credit rotated in a wheel of international scale, while plantation products such as cotton and sugar — or slaves — circled in geared opposition. And at every step of their participation in the circulation of capital and commodities, Franklin, Ballard, and Armfield siphoned off a modicum of what they bluntly called "profit."[28]

The traders' participation in and manipulation of a series of vast networks of financial and commercial exchange meant that they were well versed in the way that the world of production, trade, and consumption worked. They accumulated knowledge and expertise, and they accumulated profits as well. By the end of the 1830s, gains from the trade had enabled Isaac Franklin to settle in Tennessee on Fairvue, one of several plantations that he now owned. This one was reputedly more impressive than his neighbor Andrew Jackson's Hermitage. At his death in 1846 Franklin's estate commanded a value of three-quarters of a million dollars despite an ongoing economic depression.[29] Ballard, meanwhile, retired to Louisville, Kentucky, with his new wife. There, he lived off the skimmings of seven plantations that he had accumulated in the Mississippi Delta during the boom decade of the 1830s and the hard times of the 1840s. With almost a thousand slaves to his name, Ballard had clambered to a pinnacle of wealth occupied by only a handful of others in the antebellum United States. The slave trade had brought these men wealth, facility and familiarity with their economic world, and status.[30]

So Ballard and Franklin, planters and traders, were hardly the socially excluded slave traders of late antebellum fictions. They handled cash and credit as insiders, and their ideas about the other commodities they manipulated illustrate beliefs implicit in the trade as a whole. In many ways, slaves moved through the circuits of trade like other early nineteenth-century goods. Certainly, traders tried to push them through in similar fashion. Of course, human beings do present particular challenges to those seeking to treat all products, in the quest for profit, as transparently fungible. In Marx's famous illustration of the commodity fetish, buyers and sellers denied the human life and labor that made a table. Once the latter became a market commodity, it then "stood up," said Marx, and talked back to human beings, "evolv[ing] out of its wooden brain grotesque ideas."[31] Such grotesque ideas, by which Marx meant buyers' and sellers' myths about the objective reality of the market and its laws of supply and demand, existed only in the minds of human beings. Enslaved people were not wooden tables and thus had their own ideas, quite different from the masters' ideas about what slaves represented in their own market world. They could not only stand up and rebuke but could resist and even kill the creators of the conditions that made them commodities, as slave owners and traders knew only too well. Thus when an 1834 traveler crossed John Armfield's path in the mountains of Virginia, as the latter marched two hundred slaves toward far-off Natchez, he noted that the trader had chained all the men together with stout precautionary iron shackles.[32]

In fact, by the end of the eighteenth century, if not before, African American culture had created families and individuals that rejected the despair that was one possible response to servitude and instead raised up children imbued with a survivalist mentality. Men and women such as twenty-one-year-old Henry Gant (cost: $450) or seventeen-year-old Charlotte McKenny (cost: $300), both shipped from Richmond by R. C. Ballard on September 27, 1831, to New Orleans on the brig *Tribune,* were themselves the products of complex human social relations. Chesapeake communities supplied Gant, McKenny, and their peers with selfhood and enabled at least some masters to see slaves as more than the socially dead creatures postulated by the ideal state of bondage.[33] Yet just as the social relations of industrial production created commodities such as Marx's table, often in the face of workers' resistance, the relations of reproduction enshrined in the slave South's law, custom, and political economy succeeded in selling human beings as goods on a market. Mothers, fathers, children, spouses, siblings, lovers, and friends could cajole, plead, and threaten in efforts to prevent the brutal division of human relationships. The history told by ex-slaves, however, contains many more separations than cases in which such pleading worked.[34] Resistance to sale was typically ineffective, especially after the expansion of new plantation regions permitted slaveowners to sell the children that law made chattel at quite a profit. The act of sale ruptured the old plantation districts' relationships of family, kinship, and community. The possibility of blacks manipulating whites narrowed radically, especially once original owners sold enslaved people to traders. Neither traders nor the frontier planters to whom they sold slaves displayed much interest in African Americans' individual or family social histories and identities. Decisively violent resistance, another possible alternative, was rare. Shackles, guns, whips, threats, isolation, division, dogs, and guards all did their work. Despite a few celebrated revolts, most enslaved people sent south and west to New Orleans were sold there to new owners not of their own choosing. The growth of the domestic slave trade after 1790 or so thus plunged the enslaved into a new round of commodification, which they had to find a way to survive.[35]

As white men, traders, and masters moved enslaved people between and onto markets, they conceived of African Americans as commodities. A transmutation of words and meanings allowed sellers and buyers to endow actual human beings with the universal and abstract qualities characteristic of the commodity. Traders such as Rice Ballard and Isaac Franklin began by drawing brutally thick lines between themselves and the goods they sold. During a cholera epidemic in Natchez, Franklin noted that the problem was not so much that some slaves were dying but that their deaths, if not properly hidden, would impede further sales: "The way we send out dead negroes at night and keep dark is a sin." Of course, slave traders did not understand their own potential demise as a mere impediment to further business or as the simple depreciation of trade goods. When Ballard heard that cholera had hit the river towns, he wrote to tell his partner to abandon his slaves to death should they become ill, rather than trying to care for them: "We had better loose [*sic*] all and begin again than loose ourselves."[36] In another case, Franklin worried about business, "not so much on his own account, as those he is conserned with," because he feared the loss of his partners' precious investments of time and money. Then he casually noted, "I sold Old Man Alsop's two scald headed boys for $800. One of them Took the Cholera the day afterwards and died and the other was very near kicking the Bucket." The individual white trader, his time, and his hard-won resources were all irreplaceable. In contrast, the partners could easily replace the black folks who made up their capital investment, so long as they had the cash required.[37]

The transformation of slaves to easily replaced, inhuman goods was part of a process one might call the deanimation of enslaved people: their reduction, in traders' words, to virtually inanimate articles. Whites held virtually every card in this game. In the letters exchanged by these traders, at least, this was no back-and-forth exchange between anxious traders and African Americans whose cooperation needed to be secured by coaxing. Those in the firm of Franklin, Armfield, and Ballard swung into the linguistic rhythms of deanimation with a coarse and practiced swagger. In March 1832, for instance, James Franklin wrote to Ballard from Natchez, eager for the next day of sales to begin: "I shall open my fancy stock of Wool and Ivory early in the morning." The younger Franklin's words evoked a peddler opening a case to display cloth and carved knickknacks, although he referred to enslaved African Americans. His "wool" suggested common racist descriptions of their hair, and his "ivory" evoked both African origins and the teeth that buyers inspected. Franklin described the enslaved as inanimate articles, stilled of life, and reduced to hair and teeth.[38]

Slavemongers also referred incessantly to men, women, and children as "stock": James Franklin reported to Ballard after reaching Natchez in the fall of 1832 that "we arrived in this place . . . with all of our stock."[39] Other references to their human merchandise underlined the deanimation inflicted in the traders' own minds. James, always a reliable font of offensive expressions, also wrote to Ballard in 1834, saying, "I suppose you are not buying any Cuffys right now." Later his uncle also used the term, reporting, "The price of Cuffy comes on whether they have fallen or not they are very high through all the country." The singular term "Cuffy" standardized the human produce shipped from the Chesapeake, using a partitive term to imply that selling slaves was no different from selling soup or lumber. The product was uniform: the main difference between one and thirty was one of quantity.[40]

To be sure, Franklin and Ballard sought a mix of types of slaves. In November 1833, Isaac Franklin complained to Richmond that "[I] Could have sold as many more if we had had the right kind, men from 8 to 900 dollars, field women large and likely from 6 to 650 dollars." He also reported "a Great demand for fancy maid[s]" as well as artisans and other skilled workers. Franklin also complained to Ballard about a recent shipment that did not meet standard size and age requirements: "Yours and Armfields was the leanest invoice I have ever received. In fact your little slim assed girls and boys are intirely out of the way and cannot be sold for a profit." Each variety was identical within itself, measured and assigned a certain dollar value to correspond to the quantity of Cuffy that he or she contained.[41]

Enslaved human beings, in the minds of those who bought and sold them, became goods easily replaced and thus valuable in proportion to their equivalency in money, the most easily transmuted commodity of all. Consider how one South Carolina planter wrote about disposing of a recalcitrant slave at a Charleston auction house: "Give Brass a new shirt and send to Robert Blacklock & Co. to be turn'd into money forthwith."[42] Brass became gold or paper, and at some point might be turned (in whites' eyes) into Brass again, but the trader would hardly care. Franklin even complained in 1834 that Ballard had taken to extreme length the propensity to see slaves as uniform commodities, imagining that all goods were not only uniform within each particular category but that the categories themselves did not differ from each other in any way. Ballard had forgotten every peculiarity of human beings as retail goods, assuming that excess inventory could be purchased at low prices when demand was dull, stored without expense or risk, and sold when prices were high again. "He said," Franklin grumbled, "he had concluded to continue purchasing at prices that were more Justifyable or profitable notwithstanding that he had been advised that we were suffering Great Losses from cholera and Small Pox and notwithstanding he had been advised of the risque."[43]

To whites in the slave market, blacks were deanimated commodities, and whites treated them as such. The humane practices of slave families and communities of the southeast and the inhumane structures of white planter law produced and reproduced enslaved African Americans ready for the slave trade, though hardly willing. Then planters and traders colluded to market as standardized what could not be standardized, to deanimate those who thought, spoke, and acted. The slave traders' success in accomplishing this mental movement created horrible consequences for the human beings packed onto slavers' brigs like cordwood, imprisoned in cholera-infested Natchez pens like cattle, or displayed on the market like wool and ivory. To be told at such a point that one was in fact only a false and not a real commodity might have been cold comfort. And even as the words of Ballard and the Franklins deanimated their own idea of the slave, fixing her in white minds as the commodity Cuffy, the traders simultaneously reanimated the lifeless commodity:

now not as individuals but as market myths. As people faced the crowd of "negro speculators" from the block, workers employed by the traders sometimes forced the slaves to dance. The "liveliness" they thus demonstrated was another one of the commodity's standard package of imagined qualities. The ex-slave William Wells Brown recalled his service to a trader at a New Orleans slave pen: "Some were set to dancing, some to singing, and some to playing cards. This was done to make them appear cheerful and happy. . . . I have often set them to dancing when their cheeks were wet with tears." Such demonstrations supposedly proved that those offered for sale were lively if not truly living—standard, acceptably happy, ready-made units of slave.[44]

The Franklins did not record any anxiety that the actual enslaved people whom they auctioned would refuse to dance while the sale proceeded. What they did worry about was a far more abstracted dance echoed by the ideal Cuffys prancing on the block: that of the reanimated yet lifeless and generalized commodity. The dealers believed that the mystical spell of the market's abstract forces affected enslaved humans as they did cotton or interest rates, creating a *fetiço* Cuffy: a made thing that capered up and down in price and quantity, dancing on strings held by the abstract forces of supply and demand, a mere particle cavorting on a price wave. Like Marx's table, slaves lived again in the minds of market-minded whites such as Ballard and the Franklins. In the twilight realm that was the grotesque half-life of the commodity, slaves rose and fell, they were "dull" or brisk, because of their relative relation to other commodities, especially credit, money, and cotton. In early 1834, Isaac Franklin reported that "the [potential] rise of slaves had been lost by the fall of cotton." James Franklin concurred, noting that "cotton is only 130 to 140 which makes Negroes dull." Even slaves already held by Deep South planters breathed air filtered through a matrix of supply and demand. In 1832, Ballard advised Franklin to slow sales until a feared cholera epidemic had run its course: "My opinion is that we had best hold on: the more negroes lost in that country, the more will be wanting if they have the means of procuring them." The number that survived or died in planters' hands would determine the price and pressure for more on the following year's market.[45]

The bourgeoisie critiqued by Marx invested the energy of belief in one linguistically mystical move. They saw products as having no relation to the expropriation of wage labor that erased goods' identities as the historical product of communal labor, clothing them instead in the abstract guise of commodities from nowhere and no-time. White men who watched and manipulated the slave market, however, invested in two such moves. First, they pretended that slaves were not alive—at least not in the sense of being living creatures with rights, social claims, and the ability to resist. Second, they reanimated the socially dead, but in a new fetishized form that allegedly responded to market forces instead of to human ones. In fact, Isaac Franklin argued, one had to subscribe to the rules of such forces, whether illusory or not, in order to succeed in the "game" (as his nephew called it) that the beliefs of commodity fetishism had constructed. Franklin esteemed his partner Ballard, for instance, as "a Gent of his known capacity in financial arrangement" because Ballard understood the rules of their fetish world. He grasped the complex links between slave supply in Virginia, credit availability in New York, cotton prices on the Liverpool market, and the prices and demand for slaves at New Orleans and Natchez. Ballard saw not enslaved people but goods that lived only in relation to abstractions of cotton and credit. Power and skill enabled the fetishizer to make his vision shape the realities of lives inhabited by some human beings. He was, as another friend described him, "a smooth hand on Cuff."[46]

Forgetting undergirded the deanimation of the enslaved and their subsequent half-life in whites' minds as Cuffy, but a sort of remembering added a spice of cruel power to the slavers' experience of manipulating commodities. Like sugar or tobacco, slaves started as luxuries and were transformed into necessities in the eyes of their users as the latter bought, sold, and consumed the former in order to raise their own social and cultural status.[47] Far more obviously than the conspicuous consumption of sugar, the idea of the slave commodity carried a frisson, an implication, of the power and pleasure — sadistic or sexual (or both) — that created the precious commodity thus consumed. Those who could view and use persons as mere objects of commerce could also exert immense power while displacing either burdens of guilt or the obligations enacted by social ties. The existence of a commercial market in human beings meant that some people could, at will, destroy the familial and social relationships that had raised an infant into a full-grown enslaved human being. Although defenders of slavery claimed that the division of families was a rare but sometimes unavoidable necessity, the ability to separate families at will was at the heart of their economic and social power. Slave buyers and masters could pocket, or consume, the profit thus produced — an almost chemical energy released by the breaking of human bonds whose fragility the law and custom of slavery enforced. Those who forgot still remembered the privilege and pleasure of destruction. More than that, some slave traders, at least, clearly enjoyed their ability to consume and digest old social worlds, forcing slaves into new, often frightening relationships. "The small fry," wrote James Franklin with apparent relish of the unsold children in his Natchez pen, "look at me as if they were alarmed and I suppose they will have some cause when F[ranklin] & A[rmfield]'s lot arrives as I am daily looking for them."[48]

Small children would be caged with strange adults whom they had never seen before. Some would be kind, some would be indifferent, and a few might be brutal. But none would be the parents or relatives from whom market transactions had separated them. James seemed to enjoy imagining their terror.

Thus the desire for slaves rested in part on the remembering of the consumption of their human relationships and also, as we have seen, on the simultaneous forgetting or denial that they were human beings created in the matrix of family and culture, rather than things in the shadow world of the market. So the gents of Franklin and Ballard, with their known capacities in financial arrangement, moved easily in the world of commodities. They deanimated and reanimated the objects of their commercial dealings, broke the bonds between them, and experienced pleasure from the power thus exercised and created. Even as slave traders saw slaves as commodities, masters had no difficulty in accommodating themselves to the dealers. Staring up at us from the words scrawled by Franklin, Ballard, and company, we find evidence that their business represented an irruption of commodity fetishism—that supposed classic marker of capitalist cultural epistemology—within the heart of the allegedly anticapitalist South. The southern men who supplied migrant planters with the laborers necessary to extend the plantation system to its height of antebellum power were, in their prejudices and perceptions, further astray in the mist of commodity fetishism than the most capitalistic Yankee cotton mill magnate.[49]

The trade signaled another irruption as well. Among themselves, the members of the firm Franklin, Ballard, and Armfield did not assume that participation in the slave trade made them only "pirates" or "robbers." They were something else as well. In a March 1832 letter to R. C. Ballard, James Franklin wrote of what he feared were grim economic prospects for himself and his partners: "We anticipate tolerably tough times this spring for one-eyed men."[50] The traders' economic pessimism is misleading. They usually did well so long as they could collect even a portion of their accounts payable. But who, or what, were "one-eyed men"? Both the older and the younger Franklin used the phrase to describe themselves, their associates, and indeed all white men who bought or sold on the slave markets of the South. Isaac Franklin told Ballard in 1833 that he had "met with the robbers but has bore up as well as a One Eyed Man could well do."[51] In another case, James Franklin used it almost as a term of contempt. Worried about the slow state of the market in Natchez and the rampant cholera that was killing off his "stock," he looked for a buyer with peculiar vision. Single-minded and single-visioned, this half-blind viewer with an eye for purchasing would overlook as peripheral the disease-ridden state of the slaves Franklin had to sell: "I am in hopes that all the fools are not dead yet and some one-eyed man will buy us out yet." And in other cases, to call someone or oneself a one-eyed man was clearly to acknowledge participation in the slave market as either supplier or customer. "The way your Old one-eyed friend looked the pirate," wrote Isaac Franklin, referring to himself, and showing little desire for absolution, "was a sin."[52]

One-eyed men, of course, are kings in the land of the blind. But there are other one-eyed men in the metaphorical world. The phrase appears in eighteenth-century slang as a synonym for the penis.[53] Quite clearly, it survived in that incarnation into the nineteenth century (and remains current today), for these words from a letter written by James Franklin reveal his own phallic representation: "I have seen a handsome girl since I left V[irgini]a that would climb higher hills and go further to accomplish her designs than any girl to the North & she is not too apt to leave or loose her gold[.] The reason is because she carries her funds in her lovers purse or in Bank & to my certain knowledge she has been used & that smartly by a one-eyed man about my size and age, *excuse my foolishness.* In short I shall do the best with and for the fancy white maid and excellent cook that I can."[54] Franklin's extended metaphor tells a lyricized version of the rape of the light-skinned "fancy white maid" by a phallic "one-eyed man" and leads one into the complex of remembering and forgetting that structured these slave traders' understandings of sexuality and self. The first sentence leaves open the possibility that the "handsome girl" from Virginia might be free and white. Yet we find that she is "not to apt to leave or loose her gold" for she carries her "funds" in her "lovers purse or in Bank." We can interpret the last phrase in two noncontradictory ways. The reference to a lover's purse might mean that the woman's lover carries money to spend at her discretion, in an attempt to win her favor, or perhaps she (were she free) seeks to marry a lover with a purse full of funds. But in a world where men bought enslaved women for the purpose of sex, the funds in question were more likely the purchase price of the woman and thus obviously rested in the purse or bank of her future owner and "lover." And this value was likely to be considerable, since Franklin's immediate reference to the "fancy white maid" reveals that she was in fact the "handsome girl" of the rest of the paragraph.

The second interpretation of the "lovers purse" notion reinforces the supposition that the woman at hand was enslaved: the lover's purse is a multilayered metaphor that draws on a common slang term for the vagina. The girl carries her funds in her "lovers purse" because her high market value derives directly from her exploitable sexuality. Here, Franklin locates that specifically in her genitalia, but she is not apt to "leave or loose" that gold so long as she remains female, "fancy," and sexually available to white slave traders or purchasers. The absence of the possessive apostrophe in Franklin's formulation only adds to the complexity of the metaphor. Whether lover's purse (a purse belonging to a lover) or lovers' purse (a purse in which to place the penises of potentially multiple lovers), the handsome girl's sexual accessibility to himself and other white men was for James Franklin the key to her value.

In fact, as he goes on to brag, in no sense has the purse remained closed to him. In the sense of the literal purse or bank account of her future purchaser, Franklin would soon enough receive a payment from "her" funds. But he claimed that he had already enjoyed some of her sexual and economic value ("to my certain knowledge she has been used & that smartly by a one-eyed man about my size and age"). The symbol of the one-eyed man was replete with simultaneous meanings. Franklin boasted of the accomplishments of his penis but also of his accomplishments as a penis. He knew that the handsome girl had been sexually "used," for he, himself the one-eyed man, had already had sex with her. Franklin had already "do[ne] the best with" her that he could, thus showing himself to be a "one-eyed man."[55]

This key unlocks important additional implications buried in several of the cited occasions of the phrase. When James Franklin hoped that "all the fools are not dead and some one-eyed man will buy us out yet," he counted on sexual desire to overcome economic reasoning. He hoped that some white man would buy Franklin's remaining stock of slaves, especially the female ones. But Isaac Franklin also called himself a one-eyed man. His idea of his own character, his metaphor for himself as a participant in the buying, selling, and raping of enslaved people, was plainly phallic. He, his partners, and his buyers were all one-eyed men together. Like ideas about honor and manhood, independence, and whiteness, the collective sexual aggressiveness enabled and valorized by the slave trade helped form a group identity for slaveowning white men. Market participants were all greedy for male and female labor in the fields and for reproductive labor in the slave quarters but also for fancy maids. So greedy were they, in fact, that such men spoke of themselves as if they were animated, erect penises, one-eyed men watching for mulatto women to rape.[56]

Thus at the heart of the trade's remembering and forgetting was another form of consumption, one that helped form traders' and planters' deepest concepts of themselves as sexually active men and as individual members of a class produced by and producing a history. A historically specific form of sexual fetishism worked together with commodity fetishism in an era of rapid plantation expansion, amplifying and accelerating each other's force, creating a powerfully charged set of meanings that reveal slavery's multiple attractions for its white participants. The trade and consumption of enslaved human beings promised powerful gratifications of the senses and the self, implying psychological and physical — including explicitly sexual — pleasures. For along with other whites throughout the Anglo-Atlantic world, the men of the firm of Franklin, Armfield, and Ballard remembered, consciously and unconsciously, the sexual coercion of black women when they spoke or thought about slavery and the slave trade.

The white world's obsession with black female sexuality began, of course, long before the U.S. domestic slave trade or the United States itself. From the beginning of the European-African encounter, attempts to claim that black female bodies were disgusting because they did not obey European gender roles rang hollow.[57] During the seventeenth-century rise of the plantation complex, black women became by law the sexual prey of all white men. Later, would-be patriarchs of the eighteenth century, such as Virginia's William Byrd II, attempted to exert sexual control over black women as part of wider projects of household and self-dominion.[58] By the nineteenth century, the belief that black women were inherently sexually aggressive, in contrast to allegedly chaste white females, increased their attractiveness to white men, even as white men publicly proclaimed their disgust with African American women and their love for the pure and passive belle. Many encounters, rather than a single Freudian trauma of infantile sexuality, shaped the complex obsession with black women. Then the rejected black female body returned in the fixation on the fancy maid.[59]

The rise of the domestic slave trade after 1790 as new lands opened up in the South and new demands for plantation produce — namely, cotton — arose in the Atlantic world produced a particular commercialized category of enslaved women that focused white fixations. Within the trade, light-skinned or mulatto fancy maids became to many white men the perfect symbols of slavery's history, while also ensuring that being "a smooth hand with Cuff" helped make one a one-eyed man. To men such as the slave traders discussed here, women such as the Charlottesville maid evoked a process of power and pleasure, remembered and forgotten in an ambiguous, simultaneous experience parallel to that which characterized the traders' commodity-fetish relation to "Cuffy." Indeed, coercion, the trade, and the pairing of sexual imagery with women of mixed African and European ancestry were always close companions. Northern and British visitors to pre–Civil War New Orleans rarely failed to write about "yellow" women, fancy maids, and nearly white octoroons sold as both house servants and sexual companions. Some observers claimed to have knowledge of special auctions at which young, attractive, usually light-skinned women were sold at rates four to five times the price of equivalent female field laborers. Travelers and other writers constantly returned to the

simultaneously offensive and exciting sight of coerced interracial sex, especially between white men and light-skinned fancy women.[60]

The oft-repeated term "fancy" significantly united the themes of speculation
in the boisterous markets of the new commercial economy and sexual pleasures bought and sold. In the slang of antebellum Wall Street, "fancy stocks"
were those of purely commercial value, scandalous in their speculative nature,
"wholly wrapped in mystery," as one 1841 commentator had it. Some were
certainly the flimsy bank bonds of frontier South states such as Louisiana and
Mississippi, issued in the 1830s to raise capital that financed planters' purchases of slaves and land. The causal proximity of such stocks to the slave
market is perhaps no mere accident. Fancy maids, like fancy stocks, were
objects of speculation. Yet American society, still groping through its transition to a state in which the market would be all in all, still half-believed that all
goods should be priced by their intrinsic values. The apparently mysterious
and uncertain nature of both fancies revealed the uneasy bargains made with
the fiction of commodification. What—if anything—lay hidden behind the
value attached to a fancy stock by the ups and downs of supply and demand on
Wall Street? Its attractiveness lay in its brassy nature, the unconcealably arbitrary character of its value, assigned only by the magical thinking of the market. Like fancy stock, the value of a fancy maid was also arbitrary when
compared to the monetary value of her productive labor. Yet the origin of her
market-assigned price in the power to coerce sexuality was lewdly plain to all
one-eyed men who cared to titillate themselves. She was neither precisely
black nor white and neither field labor nor house hand but rather the "fancy"
of the market for selling the right to rape a special category of women marked
as unusually desirable.[61]

Slave traders and other one-eyed men singled out these women in particular,
and the Franklins and Ballard assumed that because of their possession of such
women they were one-eyed men, because slave traders' violence represented
and reenacted their own historically created identities. As historical practice,
sexual violence was depressingly common: an inescapable itch for whites who
discussed slavery, an everyday wound inflicted on people bought and sold as
commodities. Abundant testimony by ex-slaves and white participants confirms the ever-present sexual coercion of the traders' yards. For many, slave
and free, the act of rape signified the slave trade and even slavery itself.[62]
The correspondents of Franklin, Ballard, Armfield, and company revisited the
topic incessantly. Isaac Franklin was, of course, eager to see Ballard's Charlottesville maid. A few months after the older Franklin twice requested that
Ballard send the woman out to New Orleans, James Franklin told Ballard that
Uncle Isaac had sent a slave on to Natchez for the younger man's use. Perhaps

they spoke of the same woman: "The Old Man sent me your maid Martha. She is inclined to be compliant." Earlier, James had written about another light-skinned enslaved woman shipped by the partners to Natchez, "I will do the best with and for the fancy white maid and excellent cook I can." And, James reported, his uncle Isaac was staying out late every night, engaged in "very boyish" behavior with some women, probably from their stock.[63]

A caveat should remind us of the possible wider stakes of the argument: although commentators described slave traders as the most dissolute members of white southern society, their eager desire to buy, use, and circulate enslaved women in sexual service hardly distinguished them from planters. Traders catered to the desires of planters when they selected and marketed fancy maids. Women such as "the fair maid Martha . . . and our white Caroline" — both for sale by Isaac Franklin at Natchez in May 1832 — were so light-skinned that they were called white by the traders, although their legal blackness was clearly understood by all. They were typically young, attractive, and trained for servitude in the house. Even at high prices, reported Isaac Franklin in 1833, "there are great Demand for fancy maid [*sic*]." He told Ballard that he needed more such women to supply a growing market: "I do believe that a Likely Girl and a good seamstress could be sold for $1100," or twice the going rate for female field hands.[64]

The focus by slave traders on particular women such as one called Lucindy, whom Isaac Franklin impregnated and then passed on to a Louisville friend when his own impending marriage rendered her presence inconvenient, might lead one to believe that the sharpness of desire made them distinct individuals in the minds of whites.[65] Ex-slaves' memories and contemporary documents generated by whites reveal that planters selected some enslaved women for the specific purpose of sexual service.[66] Ballard sold a woman named Maria to a Mississippi planter named L. R. Starks in 1833. She was not happy with the arrangement that Starks had in mind, but soon something brought her around to his way of thinking: "M[a]ria seems much pleased with me and looks much better than when I made the purchase." Perhaps Maria discovered a way to leverage Starks's desires into something of supreme importance to her. Or perhaps Starks had discovered another sword to suspend above her head: "She is very desirous I should get her son. I therefore will take him if you will send him."[67] Although some enslaved women maneuvered to turn white male desires to their own or others' protection, traders and masters maneuvered as well. The stark imbalance of power meant that women such as Maria chose, at best, between negotiated surrender on one hand and severe punishment and possible death on the other. So a different woman named Maria may have found in 1848, when Ballard's later business partner had her flogged repeatedly until she was maimed and sterile — all, it seems, for refusing his advances. As one ex-slave remembered: "I can tell you that a white man laid a nigger gal whenever he wanted."[68]

Such men were not interested in a particular Maria or a specific Lucindy but in their own fancy. The category of fancy maid did not open a way for women to make white men see them as people whose opinions must be considered. Instead, white men were intent on forgetting any fears of weakness implied by sexual need and directing their desires toward particular women whose fates they controlled. They erased dependence in a blur of self-controlled pleasure. Their occasional miming of some of the conventions of romance may have enabled some to forget their own control over the entire fancy maid scenario. More often, as the letters of the Franklins and Ballard show, they reveled in their power. And when women such as Lucindy tried, as a tactic of self-defense, to create lasting emotional bonds from sexual encounters, they often found that white men readily discarded enslaved concubines and even their own children.[69] Nor did the manipulation of fancy maids re-create traders and planters as one-eyed men because white men were simply more attracted to light-skinned women than to dark-skinned women. The Franklins and Ballard, and others, could have talked about white prostitutes or waxed lyrical about the rapes of dark-skinned women. The latter were certainly a part of life in the slave pens. Indeed, despite the frequent efforts of white society to identify light-skinned women of mixed African and European descent as more attractive than their darker sisters, white men have constantly pursued the latter group as well. This, of course, helps explain how the United States became the home of so many light-skinned blacks.[70] Instead, the affinity of one-eyed men for fancy maids arose from the ways in which the former attributed to the latter an identity that both forgot and remembered the long history of sexual violence and fetishism. The presence of light-skinned women for sale seemingly spurred white men to spill out a whole set of ideas about available and abusable sexuality. The metaphorical and actual uses that the white world sought, with a winking leer, to impose on such women coyly revealed meanings that shot through the entire domestic trade.[71]

Within the remembering and forgetting that made such women impassioned objects, one can find several relationships that explain the disconcerting contiguity of one-eyed men to fancy maids in these particular traders' words. First, an anxiety caused by the specific cultural history of the early nineteenth century suggests something that sounds like the classically Freudian sense of sexual fetishism, although the castration anxiety he and many other interpreters of fetishism privileged cannot lift all of the weight of meaning that rested on images of fancy maids and one-eyed men.[72] These traders referred to light-skinned and mulatto female slaves in terms that burlesqued the advancing ideal of female domesticity. The high price of one "Yellow Girl" named Charlott, $900 in 1834, came in part from a background that equipped her to mime the conventions of the polite and proper parlor, the centerpiece of a domestic sphere increasingly dominated by female moral and cultural taste. Of Charlott, Isaac Franklin noted, "you mentioned that you purchased her from some *Branch* of the Barber [Barbour] family . . . the respectability of that family will have great effect."[73]

The "Yellow Girl" would not carelessly break the china or embarrass one before a guest. Yet her high price revealed and also concealed, in true fetish fashion, that for many white men she probably represented not a serving maid but a fancy. Her value to these particular men was her fetishized use: subject to their sexual assault, she represented for them a hostile satire of the parlor ideal, a rebuke of and a recourse against uppity white women. Traders' words described Charlott and others in ironic terms and phrases that mocked the language of polite, feminine, and white domesticity. Isaac and James Franklin underlined the words "The fair maid Martha" in a letter to Ballard, mocking proper literary-romantic descriptions of white heroines. Black women, however, were antiheroines. Women such as Martha, forwarded by Isaac Franklin to his nephew, were not allowed, despite their light skin, to remain maids. Direct or implied force "inclined [them] to be compliant" and thus recast men as still in control of both economic household and cultural home. On the other hand, the existence of fancy maids saved the one-eyed man by preventing the loss of power threatened by even modest and largely symbolic increases in female moral and cultural authority.[74]

Second, a conglomeration of then-current gendered ideas about independent manhood made it unlikely that Isaac and James Franklin or R. C. Ballard would have completely enjoyed the explicit negotiations necessary for access to heterosexual relationships with free women.[75] White men struggled to chalk out proofs of their manhood by means of various cultural formulae in the American South in the early 1830s. Some were obsessed with honor and independence in a slavery-based society, others with the delusion of independent action, self-creation, and personal autonomy created by the market fictions of commodity fetishism, and still others with political republicanism. Often, the same man played several of these language games at once. We can see the independent man in the image of the duelist facing down a pistol or the candidate proclaiming his rejection of all outside influence on his political independence. But we can also see this ideal in the land pirate or the robber or in the obsession of Isaac Franklin with beating his competitors to the Natchez market. For such a man, the coercion of sex from the enslaved, at least at one

level, obviously evaded the problem of explicit negotiation and its acknowledgment of incomplete independence. A purchase of a human being seen as a
commodity with no entangling social ties, purely represented by price, could
be imagined as the self-controlled consumption of sexual pleasure. The assertion of complete independence that such rapes represented denied dependence
on women and also on the enslaved of African descent.

Yet the specific white focus on fancy or obviously mixed-race women relentlessly returns us to the place of history, especially its memory and its understanding, as the remembering that was present in the traders' sexual fetishes.
The exploitation of enslaved women of African and mixed African-European
backgrounds was a part of plantation society long before the ideology of
sentimental feminine domesticity ever could have unleashed male anxieties.
And the same exploitation contributed, in ways not yet sufficiently investigated by cultural historians, to the ideal of the independent master.[76] The
traders' own words remind us that land pirates believed that they became one-
eyed men by the rape of women who symbolized the past, present, and future
of slaveowning men. This becoming was a not-so-secret history that mixed
anxiety and pleasure, attraction and control. Fancy maids, more than other enslaved women, embodied a history of rape in the pre-emancipation nineteenth-
century South, one that reveals white anxieties about dependence on blacks
but allowed white men to assert and reassert their power and control.

People of mixed racial heritage, or mulattoes, symbolized the dependence of
white men on black labor, both in the field and in the bed. Marked by their very
skin color and other features as products of the white-black encounter in the
South, mulatto women were obviously white and not white, like "our white
Caroline." They were products of the long encounter between white exploiters
of labor and black sources of labor, productive and reproductive. Their commodification reminded all that in the South, every child of an enslaved mother
was some form of slave laborer, an arrangement that enabled plantation slavery to function. Every enslaved man, woman, and child was a repository of
reproductive capital and a source of production. The white political economy
of the South would have collapsed without the legal and cultural fictions that
assigned the mulatto and other children of African women to the created
categories "black" and "enslaved." Women such as Martha and Charlott also,
in their phenotypes, illustrated the long past of white sexual assault. Mulatto
women thus embodied white dependency and white power and offered men
the chance to recapitulate and reexamine the past that had produced both
white power and mixed-race individuals. Unwillingly, such women introduced
a pornographic history, one that was obscene yet for that very reason more
lusted-after, into the parlors, bedrooms, and above all, the markets of the elite

white man's world. They made flesh the years of white men's desiring and depending on women (and men) who were supposedly less than civilized, Christian, or human.

If the presence of mulattoes' poorly concealed dependence, in the past and the present, on black labor, the presence of fancy maids allowed white men to remember and reassert a sort of control over past and present. The history of rape, obvious to all though openly spoken of by few, was the remembered meaning of the fetish of the fancy maid in the white male mind. Assaults repeated and thus confirmed a history that had produced white men who bought and sold black women and men and had made mulattoes as well. The historic penis, the one-eyed man, of earlier generations had in fact fathered the fancy maid—creating in the flesh a symbol of the history of coerced sexuality to which white men such as the slave traders could return at will. Like the Freudian fetishisms that do not produce neuroses, this symbolic relationship was the sexualized prose of the slave traders' world. It worked for them.[77]

The acts of coercion affirmed and re-created the rampant one-eyed man. Thus white slaveowners pleasured themselves with bodies marked by the past of their own power as a class; they had sex with the living proofs of their own histories. Their assaults repeated the originating acts of their own class and their own power, controlling past and future. Forgetting the human soul of the mulatto body, the Franklins, Armfield, and Ballard coupled instead with the history of rape. Their white male bodies also reenacted earlier acts in that history, with their penis as the symbol, the weapon, of white authority. When such men fathered mixed-race children, they readied a new generation for the market in commodity and sexual fetishes. As one formerly enslaved woman recalled: "They was glad of it . . . [they would] be glad to have them little bastards, brag on it."[78] They inflicted themselves on people seen as material representations of their own past and, in so doing, generated personal, collective, and economic futures.

Thus the obsession with fancy maids evolved out of histories personal and social. Light-skinned and mulatto women symbolized for traders and planters the claimed right to coerce all women of African descent. Such men reveled in the acts of purchase and sale. To them, one act symbolized another, sliding together in a cloud of buying, selling, raping, and consuming. Midas-like, their possession of the lover's purse turned the contemplation of the slave as commodity into the one-eyed man's pawing over the gold of her value, and vice versa. All forms of domination of enslaved women, and men as well, made the trader feel like a penis—the source of his own self-controlled pleasure, the progenitor of his own history, in short, a veritable one-eyed man. At the same time that he remembered and reasserted his power, he forgot the specter of castration or other forms of loss of masculine and masculinizing power, of course, but more important, the source of his power in past and present dependence on the human beings whom he would prefer to see as commodities.

The only distinction between commodity and sexual fetishization in this history of the slave trade comes from our own habit of intellectually separating economic desires from those of sexuality, our own kind of remembering and forgetting. The two sets of desires were remarkably compatible, and, indeed, the commodity and the sexual fetish were ultimately the same for such men. Slave women were so vulnerable to sexual assault — in the sense that they had no legal recourse and usually few other means of resistance — because they could be sold, and they were such desirable purchases in part because they could be raped. Put another way, in the creation of the commodity fetish, the object becomes understood as its market-given value. If the slave market valued fancy maids for their sexual desirability and enforced availability, what was the value, to white men, of their "gold," to quote James Franklin again? The commodification of black bodies meant that for white men, sexuality of a particular sort — the promise and the pleasure of rape — irradiated the enslaved human commodity, especially women, in the eyes of one-eyed men. White men repeated the acts of a history of rape and found them pleasurable and powerful. Despite the resistance of many enslaved African and African American women, these acts reasserted slaveowners' authority over women such as Charlott, Martha, and Caroline and also over all enslaved African Americans, male and female. Yet neither dependence nor control was absolute. One could even argue that the physical and symbolic or psychological pleasures of coerced sexuality were addictive, creating a psychological dependence on being able to assert sexual power over such women. Neither could have been present without the other. Such is the ambiguity of the fetish relationship.[79]

I have tried to limit my discussion to a few men and to a few years. But the intersection between racial slavery, the commodification of human bodies, and the fetishization of raped women of African descent in the Atlantic world was, by the 1830s, an old story being played out in new ways. The long and inarguably linked histories of white-on-black rape and the various slave trades lead me to raise a few final and frankly speculative questions, which must be tested elsewhere. First, one might hypothesize that, over the long centuries of the Atlantic slave plantation complex, the association of coerced sexuality with enslaved women added significantly to whites' experience of excitement and power in the trade in all things related to slaves and slavery. The image of sexual power without restraint was everywhere: one-eyed men stalked the landscape of slavery in the white mind of the Atlantic world, and in some ways they still do. The message that African women were commodities, often raped by white men, added a taste of secondhand sexual power without restraint, a glimpse of the pure consumption of human beings, to the unconscious and conscious minds of many consumers. From sugar to investment in planter-dominated banks to, of course, the trade in slaves itself, the whole plantation complex stank of the arousal of rape. Even the abolitionist movement leaned on the prurient imagery of sexual coercion to generate opponents of slavery both repelled and fascinated by the institution's sexual abuses.

The plantation complex's sexual relationships, which ultimately produced white male masters, were hidden but not hidden. Franklin and Ballard were, perhaps, unusual only because they actually spoke the unspoken messages that so pervaded everything having to do with slavery and the massively profitable plantation sector. But what does that pervasiveness signify? Mintz implies that the evolution of sugar into a highly fetishized commodity not only influenced the tandem developments of industrialization and imperialism (including plantation slavery) but also shaped the growth of the modern concept of the commodity itself. Could the complex fetishization of enslaved Africans have played a similar, simultaneous role? We have plenty of books about the Atlantic slave trade — experiences, numbers, and social results. But what of the meaning of the trade for the whites who participated in, directed, and profited from it? What of those who supported it, opposed it, or simply heard of it? Slaves, along with sugar, may have been the first modern commodities. They were people converted into symbols and objects of economic power, social status, and psychosexual fulfillment. Violent eroticism fetishized commodity fetishism, making all commodities taste a bit of the social and sexual relationships of slavery and the slave trade. After turning humans into Cuffy, wool and ivory, and fancy maids, and for some, transforming the self into a one-eyed man, perhaps we have made additional commodifications — credit, labor power, labor product, salvation, government services, hope, justice, information — easy.

In the end, even the potential for fetishizing the term "fetish" may serve a rhetorical purpose. How else can we evoke the terrible alchemy that allowed so many people to enjoy and deny, simultaneously, the exploitation of human sexuality that glowed like an aura from each plantation commodity? So the history of commodities begins with a slave trader or master's imagined or retold rape of an enslaved woman; the history of slavery is the history of humans commodified and fetishized, charged by their buyers and sellers with a number of passionate meanings. The history of freedom, which must be told elsewhere, is in no small part the history of blacks' resistance to the attempt to make them the fetish objects of white desires.

Notes

The author is a member of the Department of History at Cornell University. He would like to thank the following persons for assistance and criticism: Ligia Aldana, Stephanie Baptist, Jeff Brosco, Stephanie M. H. Camp, Kenneth Goodman, Walter Johnson, James Lake, Russ Castronovo, Drew Gilpin Faust, Charles Rosenberg, Lee Sorenson, Phillip Troutman, and the editorial board and anonymous reviewers of the *American Historical Review.* Richard S. Dunn and the McNeil Seminar for Early American Studies provided important feedback and encouragement, and Mimi Miller and the Historic Natchez Foundation, and Steven Engle and the Department of History at Florida Atlantic University, granted additional opportunities to present and discuss papers on this topic. He is also extremely grateful to John White and Laura Clark Brown of the Southern Historical Collection at the University of North Carolina and to Tim Pyatt, now of Duke University, for the many ways in which they facilitated the research that led to this essay. This essay was originally published in *The American Historical Review,* 106 (December 2001), 1619–1650, and is reprinted by permission.

1. I. Franklin to R. C. Ballard, January 11, 1834, folder 13, Series 1.1, Rice Ballard Papers, Southern Historical Collection, University of North Carolina, Chapel Hill (hereafter Ballard Papers). See Wendell Holmes Stephenson, *Isaac Franklin: Slave Trader and Planter of the Old South, with Plantation Records* (Baton Rouge: Louisiana State University Press, 1938); Phillip D. Troutman, " 'Fancy Girls' and a 'Yellow Wife': Sex and Domesticity in the Domestic Slave Trade," unpublished paper presented at the Southern Historical Association, Louisville, Ky., November 10, 2000. For other references to the firm of Franklin and Armfield or that of Franklin and Ballard, see George W. Featherstonhaugh, *Excursion Through the Slave States,* 2 vols. (London: Murray, 1844), 1:51–70; E. A. Andrews, *Slavery and the Slave Trade in the United States* (Boston: Light and Stearns, 1836), 135–53; William Jay, *A View of the Action of the Federal Government in Behalf of Slavery* (New York: American Anti-Slavery Society, 1839), 75, 84, 86; E. S. Abdy, *Journal of a Residence and Tour in the United States of North America, From April, 1833, to October, 1835* (London: Murray, 1835), 2:179–80; Frederic Bancroft, *Slave Trading in the Old South* (Baltimore: Furst, 1931), 59–60, 64, 275–76, 304; Michael Tadman, *Speculators and Slaves: Masters, Traders, and Slaves in the Old South* (Madison: University of Wisconsin Press, 1989), 80–81, 84, 104, 107; Ariela Gross, "Pandora's Box: Slavery, Character, and Southern Culture in the Courtroom" (Ph.D. diss., Stanford University, 1996), 235–246; William Calderhead, "The Role of the Professional Slave Trader in a Slave Economy: Austin Woolfolk, A Case Study," *Civil War History* 23 (September 1977): 195–211; and Calderhead, "How Extensive Was the Border State Slave Trade? A New Look," *Civil War History* 18 (March 1972): 42–55.

2. See Elizabeth Fox-Genovese, *Within the Plantation Household: Black and White Women in the Old South* (Chapel Hill: University of North Carolina Press, 1988), 98;

Eugene Genovese, *Roll, Jordan, Roll: The World the Slaves Made* (New York: Pantheon, 1974), perhaps most explicitly on 96–97; and Genovese, "The Logical Outcome of the Slaveholders' Philosophy: An Exposition, Interpretation, and Critique of the Social Thought of George Fitzhugh of Port Royal, Virginia," in *The World the Slaveholders Made: Two Essays in Interpretation* (New York: Pantheon, 1969), 118–244; Jeffrey R. Young, *Domesticating Slavery: The Master Class in Georgia and South Carolina, 1670–1837* (Chapel Hill: University of North Carolina Press, 1999).

3. See Tadman, *Speculators and Slaves;* Walter Johnson, *Soul by Soul: Life Inside the Antebellum Slave Market* (Cambridge: Harvard University Press, 1999); Steven Deyle, "'The Irony of Liberty': Origins of the Domestic Slave Trade," *Journal of the Early Republic* 12 (Spring 1992): 37–62; Phillip D. Troutman, "Slave Trade and Sentiment in Antebellum Virginia" (Ph.D. diss., University of Virginia, 2000).

4. Recent scholarship has revived the earlier claims of Eric Williams and others to reemphasize the role of slavery and slave trades in making capitalist and consumerist society: Robin Blackburn, *The Making of New World Slavery: From the Baroque to the Modern, 1492–1800* (London: Verso, 1997); but see Eric Williams, *Capitalism and Slavery* (Chapel Hill: University of North Carolina Press, 1944); Barbara Solow and Stanley Engerman, eds., *British Capitalism and Caribbean Slavery: The Legacy of Eric Williams* (Cambridge: Cambridge University Press, 1987).

5. Carlo Ginzburg, *The Cheese and the Worms: The Cosmos of a Sixteenth-Century Miller,* trans. Anne and John Tedeschi (Baltimore: Johns Hopkins University Press, 1980), xxi.

6. Historians have now begun to address the experience of sexual abuse in slavery, which was traumatic and extensive, as African American vernacular history had long since told anyone willing to listen. See Pauli Murray, *Proud Shoes: The Story of an American Family* (New York: Harper, 1956), 33–54; Paul Escott, *Slavery Remembered: A Record of Twentieth-Century Slave Narratives* (Chapel Hill: University of North Carolina Press, 1979), 46–47; Deborah Gray White, *Ar'n't I a Woman? Female Slaves in the Plantation South,* 2d ed. (New York: Norton, 1999), esp. 27–46; Angela Y. Davis, *Women, Race, and Class* (New York: Random House, 1981), 3–29; Brenda Stevenson, *Life in Black and White: Family and Community in the Slave South* (New York: Oxford University Press, 1996), 236–38; Stephanie M. H. Camp, "Viragoes: Enslaved Women's Everyday Politics in the Old South" (Ph.D. diss., University of Pennsylvania, 1998), chap. 1; John Blassingame, *The Slave Community: Plantation Life in the Antebellum South,* 2d ed. (New York: Oxford University Press, 1979), 154–56, 172–73; Hortense Spillers, "Mama's Baby, Papa's Maybe: An American Grammar Book," *Diacritics* 17 (Summer 1987): 65–81; Darlene Clark Hine, "Rape and the Inner Lives of Black Women in the Middle West: Preliminary Thoughts on the Culture of Dissemblance," *Signs* 14 (Summer 1989): 912–20; Catherine Clinton, "Caught in the Web of the Big House: Women and Slavery," in *The Web of Southern Social Relations: Women, Family, and Education,* ed. Walter J. Fraser Jr., R. Frank Saunders Jr., and Jon L. Wakelyn (Athens: University of Georgia Press, 1985), 19–34; Clinton, *The Plantation Mistress: Women's World in the Old South* (New York: Pantheon, 1982), 212–13, 220–21; Saidiya Hartmann, *Scenes of Subjection: Terror, Slavery, and Self-Making in Nineteenth-Century America* (New York: Oxford University Press, 1997), 79–112; Martha Hodes, *White Women, Black Men:*

Illicit Sex in the Nineteenth-Century South (New Haven: Yale University Press, 1997), 1–9; Adele Logan Alexander, *Ambiguous Lives: Free Women of Color in Rural Georgia, 1789–1879* (Fayetteville: University of Arkansas Press, 1991), 63–66, 78–79, 86–89; Carolyn J. Powell, "In Remembrance of Mira," in *Discovering the Women in Slavery: Emancipating Perspectives on the American Past*, ed. Patricia Gordon (Athens: University of Georgia Press, 1996), 47–60; Victoria E. Bynum, "Misshapen Identity: Memory, Folklore, and the Legend of Rachel Knight," in Gordon, *Discovering the Women in Slavery*, 29–46; Hélène Lecaudey, "Behind the Mask: Ex-Slave Women and Interracial Sexual Relations," in Gordon, *Discovering the Women in Slavery*, 260–77; Thelma Jennings, "'Us Colored Women Had to Go Through a Plenty,'" *Journal of Women's History* 1 (1990); Harriet Jacobs, *Incidents in the Life of a Slave Girl, Written by Herself*, ed. and intro. Jean Fagan Yellin (Cambridge: Harvard University Press, 1987); Johnson, *Soul by Soul*; and Nell Irvin Painter, "Soul Murder and Slavery: Toward a Fully Loaded Cost Accounting," in *U.S. History as Women's History: New Feminist Essays*, ed. Linda K. Kerber, Alice Kessler-Harris, and Kathryn Kish Sklar (Chapel Hill: University of North Carolina Press, 1995), 125–46.

But desire and rape are not seen as central pillars of the institution of slavery in most works that focus on white slave owners, mistresses, and traders. Exceptions include Drew Gilpin Faust, *James Henry Hammond and the Old South: A Design For Mastery* (Baton Rouge: Louisiana State University Press, 1982), 86–87, 314–20; Walter Johnson, "The Slave Trader, the White Slave, and the Politics of Racial Determination in the 1850s," *Journal of American History* 87 (June 2000): 13–38; Johnson, *Soul by Soul*; and some hints from Bertram Wyatt-Brown, *Southern Honor: Ethics and Behavior in the Old South* (New York: Oxford University Press, 1982), 308–324. But usually, even historians who acknowledge the occurrence of rape are more descriptive than analytical: Bancroft, *Slave Trading in the Old South*, 328–34; Edmund L. Drago, *Broke by the War: Letters of a Slave Trader* (Columbia: University of South Carolina Press, 1991); Tadman, *Speculators and Slaves*, 184. For resistance to the use of sexuality and desire as categories of historical explanation, one need look no further than the debates surrounding Thomas Jefferson's affair with Sally Hemings: Virginius Dabney, *The Jefferson Scandals: A Rebuttal* (New York: Dodd, Mead, 1981); Joseph J. Ellis, *American Sphinx: The Character of Thomas Jefferson* (New York: Knopf, 1996), 216–19, 303–307; Ellis, "Jefferson: Post-DNA," *William and Mary Quarterly*, 3rd ser., 57 (Jan. 2000): 125–138; Annette Gordon-Reed, *Thomas Jefferson and Sally Hemings: An American Controversy* (Charlottesville: University Press of Virginia, 1997); Jan Ellen Lewis and Peter S. Onuf, eds., *Sally Hemings and Thomas Jefferson: History, Memory, and Civic Culture* (Charlottesville: University Press of Virginia, 1999).

7. For examples, see Bancroft, *Slave Trading in the Old South*, 314.

8. The quotation is taken from Emily Apter, *Feminizing the Fetish: Psychoanalysis and Narrative Obsession in Turn-of-the-Century France* (Ithaca: Cornell University Press, 1991), 3. See Michael Leiris, "Alberto Giacometti," *Documents* 1, no. 4 (1929): 209, translated by James Clifford in *Suffer*, no. 15 (1986): 39; cf. Jean Baudrillard, *For a Critique of the Political Economy of the Sign*, trans. Charles Levin (St. Louis: Telos, 1981); William Pietz, "The Problem of the Fetish, I," *Res* 9 (Spring 1985): 5–17; Pietz, "The Problem of the Fetish, II," *Res* 13 (Spring 1987): 23–46; Patrick Brantlinger, *Fic-*

tions of State: Culture and Credit in Britain, 1694–1994 (Ithaca: Cornell University Press, 1996).

9. For this account of the etymology of "fetish," see Anne McClintock, *Imperial Leather: Race, Gender, and Sexuality in the Colonial Conquest* (New York: Routledge, 1996), 185–87; Pietz, "Problem of the Fetish, II"; Emily Apter and William Pietz, eds., *Fetishism as Cultural Discourse* (Ithaca: Cornell University Press, 1993). For Marx's account of commodity fetishism, see Karl Marx, *Capital,* trans. Ben Fowkes (New York: Vintage, 1976), 1:163–78; and Michael Taussig, *The Devil and Commodity Fetishism in South America* (Chapel Hill: University of North Carolina Press, 1980).

10. Sigmund Freud, 'Fetishism," in *The Standard Edition of the Complete Psychological Works of Sigmund Freud,* ed. James Strachey (London: Hogarth, 1953–74), 21:152–58; and Freud, "The Sexual Aberrations" in "Three Essays on Sexuality," *Standard Edition* 7, esp. 152–55. This example comes from Freud, "Fetishism," 155.

11. Those who still insist that psychoanalytic theories refer only to the individual and not to culture might revisit Peter Gay, *Freud for Historians* (New York: Norton, 1985), esp. 144–180.

12. For some explanations of this process, see Winthrop D. Jordan, *White over Black: American Attitudes Towards the Negro, 1550–1812* (Baltimore: Penguin, 1968); Kathleen M. Brown, *Good Wives, Nasty Wenches, and Anxious Patriarchs: Gender, Race, and Power in Colonial Virginia* (Chapel Hill: University of North Carolina Press, 1996), 37–41, 109–16, 207–11, 355–57; Jennifer L. Morgan, " 'Some Could Suckle over Their Shoulder': Male Travelers, Female Bodies, and the Gendering of Racial Ideology, 1500–1770," *William and Mary Quarterly,* 3rd ser., 54 (January 1997): 167–92.

13. Luce Irigaray, *This Sex Which Is Not One,* trans. Catherine Porter with Carolyn Burke (Ithaca: Cornell University Press, 1985).

14. McClintock, *Imperial Leather,* 181–203 (for "impassioned object"); Pietz, "Problem of the Fetish, I"; John Hoberman, *Darwin's Athletes: How Sport Has Damaged Black America and Preserved the Myth of Race* (Boston: Houghton Mifflin, 1997); David Shields, *Black Planet: Facing Race During an NBA Season* (New York: Crown, 1999).

15. Sidney Mintz, *Sweetness and Power: The Place of Sugar in Modern History* (New York: Viking, 1985), 43. Compare Johnson's citation (*Soul by Soul,* 111–12) of Chancellor Johnson of the South Carolina Supreme Court, who denied slaves' commodity status. Johnson's discussion of planters, slave traders, and slaves' commodity status emphasizes differentiation between slaves and the breakdowns and contradictions in whites' invocation of commodity and market myths to describe the enslaved (ibid., 111–12). It should be quite obvious that on this point I disagree with his marvelous book: I see white slave traders' and buyers' attempts, at least those documented in the Ballard Papers, to understand enslaved human beings as denatured commodities as successful on their own terms. Breakdowns occurred and contradictions existed. But whites also thought of and treated the enslaved as commodities, almost whenever it suited their purposes to do so. Fetishism, in fact, thrived on contradictions.

16. The historiography of the trade includes U. B. Phillips, *Life and Labor in the Old South* (Boston: Little, Brown, 1929), 155–59; Tadman, *Speculators and Slaves;* Deyle, "Irony of Liberty"; Bancroft, *Slave Trading in the Old South;* Winfield Collins, *Domestic*

Slave Trade of the Southern States (New York: Broadway, 1904); Johnson, *Soul by Soul;* Troutman, "Slave Trade and Sentiment."

17. See the description of Armfield himself in Featherstonhaugh, *Excursion Through the Slave States,* 1:151–70. The process of depicting the slave trader, not the slave buyer, as the problem began by the 1820s at the latest. See Robert H. Gudmestad, *A Troublesome Commerce: The Transformation of the Interstate Slave Trade* (Baton Rouge: Louisiana State University Press, 2003).

18. See D. R. Hundley, *Social Relations in Our Southern States* (New York: Price, 1860), 139–47. For a few examples of northerners' obligatory discussion of mulatto women and sexual slavery, see H. Mattison, *Louisa Picquet, the Octoroon: A Tale of Southern Slave Life,* in *Collected Black Women's Narratives,* ed. Anthony G. Barthelemy (New York: Oxford University Press, 1988); J. H. Ingraham, *The Quadroone; Or, St. Michael's Day* (New York: Harper, 1841); Abdy, *Journal of a Residence and Tour,* 2:100; Jay, *View of the Action of the Federal Government,* 67–73, 89; Harriet Martineau, *Society in America* (New York: Saunders and Otley, 1837), 2:106–36; Henry Wadsworth Longfellow, "The Quadroon Girl," in *Poems on Slavery* (1842; reprint, New York: A. L. Burt, 1901), 221–23.

19. The quotation is taken from I. Franklin to R. C. Ballard, June 11, 1833, folder 11; cf. I. Franklin to R. C. Ballard, December 8, 1832, folder 8; I. Franklin to R. C. Ballard, April 9, 1834, folder 11, all in Ballard Papers.

20. I. Franklin to R. C. Ballard, December 8, 1832, folder 8; I. Franklin to R. C. Ballard, April 9, 1834, folder 11 (for "pirates"); I. Franklin to R. C. Ballard, January 29, 1833, folder 10 (for planters as "robbers"); I. Franklin to R. C. Ballard, April 9, 1834, folder 11 (for "land pirates"); I. Franklin to R. C. Ballard, March 11, 1834, folder 13 (for "shavers"); all in Ballard Papers.

21. John Brown, *Slave Life in Georgia: A Narrative of the Life, Sufferings, and Escape of John Brown, A Fugitive Slave,* ed. F. N. Boney (Savannah: Beehive, 1972), 19; W. Reeves to R. C. Ballard, November 27, 1832, folder 8, Ballard Papers.

22. A minority of slavery's critics stridently agreed: planters were no better than the much-maligned traders. Thus Harriet Martineau wrote: "Every man who resides on his plantation may have his harem, and has every inducement of custom, and of pecuniary gain, to tempt him to the common practice." Martineau, *Society in America,* 2:112.

23. Stephenson, *Isaac Franklin,* 14–16.

24. Ibid., 22–33; for histories of this massive regional expansion, see Christopher D. Morris, *Becoming Southern: The Evolution of a Way of Life, Warren County and Vicksburg, Mississippi, 1770–1860* (New York: Oxford University Press, 1995); Joan Cashin, *A Family Venture: Men and Women on the Southern Frontier* (New York: Oxford University Press, 1991); Ann Patton Malone, *Sweet Chariot: Slave Family and Household Structure in Nineteenth-Century Louisiana* (Chapel Hill: University of North Carolina Press, 1992); Daniel Dupre, *Transforming the Cotton Frontier: Madison County, Alabama, 1800–1840* (Baton Rouge: Louisiana State University Press, 1997); Steven Deyle, "The Domestic Slave Trade in America" (Ph.D. diss., Columbia University, 1995); Troutman, "Slave Trade and Sentiment"; Edward E. Baptist, *Creating an Old South: Middle Florida's Plantation Frontier Before the Civil War* (Chapel Hill: University of North

Carolina Press, 2002). For the New Orleans market's central place in the interstate trade, see Johnson, *Soul by Soul;* Bancroft, *Slave Trading in the Old South,* 312–38.

25. R. C. Ballard & Co. Invoice Book, folder 417, vol. 2; R. C. Ballard & Co., Slaves Bought, 1832–1834, folder 420, vol. 4; [Enclosures in Vol. 4], folder 421, all in Ballard Papers.

26. J. G. Blakey to R. C. Ballard, June 17, 1834 ("to be laid out"), J. G. Blakey to R. C. Ballard, July 24, 1834 ("three brothers"), J. G. Blakey to R. C. Ballard, August 6, 1834 ("great many buyers"), all in folder 15; I. Franklin to R. C. Ballard, February 7, 1834, folder 13 (for the *Tribune*), all in Ballard Papers; Bancroft, *Slave Trading in the Old South,* 275–76.

27. I. Franklin to R. C. Ballard, January 9, 1832, and I. Franklin to R. C. Ballard, January 18, 1832 (attempts to adjust to Louisiana law), both in folder 4; I. Franklin to R. C. Ballard, March 11, 1834, folder 13; I. Franklin to R. C. Ballard, May 13, 1834, folder 14, all in Ballard Papers. For the law, see Collins, *Domestic Slave Trade,* 127–28. Collins cites *Acts of Extra Sess. of 10th Leg. of La.,* p. 4; Hurd, vol. 2, p. 162; and *Laws of La.,* 1834, p. 6.

28. For the factorage system, see Harold Woodman, *King Cotton and His Retainers: Financing and Marketing the Cotton Crop of the South, 1800–1925* (Lexington: University of Kentucky Press, 1968); R. C. Ballard to Messrs. Franklin, Ballard, & Co., September 7, 1832, folder 7; I. Franklin to R. C. Ballard, March 11, 1834 (amount of money credited to accounts receivable), folder 13, Ballard Papers. For the investment of the larger southern financial system in interregional slave trading, see "An Abstract of the lists of debts owed to the Bank of Virginia," enclosed in B. Tait to R. C. Ballard, May 1, 1838, folder 24, Ballard Papers.

29. Stephenson, *Isaac Franklin,* 11–12. One of Franklin's plantations on the Mississippi River, Angola, in Louisiana's West Feliciana Parish, has been since the early twentieth century the site of the notorious Louisiana state prison and labor camp of the same name. His home there has recently been excavated.

30. See Collection Overview and Series 1.2, Ballard Papers. Ballard, however, continued to trade slaves on a smaller scale: cf. interview with Lucy Thurston in George Rawick, ed., *The American Slave: A Composite Autobiography,* supplement, ser. 1 (Westport, Conn.: Greenwood, 1977), vol. 10, pt. 5, 2112; and ser. 1.3, Ballard Papers.

31. I borrow Marx's famous imagery; see Marx, *Capital,* 1:163–64.

32. Featherstonhaugh, *Excursion Through the Slave States,* 1:120–24. See Edward D. Jervey and C. Harold Huber, "The Creole Affair," *Journal of Negro History* 65 (Summer 1980): 196–211.

33. For McKenny and Gant, see Invoice Book, folder 417, Ballard Papers. For historiography on the development of the black community in the Chesapeake see Allan Kulikoff, *Tobacco and Slaves: The Development of Southern Cultures in the Chesapeake* (Chapel Hill: University of North Carolina Press, 1986), 335–80; Stevenson, *Life in Black and White;* Philip D. Morgan, *Slave Counterpoint: Black Culture in the Eighteenth-Century Chesapeake and Lowcountry* (Chapel Hill: University of North Carolina Press, 1998), 498–558, esp. 519–22; For the concept of "social death," see Orlando Patterson, *Slavery and Social Death: A Comparative Study* (Cambridge: Harvard University Press, 1982).

34. The WPA ex-slave narratives (Rawick, *American Slave*, ser. 1 and 2 and supplements to ser. 1 and 2, and Charles L. Perdue Jr., Thomas E. Barden, and Robert K. Phillips, eds., *Weevils in the Wheat: Interviews with Virginia Ex-Slaves* [Charlottesville: University Press of Virginia, 1992]) are filled with far more accounts of such separations than of successful negotiations.

35. Few families remained intact in the domestic slave trade, despite protestations of proslavery paternalists and modern-day moderators to the contrary: contrast Robert W. Fogel and Stanley Engerman, *Time on the Cross: The Economics of American Negro Slavery* (Boston: Little, Brown, 1974), esp. 49, with Paul David et al., *Reckoning with Slavery: A Critical Study in the Quantitative History of American Negro Slavery* (New York: Oxford University Press, 1976), 94–133, and Tadman, *Speculators and Slaves,* 163–78.

36. I. Franklin to R. C. Ballard, December 8, 1832 ("the way we send"), and R. C. Ballard to I. Franklin, December 2, 1832 ("we had better loose"), both folder 8, Ballard Papers.

37. I. Franklin to R. C. Ballard, June 11, 1833, folder 11, Ballard Papers.

38. J. Franklin to Messrs. R. C. Ballard & Co., March 4, 1832, folder 5, Ballard Papers.

39. J. Franklin to R. C. Ballard, October 5, 1832, folder 8; compare I. and J. Franklin to R. C. Ballard, May 13, 1832, folder 6; I. and J. Franklin to R. C. Ballard, October 25, 1833, folder 11, all in Ballard Papers. For this sort of language in the law and other forms of discourse, see Spillers, "Mama's Baby, Papa's Maybe," 79.

40. "Cuffy" was a slang name for any black person. See J. E. Lightner, ed., *Random House Historical Dictionary of American Slang* (New York: Random House, 1994), 1:538; J. Franklin to D. Ballard, March 7, 1834, folder 13; I. Franklin to R. C. Ballard, September 27, 1834, folder 15, R. C. Ballard Papers. For a similar use of the term, see J. W. Paup to E. B. Hicks, October 13, 1842, E. B. Hicks Papers, box 1, folder 1830–1846, Perkins Library Special Collections, Duke University, Durham, North Carolina; or Abraham Lincoln, "Draft of a Speech" (late December 1857), in *Lincoln: Selected Speeches and Writings* (New York: Vintage/Library of America, 1991), 124.

41. I. Franklin to R. C. Ballard, November 1, 1833, folder 12; same to same, December 8, 1832 (for "in fact"), folder 8, Ballard Papers.

42. J. H. Easterby, *The South Carolina Rice Plantation as Revealed in the Papers of Robert F. W. Allston* (Chicago: University of Chicago Press, 1945), 194; compare 426. See Norrece T. Jones, *Born a Child of Freedom, Yet a Slave: Mechanisms of Control and Strategies of Resistance in Antebellum South Carolina* (Middletown, Conn.: Wesleyan University Press, 1990), 41.

43. I. Franklin to R. C. Ballard, March 18, 1834, folder 13, Ballard Papers.

44. William Wells Brown, *Narrative of William W. Brown, a Fugitive Slave,* ed. William Andrews (New York: Oxford University Press, 1993), 45.

45. R. C. Ballard to I. Franklin, December 2, 1832, folder 8 ("my opinion"); I. Franklin to R. C. Ballard, March 18, 1834, folder 13 ("the . . . rise"); J. Franklin to R. C. Ballard, November 13, 1833, folder 12 ("Cotton is"); cf. I. Franklin to R. C. Ballard, November 7, 1833, folder 12; I. Franklin to R. C. Ballard, September 27, 1834, folder 15; I. Franklin to R. C. Ballard, May 31, 1831, folder 1, all in Ballard Papers.

46. J. Franklin to R. C. Ballard, January 18, 1832, folder 4 ("game"); I. Franklin to R. C. Ballard, March 18, 1834, folder 13 ("Gent of his known capacity"); J. Cage to W. Cotton, August 27, 1839, folder 28 ("smooth hand"), all in Ballard Papers.

47. On the history of commodities, see Mintz, *Sweetness and Power*; Jordan Goodman, Paul E. Lovejoy, and Andrew Sherratt, eds., *Consuming Habits: Drugs in History and Anthropology* (London: Routledge, 1995).

48. J. Franklin to Messrs. R. C. Ballard & Co., March 4, 1832, folder 5, Ballard Papers; Mintz, *Sweetness and Power*, 101, xxix.

49. Contrast the respective roles of the trade in southern society in the pictures painted by Fred Bateman and Thomas Weiss, *A Deplorable Scarcity: The Failure of Industrialization in the Slave Economy* (Chapel Hill: University of North Carolina Press, 1981), Fox-Genovese, *Within the Plantation Household*, 37–99, Genovese, *Roll, Jordan, Roll*, or Young, *Domesticating Slavery*, with those of Tadman, *Speculators and Slaves*, Deyle, "Domestic Slave Trade," or Johnson, *Soul by Soul*.

50. J. Franklin to Messrs. R. C. Ballard & Co., March 27, 1832, folder 5, Ballard Papers.

51. I. Franklin to R. C. Ballard, January 29, 1833, folder 10; I. Franklin to R. C. Ballard, December 25, 1833, folder 12; and B. Tait to R. C. Ballard, November 25, 1838, folder 25, all in Ballard Papers.

52. J. Franklin to R. C. Ballard, May 7, 1833, folder 11 ("I am yet in hope"), and I. Franklin to R. C. Ballard, January 11, 1834, folder 13 ("looked the pirate"), Ballard Papers.

53. Lightner, *Random House Historical Dictionary of American Slang*, 2:720, lists "one eyed" plus a noun as a way to refer to the penis and cites a 1775 toast to "Adam's dagger . . . the one-eyed stag." See also Michael Moon, *Disseminating Whitman: Revision and Corporeality in* Leaves of Grass (Cambridge: Harvard University Press, 1991), 26–30, for Whitman's use of similar imagery in a different context.

54. J. Franklin to Messrs. R. C. Ballard & Co., March 27, 1832, folder 5, Ballard Papers (emphasis in original).

55. Franklin and his associates defined their essence as penile, although recent historians have argued that, before the 1890s, white men in the United States did not focus on definitions of masculinity based primarily on biology or even on private sexual behavior. Indeed, according to these and other scholars, one's ability to establish one's independence — in republican politics, in artisanal or yeoman economic self-reliance, and in the cultural performances of male defiance of authority — was the all-important basis for proving one's manliness. The definition of masculinity as an innate force in all male bodies, usually exemplified by the performance of genital heterosexuality, became more prominent in the 1880s and 1890s. Gail Bederman, *Manliness and Civilization: A Cultural History of Gender and Race in the United States, 1880–1917* (Chicago: University of Chicago Press, 1995), E. Anthony Rotundo, *American Manhood: Transformations in Masculinity from the Revolution to the Modern Era* (New York: Basic Books, 1993), and Michael Kimmel, *Manhood in America: A Cultural History* (New York: Free Press, 1996) have roughly agreed with her chronology.

56. J. Franklin to R. C. Ballard, May 7, 1833, folder 11 ("all the fools"), Ballard Papers. Rape or the threat of rape may have served to increase planters' and slave traders'

power by means of terror; Antonia I. Castañeda, "Sexual Violence in the Politics and Policies of Conquest: Amerindian Women and the Spanish Conquest of Alta California," in *Building with Our Hands: New Directions in Chicana Studies*, ed. Adela de la Torre and Beatríz M. Pesquera (Berkeley: University of California Press, 1993), 15–33; Richard D. Trexler, *Sex and Power: Gendered Virtue, Political Order, and the European Conquest of the Americas* (Ithaca: Cornell University Press, 1995). Ideas about honor did help shape group identity among planters and other wealthy southern white men in this era. See Wyatt-Brown, *Southern Honor;* Faust, *James Henry Hammond;* Kenneth Greenberg, *Honor and Slavery: Lies, Duels, Noses, Masks, Dressing as a Woman, Gifts, Strangers, Humanitarianism, Death, Slave Rebellions, the Proslavery Argument, Baseball, Hunting, and Gambling in the Old South* (Bloomington: Indiana University Press, 1996).

57. Jordan, *White over Black;* K. Brown, *Good Wives;* Morgan, "Some Could Suckle."

58. For the nonexistence of the legal category of the rape of enslaved women — in other words, the fact of its pure legality — see Thomas P. Morris, *Southern Slavery and the Law, 1619–1860* (Chapel Hill: University of North Carolina Press, 1996), 305 ("No white could ever rape a slave woman"); Melton McLaurin, *Celia: A Slave* (Athens: University of Georgia Press, 1991), 89–121; Philip Schwartz, *Twice Condemned: Slaves and the Criminal Laws of Virginia, 1705–1865* (Baton Rouge: Louisiana State University Press, 1988), 159–61; Mark Tushnet, *The American Law of Slavery, 1810–1860* (Princeton: Princeton University Press, 1981), 85–86; Genovese, *Roll, Jordan, Roll,* 33; U. B. Phillips, *American Negro Slavery* (New York: D. Appleton, 1918), 459. For the importance of sexual control over enslaved women to eighteenth-century patriarchs' efforts to define themselves as autonomous, not dependent on the consent of others for the fulfillment of their own pleasures, see K. Brown, *Good Wives,* 319–73; Kenneth Lockridge, *On the Sources of Patriarchal Rage: The Commonplace Books of William Byrd and Thomas Jefferson and the Gendering of Power in the Eighteenth Century* (New York: New York University Press, 1992).

59. McClintock, *Imperial Leather,* esp. 184. Spillers, "Mama's Baby, Papa's Maybe," 77, argues that "slavery in the United States [was] one of the richest displays of the psychoanalytic dimensions of culture before the science of European psychoanalysis began to take hold." Here she refers specifically to the tangles of interracial sexuality and genealogies. See also Painter, "Soul Murder and Slavery," and Nell Irvin Painter, "Of Lily, Linda Brent, and Freud: A Non-Exceptionalist Approach," in *Half-Sisters of History: Southern Women and the American Past,* ed. Catherine Clinton (Durham: Duke University Press, 1994), 93–109; Clinton, "Caught in the Web of the Big House," 22; James Hugo Johnston, *Race Relations in Virginia and Miscegenation in the South* (Amherst: University of Massachusetts Press, 1970); Harriet Martineau, *Retrospect of Western Travel* (London and New York: C. Lohman, 1838), 1:267–68. For Francophone parallels to English-language discourses on black female sexuality, see T. Denean Sharpley-Whiting, *Black Venus: Sexualized Savages, Primal Fears, and Primitive Narratives in French* (Durham: Duke University Press, 1999).

60. Bancroft, *Slave Trading in the Old South,* 327–33; Collins, *Domestic Slave Trade,* 105–6; Andrews, *Slavery and the Domestic Slave Trade,* 165–66; Monique Gillory, "Some Enchanted Evening on the Auction Block: The Cultural Legacy of the New Or-

leans Quadroon Balls" (Ph.D. diss., New York University, 1999); Johnson, "Slave Trader, the White Slave, and the Politics of Racial Determination"; Karen Halttunen, "Humanitarianism and the Pornography of Pain in Anglo-American Culture," *American Historical Review* 100 (April 1995): 303–34; Judith Wilson, "Optical Illusions: Images of Miscegenation in Nineteenth- and Twentieth-Century American Art," *American Art* 5 (Summer 1991): 88–107; Albert Boime, *The Art of Exclusion: Representing Blacks in the Nineteenth Century* (Washington, D.C.: Smithsonian Institution Press, 1990), 82–84. Despite evidence suggesting a white obsession with the mulatto, Eugene Genovese suggests that light-skinned women had no particular significance in the world of white meanings: "Typically, the mulatto, especially the mulatto slave, was 'just another nigger' to the whites," *Roll, Jordan, Roll,* 429; see 413–31.

61. [Frederick Jackson], *A Week in Wall Street, By One Who Knows* (New York: "The Booksellers," 1841), 83; see 80, 82; George G. Foster, *Fifteen Minutes around New York* (New York: DeWitt and Davenport, 1854), 49–50; C. G. Parsons, *Inside View of Slavery: Or a Tour Among the Planters* (New York: DeWitt and Davenport, 1855), 182; Robert Everest, *A Journey Through the United States and Part of Canada* (London: J. Chapman, 1855), 104. See also Brantlinger, *Fictions of State.*

62. John Brown remembered that in the New Orleans slave pens where he spent several months in the late 1840s, "the youngest and handsomest females were set apart as the concubines of the masters, who generally changed mistresses every week . . . the slave-pen is only another name for a brothel": *Slave Life in Georgia,* 95. Compare Moses Roper, *A Narrative of the Adventures and Escape of Moses Roper from American Slavery* (London: Darton, Harvey, and Darton, 1838), 24, 63–66; Bethany Veney, *The Narrative of Bethany Veney, a Slave Woman* (Worcester, Mass.: George H. Ellis, 1889), 29–30; McLaurin, *Celia;* Fredrika Bremer, *The Homes of the New World: Impressions of America,* trans. Mary Howitt (New York: Harper and Brothers, 1853), 1:373, 2:535.

63. I. Franklin to R. C. Ballard, November 1, 1833, folder 12 ("fancy girl"), and I. Franklin to R. C. Ballard, January 11, 1834, folder 13; J. Franklin to R. C. Ballard, March 7, 1834, folder 13 ("Old Man"); J. Franklin to Messrs. R. C. Ballard & Co., March 27, 1832, folder 5 ("very boyish"), all in Ballard Papers; Stephenson, *Isaac Franklin,* 19.

64. I. and J. Franklin to Messrs. R. C. Ballard & Co., May 13, 1832, folder 6 ("fair maid Martha"); I. Franklin to Messrs. R. C. Ballard & Co., June 8, 1832, folder 7; I. Franklin to R. C. Ballard, November 1, 1833, folder 12 ("I do believe"), all in Ballard Papers. See also J. Brown, *Slave Life in Georgia,* 19.

65. J. Cage to W. Cotton, August 27, 1839, folder 28, Ballard Papers.

66. Here are but a few examples of ex-slaves' memories of women bought specifically for sexual abuse: Rawick, *American Slave,* vol. 16, pt. 3 (Maryland), p. 54 (Richard Macks); ibid., supplement ser. 2, vol. 7 (Texas), pt. 6, 2531 (Rosa and Jack Maddox); ibid., vol. 8 (Texas), pt. 7, p. 3292 (Mary Reynolds); ibid., vol. 16, pt. 4 (Ohio), p. 104 (Julia Williams); Blassingame, *Slave Testimony,* 362; 400; McLaurin, *Celia.*

67. L. R. Starks to R. C. Ballard, February 5, 1833, folder 10; P. B. January to R. C. Ballard, October 28, 1854, folder 217; P. B. January to R. C. Ballard, November 29, 1854, folder 219, Ballard Papers.

68. J. M. Duffield to R. C. Ballard, May 29, 1848, folder 127; J. M. Duffield to R. C. Ballard, August 5, 1848, folder 131, Ballard Papers. For ex-slaves' comments on this

topic, see J. Brown, *Slave Life in Georgia*, 104, 112–13; Rawick, ed., *American Slave*, vol. 16, pt. 3 (Maryland), pp. 53, 55 (Richard Macks) for a case of resistance that ended in death; ibid., vol. 16, pt. 4 (Ohio), p. 61 (Julia King); ibid., vol. 18, p. 2; vol. 18, p. 51; supp. ser. 1, vol. 8 (Mississippi), pt. 3,p. 803 (Lucy Galloway). "I can tell you" is quoted in supp. ser. 2, vol. 7 (Texas) pt. 6, p. 2531 (Rosa and Jack Maddox), but one might just as well cite the WPA narratives, passim, because the ex-slaves are generally in agreement that force and threat made these relationships inevitable. Further limiting the ability to defend oneself against sexual aggression was the fact that the slave trade had separated Maria and her sisters from family, friends, and potential white allies. Such women were therefore more vulnerable to sexual predation — more easily seen and treated by whites as commodities — than ever.

69. J. Cage to W. Cotton, August 27, 1839, folder 28; see also V. Boyd to Col. Ballard, May 6, 1853, folder 191; C. M. Rutherford to R. C. Ballard, August 8, 1853, folder 196, all in Ballard Papers. For masters selling their own children, see Rawick, *American Slave*, 18:3, 251–52, 298; Blassingame, *Slave Testimony*, 400 (interview with J. W. Lindsay), 702–4 (Sella Martin).

70. Joel Williamson, *New People: Miscegenation and Mulattoes in the United States* (New York: Free Press, 1980); F. James Davis, *Who Is Black? One Nation's Definition* (University Park: Pennsylvania State University Press, 1991).

71. Spillers, "Mama's Baby, Papa's Maybe," 67; Abdy, *Journal of a Residence and Tour*, 179; Everest, *Journey Through the United States*, 104; Johnson, *Soul by Soul*, 113–15.

72. McClintock, *Imperial Leather*, 181–85, criticizes the overemphasis on the "authority of the castration scene"[183]; for readings of sexual fetishism that emphasize the centrality of castration anxiety, see Freud, "Fetishism"; Robert J. Stoller, *Observing the Erotic Imagination* (New Haven: Yale University Press, 1985), 35–36.

73. I. Franklin to R. C. Ballard, September 27, 1834, folder 15, Ballard Papers. See also J. Alsop to D. Ballard, February 5, 1834; I. Franklin to R. C. Ballard, January 11, 1834, both in folder 13, Ballard Papers.

74. I. and J. Franklin to Messrs. R. C. Ballard and Co., May 13, 1832, folder 6; J. Franklin to D. Ballard, March 7, 1834, folder 13 ("fair maid"), Ballard Papers. For an example of the tensions engendered in the antebellum United States by the rise of the domestic ideal, see Carroll Smith-Rosenberg, "Davy Crockett as Trickster: Pornography, Liminality, and Symbolic Inversion in Victorian America," in her *Disorderly Conduct: Visions of Gender in Victorian America* (New York: Knopf, 1985), 90–108. For southern accounts, see Painter, "Soul Murder and Slavery," esp. 136–37; and Marli Weiner, *Mistresses and Slaves: Plantation Women in South Carolina, 1830–1880* (Urbana: University of Illinois Press, 1998), 53–56.

75. It seems almost redundant to add that whereas gender and sexuality are currently seen as different categories of historical and cultural analysis, one can bear on the other: Isaac Franklin was unlikely to have considered that his gendered identity had nothing to do with his sexual practices, and vice versa.

76. See Brown, *Good Wives*, esp. 372, 328–34.

77. The motifs of incest and oedipal competition come to mind. They are beyond the scope of this essay, but recall the admonition of the 1850s proslavery theorist Henry

Hughes that "Amalgamation is incest." Hughes, *Treatise on Sociology, Theoretical and Practical* (Philadelphia: Lippincott, 1854), 240. See also Jennifer DeVere Brody, *Impossible Purities: Blackness, Femininity, and Victorian Culture* (Durham: Duke University Press, 1998), 55.

78. Rawick, *American Slave*, 18:251.

79. James Baldwin recognized the still-potent historical detritus of these white ideas in his own time in his short story "Going to Meet the Man" (1965). For a view of fetishization that examines consequences and responses among African Americans in the nineteenth century, see Robert Reid-Pharr, "Violent Ambiguity: Martin Delany, Bourgeois Sadomasochism, and the Production of a Black National Masculinity," in *Representing Black Men*, ed. Marcellus Blount and George Cunningham (New York: Routledge, 1996), 73–94. For the early twenty-first century see Greg Tate, ed., *Everything But the Burden: What White People Are Taking from Black Culture* (New York: Broadway Books, 2003).

9

Grapevine in the Slave Market
African American Geopolitical Literacy and the 1841 *Creole* Revolt

PHILLIP TROUTMAN

In November 1841, a group of at least nineteen enslaved African American men held aboard the brig *Creole* effected a successful inversion of United States slave traders' network of communication and transportation. Bound from the Chesapeake to New Orleans in the domestic U.S. slave trade, they violently captured control of the ship and forced the crew to chart a course for Nassau, Bahamas. There, with the aid of black Bahamians and British colonial officials, they gained freedom along with all but five of their enslaved shipmates, 130 in all. White contemporaries tended to view the *Creole* "incident" in terms of its contribution to an international trade conflict between the United States and Great Britain. Its chief historian, Howard Jones, has made clear its importance in that regard. The revolt, however, is at least as important for what it illustrates about how enslaved African Americans worked to acquire, disseminate, and apply geographic and geopolitical knowledge and information — what I call geopolitical literacy — and what that might mean for their broader Afro-American consciousness. By contrast to the more famous bid for freedom carried out in 1839 by kidnapped Mendi aboard the Cuban schooner *Amistad,* the *Creole* revolt was successful in its initial stage. Key to these rebels' remarkable (and unique) success were their ability to create and articulate conceptual maps of slavery and freedom in the African Atlantic and their application of navigation skills to transgress the boundaries of that political landscape.[1]

The *Amistad* Africans, like all those enslaved for the transatlantic trade, had been alienated from their known world and were unfamiliar with the maritime geography of the Americas. Vulnerable to duplicity on the part of their captive crew, they found themselves directed not east, back to Africa, as they had demanded, but rather north, up the American coast. The African Americans aboard the *Creole,* by contrast, knew their geopolitical context, knew where to find freedom within it, and knew how to effect their passage there. Although alienated from their families and communities by the interstate slave market, the *Creole* rebels nonetheless remained within the larger world of American slavery made known to them by their use of the grapevine and made navigable by their maritime skills. They operated a covert network of information and knowledge across and within the overt networks of commerce built by interstate slave traders, then used that information to carry out the most successful African American attempt at freedom in the history of the United States before the Civil War.

The *Creole* revolt exposes the ways people and knowledge moved in and out of what we usually think of as the bounded spaces of American slavery and even within the most tightly controlled spaces of incarceration, the holding cells of the domestic slave trade. When one was a slave, one was in the slave market. That was the meaning of the chattel principle, as African American autobiographers made clear again and again.[2] Yet many historians continue to marginalize the slave market as a sideshow, as if it were somehow peripheral to slavery. Most studies of slavery in the United States have focused on master-slave relations or on slave community in spaces conceived of as bounded and often rather static. Forced and willful migration within the system has rarely been fully incorporated into our understanding of slavery.[3]

Slavery, however, was a system of forced migration as well as of forced labor. Chattel slavery defined slaves as moveable personal property, and slaveholders effected both short- and long-distance slave migrations by means of hire, sale, and bequeathal. On the eighteenth-century Virginia frontier, as planters claimed more land and ordered it cleared for agriculture, the forced migration of slaves took place first across relatively short distances, from county to county, but increasingly across broader spaces, from the Tidewater region to the Piedmont. In the decades following the revolution, Americans conquered and seized Native lands west of the Alleghenies and across to the Mississippi Delta, where cotton could be grown in abundance. Between 1790 and 1860, planters and commercial traders forced the migration of 1.1 million enslaved African Americans from the eastern seaboard and upper south states to these plantation frontiers. This represented more than twice the number of Africans carried to mainland North America in the previous century. Migrating planters moved significant numbers of slaves in at least fragments of families and partial communities, but more often and especially after 1830, enslaved migrants were sold to commercial traders, who moved people more often than not as individuals, not families.[4]

The slave market constituted an elaborate network, a web across which men of means moved money, information, and people. Its tendrils followed the lines of other commerce: rivers, roads, canals, coastal shipping lanes, and financial channels. Slave traders strengthened and extended those traditional lines of commerce, thickening and expanding the bands of that web. In their attempts to conquer space, to rationalize the southern labor market, and to turn a profit, the traders and the planters who sold to them created a market revolution in slavery. The slave market connected Philadelphia banks to Richmond slave trading houses to Natchez sales depots. It connected coastal ports with each other and with the hinterlands, both in the upper south regions of slave labor supply and the lower south regions of demand for slave labor. And it created social dislocations among the migrant laborers that matched those of the market revolutionary North.[5] Tellingly, it is historians of the family who have understood most fully the impact of the market revolution in slavery on African American life. By continually extending the plantation frontier across the southwest, and by moving slaves through the market to get them there, slaveholders and traders put African American families through traumatic cycles of consolidation and dispersal of families and communities.[6]

Migration held other cultural implications as well. African Americans created their own networks at the same time, covert ones that overlay and undercut slaveholders' overt web of commerce. Julius Scott and Jeffrey Bolster have each made clear the importance of sailors and the fluidity of maritime communications in helping create a broad network of African American communication throughout the Caribbean basin and southern Atlantic. This loose network stretched up the North American coast and across the Gulf of Mexico, connected by sailors, stevedores, and other workers in and on vessels and by slaves transported from place to place. As people moved, they carried with them news, information, ideas, and knowledge, transmitting it from port to port. In Scott's apt phrasing, the "common wind" of African American mobility swept across broad geographical divides, even under slavery.[7] Moses Grandy, for example, lived near Elizabeth City, North Carolina, on the Albemarle Sound. His brother was enslaved to a ship captain and traveled frequently to the West Indies but visited Moses from time to time. As a boatman himself, Moses plied coastal waterways north to the James River in Virginia and south to Ocracoke in North Carolina, a distance of about 150 miles. The Grandy brothers represented precisely the kind of conduit by which news moved across the waters, linking the Caribbean to the coastal United States.[8]

On the North American mainland, through men such as Moses Grandy, this network reached deep inland via coastal waterways and navigable rivers such as the James and the Mississippi. It stretched across the land by means of what contemporaries called the "grapevine." Whereas women often stood at the hub of this system, men more often constituted the spokes because they were generally more mobile, both by force and by will, than women. Men were more likely to be the visiting spouse in interplantation marriages, and they were more likely to "lay out," or flee as fugitives. They were more likely than women to be hired out or sent on errands off the plantation. As boatmen, herdsmen, wagon drivers, and other mobile African Americans traveled as part of their employment, they moved among slaves bound more tightly by masters' geography. They shared selectively their knowledge of the wider world. In this way, the grapevine infiltrated every plantation.[9] These networks carried information from plantation to plantation and neighborhood to neighborhood, even in places where only a few individuals might have been allowed mobility. More than one former slave compared it to that most modern of antebellum inventions, the telegraph. Booker T. Washington wrote that during the Civil War slaves "kept themselves informed of events by what was termed the 'grape-vine' telegraph." The North Carolina fugitive J. W. C. Pennington went further, arguing that not even telegraph wires, which flashed news at "the speed of lightning," could match the efficiency and reach of the African American grapevine. White people knew about it, too. The Virginia planter W. W. Gilmer claimed that "Adams & Co.'s Express can't beat [the slaves] in the transmission of all sorts of reports; they travel from ten to thirty miles in a night."[10]

This was a geographical literacy in the sense that it represented words in motion, news and information categorized and passed on surreptitiously across the space of slavery. It was also a geopolitical literacy in that it represented a mode of gathering and transfer of knowledge about the abstract but quite real boundaries that defined legal slavery and freedom in the Americas. The invocation of "literacy" does not necessarily mean that these men were literate in the strictest sense, namely, that they could read and write, but it does imply that they drew on cognitive patterns that we associate with literate people. Theirs was largely an oral culture, which Walter Ong defines in part as "conservative or traditionalist," as "situational rather than abstract," and as "aggregative rather than analytic."[11] Others have challenged Ong's dichotomy between oral and literate cognition. And for African Americans, even in slavery, it was also a world informed by an understanding of the power of literacy and shaped by contact with literacy, whether casual or sustained, overt or surreptitious. The *Creole* insurgents demonstrated their participation in a semiliterate world in discrete acts such as reading a compass. They drew from both oral and literate modes of thought in conceiving a broad mental map of slavery and freedom in the Atlantic.[12]

Geopolitical literacy, like alphabetic literacy, represented specialized skills that were not only difficult to obtain and use under slavery but were also differentiated in that difficulty. In the nineteenth century generally, reading and writing were taught separately, so that people who could read often could not write. In the case of U.S. slavery in particular, as Jennifer Monaghan shows, whites attributed different types of power to reading and to writing, and African Americans gained different types of power from each. Whites associated writing with commerce and mobility and usually considered it a potentially dangerous tool in the hands of slaves, more so than reading, which whites invested with evangelical associations. Thus, geopolitical literacy for African Americans in slavery was shaped by and around the power wielded by slaveholders. Enslaved readers and writers had to navigate what Bruce Fort has called a "politics of literacy" that both master and slave understood: gaining reading and especially writing skills meant gaining a kind of power slaveholders did not want slaves to possess.[13] The same might be said of geopolitical literacy. It was easier, though by no means less dangerous, to "read" the social and political landscape than to "write" on it by changing it or by escaping master's landscape altogether.

The power in geopolitical literacy flowed along other axes as well, however. Exercise of that power in an attempt to escape, for example, could prove highly risky. Only certain people could be trusted with information or with one's life. The grapevine, then, was laced with secrecy and distrust. Its oral operation meant that certain information might be kept out of the wrong hands, but that meant that people had to make decisions about whom to trust with what information.[14] By connecting black people across political landscapes, the grapevine constituted a potent tool for undermining slaveholders' control over the landscape, and it contributed to the creation of a broad Afro-American consciousness extending across the Caribbean basin. But at the same time, on an individual level, the grapevine could help undermine trust among African Americans. All these tensions are evident in the *Creole* rebels' use of the grapevine in the slave market.

Knowledge about the relations between places and between people across those spaces had long helped build community under slavery in North America. Allan Kulikoff has shown that within the Virginia Tidewater region in the eighteenth century, forced separations and relocation ironically helped foster broader interplantation communities. Despite the dispersal of plantation households, Africans and African Americans traveled between them, with or without masters' permission, beating down a network of paths forming communities recognized as neighborhoods that stretched for miles. These were relatively short-distance dislocations and migrations, however. Julius Scott argues more broadly that the "common wind" of maritime communications in the revolutionary Atlantic facilitated the creation of an Afro-American consciousness that not only crossed political boundaries but was also political in its own right. This broader network, like the local branches of the grapevine, was an especially male one, as men's work in slavery more often required their travel and as men more readily than women found political voice in European American venues. Paul Gilroy points to literate travelers, especially men such as Olaudah Equiano, Robert Wedderburn, and Martin Delaney (but also Phyllis Wheatley), as among the most cosmopolitan exemplars of an Afro-Atlantic consciousness. If most ordinary black travelers did not formulate a specific racial or pan-African nationalism in the antebellum period, they did imagine themselves into larger communities (to paraphrase Benedict Anderson) based not only on literal connections but also on common experiences, assumptions, and cultural practices as people of African descent enslaved in the Americas.[15] Physical migration and grapevine communications were key to that sense of shared identity.

African Americans did not do this uniformly or uncritically, however. As Walter Johnson has noted, this process necessarily rode on a highly unstable and potentially risky "infrapolitics" of information-sharing among blacks.[16] The broad diversity of experiences under slavery and the diversity of strategies of surviving or resisting slavery's many oppressions meant that enslaved individuals in discrete situations might act at cross purposes. This infused their use of the grapevine with a certain level of distrust. This caution was made manifest in how people chose whom to believe and whom not to believe, how they substantiated or corroborated rumors in order to create a body of useful information, and how they decided, in turn, whom to entrust with that information. As the term "infrapolitics" might imply, the devil was in the details of individual interactions.

The details of the *Creole* revolt reveal how under exceptional conditions, African Americans not only "read" the geopolitical landscape but also "wrote" themselves across geopolitical boundaries and out of slavery. The accounts of witnesses (*Creole* crew members and cohorts of the slave traders), though self-serving, hint at the complicated and, in instances, compromised collective consciousness held by the African Americans who implemented the revolt and those who benefited from it. Our attention to the grapevine in the slave market is key. The men plotting escape aboard the *Creole* probably left Virginia with key bits of geopolitical knowledge already acquired, perhaps while being held in the confines of Richmond's slave jails. They apparently knew about emancipation in the British colonial islands, and they certainly knew about a specific case like their own in which U.S. slaves went free in Nassau.

Afro-Virginians had long been cognizant of the larger Afro-American world in the Caribbean. News of the Haitian Revolution (1794–1804) had reverberated throughout the Caribbean rim, including the Chesapeake, to which thousands of white and black refugees had fled. Knowledge about Haiti's black revolution informed Afro-American culture, perhaps even influencing Gabriel's conspiracy in Virginia in 1800. Although African Americans had to sift any information about Haiti through the sieve of proslavery propaganda about the supposed chaos of freedom there, Haiti remained an important touchstone for their thinking about freedom, and it helped keep the Caribbean at large within their scope.[17] In 1829, slaves aboard the schooner *Lafayette*, bound from Norfolk to New Orleans, rose in an unsuccessful revolt. We cannot know whether these rebels intended to head for the black republic in the Caribbean (or indeed, whether they took any ironic inspiration from the republican namesake of their vessel). But three years earlier, a Baltimore trader's slaves, bound for Georgia on board the *Decatur,* seized control of that ship and did demand to go to Haiti. News of these and other episodes in the coastal U.S. slave trade may have passed through the grapevine, resonating in the *Creole* rebels' memories and heightening their awareness of opportunities for freedom in certain specific Caribbean locales. Slaves from the United States had already found freedom in the Bahamas, not by their own design but by sheer luck and the actions of Bahamians. In 1830 or 1831, the *Comet,* out of Alexandria, Virginia, ran aground on the False Keys; wreckers from Nassau freed its 164 enslaved passengers. In 1835, the *Enterprise,* sailing from the District of Columbia, put into Nassau seeking shelter from a storm. Local activists successfully pressed the courts to free the seventy-eight enslaved passengers. Finally, and most important, less than a year before the *Creole* uprising, in October 1840, the schooner *Formosa* (referred to as the *"Hermosa"* in Senate documents) ran aground on the Spanish key of Abaco. Bahamian wreckers rescued the passengers — including thirty-eight enslaved African Americans who were being shipped by a Richmond trader and who were not returned by the British colonial government.[18] Word of their emancipation reached the enslaved population in Virginia.

The *Creole* insurgents knew about the *Formosa* slaves' liberation in the Bahamas, and they knew and recited the important details to their captive crew. The rebels referred to the *Hermosa*. They made reference to Abaco (mistaking it for the destination) and to "British islands," as opposed to those under other colonial powers.[19] Two of the revolt's leaders, Ben Blacksmith and Doctor Ruffin, made it clear to the ship's crew that "they did not want to go anywhere else but where Mr. Lumpkin's negroes went last year."[20] This clarifying detail was important to them. It was intended to leave no doubt in the minds of the captive crew as to their intended destination. It was the kind of detail that might have been repeated in the multiple tellings of the story, as suggested by its appearance as a narrative fragment. It was also underscored in the *Creole* rebels' own experience in the Richmond jails, for they too were, in a sense, "Mr. Lumpkin's." The Richmond slave trader Robert Lumpkin does not in fact appear to have been the owner of the people aboard the *Formosa,* but he did professionally incarcerate people being moved by other traders. By 1844, three years after the *Creole* revolt, he had established the commercial jail compound for which he became famous (and infamous) in the trade in the 1850s.[21] The *Creole*'s crew identified many of the enslaved people aboard as being sent by Lumpkin, although these people were owned by other traders. They too might have identified the *Formosa* slaves held by Lumpkin as "Lumpkin's negroes."

The Lumpkin connection was potentially critical in the grapevine. The *Creole* rebels may very well have learned about the *Formosa* escapees — or at least confirmed or augmented their knowledge about them — while in Robert Lumpkin's possession in Richmond. Lumpkin and the other traders would have been seething at their loss and at Britain's refusal to recognize their "legitimate" trade. Guarded as they may have been in the presence of enslaved servants and inmates of the jail, their complaints must eventually have reached the ears of those in Lumpkin's charge. There, where men and women from different parts of Virginia, Maryland, and North Carolina were forced to gather for up to two months awaiting passage to New Orleans, news of an event such as the *Formosa* rescue might percolate for months or years after the fact. In the case of the *Creole* slaves, the news about the *Formosa* was less than a year old.[22]

How the grapevine could work in such a tightly controlled space is demonstrated by the famous case of Anthony Burns. In 1854, Burns found himself sitting in Robert Lumpkin's jail compound, like the *Formosa* and *Creole* prisoners more than a decade earlier. He had escaped from Virginia to Boston but was caught, put on trial, and returned to Richmond. There he was incarcerated in the attic of Lumpkin's male slave barracks.[23] Isolated in this garret cell, Burns quickly moved to gain access to his fellow prisoners below and to the larger world outside. He bored a hole in the floor and through this tiny portal he opened up a bartering relationship with the others.[24] To the other detainees, he provided tales of his escapade. His abolitionist biographer, Charles Stevens, wrote evocatively that "he was their Columbus, telling them of the land, to them unknown, which he had visited," both "inspiring" them with the free land's promise and warning them of the pitfalls of getting there. Stevens pictured Burns rather romantically as the geographer, the explorer, the raconteur. To Burns's listeners he may well have been these things. At the same time, his stories held pragmatic information for the listeners, and the storytelling events had utility for Burns. They helped him bond with his fellow inmates, from whom he gained tobacco, outside information, and, perhaps most important for him, ink.

With the pen and paper he had already smuggled in his clothing (exactly how he managed to do this Stevens did not fully explain), Burns was now able to write letters, which he dropped surreptitiously to black passers-by in the alley below. By such tenuous and dangerous means, he managed to get at least two letters through to the post office. Lest we think Stevens's account melodramatic on this score, in the letter that remains extant Burns wrote to his chief counsel in Boston, Richard Henry Dana, indicating his own moral geopolitics: he pled with Dana to buy him out of Virginia, a "Land of death." In another letter, he wrote his master to complain of harsh treatment in Lumpkin's jail. The white man's response indicated the power he knew literacy could hold over slavery's political geography: he came and took away Burns's pen, ink, and paper.[25]

The grapevine potentially wound into Lumpkin's domestic space, however, and Burns worked to establish contact with two women there. This trader and professional jailer, who separated countless African American families, held his own family in slavery. Beginning in the 1830s, a mixed-race woman named Mary F. Lumpkin, whom Robert Lumpkin legally owned, bore him five children whom he recognized as his heirs.[26] Mary recognized Burns's literacy and brought him a "testament and a hymn-book." According to Stevens, Lumpkin also held a concubine (whom Stevens described as "black" as opposed to Mary Lumpkin's "yellow"); she lived in the garret of the Lumpkin house, right next to the barracks. She "manifested a friendly spirit toward the prisoner," and across that empty space, from garret window to garret window, this woman "contrived to hold conversations" with Burns. Surely he sought news and information from these African American women intimate to the Lumpkin household. In fact, when Lumpkin found out about the communications with the concubine, he put a stop to them. Stevens suggested that Lumpkin did this out of jealousy, but it was also surely to nip this budding tendril of the grapevine.[27]

Anthony Burns's surreptitious communications with his fellow inmates, with African American members of Lumpkin's household, with his master, and with his Boston attorney—all while kept in solitary confinement in an attic cell—testifies to Lumpkin's inability to gain total control over information coming in and out of his jail, much less that being passed down among inmates within its confines. This network was the same one to which the *Creole* conspirators had access while in the possession of Lumpkin over a decade earlier and by which they could very well have gained or at least augmented the knowledge they had about the *Formosa* and its passengers.

The possibility that the *Creole* conspirators had an inside informant is an intriguing one. Before the revolt, Madison Washington had been serving as an enslaved "steward," a position that perhaps gave him access to conversations between traders.[28] Witnesses also named as one of the insurgents Robert Lumpkin (sometimes Lumpkins), who was also called Lumpley (or Lumley). This man could have taken this name as a nomme de guerre, an ironic stab at the white man who had incarcerated them in Richmond.[29] But his name might instead reflect a more extended intimacy with the household of his namesake. The trader Lumpkin recognized in his will five children of Mary F. Lumpkin, but there may indeed have been other African American Lumpkins, other children of Mary or of a concubine, or perhaps a nonrelative taking the name Lumpkin. If such a household member were to fall calamitously out of favor with the slave trader, he could easily have disposed of that person in the market. If this African American Robert Lumpkin had been an intimate of the white Robert Lumpkin's household, he would have been in a good position to overhear discussion of business matters such as that of the *Formosa* case. If so, he could have been a conduit of that crucial bit of knowledge.

Whatever their source of information about the *Formosa,* the *Creole* rebels were better informed than some of the British in Nassau. Twelve British colonial officials and servicemen in the Bahamas testified about their knowledge of interaction with ships entering the Bahamas with U.S. slaves aboard. All but one were in a position to have heard about the *Formosa* and possibly of the earlier cases. Asked whether they knew of any American ships other than the *Creole* entering British West Indies waters from which American slaves gained their freedom, only four witnesses said that they did. Knowledge about the *Formosa,* which the conspirators aboard the *Creole* had actively sought, confirmed, and carefully remembered, was scarcely of any importance to most of these white men in Her Majesty's service.[30]

Knowledge could be political, especially when the stakes were so high. Only viable, reliable information about the geopolitics of slavery and freedom in the

Caribbean could inspire any realistic attempt at escape. Wherever the rebels may have acquired their knowledge, they must have corroborated information from various sources, weighing the relative value of vague rumors, overheard conversations, and gleanings from political and business news. Moreover, as they came together in conspiracy to use that knowledge, they must have moved with great trepidation and yet daring. The nineteen or more men who conspired to take control of the *Creole* most likely did not know each other before their incarceration in Richmond or Norfolk. They very quickly had to assess one another's knowledge, reliability, ability, and commitment. They also had to keep potential informants from having access to the conspiracy. Surely others knew about their plan and worked to keep it a secret.[31] In fact, several more African Americans were named by witnesses as participants in the revolt, and even the British official greeting them in Nassau recognized that the nineteen were those "identified as taking the *most* active part." But the conspirators did not necessarily trust the rest. After the revolt, the rebels removed the gratings over the hatches but made most of the African Americans stay below deck. This was perhaps merely a pragmatic measure, but according to one white witness, the rebels also "ordered them about as if they were their masters."[32]

More important, differences among the conspirators put their success in jeopardy. It is not at all clear that the four leaders named by the crew (Madison Washington, Ben Blacksmith or Johnstone, Elijah Morris, and Doctor Ruffin) initially agreed on the ultimate plan or on who held final authority. They variously ordered the sails hoisted up, then taken in, then finally up again, leaving the crew wondering exactly who was in charge. According to one captive crew member, Morris said he thought he and his co-conspirators would probably "rise again amongst ourselves."[33] Deciding on their destination threatened to split the revolt. Madison Washington, whom Frederick Douglass later lionized in fiction as a revolutionary,[34] first insisted that the rebels direct the ship to Liberia. This signaled his broader consciousness of the Atlantic passage and perhaps something of his political or religious consciousness as well. He had reportedly escaped to the North and conversed with abolitionists before being recaptured on returning to Virginia. Perhaps he was influenced by African American colonizationist thought like that of Paul Cuffee and Lott Cary. The latter, from Virginia, died in 1828 but gained posthumous notoriety in the mid-1830s.[35] Following Washington's course of action, however, would surely have led to disaster for all aboard the ship. One of their white hostages, William Merritt, who before the revolt had been charged with "managing" a group of them in transit, informed Washington and the others that the ship did not carry enough provisions to make it to Africa. Skilled in making these maritime estimates, or at least in evaluating this white man's estimate, they did not make the mistake of the *Amistad* Africans. But they perhaps risked the cohesion of the rebellion. The others, after all, believed the white man and took his advice against Madison Washington's bid for Liberia. Had Washington not assented to their reading of the white man's perception of their navigational predicament and to the others' preference for Nassau, it could have meant trouble for the rebellion. In resolving this potential crisis in unity, the *Creole* rebels drew not only on this geopolitical knowledge but also on their maritime knowledge and, in the end, their judgment about a white man's trustworthiness and his seafaring knowledge.

Their need of the white hostages, however, pointed to a deficiency in the African Americans' navigational literacy. According to the testimony, this man showed them the charts and "read to them the Coast Pilot," describing landmarks on the way to the port of Nassau. This revealed that they could not read the coast pilot.[36] They had to work to overcome this, and they did so with threats of further violence. They promised him his life in exchange for navigating the *Creole* safely to freedom.[37] They still knew they had to verify this man's continued honesty, however. Here their navigational skills came into play in a crucial way. According to witnesses, two of the rebels, Doctor Ruffin and George Portlock, "knew the letters of the compass" and apparently taught some of the others. Three of the men — Washington, Elijah Morris, and Ruffin — kept a vigilant eye on their white hostage and on the compass. To prevent the passing of any secret messages among the crew, Washington and Blacksmith prohibited anyone from speaking in any language they could not comprehend. Finally, Portlock provided a further check, drawing on his oral and not his literacy skills. He had been to New Orleans before and claimed to know the route. If any of the *Creole* crew members deceived them (as the *Amistad* crew had the Mendi), Portlock presumably would recognize the landmarks and foil any such counterplot.[38]

Portlock was confident in his memory, and the crew seemed to believe him. Since he knew the compass, he likely knew other navigational skills, and his ability to read and remember landscape cues may have been quite sharp. Even if he had been to New Orleans only once, if he had realized that a mental map of the gulf coastline would be useful, he would have worked to commit those landmarks to memory. The ex-slave Charles Ball had taken the same tack, as he detailed in his autobiography. Sold from his wife and children in Maryland to a Georgia trader, he worked on his forced march to memorize the landmarks so that he could follow them back home one day.

I had endeavoured through the whole journey, from the time we crossed the Rappahannock river, to make such observations upon the country, the roads we travelled, and the towns we passed through, as would enable me, at some future period, to find my way back to Maryland. I was particularly careful to note the names of the towns and villages through which we passed, and to fix on my memory, not only the names of all the rivers, but also the position and bearing of the ferries over those streams. . . . By repeatedly naming the rivers that we came to, and in the order which we had reached them, I was able at my arrival in Georgia, to repeat the name of every considerable stream from the Potomac to the Savannah, and to tell at what ferries we had crossed them.

Ball's 1837 narrative accordingly read like a gazetteer, naming each river his chained gang crossed: the Patuxent, the Potomac, the Rappahanock, the Matapony, the North Anna, the South Anna, the James, the Roanoke, and the Yadkin. Later escaping from Georgia, Ball navigated by the stars and the sun, read landmarks such as hills, swamps, roads, and hamlets, and gained further geographic information by listening in to conversations along the roadside. He recounted crossing the Apalachie, Oconee, Savannah, Catawba, Yadkin, and Appomattox rivers before finding his original route; he then retraced his way back across the James, Pamunky, Matapony, Potomac, and Patuxent rivers.[39] Aboard the *Creole*, George Portlock claimed the same capacity to "fix in his memory" the important landscape features marking the coastal route to New Orleans. Members of the captive crew, themselves perhaps possessing these same skills, gave him the benefit of the doubt.

In their use of the grapevine, the African Americans aboard the *Creole* had read the geopolitical map of the Caribbean and had learned of a place where British law would render them free. But they were not only right about the colonial and abolitionist geopolitics of those in power. They were also right about the people they conceived of as their fellow African Americans in the Bahamas. Clearly, the Bahamians identified with them, and vice versa. One man did so through quite literal connections. A crew member of the pilot boat that greeted the *Creole* told the refugees that "he came out from Charleston, and that he got free by coming out there in that way." This immediate confirmation of the success of their plan led to the Americans' open embrace of the Bahamians. According to a white witness, when the black crew of the pilot boat boarded, some of the *Creole* refugees "kissed the negroes that came on board and said, you are my brothers, &c. The negroes of the Creole laughed, and appeared much rejoiced, particularly those who heard the negro say, that he had got free in that way."[40]

It was not only this fellow refugee who identified with the rebels. As

Roseanne Adderley makes clear, local fishermen and other black British subjects in Nassau helped ensure the *Creole* refugees' freedom by surrounding the vessel, keeping vigil, ferrying them to shore, and helping them disperse to Jamaica and elsewhere.[41] Further, when Merritt, the former manager, went ashore, he discovered how far knowledge of the *Creole*'s arrival had been transmitted and how deeply committed to the refugees' cause locals had already become. Merritt recounted that he and the American consul "went into a number of places, and saw arms and muskets, and tried to buy them, but the people refused to sell them." He "could not purchase any at all."[42] The grapevine operated in and about Nassau, too, of course, and it informed people's consciousness. The locals probably knew about the *Formosa* incident of the previous year, and hearing news of yet another ship with enslaved African Americans was enough immediately to reaffirm notions of identity with American refugees from slavery. They did not necessarily have to meet them or even see the ship in the harbor. Word was enough.

The sense of camaraderie between the Americans and the Bahamians, however, was not absolutely uniform, and the politics of knowledge about the place itself complicated things for a handful of the refugees in particular. According to William Merritt, five African Americans (four women and a child) "did not like the island, as the negroes there appeared to be very poor, and with nothing to wear or eat." These women had not even stepped ashore, however, and could have seen only the Bahamians who had boarded the ship or come alongside. If these *were* the women's notions, they had come mainly from Merritt. But however self-serving Merritt's propaganda about freedom in the Bahamas, he may not in fact have completely misrepresented the women's sentiments in his later testimony, for he also noted, perhaps without realizing its implications, that the women said that "if they could have [freedom] in their own country, they would like it very well." Merritt in fact used this as an enticement, telling one woman, Mary, that he thought her master might free her if she continued on to New Orleans. Mary, however, had to weigh this faint hope against information she received from one of the white colonial officers. This man, Merritt testified, had been "conversing secretly" with the African American women on the *Creole* and had told Mary that if she returned to the United States that "she would be punished for the deeds, that the others had committed." Merritt, on the other hand, "tried to persuade her out of that notion."[43]

The grapevine was often riddled with unsubstantiated rumor and intentional misinformation. Those not in control of the revolt had to weigh their own imperfect knowledge about the rebels' chosen destination in order to decide how to act once they arrived. For some of them, their prospects in this unknown land may have been intimidating enough (though no less intimidating than the equally unknown land of, say, Mississippi). Moreover, having been removed from the network of any known grapevine at home, Mary had access only to these dubious sources of information. In the end, she returned to the United States. Perhaps she thought, "better the devil you know than the devil you don't." Or perhaps family ties bound her there. Mary was in a discrete minority, however. The remaining 111 disembarked in Nassau and, along with the nineteen named conspirators (who were detained only briefly), dispersed themselves in the British colonies, just as the lucky *Formosa* refugees (and others) had done before them. Whatever information, misinformation, and rumor they had access to, they tended to trust the inclinations of the insurgents who had made the decision to carry them to Nassau and the helpful black Bahamians eager to welcome them. In the face of this movement ashore, Mary's decision isolated her both physically and ideologically from the rest of the *Creole*'s passengers and their local liberators. The Bahamians disapproved and let her know in no uncertain terms.

Thus, deploying their geopolitical literacy, the *Creole* insurgents successfully read the landscape and wrote on it — transgressing the geopolitical boundaries that were supposed to keep them in slavery (and creating, as Howard Jones has shown, an international "incident" over commerce).[44] Unlike the kidnapped Africans aboard the *Amistad,* who were thoroughly cut off from their known networks of meaningful knowledge, these African Americans knew something of the landscape of freedom and slavery in the Americas. They did not try to go north; perhaps understanding the legal "legitimacy" of the coastal trade, they knew they would not find freedom there. They did not attempt the trip to Africa on short provisions. Though none of them mentioned the *Amistad,* it is conceivable that they had heard about that case. Regardless, the *Amistad* was clearly not their model. Instead they drew on knowledge of the *Formosa* slaves' escape in the Bahamas, and they used their maritime skills to prevent the crew from turning the compass against them. This magnificent use of the grapevine in the slave market was indeed exceptional. Yet in its exceptionality it highlights the features of the grapevine that traced commercial networks within the enslaved landscape out of which the *Creole* people had passed.

The story of Isaac Williams and Henry Banks illustrates the importance and tenuous nature of geographic literacy. It shows how the grapevine wound its way into the slave jails, how it was tainted with distrust, and how fugitives used broader geopolitical knowledge in their escape. In the fall of 1854, Williams met Banks in the Fredericksburg, Virginia, slave-holding pen of the trader George Ayler. Banks had already been caught once before after several months' sojourn in an attempt to escape, and geopolitical ignorance had done him in. He said he "had heard tell of a free country — but I did not know where it was, nor how to get there." He apparently had learned more about it along the way, however, for on making it to Washington, D.C., he boarded a ship whose white captain claimed to be headed for Boston. Instead the captain turned him in; such was the danger in trusting new informants. A third man, George Snowden, joined Williams and Banks in the cell. Williams and Banks plotted to escape, but, as Williams later recalled, "We were afraid to let George know, for fear he would betray us." Williams did not explain why they did not trust Snowden, but having once been betrayed by fellow slaves, he perhaps read something in Snowden's countenance that he did not like. By contrast, Banks's experience in laying out, which would also indicate his local geographical knowledge and his obvious willingness to take risks, surely helped convince Williams of Banks's trustworthiness. The two men deceived Snowden by their escape and came to trust each other greatly during two months of lying low near Williams's home plantation, but there they were recaptured.

Escaping once again, on the run, they met a third fugitive, Kit Nichols, whom they likewise trusted and who joined them. The three took a different path now, using commercial links to the North to effect their escape from slavery itself, not only the slave trader. They headed for Warrenton, found the railroad line, and "footed it" to Alexandria. Just before entering Washington, D.C., they asserted a different geopolitical posture. Rather than sneaking like fugitives, they strutted into the bourgeois town, all three smoking cigars while Williams "walked on, swinging a little cane." This behavior, they must have known, would situate them in locals' minds not as fugitives from the plantation districts but as urbane free blacks or hirelings. Geopolitical literacy meant not only getting to the city but acting as if one belonged there. Back in rural Maryland, they again followed the rails to Baltimore, spotted the train bound for Philadelphia, and followed those tracks to freedom. Commerce, as these men understood, knew no bounds.[45]

Williams, Banks, and Nichols, like the *Creole* conspirators, seized on larger geopolitical and navigational information and bore out what slaveholders and slave traders already knew: that enslaved people, especially those close to the trade, knew far more than traders wished or could control. Commercial traders were especially aware of their enslaved servants' access to the networks of trade. The slave trader James Mitchell indicated his own knowledge of networks of information operating within the commercial slave jails. When he sent an escapee to fellow trader Richard H. Dickinson to hold for resale, he warned Dickinson to "be perticular when you get him in possession." Confine him "at once," Mitchell instructed, "and suffer no servants to see him while in your possession." His precaution was warranted. Charles Gilbert, a man incarcerated for sale by Benjamin Davis, learned of a local Underground Railroad ship captain while in the trader's possession.[46]

African Americans whose work in slavery involved navigation or proximity to commercial activity were in especially good positions to tap networks of knowledge and aid in order to escape. Just as watermen carried news between otherwise isolated populations, slave traders' trustees could be conduits between the incarcerated and the outside world.[47] They could also use that access to information for themselves. According to the Underground Railroad agent William Still, a man named Robert M'Coy had been held by the Norfolk trader and jailer William W. Hall and therefore had "possessed vary favorable opportunities for varied observation and experience relative to the trader's nefarious business." M'Coy used that access and his skills to tap into the Underground Railroad network, and when Hall threatened to sell him away, M'Coy seized on all his geographic knowledge and fled, probably by ship, to Philadelphia, where he contacted Still. M'Coy's wife, evidently privy to the same information and network of helpers, soon followed.[48]

Traders, however, commanded their own network of information, which they used to counter the actions of people like the M'Coys. In 1848, after a barber owned by Robert Lumpkin escaped, the Lynchburg trader Seth Woodruff wrote to the trader R. H. Dickinson of Richmond with news that the man had been seen cutting hair in Rochester, New York. Woodruff had his own issue to press, however. "I have a letter in my possession from my Boy" Creed, he complained, "which was written from New York." Creed had apparently made it down the James from Lynchburg to Norfolk, a distance of about 250 miles, and there had hopped aboard a northbound steamer. He had written to flaunt his escape, telling Woodruff that he was now headed for Boston. Whether this was Creed's intended destination or not, he surely meant to raise the ire of Woodruff by invoking the seat of abolition. He knew the trader's geopolitical outlook. For his part, Woodruff was furious and wanted Dickinson's help in finding out which ship captain had run slavery's blockade on African American egress.[49]

While we cheer the actions of people such as Creed or Anthony Burns, we must dampen that enthusiasm with the understanding of why those actions merit our attention. Traders operating the domestic U.S. slave trade generally succeeded in controlling the networks of commerce by which they moved those many thousands to the cotton kingdom. They generally remained safe in their assumptions that no one would challenge the legitimacy of their trade or turn the tables against them. In fact, the captain of the *Creole* felt confident enough in his trade that he had his wife, daughter, and a niece on board. Surely he would not knowingly have risked their lives. Surely he did not think his ship could be turned into a powder keg. Moreover, slaveholders generally succeeded in imposing their geopolitics on the enslaved by means of the violence of separation, the imposition of geographic ignorance, overt control over lines of communication, and overt political power, all serious obstacles to the kind of action the conspirators took aboard the *Creole*. Long-distance interstate slave traders and the slaveholders who sold to them succeeded in alienating African Americans from their known networks of information and support. Removal from neighborhoods and from webs of kin, friends, and masters repeatedly reenacted and reinforced the process of enslavement.

Forced alienation threw most people transported by traders into a geographic vacuum from which they could only emerge after establishing new networks in their new locales. Many forced migrants thus suffered "social death," losing all contact with those who peopled their former lives. Most enslaved African Americans were prevented from gaining knowledge of the geography beyond their own network of neighborhoods. Many people wanting to leave did not know where to go. Geopolitical fluency was a rare achievement indeed. As the ex-slave Leonard Black put it with considerable understatement, "Slavery is as ill adapted for obtaining this kind of knowledge as all other kinds."[50]

Slaveholders worked to control the passage of geopolitical information, as would-be fugitives understood painfully well. Written passes and white patrols had long served as a check on unauthorized movement by African Americans to pass information,[51] but modern means of communication often stood as emblematic of masters' power to conquer space. The fraternity of slave traders was sustained in part by the United States mail service, as the letters from Woodruff and others testify. Masters had other means as well. The fugitive Isaac Williams remembered how one master had told his slaves that "times were so straight with the telegraph and railway" that escape was nearly impossible.[52] William Grose gave an equally vivid image of lines of communication interfering with his escape, bearing directly on his state of mind. He drew an explicit contrast between the modern speed of telegraphed information and the languid pace of his own more conventional modes of travel: "At one time I was on a canal-boat — it did not seem to go fast enough for me, and I felt very much cast down about it." Plodding along on foot, he felt "a heavy load"; he "would look up at the telegraph wire, and dread that the news was going on ahead" of him. Finally, he recalled, he "came to a place where the telegraph wire was broken, and I felt as if the heavy load was rolled off me."[53] Although he followed the paths of modern commerce and communication in his escape from slavery, he saw them ultimately as oppressive, not liberating. The technology at masters' disposal could straighten out time itself.[54]

Finally, slaveholders had a lock on state power, which, especially after passage of the Fugitive Slave Act of 1850, included the power of the federal government. As Frederick Douglass put it in his fictional account of the *Creole* revolt, the "swagger" and "whip" went a long way toward intimidating enslaved men in places "where you have the sympathy of the [white] community, and the whole physical force of the government, State and national, at your command; and where, if a negro shall lift his hand against a white man, the white community, with one accord, are ready to unite in shooting him down. . . . It is one thing to manage a company of slaves on a Virginia plantation, and quite another thing to quell an insurrection on the lonely billows of the Atlantic, where every breeze speaks of courage and liberty." As Douglass's fictionalized Madison Washington declared, "You cannot write the bloody laws of slavery on those restless billows. The ocean, if not the land, is free." Virginia's landscape was inscribed within the national legal and political geography; it stood in stark contrast to Douglass's idealized freedom of the open sea, where a masculine natural law ruled.[55] The sea, of course, was neither free nor immune to the laws of nations. The African Americans aboard the *Creole* knew this well. It was only by passing into territory ruled by British colonial law that they had found freedom.[56]

The ongoing process of forced migration simultaneously created a need for and, to a certain degree, allowed for geopolitical literacy. It is impossible to comprehend slavery without an acknowledgment of these two entangled networks: the grapevine and the slave market. Many studies of slavery invoke a bounded sense of place by focusing on social relations within the confines of the plantations. We cannot understand those places, however, without seeing the networks that connected them to each other and to worlds beyond and the forces that carried people and information across those networks. Social relations were not played out on a static field. Slavery was always in motion. This was ensured by the chattel principle: slaves as moveable personal property. Enslaved people moved around, both by force and by will. They carried information, rumors, knowledge about the places they had been to and seen or about those they had heard about from others. Some called that covert network of information the "grapevine." Others compared it to that most modern of antebellum inventions, the telegraph. Like the telegraph, it could speed information across spaces even when individuals carrying the information did not travel the entire distance. And like a grapevine, it could reach just about anywhere, even — and perhaps especially — inside the most guarded nooks and crannies of the slave market.

The grapevine was such that news of the Haitian Revolution and of ships such as the *Formosa* reached enslaved people as far north as the Chesapeake.

The grapevine that informants articulated, reshaped, and relied on helped them see worlds far beyond local plantation neighborhoods. Individual migrations tied together the territories they crossed, from the Chesapeake to the Mississippi Delta to the Caribbean. That network of knowledge and information, spun out across the avenues of slaveholders' commerce, helped shape enslaved African Americans' consciousness and action.

The *Creole* revolt also suggests that geographic literacy — in the form of the grapevine woven across the slave market — helped shape African Americans' historical consciousness. Tamara Giles-Vernick argues that Banda people in Central Africa today think of history spatially rather than temporally, as a series of "past places" linked mnemonically to each other and to the present by roads and other physical landmarks. She concludes that during the long processes of enslavement and colonial rule, Banda people's "continued movement over roads provided them with a more spatial means of expressing and experiencing their connections to past spaces, knowledge, and peoples."[57] Such was the case, too, in the era of the American slave market revolution. Forced migration ironically forced African Americans take a broader view of the social landscape than more settled people would have needed to. Family histories constituted maps of the forced migration, as people kept track of kin who had been sold away by naming their children after them. Their autobiographies represent an inversion or even, as Lisa Brawley argues, a perversion of bourgeois American travel literature, their life histories in slavery mapping the venues and avenues of force in the land of the free.[58]

For some, even half a century after emancipation, slavery was less a past era than a past place. The places were still there, connected to their past by the immediacy of contemporary landmarks representing the same racist power. African Americans interviewed in the twentieth century used landmarks such as slave auction blocks and Confederate statues (the latter often having replaced the former on the same sites) to anchor their memories of events and the moral implications of their stories. Virginia Hayes Shepherd recalled in 1937 that Norfolk's auction block "was right down there between the Portsmouth Ferry and the Monument." This Confederate obelisk (erected in 1898), she asserted, "stands for all the devilment and cruelty that was done to the Negro during the days of slavery." Charles Grandy held a similar view of that same monument, informed by experiences that began on that site and continued throughout his life. At the age of two months, he said, he was "brung to Norfolk an' sol' down Mississippi wid my mother." In 1937, he lectured his interviewers, "Know dat statue over yonder by Portsmouth Ferry[?] De man on top dar pointin' south. Know what it mean? 'Carry de nigger down South ef you wanna rule him.' "[59] Here the mnemonic patterns of oral culture were overlaid with the physical experience of dislocation, creating a vision of power played out across southern space. Shepherd and Grandy mnemonically conflated these physical landmarks—the auction block and the monument that replaced it—and used them to read the racist landscape through which they had moved. Theirs was a particularly apt analysis of Norfolk's role in the slave trade from the Chesapeake to New Orleans, the route from which the *Creole* insurgents departed so deftly and so violently.

Slavery was always in motion. Slaves were always in motion. The slave market and the grapevine provided the conduits across which enslaved and enslaver played out many of their conflicts. Geopolitical literacy held consequences for both. The *Creole* revolt lived in the memories of slave traders and surely of African Americans as well. Shippers in the coastal trade took heed of what geopolitical knowledge they thought their prisoners might possess and the lengths to which African Americans might go in order to use that information. William Grose described only briefly his forced journey in 1849 or 1850 from the Chesapeake to New Orleans, but he gave one especially prescient detail: "There were about seventy of us, men, women, and children shipped to New Orleans. Nothing especial occurred except on one occasion, when, after some thick weather, the ship came near an English island: the captain then hurried us all below and closed the hatches. After passing the island, we had liberty to come up again."[60]

Only a recognition of African Americans' geographic literacy and the historical memory of the *Creole* and other like incidents could have warranted such action. That same recognition of the grapevine and of the slave market must inform our own historical work in reinterpreting slavery. We need to see the dynamic, even chaotic system of forced migration that African Americans understood slavery to be, as well as the complex ways enslaved people worked to read their geopolitical landscape and to write their lives on it.[61]

Notes

My sincere thanks to Edward Baptist and Walter Johnson for their challenging comments on drafts of this essay and to others who responded to versions that I presented in the following venues: a Mellon Fellow writing workshop, Duke University, Durham, North Carolina, October 2003; the annual meeting of the Organization of American Historians, Washington, D.C., April 2002; the Seventh Annual University of Houston Black History Workshop, Houston, Texas, March 2003; and the annual meeting of the Southern Historical Association, Houston, Texas, November 2003. Thanks, too, to Edward Ayers, who read this essay in its embryonic form as a rump (and, on his advice, deleted) chapter of my 2000 dissertation.

1. Nineteen men named as insurgents were detained briefly in Nassau before being

released by the court; several others were variously named by witnesses as participants in the revolt but were not detained with the nineteen. Five slaves returned to the United States aboard the ship. For the basic narrative, see Howard Jones, "The Peculiar Institution and National Honor: The Case of the *Creole* Slave Revolt," *Civil War History* 21 (March 1975): 28–33; Edward D. Jervey and C. Harold Huber, "The *Creole* Affair," *Journal of Negro History* 65 (Summer 1980): 196–211. Accounts of the *Creole* crew members are published in Sen. Docs. no. 51, 27th Cong., 2nd sess., 1842, vol. 2, pp. 1–46. Lawsuits emerging from the insurance claims made on the *Creole* slaves are documented in Louisiana Commercial Court (Orleans Parish), "Suits relating to the slave mutiny aboard the *Creole, 1841*," Docket Nos. 4408, 4409, 4410, 4411, 4413, 4414, 4419, microfilm, New Orleans City Archives, New Orleans Public Library. For the terms and justification for the negotiated British settlement, see Sen. Docs. no. 103, 34th Cong., 1st sess., 1855, vol. 15, pp. 52, 241–245. For a critical account of the contemporary public rhetoric about the events, see Maggie Sale, *The Slumbering Volcano: American Slave Ship Revolts and the Production of Rebellious Masculinity* (Durham: Duke University Press, 1997), 122–129, 130–132, 141. For similarities and differences between the *Creole* and *Amistad* incidents, see Jones, "Peculiar Institution and National Honor," 34–35, and Sale, *Slumbering Volcano*, 120–121, 144. See also George Hendrick and Willene Hendrick, *The* Creole *Mutiny: A Tale of Revolt Aboard a Slave Ship* (Chicago: Ivan R. Dee, 2003); Alice Lee Anderson, "The *Creole* Affair: Climax of the British-American Fugitive Slave Controversy, 1831–1842," M.A. thesis, Old Dominion University, 1970; Walter Johnson, *Soul by Soul: Life Inside the Antebellum Slave Market* (Cambridge: Harvard University Press, 1999), 72–76.

2. J. W. C. Pennington said it best: "The being of slavery, its soul and body, lives and moves in the chattel principle, the property principle, the bill of sale principle; the cartwhip, starvation, and nakedness, are its inevitable consequences to a greater or less extent, warring with the dispositions of men." Pennington, *The Fugitive Blacksmith; or Events in the History of James W. C. Pennington, Pastor of a Presbyterian Church, New York, Formerly a Slave in the State of Maryland, United States,* 2nd ed. (London: Charles Gilpin, 1849), iv–v. Electronic edition in Documenting the American South, University of North Carolina at Chapel Hill Libraries, //docsouth.unc.edu/neh/penning49/penning49.html (accessed 3 June 2002). On African American autobiographical interpretations of the slave market, see Phillip Troutman, *Sentiment in the Market Revolution* (University of Florida Press, forthcoming).

3. Particularly deficient in this regard is Eugene D. Genovese, *Roll, Jordan, Roll: The World the Slaves Made* (1972; reprint, New York: Vintage Books, 1976); the book's treatment of the domestic slave market and forced migration is limited to roughly a dozen pages: 125, 332, 372, 416–417, 419, 452–453, 471, 485, 625. The quantitative work demonstrating the pervasiveness of slave sale and family separation has generally not been incorporated into the broader historiography of life under slavery. (But see, e.g., James Oakes, *Slavery and Freedom: An Interpretation of the Old South* [New York: Vintage, 1991], 99–101.) For that quantitative work, see Herbert Gutman and Richard Sutch, "The Slave Family: Protected Agent of Capitalist Masters or Victim of the Slave Trade?" in Paul A. David et al., *Reckoning with Slavery: A Critical Study in the Quantitative History of American Negro Slavery* (New York: Oxford University Press, 1976), 94–

133; Michael Tadman, *Speculators and Slaves: Masters, Traders, and Slaves in the Old South* (Madison: University of Wisconsin Press, 1989); Richard Holcombe Kilbourne Jr., *Debt, Investment, Slaves: Credit Relations in East Feliciana Parish, Louisiana, 1825–1885* (Tuscaloosa: University of Alabama Press, 1995), 49–50; Thomas Russell, "South Carolina's Largest Slave Auctioneering Firm," *Chicago-Kent Law Review* 68 (1993): 1161–1209; Thomas D. Russell, "Sale Day in Antebellum South Carolina: Slavery, Law, Economy, and Court-Supervised Sales," Ph.D. diss., Stanford University, 1993; Donald Sweig, "Reassessing the Human Dimension of the Interstate Slave Trade," *Prologue: The Journal of the National Archives* 12 (Spring 1980): 5–21.

4. Allan Kulikoff, *Tobacco and Slaves: The Development of Southern Cultures in the Chesapeake, 1680–1800* (Chapel Hill: University of North Carolina Press, 1986), 141–148, 342, 362; Philip D. Morgan, "Slave Life in Piedmont Virginia," in *Colonial Chesapeake Society*, ed. Lois Green Carr, Philip D. Morgan, and Jean B. Russo (Chapel Hill: University of North Carolina Press, 1998); Kulikoff, "Uprooted Peoples: Black Migrants in the Age of the American Revolution, 1790–1820," in *Slavery and Freedom in the Age of the American Revolution*, ed. Ira Berlin and Benjamin Hoffman; Adam Rothman, "The Expansion of Slavery in the Deep South, 1790–1820," Ph.D. diss., Columbia University, 2000; Edward E. Baptist, *Creating an Old South: Middle Florida's Plantation Frontier Before the Civil War* (Chapel Hill: University of North Carolina Press, 2002); Tadman, *Speculators and Slaves*, ch. 2; Jonathan Pritchett, "Quantitative Estimates of the United States Interregional Slave Trade, 1820–1860," paper presented to the Social Science History Association Annual Meeting, Chicago, Illinois, 21 November 1998; Robert H. Gudmestad, *A Troublesome Commerce: The Transformation of the Interstate Slave Trade* (Baton Rouge: Louisiana State University Press, 2003). Baptist is keen to point out that, contrary to Tadman's assumptions, migrating planters (like traders) skewed age and sex ratios of migrant populations, selecting for young slaves, especially men. They also separated family ties whenever they moved, sold, or bought, slaves.

5. On the slave market's articulation in the broader market revolution, see Troutman, *Sentiment in the Slave Market Revolution*. Harry L. Watson is among the few historians to recognize the slave market's role in the U.S. market revolution. See Watson, "Slavery and Development in a Dual Economy: The South and the Market Revolution," in *The Market Revolution in America: Social, Political, and Religious Expressions, 1800–1880*, ed. Melvin Stokes and Stephen Conway (Charlottesville: University of Virginia Press, 1996), 43–73. By contrast, see Douglas R. Egerton, "Markets Without a Revolution: Southern Planters and Capitalism," *Journal of the Early Republic* 16 (Summer 1996): 207–221. Walter Johnson dissolves historians' traditional separation of culture from the market in regard to slavery; see *Soul by Soul*, ch. 3. On the general operation of the domestic U.S. slave market in the nineteenth century, see Frederic Bancroft, *Slave Trading in the Old South* (1931; reprint, Columbia: University of South Carolina Press, 1996); Tadman, *Speculators and Slaves*; and Steven H. Deyle, "The Domestic Slave Trade in America," Ph.D. diss., Columbia University, 1995.

6. Herbert G. Gutman, *The Black Family in Slavery and Freedom, 1750–1925* (New York: Pantheon, 1976), esp. chs. 3 and 4, and on cycles of family consolidation and separation, 129–132, 151–154; Deborah Gray White, *Ar'n't I a Woman? Female Slaves in the Plantation South* (New York: Norton, 1985); Brenda E. Stevenson, *Life in Black*

and White: Family and Community in the Slave South (New York: Oxford University Press, 1996); Ann Patton Malone, *Sweet Chariot: Slave Family and Household Structure in Nineteenth-Century Louisiana* (Chapel Hill: University of North Carolina Press, 1992); Cheryl Ann Cody, "Naming, Kinship, and Estate Dispersal: Notes on Slave Family Life on a South Carolina Plantation, 1786 to 1833," *William and Mary Quarterly* 39 (Jan. 1982): 192–211; Cody, "Sale and Separation: Four Crises for Enslaved Women on the Ball Plantations, 1764–1854," in *Working Toward Freedom: Slave Society and Domestic Economy in the American South*, ed. Larry E. Hudson Jr. (Rochester: University of Rochester Press, 1994), 119–142. Edward Baptist reinterprets slavery and antebellum southern society in light of forced migration and the plantation frontier: Baptist, *Creating an Old South*, esp. chs. 3 and 7. Walter Johnson uses the narrow aperture of the New Orleans slave pens as a lens through which to refocus our attention on the implications that speculation (traders', buyers', slaves') holds for the meaning of chattel slavery broadly: Johnson, *Soul by Soul*.

7. Julius Scott, "The Common Wind: Currents of Afro-American Communication in the Era of the Haitian Revolution," Ph.D. diss., Duke University, 1986; Scott, "Afro-American Sailors and the International Communication Network: The Case of Newport Bowers," in *Jack Tar in History: Essays in the History of Maritime Life and Labour*, ed. Colin Howell and Richard Twomey (Fredericton, N.B.: Acadiensis Press, 1991); W. Jeffrey Bolster, *Black Jacks: African American Seamen in the Age of Sail* (Cambridge: Harvard University Press, 1997). For an interesting parallel among free white Francophones in the Revolutionary-era Atlantic, see R. Darrell Meadows, "Engineering Exile: Social Networks and the French Atlantic Community, 1789–1809," *French Historical Studies* 23:1 (2000): 67–102.

8. Moses Grandy, *Narrative of the Life of Moses Grandy, Late a Slave in the United States of America* (London: C. Gilpin, 1843), 13, 14. Electronic edition in Documenting the American South, //docsouth.unc.edu/grandy/menu.html (accessed 21 July 2002).

9. White, *Ar'n't I A Woman?*, 131–132; Leni Ashmore Sorensen, " 'So that I get her again': African American Slave Women Runaways in Selected Richmond, Virginia Newspapers, 1830–1860, and the Richmond, Virginia Police Guard Daybook, 1834–1843," M.A. thesis, College of William and Mary, 1997. David S. Cecelski, *The Waterman's Song: Slavery and Freedom in Maritime North Carolina* (Chapel Hill: University of North Carolina Press, 2001) esp. 264 n73, 267n73, and for more on Moses Grandy in the North Carolina and Virginia maritime context, see 27–56; Thomas C. Buchanan, "The Slave Mississippi: African American Steamboat Workers, Networks of Resistance, and the Commercial World of the Western Rivers, 1811–1880," Ph.D. diss., Carnegie Mellon University, 1998; Douglas R. Egerton, *Gabriel's Rebellion: The Virginia Slave Conspiracies of 1800–1802* (Chapel Hill: University of North Carolina Press, 1993), 119–123; Bruce G. Terrell, "The James River Bateau: Nautical Commerce in Piedmont Virginia," *Virginia Cavalcade* 38:4 (1989): 180–191. Fanny Kimball remarked on slaves' knowledge of the sea islands waterways; see Jacqueline A. Bindman, " 'The Outer Bounds of Civilized Creation': Power, Space, and Meaning on an Antebellum Sea Island," paper presented to Southern Historical Association Annual Meeting, Little Rock, AR, 1 Nov. 1996. On African Americans as seamen more generally, see also Martha S. Putney, *Black*

Sailors: Afro-American Merchant Seamen and Whalemen Prior to the Civil War (New York: Greenwood Press, 1987); and James Barker Farr, *Black Odyssey: The Seafaring Traditions of Afro-Americans* (New York: Peter Lang, 1989).

10. Booker T. Washington, *Up from Slavery* (1901; reprinted in Documenting the American South, http://metalab.unc.edu/docsouth/, 1997), 8l; J. W. C. Pennington, *A Narrative of Events of the Life of J. H. Banks, an Escaped Slave, from the Cotton State of Alabama, in America* (Liverpool, 1861), quoted in *Puttin' On Ole Massa: The Slave Narratives of Henry Bibb, William Wells Brown, and Solomon Northup,* ed. Gilbert Osofsky (New York: Harper and Row, 1969), 26; W. W. Gilmer, "Management of Servants," *Southern Planter* 12 (April 1852): 106–107, quoted in James O. Breeden, *Advice Among Masters: The Ideal in Slave Management in the Old South* (Westport, Conn.: Greenwood Press, 1980), 44.

11. Ong's emphasis is on the gulf between literate cultures and "primary oral cultures"—those with no knowledge of literacy. But Jacqueline Jones Royster defines "literacy" far more broadly than does Ong to include the capacities of orality as well: "the ability to gain access to information and to use this information variously to articulate lives and experiences and also to identify, think through, refine, and solve problems, sometimes complex problems, over time." Walter J. Ong, *Orality and Literacy: The Technologizing of the Word* (New York: Methuen, 1982), 36–57; Ong, "Writing Is a Technology That Restructures Thought," in *Literacy: A Critical Sourcebook,* ed. Ellen Cushman et al. (New York: Bedford/St. Martin's, 2001), ch. 1; Royster, *Traces of a Stream: Literacy and Social Change Among African American Women* (Pittsburgh: University of Pittsburgh Press, xxxx), 45.

12. Walter Ong, Jack Goody, and others hold oral cultures to be more restricted than literate ones in the cognitive capacity they offer for abstract thought, formal logic, and critical analysis and that acquiring literacy (as a society or as an individual) fundamentally changes cognition. Goody has argued more recently that in semiliterate societies there is "feedback" between the literate and the oral "registers" of communication, so that nonliterate people with some proximity to literacy might adopt aspects of literate modes of thought even when they do not learn to read and write. Jack Goody, *The Interface Between the Written and the Oral* (New York: Cambridge University Press, 1987), 262–264, 266–272, 274–289. John Halverson provides a critical overview of this literature in "Goody and the Implosion of the Literacy Thesis," *Man* 27 (June 1992): 301–317. Other specific challenges to Goody and Ong include Peter Wogan, "Perceptions of European Literacy in Early Contact Situations," *Ethnohistory* 41 (Summer 1994): 407–429; D. H. Green, "Orality and Reading: The State of Research in Medieval Studies," *Speculum* 65 (April 1990): 267–280; Karen Schousboe and Mogens Trolle Larsen, eds., *Literacy and Society* (Copenhagen: Center for Research in the Humanities, Copenhagen University, printed by Akademisk Forlag, 1989); Elizabeth McHenry and Shirley Brice Heath, "The Literate and the Literary: African Americans as Writers and Readers—1830–1940," in *Literacy: A Critical Sourcebook,* ed. Ellen Cushman et al. (New York: Bedford/St. Martin's, 2001), ch. 15; Shirley Brice Heath, "Protean Shapes in Literacy Events: Ever-Shifting Oral and Literate Traditions," in *Literacy: A Critical Sourcebook,* ed. Ellen Cushman et al. (New York: Bedford/St. Martin's, 2001), ch. 26. But for a

reiteration of the importance of distinctions between orality and literacy, see Jeff Guy, "Making Words Visible: Aspects of Orality, Literacy, Illiteracy, and History in Southern Africa," *South African Historical Journal* 31 (November 1994): 3–27.

13. Jennifer Monaghan, "Reading for the Enslaved, Writing for the Free," *Proceedings of the American Antiquarian Society* 108 (1998): 309–341; James Bruce Fort, "The Politics and Culture of Literacy in Georgia, 1800–1920," Ph.D. diss., University of Virginia, 1999.

14. Johnson, *Soul by Soul*, 72–76.

15. Kulikoff, *Tobacco and Slaves,* 320–321, 339–340, 359–364; Scott, "Afro-American Sailors" and "Common Wind"; Paul Gilroy, *The Black Atlantic: Modernity and Double Consciousness* (Cambridge: Harvard University Press, 1993), 12–13, and on Martin Delaney, 17–29. Of course, notions of race differed across the diaspora, and they changed as people moved among different diasporic locations; Gilroy emphasizes this cosmopolitan nature of Black Atlantic consciousness. Similarly, Africans and African Americans also contributed to a class-based political consciousness among sailors, who were a "motley" crew of diverse ethnic, racial, and national origins. See Peter Linebaugh and Marcus Rediker, *The Many-Headed Hydra: Sailors, Slaves, Commoners, and the Hidden History of the Revolutionary Atlantic* (Boston: Beacon Press, 2000), 212–213, 165–167; on Robert Wedderburn as a pan-Atlantic (not pan-African) revolutionary, see ch. 9. See also Sidney W. Mintz and Richard Price, *The Birth of African-American Culture: An Anthropological Perspective* (1976; reprint, Boston: Beacon Press, 1992); Benedict Anderson, *Imagined Communities: Reflections on the Origin and Spread of Nationalities* (London: Verso, 1983).

16. Johnson borrows the notion of "infrapolitics" from James C. Scott and from Robin D. G. Kelley, using it to emphasize both how African Americans' individual conflicts with masters could help create a common black identity and how that common identity could be undermined by distrust among African Americans. By contrast, Patricia Turner focuses on rumors (about conspiratorial white malevolence toward black people) that went relatively unchallenged among many Africans and African Americans. She follows Gordon W. Allport and Leo Postman in defining rumor as "a specific proposition for belief, passed along from person to person, usually by word of mouth, without secure standards of evidence being present." Interestingly, a rumor about whites' cannibalism helped spur the Amistad Africans to action. Johnson, *Soul by Soul*, 49, 72–76, 234 n60; Turner, *I Heard It Through the Grapevine: Rumor in African-American Culture* (Berkeley: University of California Press, 1993), 4 (quoting Allport and Postman), 14.

17. James Sidbury, "Saint Domingue in Virginia: Ideology, Local Meanings, and Resistance to Slavery, 1790–1800," *Journal of Southern History* 63:3 (1997): 531–552; Sidbury, *Ploughshares into Swords: Race, Rebellion, and Identity in Gabriel's Virginia, 1730–1810* (New York: Cambridge University Press, 1997), 39–48, 97; Egerton, *Gabriel's Rebellion,* 48–49; Scott, "Afro-American Sailors," 44; Scott, "Common Wind," 276, 283–284, 291, 308. Haiti remained in African American consciousness, as evidenced by (and surely aided by) the emigration of about two thousand black settlers from the United States to Haiti in the 1850s and 1860s. Chris Dixon, *African America and Haiti: Emigration and Black Nationalism in the Nineteenth Century* (Westport: Green-

wood Press, 2000); Alfred N. Hunt, *Haiti's Influence on Antebellum America: Slumbering Volcano in the Caribbean* (Baton Rouge: Louisiana State University Press, 1988).

18. Other sources refer to the *Formosa*, but the name *Hermosa* is used in Sen. Docs. no. 103, 34th Cong., 1st sess., 1855, vol. 15, and Sen. Docs. no. 51, 27th Cong., 2nd sess., 1842, vol. 2. See Jones, "Peculiar Institution and National Honor," 35; Bancroft, *Slave Trading in the Old South,* 41; Wendell H. Stephenson, *Isaac Franklin: Slave Trader and Planter of the Old South* (Baton Rouge: Louisiana State University Press, 1938), 40–41n, 52n (quoting *Niles' Weekly Register* 37 [1829–1830]), 328; John R. Spears, *The American Slave-Trade: An Account of Its Origin, Growth, and Suppression* (Williamstown, Mass.: Corner House, 1978), 176–179. George Anderson, attorney general for the Bahamas, mentioned the *Comet* and the *Enterprise* by name in his testimony; he knew the *Formosa* case by its circumstances, and he mentioned yet another American ship, the *Encomium,* whose enslaved passengers went free in Nassau sometime in the 1830s. *Thomas McCargo v. The New Orleans Insurance Company, In the Commercial Court of New Orleans,* #4409 (1841), microfilm, printed testimony of George Campbell Anderson, 78–79.

19. It may be significant that they asked to go to a British island and not to Haiti. Perhaps the screen of proslavery cant about the barbarity of freedom in Haiti had filtered out any reliable information. Knowledge about Britain's colonial emancipation policy was far more recent and perhaps more relevant information in 1841.

20. Sen. Docs. no. 51, 27th Cong., 2nd sess., 1842, vol. 2, p. 40; Sen. Docs. no. 103, 34th Cong., 1st sess., 1855, vol. 15, pp. 52, 57, 228–240.

21. Richmond City Deed Book 53, p. 155, microfilm, Library of Virginia.

22. Herbert Freudenberger and Jonathan Pritchett found that slaves shipped by traders from Virginia to New Orleans in 1830 spent between two and four months confined by traders between date of purchase and resale. A sample of ten slaves from Richmond spent an average of 28 days waiting to board, 21 days en route, and 35 days in New Orleans (84 days total). A sample of seventy-seven slaves from Norfolk spent an average of 55 days waiting to board, 19 days en route, and 44 days in New Orleans awaiting sale (118 days total). As in the *Creole* case, ships might originate in Richmond and take on more enslaved passengers in Norfolk. Herbert Freudenberger and Jonathan B. Pritchett, "The Domestic United States Slave Trade: New Evidence," *Journal of Interdisciplinary Studies* 21 (Winter 1991): 467–470; 471, table 5.

23. My discussion here and below of Burns's time in Lumpkin's jail necessarily relies on Charles Stevens, *Anthony Burns: A History* (Boston: John P. Jewett, 1856), 187–194; electronic edition in Documenting the American South, //docsouth.unc.edu/stevens/stevens.html (accessed 21 June 2002). My understanding of the layout of Lumpkin's jail compound relies on Bancroft, *Slave Trading in the Old South,* 102–103, and especially Charles H. Corey, *A History of the Richmond Theological Seminary,* 42–50, 54–58, 69–84. For the most comprehensive account and context of the entire Burns affair, see Albert J. Von Frank, *The Trials of Anthony Burns: Freedom and Slavery in Emerson's Boston* (Cambridge: Harvard University Press, 1998); on Stevens, see 302.

24. Harriet Jacobs's autobiography resonates strongly with the Burns biography. Jacobs deftly exploited the double meaning of "loophole" as a garret hiding place (unlike

Burns's garret, a holding place) and as a small portal through which to gain access to the outside world. The hole she drilled gave her limited but crucial knowledge of goings-on outside her garret, much as it had for Burns. See Harriet A. Jacobs, *Incidents in the Life of a Slave Girl; Written by Herself* (1861, orig. edited by L. Maria Child, reprint edited by Jean Fagan Yellin [Cambridge: Harvard University Press, 1987]), 115–116; for Yellin's etymological amplification, see 277n. My thanks to Eric Lott for pointing to the importance of Jacobs's "loophole."

25. Burns to Dana, 25 August 1854, Massachusetts Historical Society, reprinted in Von Frank, *Trials of Anthony Burns*, 287–288.

26. I examine Lumpkin's domestic relations more closely in *Sentiment in the Slave Market Revolution*. See Richmond City, Hustings Court, Will Book 24, pp. 419–422 (my thanks to Josh Rothman for providing me with a copy). The birth dates of the children are estimated from U.S. Bureau of the Census, 1840 manuscript population schedule for Henrico Co., VA, p. 149, and from Richmond City, Personal Property Tax books, 1841–1866.

27. Stevens, *Anthony Burns*, 192–193.

28. Johnson, *Soul by Soul*, 241 n73.

29. Ronald Seagrave, telephone conversations with author, Sergeant Kirkland's Museum and Historical Society, Fredericksburg, Virginia, June 2000.

30. *McCargo v. New Orleans Insurance Company*, #4409, printed testimony of William Hamilton, John Pinder, William Dalzell, John Burnside, John Grant Anderson, James Mends, John Warren Glubb, Lionel Fitzgerald, William Murray, Stephen Hill, Henry Cobbe, and George Campbell Anderson, 13, 20, 28, 35, 41–42, 47, 51, 55, 58, 62–63, 68, 78–79.

31. Johnson recognizes the likelihood of wider complicity in the conspiracy, but he does not discuss potential divisions among the African Americans on board; *Soul by Soul*, 76.

32. *McCargo v. New Orleans Insurance Company*, printed testimony of William H. Merritt, 11, 12; see printed testimony of J. D. McCargo [the slave trader plaintiff's nephew], 39.

33. Sen. Docs. no. 51, 27th Cong., 2nd sess., 1842, vol. 2, pp. 33, 40.

34. Frederick Douglass, *The Heroic Slave, in Autographs for Freedom*, ed. Julia Griffiths (Boston: J. P. Jewett, 1853), 174–239, electronic edition in Modern English Collection, University of Virginia Etext Center, //etext.lib.virginia.edu/toc/modeng/public/DouHero.html (accessed 3 June 2002). On Douglass's use of Madison Washington as American revolutionary, see Sale, *Slumbering Volcano*, ch. 5.

35. On Madison Washington, see Hendrick and Hendrick, Creole *Mutiny*. See also Ralph Randolph Gurley, "Sketch of the Life of the Rev. Lott Cary," in *Life of Jehudi Ashmun, Late Colonial Agent in Liberia. With An Appendix, Containing Extracts from his Journal and Other Writings; With a Brief Sketch of the Life of The Rev. Lott Cary* (Washington, DC: James C. Dunn, 1835), electronic edition in Documenting the American South, //docsouth.unc.edu/gurley/menu.html (accessed 3 June 2002); James Barnett Taylor, *Biography of Elder Lott Cary, Late Missionary to Africa. With an Appendix on the Subject of Colonization, by J. H. B. Latrobe* (Baltimore: Armstrong and Berry, 1837), electronic edition in Documenting the American South, //docsouth.unc.edu/neh/taylor/

taylor.html (accessed 3 June 2002). Note that the pan-Africanist "back to Africa" movement was generally a late nineteenth- and early twentieth-century phenomenon. Antebellum African Americans generally opposed the colonization movement, and those who went to Liberia found themselves poorly supported by their sponsors. Kwame Anthony Appiah, *In My Father's House: Africa in the Philosophy of Culture* (New York: Oxford University Press, 1992); Alison Goodyear Freehling, *Drift Toward Dissolution: The Virginia Slavery Debate of 1831–1832* (Baton Rouge: Louisiana State University Press, 1982), ch. 7; and *Dear Master: Letters of a Slave Family*, ed. Randall Miller (1978; reprint Athens: University of Georgia Press, 1990), pts. 1 and 3.

36. David Cecelski notes that in coastal North Carolina, ship captains often relied on pilot boats, many operated by African Americans, to guide them through the shoals; even the ability to read a printed coast pilot or chart was often not enough. Cecelski, *Waterman's Song*, 260–261, n1.

37. Sen. Docs. no. 51, 27th Cong., 2nd sess., 1842, vol. 2, pp. 24, 40.

38. Ibid., pp. 17, 21, 29, 23–34, 40–41.

39. Charles Ball, *Slavery in the United States: A Narrative of the Life and Adventures of Charles Ball, a Black Man, Who Lived Forty Years in Maryland, South Carolina and Georgia, as a Slave Under Various Masters* (New York: John S. Taylor, 1837), 48–49. Electronic edition in Documenting the American South, //docsouth.unc.edu/ballslavery/ball.html (accessed 21 June 2002).

40. *McCargo v. New Orleans Insurance Company*, printed testimony of Jacob Leidner, 1–2.

41. Roseanne M. Adderley, "The *Creole* Slave Ship (1841) as a Study of Social and Cultural Contact Within the Wider African Diaspora," paper presented at the Organization of American Historians Annual Meeting, Washington, D.C., April 2002. Perhaps maritime traditions of mutual aid also contributed to the Bahamian willingness to help these refugees. On African American maritime workers aiding fugitives in coastal North Carolina, see Cecelski, *Waterman's Song*, 141–142.

42. *McCargo v. New Orleans Insurance Company*, printed testimony of William Merritt, 10.

43. Merritt said that the locals "cursed" the five who stayed on board and that there were rumors of their attacking the ship; colonial officials said that there were no threats made and that they immediately halted the local boaters' effort to get the other five to come ashore. Ibid., printed testimony of William Merritt, 9–10, 13, 14, 20; printed testimony of William Hamilton, 9, 11.

44. Although Britain had paid compensation for slaves freed in Nassau before its 1833 Emancipation Act, it refused to pay for those marooned thereafter, and in 1841, the question still remained open on the *Formosa* case and would so until 1855. Jones, "Peculiar Institution and National Honor," 28, 35.

45. The Williams and Banks interviews are in Benjamin Drew, *A North-Side View of Slavery: The Refugee; or The Narratives of Fugitive Slaves in Canada Related by Themselves* (Boston: John P. Jewett, 1856), 60–61, 65–66, 75, electronic edition in Documenting the American South, //docsouth.unc.edu/neh/drew/drew.html (accessed 3 June 2002). Any other details about the escape that Williams, Banks, and Nichols (whom Drew also interviewed) may have revealed to Drew were elided in the published volume.

46. James Mitchell to [R. H.] Dickinson, 3 Aug. 1848, R. H. Dickinson & Brother correspondence, [1846–1865], Slavery in the United States Collection, American Antiquarian Society (hereafter AAS); William Still, *The Underground Railroad: A Record of Facts, Authentic Narratives, Letters, &c.*, 2d ed. (Philadelphia: People's Publishing, 1879), 235–236, 274.

47. Cecelski, *Waterman's Song,* 141–143; Johnson, *Soul by Soul,* 167– 170.

48. Still, *Underground Railroad,* 274–275.

49. Seth Woodruff to R. H. Dickinson, 15 Aug. 1848, AAS.

50. Since American forced migrants remained within their broader Afro-American context, the "social death" imposed by the American domestic slave trade was not as complete as that which Orlando Patterson identifies with certain forms of African slavery and with the transatlantic trade. Patterson, *Slavery and Social Death: A Comparative Study* (Cambridge: Harvard University Press, 1982). See Leonard Black, *The Life and Sufferings of Leonard Black* (New Bedford, MA: Benjamin Lindsey, 1847), 33–34, quoted among other examples of geographic ignorance in Gilbert Osofsky, ed., *Puttin' on Ole Massa: The Slave Narratives of Henry Bibb, William Wells Brown, and Solomon Northup* (New York: Harper and Row, 1969), 17.

51. Sally E. Hadden, *Slave Patrols: Law and Violence in Virginia and the Carolinas* (Cambridge: Harvard University Press, 2001).

52. The Williams interview is in Drew, *North-Side View of Slavery,* 58.

53. The Grose interview is in ibid., 85–86.

54. On masters' efforts to do just that, see Mark W. Smith, *Mastered by the Clock: Time, Slavery, and Freedom in the American South* (Chapel Hill: University of North Carolina Press, 1997).

55. Douglass, *Heroic Slave,* 227–228, 237.

56. This was certainly the perspective of British officials in Nassau, and it was represented in the attention given to their nomenclature during the insurance trials; the trader's witnesses referred to the African American people aboard the *Creole* as "slaves," and the British officials designated them "colored passengers." *McCargo v. the New Orleans Insurance Company,* printed testimony of William Merritt, 15; printed testimony of George Campbell Anderson, 78; printed testimony of John Pinder, 21–22; printed testimony of William Dalzell, 27, and esp. 29.

57. Giles-Vernick does not comment on whether this spatial way of thinking is peculiar to orality or whether it may have been influenced by Francophone literacy. Tamara Giles-Vernick, "Na Lege ti Gueriri (On the Road of History): Mapping Out the Past and Present in M'Bres Region, Central African Republic," *Ethnohistory* 43 (1996): 247–275, quotation at 257–258.

58. Gutman, *The Black Family in Slavery and Freedom*; Lisa C. Brawley, "Fugitive Nation: Slavery, Travel, and Technologies of American Identity, 1830–1860," Ph.D. diss., University of Chicago, 1995, introduction and ch. 4.

59. The Charles Grandy and Virginia Shepherd interviews are in *Weevils in the Wheat: Interviews with Virginia Ex-Slaves,* ed. Charles L. Perdue Jr., Thomas E. Barden, and Robert K. Phillips (Charlottesville: University Press of Virginia, 1992), 115, 257. On the monument's construction and for images of the site of the market, ferry, and monument,

see *Through the Years in Norfolk* (Norfolk: Norfolk Advertising Board, 1936 [1937]), 39, 72–73.

60. The Grose interview is in Drew, *North-Side View of Slavery,* 84.

61. Stephanie Camp's work is exemplary in this regard. See " 'I Could Not Stay There': Enslaved Women, Truancy, and the Geography of Everyday Forms of Resistance in the Antebellum Plantation South," *Slavery and Abolition* 23 (December 2002): 1–20; and Camp, "The Pleasures of Resistance: Enslaved Women and Body Politics in the Plantation South, 1830–1861," *Journal of Southern History* 68, no. 3 (August 2002): 533–572. See also John Michael Vlach, *Back of the Big House: The Architecture of Plantation Slavery* (Chapel Hill: University of North Carolina Press, 1993); Vlach, "Not Mansions . . . But Good Enough: Slave Quarters as Bi-Cultural Expression," with commentary by Brenda Stevenson, in *Black and White: Cultural Interaction in the Antebellum South,* ed. Ted Ownby (Jackson: University of Mississippi Press, 1993), 89–124.

10

The Fragmentation of Atlantic Slavery and the British Intercolonial Slave Trade

SEYMOUR DRESCHER

I

By the middle of the eighteenth century the expansion of the plantation complex in the Americas was firmly linked to transplanted Africans' labor. This system transcended the division of the Atlantic world into six "imperial" economies (British, Portuguese, French, Spanish, Dutch, and Danish). In one way or another, these contending polities attempted to benefit from the transatlantic traffic by taxation, subsidization, reexportation, or the creation of facilities for the convenience of foreign slavers. Even the exigencies of war allowed room for the system to function. Slaveholders in conquered islands were encouraged to continue business as usual, often under their own legal systems. Indeed, foreign conquest could mark defining moments in the expansions of Atlantic slavery. The British conquest of Havana during the Seven Years' War temporarily shattered the Spanish imperial Asiento system in Cuba. The labor of at least four thousand slaves, introduced during eleven months of occupation, set the stage for a new phase of plantation development in that island.[1] Until the 1770s, all the European imperial systems remained permeable by a ubiquitous system of commercial agriculture that drew on fresh supplies of enslaved Africans. As Joseph Inikori notes, the Atlantic in the seventeenth and eighteenth centuries was "a common market of sorts," and the slave trade of the early modern period was possibly the most "international" activity of the preindustrial era.[2] Before the beginning of America's struggle for independence in the 1770s there were only two major constraints on the expansion of transatlantic slavery: Unrestricted slavery could only be practiced by Europeans on non-Europeans in areas outside of northwestern metropolitan Europe "beyond the line," and Europeans themselves were unenslavable anywhere in regions they dominated on either side of the Atlantic.

The initial fissures in the Atlantic system, fostered by colonial revolutions, were significant but incomplete.[3] The first extended break in the uninterrupted flow of Africans to New World plantations followed the closure of colonial mainland ports to British slaves on the eve of the American Revolution. Britain's defeat divided the largest slave system in the New World but did not end the flow of Africans to either fragment. Although some historians regard the split as a boon to Anglo-American antislavery, easing the task of British abolition in particular, the inference is dubious. If the British Empire lost more than half of its plantations and their slaves in 1783, British abolitionism had also lost its strongest overseas political constituencies supporting curtailment of the Atlantic slave trade. Indeed, the loss of the thirteen mainland colonies enhanced the relative imperial value of the colonies that were most dependent on the indefinite importation of Africans for economic expansion. It is hardly coincidental that for at least two decades after Yorktown, postrevolutionary British governments placed a high priority on first securing and then expanding their West Indian plantation system. The West Indies became, as never before, not only the jewel in the imperial crown "but now virtually the crown itself."[4] The imperial Parliament simultaneously committed itself to a limited role in the internal affairs of the slave colonies. As late as the 1780s, occasional suggestions for transforming the labor system of the plantation complex received short shrift from all imperial authorities.

The conjunction of the French wars and the French Caribbean slave uprisings in the 1790s constituted a more direct challenge to the Atlantic slave system than the American Revolutionary War. Haitian independence in 1804 permanently eliminated the largest prerevolutionary destination for Africans in the Caribbean. Yet the great St. Domingue slave revolution of the 1790s encouraged compensatory expansions of plantation regimes throughout the Caribbean rim.[5] By the middle of the first decade of the nineteenth century the political configuration of the plantation complex had changed far more dramatically than during the decade after 1775. Planters in the United States had displaced their French Caribbean counterparts among the major New World importers of slaves. Spanish-ruled Cuba had become the fourth-largest recipient of slaves in the Atlantic plantation complex. Only the British and Brazilian slave systems remained unchanged in their dominant positions as importers of Africans. (See table 10.1.)

Thus as they began their final assault on the African slave trade in 1804, the British parliamentary abolitionists, dubbed "the Saints" by their opponents, were aware that slavery had lost none of its dynamic potential. Vast undeveloped lands in the Caribbean rim still beckoned metropolitan capital and African labor. British slavers, still the principal carriers of slaves from Africa, were on the verge of a new era of expansion. In 1800 British abolitionists could hope to impose imperial limitations on Atlantic slavery only at its margins, by limiting British colonial potential for growth. During the decade 1794–1804 British acquisitions of new colonies threatened to shatter the tenuous abolitionist assertion that the British tropical frontier was near its "natural limits" and a "natural rate" of slave reproduction.[6]

In 1801, Parliament prepared to welcome peace with France for the first time in almost a decade. William Wilberforce sorrowfully noted that newly acquired Trinidad would require the acquisition of a million slaves, postponing the "natural limits" of the British slave frontier for a century. The following year George Canning made the same point in comparative terms when he opposed the opening of prime Crown land in Trinidad to sugar planting. The island, he warned the House of Commons, had almost as much undeveloped acreage fit for cane as did Jamaica. The latter colony held more than a quarter of a million slaves compared with Trinidad's ten thousand. Jamaica had imported nearly seven hundred thousand Africans over the course of a century in order to reach a slave population of only two hundred fifty thousand. It was clear that Trinidad alone could move up to another million coerced Africans into the Middle Passage.[7]

Britain's reconquest of Demerara soon after the resumption of hostilities with France in 1803 elicited a public cry of despair from James Stephen, the most influential political strategist among the abolitionists during the five years before abolition of the slave trade. He saw his country "still given up without remorse to the unbridled career of slave trading speculators. . . . The monster, instead of being cut off, as the first burst of honest indignation promised [in 1792], has been more fondly nourished than before, and fattened with fuller meals of misery and murder, into far more than his pristine dimensions." Three years later, on the verge of abolitionist victory, Wilberforce warned his constituents that most established West Indian proprietors were "prompted by a true persuasion that abolition will materially lessen their gains." He had "no hope of the West India body's opposition to abolition ending of its own accord as long as there remained cultivable land in the western hemisphere."[8]

Table 10.1. *Average Annual Movements of Slaves to the Principal Importing Areas of the Americas, 1804–1839 (thousands)*

(1)	(2)	(3)	(4)	(5)
		All Areas		
		British West India	Spanish	
ca. 1804–5	U.S. (all)	(all)	America	Brazil
	17.9	24.9	12.5	23.3
		Demerara/Trinidad		
ca. 1804–5	U.S. (all)	/Jamaica	Cuba	Brazil
	17.9	17.0	9.3	23.3
		Frontier Areas		
1808–33	Importing states	Demerara/Trinidad	Cuba	Brazil
	16.2	0.8	12.3	34.8
1814–39	Importing states	Demerara/Trinidad	Cuba	Brazil
	20.7	0.9[a]	15.6	37.5
Total net migration, 1814–39	516.6	23.3	390.8	937.5

[a]This figure includes free migrants after 1834. *Sources:* Column 1: R. W. Fogel, "Revised Estimates of the U.S. Slave Trade and the Native-Born Slave of the Black Population," in *Without Consent or Contract: Evidence and Methods,* ed. Fogel et al. (New York: Norton, 1992), pp. 53–58; Michael Tadman, *Spectators and Slaves: Masters, Traders, and Slaves in the Old South* (Madison: University of Wisconsin Press, 1989), p. 12, table 2.1; column 2: S. Drescher, *Econocide: British Slavery in the Era of Abolition* (Pittsburgh: University of Pittsburgh Press, 1977), p. 95, table 23; David Eltis, "The Traffic in Slaves Between the British West Indian Colonies, 1807–1833," *Economic History Review* 25(1) (February 1972): 55–64, 58, table 1; B. W. Higman, *Slave Populations of the British Caribbean, 1807–1834* (Baltimore: Johns Hopkins University Press, 1984), pp. 417–18, 430, tables S1.2, S1.20; Bonham C. Richardson, *Caribbean Migrants: Environment and Human Survival on St. Kitts and Nevis* (Knoxville: University of Tennessee Press, 1983), p. 88, table 4; *Parliamentary Papers,* 1845 (426), 31:329 ff., Census of the West Indies 1844; column 3: David Eltis, *Economic Growth and the Ending of the Transatlantic Slave Trade* (New York: Oxford University Press, 1987), pp. 245, 247, tables A.2, A.4; Column 4: Ibid., pp. 243–44, table A.1.

II

Between 1788 and 1807, abolition of the intercontinental slave trade was one of the most continually debated issues in the imperial Parliament. Year after year the House of Commons divided, often very narrowly, over bills and resolutions linked to that issue. Successive parliamentary committees heard testimony and gathered mountains of evidence. Waves of petitions to Parliament attacked the trade. Abolition became campaign fodder in hotly contested elections to Parliament. Its abolition of the African slave trade was a fatal blow to Britain's position as the leading carrier of African slaves.

The potential for British colonial slavery's expansion had not, however, been entirely eliminated. There was still the question of the internal mobility of British Caribbean slavery, although before closing the Atlantic traffic, abolitionist pressure had succeeded in restricting it. Imperial policy concerning that traffic began, almost imperceptibly, with an administrative Order-in-Council in October 1805, more than two years before the Slave Trade Abolition Act took effect. William Pitt's last administration issued this Order-in-Council in order to limit the flow of slaves to the newest British slave frontiers. These limits were reconfirmed by the Abolition Acts of 1806–7.

All subsequent revisions, culminating in the Slave Trade Law Consolidation Act of 1824, passed through Parliament with a minimum of discussion. Except for a single brief exchange, unrecorded in *Hansard's Parliamentary Debates,* the entire subject escaped the attention of the broad reading public.[9] There were no major petition campaigns for or against the regulation or abolition of the intercolonial trade. The Caribbean traffic was overshadowed by successive campaigns to reduce the Atlantic slave trade, to prevent the illicit flow of Africans to the British colonies, and to accelerate the at first gradual, and finally the immediate, emancipation of British slaves.

In order to prevent smuggling of new slaves from Africa under the guise of intercolonial traffic, after 1807 slaves could no longer be carried from colony to colony without a license from the colony of departure. If the receiving area was a newly acquired colony, the slaveholder needed a second license from the colony of destination. As a further check on transatlantic traffickers, annual importations to the new colonies were limited to a maximum of 3 percent of the slave population of that colony. Finally, and crucially, imports could not exceed the actual annual decrease of slaves in those colonies. Even in the event of an epidemic in Trinidad and Demerara, these new British colonies could import no more than three thousand slaves per year, less than one-third of their preabolition rate. Any major frontier boom was preemptively prohibited, and the effective expansion of the British slave frontier in an open slave market was already at an end.[10]

After 1805 British frontier planters could no longer hope to acquire so much as half of Havana's annual slave imports, not to mention still larger slave imports into Brazil. The results of Britain's combined policy of transatlantic abolition and transcaribbean regulation can be seen in tables 10.1 and 10.2. From 1808 until British emancipation in 1833, its two new sugar colonies received a combined average of well under a thousand slaves per year, a situation that continued beyond emancipation until the end of "Apprenticeship" in 1838. During the same generation, Cuba was annually importing seventeen times as many enslaved Africans. Even the United States, which also legally closed its territory to African slaves in 1807, saw greater growth in its slave population. Slavery on the mainland had long been expanding more rapidly by natural growth than from fresh African imports. The slave-importing southern states received slaves at twenty-three times the rate of slaves reaching the British frontier. Brazil, like Cuba, continued to rely on Africa for its slave labor growth and outdid the British colonies by the greatest margin. From 1808 to 1833 more than forty slaves were landed in Brazil for every slave arriving in Trinidad and Demerara.

The relative outcome was a foregone conclusion. In 1808 Britain's importing frontier colonies contained about 107,000 slaves. By the early 1830s that number had dwindled to 85,000. By contrast, Cuba's slave population at the beginning of its peak quinquennium of African importation (1816–1820) was already twice that of Trinidad and Demerara. Ten years later, Cuba's slave population was triple that of the two British colonies. The slave frontier of the American South expanded still more dramatically. In 1810 slave-importing U.S. states and territories had a combined population of 204,500, almost twice that of Trinidad and Demerara. By 1830 the same states, plus Arkansas and Florida, contained 697,000 slaves, or more than seven and a half times the combined slave populations of Trinidad and Demerara. Brazil's sparser and less reliable estimates do not permit the same comparison on the eve of British slave emancipation (see table 10.2).

The differentiation between the British Caribbean and the other plantation zones continued to deepen during the Apprenticeship years (1834–1838) and into the 1840s. Indeed, the difference between the effective labor power available to British planters and to the others was far greater than the raw numbers suggest. Barry Higman notes that between abolition and emancipation in Demerara, "the 30–40 years group was modal until 1826, when it was replaced by the 40–50 age group. During the same period the cohort over

Table 10.2. *Slave Populations in Major Plantation Zones,*
1800–1864 (thousands)

	(1)	(2)	(3)	(4)
		British Caribbean		
	United States	(including conquests)	Cuba	Brazil
Year	1800	1800		
Number	1,191	765		
Year	c. 1817	1817	1817	
Number	1,435	746	199	
Year	1820	1820		
Number	1,538	733		
Year		1823		1823
Number		717		1,148
Year		1827	1827	
Number		700	287	
Year	1830	1830	1830	
Number	2,009	685	310 (359)[a]	
Percentage change, 1817–1830	+31	−8	+55	
Year			1846	
Number			324	
Year	1850			c.1850
Number	3,204			c. 1,875–2.250
Year	1860			
Number	3,954			
Year			1862	
Number			369	
Year				1864
Number				1,715

See notes on facing page

50 years old increased its share of the slave population from 4.3% in 1817 to 14.1%, while the share of slaves under 10 years decreased from 22.3 to 18.7 percent."[11]

Between 1821 and 1835, 18 percent of Africans purchased in Cuba were under fourteen years old, 78 percent were between fifteen and forty, and only 4 percent were over forty. The age pyramid of African slaves in 1823–44 clearly reflects the role of the African trade in keeping Cuba's modal group well within the twenty-to-forty-year-old range.[12] Between 1808 and 1839 the new British colonies were demographically hobbled. They could not match their African-importing competitors (Cuba and Brazil) in expansion or in age and gender profiles for maximum labor efficiency. Nor could they match the ability of their counterparts in the American South to draw on older contiguous areas of slavery with high natural rates of population growth.

The cumulative impact of British imperial constraints was considerable. When emancipation was enacted by the government in 1833, slave owners were offered different rates of compensation for slaves held in each colony. These rates were designed to reflect a proportion of the average market value of slaves in each colony between 1823 and 1830. (See table 10.3.) Note that the average rate of compensation in the three most highly rated British colonies was more than three and a half times that offered in the lowest three. Owners of sugar plantations in Demerara received nearly three times as much compensation per field slave as did owners of sugar plantations in the sugar island of St. Kitts.

Once again, the intercolonial productivity gap indicated by these valuations was not only wide but widening in the final decades before emancipation. From 1815 to 1819, the ratio of tons of sugar produced per slave in the four

---

continued from facing page

[a]All Spanish Caribbean. *Sources:* Column 1: *Preliminary Report on the Eighth Census* (Washington, D.C.: GPO, 1862), p. 7; column 2: Higman, *Slave Populations of the British Caribbean* (Baltimore: Johns Hopkins University Press, 1984), pp. 417–18; S. Drescher, *Econocide: British Slavery in the Era of Abolition* (Pittsburgh: Pittsburgh University Press, 1977), p. 34; column 3: Laird W. Bergad et al., *The Cuban Slave Market, 1790–1880* (New York: Cambridge University Press, 1995), p. 39; Stanley L. Engerman and B. W. Higman, "The Demographic Structure of the Caribbean Slave Societies in the Eighteenth and Nineteenth Centuries," in *General History of the Caribbean*, vol. 3, *The Slave Societies of the Caribbean* (London: UNESCO Publications, 1997), ed. Franklin W. Knight, pp. 45–104, esp. 50–52, table 2.1; column 4: Leslie Bethell and José Murillo de Caravalho, "Brazil from Independence to the Middle of the Nineteenth Century," in *The Cambridge History of Latin America*, vol. 3, *From Independence to c. 1870*, ed. Leslie Bethell (Cambridge: Cambridge University Press, 1985), pp. 679, 747.

Table 10.3. Ranking of Colonies by Average Compensation Payments per Slave, 1834 (£ sterling)

Employed slaves		Children under 6 years		Predial unattached field laborers	
British Honduras	60.9	Trinidad	22.2	British Honduras	82.0
British Guiana	58.5	British Honduras	21.6	British Guiana	65.2
Trinidad	55.5	British Guiana	19.0	Trinidad	49.2
St. Vincent	30.6	St. Vincent	10.9	Jamaica	37.2
Grenada	30.0	Grenada	10.3	St. Vincent	35.7
St. Lucia	29.9	St. Lucia	8.4	Grenada	34.4
		Jamaica	7.7	St. Lucia	33.5
Barbados	24.9				
Jamaica	22.9	St. Kitts	5.6	Barbados	29.1
Dominica	22.7	Tobago	4.8	Dominica	26.8
Tobago	22.3	Dominica	4.6	Tobago	26.5
Nevis	21.4	Bahamas	4.4		
Montserrat	20.0	Nevis	4.0	Montserrat	22.8
St. Kitts	19.0	Barbados	3.9	Nevis	22.7
Antigua	17.8	Virgin Islands	3.3	Antigua	22.6
Virgin Islands	16.3	Montserrat	2.5	St. Kitts	22.3

Source: As calculated by B. W. Higman, *Slave Populations of the British Caribbean* (Baltimore: Johns Hopkins University Press, 1984), table 4.3, p. 79.

most productive colonies to the amount produced in the four least productive was 2:1. By 1834 the ratio of most to least productive colonies was more than 3:1.[13] In the United States, with an unrestrained interregional market in slaves, the differential was much narrower. In the period 1830–1834, prices for field hands were only 1.8 times higher in New Orleans than they were in Richmond.[14] Because prices in Cuba and Brazil were determined by the large flow of Africans to these slave-based economies, the regional price spread within these economies was much narrower than in the British Caribbean.[15]

In the case of the British colonial slave frontier, the total loss of its African labor reservoir seems to have been far more important than the subsequent impediments to the intercolonial trade. Barbados alone was able to produce a considerable surplus of slaves between abolition of the slave trade and emancipation. In the brief period when the flow of British slaves was least constrained by imperial quotas (1818–1825), Barbados's population increased by fewer than twenty-five hundred slaves. Had Barbados desired to play Virginia to the British Caribbean before 1840, it could not possibly have filled the role of the upper and middle South as a reservoir for the "new" colonies. Barbados was only to become a substantial source of outmigration after the end of Apprenticeship. According to Barry Higman, there is no evidence to suggest that Barbadian population growth "was engendered by the masters to feed a supply of slaves to the new colonies" (the so-called breeding thesis). Moreover, unlike those of the Chesapeake, Barbados's slave exports would necessarily have contributed directly to the growth of a competitor producing the same product for the same market. Intercolonial restrictions doomed parts of the British slave colonies to a diminishing competitive capacity.[16]

III

There were other marked differences between the United States and British interregional slave movements. With minor exceptions, in the United States, the decision to trade in or to accompany slaves was made by the individual slaveholder. He or she was constrained only by the balance of personal scruples and self-interest. British West Indians, whether as potential sellers, buyers, or migrants, were hemmed in by public authority at both ends of regional exchanges. Beginning in 1818, at the very moment when the intercolonial trade became numerically unfettered (with the removal of the 3 percent cap on imports), a more inhibiting limitation was included in the Amending Acts of 1818 and 1819. Indirectly violating the taboo against interfering in the proprietary relationship between masters and slaves, the government now took successive steps toward submitting slaveholders to public authority. All population transfers now had to be registered at a centralized agency in the metropolis. No transfers could be disadvantageous to the affected slaves or result in the breakup of family groups, including children under fourteen years of age.[17]

This exercise of public scrutiny was without parallel in the contemporary transatlantic slave trades or the United States interstate slave trade.[18] The violent destruction of family units was always one of the major targets of antislavery agitation. The domesticity criterion apparently worked in this case. Masters who imported slaves to the new colonies failed to maintain the high ratios of males to females previously typical of the Atlantic trade. Nor did they sustain the age structure achieved by purchasers of Africans. Higman concludes that importers of British slaves were "unable to fulfill their desire for a demographically selective movement."[19] The prerequisite of family cohesion probably also accounted for the fact that most slaves moved in large units. A single planter was responsible for more than half of the total movement from the Bahamas to Trinidad. Small groups of slaves and those transferred singly were mostly urban and domestic slaves. Migrants probably accounted for very few of the agricultural slaves most desired by planters in ·the new sugar colonies. Because proprietors moving large collectivities of slaves had the best chance of obtaining licenses at both ends of the transfer, most slaves transferred between British colonies were not traded. They accompanied their masters. This pattern made the British intercolonial migration after 1808 completely different from the Iberian transatlantic trade and, to a much more disputed extent, from the domestic slave trade in the American South.[20]

During the last decade of British colonial slavery, the welfare clauses apparently amounted to virtual abolition. After 1825, it was nearly impossible to move large units of field slaves from one colony to another. In 1828 a Barbadian planter requested permission to relocate his slaves to Trinidad. He argued his case on welfare grounds alone. In turn, the Privy Council of Barbados refused the planter's request on the same grounds: "We cannot in candor pretend that the population has yet arrived at that degree of density which renders such removal 'essential to the well being of the slaves.' " When Barbadians, with five hundred slaves to the square mile, could not be convinced to send slaves to a low-density colony with a decreasing slave population, the council seemed to have raised the hurdle to transferring slaves well beyond the level of normal demographic or economic reasoning.[21]

It remains unclear whether an unrestricted traffic in slaves between 1808 and 1833 would have led to large transfers between colonies, except in the case of groups accompanying their masters. Owners of marginal plantations in established islands were fearful of failing to sustain viability because of their ever-dwindling labor forces. At the end of the bound labor era in 1838, until they were overruled by London, sugar islands with the least productive plantations desperately attempted to legislate severe restrictions on the departure of their ex-slaves.[22] Well before emancipation, the lid was already so tightly sealed on intercolonial transfers of any kind that Trinidad and Demerara registered a net outflow of forty-five slaves for the five years preceding emancipation. The abolitionist strategy of incremental infringement of slave movement was more than successful. By 1831 it was unlawful to travel within the island of Jamaica offering slaves for sale.[23]

As one might imagine, the population-at-risk rate for long-distance removal in the British Caribbean was relatively low. The total number of slaves involved in the intercolonial traffic between 1808 and emancipation amounted to only 3.4 percent of the total population of the British Caribbean in 1817. By contrast, using the same base year, the total proportion of slaves at risk for interstate movement in the United States was seven times as great.[24] In the African-dominated Cuban slave market, the number of slaves imported from 1811 to 1830 was actually greater than the entire slave population of the island in 1817. Quite apart from Africans or Creoles sold or resold within Cuba, more than half of the slaves on the island had already been uprooted once in their lives and were certainly victims of family destruction at the African end of slave trade.

The British separation of slave colonial populations into closed enclaves had important economic repercussions. The French wars and the Caribbean revolutions had opened new opportunities for the cultivation of coffee and cotton as well as of sugar. In 1770, sugar accounted for 89.4 percent of the combined value of British Caribbean exports of these products to Great Britain. By 1786 the share of coffee and cotton had risen to 28 percent. By 1806 their combined share reached 39 percent. For the British Caribbean this represented a diversification in staple production unequaled since long before the French Revolution. During the fifteen years from the beginning of the Anglo-French wars in 1793 to British abolition of the slave trade, coffee was the most rapidly expanding commercial crop in the British colonies. As David Eltis calculates, production may well have amounted to half of the world's output by the early nineteenth century. After 1808 the significance of British colonial output as a share of total world production diminished almost as rapidly as it had grown. In the period 1821–25, the British West Indian share of the combined Cuban, Brazilian, and British Caribbean coffee exports was 37 percent. By 1830 the British colonial share had dropped below 22 percent.[25]

Within each British colony planters had to make hard choices about the allocation of their slowly diminishing and aging labor forces. In old as well as new colonies, planters shifted slave labor toward the production of sugar. In the frontier sugar colonies planters moved most rapidly toward the cultivation of cane. In 1810 Trinidad and Demerara planters employed 57 percent of their combined slave workforce in growing sugar. By 1830 that share had increased to 76 percent. Note that the ending of the intercolonial trade may have worked to the detriment of individual slaves within the new colonies as they were shifted from coffee groves and cotton fields to the more arduous work of producing sugar. The same holds true for the practice of keeping women in field labor.[26] Abolitionists obviously found it easier to block interisland movement than to create legal and procedural mechanisms to hold down the transfers of slaves from coffee to sugar plantations. In this process, the best that abolitionists could do was to attempt to use the high deficit rates in the new sugar colonies as grist for amelioration propaganda and for emancipation efforts.

IV

Of the American plantation systems on the eve of the American Revolution, the largest were the British, the Portuguese, and the French. By the revolutions of 1848, the leading plantation systems were the fragments of the old imperial settlements that had preserved slavery and the traditional means to expand their labor forces into new plantation areas. Without the closure of its slave trade (and later of slavery itself), the British fragment of the plantation complex probably would have remained among the nineteenth century's top four plantation systems. The British Caribbean certainly would not have lost ground as quickly as it did to the other systems. Slave trade abolition (in 1806–7) and emancipation (in 1834–38) played a far larger role in weakening the British component than did any of the subsequent metropolitan constraints on intercolonial movements. The British planters did not, of course, yield without a struggle. After 1808, they switched more labor and capital to the more profitable sugar economy. They managed to outdo Cuba in sugar production almost until British emancipation. New technology was effectively used to increase labor productivity, especially in the large new colonies. By 1830, slaves were generally better fed and healthier than they had been during the previous century.[27]

Most of the above trends owed more to the ending of African imports than to constraints on intra-Caribbean movement. But gradual closure may have had another subtle effect on the relations between slaves and masters in the final decades of the institution.[28] Well before the intercolonial movement of field slaves came to a virtual halt during the late 1820s, masters had lost one of their most precious weapons: the power to arbitrarily detach and exile troublesome individual slaves at minimal economic loss. The planters' ability to sell a slave "south," without consideration for family integrity, was one of their major threats against resisters or potential leaders in collective bargaining situations. A number of recent accounts of slavery in the British Caribbean note the growth of a new balance of bargaining power between slaves and masters in the decades before emancipation. For example, J. R. Ward concludes his "balance sheet" of the process of amelioration with the observation that, despite improvements in the slave regime, Jamaican planters had failed as a class to establish the sense of uniformity and routine so essential for equilibrium in slave societies. Others, including Mary Turner, Michael Craton, and Howard Johnson, have found that conditions of labor, and slave life in general, were rapidly changing. Just as the terms of servitude were being renegotiated at an accelerating pace, and just as the whip came under ever-closer metropolitan scrutiny, the possibility of "long-distance discipline" disappeared from the planters' arsenal. Higman's survey of incentives to slave labor in the British Caribbean does not even allude to the concept.[29]

What has been still less remarked by historians is that the planters fell equally silent in Parliament about this aspect of their property rights. The Slave Trade Consolidated Bill of 1824 stirred the only notice on record of the obviously tightening restrictions on the planters' right to remove their slaves from a colony. During the bill's final reading in the House of Lords, a traditional opponent of slave trade abolition expressed concern that one clause in particular impinged on the planters' right not only to trade but to move his own chattels between islands without London's permission. Another peer noted that the bill's new restrictions on the movement of chattels were clearly crossing the once-sacrosanct limit on direct parliamentary interference with slaveholders' property rights in their chattels.[30] Yet all speakers noted that the West India interest itself had abstained from any formal protest. Therefore the short parliamentary discussion about the clause was framed exclusively in terms of its putative impact on the welfare of the slaves. By 1824, at the highest level of metropolitan political discourse, planter profitability was off-limits in considering the movement of slaves between colonies.

West Indian planters, choosing their battles with care, no longer contested parliamentary limits on slave owners' authority to transfer their slaves. Within the colonies, however, masters had no choice but to formally negotiate with their slaves. Movement beyond a colony now had to be presented to their own slaves as an inducement to voluntary movement. By 1827 a Tortola slaveholder, fearful of provoking a bloody uprising, had to request the mediation of Methodist preachers to try to persuade his slaves to accept resettlement in Trinidad. By then, of course, intercolonial movement was no longer a "trade" in any meaningful sense of the term. Indeed, ten years later the planters showed how well they had learned the abolitionist language of family values. At the end of Apprenticeship some colonial legislatures enacted laws restricting the movement of ex-slaves from their islands. Freed blacks who wished to leave had to prove first that they had "no aged or infirm Father, or Mother, Wife, or infant child, legitimate or illegitimate . . . who may or ought to be dependent on him for support." In the discourse about restrictions on migration, the welfare of the laborers was now the acknowledged priority in determining policy decisions about the intercolonial moment of slaves.[31]

V

Three other aspects of the British Caribbean trade might profitably be addressed in comparative context. First, did the inhibition of colonial slave transfers strengthen or weaken the system's ability to withstand the onslaughts of abolitionists in favor, first, of gradual and then of immediate emancipation? Restraints on the movement of slaves brought them a step closer to the status of European serfs, an avowed aim during the "gradualist" phase of British abolitionists' agitation for emancipation, led in Parliament by Fowell Buxton. A total freeze on the removal of slaves from their colonies of settlement topped Buxton's list of recommendations to the government regarding ameliorations in the mid-1820s. One irony of this campaign was that contemporary attacks on the inefficiency of serfdom in Europe and the Poor Laws in England emphasized the immobility of the labor force under serfdom. The restriction of slave sales within individual colonial markets probably reduced the efficiency and raised the costs of producing tropical products. Insofar as slave immobility increased the distress of the least efficient Caribbean planters, it probably contributed to the image of British slavery as a doomed institution on the eve of emancipation.[32]

Yet intercolonial restraints on slave mobility were never as crucial or as harmful to British planters as was the closure of Africa. This may be inferred from their low-key or no-key opposition to ever-tightening constraints after 1818. By contrast, other interregional slave flows, as in the southern United States after 1808 and in Brazil after 1850, seem to have produced or exacerbated differences in regional commitments to defend slavery. In this respect the British slave colonies never broke ranks as sharply in the 1830s as did some northeastern provinces in Brazil in the 1880s over emancipation or as did some upper south states in the 1860s over secession. There may be some analogue in planter-slave relations between the situation of slaveholders in certain southern border states in 1861 and nonsugar British slave colonies (the Bahamas, the Virgin Islands) in 1833. In both "marginal" areas the process of renegotiating the terms of labor seems to have progressed furthest prior to the threat of immediate emancipation. Yet this analogy, too, argues against assigning great causal significance to the rate of British intercolonial movement.

Second, as in the other three frontier zones, the British plantation complex might have expanded somewhat more rapidly, if still modestly, had the new colonies been allowed free access to all British imperial slaves. Such growth would almost certainly not have deferred metropolitan British moves toward emancipation. Although the domestic slave trade in the United States clearly sustained slave prices in the upper south at a higher level than would have been possible without such a trade, the principal benefit of the interstate movement was probably less economic than political. It expanded the representation of slave interests in the federal legislature, probably compensating for the erosion of commitment to slavery in the border slave states between 1808 and 1860. In the British Caribbean larger intercolonial transfers of slaves to new but unrepresented Crown Colonies would not have enhanced the political weight of Trinidad or Demerara in London as much as it did that of the new states of the cotton South in Washington.

Finally, in terms of the racial dimension of British Atlantic slavery, easier slave mobility probably would have been equally inconsequential. Of the big four plantation complexes at the end of the Napoleonic wars, the British zone was different in one important respect. Apart from the remote danger of a successful slave revolution, in no part of the British empire did the threat of interisland movement have the same racial significance. In the minds of British politicians and Caribbean planters the potential sources of new colonial labor were primarily non-European. Some white inhabitants of Cuba and Brazil plausibly advocated curtailing the slave trade in order to prevent "Africanization." In the United States a powerful movement even hoped to reverse the prior results of African migration.[33] No imaginable policy could have altered the Africanization of the old British Caribbean colonies, a process virtually completed a full century before abolition of the slave trade.[34] After the ending of slavery, postemancipation experiments to lure white labor into the British Caribbean were of minimal demographic impact.

The absence of racial-communitarian arguments in British planter propaganda is consequently not surprising. In their worst nightmares West Indian and metropolitan conservative interests imagined an anarchic Haitian archipelago displacing the ordered cane fields of the old regime. Visionary abolitionists correspondingly envisioned millennial communities spreading the seeds of civilization and love from free-labor and low-crime Caribbean utopias to the heart of Africa. But neither of these scenarios envisioned the West Indian colonies as predominantly inhabited by fair-skinned descendants of Europeans.[35] The allure of community-building racial migrations that beguiled white Cubans, Brazilians, and, above all, North Americans found little echo in either Britain or the West Indies. In the British orbit, slavery had to stand or fall unbolstered by direct appeals to "whiteness" as a source of political mobilization. In this respect, the British colonies remained unalterably Afro-American between the rise of abolitionism in 1787 and the end of Apprenticeship half a century later.

Conclusion

The closure of the British intercolonial slave trade between 1808 and 1830 was an exercise in compartmentalization and compression. Abolitionists quickly discovered that rights in persons in the Atlantic system were most vulnerable when they crossed geographical and political boundaries. The "Middle Passage" was the broadest, clearest, most casually accepted of these boundaries. The twenty-year battle in Britain over the fate of its Atlantic slave trade gave abolitionists the opportunity to extend and to refine the act of boundary-drawing. When thwarted in their initial attempts to blockade the entire route between Africa and British America, they moved (1794, 1806) to draw new lines: to abolish the British trade to "foreign" colonies within the Americas, to "new" areas of old colonies (1797), and to newly conquered colonies (1802, 1805, 1806). These encroachments must be seen as part of a larger Atlantic strategy. As early as 1791 abolitionists received a charter to exempt the Sierra Leone from slaving. They unsuccessfully sought to extend that zone to a vast stretch of the African coast in 1799. After 1808 British governments negotiated geographic limits on Luso-Brazilian and Hispano-Caribbean legal slave traders. In every part of the Atlantic system, from Chile to West Africa to Russia, British governments scrambled to amass bilateral or multilateral treaties banning the slave trade in one area after another. Anglo-American abolitionists even took at least ideological advantage of the state-creating power of the U.S. Constitution to portray the movement of southern slaves across state boundaries as a long-distance slave trade, analogous in every respect to the great Middle Passage. Thus, each demarcation created by Western power or culture was integrated into an abolitionist cartography of emancipation. What had been simply "beyond the line" within the Atlantic imperium in 1770 was resolved, line by line, in the century that followed.[36]

Notes

This chapter benefited from suggestions by Stanley Engerman and Walter Johnson. I also thank the other participants in the Domestic Passages conference, and especially Steven Mintz, for comments on the original version of this paper.

1. Laird W. Bergad, Fe Iglesias Garcia, and María de Carmen Barca, *The Cuban Slave Market, 1790–1880* (New York: Cambridge University Press, 1995), 25.

2. Joseph Inikori, "Slavery and the Development of Industrial Capitalism in England," in *British Capitalism and Caribbean Slavery: The Legacy of Eric Williams,* ed. Barbara L. Solow and Stanley L. Engerman (Cambridge: Cambridge University Press, 1987), 79–101. See also David Eltis, *The Rise of African Slavery in the Americas* (Cambridge: Cambridge University Press, 2000), 136. Eltis notes that there were "market

imperfections" between major mercantilist entities as well as within the limits of sovereignty. On the volume and distribution of the slave trade, see David Eltis, Stephen D. Behrendt, David Richardson, and Herbert S. Klein, *The Trans-Atlantic Slave Trade: A Database on CD-ROM* (New York: Cambridge University Press, 1999). Dale Tomich sees the age of revolution as marking a transition from mercantilist imperial aggregation to global integration. "The 'Second Slavery': Bonded Labor and the Transformation of the Nineteenth-Century World Economy," in *Rethinking the Nineteenth Century: Contradictions and Achievements,* ed. Francisco O. Ramirez (New York: Greenwood Press, 1988). This was less obviously the case, however, in the coerced migration of African labor. The British Navigation Acts and the French *exclusif* do not seem to have had a major influence on the rate of growth of the prerevolutionary Anglo-French slave sectors. On the African coast as a whole, African and European slave traders did not have much in the way of long-term market power over others.

3. For the case of the American Revolution, see Christopher L. Brown, "Empire Without Slaves: British Concepts of Emancipation in the Age of the American Revolution," *William and Mary Quarterly,* 3rd ser., 56, no. 2 (April 1999): 273–306.

4. Michael Duffy, "The French Revolution and British Attitudes to the West Indian Colonies," in *A Turbulent Time: The French Revolution and the Greater Caribbean,* ed. David Barry Gasper and David Patrick Geggus (Bloomington: Indiana University Press, 1997), 78–101, quoted on p. 79. See also Duffy, "World-Wide War and British Expansion, 1793–1815," in *The Oxford History of the British Empire,* vol. 2, *The Eighteenth Century,* ed. P. J. Marshall (New York: Oxford University Press, 1998), 184–195; and Duffy, *Soldiers, Sugar, and Seapower: The British Expeditions to the West Indies and the War Against Revolutionary France* (Oxford: Clarendon Press, 1987), 5–16. On decennial movements of Africans in British and Colonial ships to America, see David Richardson, "The British Empire and the Atlantic Slave Trade 1660–1807," in *The Oxford History of the British Empire,* vol. 2, *The Eighteenth Century,* ed. P. J. Marshall (New York: Oxford University Press, 1998), 440–464. See also the British perspective on the process a century after the founding of the British abolitionist movement: "England, which had recently lost her thirteen colonies on the North American continent, and had not yet acquired Ceylon or the Cape of Good Hope, whilst her dominion in the East Indies was restricted and precarious, whilst Canada was unpeopled, and Australia unexplored, clung the more closely to the islands which were then the richest part of her colonial empire." "The English in the West Indies," *Edinburgh Review* (April 1888): 320.

5. For an overview of the French and Caribbean ruptures of the 1790s, see David Geggus, "Slavery, War, and Revolution in the Greater Caribbean, 1789–1815," in *A Turbulent Time: The French Revolution and the Greater Caribbean,* ed. David Barry Gasper and David Patrick Geggus (Bloomington: Indiana University Press, 1997), 1–50.

6. Seymour Drescher, *Econocide: British Slavery in the Era of Abolition* (Pittsburgh: University of Pittsburgh Press, 1977), 71–76, 92–112.

7. See *Cobbett's Parliamentary History* 36 (1801–1803), col. 143, Wilberforce, November 3, 1801; ibid., cols. 854–76, Canning May 27, 1802. Wilberforce also projected the need for another six hundred thousand slaves to develop Jamaica's uncultivated land. *A Letter on the Abolition of the Slave Trade, Addressed to the Freeholders and Other Inhabitants of Yorkshire* (London: T. Cadell and W. Davies, 1807), 291.

8. James Stephen, *The Opportunity, or Reasons for an Immediate Alliance with St. Domingo* (London: J. Hatchard, 1804), p. 137. See Wilberforce, *Letter on the Abolition of the Slave Trade*, 28, 290. See also Drescher, *Econocide*, 98, 243n16.

9. *Times* (London), June 22, 1824, reporting the discussion in the House of Lords, June 21, 1824.

10. See Roger Anstey, *The Atlantic Slave Trade and Abolition, 1760–1810* (Atlantic Highlands, NJ: Humanities Press, 1975), 348–349; and David Eltis, "The Traffic in Slaves Between the British West Indian Colonies, 1807–1833," *Economic History Review* 25, no. 1 (February 1972): 55–64, esp. 55–57.

11. B. W. Higman, *Slave Populations of the British Caribbean, 1807–1834* (Baltimore: Johns Hopkins University Press, 1984), 142. See Stanley L. Engerman and B. W. Higman, "The Demographic Structure of the Caribbean Slave Societies in the Eighteenth and Nineteenth Centuries," in *General History of the Caribbean*, vol. 3, *The Slave Societies of the Caribbean*, ed. Franklin W. Knight (London: UNESCO/Macmillan, 1997), 45–104.

12. See Manuel Moreno Fraginals, "Africa in Cuba: A Quantitative Analysis of the African Population in the Island of Cuba," in *Annals of the New York Academy of Sciences*, vol. 292, *Comparative Perspectives on Slavery in New World Plantation Societies,* ed. Vera Rubin and Arthur Tuden (New York: New York Academy of Sciences, 1977), 187–201.

13. This is calculated from Higman, *Slave Populations,* 51, table 3.4.

14. This is calculated from Richard Evans Jr., "The Economics of American Negro Slavery," in *Aspects of Labor Economics* (Princeton: Princeton University Press, 1962), 199, table 8.

15. Laird Bergad et al. *Cuban Slave Market,* treat the slave markets of Havana, Santiago, and Cienfuegos as a single market.

16. Higman, *Slave Populations,* 81, 260, 348–349. If, economically speaking, "the Old South in the U.S. had no stake in the New South," Barbados had even less of a stake in the "New British South." See Lawrence J. Kolikoff and Sebastian E. Pinera, "The Old South's Stake in the Interregional Movement of Slaves, 1850–1860," in *Without Consent or Contract: Technical Papers,* 2 vols., ed. Robert W. Fogel and Stanley L. Engerman (New York: Norton, 1992), 1:80–94. On slave "breeding" in the United States, see Robert W. Fogel and Stanley L. Engerman, "The Slave Breeding Thesis," in ibid., 2:455–472.

17. See Eltis, "Traffic in Slaves," 57. Slaveholders also had to post bond in order to move families and had to ensure their comfortable passage. See Higman, *Slave Populations,* 80.

18. As in the British Caribbean after abolition of the transatlantic trade, slaves of Dutch colonies were asked whether they agreed with their master's intended destination. Curaçao's slaves apparently did not wish to go to Suriname, the principal Dutch sugar colony. Two-thirds of the movement of slaves from Curaçao was to Puerto Rico, beyond the Dutch orbit. More heavily female than the British migration (with a female-male ratio of 2:1) and moving in small groups, most slaves moved to do domestic work. Whatever the difference between the two Caribbean interregional flows, both received few of the agricultural laborers most in demand by planters. Like their British counterparts, Dutch ex-masters would follow their British predecessors in seeking bonded laborers from Asia

to replace their emancipated Caribbean slaves. See W. E. Renkema, "De export van Curacaose slaven, 1819–1847," in *Excercities in on verleden: Twaalf opstellen over economische en sociale geschriedenis van Nederland en de kolonien, 1800–1950*, ed. P. Boomgaard et al. (Assen: Van Gorcum, 1981), 188–208. I thank Pieter Emmer for bringing this essay to my attention.

19. Higman, *Slave Populations*, p. 82.

20. Compare Tadman, *Spectators and Slaves: Masters, Traders, and Slaves in the Old South* (Madison: University of Wisconsin Press, 1996), for the United States, with Robert Wayne Slenes, "The Demography and Economics of Brazilian Slavery, 1850–1888," Ph.D. diss., Stanford University, 1975, 145–146.

21. B. W. Higman, "Slavery and the Development of Demographic Theory in the Age of the Industrial Revolution," in *Slavery and British Society, 1776–1846*, ed. James Walvin (London: Macmillan Press, 1982), 164–194, 190. See Higman, *Slave Populations*, 81. Nor were the blows to the planters forgotten. At the steepest decline of their economic fortunes, in 1847–1848, planters dated the depreciation of the prices of their slaves from the welfare-driven restrictions of intercolonial slave transfers in 1823. See *Parliamentary Papers* 1847–48, no. 23, vol. 4, p. 43, Supplement, 8th Report, 1848. Thereafter, the price of slaves in the old colonies such as Jamaica, Antigua, and Barbados fell by 50 to 70 percent compared with the price of slaves in the sugar zones of British Guiana, Trinidad, and the United States.

22. On attempts by the legislatures of St. Kitts and of Nevis to prevent emigration by ex-slaves, see Bonham Richardson, *Caribbean Migrants: Environment and Human Survival on St. Kitts and Nevis* (Knoxville: University of Tennessee Press, 1983), 81–88.

23. Higman, *Slave Populations*, p. 430, table S1.20; Higman, *Slave Population and Economy in Jamaica, 1807–1834* (Cambridge: Cambridge University Press, 1976), 63.

24. Compare Eltis, "Traffic in Slaves," 59, with Tadman, *Spectators and Slaves*, 45, for the American South. During the period 1808–1830, 264,200 African slaves entered Cuba. This is 133 percent greater than the number of slaves in the island in 1817, although this may have reduced the corresponding proportion of Creoles otherwise at risk for sale. Since 64 percent of the slaves sold in Cuba between 1820 and 1835 were Africans, I estimate that the number of Creoles sold between 1808 and 1830 was 95,100 (264.2 × 0.36). This would mean that about 48 percent of Cuban Creole slaves were at risk for sale during the period 1808–1830, about fourteen times the interregional sale rate for British Caribbean slaves. (See Bergad et al., *Cuban Slave Market*, 43). The direction of the small Spanish intercolonial trade after 1848 was into, rather than out of, Cuba. See Joseph C. Dorsey, "Seamy Sides of Abolition: Puerto Rico and the Cabotage Slave Trade to Cuba, 1848–73," *Slavery and Abolition* 19, no. 1 (April 1998): 106–128.

25. See David Eltis, *Economic Growth and the Ending of the Transatlantic Slave Trade* (New York: Oxford University Press, 1987), 294n6; Drescher, *Econocide*, 88–90; and Drescher, "The Decline Thesis Since Econocide," *Slavery and Abolition* 71, no. 1 (May 1986): 3–24, esp. p. 103, table 4.3; reprinted in Drescher, *From Slavery to Freedom: Comparative Studies in the Rise and Fall of Atlantic Slavery* (London: Macmillan, New York: New York University Press, 1999), 87–115.

26. Higman, *Slave Population*, pp. 66–71.

27. J. R. Ward, *British West Indian Slavery, 1750–1834: The Process of Amelioration*

(Oxford: Clarendon Press, 1988), 272–273. For a short while the trend accelerated after emancipation.

28. Higman, *Slave Populations*, 199–204, 219–221, 224, 242–247.

29. On slaves' bargaining power, see Ward, *British West Indian Slavery*, p. 232. On evolving conditions of slave labor and life see, inter alia, Mary Turner, ed., *From Chattel Slaves to Wage Slaves: The Dynamics of Labour Bargaining in the Americas* (London: James Currey, 1995); Michael Craton, *Testing the Chains: Resistance to Slavery in the British West Indies* (Ithaca: Cornell University Press, 1982); Howard Johnson, *The Bahamas in Slavery and Freedom* (London: James Currey, 1991). On incentives and discipline, see Higman, *Slave Populations*, 199–204, 242–247.

30. See *Times* (London), June 23, 1824, esp. the speech of the Earl of Westmoreland, a diehard defender of the British Atlantic slave trade before 1807.

31. Eltis, "Traffic in Slaves," 61. See also Richardson, *Caribbean Migrants*, 82.

32. See *Parliamentary Debates*, 2nd ser., vol. 6 (Feb–April, 1822), April 1, 1822, col. 1426, for Fowell Buxton's motion in favor of *adscripti glebe* status for West Indian slaves. On conceptualizations of serfdom and slavery see Steven Mintz, "Models of Emancipation During the Age of Revolution," Slavery and Abolition 17, no. 2 (August 1996): 1–21. Adam Smith was unequivocal: "Whatever obstructs the free circulation of labour from one employment to another obstructs that of stock likewise": *An Inquiry into the Nature and Causes of the Wealth of Nations* (New York: Modern Library, 1994), 156. In this respect both serfdom and England's Poor Laws of Settlement were less efficient than chattel slavery. It was assumed that freedom for serfs in Europe would induce labor mobility. See Richard Jones, *Peasant Rents: An Essay on the Distribution of Wealth* (London, 1831; reprint, New York: Macmillan, 1897), 29. John Stuart Mill saw the ban on the intercolonial trade as driving planters in the older colonies to ruin, because they could not relocate to areas where their slaves would have been worth up to three times as much. See Mill, "The Sugar Refinery Bill and the Slave Trade," *Examiner*, 18 September 1831, 594–95, reprinted in *Collected Works of John Stuart Mill*, vol. 23, *Newspaper Writings*, ed. Ann P. Robson and John M. Robson (Toronto: University of Toronto Press, 1987), 347–50. Another major political economist, J. R. McCulloch, viewed imperial restrictions as a serious impediment to the planters of the small islands such as Tortola. Restrictions prevented the planters from efficiently deploying capital and industry. McCulloch pointedly contrasted this constraint with the virtual absence of such restrictions in the United States. He hypothesized that the welfare of the slaves might be made the means of accelerating manumission provisions for slaves in exchange for increased freedom for planters to move them between colonies. See [J. R. McCulloch,] "Colonial Policy—West Indian Distress," *Edinburgh Review* 54 (December 1831): 330–351, esp. 350. The suggestions of Mill and McCulloch were clearly applications of free trade concepts to the question of the movement of West Indian slaves.

The Colonial Office did not fully recognize the impact of their welfare criteria on the immobilization of sunken slave and nonslave capital in the Caribbean. Earl Bathurst assumed that merchants and planters were free to withdraw their capital and employ it elsewhere. The obstacles to intraisland slave movement undermined that possibility as early as 1808, and the devaluation progressed into the 1840s. See Earl Bathurst to Robert Wilmot-Horton, 6 November 1826, in the Wilmot-Hornton Papers, Mitchell Library,

State Library of New South Wales, as quoted in Neville Thompson, *Earl Bathurst and the British Empire, 1762–1834* (Barnsley, South Yorkshire: Leo Cooper, 1999), 179. In retrospect, the movement of slaves from the older plantations following the end of Apprenticeship was identified as causing "the ruin of the planters of the old windward and leeward islands, and the abandonment of those colonies as places of trade." See *Times* (London), September 23, 1840, p. 4, col. d.

33. For the prospects and politics of "whitening" in Brazil, see Celia Maria Marinko de Azevedo, *Onda Negra, Medo Branco O negro no imaginário das elites—Século XIX* (Rio de Janeiro: Paz e Terra, 1987), 59 ff.; for Cuba, see Christopher Schmidt-Nowara, *Empire and Antislavery: Spain, Cuba, and Puerto Rico* (Pittsburgh: University of Pittsburgh Press, 1999), 27–32; for the United States, see William W. Freehling, *The Reintegration of American History: Slavery and the Civil War* (New York: Oxford University Press, 1994), chs. 1, 7, 8. For perceptions of the Caribbean as irrevocably black, see Alexis de Tocqueville, *Democracy in America,* trans. Arthur Goldhammer (New York: Library of America, 2004), 413; Edward B. Rugemer, "The Southern Response to British Abolitionism: The Maturation of Proslavery Apologetics," *Journal of Southern History* 70, no. 2 (May 2004): 221–248, esp. 233.

34. The very terms of the "deficiency" laws in the Caribbean conceded the ineluctability of a black majority.

35. On the abolitionists' imagined postemancipation communities, see David Brion Davis, *Slavery and Human Progress* (New York: Oxford University Press, 1984), 126.

36. With regard to the British intracolonial slave movement, antislavery reached its apogee on the eve of British colonial emancipation. When Berbice merged with Demerara in 1831 to form British Guiana, Berbice continued to be considered a separate colony for purposes of slave transfers. Fragmentation trumped annexation. On the role of "the line" in the history of slavery and abolition see Seymour Drescher, *From Slavery to Freedom,* 19–24, 402–407, 434–435; David Brion Davis, "Looking at Slavery from Broader Perspectives," *American Historical Review* 105, no. 2 (April 2000): 452–465, esp. 458–459; Eliza H. Gould, "Zones of Law, Zones of Violence: The Legal Geography of the British Atlantic, circa 1772," *William and Mary Quarterly,* 3d ser., 40, no. 3 (July 2003): 471–510; and Lauren Benton, *Law and Colonial Cultures: Legal Regimes in World History, 1400–1900* (New York: Cambridge University Press, 2002).

"An Unfeeling Traffick"

The Intercolonial Movement of Slaves in the British Caribbean, 1807–1833

HILARY MCD. BECKLES

Many debates serve to illuminate the forces that brought about the dismantlement of chattel slavery in English Caribbean colonies. None, however, reveals as clearly the tensions and contradictions inherent to the slave system as that concerning the intercolonial movement of enslaved persons during the years between the 1807 abolition of the transatlantic slave trade and the 1833 emancipation legislation. The transfer of enslaved persons from one colony to another was represented as an extension of the transatlantic slave trade. Its expansion was encouraged by slaveowners was but anathema to abolitionists.[1]

After 1807 stakeholders of the plantation system were divided with respect to its economic condition, viability, and responsiveness to meaningful social reform. The enslaved population also took the opportunity to press its opinions. It emerged a major focus of policy formulation. In some instances slaves successfully challenged slaveowners' rights by protesting relocation proposals. In this regard they welcomed the imperial campaign to promote amelioration strategies.[2]

Intense political debate and acrimony surrounded what were in fact market forces seeking to bring equilibrium to uneven resource distribution within the regional economic environment. In 1815, for example, Governor Ralph Woodford of Trinidad wrote that "the average price of slaves is four hundred dollars for an able negro, ready money, . . . small gangs of slaves are procurable from Dominica where the lands are worn out and they are starved by hurricanes, and they are sold here for 360 dollars at one and two years credit. 600 and 800 and even 1000 dollars are given for masons, boilers, etc."[3] He noted, furthermore, that the collapse of St. Domingue, the region's largest sugar producer, following the 1790s antislavery revolution and the emergence from its political ruins of the Independent State of Haiti there in 1804 was a seminal moment. It opened up the sugar market to new producers and stimulated greater demand for slaves in newly acquired colonies such as Trinidad and Demerara. These and related circumstances, moreover, illustrated the degree of market responsiveness and sensitivity within the slave economy. They also reflected the extent to which its internal social relations and external commercial connections had been politicized by the emancipation discourse.

Primarily for financial reasons, the abolition of the slave trade was welcomed by some planters in the smaller traditional colonies, most notably Barbados.[4] The fear in these territories of competition from sugar producers in larger colonies, particularly those acquired during the imperial rivalries in the era of abolition, was real enough. But abolition was dreaded in Jamaica and indeed in all the large colonies. Planters who invested in nonsugar crops were quickest to resign themselves to a gradual demise. This range of attitudes and positions fueled regional and imperial politics and provided much of the evidence and arguments used on both sides of the debate.

Despite the intensity of the discussion and its implications for an effective understanding of the process of reform that culminated in general emancipation, this subject has attracted few detailed assessments since the initial presentation by Lowell Ragatz in 1933. Eric Williams's (1942) analysis focused on the persistence of localized slave trading as evidence of the ideological crisis and political duplicity of British abolitionists.

David Eltis (1972), in challenging Williams's approach and specific concerns, addressed the details of legislative deficiencies and administration while setting out the quantitative framework of the migration. Other scholars, most notably Barry Higman (1984) and Meredith John (1988), both of whom offered important adjustments to aspects of Eltis's calculations, have made significant contributions while participating in debates about the wider issues associated with the economic and demographic patterns that characterized the emancipation process.[5]

The pattern and volume of intercolonial transfers were determined by the level of demand across the region and were reflected in economic and demographic trends. Net exporters tended to be the smaller colonies where the sugar sector was in decline or where the nonsugar sector of the economy was in crisis. Net importers were generally the larger sugar colonies. The movement was away from the smaller sugar economies and nonsugar sectors. Barbados and the Leeward Islands (St. Kitts, Antigua, Nevis, and Montserrat), where soils were exhausted and labor productivity was low, in addition to the Windward Islands (Grenada, Dominica, St. Lucia, and St. Vincent), where the nonsugar sector had gained ground, supplied slaves to the frontier colonies of Trinidad and Guiana (Demerara and Essequibo in particular).

The Windward Islands, ceded from France to Britain after the Seven Years' War in 1763, constituted a primary net exporter. They were part of a wider trend, including the Bahamas, that saw the movement of slaves away from the nonsugar sector — coffee, cotton, cattle, and towns — toward the sugar sector. This movement took place between and within colonies such as Jamaica. Although the Jamaican sugar sector was a significant market for slaves from the Bahamas, it also attracted slaves from other parts of the rural economy, as well as from the urban and domestic sectors.[6]

In addition, net-importing colonies were generally those with slave populations that were experiencing systematic natural decline on account of relatively greater mortality rates. They were least likely to have population structures conducive to natural growth. Neither were slave management policies supportive of reproduction. Trinidad, for example, possessed more arable acreage than all the smaller colonies combined. According to William Wilberforce, it required a million slaves, over the course of a hundred years, in order to maximize its sugar-producing capacity.[7]

Wilberforce's estimate was based on the observation that Jamaica, with a comparable amount of prime sugar lands, had imported at least a million slaves under British rule since 1655 but had less than half that number when the trade was abolished. The new colonies had a mere 105,000 slaves between them (Demerara and Essequibo had 80,000, and Trinidad 25,000) in 1807 and were restricted to importing fewer than 4,000 per year, less than 30 percent of the rate in 1806, when the act was passed.[8]

The majority of slaves in Trinidad were therefore employed on plantations. Export agriculture was the main reason for Britain's considerable interest in the colony. According to Meredith John: "In 1808, there were 3,680 urban slaves and 18,303 plantation slaves . . . in Trinidad. Thus plantation slaves constituted 83% of the total slave population. In 1811, there were 3,891 urban slaves and 17,397 plantation slaves in Trinidad, so plantation slaves constituted 82% of the total slave population." Plantations produced mostly sugar. Of the 17,087 plantation slaves on the island in 1813, noted John, 12,256 worked on plantations that grew sugar as their sole commercial crop;

Table 11.1. Natural Change (per 1,000) in Slave Populations in Old and New Sugar Colonies, 1815–22

Colony	Year	% Change
Barbados	1817–20	+4.4
Montserrat	1817–21	+0.5
St. Kitts	1817–22	−5.7
Antigua	1817–21	−4.3
Jamaica	1817–20	−0.7
Trinidad	1816–19	−18.5
Demerara-Essequibo	1817–20	−9.8

Source: B. W. Higman, *Slave Populations of the British Caribbean, 1807–34* (Baltimore: Johns Hopkins University Press, 1984), pp. 308–310.

1,146 slaves tended coffee, 1,1040 grew cocoa, 779 produced foodstuffs, and 506 cultivated cotton.[9]

The settlement of Demerara in 1803, during the war with the French, availed the English of sugar lands greater than those on offer in Trinidad and Jamaica. Demerara had the lowest per capita slave population and the second highest negative growth performance among the enslaved population (see table 11.1). This development caused considerable anxiety within the anti-slavery camp. It was believed that the two new colonies would stimulate renewed confidence in the slave economy and spiral demand for slaves.

Furthermore, legislators who supported the abolition agenda, no matter how conceived, understood that the expansion of the sugar frontier could endanger much of what was done by way of ameliorating the conditions of slaves. In general, they feared that the enormous injection of fresh acreage into the plantation economy would relegate emancipation considerations to the bottom of imperial concerns for at least fifty years. It was for this reason that the Pitt government, in seeking to keep faith with Wilberforce, agreed in 1805, two years before the seminal legislation, to limit the ability of these colonies to acquire slaves.

The influential Barbadian sugar producers were divided. They had within their ranks a minority that saw a brighter future in migrating to the new colonies. But most saw the new spaces as presenting competition in the years ahead and wished them closed. Barbados alone was experiencing sustainable growth among the slave population in 1807. Table 11.2 shows that the colony had been a steady exporter of slaves for at least two decades, mostly to the

Table 11.2. Slave Imports and Exports in Barbados, 1788–1804

Year	Imports	Exports
1788	1,585	1,270
1789	556	490
1790	131	91
1791	426	310
1792	744	590
1793	1,438	1,107
1794	1,218	943
1795	2,059	1,729
1796	3,582	3,280
1797	3,462	2,895
1798	3,244	2,786
1799	1,968	1,491
1800	830	796
1801	—	—
1802	608	400
1803	3,177	2,498
1804	999	874
Total	26,027	21,550

Source: Governor Seaforth to the Earl of Camden, 7 Jan. 1805, C.O. 28/72, f. 55, Public Records Office, London.

Windward Islands, where merchants and planters had been making important capital investments.

In this regard Barbados established a reputation for being "overstocked" with slaves and was expected in some quarters to supply its needy neighbor.[10] But while colonists there were looking for new opportunities in neighboring frontier colonies, they were also keen to protect the competitive standing of what they had already created. The impact of the 1807 legislation, then, varied considerably within and between colonies. Abolition subverted the enormous economic capacity of Trinidad and the Guianas. Neither emerged as a large-scale sugar producer surpassing Jamaica, Britain's prized plantation. Jamaica was weakened but was expected to survive by introducing labor management measures in order to increase both production and productivity.

Uneven economic conditions were reflected in the price and productivity differentials between net-exporting and net-importing colonies. This circumstance contributed principally to the general direction and volume of trans-

Table 11.3. Slave Population of Guiana, 1762–1812

Year	Essequibo	Demerara	Berbice
		Region	
1762	2,571	1,648	4,077
1782	8,700	12,559	7,000
1796	n.a.	n.a.	8,232
1812	18,000	47,000	25,169

Source: Alvin Thompson, *Colonialism and Underdevelopment in Guyana, 1580–1803* (Bridgetown: Carib, 1987), p. 93.

fers. Slaveowners in the Windwards and the Leewards were among the first to admit that their soils were exhausted by sugar monoculture and that the proximity of abundant fertile soil was a major attraction. Planters in the Windward Islands in particular did not feel confident in post-1807 conditions, and many folded up their operations and looked to sell slaves in Trinidad.[11]

As part of the campaign to attract new investments from the older colonies, as well as from Europe, sugar producers in the Guianas and Trinidad highlighted their advantage in labor productivity, which they measured in tonnage of sugar output per slave. Although they also emphasized superior sugar yield per acre, the focus was on labor because this was the scarce factor of production. By drawing attention to low slave prices in the older colonies and showing considerably higher prices in their economies, they hoped to sponsor a significant transfer business.[12]

Settlers in Demerara also boasted such advantages over colleagues in Berbice, which had been a major Dutch sugar colony during the eighteenth century. Significant inflows from Berbice contributed to the absolute growth in the slave population after 1807. The colony also benefited as a result of transfers from the islands, some coming from as far away as the Bahamas. Table 11.3 shows that the relative increase was greater in Demerara, a reflection of the widespread expectation that the sugar sector would yield much greater profits than could reasonably be imagined in the islands.

Relative to earlier intercolonial migration, the number of slaves transferred after 1807 was substantial. In no way was it comparable to the annual input from the transatlantic slave trade. In the decade before 1807, the sugar colonies imported heavily from Africa. Even the Bahamas, which was not a sugar colony but relied on minor crops such as cotton and sponges, was a major importer, although a significant share of imports were reexported. Jamaica was heavily dependent on the African market, as were the new colonies of Trinidad and Guiana.

According to Philip Curtin, Trinidad imported 12,400 slaves in the years between 1797 (the year of its attachment by the British) and 1807. Higman considers Curtin's figure a significant underestimation of the volume. He noted that at least 9,000 were imported from Africa in the years 1802, 1803, and 1805. Furthermore, he asserted that the vast majority of slaves in the newer colonies on the eve of the 1807 abolition were recent African imports.[13]

After 1807 these newer colonies continued to experience rising demand for slaves that could only be legally met by intercolonial transfers. Williams deduces from the fragmented evidence that at least thirteen thousand slaves were imported into the Guianas and Trinidad between 1808 and 1825 and that most of these came from Barbados and the Windward Islands. He emphasizes the inability of the data to yield an accurate count but draws attention to the increasing volume over time and the lack of political will within colonial administrations to clamp down on expansion.[14] Higman concludes that about twenty thousand enslaved persons were transferred to the newer colonies during the period and suggests that although the figure was considerable in the context of policy and legislative actions against slave trading, it was not large enough to have a transformative impact on general demographic and economic trends within the regional slave system.[15]

Slave transfers were never sufficiently large to act as a stabilizing or reversing factor in the negative growth performance of net-importing colonies. At no stage did the aggregate number of slaves transferred exceed 5 percent of the total slave population in any of these colonies. Neither did a colony export more than 10 percent of its slave population during the period. According to Eltis, "In the busiest single year, 1816, less than 0.5% of the slave population was involved. In Berbice, the Bahamas, and Dominica, none of which contained very large numbers of slaves, exports were never more than 5% percent of the slave population in the twenty-two-year period."[16] Less is known about the profiles of transferees, but there is enough evidence to show that their impact on the demographics was negligible in terms of general trends and patterns.

Eltis, too, acknowledges the limitations of the data. He concludes, nonetheless, that more than "22,000 slaves were shipped between the various British West Indian colonies in the twenty-three years after the abolition of the African Slave Trade." Table 11.4 illustrates the distribution of these transfers, but Eltis tells us something important: "Only three colonies had net imports on a signifi-

Table 11.4. Movements of Slaves Between the British Caribbean Colonies, 1808–30

	Imports			Exports		
	1 Mar. 1808 to 31 Dec. 1814	1 Jan. 1815 to 28 Feb. 1825	1 Mar. 1825 to 30 July 1830	1 Mar. 1808 to 31 Dec. 1814	1 Jan. 1815 to 28 Feb. 1825	1 Mar. 1825 to 30 July 1830
Tobago		136	45		18	49
Demerara	312	7,350			60	238
Berbice	49	518	125	83	3,505	80
St. Kitts	55	51	17	114	239	30
St. Lucia		85	0		26	0
Trinidad	353	5,843	672	103	103	
Dominica	0	4	27	293	2,982	81
Grenada	30	220	10	82	834	12
St. Vincent	459	1,692	0	321	833	0
Barbados	0	148	26	8	263	348
Antigua	7	74	0	129	99	0
Jamaica	17	1,888	5	890	848	8
Bahamas	0	97	44	0	3,087	34
Subtotal	1,282	18,106	971	2,023	12,897	880
Total for 1808–30		20,359			15,800	

Source: David Eltis, "Traffic in Slaves Between British West Indian Colonies, 1807–1833," *Economic History Review* 25 (1972): 55–64.

cant scale. The three, Demerara, Trinidad and St Vincent, attracted imports from all across the Caribbean, but in each case there were one or two colonies which supplied the vast majority of the imports: Demerara drew heavily from Berbice, and less heavily from the Bahamas and Dominica; Trinidad's main sources were Grenada and Dominica and to a lesser extent Barbados; St Vincent's inflow came largely from Dominica and the Bahamas."[17] Custom House records for Trinidad show double-digit import levels for the years 1813–1816 coming from twelve colonies. These data are presented in table 11.5.

Significantly, neither Williams nor Eltis includes in his calculations the thousands of "liberated Africans," persons captured on the seas from illegal slavers by the British Navy and employed as apprentices in labor-starved colonies.

Neither has there been an attempt to estimate the number of slaves who were smuggled between colonies. Yet widespread allegations of extensive

Table 11.5. Sources of Trinidadian Slave Imports, 1813–16

Colony	1813	1814	1815	1816
Antigua	2	—	20	18
Barbados	4	11	41	65
Bermuda	7	3	11	1
Dominica	—	67	413	167
Grenada	15	44	245	324
Guadeloupe	5	38	24	159
Martinique	6	91	11	2
St. Kitts	—	—	11	5
St. Lucia	—	11	35	20
St. Martin	—	12	2	5
St. Vincent	5	5	18	29
Tobago	—	3	6	11

Source: Colonial Office Papers, C.O. 295/55, ff. 355–356, Public Records Office, London.

smuggling should indicate that it might have been larger in volume than legal transfers. Most colonies reported cases of smuggling from colonies across, as well as within, imperial lines.

Governors frequently reported cases in which local officials were in sympathy with sugar planters and condoned the breach of law. Ragatz concludes that in most cases "sensational allegations" of rampant smuggling, when investigated, "appear to have been barren of results." Williams, however, suggests that the payment of one guinea per head to the chief custom officer for each slave forfeited was a part of an attempt by the governor to suppress the illegal activity that might have been running ahead of legitimate commerce.[18]

Several laws were passed by the British Parliament in order to reduce and control the movement of slaves between colonies. The result was a network of interconnected laws passed over the course of two decades. The 1806 Act to Prevent the Importation of Slaves focused directly on slaves supplied from Africa. It did not outlaw the movement of slaves between colonies but established a licensing arrangement that monitored and restricted such transfers.

In this way Parliament made provision for local adjustments to the secondary labor market. It identified a number of special circumstances under which transfers would be exempted. A license was to be acquired from the local government in order to take a slave out of the colony, and the owner of the slave was required to post a bond for the slave named. In order to facilitate the normal migrations of free persons between colonies, legislators exempted free persons who carried up to two slaves provided that they were household servants, sailors, or fishermen, and their names registered with the captain as passengers.

An additional provision was made to further burden persons who wished to transfer slaves into Trinidad and Demerara. A license also had to be acquired from the governor of the importing colonies. Furthermore, a limit was placed on the ability of these colonies to accommodate incoming slaves. A ceiling was set to contain the annual inflow at no more than three per hundred of the existing slave population. This meant that a governor was expected to constantly review the changing demographics of the slave population in order to effectively implement the policy.[19]

Williams makes much of the evidence that suggests how imperial policy was conceived to encourage subversion of the law by means of the compliance and corruption of local officials. He stresses that legislators were not concerned unduly with this aspect of the slave trade. Knowing the difficult and awkward positions governors generally occupied in these colonies, he implies that legislators might have established the machinery with the expectation that breaches would be defended locally.

Eltis states the case in different terms. He focuses on an imperial tendency to develop policy more for the protection of British capital than to enhance the well-being of the enslaved population. A major concern was that postwar negotiations would lead to the return of these colonies to their former imperial owners. By the signing of the postwar treaty Trinidad and Demerara were ceded to Britain. This outcome removed doubts about the future of capital investments and facilitated the expansion process.[20]

The 1806 act, then, was not intended to stem the flow of slaves between colonies. What alarmed those who lobbied against the slave trade, however, was evidence showing that the smuggling of slaves into these colonies was also done with the support of local officials. Shutting down the Atlantic trade was the top priority for British legislators. But this objective made it necessary to push another bill through Parliament in 1811 making the illegal trade in enslaved Africans a felony.

It is possible that more slaves were smuggled across imperial lines than were legally transferred between colonies. But neither the 1807 act nor the 1811 act developed serious penalties to combat the continuous expansion of the intercolonial trade. Slavers argued that such laws would not be acceptable and that the imperial government could not break their resolve to reject restrictions on the enjoyment of their property rights in slaves. Cases of smuggling were prosecuted under the 1806 and 1811 laws. Generally, they met with political responses and solutions that indicated the difficulties faced by the colonial judiciary in suppressing both types of slave trafficking.

Unable to stem the illegal flow in slaves and bring order to the transfer trade, abolitionists argued that slaveowners were doing all they could to subvert the law. As a result they adopted a two-part strategy. First, they suggested that a head count approach to the problem was the only reliable way to identify illegal imports and monitor the legitimacy of legal transfers. This required colonies to develop census materials in order to register the slave population in a way that would enable significant demographic changes to be identified.[21]

James Stephen, heading the campaign for the Colonial Office, called for a comprehensive, centrally organized registration system as early as 1812. By means of an Order in Council, the governor of Trinidad partially instituted such a system. According to Ragatz, "Census returns for 1811 had shown an official total of 21,288 slaves in the colony; the first registration of 1813, four and a half thousand more — 25,717. This increase was seized upon . . . as proof that extensive smuggling had taken place and became the basis for a four year long struggle to establish compulsory registration in all the Caribbean possessions."[22]

Slaveowners disagreed with Stephen's conclusion and used public institutions as sites of opposition. They foregrounded the argument that the required registration of all slaves was part of the abolitionists' plan to push through a bill for general emancipation. This argument posed a special political problem for the Barbadian slavers. They had used it to explain the large-scale uprising of their slaves in April 1816. In their opinion, the rebels had acted in support of the abolitionists who had secured the support of the monarch for general emancipation.[23] The slaves in turn had articulated the view that their rebellion was an attempt to implement the royal wish as expressed by abolitionists. Slavers, then, in defending their interests, were providing ideological ammunition to the enslaved for their emancipation campaign.

The second approach was to gradually reduce the size of legal transfers by further narrowing the band of select categories. This meant new legislation, because previous acts were considered too generous. Two separate acts passed in 1818 and 1825 sought to address this concern by targeting occupational groups who could be legally transferred rather than imposing numerical limits. These laws provided that only domestic slaves, sailors, and fishermen could be exempted from the licensing arrangement.

At the same time the 1818 act relaxed the provision that new colonies could import annually under license from old colonies a number of slaves up to 3 percent of the existing slave population. The argument used by legislators was that the removal of the cap was in the interest of the slaves. Such transfer, the act stated, might tend to ameliorate the material condition of slaves in economically depressed colonies. This adjustment reflected slaveowners' reasoning that in the crisis-ridden nonsugar sector in colonies such as the Bahamas and Dominica, slaves were experiencing severe hardship, and only their removal to more prosperous areas could prevent catastrophic disaster.

The 1825 Consolidated Slave Act, with which the imperial government legally declared its policy of gradual emancipation, formally tied applications for slave transfers to the amelioration project. The focus shifted away from occupational groups and limits to the nature of the impact of relocations on the slaves. According to the terms of the act only the British Privy Council could issue import licenses, and it was expected to do so only on the submission of evidence that the slaves would benefit. The law obliged slaveowners, furthermore, to provide a bond as evidence of commitment to keep families intact and that slaves would travel in relative comfort.

The enslaved community held views regarding transfers that were articulated with much the same passion and precision as those of the free community. There was no single, simple opinion among its members, who could be grouped into three broad categories. First, some slaves were assertive proponents of amelioration policies and resisted attempts to restructure and disrupt their social lives by relocation. They were keen to report objections to magistrates when family members were slated for relocation. Often, they confronted owners in large groups when told of transfer proposals.[24]

Estate and court records, for example, reflect the link between the social instability associated with transfers to frontier colonies and marronage. Slaves knew as well as whites that Trinidad and Demerara were experiencing considerably higher mortality rates and were notorious as places where the work regime was harsh as well as deadly. Soggy, waterlogged valleys and plains, in addition to swamplands, were being drained and prepared for sugar cultivation. Slaves knew of the debilitating work this project entailed. Their health experiences and medical culture had taught them to avoid areas such as these that were infested with mosquitoes.

Second, slaves understood the hardships related to subsistence in some colonies, particularly in the Windward Islands. Part of the push from these colonies, then, was the crisis of subsistence that produced among some slaves a keen material interest in relocation. Flight from hardship, therefore, was not confined to whites. Furthermore, there were instances in which slaveowners and slaves agreed to approach resettlement jointly with enthusiasm.

The third category included slaves who were a part of the normal clandestine movement between colonies. They knew the physical landscape and general living conditions across the region in as much detail as did members of the free community. Island-hopping slaves, including fugitives from the law, had established a survival network that operated between colonies. The knowledge they gained was shared with the enslaved community and was a feature of its social and political life.

The flexible aspect of slave relations in these colonies enhanced mechanisms whereby slaves were allowed to "freely" travel between colonies looking for work or selling goods. Barbadian hucksters and artisan slaves, for example, who were "self employed" and who paid a part of their income to owners, were keen travelers between colonies in search of better wages and prices. Slaves, then, held a range of opinions regarding resettlement. The evidence in general suggests, however, that the majority held reservations about it and were likely to protest relocation.[25]

Abolitionists in the Colonial Office would instruct governors to enforce the law by ensuring that voyages made between colonies to transfer slaves in no way resembled the Atlantic crossing. This meant that slaves were to be treated as passengers rather than cargo. The assurance, however, could not be given. With the opening of frontier colonies slaveowners began the practice of using the transfer mechanism as a form of punishment for rebellious or insubordinate slaves. Part of the punishment was shipment in chains. Being sold "overseas" during this period, therefore, was a part of the reign of terror that owners considered an effective strategy. Such concerns informed the decision of Parliament to outlaw after 1828 all transfers except for fishermen, sailors, and domestics accompanying their owners. But, critically, there continued to be no obligation on owners to take these slaves when they returned to their homes.

After 1828, a greater onus was placed on persons wishing to transfer a slave to show evidence of ownership or legitimate possession, residency in the colony from which the slave was being removed, that the slave was attached as a servant companion of the person in whose name the license was issued, and that the two were to travel on the same vessel. This approach proved equally open to abuse. According to Williams, an interesting question arose as to whether infants, much in demand, could properly be considered domestics within the meaning of the act.[26]

For all practical purposes the 1828 regulation was of little avail. The evidence from Trinidad and Demerara indicates that there was widespread violation of its provisions. Customs officers seemed quite amused, notes Williams, by the arrival of a stream of "domestics" ostensibly in the employ of ladies and strangers. Many of these blacks were sold to persons willing to take the risk of traveling with them, while those who could not attract buyers were left behind.[27]

Williams's conclusion that the degree of fraud was large is borne out by the descriptions presented to the Colonial Office by governors. With respect to Barbados, Governor Lyon was satisfied that many slaves taken to Trinidad were not kept in the domestic service of persons they accompanied but were bound for resale or conversion to plantation labor. In his judgment, there was little more that could be done to stop this movement, described by a colonial official as "an unfeeling traffick," so long as the owner of a slave could obtain twice or three times the price by selling the slave in frontier colonies.[28]

Not surprisingly, Demerara and Trinidad became net importers in the decade between 1818 and 1828. Higman shows that the former achieved a net import balance of seventy-five hundred between 1808 and 1828 and the latter secured a net import balance of about six thousand between 1813 and 1825. The principal net exporters were the Bahamas, Berbice, Barbados, and Dominica. Net importing colonies did not report satisfaction that the labor shortage was impacted, and there continued to be a feeling in the exporting colonies that there was insufficient work to productively employ the enslaved labor force.[29]

The number of enslaved persons transferred to the newer colonies, therefore, was insufficient to alter in any meaningful way the principal demographic features of any one colony. Slaveowners were unable to control the composition by age and sex of transfers. Certainly, they would have preferred to import a predominately male labor force for the development of plantation infrastructure. Lacking selective control for age and sex, slaveowners did not consider the transfer business efficient, and they much preferred the range of choice available within the Atlantic trade before 1807.[30]

Trinidad's statistics for the peak period of 1815–25 show the ineffectiveness of transfers with regard to these factors. For a sample of 538 enslaved persons transferred from the Bahamas to the colony in 1822, the ratio of males to females was 107:100. For the Bahamas at the time of export the sex ratio was 104:100. Furthermore, with respect to the 2,500 enslaved persons imported into Trinidad between 1822 and 1825, there were 115 males to 100 females, and for the colony as a whole there were 124. Higman concludes from these data that although the slaveowners were able to attract a relatively large number of men from the older colonies they did less well than when they had participated in the Atlantic trade.[31]

An important reason for insufficient cohort control was that most of the slaves transferred into Trinidad came from a few large plantation properties and from the urban sector in exporter colonies. It was the norm for entire groups of slaves to be transferred from a given plantation with no regard to gender or age differences. In the case of Barbados, the majority of slaves transferred between 1817 and 1820 originated in Bridgetown, the capital, and its environs. After 1825, when mainly domestics were exported, the parish of St. Michael, which hosted Bridgetown, was a principal exporter of the larger female component.[32]

Stephen was keen to show that such slave transfers were not directed at the expansion of the sugar sector, as argued by investors in frontier development, but was an aspect of the legacy of mercantile speculation associated with slave trading. His findings regarding illegal transfers were presented to the government as part of an effort to show the importance and wisdom of a compulsory registration policy. He relied on informed persons in the colonies to supply the data that he shared with Parliament. In 1828 he told the government: "There appears very strong grounds for suspecting that the great comparative value of slaves in Trinidad has tempted many persons to make fraudulent importations from Barbados, by attributing the character of domestics to slaves whom it was never intended really to employ in that capacity." Data for Trinidad show that of 266 slaves who were imported from Barbados under license in 1827, 204 were no longer in the employ of the person in whose name the license was issued. Another group of 81 were doing jobs that fell outside the category of "domestic."[33]

Slaveowners and their legal representatives contested as best they could efforts by the imperial government to impose such restrictions on their right to use their chattel in a manner beneficial to themselves. They objected to being defined as legal offenders by imperial officials who assumed that each change of a slave's occupation was done in an attempt to subvert the law. Rising to their defense, Attorney General Henry Fuller of Trinidad told them that no law existed in the colony to prevent their redeployment of slaves from domestic service to field gangs. Many domestics, he said, preferred life on the plantation to life in the towns, and many did not consider the seasonal nature of field work more burdensome than housework.[34]

Similarly, a customs official in Barbados, disputing the governor's claim that the trade in domestics to Trinidad was in fact a covert traffic in field hands, argued that were the numbers large the slaves themselves would have objected. In 1829 the controller of customs, while objecting to this allegation, reminded the governor that slaves in Trinidad and Guiana, unlike their counterparts on the island, were invested with the power to appeal to the protector of slaves, a public official who survived the changeover from Spanish to English law. On being informed of such a facility, a Colonial Office spokesman replied that local domestic slaves would carry the greater burden since they would be sent to the fields in order to make room for imported domestics.[35]

In Barbados, the 1829 Franklin case gained notoriety throughout the region because it symbolized slaveowners' views concerning the use of legislation to control and limit the intercolonial transfer of slaves. For Williams, the case indicated the lengths to which slaveowners went in opposition to antislavery policy and imperial officials in the colonies. On the surface the case began like many others. Franklin, described in the records as a modest slaveowner, received various licenses in order to ship fourteen of his slaves to Trinidad. He indicated that they were to travel with his family.[36] These persons, most of them children, were not put to domestic work. Franklin was adjudged to have violated the law, an offense for which he was imprisoned.

The trial by grand jury predictably led to Franklin's acquittal. His peers took the view that a slaveowner should not be presumed a criminal for altering the nature of his slaves' occupation. Empowered by the verdict, Franklin secured substantial funding to bring a suit against the magistrate who signed the documents under whose terms he was sent to prison. Significant sections of the colonial elite, many lawyers included, rallied to his aid in seeking damages to the value of £5,000 pounds (colonial currency) for false imprisonment.[37]

News of the case reached neighboring colonies and was widely reported in the press. Franklin was described by the governor as a "man of straw" who was backed by men of substance whose interest it was to create a "system of intimidation" and "embarrass the Government" in order to compromise and repress the "efforts of public officials . . . in the prosecution of offenders." The Colonial Office understood all too well that Franklin was a front and that the struggle "had really been waged with the Officers of Customs rather than with him."[38]

The battle, though, was much wider in scope. The field of contest was the very future of British slavery in the Caribbean. Imperial interests were still in a celebratory mode with respect to the bounty represented by two large frontier colonies. Some slaveowners in the "old" colonies were anxious to take the new breath of life offered by large tracts of fertile soil. The frontier had obvious economic attraction for investors. The collusion of imperial and colonial interests in this regard seemed sufficiently compelling to allow the market to determine the outcome.

Abolitionists, however, had other ideas. They saw the potential in these colonies for a grand revival of interest in colonial slavery and used the practice of intercolonial transfers of slaves to test the durability and depth of their support in the British legislature. They were determined to limit the ambitions of slavers who saw in the frontier colonies a new lease on life. The old colonies, they knew, ran the risk of dying on the vine unless they could wean themselves from any kind of slave trading, and the new colonies would not be allowed to make a case for rolling back the abolitionist policy.

The slaves, too, had their say in determining the outcome of the debate and the formulation of ameliorative legislation. They knew the limitations of their political voice but in general turned their faces against the new colonies until slavery was abolished. The point was not lost on slaveowners that the post-1807 movements of slaves were taking place within a charged political environment that featured not only imperial rivalry but an upsurge in the number and frequency of slave rebellions in the aftermath of the Haitian revolution.

Barbados, considered the "safest" of England's colonies on account of not having experienced a rebellion in the "long" eighteenth century, had its first slave war in 1816. Demerara followed in 1823, and reports of the connection between these rebellions informed popular understanding of slaves' intercolonial linkages. Both rebellions were associated, at least in the slaves' minds, with the idea that registration procedures were a prelude to emancipation. This was the slaveowners' own line, and they had been hooked by their slaves. When slavery was finally abolished, blacks in Barbados migrated by the thousands to Guiana and Trinidad in search of new opportunities for self-empowerment. The colonial government was forced to pass antiemigration legislation to stem the tide for fear of having the local labor force decimated.[39]

The intercolonial slave trade, then, raised more ideological issues in political fora than it resolved economic problems on the frontier. Abolitionists may have had their finest hour in effectively marginalizing the new frontier within the empire. They ensured that the expansionist possibilities of newly acquired colonies did not rise on the basis of an emerging slave system in the way that was the case in Cuba at the same time. For this important reason it would not be accurate to say that the intense debate and the many legislative interventions were much ado about little.

Notes

1. See David Eltis, *The Rise and Fall of African Slavery in the Americas* (Cambridge: Cambridge University Press, 2000); Seymour Drescher, *Econocide: British Slavery in the Era of Abolition* (Pittsburgh: Pittsburgh University Press, 1977); Drescher, *Capitalism and Anti-Slavery: British Mobilization in Comparative Perspective* (Oxford: Oxford University Press, 1986); David Geggus, "Slavery, War, and Revolution in the Greater Caribbean, 1789–1815," in *A Turbulent Time: The French Revolution and the Greater Caribbean,* ed. David B. Gaspar and David Geggus (Gainesville: University of Florida Press, 1997), pp. 1–50; B. W. Higman, *Slave Populations of the British Caribbean, 1807–34* (Baltimore: Johns Hopkins University Press, 1984); Sidney Mintz, "Models of Emancipation During the Age of Revolution," *Slavery and Abolition* 17, no. 2 (1996): 1–21.

2. J. R. Ward, *British West Indian Slavery, 1750–1834* (Oxford: Oxford University

Press, 1988); Hilary Beckles, *Natural Rebels: A Social History of Enslaved Black Women in Barbados* (New Brunswick: Rutgers University Press, 1989).

3. See Governor Woodford to Colonial Office, 15 Oct. 1815, C.O. 2^{95}/37, Public Records Office, London.

4. See Hilary Beckles, *Natural Rebels;* Beckles, *Black Rebellion in Barbados: The Struggle Against Slavery, 1627–1834* (Bridgetown, Barbados: Antilles, 1985); Karl Watson, *Barbados: Civilised Isle: A Social History* (Bridgetown, Barbados: n.p., 1979).

5. Lowell J. Ragatz, *The Fall of the Planter Class in the British Caribbean, 1763–1833* (New York: Octagon Books, 1977), pp. 385–407; Eric Williams, "The British West Indian Slave Trade After Its Abolition in 1807," *Journal of Negro History* 27 (1942): 175–91; David Eltis, "Traffic in Slaves Between British West Indian Colonies, 1807–1833," *Economic History Review* 25 (1972): 55–64; Higman, *Slave Populations,* pp. 80–99; A. Meredith John, *The Plantation Slaves of Trinidad, 1783–1816* (Cambridge: Cambridge University Press, 1988), pp. 44–61, 164–167; George Roberts, "Movements in Slave Populations of the Caribbean During the Period of Slave Registration," in *Comparative Perspectives on Slavery in the New World Plantation Societies,* ed. V. Rubin and A. Tuden (New York: New York Academy of Science, 1977), pp. 145–60; Robin Blackburn, *The Overthrow of Colonial Slavery, 1776–1848* (London: Verso, 1988), pp. 316–326.

6. Higman, *Slave Populations,* pp. 80–82; Beckwith to Collector and Comptroller of Customs, Nov. 22, 1810, C.O. 2879; Proceedings Under the Abolition Laws; Letters from Collector of Customs, Demerara, to Commissioners of Customs, London, June, 1831; Colonel Codd to Sec. Bathurst, Nov. 18, 1813, C.O. 1^{11}/16, all in Public Records Office, London.

7. See Seymour Drescher, "The Fragmentation of Atlantic Slavery and the British Inter-colonial Slave Trade, 1805–1839," paper presented at the conference "Domestic Passages: Internal Slave Trades in the Americas, 1808–1888," Yale University, Oct. 22–24, 1999.

8. Ibid.; see also Higman, *Slave Populations,* pp. 88–92.

9. John, *Plantation Slaves of Trinidad,* pp. 47–57; Registrar of Slaves' Report of Slave Exports from Trinidad, 1813–18, C.O. 2^{95}/55, f. 356, Public Records Office, London.

10. Higman, *Slave Populations,* p. 87; Williams, "British West Indian Slave Trade," p. 176.

11. See speeches by Ellis, *Parliamentary Debates,* 2:652, June 30, 1804; Beckwith to Collector and Comptroller of Customs, Nov. 22, 1810, C.O. 28/79, Public Records Office, London.

12. *The Speeches of the Rt. Hon. William Huskisson with a Biographical Memoir* (London: n.p., 1831), 3:610; Colonel Codd to Bathhurst, Nov. 18, 1813, C.O. 1^{11}/16, Public Records Office, London; Evidence of John Mayers, Agent for Barbados, House of Commons Sessional Papers, 1831–32, no. 381, p. 15.

13. Philip Curtin, *The Atlantic Slave Trade: A Census* (Madison: University of Wisconsin Press, 1969), p. 68; Higman, *Slave Populations,* p. 78.

14. Williams, "British West Indian Slave Trade," p. 178.

15. Higman, *Slave Populations,* p. 81.

16. Eltis, "Traffic in Slaves," p. 59.

17. Ibid., p. 57.

18. Ragatz, *Fall of the Planter Class*, p. 393; Williams, "British West Indian Slave Trade," pp. 176–181.

19. See Eltis, "Traffic in Slaves," pp. 55–58.

20. Williams, "British West Indian Slave Trade," pp. 178–182; Eltis, "Traffic in Slaves," pp. 55–58.

21. Williams, "British West Indian Slave Trade," pp. 178–182; Eltis, "Traffic in Slaves," pp. 55–58.

22. Ragatz, *Fall of the Planter Class*, p. 390; see James Stephen, *Reasons for Establishing a Registry of Slaves in the Colonies* (London: Smith, 1815), pp. 22–28, 83–107; Stephen, *A Defence of the Bill for the Registration of Slaves* (London: Smith, 1816).

23. *A Review of the Reasons Given for Establishing a Registry of Slaves in the British Colonies* (London: n.d.); *Arguments in Support of the Proposed Bill for the Registration of Slaves in the West Indian Colonies* (London, 1817).

24. The case of Barbados slaves was set out in Andrew Pankhurst to Governor Grant, Aug. 13, 1829, C.O. 2⁹⁵/₈₁, Public Records Office, London.

25. See Higman, *Slave Populations*, p. 84.

26. Williams, "British West Indian Slave Trade," p. 179.

27. Ibid.

28. Grant to Murray, July 10, 1829, C.O. 2⁹⁵/₈₁, Public Records Office, London; Williams, "British West Indian Slave Trade," p. 188.

29. Higman, *Slave Populations*, p. 80.

30. Ibid., p. 82.

31. Ibid., pp. 82–83.

32. Ibid.

33. Stephen to Twiss, Oct. 17, 1828, C.O. 2⁹⁵/₇₉, Public Records Office, London; Williams, "British West Indian Slave Trade," p. 181.

34. Williams, "British West Indian Slave Trade," p. 181.

35. Bowell to Murray, Aug. 25, 1828, C.O. 2⁸/₀₂, Public Records Office, London.

36. See documents relating to this case in Attorney General of Barbados to Governor Lyon, June 25, 1829, C.O. 2⁸/₁₀₃, Public Records Office, London.

37. Stephen to Twiss, March 10, 1830, C.O. 2⁸/₁₀₆, Public Records Office, London.

38. Lyon to Murray, Sept. 28, 1830, C.O. 2⁸/₁₀₅; Lyon to Goderich, April 3, 1831, C.O. 2⁸/₁₀₇; Stephen to Twiss, March 10, 1830, C.O. 2⁸/₁₀₆, Public Records Office, London.

39. Hilary Beckles, "Emancipation by Law or War? Wilberforce and the 1816 Barbados Slave Rebellion," in *Abolition and Its Aftermath, 1790–1916,* ed. David Richardson (London: Frank Cass, 1985), pp. 80–105.

12

The Kelsall Affair
A Black Bahamian Family's Odyssey in Turbulent 1840s Cuba

MANUEL BARCIA PAZ

I have good authority for saying that there are many estates in this island where the English language alone is spoken amongst the slaves, thus clearly showing their origin; and I have no doubt that if I made subject of nego-tiation, every one of those unfortunates would be rescued from bondage, wherein they are now illegally suffering.

—*Joseph T. Crawford*

On 25 May 1844, the commander in chief and governor of the Bahamas, Major General Sir Francis Cockburn, wrote a letter to the British consul in Havana, Joseph Tucker Crawford. The aim of this message was to inform him about some individuals from the Bahamas who remained in slavery in Cuba after they had been freed in 1822. This letter marked the beginning of a turbulent affair involving Crawford, Cuban governor Captain General Leo-poldo O'Donnell, and the Bahamian slaveholders in the eastern neighborhood of Candelaria who kept the said free persons in slavery. This was a minor episode in the fight between two of the empires interested in the destiny of the "ever faithful island of Cuba."[1]

Cockburn's request arrived in Cuba in the midst of the repression of a black conspiracy known as La Escalera, which had been uncovered only six months earlier by the Cuban landowner Esteban Santa Cruz de Oviedo in his *ingenio* (sugar mill) Santísima Trinidad. By June 1844 a large number of free and enslaved blacks were awaiting a verdict in jail. Meanwhile, some others had managed to flee, but many died every day because of the severe punishment they received from colonial public prosecutors.

By June 1844 the most renowned leaders were executed, among them the famous mulatto poet Gabriel de la Concepción Valdés, also known as Plácido. In those days even the British officials in Havana were vulnerable to the Cuban government's response to the slave conspiracy. James Kennedy, a judge in the Court of Mixed Commission, which had been established in the Cuban capital, was publicly accused of being one of the masterminds of the conspiracy together with the former British consul David Turnbull.[2] Crawford had also spent the first half of 1844 in a difficult struggle with Spanish authorities to free a few imprisoned British citizens accused of instigating the conspiracy among the blacks.[3]

During this period the entire island was plagued by problems. Eyewitnesses' testimonies offer a clear vision of the precarious order existing in the colony in 1844, usually remembered as "the year of fear," "the year of the whip," or "the year of La Escalera." The testimony of a Tarragona infantry regiment's attorney, a second lieutenant named Rosendo Armada, was perhaps the first to reproach such butchery. Armada criticized the whole Spanish penal system by suggesting that the conspiracy never existed except in the minds of the authorities. His "here and there" is today a precious resource for appreciating the realm of death surrounding him at that hour: "Here were put in the prisoners' mouths words they never said; there appeared partial agreements, mistakes and indignities; here emerged the excessive use of alcohol, transforming the orderly proceedings into dangerous ones; there were gifts, blackmails, violent acts, knocks, shameful ways, papers which came up from the same inexhaustible source of evil, in order to capture notoriety sustained on the blood."[4]

It was in this context that Cockburn's dispatch arrived in Cuba, containing in the same envelope a few copies of manumission certifications signed in the Bahamas on 14 March 1822 by Mary Elizabeth Kelsall, then a widow from New Providence.[5] These originals had been sealed in the presence of a friend, Samuel Chapman, and the widow's son-in-law Joseph Eysing. Registered copies of the documents remained in the Bahamas while the witnesses traveled to Cuba together with Mary Elizabeth Kelsall and her slaves. These men, who had received their "freedom" that day, were all brothers, and their names were Nat, Cuffee, John, Newton, Billy, and Daniel Kelsall.[6] Although the six men had been officially freed on that long-ago morning, five of them had remained in slavery for a period of more than twenty years.

Soon after granting freedom to her slaves, Mary Elizabeth Kelsall and her family had emigrated to Cuba, taking advantage of the opportunities offered by the Cuban civil authorities' policy of encouraging white immigration. The widow's slaves — even those who had been freed in March 1822 — came with her to Cuba, leaving behind a place in which the institution of slavery was under daily attack from the British abolitionist movement. The Cuban government's promotion of this kind of emigration appeared to these Bahamian slaveowners as an opportunity to conserve their wealth and security, which were based on their slaves' labor.

It seems that the six brothers did not realize that they had attained their freedom before a public official in Nassau. This assumption is reinforced by the fact that, once in Cuba, they were eventually separated and sold by their Bahamian owners. If they had had knowledge of their condition as freed men, one would assume that they would have fought for their freedom, but they never did.

Mary Elizabeth Kelsall died less than two years after she signed their liberation documents in the Bahamas. With her death the last hopes of the Kelsall brothers to know about their real situation disappeared. Twenty years later, they learned the truth.

We can only imagine what they felt when the truth was revealed to them. Legally free for more than two decades, these men had lost their youth working as slaves for cruel masters. All of them gave the same testimony when their case eventually came to trial: they never knew about their emancipation. Furthermore, they recalled that all of them were obliged to sign, while they were still in Nassau, a document appointing them to work as apprentices in Cuba.

Indeed, they had been trapped. They had signed by drawing a cross, a custom for those who could not read and write at that time, but they were not informed about the document they signed. One of them, Newton, said to the governor of Holguín, who interrogated him, that "in the Bahamas, two or three days before they came to Cuba, he had to draw a cross in a document, and when he asked about it to his owner Mary Elizabeth Kelsall, she told him that at that time he should not know anything about such document, but much later on."[7]

The plan that the white Kelsalls had conceived was to liberate their slaves and, at the same time, to keep them bound by contract as apprentices. At this point a difficult question arises: Why did Mary Elizabeth Kelsall behave in such a secretive and contradictory way? First, she was a planter who, like many others, observed the collapse of the formerly promising cotton economy in the Bahamas with regret. This collapse had a significant effect on her life because she was obliged to move from her Hermitage, her declining farm in Little Exuma, to New Providence and to begin there an austere new life.

Second and more important, when Kelsall decided to emigrate, she was no doubt reacting against the slave registration system that had been put in place in the Bahamas in 1822. As with many other slaveowners there, she found a way to take her remaining slaves to Cuba. According to David Eltis, a substantial percentage of Bahamian slaves were transferred to Cuba and other territories before an efficient registration system disclosed the traffic and the imperial government moved to stop it.[8]

In the Bahamas many slaveowners invented ways to abduct their own slaves and send them to other lands. New regulations allowed the slaveowners to transport only two slaves with them when emigrating from the islands. Craton and Saunders state that "some planters were persuading their friends to take pairs of slaves to Cuba for them or even hiring free coloured for the purpose."[9] What Mary Elizabeth Kelsall did, then, was to free her slaves with the clear intention of evading the law.[10]

The first two years they spent in Cuba were quite normal. After Mary Elizabeth's death, however, things drastically changed. The good treatment that had been given to the slaves on the farm where they began their lives in their new country became a regime of rigid discipline. As Newton Kelsall told the story of his life before the governor of Holguín, he related that during those years they "experienc[ed] a bad treatment after his mistress's death, he did not want to serve her daughter anymore, and subsequently he spent two or three weeks looking for a new master. Later he came back to the house and, soon after, thanks to D. José de la Cruz Castellanos, her owner Mrs. Eysing sold him to his present owner."[11]

Newton's story was not as simple as it seemed or as the deposition records it. At least six years passed between Mary Elizabeth Kelsall's death and Newton's sale. Only on 26 May 1831 did Newton achieve his goal when another foreign planter, John Bush, purchased him.[12] In order to gain his release from Henrietta Eysing's claws, Newton had spent his time doing all his tasks as badly as possible and eventually becoming a *cuatrero,* or horse thief. Although the authorities never proved anything against him, Henrietta Eysing was ordered to sell him as far away from her farm as she could, offering Newton the opportunity he was looking for.

The rest of the clan — with the exception of Daniel — remained under Henrietta and Joseph Eysing's rule. Although the farm turned out to be one of the most important in the Candelaria district, several inopportune episodes led to its owners' unwanted end. In a pathetic letter to the governor of Holguín written in August 1844, Henrietta Eysing detailed the account of her family and her slaves since the moment they decided to immigrate to Cuba. According to her, they had lived peacefully in the Bahamas until 1821, when they received the various royal decrees of Ferdinand VII of Spain, published between 1815 and 1817, inviting white immigration to Cuba.

At that moment, her mother Mary Elizabeth and her husband Joseph Eysing decided to take advantage of the circumstances.[13] Eysing came to Holguín and, after an interview with the former governor, Francisco de Zayas, he went back to Nassau with the intention of liquidating the family business in the Bahamas and moving to Cuba. They emigrated in April 1822. Less than two years later Mary Elizabeth Kelsall died, leaving her daughter as her only heir. Shortly afterwards the house was invaded by six thieves who plundered the family's most valuable things and stabbed Joseph Eysing, wounding him seriously. He died in 1832 from complications of the injuries he received in the robbery.[14]

The Eysing family's calamities did not end there. Before Joseph's death, the house caught fire a couple of times. On the second occasion they lost everything the thieves had left behind: commodities, official papers, clothes, furniture, and so on. These, then, were the conditions Henrietta faced in 1844. Several slaves and a prosperous farm were all she had left, but they provided her with everything she and her children needed to live. Now we are able to understand why she complained when she received notice of Governor Cockburn's request.[15]

When the Cuban governor, Leopoldo O'Donnell, received the letter of the Bahamian governor, Francis Cockburn, the Kelsall affair already had a well-known history. On 16 July 1842, the British abolitionist and former consul at Havana, David Turnbull, had written to Cockburn explaining how he uncovered evidence of the fraud in the eastern Cuban district of Holguín. Turnbull wrote that after several days' labor in the Bahamas, he had discovered a few documents of manumission sealed in Nassau in the remote year of 1822. With the information in his hands Turnbull traveled to the town of Gibara, close to Holguín, where he began an exhaustive search for the named individuals.[16]

Finally, with information from two British farm workers, Turnbull found one of the freed men, Daniel Kelsall, in the sugar mill La Caridad, owned by Henry Wood, a planter from the Bahamas who had bought him a few years earlier from a man named Patterson.[17] Once he met Daniel, Turnbull asked him a few questions to ascertain identity and left Gibara completely persuaded that he had met the real Daniel Kelsall.[18] A couple of months earlier, Turnbull had been in touch with Eliza Burnside, Daniel's wife, who made a trip to Nassau to make a declaration about the status of her husband.[19] With both the certified deposition of Daniel's wife and the transcript of his interview with him, Turnbull compelled the British government to demand his freedom from the Spanish government.

In February 1843, Crawford wrote to the earl of Aberdeen to acquaint him with the case of Daniel Kelsall and several other Bahamians enslaved in Cuba. Crawford had already presented his demand that they be freed to Captain General Jerónimo Valdés. Governor Valdés at first maintained a rigid position regarding the demands, but later he acceded to a hearing of their case. But the matter was more complicated than it seemed, according to Crawford, for "here [in Cuba] we can effect nothing, however, just our pretensions, because where the liberation from slavery of so many labourers is involved, the whole power and influence, and I may add, the wealth of the proprietors of the island generally, will be employed to sway the authorities."[20] In the same letter Crawford pointed out that the number of persons taken illegally from the Bahamas to Cuba reached "several thousands." Crawford's efforts on their behalf were firm enough to obtain the freedom of several of those enslaved men.[21]

Regarding the liberation of Daniel Kelsall, Crawford complained on 5 June 1843 that many of his efforts had been futile. For more than six months he had written repeatedly to Valdés, receiving promises but no action. By June, however, there was reason for hope. In a letter to Aberdeen the British consul alluded to the attitude of Valdés, who after "many months" had written to the governor of Santiago de Cuba, asking for his collaboration in the emancipation of Daniel Kelsall.[22]

The legal process that followed was irregular, and complications postponed disposition of the matter for a few months.[23] But it finally concluded with the liberation of Daniel Kelsall in January 1844. After more than a year of complaints, newspaper advertisements, and international reports, Daniel Kelsall departed for the Bahamas aboard the steam packet *Teviol* on 10 May 1844.[24]

One year later Crawford began a new struggle for the rest of the Kelsall family. A few questions remain, however. Why did the other Kelsall brothers never complain about their status? How were they held as slaves for so many years without causing a scandal? Did they know about their condition as freedmen? What mechanisms were used by the colonial authorities, the British consulate, the slaveowners, and the Kelsall brothers in order to achieve their respective aims?

In 1844 Henrietta Eysing declared that—in spite of the fact that her husband had witnessed the formal act emancipating the Kelsalls—she never knew anything about their freedom. Of her own innocence she said: "Busied only in my domestic concerns and in the preparations to the transit to Cuba . . . I merely heard that my mother decided to emancipate some of her slaves."[25] She nevertheless admitted that she knew about a certain letter of commitment that the slaves had signed in the Bahamas engaging them as apprentices under their former owner's supervision for the next twenty or twenty-five years. To Cockburn's inquiries she replied that together with the letters of manumission he should have sent the commitment to apprenticeship signed by her slaves.

This suggests that she actually had known about her slaves' freedom all those years. But the game was turning against her. This time Cuban authorities had decided to resolve the affair as soon as they could. Consequently, Governor O'Donnell tried to speed the process in order to satisfy the British demands.[26]

Only a month later, Henrietta Eysing was ordered to present herself together with her slaves before the Court of Justice of the city of Holguín. The court also called Samuel Chapman, an old friend of the white Kelsalls and probably the only individual alive who had been present in the notary's office in Nassau for the declaration of freedom to Mary Elizabeth Kelsall's slaves.

On 31 July 1844, both Chapman and Eysing went before the court, accompanied by the group of illegal slaves. Chapman confirmed the 1822 award of manumission, and Eysing said that those blacks were from her mother and that accordingly she could not affirm whether they were free. She remarked further that Nat's son, Federico, was the son of a Creole mulatto woman named Teresa, purchased by her in Holguín a few years earlier. Concerning Eve, Cuffee's wife, and their ten children, she proclaimed that all of them were her slaves and that there was no evidence to the contrary. To support these arguments, Eysing claimed her right of ownership of the children of Teresa and Eve, reinforcing her position with the argument that Cuffee and Eve had never married and that therefore all of their children were illegitimate and so necessarily followed the condition of their mother.

Following the hearing the lieutenant governor of Santiago de Cuba wrote to O'Donnell suggesting that he provide some kind of protection to Henrietta Eysing and her property, which in this case meant her slaves.[27] O'Donnell, in turn, ordered the third counsellor of the colonial government, Fernando O'Reilly, to make a detailed report about the status of the Bahamian slaves.[28]

O'Reilly's report about the disagreement between the Kelsall-Eysing family and the British consul in Havana revealed a detailed understanding of the case. O'Reilly carefully examined every particular and supplied a well-balanced final report. According to him, it was evident that the documents presented by Crawford corroborated the claim that in 1822 Mary Elizabeth Kelsall had declared all the Kelsall brothers to be free. In addition, O'Reilly asserted that the supposed agreement signed by the Kelsall brothers after they were freed, even if it existed, would not be considered valid because it was based on falsehood and intentional prevarication. No doubt O'Reilly saw in this action a clear violation of Bahamian law. His words were clear enough: "If the compromise was signed before their manumission, the second act annulled the first; meanwhile, if it was signed after, it could not be considered authentic at all, because the freedom was a right that had preference over the others, and it could never be admitted such a mockery as to make a man free and at the same time abuse of [sic] the influence of the lordship and the sense of gratefulness to return him to slavery."[29]

O'Reilly congratulated himself and the Spanish legal system because it did not support the mistreatment and abuses observed in other parts of the Americas regarding slaves, not even in those, apparently, where slavery no longer existed. In order to maintain his theory, he cited the Black Code, approved only two years earlier by the Cuban colonial government, which sanctioned amelioration of slaves' way of life.[30]

In so doing, he conveniently forgot the reality in which he was living from day to day. The repression of hundreds of supposed rebel slaves, characterized by punishment and death, did not harmonize with O'Reilly's words. Whereas he was trying to protect the rights of the Kelsall brothers, he could not forget his responsibilities as an official of the colonial government of the island.[31] The last sentence of his report, however, was definitive: "The letter of freedom given by Mary Elizabeth Kelsall is pure, absolute and without condition, and according to this letter the individuals who are mentioned on it are free."[32] Soon afterward, O'Reilly recommended that O'Donnell release immediately the illegal slaves with the help of the British vice consul at Santiago de Cuba, James Forbes.

Before writing to Forbes, O'Donnell wrote to Crawford to inform him of O'Reilly's opinion. Crawford replied with a salute to the final agreement between Cuban authorities and the British consular office. On 19 September he drafted another message to O'Donnell in which he wrote: "It will afford me very great pleasure to lay before Her Majesty's Government Your Excellency's most just determination upon the lucid opinion which has been delivered by the 3rd counsellor general upon my claim and the evidence attached for the liberation from slavery on this island of Nat, Cuffy, John, Newton and Billy Kelsall."[33]

According to Crawford, O'Reilly's response to Henrietta Eysing's claims about the apprenticed condition of the Kelsall brothers was "most honourable." Crawford, however, was not completely satisfied and soon petitioned the Cuban government so that Cuffee's wife Eve and her large family, and the son of Nat, should be liberated as soon as he could obtain evidence of their freedom.[34]

Once the lieutenant governor of Holguín, Francisco Moreno, received a copy of O'Reilly's message, he sent the five Kelsall brothers under custodianship to Santiago de Cuba. There they waited in jail for Forbes, who received orders to send them all to a place outside Cuba.[35] A few days later, Crawford wrote again to O'Donnell to notify him that Forbes "was prepared to receive them and having my instructions proposed to them to elect for themselves to return to the Bahamas or to go to Jamaica. They chose the latter destination as Mr. Forbes accordingly informed me."[36]

At the same time, Forbes began the procedures for obtaining passports for the Kelsall brothers. Pedro Becerra, the new lieutenant governor of Santiago de Cuba, permitted them to receive five tickets to Jamaica. The five Kelsalls traveled to Jamaica that same week.[37] Although they were separated from their wives and children, who remained in Candelaria, the Kelsall brothers gained their freedom after more than twenty years of illegal enslavement. In January 1845 Crawford wrote to O'Donnell announcing, "In obedience to instructions which I have received from the Right Honourable, the Earl of Aberdeen, I have the honour of expressing to Your Excellency the satisfaction felt by Her Majesty's Government at the accomplishment of this act of justice."[38]

But Crawford knew very well that the struggle had just begun. In the following years he continued complaining about the fortune of the relatives of the brothers who were still held in slavery and were now isolated from them because of the Cuban government's determination to expel all foreigners *de color* after the uncovering of the 1844 conspiracy.

According to the Reglamento de Policía issued by Captain General Jerónimo Valdés in 1842, and as part of the repression of the conspirators of La Escalera, O'Donnell had delivered an order to banish from Cuba all the colored freemen in April 1844. He had given the ousted men two weeks to sell their properties and depart from the island. Beginning in the first week of May, in spite of Crawford's complaints, a large number of foreign blacks and mulattos were driven out of Cuba.[39]

This meant that the Kelsall affair continued for both Crawford and O'Donnell. In July 1845 Crawford wrote O'Donnell to make several more complaints about other Bahamian citizens who were brought to Cuba as slaves. One of them was a black woman named Dido, who was curiously in the same situation as the Kelsall brothers and was owned by the same person, Henrietta Eysing. The rest of the illegal slaves he mentioned were John Kelsall's wife,

Polly Gaythorne, owned by Ventura Cardel, and some other men and women from Nassau held in Candelaria by Samuel Driggs.[40] Furthermore, Crawford mentioned the intention of Nat Kelsall to claim his ten-year-old son Federico, who remained in slavery on Eysing's farm. According to Crawford, Manuel and Ventura Cardel owed Nat two hundreds dollars that he wished to use to purchase his son's freedom.[41]

To accelerate the process, O'Donnell assigned the case to the well-informed magistrate Fernando O'Reilly. This official, whom British diplomats thought of as a proper and wise man, reviewed the new cases that O'Donnell sent him, but this time his verdict was not as pleasant as it had been in the case of the five Kelsall brothers. O'Reilly opined that in the new case all the evidence supported the slaveholders settled near Holguín. He took care to state that in the earlier case he had approved the petitions because the British consul had handled it himself in harmony with the law. But this time O'Reilly declared the request unfair, and in the specific case of Nat's son he suggested that Nat submit a legal demand before the corresponding ordinary tribunal.[42] Although it is impossible to know with certainty what happened to Nat and Federico in the following years, it seems possible that they were able to reunite shortly afterwards.[43]

The following year the problem still remained, with direct implications for the British and the Spanish central governments. In May 1845, Cuffee Kelsall invoked the intervention of British authorities to obtain the liberation of all relatives still enslaved in Cuba. Cuffee wrote an emotional letter to Lord Grey, the head of the Colonial Office in London, in which he begged him to rescue his family. According to the Spanish consul at Kingston, the Court of Commerce of that city, had aided Cuffee, showing that more than a simple desire was hidden behind those paragraphs.[44] Going beyond his original demand, Cuffee attacked the illegal emigration to Holguín from the Bahamas in the 1820s, arguing, "Twenty five years ago, when colonies and slaveholders were under the influence of a panic due to the apprehension that they would be soon deprived of their slaves' services without indemnification, a large number of them in straight contravention of British statutes to suppress the slave trade, were induced to emigrate together with their slaves, and more especially those who lived in the Bahamas, to the nearby colony of Cuba."[45]

In order to reinforce his allegations he shared his own experience in Cuba, from which he had been removed for three years. He attested to several efforts to establish a correspondence with Eve and his children since that unfortunate moment, but all of them had been fruitless. The district of Candelaria, Cuffee testified, "is almost completely inhabited by both the victims of the intercolonial traffic and the African traffic." He added, "The English language is common there where it is even spoken by Spaniards and African slaves, and it is well known in the whole jurisdiction."[46] In Cuffee's testimony we see the final context of the Kelsall affair: a vigorous internal trade in free people stolen from the Bahamas alongside the ongoing (and, after the Treaty of 1817, illegal) African trade.

In spite of his complete loyalty to the Spanish side, the new governor of Holguín, José Marcial, mentioned some irregularities in responding to Cuffee Kelsall's petition. Marcial supported Henrietta Eysing's property rights, but he asserted that "in harmony with the slave's attestations, when they were brought to this Island by their owners, they were promised they would be liberated after ten years of servitude, a promise that was not realized."[47] In addition, his letter revealed that many more slaves were abducted from the Bahamas at the same time the Kelsalls were.

Satisfied with the governor of Holguín's actions, O'Donnell forwarded the problem to Major Melitón Balenzástegui, the officer who replaced O'Reilly after his premature death. He determined that "there is no right to accede to what Cuffee, husband of Eve and father of her ten children, asked for, so all them should stand as it is instituted by the law," which meant, no doubt, as slaves on their owner's farm.[48] The new captain general of Cuba, Federico Roncali, count of Alcoy, who had just arrived in Havana, received this letter. To speed up the resolution he sent all the documents generated during the process to the Ministry of State, closing in this way a long and complicated affair. The last attempt of the Kelsalls to obtain freedom for all their relatives was concluded.[49]

After more than six years of struggle, the majority of the members of the black Kelsall family remained enslaved. Henrietta Eysing died in about 1849. This circumstance might have changed things for the separated family, although no information confirming this has been found. The Kelsall affair is a clear example of the injustices that prevailed in Cuba in an age marked by repression of and control over the black population.

In spite of the British criticism of the Spanish policy, the district of Candelaria kept a large number of slaves born in the Bahamas, a territory where slavery was legally abolished in 1834. The expulsion of Turnbull in 1842 and the consistent accusations against his successor, Crawford, are transparent examples of the real intentions of Cuban authorities in this period.[50]

O'Donnell's government hardly maneuvered to weaken the British position. This rough policy, supported by colonial laws, answered both to Cuban authorities and to the "prestigious neighbors" who were no doubt the most faithful guardians of the status quo.

The Cuban government's disposition of all matters related to the slaves were promulgated with the aim of exorcising—from the officials' minds at least—the always present danger of a general slave uprising on the island. The British emancipation policy was much more dreadful than the slave rebellions themselves, and consequently British representatives and neighbors on the island became favorite targets of the Cuban authorities. This is why tensions between the two empires, far from being relieved, remained constant and vivid.

Meanwhile, British consular officials in Cuba, deeply influenced by the antislavery movement, took on a dual role. They were official agents of the British government at the same time they were nonofficial agents of the British Anti-Slavery Society. They conspired with Cuban whites, free blacks, and slaves, distributed propaganda against Spanish slavery and established operational bases in Nassau and Kingston, challenged Cuban authorities again and again, and even disobeyed their orders when they dealt with British citizens. From their precarious position, Turnbull, Crawford, and their team became a source of great trouble to Cuban governors in the 1840s. Even in cases—such as the Kelsall affair—in which British officials were unable to succeed completely, their acts of open defiance constituted a way to denounce the illegalities and to resist the colonial policy with regard to the slave trade and to the slave system itself.

Notes

I wish to acknowledge the help I received from friends and colleagues who were disposed to give me critiques and comments. I am truly grateful to Carmen Cabrera, Luz M. Mena, Manuel Rodríguez, Jonathan Curry-Machado, Tom Goddard, and especially David Geggus and Michael Craton.

1. A few works that treat this time and its problems include Franklin W. Knight, *Slave Society in Cuba During the Nineteenth Century* (Madison: University of Wisconsin Press, 1970); David R. Murray, *Odious Commerce: Britain, Spain, and the Abolition of the Cuban Slave Trade* (Cambridge: Cambridge University Press, 1980); Robert L. Paquette, *Sugar Is Made with Blood: The Conspiracy of La Escalera and the Conflict Between Empires over Slavery in Cuba* (Middletown, Conn.: Wesleyan University Press, 1988); Rodolfo Sarracino, *Inglaterra: Sus dos caras en la lucha cubana por la abolición* (Havana: Editorial Letras Cubanas, 1989). The best studies of slavery in the Bahamas that I have found are David Eltis, "The Traffic in Slaves Between the British West Indian Colonies, 1807–1833," *Economic History Review* 25:1 (1972): 55–64; Michael Craton, *Testing the Chains: Resistance to Slavery in the British West Indies* (Ithaca: Cornell University Press, 1982); Michael Craton, "Changing Patterns of Slave Family in the British West Indies," *Journal of Interdisciplinary History* 10:1 (1979): 1–35; Michael Craton and Gail Saunders, *Islanders in the Stream: A History of the Bahamian People* (Athens: University of Georgia Press, 1992), vol. 1.

2. David Turnbull was the British consul at Havana between 1841 and 1842. There was evidence to accuse him of being one of the heads of the conspiracy. Francis Ross Cocking, his personal assistant and the most probable link between Turnbull and the rebels, was not accused at all. See Paquette, *Sugar Is Made with Blood*, 131–157; Sarracino, *Inglaterra*, 15–41; and Manuel Barcia Paz, "Entre Amenazas y Quejas: Un acercamiento al papel jugado por los diplomáticos ingleses en Cuba durante la conspiración de La Escalera," *Colonial Latin American Historical Review* 10:1 (2001): 1–25.

3. British officials often were considered undesirables by the Spanish colonial government in Cuba. Their continuous disapprovals were the source of several disagreements between Spain and Great Britain. Among the most relevant were Henry T. Kilbee, W. S. Macleay, Richard R. Madden, Charles Tolme, Campbell J. Dalrymple, James Kennedy, Francis Ross Cocking, David Turnbull, and Joseph T. Crawford.

4. Quoted in Comisión Militar, 76/1, Archivo Nacional de Cuba (hereafter ANC).

5. Henrietta Eysing (née Kelsall) was born in South Carolina around 1786. When she was four, her mother, Mary Elizabeth Kelsall, traveled with her to the Bahamas, where they settled. Michael Craton and Gail Saunders studied their lives as an example of the loyalist families in the Bahamas. For these scholars the Kelsalls were the "quintessential Bahamian Loyalist family." In their study, the authors mention a still unpublished compilation of letters of Mary Elizabeth and Henrietta Kelsall titled "Henrietta, My Daughter," edited by Mary K. Armbrister. These letters, together with the study of Craton and Saunders, probably contain the most relevant information about the Kelsalls' past in the Bahamas. See Craton and Saunders, *Islanders in the Stream*, 232–243.

6. The widow's will was transcribed by the registrar of records of the Bahama Islands, Charles Roger Nesbitt, who certified the validity of the act of manumission in book R/3, p. 7 of the records in his custody.

7. Deposition of Newton Kelsall, Gobierno Superior Civil, bundle 850, file 28640, ANC.

8. Eltis, "Traffic in Slaves," 55–64. I appreciate the help of David Geggus regarding this point since it was he who suggested this article to me. See also Craton and Saunders, *Islanders in the Stream*, 221–25.

9. Craton and Saunders, *Islanders in the Stream*, 225.

10. Ibid. Craton and Saunders used a quite similar example when they wrote that in such ways "an Exuma planter, William Forbes, had already transferred at least twenty-nine of his slaves and could not be extradited for any offense."

11. Deposition of Newton Kelsall.

12. Deposition of John Bush, Gobierno Superior Civil, bundle 850, file 28640, ANC. According to Bush's declaration, he paid 325 pesos for Newton. Once he knew about the real status of his servant, he wished him all the best, and afterwards he filed a claim for the money he paid in this fraudulent exchange.

13. A German national, Joseph Eysing served in his youth as a captain in the Second West India Regiment during the Napoleonic War. He married Henrietta Kelsall on 18 April 1814. Craton and Saunders, *Islanders in the Stream*, 237.

14. Ibid., 238.

15. Henrietta Eysing to Lieutenant Governor of Holguín Francisco Moreno, Candelaria, [13] August 1844, Gobierno Superior Civil, bundle 850, file 28640, ANC.

16. Turnbull's behavior provoked panic among the Bahamian slaveowners who had settled in Holguín. Fourteen of them wrote a melodramatic letter to Governor Jerónimo Valdés asking for his protection against Turnbull's attacks. The fact is that Turnbull was uncovering many illegal slaves in the region. They complained just because they feared becoming victims of Turnbull's investigations. Notwithstanding, Henrietta Eysing was not among the planters who signed the document. Bahamian Slaveowners to Captain General Jerónimo Valdés, Holguín, December 1842, Gobierno Superior Civil, bundle 941, file 33191, ANC.

17. A few months later, both Henry Wood and Daniel Kelsall were summoned by Santiago de Cuba's authorities in the city newspapers. *El Diario Redactor,* 4 July 1843, vol. 10, no. 1180, p. 4. James Patterson had purchased Daniel Kelsall several years earlier from Eysing. Wood and Patterson signed the letter to Valdés.

18. David Turnbull to ?, Nassau, 16 November 1842, Gobierno Superior Civil, bundle 850, file 28617, ANC.

19. Declaration of Eliza Burnside, issued in Nassau, 24 August 1842, Gobierno Superior Civil, bundle 850, file 28617, ANC. This document was certified by C. R. Nesbitt on 3 October 1842.

20. Crawford to Lord Aberdeen, Havana, 19 February 1843, *British and Foreign Anti-Slavery Reporter* (hereafter *BFASR*) 5:26 (25 December 1844): 234.

21. Crawford's temperament was much more efficacious than that of his predecessor, David Turnbull, who as a result of his merciless attacks on Spanish rule was expelled from the island in 1842.

22. Crawford to Lord Aberdeen, Havana, 5 June 1843, *BFASR* 5:26 (25 December 1844): 234.

23. Gobierno Superior Civil, bundle 850, file 28617, ANC. For instance, a grave mistake was made in the first translation of the legal documents sent from the Bahamas when the experienced official Luis Payne recorded the date as 1842 instead of 1822. Other small problems arose in Havana because of the counsellor Fernando O'Reilly and in Holguín and Santiago de Cuba with the legal procedures.

24. Gobierno Superior Civil, bundle 850, file 28617, ANC. From the Bahamas, Daniel Kelsall traveled to Jamaica. A few months later, when the turbulent events started again in 1844, this time with the rest of Daniel's family, Governor O'Donnell commented in a letter to the governor of Santiago de Cuba that Daniel Kelsall had been released and sent to Jamaica soon afterward. O'Donnell to Cayetano de Urbina, Havana, 22 June 1844, Gobierno Superior Civil, bundle 850, file 28640, ANC.

25. Henrietta Eysing to Lieutenant Governor of Holguín Francisco Moreno, Candelaria, [13] August 1844, Gobierno Superior Civil, bundle 850, file 28640, ANC.

26. Ibid.

27. Cayetano de Urbina to O'Donnell, Santiago de Cuba, 25 August 1844, Gobierno Superior Civil, bundle 850, file 28640, ANC.

28. Fernando O'Reilly was a well-positioned Cuban Militar official. A member of a prestigious family, he became magistrate of the Real Audiencia of Puerto Príncipe on 25 April 1843. In August of the same year he was designated lieutenant governor general and counsellor of the colonial government. He died three years later. The novelist Cirilo Villaverde, who probably knew him very well, used him as one of the characters in the

most important Cuban novel of the nineteenth century. Villaverde assigned him the role of a close friend of the protagonist, Leonardo Gamboa, and depicted O'Reilly as a rude and resolute man. Cirilo Villaverde, *Cecilia Valdés o la Loma del Angel* (Lima: Talleres gráficos Torres-Aguirre, 19[56]).

29. Report of the Third Counsellor Fernando O'Reilly, Havana, 9 September 1844, Gobierno Superior Civil, bundle 850, file 28640, ANC.

30. The Reglamento de Esclavos, also known as the Black Code of 1842 and as the Code of Valdés, remained in force only until 1844. Then, Governor O'Donnell promulgated a new black code known as the Ordenanzas de 1844. This document drastically changed all the provisions in favor of slaves announced in the former code. An analysis and a comparison of both codes, as well as their entire texts, can be found in Manuel Barcia Paz, *Con el Látigo de la Ira: Legislación, Represión y Control en las Plantaciones Cubanas* (Havana: Ciencias Sociales, 2000). Other studies include Rafael María de Labra, *Los Códigos Negros: Estudio de Legislación Comparada* (Madrid: Imprenta de Aurelio J. Alaria, 1879); Fernando Ortiz, *Los Negros Esclavos* (Havana: Ciencias Sociales, 1976); Leví Marrero, *Cuba: Economía y Sociedad* (Río Piedras, P.R.: Editorial Playor), vol. 13; Gloria García, *La Esclavitud desde la Esclavitud: La visión de los siervos* (Mexico, D.F.: Centro de Investigación Científica Ingeniero Jorge L. Tamayo, 1996).

31. Like many other distinguished colonial officials, O'Reilly had to choose between honor and social status. Because La Escalera offered an opportunity to rise through the ranks of the army, most of the young prosecutors tried to advance in rank, whereas most of the elder officials had to face a huge paradox in which their honor and prestige were threatened by repression and death. They saw themselves as being in the eye of the tempest, surrounded by a ceaseless wall of wind with no way out. The second counsellor in O'Donnell's government, Blas Osés, had to face a similar situation. Although Osés was an old friend of the most progressive Cuban men, he signed several documents condemning the conspirators. He—like O'Reilly—became a supporter of O'Donnell's policy.

32. Report of the Third Counsellor Fernando O'Reilly, Havana, 9 September 1844, Gobierno Superior Civil, bundle 850, file 28640, ANC.

33. Crawford to O'Donnell, Havana, 19 September 1844, Gobierno Superior Civil, bundle 850, file 28640, ANC.

34. Ibid.

35. Francisco Moreno to Pedro Becerra, Holguín, 12 October 1844, Gobierno Superior Civil, bundle 850, file 28640, ANC.

36. Crawford to O'Donnell, Havana, 2 November 1844, Gobierno Superior Civil, bundle 850, file 28640, ANC.

37. Pedro Becerra to O'Donnell, Santiago de Cuba, 18 November 1844, Gobierno Superior Civil, bundle 850, file 28640, ANC.

38. Crawford to O'Donnell, Havana, 22 January 1845, Gobierno Superior Civil, bundle 850, file 28640, ANC.

39. Gobierno Superior Civil, bundle 850, file 28634, ANC. All of the correspondence between Crawford and O'Donnell concerning this disposition is located in this file.

40. Crawford to O'Donnell, Havana, 18 July 1845, Gobierno Superior Civil, bundle 850, file 28640, ANC.

41. Ibid. Crawford dramatically stated that "this sum of 200 dollars the poor man is very willing to sacrifice in order to obtain the freedom of the son of Teresa."

42. O'Reilly to O'Donnell, Havana, 20 February 1846, Gobierno Superior Civil, bundle 850, file 28640, ANC.

43. When Nat's brother Cuffee started a legal procedure against his former owner, he did not mention Nat's separation from Federico. This could be evidence of the final solution of this case.

44. Juan del Castillo to the Ministry of State, Kingston, 22 September 1847, Gobierno Superior Civil, bundle 946, file 33340, ANC.

45. Cuffee Kelsall to Lord Grey, Kingston, 10 May 1847, Gobierno Superior Civil, bundle 946, file 33340, ANC.

46. Ibid.

47. José Marcial to O'Donnell, Holguín, 6 February 1848, Gobierno Superior Civil, bundle 946, file 33340, ANC.

48. Melitón Balenzástegui to O'Donnell, Havana, 24 February 1848, Gobierno Superior Civil, bundle 946, file 33340, ANC.

49. Alcoy to the Ministry of State, Havana, 29 April 1848, Gobierno Superior Civil, bundle 946, file 33340, ANC.

50. Gobierno Superior Civil, bundle 946, file 33340, ANC. In 1844, regarding Crawford, O'Donnell stated to the governor of Matanzas, Antonio García Oña, that they should be prepared for any sort of reaction by the British government because it could be provoked by "the spirit of resentment and hostility that encouraged that Consul." O'Donnell to García Oña, Havana, 4 November 1844. A few months later he wrote to the Ministry of State that he had "constant [proof of] his evil faithfulness and perfidious proceedings." O'Donnell to the Ministry of State, Havana, 4 January 1845.

13

Another Middle Passage?
The Internal Slave Trade in Brazil

R I C H A R D   G R A H A M

Brazil imported more slaves from Africa than any other country, and slavery persisted in Brazil until 1888, that is, long after it had been abolished elsewhere in the Americas. Its experience differed from that of other slave-holding countries in other ways as well and certainly differed in the course of its internal slave trade. In the first half of this chapter I examine how many slaves were involved in the Brazilian trade, who was traded, where they came from, and where they went. Such an approach is useful as far as it goes because it suggests patterns not necessarily visible at the time. I press on, however, for we must also ask the truly important question: What did the slave trade mean for the human beings who were traded? The answer cannot be a tidy general-ization, for enormous variety characterized them, and it is the range of human experience that makes history most revealing. So I look at particular individ-uals and consider the realities of the slave trade for each of them. From the juxtaposition of these two kinds of material — quantitative and qualitative, general and specific — I draw the conclusion that the internal slave trade con-tributed powerfully to hastening slavery's abolition in Brazil. In making this argument I find the role of the slaves themselves to have been particularly important. The heightened resistance of slaves who had been torn from famil-iar contexts and old social ties undermined the authority of slaveholders and encouraged slaves in forcing their own liberation by means of direct action. They were more than chattel.[1]

Before 1850

When scholars have spoken of the internal slave trade in Brazil they have usually meant the nineteenth-century shift in slaves — many of them born in Africa — from the old sugar regions in the Northeast to the newly prosperous coffee areas of the Southeast after the end of the transatlantic slave trade in 1850. But the movement of slaves from region to region had much earlier precedents. By at least the beginning of the seventeenth century, traders were shipping Indian slaves to the rich sugar-producing regions of Bahia and Pernambuco from various Brazilian ports, principally from the Amazon region including Maranhão and, to a lesser extent, from São Paulo (see fig. 13.1). In a single western expedition in 1628–30 Indians enslaved by the *paulistas* reportedly numbered thirty thousand to sixty thousand, and some of them (the sources do not specify how many) went northward to sugar estates. Even earlier, Indian slaves captured in southernmost Rio Grande do Sul were shipped northward along the coast to Rio de Janeiro. Although we know that some Indian slaves were marched overland from Maranhão to Pernambuco, a more common pattern relied on sailing vessels. In June 1636 a partnership in Belém (at the mouth of the Amazon River), following what seems to have been its well-established practice, shipped nine hundred Indians southward on two ships. Sometime during the period when the Dutch West India Company ruled Pernambuco (1630–54), an influential Dutchman urged it to expand its control into Maranhão precisely in order to take charge of the Indian slave trade. And when the Dutch occupied Angola from 1641 to 1647, cutting off the normal supply of slaves from Africa to Bahia, the Bahian demand for Indian slaves increased sharply.[2]

Planters generally preferred African slaves to Indians for several reasons. Most important, they were more resistant to Old World diseases and could be expected to render more years of labor. In addition, Africans were less likely to flee into the hinterland at the first opportunity, more familiar with agricultural labor in a fixed locality (especially the men), and possibly more accustomed to the notion of personal servitude. Yet Indian slavery remained a reality in Brazil even after its final prohibition in the eighteenth century. Called *administrados* instead of slaves, Indian workers were nevertheless bought and sold as merchandise, inherited, and hunted down when they escaped well into the nineteenth century.[3] Long-distance trade in them, however, seems to have almost ended in the middle of the seventeenth century with the massive importation

Figure 13.1. Provinces of Brazil in the Mid-Nineteenth Century.

of Africans. As Fernando Novais points out, there had never been an en-
trenched merchant community committed to fostering a trade in Indians as
there was for the African trade, to which Luiz Felipe de Alencastro has added
the specific argument that the slave trade, like any other, required goods in
return, goods that could most easily be supplied by the Portuguese merchants
to whom the Crown had granted a monopoly of overseas trade. Alencastro
also notes that among the Indians there was no notion of capturing members
of other tribes for sale to the Portuguese, in sharp contrast to the situation
in Africa.[4]

The enormous number of Africans forcibly transported to Brazil has been
thoroughly calculated elsewhere, especially by Philip Curtin and David Eltis. It
is estimated that about four million arrived there over the course of three

centuries, compared to about 560,000 transported to British North America; the Brazil trade accounted for almost 40 percent of all those shipped out of Africa. The sugar plantations of Bahia and Pernambuco remained the principal destination of slaves until 1700, but some went elsewhere.[5] In fact, the flow of slaves within Brazil reversed course when Africans replaced Indians: from Salvador, the great entrepōt, African slaves were transshipped northward to Maranhão and Pará; from there merchants sent them up the Amazon River and its tributaries all the way to the far-off mines of Mato Grosso. One result was to extend slaves and slave ownership throughout the entire colony. Still, the numbers making this internal migration were relatively few: Those going to Pará have been estimated at no more than five hundred per year during the eighteenth century.[6]

The late seventeenth-century and early eighteenth-century discovery of gold and diamonds deep in the forests of south-central Brazil attracted a rush of people to Minas Gerais. Some sugar planters in the northeastern part of the colony abandoned their long-established estates and moved to the mining region, taking their slaves with them, but slaves from the Northeast arrived in Minas Gerais mainly by way of slave traders. In some cases these traders marched their human property overland from the Northeast, a distance of at least seven hundred miles, despite the danger of Indian attack. Even more numerous among the slaves headed for the mines were those who arrived from Africa at Rio de Janeiro and were then sold to middlemen who similarly marched them in convoys to the interior. Between 1695 and 1735 Minas Gerais was transformed from a zone inhabited almost entirely by nomadic Indians into one where more than 96,000 black slaves labored at many tasks, most in mining. Almost 90 percent of them were African-born.[7] In short, slaves had long been traded within Brazil, some over very long distances, whether they had first also been transported from overseas or not.

The most important market consideration was always the cost of a slave and, as long as slaves could be purchased from Africa for a small price, the incentive for moving slaves who had already been settled in one place within Brazil remained relatively minor. But this situation eventually ended. In 1831, as a result of commitments made earlier with the British in order to secure recognition of Brazil's independence from Portugal, the Brazilian parliament passed a law freeing any slave brought into the country after that date and imposing various penalties on those involved in the trade. But locally elected officials were reluctant to investigate and press charges, and juries adamantly refused to convict or to accept as valid the evidence presented by prosecutors, so the government soon abandoned any effort to apply the law.[8] In 1850, however, partly as a reaction to the flood of newly arrived slaves and the consequent fear of slave unrest, partly as an effort to wipe out debts owed by planters to slave traders for the purchase of illegally imported slaves, and largely because the British threatened Brazil's national sovereignty by seizing Brazilian ships even within Brazilian waters if they were suspected of engaging in the nefarious business, the Brazilian government took action effectively to end the transatlantic trade. It issued a new law placing the responsibility for enforcement in the hands of the navy, thus removing the right to a jury trial from those accused of slave trading. The law also imposed higher penalties on violators and deported foreigners (read: Portuguese) who engaged in the trade, thus hindering their collection of debts.[9] At first some ships still landed clandestinely on the coast bearing their dreary cargoes, which were, in the words of one contemporary, "taken to the interior along impenetrable paths and unknown shortcuts."[10] But the government held firm to its determination and, as a class, planters—many of whom were members of parliament or in the cabinet—put up no organized opposition.

Trade Patterns

Once the government actually suppressed the overseas trade in the early 1850s, the only slave trade was an internal one. Inevitably, given the enormous number of Africans within the country, many of those moved from one province to another had already suffered the transatlantic trade. Twenty-eight percent of those arriving in Rio de Janeiro from the Northeast whose numbers were recorded for some months in 1852 had been born in Africa, and one may suppose that some of those reported as Brazilian-born were actually African but imported after 1831, when such imports had become illegal. Over time the proportion of creoles (slaves born in Brazil) in the trade increased and, eventually, as Africans became older, creoles were almost the only slaves worth shipping from province to province.[11]

By the middle of the nineteenth century the coffee economy of Rio de Janeiro Province was booming, soon to be followed by that of São Paulo, and it was to these areas that slaves were principally transferred. Naturally, the fact that there were several export crops in Brazil and the fact that their profitability did not increase and decrease in tandem provoked variations in this flux of slaves from one region to another. On the whole, however, they were funneled to the ports of Rio de Janeiro and Santos from the less profitable sugar-producing Northeast—the predominant source—or northward from Rio Grande do Sul, where the salted beef business was in decline. Given the lack of good inland roads, the principal route for the trade remained a coastwise one; for the Africans it extended some of the trauma of their earlier middle passage across the Atlantic. Surviving police records of slaves arriving in Rio de Janeiro City in 1852 show that three-quarters of the ships carrying them came from ports north of Rio, and 83 percent of the Brazilian slaves for whom these records indicate the province of birth were born in the Northeast. Evidence from later periods confirms this region as the source of most slaves sent to Rio de Janeiro from elsewhere in Brazil, although as a proportion of its slave holdings, Rio Grande do Sul exported more than did the Northeast.[12]

Another region to which slaves were taken was Minas Gerais. There has been considerable disagreement among historians about the extent of this trade, especially for the peak period of the 1870s, and contrary arguments have been advanced by Robert Slenes, Roberto Borges Martins, Douglas Cole Libby, and Laird W. Bergad, all of whom have some connection to North American cliometrical traditions.[13] It is safe to conclude that for that decade, slave traders introduced thousands of slaves into the region.

Quantitative data for the overall internal slave trade after 1850 are notoriously imprecise when they appear at all, but its volume was definitely smaller than that of the earlier overseas one. A contemporary statistician calculated the average number of slaves traded each year from the Northeast to Rio de Janeiro in the 1850s at 3,439, and he supposed that another 1,500 or so arrived with their owners or came from the southern parts of the country.[14] The historian Herbert Klein concludes that these figures are believable and that, if shipments of slaves to the port of Santos are added, it is likely that in the 1850s and 1860s the number coming from the Northeast averaged 5,000 to 6,000 per year, compared to the 24,000 per year brought from Africa to all ports of Brazil during the two preceding decades. The number of those in the internal slave trade decreased somewhat in the 1860s because the U.S. Civil War encouraged cotton production to compensate for the scarcity of American exports to England, and producers in the Northeast therefore once again placed a high value on their slaves. But the interprovincial slave trade became much more intense in the 1870s, when the international price of cotton and sugar declined precipitously while that of coffee shot up. Slenes has estimated the number of slaves traded during that decade at 10,000 per year, that is, almost double the earlier level. He concludes that 200,000 slaves were traded and moved from one province to another after 1850. In addition, within each province a great movement of slaves occurred from the cities, from general farming areas, and from the gold and diamond fields (where the veins had run out) to export-focused plantations. Robert Conrad supposes that if this intra-provincial trade were also tallied, the number of those in the internal trade would be double the above estimates.[15] Such a large movement of people would have had a significant impact on the demographic and cultural makeup of the country.[16]

It has been calculated that any one slave's chance of being swept up in the Brazilian interprovincial trade in any year during the 1850s and 1860s was 0.4 percent, but that chance apparently became much greater in the 1870s. We have no study for Brazil like the one done by Michael Tadman for the Old South in the United States (nor could there be, for lack of comparable census data). He shows that the chance of having been separated from a spouse sometime during one's life was 10 or 11 percent for slaves aged forty-five to fifty-four.[17] The absolute number of those moved from state to state in the United States (742,000) impressively overshadows the numbers in Brazil (somewhat more than 200,000).[18]

On the whole, the slaves shipped south from the Northeast did not come from sugar plantations. Because sugar exports from the Northeast were no longer expanding, there is a misconception that it was the sugar planters who sold their workers southward, but that was not usually the case. The most important sources over the long term for the new slave trade were the small- and medium-sized farms. A British consul reported in the 1860s that agents scoured the countryside, buying up slaves from indebted small proprietors. In the following decade a Brazilian observer complained that "agents, intermediaries, carry out this trade; they go from the South to the northern provinces, traversing them every which way . . . rounding them up like sheep." The historian Stanley Stein interviewed a former slave in Rio de Janeiro Province who related how in the early 1880s he had come from a castor bean and cotton farm in Maranhão.[19] In addition, a significant shift in the concentration of the slave population within Minas Gerais accompanied the spread of coffee plantations in the southeastern part of the province from the late 1860s and into the 1880s; the agricultural and stock-raising areas of the province and the mining districts (that is, the noncoffee regions) lost slaves, while the coffee counties increased their share of the provincial slave population from 24 percent to 31 percent between 1873 and 1886.[20] So it was not, in the first instance, the sugar planters who coped with a diminished slave labor force.

It is true, however, that in the late 1870s a terrible drought seared the interior of some northeastern provinces, producing both a flood of free migrants to the coastal sugar zones in search of employment and a fire sale of slaves from the dryer regions. The province of Ceará, not in the sugar zone, was one of the most devastated by drought; it sent thousands of slaves southward; more were transferred during the 1870s than from any other single province except Rio Grande do Sul. And as a result of the drought,

Pernambuco sugar planters do seem to have lessened their reliance on slave laborers, turning especially to *moradores,* that is, to free or freed persons to whom the planter granted the use of some unneeded land in exchange for occasional services, especially at harvest time, and who represented no burden to him when business slowed.[21] More research needs to be done to explore the dimensions of this phenomenon and to discover whether, indeed, in this province at this time, large sugar planters sold their slaves. In Bahia, however, we know that prosperous planters for a long time managed to keep up the number of slaves on their estates by buying slaves from the cities, from small farmers, and from less successful planters. What hindered the less successful ones was the rapid increase in prices so that some could not afford to buy new slaves from traders who got better deals by selling them south.[22]

One result of rising prices was the concentration of slave ownership in fewer hands, as the less well-off sold their slaves to wealthier buyers. The price of slaves in western São Paulo was more than twice that paid for them in interior Bahia. In this way the trade altered somewhat the pattern of wide distribution dating back to colonial days. Another consequence was the lower proportion of slaves in the cities.[23] Insofar as the ownership of slaves was increasingly concentrated in fewer hands and in rural areas rather than urban centers, the institution of slavery itself could count on fewer enthusiastic supporters.

Provincial legislators in Bahia attempted to help the planters there by adopting various measures to encourage urban slave owners to divest themselves of their slaves and make them available to planters. Sometimes such measures were cloaked in the discourse of progress and humane concern, as happened in Salvador. Already in 1848 the Salvador municipal council had levied a tax on any slaves engaged in rowing the lighters in this active port city, and in 1850 it had forbidden them to do so altogether. Within a few years slaves had also been denied work as stevedores.[24] The motivations behind these actions are complex. The provincial president explained that such measures would not only funnel slaves into work on the sugar plantations but would also prevent slaves from concentrating at the capital; doubtless he still remembered the events that occurred when he had been the police chief of the province at the time of the famous "malê" revolt of Africans in 1835.[25] Urban residents crowed that this measure helped free workers find employment, a step toward the future.[26] The effect, however, was to transfer urban slaves to field work. (We may presume that urban slaveholders would just as soon sell their slaves to sugar planters in the surrounding regions as to long-distance slave traders, depending entirely on the price they were offered.)

In the first years of the new slave trade the sale of urban slaves into the interprovincial trade outpaced that of those from agricultural zones. Some data for 1854 from Bahia, for instance, demonstrate that almost 60 percent of the slaves exported from that province came from cities and towns. It is suggestive that, right after 1850 at least, 23 percent were workers with urban skills. It may be that at this early point in time there was still a strong demand for them within prosperous Rio de Janeiro City. A typical advertisement placed in a Rio de Janeiro paper in 1854 spoke of "slaves . . . recently arrived from the North, handsome and young, including a goldsmith, a lovely creole woman, an 18 or 20 year old skilled mulatta, a black baker and oven-master, a . . . 17 year old male just right as a page, and other blacks and young boys."[27]

Yet from Rio de Janeiro City, as in Salvador, slaves were eventually sold in large numbers to the rural counties of the surrounding province. Between 1864 and 1874 the number of slaves in the city of Rio de Janeiro declined by 53 percent, whereas their number in the province of Rio de Janeiro remained virtually the same as before, despite deaths and manumissions. During the following ten years the province lost slaves as well, but the 14 percent decline in their number significantly trailed the city's 32 percent loss. Meanwhile slaves from the Northeast continued to flow through the city to the countryside in even higher numbers than in earlier decades, and it is impossible to distinguish those who were employed at least for a while in the city from those who were immediately bought up by planters from the city's many traders at their large and small warehouses and yards. Data on slave sales in two coffee-producing counties in the Paraíba Valley show a sharp increase in the number originating in the Northeast.[28] In 1879 the provincial president asked each county judge who supervised the slave registers to prepare data on the number of slaves within the county and the reason for the increase or decrease since the base year of 1872–73. Although some counties lost slaves because they had been moved away (as distinct from decreases due to death or manumission) and others gained them, taking all counties together they showed a net increase from migration of 16,016.[29]

We do not know the sex ratio among those sold out of the city, but probably more men than women were sent to the plantations. Women had been present in the transatlantic slave trade partly because of decisions made in Africa by other Africans,[30] but it is notable that even among Brazilian-born slaves shipped to Rio de Janeiro from elsewhere in Brazil, most were men. It is possible that the large proportion of women in domestic service could have led sellers to prefer to dispose of the men, but the demand for agricultural workers in the South is a more likely explanation. In a sample examined by Klein of 978 slaves arriving in Rio in 1852, the ratio of men to women was 182 to 100, and Conrad cites an 1856 British consular report prepared in Pernambuco on the export of 606 slaves (probably both African-born and creole) in which the ratio was an even more skewed 209 to 100. By 1884 the total slave population of the country was 53 percent male, but in that year males in the coffee-producing provinces accounted for 55 percent, those in the exporting provinces of the Northeast, only 49 percent.[31] In short, women remained behind while men were sent south.

Still, this nefarious trade included many women. If the proportion set in 1852 continued to hold (35 percent female), that would mean that thirty-five hundred slave women were arriving annually in Rio by the 1870s. Of these, many, perhaps most, ended up as domestics, whereas others were intended to be used as prostitutes. Sandra Lauderdale Graham notes that at least one importer in Rio de Janeiro specialized in supplying brothels. In such cases the women went to the madams almost immediately upon arrival, although others languished at the dealer's for weeks or months until they were placed, sometimes in the hands of a small-time owner who relied on the income of a single slave prostitute to augment a meager income. Buyers doubtless probed and inspected them with even more care and with different criteria than for other slave purchases they might make. Importers normally stated that the women were employed as domestic servants, but in 1871 the police found many slave women "placed at the window for a price"; those who were freed as a result of the ensuing furor were young mulattas almost all of whom had come from northeastern provinces.[32]

Most of the slaves caught up in the internal trade, whether men or women, were of working age. Both Klein's and Conrad's samples show that 84 to 86 percent were between the ages of ten and forty. Klein's sample displays a marked concentration (38 percent) of slaves in their twenties, whereas Conrad's sample is younger, with 57 percent between eleven and twenty and another 14 percent between five and ten years of age. Figures on sales into the interprovincial trade from interior Bahia from 1874 to 1884 show that two-thirds of these slaves were between eleven and thirty years old. It is possible that children were often not counted or were greatly undercounted, but it is perhaps more likely that the low price to be had for very young children did not compensate for the cost of transporting them.[33] If this was the case it meant an even greater likelihood of heart-rending separations, all too common to begin with.

The fact that slaves were treated as property before the law meant that commercial rules governed the trade in slaves and that their sale was subject to a tax, calculated at half the rate levied on sales of real estate. Since a slave involved in the trade went from hand to hand (for instance, from seller to slave trader in Salvador to the captain of a ship bound for Rio de Janeiro to another trader there to someone conducting the slaves to an interior town and finally to a coffee planter in need of workers), such a tax would have been prohibitive if levied on each transaction. Instead, the seller, in exchange for adequate compensation, issued a power of attorney to the first trader, giving him the right to sell the slave or grant similar powers of attorney to others. These legal instruments could then be passed on and on until reaching the final buyer. Only then did the purchaser pay the tax.[34]

Restrictions on the Trade

In contrast to the governmental effort to encourage trade from city to surrounding region, attempts to restrict the sale of slaves across provincial borders had a long history in Brazil, beginning in 1700, when, fearing a decline in sugar production, the Crown forbade planters to sell their slaves to miners in Minas Gerais. Such a law proved unenforceable, as one governor soon pointed out, and the Crown revoked it in 1709.[35] In the nineteenth century, when economic and political elites in the Northeast feared that urban slave owners would sell all their slaves south to the burgeoning coffee plantations of Rio de Janeiro or São Paulo rather than to local sugar planters, they attempted similar measures. Several northeastern provinces imposed taxes on the export of slaves. In Bahia persons who left the province with their own slaves as personal servants had to post bail, which would be lifted only if within forty days they presented a certificate from the chief of police of the other province certifying that said slaves were employed "in the service" of the person who took them. Because these provincial export taxes had minimal effect, João Maurício Wanderley (later the barão do Cotegipe), owner of an important sugar estate in Bahia and a rising political force there, having been elected to the national parliament, proposed a bill in 1854 to apply the antitrading law of 1850 with all its punitive clauses to the interprovincial slave trade within Brazil as well. The bill provoked a vigorous debate and suffered defeat, but its purpose was clear: to block the flow of slaves from the Northeast to the Southeast.[36]

Eventually planters in the Southeast became concerned with the quickening flow of slaves to their provinces. As early as 1871 a provincial legislator in São Paulo proposed imposing a heavy tax on their importation. Although the bill got nowhere at that time, by the end of the decade a majority of the assemblymen approved it. The provincial president at first vetoed the measure, but he changed his mind when leading planters of the coffee-rich district of Campinas lobbied on its behalf. The measure more than doubled the price of a slave.

The motivation behind their seemingly puzzling action is the subject of some controversy, and the debates in the São Paulo legislature supply plenty of ammunition for all sides. Paula Beiguelman places the decision within the context of an expanding demand for workers in the newest coffee regions of São Paulo Province, where, she believes, would-be planters foresaw that only a supply of European immigrants would be sufficient to satisfy their needs. Since they recognized that such immigrants would be reluctant to move to Brazil if they would have to work alongside slaves, these landowners supported the incipient abolitionist movement and sought, as a first step, to restrict the flow of slaves from the Northeast into their region. They found allies among planters in the oldest coffee-planting area of the province (well supplied with slaves), who wished to increase the price of slaves and thus the value of their "stock." That, she says, explains the imposition of the prohibitively high tax on imports of slaves into the province. Conrad argues, on the contrary, that the real purpose of these actions was to prevent the Northeast from becoming free of slaves and then pressuring the Southeast to abolish the institution. Dismissing the occasional speeches of assemblymen who supported the bill by denouncing slavery, Conrad insists that the purpose of the law was, rather, to preserve it. Celia Maria Marinho de Azevedo focuses on the speakers who expressed their fear that a flood of slaves would overwhelm slave owners by their sheer number. She notes that when a lawmaker argued that the tax would diminish "this leprosy that comes to us from the northern provinces," he did not refer to the institution of slavery but to the slaves themselves and the supposed characteristics of blacks. Fear of rebellion drove the representatives of slaveowners to end the importation of more slaves, despite their need for laborers in a booming economy.[37] Her data and other evidence discussed below lead me to agree with this last argument. I would add, however, that slaveowners recognized that the slave trade exposed the truly dehumanizing nature of slavery to public view, negating their attempt to portray it (to others and to themselves) as merely a form of labor with many saving graces, characterized by benevolent paternalism in which punishment was applied as a useful corrective and last resort. It was impossible to maintain that myth in the face of slaves in chains on ships, in the streets, at the slave markets, or trekking to the interior — and, because an abolitionist movement was being organized in the cities for the first time, maintaining that myth was more important than ever. In any case, São Paulo, Minas Gerais, and Rio de Janeiro Provinces all imposed such taxes as to virtually forbid the importation of slaves from other provinces in late 1880 and early 1881 and thus end the interprovincial trade in human beings.[38]

At the national level some legislators also urged measures to forbid the interprovincial slave trade, in effect returning to the proposal made by Cotegipe in 1854. In 1877 a well-known jurist and legal commentator, Agostinho Marques

Perdigão Malheiro, spoke in parliament to urge that trading in slaves (buying in order to resell, acting as a middleman), whether between provinces or within them, be made illegal. The abolitionist Joaquim Nabuco in 1880 urged that slaves transported from one province to another overland be declared free and that all slave traders be heavily taxed, in order "to close once and for all these markets of human flesh . . . these sources of corruption." As one might surmise, these two speakers opposed slavery, Nabuco as a radical, Perdigão Malheiro as a moderate. But a similar bill was introduced at the same time by Antōnio Moreira de Barros, who belonged to one of the major coffee-planting families and was known for his strident opposition to abolition.[39] Finally, in 1885 a law actually was passed freeing any slave moved from one province to another. Since the major slave-importing provinces had already crippled the internal trade, the measure had only a small effect on most of the trade. But the Conservative ministry in charge of implementing this law, to the astonishment of the opposition and the satisfaction of many coffee planters, declared that in this one instance the city of Rio (a kind of federal district since 1834) would be considered part of the surrounding province of Rio de Janeiro. The city lost a large proportion of its slaves between 1885 and 1887, probably because of sales to plantations.[40]

The Trade as Experience

The experiences of slaves caught up in the internal trade were never good ones. Many walked long distances to northeastern ports for shipment south and then again from Rio de Janeiro or Santos to the coffee plantations, always under the watchful gaze of a driver. Others went overland the entire way at least to Minas Gerais.[41] Slaves were uncertain as to their fate, all the more so because they passed from hand to hand and not from original owners directly to new ones, which would have been bad enough. The former slave interviewed by Stein recounted how in the 1880s he had been bought by an itinerant trader in Maranhão who had taken him as far as the city of São Luiz; there the trader had sold him to a merchant for transshipment to Rio, where he had been warehoused until an upland coffee planter purchased him and sent him by train to the county seat, where he was subsequently called for and taken to the plantation.[42] He was luckier than most: only the wealthiest planters came to Rio to make their purchases. Most relied on upland middlemen who had contact with fellow merchants in Rio or on mule drivers who delivered coffee in Rio and brought back slaves on consignment for eventual sale. In such a case the slave's future remained in agonizing doubt as a succession of strangers took possession of him or her. All this must have seemed especially frightening for all the Africans who once again confronted a ship for transport to a distant port.

In 1852 slaves were typically shipped from port to port within Brazil in small groups, often in lots of four or so, that is, presumably along with other commercial cargo, not on slaving ships. An 1854 newspaper in Salvador advertised the departure for Rio of a barque that "has good rooms both for passengers and slaves" and a schooner that "takes on small cargo and slaves." By the 1870s, however, much larger numbers of slaves traveled together on a ship. Slenes has found examples of 51, 78, and 232 slaves carried on a single ship in the interprovincial trade. Still, in 1880 a passenger complained that "one cannot travel on the [steam] packets of the Brazilian Company except in the company of this human cargo destined for sale in the South." So ships used strictly for slaving do not seem to have been common.[43] A trip by sea from Bahia to Rio lasted approximately four days by steamship (the preferred mode of transportation by the 1870s), much less than the six weeks or so that the trade from Africa had required, although the slaves were perhaps still chained. And, as a nineteenth-century author who compared the two trades grimly reminded his readers, a very large proportion of those transported across the Atlantic had died in the process of becoming acclimatized and reconciled to their new situation; he assumed that this did not occur to the same degree among those transported within Brazil, where the disease environments did not change much and the language barrier was virtually absent. Nevertheless, even in the 1850s the trade was described by Cotegipe as a repugnant business. He said it was a horror "to see children yanked from their mothers, husbands separated from wives, parents from children! Go to the [slave market] and you will be indignant and stricken with the spectacle of so much misery!"[44]

Once slaves arrived in Rio de Janeiro City, the businessmen to whom they were consigned often treated them badly. A government official described how the biggest dealer, Antonio Gonçales Guimarães, crowded them into a small space, causing many to become ill, and concluded that, although his enterprise was one of the best around, it still "left a great deal to be desired." Another dealer, a partner in the trading firm Duarte, Fonseca, and Company, who received slaves from several northeastern and northern provinces, claimed that he "dressed, fed, lodged, and treated [them] in the best possible manner," even sending sick ones to the hospital. Yet of thirty-eight slaves he received in one shipment from the province of Ceará in 1879, twenty-two died while in his care.[45]

As noted above, from the ports of Rio de Janeiro or Santos slaves were forced to walk long distances to interior plantations in São Paulo, Minas Gerais, or the province of Rio de Janeiro. Sidney Chalhoub recounts how one slave-trading transaction went awry in 1870 and ended up in court. Through this story we can glimpse something of the business. José Moreira Veludo set up a temporary partnership with Francisco Queiroz to transport slaves from the city of Rio to Minas Gerais and sell them there. Both of these men were Portuguese, but Veludo supplied the capital and the slaves and Queiroz, whose normal occupation was that of store clerk, entered the deal by providing the labor. Queiroz set off from Rio with twenty-four slaves, both men and women, three mules, a change of clothes for the slaves, cloaks, sleeping mats, a boiling pot, cups, plates, coffee, sugar, and other foodstuffs (probably manioc meal and dried meat). He left in May and came back in August, having sold twenty slaves, returning with four still unsold. Some of the buyers later claimed that they had received defective merchandise, such as a slave who suffered from gout and said he had been treated for it for at least five years.[46] Gouty or not, he and his companions had gone on foot a distance of 125 miles, over an escarpment that rises from sea level to eight hundred meters. Queiroz had doubtless ridden one of the mules, and the slaves had probably been forced to carry some of their food and equipment. It is reasonable to expect that most slaves who did not remain in the city moved in this fashion to the landed estates that were to be their new homes, even if in later times some part of the voyage could be made by train.

A productive way to think about the meaning of slaves' experience of the trade is to consider some individual cases, remembering that there is no such thing as a "typical" individual. The stories emerging from the judicial records in Rio, first used by Sandra Lauderdale Graham, then by Sidney Chalhoub, and subsequently by many other historians, could doubtless be multiplied not only in that city but in other places, including small towns, where notarial records are often more accessible than historians once thought. When enough of these have been collected, we may begin to draw overall conclusions, being cautious, however, to focus not on some imagined sociological mean but on the limits of the possible. Meanwhile, it is useful to consider a number of individuals swept up in the interprovincial slave trade.

Cypriano, a Yoruba-speaking African, was caught up in the internal slave trade before 1850. According to his master's testimony, he had arrived in Salvador from Africa in 1827 and been baptized as Cypriano two years later. He was first apprenticed to a barber, apparently unsuccessfully, and then his master put him to work as a clerk in his store. Cypriano, said his owner, "pretended" to be too slow-witted to carry out his duties, so in 1834 his master consigned him for sale to the captain of a ship headed for the southern province of Rio Grande do Sul. There, however, zealous officials apprehended him on suspicion of having arrived from Africa "after the prohibition of the slave trade" in 1831. He testified that he had arrived just "nine moons" before being sent to Rio Grande do Sul, that he had never been baptized at all, although his fellow slave at the store had taught him to pray, and that, before being shipped south, his only tasks had been to carry firewood and perform other porterage on the streets of Salvador, that is, not in close proximity to his master as an apprentice. Witnesses vouched for the veracity of the owner's account, but no one besides Cypriano himself spoke on his behalf. The jury preferred to believe the master's story and Cypriano returned to slavery, though whether this was in Rio Grande do Sul or in Salvador is not clear.[47] His hopes, raised by state action, were dashed by the state officials.

Luiz Gama had a very different experience. His mother was an African woman already freed at the time of his birth in Salvador. Implicated in plotting a revolt, she was forced to flee the city, leaving Luiz behind. When his Portuguese father fell on hard times, he illegally sold Gama into slavery at the age of eight, and the boy was taken to Rio, then to Santos, and finally on foot to São Paulo City, where he worked as a servant at a boarding house. Befriended by a boarder, he learned to read and write. At age seventeen he ran away, enlisted in the army, rebelled at its discipline — which reminded him of slavery — and was dishonorably discharged. He then found employment as a typesetter and soon began to write articles, signing his column "Afro." Eventually he became a newspaper editor and a poet and joined the ranks of the abolitionists. He proved in court that he had been born free. In doing so, he learned the elements of lawyering, a knowledge he put to work for other African Brazilians, securing the freedom of numerous slaves in the late 1870s by getting the courts to acknowledge that all those imported after 1831 were legally free along with their descendants.[48] He clearly identified with others whose plight resembled his.

Honorata was brought by her mistress, a laundress, from Bahia in the early 1860s and was forced into prostitution at the age of twelve. By the time she was nineteen, Honorata was sometimes expected to fend for herself, paying a specified weekly sum to her mistress but otherwise finding her own housing, clothes, food, and customers. (Self-hiring was a common practice for skilled slaves, whether male or female, sometimes allowing slaves to earn enough extra to eventually buy their freedom.) When Honorata contracted a chest ailment, perhaps tuberculosis, and sought the aid of her owner, the latter, rather than providing medical attention, ordered her to be beaten. Like all prostitutes she was particularly vulnerable to venereal disease. On the other hand, Honorata could count on a coachman to lend or give her money to satisfy the demands of her mistress when she had not secured the necessary earnings and on her male customers for support in her eventual effort to secure legal freedom. "Respectable" slave owners saw the prostitution of slaves as a threat to the institution and occasionally cracked down on the small-time madams who forced their slaves into the practice.[49]

Corina, a mulatta, was sold into the trade from Bahia at the age of twenty in March 1867 and was soon afterward purchased from a dealer in Rio de Janeiro City by a middle-aged black female brothel owner, well known for her collection of "extremely beautiful . . . mulatta slaves . . . all of them more or less light skinned, . . . all young, almost fledglings." Corina did not remain young for long. When she gave birth, her child was taken from her within days and delivered as a foundling to the public orphanage so that she could continue "to provide her services." Corina was treated for several festering syphilitic sores on her legs and the inside of her upper thighs, an inflammation of the lymph glands on the side of her neck, and several skin eruptions. While she was still attractive, her days stretched from the late mornings until 2:00 or 3:00 A.M., yet she was able on her own to gather at least three-quarters of her sale price as she strove to purchase her freedom.[50] What kind of freedom that would have been, given her illness, we can only imagine. We also cannot know how many of the perhaps thirty-five hundred slave women shipped every year from the Northeast shared Corina's fate, but we know she was not alone.

The desire to return north to their familiar locations surfaced as a common theme among slaves in and around Rio de Janeiro. A young creole slave sent there from Salvador in the early 1870s and then sold to a coffee planter in the interior tried unsuccessfully to retrace his trajectory. Braulio, son of the slave woman Severina, had been a feisty child who wounded another boy and was later understood to "procede [so] badly" that at one point the police had to be called in to punish him. Chalhoub describes how his fate worsened at the death of his master. This "dark mulatto" was placed in the hands of a slave-trading firm in Salvador along with his mother and brother, but although they went to far-away Rio Grande do Sul, Braulio was shipped to Rio city and then transferred to the coffee-planting county of Valença in Rio de Janeiro Province. Not surprisingly, he did not please his new master, who put him up for sale. After being the property of several others, he fled back to Rio, where he passed himself off as free, taking up the trade of carpenter. The scars on his ankles made by iron stocks betrayed him, and the police apprehended him on suspicion of being a slave. When his owner visited Rio, he knew to go by the jail to see if any escapees were there and easily picked Braulio out of a line-up. At this time Braulio had not yet reached the age of twenty-one. At the first chance he got after being returned to his master, Braulio plunged a file used in making bone toothpicks into the man's chest, later admitting that he intended to murder him because his owner was extremely violent and had already killed two slaves who disobeyed him. Braulio stated that he would prefer the death penalty to further subjection to this man.[51] By such actions Braulio had challenged not just his master but slavery itself and the institutions designed to protect it. For him, and perhaps for others, death could be no worse than slavery. Once that decision had been made, the establishment was defanged.

In 1878, at the age of twenty-seven, the slave Serafim, born to an African couple in Alagoas, was shipped south aboard a steamship along with six other slaves. Two slave traders, one in Alagoas, the other in Rio de Janeiro, handled the transfer. Whereas the other slaves found ready buyers, Serafim managed to display his unsuitability for any employment, insisted that he be sent back to Alagoas, and eventually sickened and had to be treated at the hospital. Later he attacked a fellow slave, and the trader called in the police; it took two policemen to subdue him and carry him away. Another trader eventually took him to Minas Gerais and sold him to Domingos Pedro Robert, the son of a Frenchman, for work in coffee fields. Serafim soon ran away, back to Rio de Janeiro, traveling at night on foot and being fed by slaves on other plantations who took that risk and must have approved of his enterprise. In 1884 Serafim was arrested in Rio for fighting with a coachman and a policeman. He declared readily that he was Robert's slave, but Robert preferred to abandon him — thus making him free — than to expend the sum needed to recover and return him to Minas, a sum that, Robert judged, exceeded Serafim's value.[52] In effect, Robert had been defeated. How many other masters had also seen the futility of their effort to maintain authority?

Sale almost always marked a moment of wrenching separation and grief. As one reformer put it, "What once was done to Indians, is now done with [black] slaves, so inhumanely and barbarously yanked from their place of birth, their loves, their families."[53] Those transported found themselves isolated from their accustomed human contacts. The strangeness of the new setting they encountered can only have added to their dismay. Mothers, sisters, mates, and children left behind must have been devastated by the gaping absence of those sent away. An extreme case is recounted by Hebe Maria Mattos de Castro: the slave woman Justina, besides caring for her three children, also took care of the child of another woman who had been sold into the trade, leaving her child behind; when Justina believed the same fate was about to befall her, she drowned her children and attempted suicide.[54] She, too, because of the internal slave trade, ended up casting an intolerable light on the horrible reality of slavery itself.

Nowadays it hardly needs repeating that slaves greatly valued family ties. As a former slave put it in 1835, he had "a home, children, and all else that mattered in life" and did not want to be forcefully removed from Bahia. One evidence of such commitment to family is that, once freed, family members made strenuous efforts to reestablish links with those from whom they had been separated by sale. It was particularly difficult to do so if a slave had been sold not to a neighboring plantation where the possibility of contact existed but to a trader who shipped him or her off to a distant region. Maria Ana de Souza do Bomfim, a mother who had been freed in Bahia, went to Rio de Janeiro in 1868 seeking her daughter Felicidade, who had been sent there as a slave. Lauderdale Graham explains that by the time Maria Ana reached Rio her daughter had been passed on to a buyer in Minas Gerais. The mother then contracted with a Rio slave dealer, paying him to go to Minas Gerais to find Felicidade, buy her, and bring her to Rio, where Maria Ana would pay for her freedom in installments. This plan succeeded until the mother failed to make two payments and a court battle over Felicidade's status resulted. Her mother finally established that Felicidade was in effect *coartada,* that is, freed conditionally with the obligation to make payments until completing her sale price, and the court ruled that these payments could be converted to an obligation by the mother and daughter to render service for a period of three years. Felicidade's master agreed to this solution because, he said, of the "spirit of insubordination by which she is naturally possessed."[55] Maria Ana's search and perseverance were at last rewarded, and her daughter's insubordination, recognized as "natural," could only mean a questioning of the system's viability.

In the 1820s Maria Lourindo and her husband Casemiro had been the slaves of a Pernambuco sugar planter from a distinguished family. This did not keep them from being separated from their daughter Victoriana; a trader shipped mother and father to Rio Grande do Sul, but the fate of their daughter remained a mystery. Thirty years later the widowed mother, now freed, placed an advertisement in a Pernambuco newspaper, hoping to find Victoriana or her children, if there were any.[56] We do not know whether she succeeded in locating the daughter, but her effort speaks of the devastating effect of the internal slave trade and a mother's persisting affection. Given the importance of such family connections, breaking them had serious personal and social consequences.

For a slave to be sold for shipment from the city to an interior plantation or from city or farm to another province was understood by slave and master alike as a punishment. It was not done lightly. The one occasion before 1850 when slaves were shipped from Bahia to Rio de Janeiro in relatively large numbers was just after the malê revolt in Salvador in January 1835. Carlos Eugênio Líbano Soares shows that 98 such slaves, only two of whom had been born in Brazil, arrived in Rio from Bahia on one ship, and João José Reis has counted up 380 slaves sold out of Bahia by April of that year.[57] True, slaves often wished to be sold to any other master to escape the control of an extremely harsh one, and some others identified the specific person to whom they wanted to be transferred. But I have found no evidence of any slave asking to be sold into the impersonal slave trade. On the contrary, I found at least one slave so incensed when his mistress told him he would be sold that he attacked and tried to kill her, and Reis discusses an entire group of slaves who rebelled (unsuccessfully) when their master announced his decision to sell them into the interprovincial trade.[58]

Some slaves moved from one plantation or region to another in the company of their master and presumably with most of the other slaves with whom they had worked as part of an entire household, including their wives and children. We have seen that some such movement occurred in the eighteenth century between the sugar-producing Northeast and the mining areas of Minas Gerais, and some slaveowners from Minas Gerais moved into Rio de Janeiro and São Paulo Provinces in the early nineteenth century to take up coffee planting. It is well known that many coffee planters — or their sons — moved from worn-out coffee fields in the Paraíba do Sul River valley in the provinces of São Paulo and Rio de Janeiro to the newly opened up center-west area of São Paulo in the 1870s, taking their slaves with them.[59] As noted above, however, this happened in Brazil much less often than in the southern United States, suggesting that the full trauma of sale was more likely for slaves within the internal slave trade in Brazil. And for those who did move with their owners, one can be sure that some of the slaves' family and friends were left behind either because they belonged to other estates or because the moving owner would dispose of the less useful slaves in a kind of "moving sale" while purchasing new ones of prime working age to take along. Moreover, as the case of Honorata demonstrates, moving with one's owner did not necessarily improve one's lot.

In addition, bondsmen were constantly being sold from plantation to plantation; if near enough to his or her former location, a slave might be able to visit husband, wife, lover, child, or parent on a day off or take time from rest, perhaps walking through the night to do so. The conditions of work in such a case may have been roughly similar. Or, if a slave moved from a sugar plantation or a mining enterprise to a relatively nearby coffee establishment, as could have happened in Rio de Janeiro Province or Minas Gerais, the work may actually have been easier. Although the personal shock caused by this trade cannot be doubted, it may have been less than the wrenching experiences of those moved far away to totally unfamiliar locales.

When the trade represented a shift from a small-time owner to a big plantation, as was particularly characteristic of the interprovincial trade, the relationship between slave and master was deeply altered. The new master could hardly be expected to know the names of a hundred or more slaves and, in any case, often relied on an overseer or at least a slave driver, intermediaries unknown in a small holding.[60] The rules of behavior and the expectations of slaves regarding a master's appropriate stance now had to be relearned. The meaning of the internal slave trade for the two hundred thousand or more slaves who, in the period after 1850, found themselves torn from familiar environments, separated from those they loved, transported long distances, and coerced to work at unfamiliar tasks by masters or overseers whom they did not know cannot be fully fathomed with the sources at hand, but we can try.

A Dangerous Trade

Relatively young, overwhelmingly male, no longer stitched into the social life of a particular place, and forcibly denied the contacts with family and friends that could have exerted a moderating influence on behavior, the transported men were probably angry, resentful, anxious, less constrained by social expectations, and certainly volatile. Males alone had always had less to lose by their active resistance. Many observers noted that newly moved slaves were more rebellious than others, being a source, as the abolitionist Joaquim Nabuco put it, of "disorder and perturbation" in the province of São Paulo and thus threatening its development, which had been so promising, he said, when it had relied predominantly on free labor.[61] In 1854 planters in one county located in the coffee-rich Paraíba River do Sul valley formed a committee to make sure every planter would be prepared for any eventual insurrection of slaves on his plantation, because the danger had increased, they believed, "now that plantations are supplying themselves with slaves from the North." A historian of Pará working close to the sources describes the creole slaves brought in from other parts of Brazil in the nineteenth century as even more "turbulent" than those from Africa.[62] It is only logical to conclude that those who had been sold away would tend to blame the system of slavery itself, for their experience not only placed slaves in a situation of hostility toward their new owners but suggested that any earlier sense that an implicit bargain had been struck with former owners was now exposed as merely a hoodwinking exercise. Masters who had purchased such slaves could sense the disquiet among them. Slaveowners, overseers, and drivers needed to know the physical and mental qualities of the slaves, and the slaves needed to have the measure of those who issued orders, sensing their moods, reading their body language. In a new relationship neither party had these advantages. For control had always been problematic, the result of an intricate if unspoken negotiation, contingent on the specific situation and ever contested.

In the regions to which slaves were now moved, all this was now in doubt, as several authors have shown, and the slaves' resistance was clearer than ever. A provincial legislator in São Paulo claimed that these slaves brought with them "vice, immorality, insubordination. . . . Those planters who buy slaves from the outside" harbored "assassins . . . in their houses." Another spoke of "the lamentable and critical situation confronted by our province, receiving daily from northern ports, not hands that come to augment its income and thus contribute to its prosperity, but, on the whole, robbers and assassins who come to unsettle the peace of the home and place [our] families and, eventually, [our] small towns in a constant state of alarm and worry." The president of Rio de Janeiro Province declared that the slaves brought south in the internal trade "brought to the plantations neither the resignation nor the contentment with their lot that are essential to good discipline," and he hoped that restricting the trade would help maintain "order and tranquility on rural establishments."[63] A study conducted by Robert Slenes for Campinas, a coffee-rich town in São Paulo Province, shows that the comparison of neighboring properties shows greater unrest in those with more slaves recently transported in the internal trade than in those with a more settled group.[64] In short, the acts of individual resistance provoked by the trauma of the internal slave trade increased the cost of supervision and security for the masters and undermined the institution of slavery itself. Both masters and their critics were aware of how precarious the old order had become.

The final abolition of slavery in Brazil in 1888 resulted from a number of factors, but one of the most important was the active resistance of the slaves themselves. Two major aspects of their role, one general, one specific, are worth highlighting. First, as just mentioned, their day-to-day recalcitrance over many years wore down the authority of the master class. Warren Dean notes that the restlessness of slaves increased after 1850, a condition that he attributes to a declining hope for manumission caused by the masters' much greater difficulty in securing new slaves after the end of the transatlantic trade and a consequent reluctance to free the ones they had. But it is also true, as Célia Maria Marinho de Azevedo shows, that just as it had once been thought that Africans were more likely to revolt than creoles, contemporaries noted that creoles who had been shipped from one province to another or from city to countryside were more prone to violence or flight than those brought up on the plantation.[65] Like the Indians referred to at the beginning of this chapter, the slaves transported in the internal trade were particularly ready to resist their plight openly and, despite having been moved, knew enough about the landscape — social rather than physical, of cities and cultivated fields rather than of forests — to subvert the rules of enslavement. Certainly the last decades of slavery saw much slave unrest and a number of murders of masters and overseers, although whether these incidents occurred more frequently than before has not been fully established. After all, everyone always says things are worse now than they were before.[66] Moreover, if selling a slave to a trader was a recognized way of getting rid of a troublesome slave, then surely the proportion of such slaves among those traded was higher than among slaves in general. Long before prices of slaves began to soar, it was not uncommon to find a case like that of João, an Angolan slave sold in Bahia in 1847 on condition of being shipped out of the province for "being suspected of having a part in the assassination of his master" or that of several rebellious slaves whom a master placed with his factor before 1806 "to be sold to Maranhão."[67] For all these reasons, the owners of slaves became increasingly concerned with issues of discipline and ever more fearful of slave behavior.

Second, in 1887 and early 1888, slaves contributed even more specifically and decisively to the final end of slavery in Brazil. A massive flight of slaves from plantations to the cities took authorities by surprise, completely overwhelming by their sheer numbers every effort to stanch the flow. By then many urban residents, including railway workers and managers, judges, professionals, bureaucrats, and soldiers, had lost faith in slavery as a solution to labor needs and refused to cooperate in upholding it, perhaps because they had witnessed too many disgusting scenes of slaves in chains on the way to upland plantations as part of the internal slave trade; some activists in the cities even encouraged the flight of slaves. At first, slaves left stealthily in the night, but soon they fled openly, sometimes confronting the authorities with firearms. Coffee planters, desperate to harvest their crop, were forced to hire runaway slaves from other plantations.[68] When the army was summoned to help maintain order, its leaders disdainfully declared that they did not wish to be charged "with the capture of poor blacks who flee slavery."[69] Faced with a fait accompli, when parliament met in May 1888, its members hastily passed a law abolishing slavery. As one legislator later explained, that law "was imposed by circumstances, dictated by . . . the planters themselves who, not being able to contain the indiscipline on the plantations nor the insubordinate slaves, went ahead of [abolitionist] propaganda, conceding full liberty to their slaves since abolitionism was at the door."[70] A former prime minister and defender of slavery exclaimed in disgust: "For what an abolition law? In fact it is done already — and revolutionarily."[71]

Despite the subsequent construction of a myth that gave principal credit for this outcome to Princess Isabel's generosity and the planters' benevolence, the story of slave activism was clearly told by Evaristo de Moraes in 1924. Still, historians including myself until recently placed insufficient emphasis on the fact that the slaves acted very much out of their own self-awareness and from their knowledge of the larger system.[72] Cleveland Donald, in his 1973 doctoral thesis and in a subsequent article, forcefully argued against the view that slaves only took action when persuaded by whites.[73] Maria Helena Machado carried the question still further in her richly researched study of secret police reports, showing that far from suddenly acting in 1887, slaves were deliberately struggling against the institution throughout the 1880s.[74] It is now impossible to discount the agency of the slaves in shaping events.

It is true that we have no firm evidence that the slaves who participated in the dramatic mass flights of 1887–1888 were necessarily those involved in the internal slave trade. But the major area of such actions was in the province of São Paulo, the province that had been most prominent in importing slaves from other regions. Another place witnessing direct action — and more spectacular because here the slaves burned the cane fields — was the sugar-producing county of Campos in the province of Rio de Janeiro described by Lana Lage Lima; it was one of the few noncoffee areas of the province to have experienced a growth in the number of slaves between 1873 and 1882. No such mass flight or generalized sabotage occurred on the sugar plantations of the Northeast, where the slaves had grown up and were more securely attached to the local society and culture.[75] I conclude that the dislocation brought on by the internal slave trade powerfully contributed to their action.

Other aspects were also important, not least of which is timing. By the late 1880s the world had changed in its attitudes toward slavery, and Brazil remained the only slaveholding country in the Americas. A long list of laws had chipped away at slavery as it was once known. The end of the transatlantic slave trade, the freeing of children born to slave mothers after 1871, and the continuing (if lessened) practice of private manumission, combined with the deaths of thousands, had shrunk the number of slaves from 1.5 million in 1874 to 723,000 in 1887.[76] The concentration of slave ownership provoked by the internal trade had significantly diminished the number of those who would be adversely affected by abolition, especially those in the growing middle class. Nevertheless, the slaves' constant push against the system in large ways and small, combined with the dramatic events of 1887–1888, cannot but be considered crucial.[77]

A growing fear among planters, especially among those in the formerly slaveholding southeastern provinces, that abolition represented only a first step toward an even more dangerous land reform greatly encouraged the growth of a Republican party and paved the way for the acquiescence of many landowners when faced with the military overthrow of the empire in late 1889.[78] Other issues were involved too, of course, but if cause and effect runs from internal slave trade to slave discontent to slave action in fleeing the plantations to abolition of slavery to the declaration of a republic — then, as I see it, the political importance of that trade was great indeed.

These outcomes could hardly have been foreseen in 1850, when the African trade came to an end, but they flowed from the subsequent action of innumerable slaveholders and traders who tore slaves away from their accustomed places and relationships within Brazil. Given the growing doubts and fissures within the community of the free about the institution itself, the internal slave trade proved a dangerous turn for the slave system. Cypriano, Luiz Gama, Honorata, Corina, Braulio, Serafim, Maria Ana, Felicidade, Maria Lourindo, and Victoriana had each, in his or her own way, suffered and reacted. Whether slaves came from city, farm, or plantation, whether they moved far or relatively near, by sea or land, the generally appalling conditions of slavery were made all the more visibly clear to slave and free alike by this new middle passage.

Notes

I thank other members of the Santa Fe Seminar for their comments on a very early version of this chapter, and I especially wish to thank Sandra Lauderdale Graham. Barbara Sommer made valuable substantive and bibliographic suggestions concerning Indians in the internal slave trade. The commentary of participants in the Yale University Gilder Lehrman Center conference on comparative internal slave trades also proved useful, but I particularly benefited from excellent comments subsequently made by João José Reis.

1. Compare David Barry Gaspar and Darlene Clark, eds., *More Than Chattel: Black Women and Slavery in the Americas* (Bloomington: Indiana University Press, 1996).

2. John Manuel Monteiro, *Negros da terra: Indios e bandeirantes nas origens de São Paulo* (São Paulo: Companhia das Letras, 1994), pp. 64, 65, 74, 76–79; João Capistrano de Abreu, *Chapters of Brazil's Colonial History* (New York: Oxford University Press, 1997), pp. 102, 105; David Graham Sweet, "A Rich Realm of Nature Destroyed: The Middle Amazon Valley, 1640–1750," Ph.D. diss. (University of Wisconsin, 1974), p. 171 n.19; Bailey W. Diffie, *A History of Colonial Brazil, 1500–1792* (Malbar, FL: Krieger, 1987), p. 258. Whether the demand in Bahia was met directly by slave raiders from São Paulo is discussed by Luiz Felipe de Alencastro, *O trato dos viventes: A formação do Brasil no Atlântico Sul* (São Paulo: Companhia das Letras, 2000), pp. 191–96.

3. Alida C. Metcalf, *Family and Frontier in Colonial Brazil: Santana de Parnaíba, 1580–1822* (Berkeley: University of California Press, 1992), pp. 49–54, 66–67, 69, 78; Monteiro, *Negros da terra*, pp. 147–52, 209–20; Marcus J. M. de Carvalho, "Negros da terra e negros da Guiné: Os termos de uma troca, 1535–1630," *Revista do Instituto*

Histórico e Geográfico Brasileiro, no. 408 (July–September 2000): 329–42. On the sixteenth-century shift from Indian to African slavery in Brazil, see Stuart B. Schwartz, "Indian Labor and New World Plantations: European Demands and Indian Responses in Northeastern Brazil," *American Historical Review* 83, no. 1 (February 1978): 43–79. The unfree labor of Indians, in one form or another, was also widespread in Spanish America, and the sale of Yaqui Indians from northwest Mexico to henequen and sugar plantations in Yucatán and Cuba occurred as late as the 1890s.

4. Fernando A. Novais, *Portugal e Brasil na crise do antigo sistema colonial* (1777–1808) (São Paulo: HUCITEC, 1979), pp. 104–5; Alencastro, *Trato dos viventes,* pp. 117–119, 126.

5. Philip D. Curtin, *The Atlantic Slave Trade: A Census* (Madison: University of Wisconsin Press, 1969), pp. 47–49, 88–89; Herbert S. Klein, *The Atlantic Slave Trade* (Cambridge: Cambridge University Press, 1999), p. 211. For a more detailed discussion of these figures see Paul E. Lovejoy, "The Volume of the Atlantic Slave Trade: A Synthesis," *Journal of African History* 23, no. 4 (1982): 473–501, and David Eltis, "The Nineteenth-Century Transatlantic Slave Trade: An Annual Time Series of Imports into the Americas Broken Down by Region," *Hispanic American Historical Review* 67, no. 1 (February 1987): 109–38.

6. Vicente Salles, *O negro no Pará sob o regime da escravidão* (Rio de Janeiro: Fundação Getulio Vargas and Universidade Federal do Pará, 1971), pp. 32, 37, 42–43, 50–51.

7. C. R. Boxer, *The Golden Age of Brazil, 1695–1750: Growing Pains of a Colonial Society* (Berkeley: University of California Press, 1964), p. 42; Laird W. Bergad, *Slavery and the Demographic and Economic History of Minas Gerais, Brazil, 1720–1888* (Cambridge: Cambridge University Press, 1999), p. 84; Kathleen J. Higgins, *"Licentious Liberty" in a Brazilian Gold-Mining Region: Slavery, Gender, and Social Control in Eighteenth-Century Sabará, Minas Gerais* (University Park: Pennsylvania State University Press, 1999), p. 74. See also Kathleen J. Higgins, "The Slave Society in Eighteenth-Century Sabará: A Community Study in Colonial Brazil," Ph.D. diss. (Yale University, 1987), pp. 73, 97.

8. Presidente da Província da Bahia to Ministro de Justiça, Salvador, 26 June, 24 July, and 22 Sept. 1834, and 14 Feb. and 7 Nov. 1835, Arquivo Nacional, Seção do Poder Executivo, Justiça, IJ1707.

9. There is a large literature on this subject, ably summarized and added to by Leslie Bethell, *The Abolition of the Brazilian Slave Trade: Britain, Brazil, and the Slave Trade Question, 1807–1869,* Cambridge Latin American Studies, no. 6 (Cambridge: Cambridge University Press, 1970).

10. José Thomas Nabuco de Araujo, quoted by Joaquim Nabuco, *Um estadista do Império,* 3rd ed. (Rio de Janeiro: Nova Aguilar, 1975), p. 197.

11. Herbert S. Klein, "The Internal Slave Trade in Nineteenth-Century Brazil: A Study of Slave Importations into Rio de Janeiro in 1852," *Hispanic American Historical Review* 51, no. 4 (November 1971): 571; this article was subsequently incorporated in Herbert S. Klein, *The Middle Passage: Comparative Studies in the Atlantic Slave Trade* (Princeton: Princeton University Press, 1978). When in the 1840s economic conditions worsened in Maranhão and Pará was booming, slaves from the former province were

traded to the latter. Some of these may have been born in Africa, but others were creoles. By 1851, just as the overseas trade was ending, the author of an anonymous letter to a newspaper editor identified himself as a sugar planter in Pará whose slaves were all "creoles from Ceará," quoted in Salles, *O negro no Pará*, p. 53.

12. Klein, "Internal Slave Trade," pp. 577, 579. Slaves exported from Rio Grande do Sul between 1874 and 1884 accounted for 14.53 percent of the slaves held there in 1874, whereas the comparable figure for the Northeast was only 6.43 percent. Naturally some northeastern provinces with relatively small holdings exported an even higher percentage, but Rio Grande do Sul was the third largest holder of slaves among exporting provinces. Robert Conrad, *The Destruction of Brazilian Slavery* (Berkeley: University of California Press, 1972), pp. 284, 290.

13. It is incontrovertible that in the early days of coffee expansion in the provinces of Rio de Janeiro and São Paulo (from the 1820s to the 1850s) some black slaves were moved out of Minas Gerais, often alongside their masters. Historians alluded to this fact without making much of it, but Roberto Borges Martins sets these scholars up as straw men to be criticized, despite acknowledging that evidence for this period is "indirect, fragmentary, and often contradictory." He concludes that, far from exporting slaves, Minas Gerais from 1800 to 1873 imported, either from Africa or from other provinces, well in excess of four hundred thousand slaves. The sources do not allow us to separate out those brought in after the end of the transatlantic trade in 1850. For the period following 1873, at the time of the first national census, Martins reverses course: Although still maintaining that Minas Gerais exported very few slaves, he argues that imports were also low and that only about seven thousand more slaves were imported than exported in the period 1873–1881. Robert Slenes had earlier alleged that in this period almost twenty-four thousand slaves came from other provinces, but Martins insisted that Slenes had underestimated the number of slaves already within the province in 1873. Robert W. Slenes, "The Demography and Economics of Brazilian Slavery, 1850–1888," Ph.D. diss. (Stanford University, 1975), p. 616; Roberto Borges Martins, "Growing in Silence: The Slave Economy of Nineteenth-Century Minas Gerais, Brazil," Ph.D. diss. (Vanderbilt University, 1980), pp. 169, 178, 212–13, 218–20 (quotation is at p. 184). A summary of Martins's argument appears in Amilcar Martins Filho and Roberto B. Martins, "Slavery in a Nonexport Economy: Nineteenth-Century Minas Gerais Revisited," *Hispanic American Historical Review* 63, no. 3 (August 1983): 537–68. For Slenes's reply see Robert W. Slenes, "Comments on 'Slavery in a Nonexport Economy,'" *Hispanic American Historical Review* 63, no. 3 (August 1983): 569, 577, and Robert W. Slenes, "Os multiplos de porcos e diamantes: A economia escrava de Minas Gerais no século xix," *Estudos Econômicos* 18, no. 3 (December 1988): 449–95. Although Martins at times seems to contradict himself, Douglas Cole Libby sometimes distorts Martins's meaning in order to criticize him. Douglas Cole Libby, *Transformação e trabalho em uma economia escravista: Minas Gerais no século XIX* (São Paulo: Brasiliense, 1988), pp. 19–21, 40. For a detailed survey of the debate see Douglas Cole Libby, "Historiografia e a formação social escravista mineira," *Acervo: Revista do Arquivo Nacional* 3, no. 1 (June 1988): 13–16. Laird Bergad's team of researchers examined more than ten thousand post-mortem inventories and many local censuses to conclude that there wasn't much significant importation of slaves into that province before 1873 (when he ends his study, despite the title of

his book): Bergad, *Slavery and the Demographic and Economic History of Minas*. Important objections have been raised, however, by Douglas Cole Libby in his review, *American Historical Review* 107, no. 1 (February 2002): 258–59.

14. Sebastião Ferreira Soares, *Notas estatísticas sobre a produção agricola e a carestia dos generos alimenticios no império do Brazil* (Rio de Janeiro: Villeneuve, 1860), p. 135.

15. Klein, "Internal Slave Trade," 568, 583; Slenes, "Demography and Economics of Brazilian Slavery," pp. 124, 135–39, 169n39; Robert W. Slenes, "Grandeza ou decadência? O mercado de escravos e a economia cafeeira da província do Rio de Janeiro, 1850–1888," in *Brasil: História econômica e demográfica*, ed. Iraci del Nero da Costa (São Paulo: Instituto de Pesquisas Econômicas, 1986), pp. 110–33; Robert Edgar Conrad, *World of Sorrow: The African Slave Trade to Brazil* (Baton Rouge: Louisiana State University Press, 1986), pp. 179, 181.

16. On the demographic effect of such a massive shift in population see Conrad, *Destruction of Brazilian Slavery*, p. 285, and Peter L. Eisenberg, "Abolishing Slavery: The Process on Pernambuco's Sugar Plantations," *Hispanic American Historical Review* 52, no. 4 (November 1972): 595. The cultural impact of the trade on Brazil can only be guessed at, but it is thought that because the late eighteenth- and early nineteenth-century trade from Africa to Bahia came mainly from African ports along the bight of Benin and the Guinea coast, where Yoruba and Fon speakers predominated, along with many Hausa, whereas in the second quarter of the nineteenth century a stream of Bantu-speaking slaves from central Africa flowed to southeastern Brazil, a massive shift of slaves from the Northeast to the Southeast in Brazil after 1850 would logically mean that religious rituals, family practices, and language patterns in the Southeast would have been affected by West African culture, even to today. See, e.g., Eduardo Silva, *Prince of the People: The Life and Times of a Brazilian Free Man of Colour* (London: Verso, 1993), pp. 48–49; on a parallel development in eighteenth-century Minas Gerais see Elizabeth W. Kiddy, "Congados, Calunga, Candombe: Our Lady of the Rosary in Minas Gerais, Brazil," *Luso-Brazilian Review* 37, no. 1 (Summer 2000): 52–53.

17. Klein, "Internal Slave Trade," 579n; Michael Tadman, *Speculators and Slaves: Masters, Traders, and Slaves in the Old South* (Madison: University of Wisconsin Press, 1989), p. 297. Also see pp. 169–70.

18. Slenes, "Demography and Economics of Brazilian Slavery," p. 145; Klein, "Internal Slave Trade," 569n. Because of rapid slave reproduction and the rarity of manumission, the total number of slaves in the United States became much greater than that in Brazil, despite the larger number of those imported to Brazil. On the other hand, the population of free and freed African Brazilians grew dramatically.

19. The British consul is cited by J. H. Galloway, "The Last Years of Slavery on the Sugar Plantations of Northeastern Brazil," *Hispanic American Historical Review* 51, no. 4 (November 1971): 589; Agostinho Marques Perdigão Malheiro, Speech, 3 July 1877, in Brazil, Congresso, Câmara dos Deputados, *Anais*, 1877, 2:23; Stanley J. Stein, *Vassouras: A Brazilian Coffee County, 1850–1900* (Cambridge: Harvard University Press, 1958), p. 72.

20. Martins, "Growing in Silence," p. 243; see also pp. 217 and 234. But compare Bergad, *Slavery and the Demographic and Economic History of Minas*, p. 118, who uses a less precise definition of "coffee zones" to say that already in 1872 [1873] they held

3 1 percent of provincial slaves. Martins is trying to make the point that the intraprovincial transfer of slaves was not as massive as earlier authors believed, but he does not deny the direction of their movement.

21. Conrad, *Destruction of Brazilian Slavery,* pp. 174–76; Conrad, *World of Sorrow,* p. 182; Galloway, "Last Years of Slavery," 601–2; B. J. Barickman, "Persistence and Decline: Slave Labour and Sugar Production in the Bahian Recôncavo, 1850–1888," *Journal of Latin American Studies* 28, no. 3 (October 1996): 614–16, 630; Martins, "Growing in Silence," p. 209.

22. Barickman, "Persistence and Decline," 595; Slenes, "Demography and Economics of Brazilian Slavery," pp. 208–13.

23. Hebe Maria Mattos de Castro, *Das cores do silêncio: Os significados da liberdade no sudeste escravista — Brasil, século xix* (Rio de Janeiro: Arquivo Nacional, 1995), pp. 104–6, 121; Erivaldo Fagundes Neves, "Sampauleiros traficantes: Comércio de escravos do alto sertão da Bahia para o oeste cafeeiro paulista," *Afro-ásia,* no. 24 (2000): 110–11. Compare the widespread ownership of slaves in earlier times, Stuart B. Schwartz, *Sugar Plantations in the Formation of Brazilian Society: Bahia, 1550–1835,* Cambridge Latin American Studies, no. 52 (Cambridge: Cambridge University Press, 1985), p. 459. Of course, many slaves were still owned by relatively poor persons; see, e.g., Sandra Lauderdale Graham, "Slavery's Impasse: Slave Prostitutes, Small-Time Mistresses, and the Brazilian Law of 1871," *Comparative Studies in Society and History* 33, no. 4 (October 1991): 669–94.

24. Câmara to Presidente da Provincia, Salvador, 21 Feb. 1850, Arquivo Municipal de Salvador, III.11 (Ofícios ao Governo, 1841–52), fol. 320v; Lei 374, 12 Nov. 1849, articles 27–28, and Lei 607, 19 Dec. 1856, article 2, *Colleção das leis e resoluções da Assemblea Legislativa e regulamentos do governo da provincia da Bahia;* Manuela Carneiro da Cunha, *Negros, estrangeiros: Os escravos libertos e sua volta a África* (São Paulo: Brasiliense, 1985), p. 96; Kátia M. de Queirós Mattoso, *Bahia: A cidade de Salvador e seu mercado no século XIX,* Coleção Estudos Brasileiros, no. 12 (São Paulo and Salvador: HUCITEC and Secretaria Municipal de Educação e Cultura, 1978), p. 279n.

25. Cunha, *Negros, estrangeiros,* p. 97; Dale T. Graden, "An Act 'Even of Public Security': Slave Resistance, Social Tensions, and the End of the International Slave Trade to Brazil, 1835–1856," *Hispanic American Historical Review* 76, no. 2 (May 1996): 269. On that earlier revolt see João José Reis, *Slave Rebellion in Brazil: The Muslim Uprising of 1835 in Bahia,* trans. Arthur Brakel (Baltimore: Johns Hopkins University Press, 1993).

26. Secretario da Policia to Presidente da Provincia, Salvador, 3 Nov. 1853, Arquivo Público do Estado da Bahia, M. 3118 (I owe this reference to Sandra Lauderdale Graham); Agentes dos remadores de saveiros to Presidente da Provincia, Salvador, 20 Oct. 1857, and Comissão encarregada do festejo dos remadores to Presidente da Provincia, Salvador, 9 Oct. 1879, both in ibid., M. 1570.

27. Slenes, "Demography and Economics of Brazilian Slavery," p. 207; Klein, "Internal Slave Trade," 574–75; *Jornal do Comércio,* 1854, quoted in Robert W. Slenes, "Senhores e subalternos no Oeste paulista," in *História da vida privada no Brasil,* ed. Fernando A. Novais (São Paulo: Companhia das Letras, 1997), 2:251.

28. Conrad, *Destruction of Brazilian Slavery,* p. 285; José Flávio Motta and Renato Leite Marcondes, "O comércio de escravos no vale do Paraíba paulista: Guaratinguetá e Silveiras na déecada de 1870," *Estudos Econômicos* 30, no. 2 (April–June 2000): 282–90.

29. Calculations are based on "Quadro estatistico da população escrava matriculada até o dia 31 de dezembro de 1878 com as alteraçoẽs occorridas até aquella data," in Rio de Janeiro (province), Presidente, *Relatorio,* 8 Sept. 1879 (Rio de Janeiro: Typographia Montenegro, 1879), appendix. The original slave register of 1872–73 was mainly complete by late 1872 because after that date planters paid an extra fee to register their slaves (and they were anxious to do so to ensure their property rights), Robert Slenes, private communication, 14 July 2000.

30. David Eltis, *The Rise of African Slavery in the Americas* (Cambridge: Cambridge University Press, 2000), pp. 105–13.

31. Klein, "Internal Slave Trade," 571; Conrad, *Destruction of Brazilian Slavery,* pp. 61, 286. See also Conrad, *World of Sorrow,* p. 175.

32. Lauderdale Graham, "Slavery's Impasse," 671–72, 681 (quotation at 680).

33. Klein, "Internal Slave Trade," 572; Conrad, *Destruction of Brazilian Slavery,* p. 61n; Neves, "Sampauleiros traficantes," 102. Also see Warren Dean, *Rio Claro: A Brazilian Plantation System, 1820–1920* (Stanford: Stanford University Press, 1976), pp. 57–58. On sales of children, compare the Brazilian case with that of the United States in Tadman, *Speculators and Slaves,* p. 171.

34. Slenes, "Demography and Economics of Brazilian Slavery," pp. 155–57, and Slenes, "Grandeza ou decadência," pp. 117–19 and 146 n.40. Slenes demonstrates that the provincial tax in Rio de Janeiro had once been a percentage of the sale price but became a fixed amount in 1859. The national tax apparently remained a percentage; see Candido Mendes de Almeida, ed., *Codigo Philippino; ou, Ordenações e leis do reino de Portugal recopiladas por mandado d'el rei D. Philippe I* (Rio de Janeiro: Instituto Philomathico, 1870), bk. 1, tit. 18, par. 9, n. 1 and appendix, p. 1387. This tax was first applied to Brazil in 1809.

35. João de Lencastre (Governor-General) to Câmara, Salvador, 30 Sept. 1700, in Biblioteca Nacional do Rio de Janeiro, *Documentos Históricos* (Rio de Janeiro: Biblioteca Nacional, 1928–60), vol. 87 (1950), pp. 34–35; Higgins, *"Licentious Liberty,"* pp. 32–36.

36. *Jornal da Bahia,* 4 Feb. 1854, p. 3; Conrad, *Destruction of Brazilian Slavery,* p. 66.

37. Paula Beiguelman, *A formação do povo no complexo cafeeiro: Aspectos políticos,* 2nd ed. (São Paulo: Pioneira, 1977), pp. 33–38; Conrad, *Destruction of Brazilian Slavery,* pp. 170–71; Célia Maria Marinho de Azevedo, *Onda negra, medo branco: O negro no imaginário das elites — século XIX* (Rio de Janeiro: Paz e Terra, 1987), pp. 112–13.

38. Slenes, "Demography and Economics of Brazilian Slavery," p. 161, n.18; on the passage of this law in Minas see Martins, "Growing in Silence," p. 212. The end of the interprovincial trade is also discussed by Emília Viotti da Costa, *Da senzala à colônia,* Corpo e Alma do Brasil, no. 19 (São Paulo: DIFEL, 1966), pp. 208–10, and Martins, "Growing in Silence," p. 230n.

39. Perdigão Malheiro, Speech of 3 July 1877, Brazil, Congresso, Câmara dos Depu-

tados, *Anais*, 1877, 2:26; Joaquim Nabuco, Speech of 4 Sept. 1880, Brazil, Congresso, Câmara dos Deputados, *Anais*, 1880, 5:36; Moreira de Barros, Speech of 12 Aug. 1880, Brazil, Congresso, Câmara dos Deputados, *Anais*, 1880, 4:194. On Moreira de Barros see Robert Brent Toplin, *The Abolition of Slavery in Brazil* (New York: Atheneum, 1972), pp. 60, 188, 233, and Conrad, *Destruction of Brazilian Slavery*, pp. 170–71.

40. Slenes, "Demography and Economics of Brazilian Slavery," p. 123; Conrad, *Destruction of Brazilian Slavery*, pp. 224, 234, 292.

41. Conrad, *World of Sorrow*, pp. 178, 180, 183; Martins, "Growing in Silence," pp. 211–12. Erivaldo Fagundes Neves makes the reasonable assumption that the five hundred or so slaves sold from an interior municipality in Bahia went overland, perhaps as far as western São Paulo. Neves, "Sampauleiros traficantes," 108.

42. Stein, *Vassouras*, pp. 72–73.

43. Klein, "Internal Slave Trade" 578–79; *Jornal da Bahia*, 22 Feb. 1854, p. 4, col. 6; Slenes, "Demography and Economics of Brazilian Slavery," pp. 150, 174–75; Joaquim Nabuco, Speech, 4 Sept. 1880, in Brazil, Congresso, Câmara dos Deputados, *Anais*, 1880, 5:35.

44. Conrad, *World of Sorrow*, pp. 171–79; Soares, *Notas estatísticas*, p. 135; Cotegipe, Speech of 1 Sept. 1854, quoted by Nabuco, *Um estadista do Império*, p. 209.

45. Quoted in Sandra Lauderdale Graham, *House and Street: The Domestic World of Servants and Masters in Nineteenth-Century Rio de Janeiro* (Cambridge: Cambridge University Press, 1988), p. 20.

46. Sidney Chalhoub, *Visões da liberdade: Uma história das últimas décadas da escravidão na corte* (São Paulo: Companhia das Letras, 1990), pp. 44–45.

47. Autuação da petição de Joaquim de Almeida, 1834, Arquivo Público do Estado da Bahia, Seção Judiciária, Auto Crime, 04/12⁸/3 (M. 3175, no. 3), fols. 7v., 10, 35v–36v., and Acareação e inquirição ad perpetuam, enclosed in ibid., but separately paged, fols. 4–4v., 6v.

48. Sud Menucci, *O precursor do abolicionismo no Brasil (Luiz Gama)* (São Paulo: Editora Nacional, 1938); Elciene Azevedo, *Orfeu de carapinha: A trajetória de Luiz Gama na imperial cidade de São Paulo* (Campinas: Editora Unicamp and Centro de Pequisa em História Social da Cultura, 1999).

49. Lauderdale Graham, "Slavery's Impasse," 669–83.

50. Ibid., 672, 674–75, with additional information about the location of the original sale gathered and gracefully shared with me by Sandra Lauderdale Graham from records of the Juizo de Direito da 2a Vara Civel, Libello de Liberdade pela escrava Corina por seu curador, defendant, Anna Valentina da Silva, Rio de Janeiro, 1869, Arquivo Nacional (Rio de Janeiro), Seção Judiciária, Caixa 1624, N. 2781. The description of the brothel is from a 1906 report by Dr. José Ricardo Pires de Almeida, quoted by Luiz Carlos Soares, *Rameiras, ilhoas, polacas . . . : A prostituição no Rio de Janeiro no século XIX*, Ensaios, no. 132 (São Paulo: Ática, 1992), p. 44.

51. Chalhoub, *Visões da liberdade*, pp. 54–56.

52. Ibid., pp. 59–65.

53. Agostinho Marques Perdigão Malheiro, Speech, 3 July 1877, in Brazil, Congresso, Câmara dos Deputados, *Anais*, 1877, 2:23.

54. Mattos de Castro, *Das cores do silêncio,* pp. 124–27.

55. Felipe Francisco Serra quoted by Reis, *Slave Rebellion,* p. 226; Lauderdale Graham, *House and Street,* pp. 81–82; Chalhoub, *Visões da liberdade,* p. 51.

56. Lauderdale Graham, *House and Street,* pp. 81, 166n76.

57. Carlos Eugênio Líbano Soares, *A capoeira escrava e outras tradições rebeldes no Rio de Janeiro (1808–1850)* (Campinas, São Paulo: Unicamp, 2001), pp. 358, 418n58; Reis, *Slave Rebellion,* p. 222. On the fear in Rio de Janeiro provoked by the arrival of slaves transshipped from Bahia, also see Flávio dos Santos Gomes, *Histórias de quilombolas: Mocambos e comunidades de senzalas no Rio de Janeiro, século XIX* (Rio de Janeiro: Arquivo Nacional, 1995), pp. 256–59.

58. Silvia Hunold Lara, *Campos da violência: Escravos e senhores na capitania do Rio de Janeiro, 1750–1808* (Rio de Janeiro: Paz e Terra, 1988), pp. 69–70, 158–63; Chalhoub, *Visões da liberdade,* pp. 68–73, 76–78; Gomes, *Histórias de quilombolas,* pp. 346–49; João José Reis, "Escravos e coiteiros no quilombo do Oitizeiro: Bahia, 1806," in *Liberdade por um fio: História dos quilombos no Brasil,* ed. João José Reis and Flávio dos Santos Gomes (São Paulo: Companhia das Letras, 1996), 355–58; Reis, *Slave Rebellion,* p. 223.

59. Costa, *Da senzala à colônia,* pp. 60–62; Pierre Monbeig, *Pionniers et planteurs de São Paulo,* Collection des Cahiers de la Fondation Nationale des Sciences Politiques, no. 28 (Paris: Colin, 1952).

60. See Mattos de Castro, *Das cores do silêncio,* pp. 129–33.

61. Joaquim Nabuco, Speech, 4 Sept. 1880, Brazil, Câmara dos Deputados, *Anais,* 1880, 5:35. The earlier influx of slaves from Bahia in 1835 was also believed by contemporaries to have led to increased rebelliousness among slaves and freed persons, Soares, *Capoeira escrava,* pp. 355–91, esp. p. 390.

62. *Instrucções para a commissão permanente nomeada pelos fazendeiros do municipio de Vassouras* (Rio de Janeiro: Typographia Episcopal de Guimarães, 1854) (Sandra Lauderdale Graham brought this source to my attention); Salles, *O negro no Pará,* p. 52.

63. Quoted, respectively, in Dean, *Rio Claro,* p. 137; Azevedo, *Onda negra, medo branco,* p. 117; and Lana Lage da Gama Lima, *Rebeldia negra e abolição* (Rio de Janeiro: Achiamé, 1981), p. 98; the last quotation also appears in Stein, *Vassouras,* p. 67n.

64. Slenes, "Grandeza ou decadência," 136.

65. Dean, *Rio Claro,* pp. 60, 127; Azevedo, *Onda negra, medo branco,* pp. 188, 190.

66. On increasing slave unrest see Maria Helena Machado, *O plano e o pânico: Os movimentos sociais na década da abolição* (São Paulo: Editora UFRJ/EDUSP, 1994); Azevedo, *Onda negra, medo branco,* pp. 116–18, 180–99; Gomes, *Histórias de quilombolas,* pp. 329–34. I do not mean to suggest that only quantitative evidence would do, however, as does Ciro Cardoso in Ciro Cardoso, Hebe Maria Mattos de Castro, João Luís Ribeiro Fragoso, and Ronaldo Vainflas, *Escravidão e abolição no Brasil: Novas perspectivas* (Rio de Janeiro: Zahar, 1988), 85–89. As I noted above, after the malê revolt of 1835 fear spread from Salvador to Rio and probably elsewhere, but no one has yet compared that period with the later one.

67. Inventário e testamento de Joaquim Teixeira de Carvalho, 1841–47, Arquivo Público do Estado da Bahia, Seção Judiciária, $^{04}/_{14}7^3/_{19}4^2/_{05}$, fols. 56, 58 (for the quotation); Stuart B. Schwartz, "Resistance and Accomodation in Eighteenth-Century Brazil: The

Slaves' View of Slavery," *Hispanic American Historical Review* 57, no. 1 (February 1977): 79.

68. On this practice on other occasions see, e.g., Flávio dos Santos Gomes, "Jogando a rede, revendo as malhas: Fugas e fugitivos no Brasil escravista," *Tempo: Revista do Departamento de História da UFF* 1 (April 1996): 89–90.

69. Moção do Clube Militar, 26 Oct. 1887, quoted by Evaristo de Moraes, *A campanha abolicionista (1879–1888)* (Rio de Janeiro: Leite Ribeiro, 1924), p. 313.

70. Mattoso Camara, Speech of 17 July 1888, Brazil, Congresso, Camara dos Deputados, *Anais*, 1888, 3:183.

71. Barão de Cotegipe to Francisco Ignacio de Carvalho Moreira, barão do Penedo, Petrópolis, 8 Apr. 1888, quoted in Renato Mendonça, *Um diplomata na côrte da Inglaterra: ão barão do Penedo e sua época*, Brasiliana, no. 219 (São Paulo: Editôra Nacional, 1942), p. 397.

72. Moraes, *Campanha abolicionista;* Richard Graham, "Causes for the Abolition of Negro Slavery in Brazil: An Interpretive Essay," *Hispanic American Historical Review* 46, no. 2 (May 1966): 123–37, also published as "As causas da abolição da escravidão no Brasil," in Richard Graham, *Escravidão, reforma e imperialismo*, Coleção Debates, no. 146 (São Paulo: Perspectiva, 1979), pp. 59–78; Costa, *Da senzala à colônia*, pp. 300–29, esp. 321–29.

73. Cleveland Donald Jr., "Slavery and Abolition in Campos, Brazil: 1830–1888," Ph.D. diss. (Cornell University, 1973); Cleveland Donald Jr., "Slave Resistance and Abolitionism in Brazil: The Campista Case, 1879–1888," *Luso-Brazilian Review* 13, no. 2 (Winter 1976): 182–93. See also Lima, *Rebeldia negra*, esp. pp. 77–151; Azevedo, *Onda negra, medo branco*, pp. 203–14; and Dean, *Rio Claro*, p. 144.

74. Machado, *O plano e o pânico.*

75. Lima, *Rebeldia negra*, pp. 98, 111–13, 126, 131, 137–39; Conrad, *Destruction of Brazilian Slavery*, p. 294; Eisenberg, "Abolishing Slavery," 587.

76. Conrad, *Destruction of Brazilian Slavery*, p. 285.

77. An alternative point of view is presented in Conrad, *Destruction of Brazilian Slavery*, who argues that by draining slaves from the Northeast, the internal trade led that region's representatives in parliament to take up the cause of abolitionism. But such legislators, who did not legally have to be from the provinces they represented and often had no ties there, were much more obligated to the prime minister, who really controlled elections, than to their voters. An analysis of voting records regarding the legislation in 1871 to free the children of slave mothers shows that the same individuals voted for and against emancipationist measures depending entirely on who was the prime minister. Finally, even if legislators had been beholden to the northeastern planters, there is little evidence that these local bosses, no matter how indifferent they may have become to the issue, ever pushed their representatives to support abolitionist measures, much less impose them on a ministry or other members of parliament, an action that, in any case, would have been unlikely to succeed given the weakened wealth and power of their region. The abolitionist movement was centered in the cities of Rio de Janeiro and São Paulo, not in the Northeast. Nowhere in Brazil was there an organized effort during 1888 to prevent passage of the abolition law or to undo it, although demands by former owners for compensation were loud and clear. On the electoral system see Richard

Graham, *Patronage and Politics in Nineteenth-Century Brazil* (Stanford: Stanford University Press, 1990), esp. pp. 71–98; on parliamentary divisions in 1871 see Guo-Ping Mao, "Homens e Cousas in the Age of Reform, Brazil, 1868–1889," Ph.D. diss. (University of Texas at Austin, 1997), p. 250; on the effort to secure compensation see the parliamentary debates in the latter half of 1888, e.g., Brazil, Congresso, Câmara de Deputados, *Anais,* 1888, 3:129, 4:441.

78. Richard Graham, "Landowners and the Overthrow of the Empire," *Luso-Brazilian Review* 8, no. 2 (Winter 1970): 44–56.

14

The Brazilian Internal Slave Trade, 1850–1888
Regional Economies, Slave Experience, and the
Politics of a Peculiar Market

ROBERT W. SLENES

One could define "internal slave trade" as the practice of selling people within the society where they reside. For analytical purposes, however, the term is more usefully reserved for a system of commerce in human beings that is relatively autonomous (with primarily endogenous determinants of prices and other characteristics) and that integrates local buyers and sellers within a region, colony, or nation, or even within an area that overlaps political boundaries, into a common market. The paradigm, of course, is the commerce in bondspeople in the American South after the abolition of the African slave trade to the United States in 1807. In Brazil, a similar mercantile system dealing in forced labor fully emerged only with the end of the African traffic to that country in 1850.[1]

In its average annual impact on the regional slave communities from which it extracted people, the Brazilian trade closely resembled the American. In other important ways, however, it was notably different. To begin with, the existence in Brazil of two strong export complexes competing for bonded labor led to the formation of regional slave markets (one in the North-Northeast and one in the Center-South; see fig. 14.1) that, although linked to each other, were themselves significantly autonomous. This finding helps explain the economic and political staying power of slavery as a national institution in Brazil through the 1870s, despite bondspeople's declining numbers after 1850 and their growing

Figure 14.1. Provinces and Regions of Nineteenth-Century Brazil. *Source:* Adapted from "Império do Brasil," in Brasil, Ministério da Agricultura, Indústria e Comércio, *Recenseamento do Brazil Realizado em 1 de Setembro de 1920,* vol. 1, *Introdução* (Rio de Janeiro: Typographia da Estatística, 1922), following 382.

concentration in the Center-South. Second, whereas the American commerce seems to have exacted a more or less steady toll from the slave population it affected (at least from 1820 on, when the documentation permits its quantification), the Brazilian trade grew considerably over time, increasingly devastating slaves' social networks and galvanizing masters' fears that in a short time only the Center-South would maintain a vested interest in chattel labor. Third, the Brazilian trade had come into existence suddenly, rather than gradually, replacing a transatlantic commerce that was not only unprecedented in size but had also helped condition the disciplinary strategies of slaveowners — who treated creoles and *ladino* (acculturated) Africans more favorably than newly imported bondspeople — and therefore slaves' expectations. Thus the new system of labor recruitment, which turned to these previously favored groups, probably contributed substantially to slave unrest.

Finally, the Brazilian internal trade developed in a context of rising national and international mobilization against slavery. This, along with the other characteristics noted above, made the commerce in human beings a focus of "political" struggle over the future of forced labor, involving masters, slaves, and other interested social groups; indeed, it could be argued that the crash of the slave market in 1881–83, reflecting a dramatic change in perceptions of "chattel futures," was more of a historical watershed than the legal landmarks that announced partial emancipation in 1871 and 1885 (freedom, respectively, for children thenceforth born to slave mothers and for sexagenarians) and complete abolition in 1888. All these distinctive aspects of the Brazilian internal trade are examined here, albeit largely from the perspective provided by research on regional slave economies and labor markets, which is considerably more abundant than work on the social and political history of this peculiar market.

The Brazilian and American Internal Slave Trades Compared: Regional Markets and Population Transfers

I have defined an "internal slave trade" as a relatively autonomous commercial system. Yet the new Brazilian internal trade that came into being in 1850 was formed by the conjunction of two regional markets that were themselves substantially autonomous. Whereas before 1850 regional slave prices moved roughly in tandem, reflecting common external determinants,[2] after mid-century their trends and fluctuations in the major coffee and sugar regions (located, respectively, in the Center-South and the Northeast) were to a considerable degree independent. To be sure, between 1850 and 1857, when coffee and sugar prices were rising, the slave price curves in both regions also increased, indeed, at about the same rate. After that, however, their trend lines sharply diverged. In Pernambuco and Bahia, the most important producers of sugar, market values of slaves moved together and clearly responded to a downward trend in the price of sugar. In Rio de Janeiro and São Paulo they also moved approximately in tandem but followed an upward trend in the price of coffee. (See fig. 14.2, which, like all subsequent graphs, has a logarithmic vertical scale; thus, different proportional changes in two curves over a given time are immediately perceived from the curves' relative slopes, with parallel slopes denoting identical rates of change.) Here is a major difference between the internal slave trades of Brazil and the United States. Ever since Ulrich B. Phillip's study of slave prices, scholars have been aware that, despite

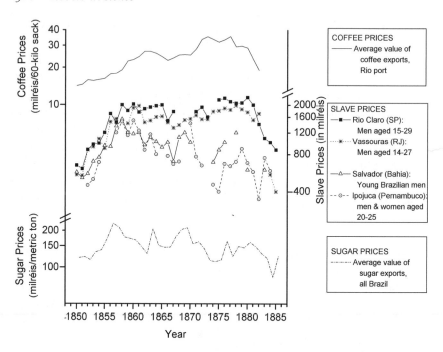

Figure 14.2. Slave Prices in Relation to Coffee and Sugar Prices: Plantation Regions of the Center-South and Northeast, *1850–1885*. *Sources and methods:* For slave prices: These are the average nominal prices (from probate evaluations for the Northeast, from bills of sale for Rio Claro, and from both sources for Vassouras) for healthy bondspeople, including skilled and domestic workers. Peter L. Eisenberg, *The Sugar Industry in Pernambuco: Modernization Without Change, 1840–1910* (Berkeley: University of California Press, 1974), 153; Maria José de Souza Andrade, *A Mão de Obra Escrava em Salvador, 1811–1860* (São Paulo: Editora Corrupio; Brasília: CNPq, 1988), 212; Warren Dean, *Rio Claro: A Brazilian Plantation System, 1820–1920* (Stanford: Stanford University Press, 1976), 55 (excluding the price for 1874, since N is only 1 and the value is clearly unrepresentative); Pedro Carvalho de Mello and Robert W. Slenes, "Características do Mercado de Escravos na Região Cafeeira: O Caso de Vassouras, 1860–1888" (1984); Pedro Carvalho de Mello and Robert W. Slenes, "Male and Female Slave Prices and the 1871 Free Birth Law in Campinas, Vassouras, and Salvador." For coffee prices: Affonso de E. Taunay, *História do Café no Brasil*, 15 vols. (Rio de Janeiro: Departamento Nacional do Café, 1939–43), 6:318–19, through 1876; C. F. Van Delden Laërne, *Brazil and Java: Report on Coffee Culture in America, Asia, and Africa* (London: W. H. Allen; The Hague: Martinus Nijhoff, 1885), 393, for 1877 onward. Calendar-year values have been estimated from fiscal-year data. For sugar prices: IBGE (Instituto Brasileiro de Geografia e Estatística), *Anuário Estatístico*, year 5, 1939–40 (Rio de Janeiro: IBGE, 1941); comparison shows this national series to be a good proxy for sugar prices in Bahia and Pernambuco, obtained from provincial presidential reports.

regional differentials, the market values of bondspeople everywhere in the Old South moved in essentially parallel curves between 1795 and 1860, and from the mid-1820s on they largely followed cotton prices.[3]

Nominal slave prices in Brazil's northeastern provinces rose rapidly during much of the 1850s and then decreased, with a particularly strong downward inflection occurring from the 1860s to the 1870s. In the coffee regions, however, the trend was for slave prices to continue rising even after the same initial period of expansion. The result was that the price differential between the markets of the Northeast and the Center-South, although always in favor of the latter, was relatively small during most of the 1850s but widened subsequently, reaching substantial levels in the 1870s.

These findings are consistent with data concerning the slave markets of the Center-South. In the provinces of Rio de Janeiro and São Paulo, the annual number of slave sales transacted (estimated from sales-tax data) closely followed the evolution of coffee exports until 1881, when the interregional trade was effectively closed by provincial levies on slave imports (see fig. 14.3). Since initial sellers and intermediaries in this commerce preferred to disguise changes of ownership as transfers of power of attorney, which were much cheaper to register as legal documents, normally it was only when the slave was finally sold to a definite buyer in the Center-South who wanted full title of property that a bill of sale was drawn up and the corresponding head tax paid.[4] As a result, the annual number of slave sales registered in the Center-South (in provinces, microregions, and localities) is a good index of the comparative robustness of the demand for bondspeople.[5] That slave sales followed the movement of coffee exports indicates that this demand, as might be expected, accompanied the growth of the regional economy's "dynamic center."

The total number of slaves entering the ports of Rio de Janeiro and Santos *a entregar,* or on consignment for sale in the market, also was closely related to the curve of coffee exports from the Center-South (fig. 14.3). Coffee exports in the 1870s were considerably above their levels for the previous two decades, especially in central-western São Paulo, and so too were the total sales of bondspeople in the two provinces and the number of entries of slaves for sale through Rio and Santos. In sum, direct data from the Rio and São Paulo markets confirm the conclusion drawn from the comparative movement of slave prices in that region and in the Northeast: the interregional slave trade to the Center-South was considerably larger in the 1870s than in the 1850s and 1860s.

My estimates of the total transfer of bondspeople to the Center-South between mid-1872 (the median date of the first national slave *matrícula,* or registry) and mid-1881 (shortly after the closing of the interprovincial trade),

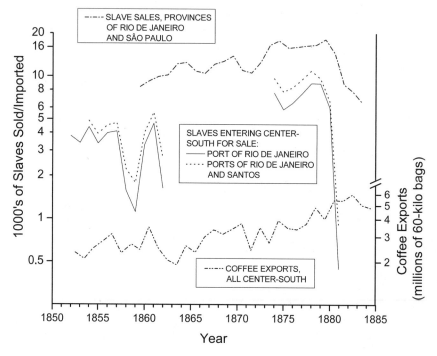

Figure 14.3. Coffee Exports from the Center-South, Slave Sales in Rio de Janeiro and São Paulo Provinces, and Slaves Entering the Ports of Rio de Janeiro and Santos for Sale, Early 1850s to Early 1880s. *Sources and methods:* Robert W. Slenes, "The Demography and Economics of Brazilian Slavery: 1850–1888," 137, 242, 598 (revised), based on slave sale and import data from provincial presidential, treasury, and police reports; data on slaves entering the port of Rio for sale (1852–62) are from British consular correspondence, and Robert Conrad, *The Destruction of Brazilian Slavery, 1850–1888* (Berkeley: University of California Press, 1972), 289; and information on coffee exports is from C. F. Van Delden Laërne, *Brazil and Java: Report on Coffee Culture in America, Asia, and Africa* (London: W. H. Allen; The Hague: Martinus Nijhoff, 1885), 394, 400–401, 411. Data are not smoothed. For slave sales (number of slaves traded): total sales tax revenue, divided by head tax. Santos data for 1876–78, 1880, and 1881 are estimated from the ratio of Santos to Rio imports in adjacent years. Santos data for 1854–62 are estimated, assuming that the ratio of imports to total slaves in São Paulo was the same as in 1874–75. Rio sales and imports for a few years without data are estimated by interpolation.

and of the various components of this interregional migration, are given in table 14.1.[6] The figures are derived from port police records, in conjunction with the global intercensal-survival method for measuring migration.[7] The total number of transfers is approximately 94,900 to 99,900.[8] Since few slaves left the Center-South for other regions, 90,000, or 10,000 a year, is a rea-

Table 14.1. Transfers of Slaves to the Center-Source, mid-1872 to mid-1881

Method of transfer	Number transferred
1. By sale (on consignment from the North/Northeast via the ports of Rio de Janeiro and Santos	67,200
2. By sale from the South, via the ports of Rio and Santos	3,800
3. By sale or the migration of masters from the South (mostly overland), not counted by the port police of Rio and Santos	17,200
4. By sale or the migration of masters overland, from the West	1,700
5. By sale or the migration of masters from the North-Northeast (mostly overland), not counted by the port police of Rio and Santos (Residual category: not directly measurable)[a]	(5,000–10,000)
Total	94,900–99,900

[a]Since the total in line 1 already significantly exceeds the estimate of net slave migration from the North/Northeast obtained by the intercensal-survival method, category 5 cannot be large. *Sources:* Port police data (lines 1 and 2) and adjusted estimates of migration obtained by the global intercensal-survival method (lines 3 and 4), from Robert W. Slenes, "The Demography and Economics of Brazilian Slavery: 1850–1888" (Ph.D. diss., Stanford University, 1976), 598, 616–617, 655.

sonable or conservative estimate of net slave in-migration (defined here as the balance of individuals actually transferred) for the nine years between mid-1872 and mid-1881. The curves of Rio and Santos slave imports and sales in earlier years, confirmed by the movement of coffee exports, suggests that the annual net number of bondspeople moved to the Center-South from other regions in 1850–63 and 1863–72 (always using the midpoint of these years as the reference point) was, respectively, about one-half and three-fourths that of the later period.[9] Thus, total net interregional transfers between mid-1850 and mid-1881 were in the neighborhood of 222,500, or about 7,200 per year for the whole period.[10]

When expressed as a percentage of the slave population affected, this latter number indicates a migrant stream that is about 76 percent of Michael Tadman's estimates for annual proportional transfers from exporting to importing states in the American South during the 1820s and 1850s.[11] (See also Chapter 6 in this volume.) Yet when only bondspeople who were moved by sale are considered, the two cases are remarkably similar.

As table 14.1 indicates, the major part of interregional slave migration from the North and Northeast of Brazil in the 1870s occurred by means of sale. Few bondspeople transferred from these regions moved with their owners. Although the evidence does not permit a separate estimate of these two categories for slaves entering the Center-South from other regions, largely overland, data from Campinas, a large slave market in central-western São Paulo, indicate that more than one-fourth of the bondspeople sold there in the 1870s from outside the Center-South were from the southernmost province of Rio Grande do Sul. It is likely, therefore, that slaves transferred overland from the South along well-established muleteer routes also were moved largely by means of sale. Although fewer data are available for the period 1850–72, the Rio port statistics for slaves imported on consignment during these years are consistent with the direct and derived labor demands from coffee production, as indicated by the curve of coffee exports; thus, in this period too, slaves would have been moved in a large measure via the trade.

If one assumes that only half of the migrants to the Center-South not included in the port police records (lines 3 to 5 in the table) came by means of sale — probably a very conservative estimate — one may calculate the proportion of migrants traded on the market in 1872–81 as at least 86 percent.[12] For the American South, Tadman has estimated that at least 61.0 percent to 69.3 percent (his figures for the 1850s and the 1820s, respectively) of bonded migrants from slave-exporting to importing states were transferred by the market.[13] Tadman's figures represent a radical revision of work by Fogel and Engerman, who had concluded that only 16 percent of slave migrants were moved via sale.[14]

When these estimates of the role of the Brazilian and American slave markets in transferring people between regions are applied to the respective total number of bonded migrants in the two countries, the results are nearly identical: 0.85 percent of slaves in American slave-exporting states (the average for the 1820s and 1850s) were sold annually to importing regions, compared to the equivalent figure for Brazil of 0.87 percent (the weighted average of the impact of interregional slave sales during the periods 1851–63, 1863–72, and 1872–81).[15] Thus, although total interregional slave transfers were relatively smaller in Brazil, the greater importance of the market there in effecting such transfers made the impact of sale on the exporting populations of the two countries virtually the same.

Two caveats must be made about these comparative estimates, however. First, the proximity of the averages conceals the fact that, whereas the impact of the trade on slave-exporting regions changed but little in the American South between the 1820s and the 1850s, it grew considerably over time in Brazil. Thus, strictly speaking, only the average for the 1863–72 period in

Brazil showed parity with the post-1820 American average. In contrast, the Brazilian average for 1850–63 was only half the overall American average, and that of 1872–81 (when 1.47 percent of the exporting population was removed by sale annually) was three-fourths again (1.73 times) the American rate of loss.[16]

The second is that, although Tadman and I use virtually the same formal definition of "exporting or importing regions" (states or provinces that were net slave-exporters or importers),[17] the very different size of these geographical areas in the two countries—the American South being much closer in scale to any one of the Brazilian regions in fig. 14.1 than to all of Brazil—creates problems for comparison. When translated into American terms, interregional transfers in Brazil were extremely long-distance movements. Since one might expect that slaveowners' opportunity costs in migrating with their bondspeople would tend to increase with the distance of the move, it is perhaps not surprising to discover that the interregional trade was even more predominant in moving bondspeople in Brazil than it was in the American South.

Indeed, a truer comparison of the relative size both of slave population transfers and of the market's contribution to their occurrence would have to include much of Brazil's intraregional slave migration—a topic visited in the next two sections of this essay. Since, as we shall see, intrarregional slave movements in the Center-South were probably more important from 1850 to 1863 than interregional transfers to that area, the difference noted above between the relative size of Brazil's trade between "regions" in those years and that of the American South in the 1820s and 1850s may have been smaller. At the same time, since intrarregional slave migration in Brazil's Center-South and Northeast, mostly by means of sale, increased considerably in absolute terms in the period after 1872, together with transfers out of the latter region, it is difficult to escape the conclusion that the overall impact of the internal trade on Brazil's "exporting populations" was especially severe in 1872–81, even in comparison to the experience of the pre-bellum United States.[18] For Tadman, the new estimates regarding the American South demolish the arguments of planters and of some historians that the peculiar institution was paternalistic. If so, the Brazilian evidence points just as compellingly—indeed, even more strongly for the 1870s—toward the same conclusion.

Slave Markets and Economies in the North and the Northeast

The data presented for the widening differential in slave prices between the Northeast and the Center-South, and for the growth of the slave market and of imports of bondspeople into the latter region, might seem to confirm the time-honored view of Brazil's internal trade as a transfer of workers from the "declining" sugar to the "booming" coffee regions and, by implication, from sugar to coffee plantations. Yet the story is considerably more complex than that. The fact that slave prices in Pernambuco and Bahia responded primarily to sugar prices, not to labor and commodity prices in the Center-South, suggests that the major component of slave demand in these northeastern provinces was that of the sugar sector. Other data further complicate the picture. If northeastern sugar prices are deflated (divided) by slave prices, one obtains a rough estimate of the movement of real sugar prices from the point of view of producers using chattel labor, or of the real value of the product of such labor — if, that is, slave productivity remained constant, an assumption that is examined shortly. On graphing this sugar-to-slave price ratio over time (see figs. 14.4 and 14.5, treating Bahia and Pernambuco, respectively) one observes that the 1850s to the early 1860s seem to have been the most discouraging years for planters. During this period, the ratio — a measure of the real value of a slave's production in sugar — fell dramatically. From then to the mid-1860s, however, this value rose substantially. During the following years, to 1881, it either remained at the mid-1860s level, albeit with large fluctuations (Pernambuco), or showed a strong decline during the late 1870s, only to rise abruptly again to its mid-1860s high points at the very end of the period (Bahia). Since technological improvements in sugar production during these decades increased slave productivity, particularly in Pernambuco,[19] both curves increasingly underestimate the real value of the chattel labor product in these provinces. Thus, Pernambuco's curve for this variable, if corrected, would tend to rise during the 1870s, whereas that of Bahia would show at least a smaller tendency to fall between about 1870 and 1878 and higher rebound values at the end of that decade.

Yet the general profiles of these curves as they are can be taken to be reliable. After 1850, sugar exports in both provinces approximately followed the trends in the sugar-to-slave price ratio. In addition, the respective curves of official slave exports from these areas[20] (presented "upside down" in the graphs so that the relation to the other variables may be more clearly perceived) tend to move in an inverse manner to trends in the other variables, particularly to those in sugar exports.[21] (Apparent anomalies in the Pernambucan curve for slave exports in the late 1850s and for the sugar-to-slave price ratio for about 1869–70 are probably the results of faulty data; see the notes to fig. 14.5.)

These curves are consistent with an interpretation that, on one hand, recognizes that the demand of the sugar sector largely determined slave prices and, on the other, also links producers' decisions to expand or reduce their acreage

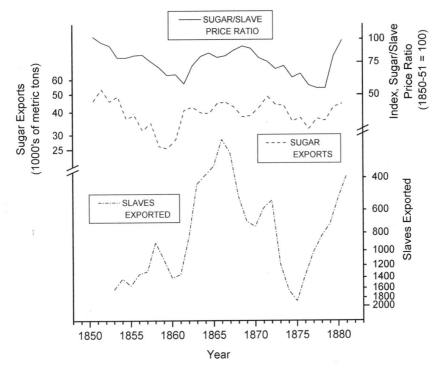

Figure 14.4. The Sugar-to-Slave Price Ratio in Bahia and Its Relation to Sugar Exports and Slave Exports, Early 1850s to Early 1880s. *Note:* All curves are smoothed (3-point adjacent averages). *Source:* Robert W. Slenes, "The Demography and Economics of Brazilian Slavery: 1850–1888," 201 (revised), using average probate evaluations of healthy young Brazilian-born male slaves with occupations in Salvador (Maria José de Souza Andrade, *A Mão de Obra Escrava em Salvador, 1811–1860* [São Paulo: Editora Corrupio; Brasília: CNPq, 1988], 212), transformed from calendar-year to fiscal-year estimates; data for missing years were interpolated from Bahian and Pernambucan slave prices in adjacent years. Data on sugar "prices" (average value of sugar exported) and on exported slaves are from Bahian presidential and police reports. For sugar exports see J. H. Galloway, "The Last Years of Slavery on the Sugar Plantations of Northeastern Brazil," *Hispanic American Historical Review* 61:4 (November 1971): 603.

in cane and to buy or refrain from buying bondspersons to their perception of the real price of sugar as measured against slave labor costs. When the sugar-to-slave price ratio fell, planters tended to reduce their acreage in cane (thus, exports of sugar declined) and bought substantially fewer slaves in the regional market, or perhaps become small net sellers of bondspeople. Slave exports then rose, but not primarily because of the sale of workers from the plantation sector; rather, it was because sellers who were engaged in other

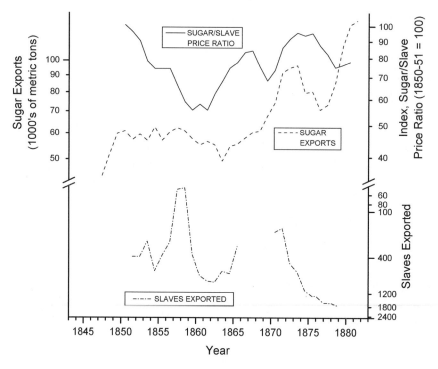

Figure 14.5. The Sugar-to-Slave Price Ratio in Pernambuco and Its Relation to Sugar Exports and Slave Exports, Early 1850s to Early 1880s. *Notes:* All curves are smoothed (3-point adjacent averages). A different logarithmic scale has been used for the slave-export data in order to fit them on the graph. Slave export figures for 1857–58 and 1858–59 seem greatly underreported (unsmoothed N = 5 and 2, respectively); likewise, the slave price for 1870 is probably exaggerated (it is higher than those in neighboring years and exceeds the Bahian price, which is unusual). Thus, much of the sharp decline in these years in the respective curves for slave exports and sugar-to-slave price ratio is apt to be spurious. Ignoring the suspected data points would make the trends of the three curves more closely correlated. *Sources:* Robert W. Slenes, "The Demography and Economics of Brazilian Slavery: 1850–1888," graph 201 (revised), based on Peter L. Eisenberg, *The Sugar Industry in Pernambuco: Modernization Without Change, 1840–1910* (Berkeley: University of California Press, 1974), 153, for slave prices (transformed here from calendar-year to fiscal-year data, with missing values interpolated from Pernambucan and Bahian prices); Paul Singer, *Desenvolvimento Econômico e Evolução Urbana* (São Paulo: Companhia Editora Nacional/EDUSP, 1968), 292, for sugar prices (average value of sugar exported), supplemented by data from provincial presidents' reports and from Instituto Brasileiro de Geografia e Estatística, *Anuário Estatístico*, year 5, 1939–40 (Rio de Janeiro: IBGE, 1941), for all of Brazil; J. H. Galloway, "The Last Years of Slavery on the Sugar Plantations of Northeastern Brazil," *Hispanic American Historical Review* 61:4 (November 1971): 603, for sugar exports; Eisenberg, *Sugar Industry,* 158; and Slenes, "Demography and Economics," 605, for slaves exported.

activities (smaller nonsugar agriculturalists and owners of urban properties) no longer found a sufficiently attractive market within the province and turned in large numbers to the interregional trade. On the other hand, when the real price of sugar — that is, the real value of the product of slave labor — rose, planters expanded their acreage in cane and exports of sugar increased; once again, as the dominant sector of demand for slaves within their region, they absorbed most of the bondspeople offered on the market. Far fewer persons were then sold to other provinces.

Is there any direct evidence that confirms this model of population movements within and from the Northeast? Herbert Klein was the first to discover such data in a detailed study of slave entries into the port of Rio de Janeiro from other provinces in 1852.[22] The occupations of these slaves (there was a relatively high percentage of artisans, or skilled workers) pointed indirectly to an urban or at least a nonplantation origin. Subsequently, I found information from the port police of Bahia showing that 59 percent of the bondspeople (with origin known) leaving that province in 1854 were from urban areas. In addition, I examined data for slave entries into and exits from Bahia's counties (*municípios*) indicating that the major losers of slaves in 1876 were nonsugar areas.[23] (The data for entries and exits [*entradas* and *saídas*] are from the official statistics on slaves who were bought, sold, or otherwise moved into and out of the counties after the national slave matrícula of 1872.) Recent research by Josué dos Passos Subrinho on the sugar province of Sergipe, just north of Bahia, confirms these results.[24] Using detailed county entry and exit data and the intercensal-survival method applied to the 1872 and 1887 slave matrículas of that province, Passos Subrinho shows that the sugar region in Sergipe had a net gain of bondspeople as a result of migration (indeed, the major sugar counties were large net importers), whereas all other regions had a net loss.

Finally, Bert Barickman conclusively demonstrates the persistence of slavery on the plantations of Bahia.[25] In the Recôncavo, the major sugar-producing area of that province, slavery continued to be the predominant labor regime on the eve of abolition, unlike the case in the equivalent plantation region (the Zona da Mata) of Pernambuco.[26] Sugar planters in Bahia were not able to find a substitute for slaves; indeed, abolition dealt a severe blow to that province's production of sugar, whereas the output of Pernambuco's industry, which had made a substantial transition to free labor, was virtually unaffected by the event.

Yet the Bahian case, combined with the other data presented here, especially those concerning the close relation between sugar and slave prices in both of these northeastern markets, suggests a reinterpretation of the Pernambucan experience. Pernambuco's transition to free labor probably was the result not of a major sale of slaves from the plantations but of the absorption of free laborers into an economy that was rapidly expanding (sugar exports from the province more than doubled between 1860 and 1880; see fig. 14.5), combined with a considerable continued influx of bondspeople into that economy, but on a scale that was insufficient to maintain the population at a steady level. To test this proposition, I examined county-level population data for Pernambuco from the slave matrículas of 1872 and 1887. Preliminary calculations are consistent with the hypothesis. The adult slave population (people over the age of fifteen) declined only 20 percent in the Zona da Mata, the sugar region, during this period, whereas it fell by about 60 percent elsewhere in the province. (During the same period, the capital, Recife, lost 88 percent of its adult bondspeople, surely indicative of the severe impact of the internal trade on urban areas.)[27]

Izabel Marson's study of the contrasting economic projects of two Pernambucan intellectuals, Joaquim Nabuco and Augusto Milet, suggests a further refinement of the interpretation of these data.[28] Milet, a spokesman for "small and medium investors, [that is, of] sugar mill owners [with fewer than twenty bondspeople] and cotton planters," noted in 1878 that Pernambucan mill owners of all sizes relied on slaves in the *engenho,* or sugar factory. Only small mill owners (proprietors of the traditional mills, or *bangüês*) still depended on slaves for work in the fields, however, since they could not attract free agricultural laborers at affordable prices. In fact, owners of the larger, more modern mills were increasingly able to dispense with both slaves and free hired laborers in the field, since they transferred to *moradores* (labor tenants, whom they were more able to attract than were the owners of bangüês) the task of planting and raising cane, while they themselves specialized in grinding it and producing sugar. The moradores used predominantly family labor; some of the more prosperous, however, may have been small slaveowners.[29] Milet's writings are consistent with the population data just reviewed. They indicate a continued demand for slaves in the sugar regions of Pernambuco during the 1870s at the same time that they point to different sectoral demands within the industry. The new evidence concerning Pernambuco may also shed light on the Bahian case, in which the modernization of the bangüê was much less advanced. Milet's description of the situation of this "middle class" (Marson's term) of small mill owners in Pernambuco may also apply to the great majority of Bahian planters and proprietors of engenhos.

My estimates of the net migration of slaves by province between 1872 and 1881 are consistent with these conclusions.[30] The provinces that lost a greater proportion of their slaves to migration in this period were nonsugar provinces that had recently acquired an important cotton-export sector (Rio Grande do Norte, Ceará, Paraíba, and Piauí). In these areas, cotton planting had enjoyed a boom during the period of high prices caused by the disruption of exports from the American South during the Civil War. When U.S. production once again entered the market in full scale in the late 1860s, Brazilian cotton prices and exports plummeted.[31] These provinces were dealt a second severe blow by the great northeastern drought of 1877–80. The economic disruption caused by both developments led slaveowners in these areas to sell record numbers of bondspeople to other markets. Probably the same occurred in parts of the interior of Pernambuco and Bahia, where cotton was a more important crop than sugar and where drought also struck. Passos Subrinho's study of Sergipe does not mention the effects of drought, but it does show that the provincial microregion that most lost slaves during this period — with a percentage decline due to migration that was approximately on a par with that of the cotton provinces mentioned above — was one in the interior that had also become an important producer of cotton in the 1860s.[32]

This evidence concerning the cotton provinces suggests a refinement of my model. The sugar regions of Bahia and Pernambuco (and probably those of Sergipe and Alagoas as well) together formed a relatively "independent" slave market, even in the 1870s, when demand from the Center-South was quite strong, in part because they were embedded in a region where other, less competitive or declining economies had created a slave labor reserve priced at bargain rates. The demand from the Center-South would have drawn bondspeople primarily from these other activities. As it did so, it must have bid overall regional slave prices up, thereby contributing to the sugar industry's labor costs. Despite this, even in the late 1870s, it had not yet destroyed the sugar industry's ability largely to determine the overall movement and trend of northeastern regional slave prices.

This reformulation of the model is confirmed by my study of the slave market of Campinas, in the heart of the coffee region of central-western São Paulo. From the mid-1860s to the late 1870s, the percentage of slaves from the northeastern sugar provinces in the total interregional trade to Campinas fell by half, from 62 percent to 31 percent, while the proportion from the northern and northeastern cotton provinces leaped from 22 percent to 39 percent. In addition, however, the proportion from the South, largely from Rio Grande do Sul, grew from 12 percent to 29 percent, with most of this increase occurring in the second half of the 1870s.[33] Southern bondspeople, traded largely overland to central-western São Paulo, probably did not have the presence in the whole Center-South that they did in the pricey market of Campinas.[34] Still, since central-western São Paulo was an important emporium, the Campinas data do permit a further fine-tuning of my model. They suggest that a reserve slave labor force, which buffered the impact of rising Center-South demand for slaves in the sugar provinces in the 1870s, not only existed in the cotton zones of the North and the Northeast but also in Rio Grande do Sul. Although the reasons for the increased southern participation in the interregional slave trade in the 1870s need further study, one thing is clear: slave prices in Rio Grande do Sul fell precipitously during the 1870s, which is consistent with the greatly increased presence of Riograndense slaves in the Campinas market in the second half of that decade. The fall in slave prices probably reflects increasing difficulties in this period of the *charque* (beef jerky) industry, which held a large number of bondspeople and had a multiplier effect on employment in the economy of Rio Grande do Sul as a whole.[35]

The discovery that sugar planters and mill owners continued to purchase slaves in the 1870s — to the point that their demand for bondspeople largely determined northeastern slave prices — may help explain why so few masters from this region "pulled up stakes" and migrated with their holdings to the Center-South. To be sure, the opportunity costs of transferring resources to a new, very distant region and into the production of a new crop (coffee) must have been high. Nonetheless, the behavior of northeastern planters and mill owners in the slave market would seem to be prima facie evidence that profits in sugar still continued to be attractive.[36] This may seem a difficult proposition to argue, in view of the bibliography on the secular decline and "decadence" of the northeastern sugar industry. My intention, however, is not to contest the difficulties confronted by owners of engenhos, particularly in Bahia, in their efforts to modernize, especially when compared to their counterparts in Cuba. What I wish to emphasize is that slaveowners' appraisals of profits rested largely on their estimates of a capitalized income stream from investments in forced labor over the coming years, which in turn were based on educated guesses about the economic and political future. Northeastern planters and mill owners had no way of predicting the disastrous fall of sugar prices in the 1880s, nor the full effects of the steep decline in the price of steel rails and equipment for central sugar factories (*engenhos centrais,* later *usinas*) that had already begun in the 1870s. These were key developments that further stimulated Cuban modernization, but less so Brazilian, and thereby dramatically increased Bahia's and Pernambuco's disadvantage in world cane sugar production in the following decades. Nor, more immediately, could planters and mill owners foresee the crash of the slave market in 1881–83, to be discussed below, and subsequent abolition in 1888.[37]

This discussion of slave population movements in the North and the Northeast has focused so far on the 1860s and 1870s, for which considerably more data are presently available. In view of the high levels of slave exports from Pernambuco and especially Bahia during the 1850s, however (figs. 14.4 and 14.5), something must be said about this earlier decade. Indeed, given the relatively small slave price differential in the 1850s between the northeastern and the central-south markets (fig. 14.2), the large outflow of slaves, at first appraisal, seems rather puzzling. I suspect that the explanation has to do with the great initial impact of the abolition of the African slave trade on small slave holdings and nonsugar properties in general.

While the African trade was still open, Brazilian buyers of slaves enjoyed comparatively low labor costs. Property in slaves was widespread, with small holdings abounding in virtually all sectors of the economy.[38] With the sudden onset of internal competition for bondspeople after 1850, the pressure on smallholders (and on many medium or large owners in nonsugar activities) must have been much more intense than it was to be in the 1870s, when truly marginal owners had long since been eliminated from the market.[39]

At the same time, although slave prices in the sugar sector were relatively high in the 1850s, the declining real price of sugar (the nominal price deflated by the cost of slave labor) meant that sugar planters were not buying large numbers of bondspeople. Indeed, the market for slaves in the Bahian sugar sector must have been especially restricted, given the 50 percent decline in sugar exports from that province during the 1850s (fig. 14.4). Furthermore, whereas slave prices in the far interior of southwestern Bahia (the county of Caitité) show a striking similarity to those in Salvador in their movements over time from mid-century to 1880 and in their annual levels after 1861, their yearly values were lower than those of the coast, especially from 1850 to 1861.[40] Although this indicates that Caitité was a part of the Bahian slave market, with the prices of bondspeople there, too, largely responding to sugar prices, it is also consistent with the hypothesis that small owners in the far interior were in a weaker position in the 1850s and more willing to sell slaves than would be the case later.

The result of all these factors was that slaves were sold in substantial numbers from Pernambuco and particularly from Bahia to the Center-South, where prices were higher and where at least certain parts of the coffee economy (especially central-western São Paulo) were expanding rapidly. Conditions specific to microregions in the interior may also have contributed to this outflow, for instance, the onset of decline in the gold-mining economy of Bahia.[41] Barickman also points to a severe drought in the Bahian backlands between 1858 and 1860, which was identified by the British consul in Salvador as obliging "many families to sell their household slaves at any price."[42] Many of these bondspeople, particularly those from the more distant Pernambuco, must have been sold to center-south markets via the coast. Yet as Robert Conrad has shown, others were sent overland, under conditions reminiscent of those in Africa and the New World during the transatlantic trade.[43]

The fact that slave exports from Bahia and Pernambuco were considerable in the 1850s — indeed, in Bahia they approached the highest levels of the 1870s — does not contradict the data showing that total slave transfers from the North and the Northeast to the Center-South were considerably lower in the earlier period. What it does suggest, in combination with that information, is that the mix of provincial origins among these forced migrants was substantially different in this earlier decade (proportionally more from Bahia and Pernambuco) than in the 1870s. Klein's data for slave entries into the port of Rio de Janeiro in 1852 support this conclusion.[44] In that year, slaves of Bahian and Pernambucan origin constituted almost half (47 percent) of the slaves coming by sea from the North and the Northeast, with Bahia alone providing 29 percent of the total. The especially large outflow of slaves from Bahia in the 1850s was certainly perceived by the province's political establishment as an economic problem. The Bahian legislature substantially raised taxes on slaves exported during this period; furthermore, it was a Bahian representative who (in 1854) introduced the only bill presented to the national Parliament before the 1880s proposing the end of the internal slave trade.[45]

Up to now, I have concentrated on the two major export sectors of the North and the Northeast — sugar and cotton — lumping all other economic activities together or even opposing sugar to nonsugar production. This is valid as a first approximation, but it does not do justice to the complexity of the northern and northeastern slave economy. Indeed, the very changes brought about by the end of the African trade probably opened up new opportunities for farmers and ranchers (particularly those with more capital and slaves) who were oriented toward the internal market. The prices of basic foodstuffs rose precipitously in the 1850s, both in the Center-South and in the Northeast, often more than slave prices.[46] Contemporaries tended to attribute this to the increasing concentration of plantation slaves in the production of export crops. Be that as it may, it would be surprising if no producers in the nonplantation sectors had been able to take advantage of the change, particularly in view of the significant presence of producers of basic foodstuffs using slave labor before 1850.[47] Indeed, Diana Galliza's study of slavery in the province of Paraíba shows that certain cattle-producing areas of the *agreste* (an intermediate region between the humid Zona da Mata and the dry interior), and of the *sertão* (backlands) itself, contained substantial concentrations of slaves, even in the 1870s.[48] And Costa's study of one locality in the Paraiban agreste demonstrates that slaves there were being transferred locally from small owners to larger proprietors raising cattle and planting diverse cash crops.[49] In sum, it would be well to heed Barickman's warnings against "plantationism" — the tendency to view Brazilian slavery as practically coterminous with the plantation — even when the focus is on the 1870s.[50]

I close this discussion of the North and the Northeast by returning to my point of departure. If the slave market of the sugar provinces was relatively independent of that of the coffee regions, this means, in effect, that even the large price differentials between them in the 1870s were generally not enough to offset substantially the cost of transferring bondspeople to the Center-South, at least in periods when the demand for chattel labor in sugar was robust. What, however, were these costs? Sea passage — as we have seen, in the 1870s most bondspeople in the interregional trade from the North and the Northeast were sent by ship — may be ruled out as a major factor. The price of passage from Salvador, Bahia, to Rio de Janeiro in 1877 for a slave sent on consignment to another merchant was between ten and fifteen milréis, at a time when the price differential between the two markets (for young slave men) was more than seven hundred milréis.[51] The price of passage probably included surveillance costs, whereas maintenance expenses on the trip, lasting as little as three days by steamer, would have been minimal.[52]

Since bondspeople usually passed through the hands of three or four intermediaries, sometimes more, the sum of the provincial taxes on slave sales could have been substantial had merchants not disguised most of these transactions as transfers of power of attorney. The number of intermediaries typically involved in the interregional trade, in combination with some evidence suggesting that exports through the large northeastern ports were concentrated in the hands of a small number of large merchants who probably had commercial contacts in Rio (and who thus may have enjoyed conditions of oligopoly),[53] may indicate that factor payments — the profits that merchants were in a position to demand — formed a very significant part of transfer costs. Unfortunately, no research has yet been focused on this question.

Data on another important cost, however, are available, namely, the taxes on slave exports commonly charged by the northern and northeastern provinces. These imposts were often high; for instance, in Bahia they fluctuated around two hundred milréis from the mid 1860s to the late 1870s.[54] Yet they were not prohibitive, certainly not during periods when demand for slaves in the sugar sectors was weak (see figs. 14.4 and 14.5). Indeed, they were important sources of revenue for the provincial governments, despite constant complaints of tax evasion.

What were legislators' intentions when this tax was first introduced and then redebated in annual discussions of fiscal policy? Bahia's secretary of the treasury answered this question in 1880, but he did so in a way that simply raises more conundrums; according to him, the export tax on slaves "constitutes one of the greatest sources of revenue that may be had, although the legislator, when he set it at a high level, was moved by the intention of creating an obstacle to the out-migration of labor necessary for our agriculture."[55] Had legislators, once frustrated, become resigned to the fact, as this statement suggests? Or did the tax levels that were voted every year represent an uneasy truce between sugar planters (or larger, more solvent slaveholders in general) who, being buyers of bondspeople, wanted to block slave exports to keep down their own labor costs and more marginal slaveowners, perhaps in combination with small and large merchants, who wished unrestricted access to center-south markets in order to reap more profits from sales? This is a significant question, for if these taxes were not prohibitive, I suspect that they nonetheless help explain the relative independence of the Pernambucan and Bahian slave markets. They may have been set just high enough to help ensure that the demand of the sugar sector in these provinces would largely determine slave prices but just low enough that provincial sellers of slaves would not face severely depressed prices when the labor requirements of sugar slumped.

Slave Markets and Economies in the Center-South

I have shown that the demand for slaves in the Center-South was substantially larger between 1872 and 1881 than in earlier years. I noted further that this demand accompanied the growth in coffee exports. The analysis may be refined, however; in fact, trends and fluctuations in the slave market were more closely related to changes in the stock of coffee planted, as measured by the export curve shifted five years to the left (five years being the time it took for coffee bushes fully to mature). The stock of coffee planted, in turn, was attuned to fluctuations in the coffee-to-slave price ratio (see fig. 14.6). This ratio is a measure of the real price of coffee (in the port of Rio de Janeiro) as deflated by slave prices (in Vassouras, province of Rio), or of the real value of the product of slave labor from the point of view of the coffee planter, again assuming constant worker productivity. When the coffee-to-slave price ratio rose, *fazendeiros* in Rio de Janeiro planted more coffee bushes, refrained from taking older, more marginal groves out of production, and began to buy or import more slaves. When the ratio fell, producers refrained from planting and stopped harvesting the reduced crops of the older groves, which caused a decline in coffee stocks (as well as current exports) and in the purchase of new slaves. Since slave productivity actually increased over time as coffee bean processing became mechanized and railroad construction reduced the need for

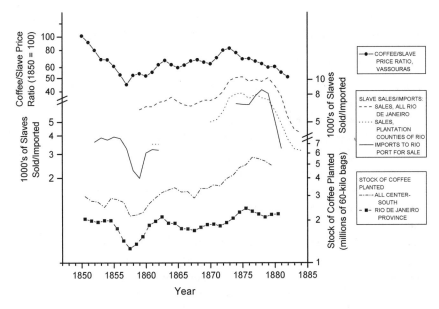

Figure 14.6. The Coffee-to-Slave Price Ratio and Its Relation to the Stock of Coffee Planted and to Slave Sales and Imports, Rio Province and Port of Rio, 1850 to Early 1880s. *Note:* All curves are smoothed (3-point adjacent averages); missing data for slave sales in Rio Province for 1864, 1868, and 1869 have been estimated by interpolation. *Sources:* Robert W. Slenes, "The Demography and Economics of Brazilian Slavery: 1850–1888," 137, 201, revised; and Slenes, "Grandeza ou Decadência? O Mercado de Escravos e a Economia Cafeeira da Província do Rio de Janeiro, 1850–1888," in *Brasil: História Econômica e Demográfica,* ed. Iraci del Nero da Costa (São Paulo: Instituto de Pesquisas Eonômicas, Universidade de São Paulo, 1986), 103–56, figure on 119, using sources cited for fig. 14.3, above.

slave muleteers, this curve (like that of the sugar-to-slave price ratio in the Northeast) should show a steeper upward inclination than it does, particularly in the 1870s, to be considered a true measure of a slave's real labor product in coffee cultivation. This, however, merely confirms the analysis, for increasing the upward inclination of the coffee-to-slave price ratio would bring it more closely into line with the curves portraying slave sales or imports and the stock of coffee planted. Note that the movement of the coffee-to-slave price ratio correlates less closely (after about 1867) with the shifted coffee-export curve for the combined provinces of Rio de Janeiro, São Paulo, Minas Gerais, and Espírito Santo (total exports from the ports of Rio and Santos) than with that for the province of Rio alone. This is because the export curve for the whole Center-South becomes increasingly affected after the mid-1860s by the rapidly expanding coffee acreage in the new zones of central-western São Paulo and the Zona da Mata of Minas Gerais, where conditions of high productivity made planters much less sensitive to fluctuations in the index of "real coffee prices" used here, which is more representative of conditions faced by planters in Rio.

During the 1860s and perhaps in the preceding decade as well, the *intra*-regional slave trade was significantly more important in bringing slaves to the coffee plantations than was the commerce between regions. In Campinas, 60 percent of all noncampineiro Brazilians sold during sample years in the second half of the 1860s came from within the Center-South.[56] In the less dynamic plantation regions of the Paraíba valley, the intraregional trade probably was even more predominant as a supplier of workers. Although Klein's assertion that the slave trade between regions was unimportant for coffee plantations before 1870 seems too strong, the evidence does support a weaker version of his argument.[57]

In the 1870s, however, the interregional trade became by far the most signif-icant supplier of slaves to the coffee regions. By the second half of that decade, in Campinas, the proportion of noncampineiro Brazilians in the market who came from areas within the Center-South had declined to 22 percent. The figures for Campinas may indicate that the intraregional trade did grow in size, in absolute terms, between the 1860s and the 1870s.[58] In relative terms, however, it seems to have retracted drastically, reflecting conditions in the North and Northeast and in the far South, which made a large number of bondspeople from these regions available at bargain prices in the 1870s.

Where were slaves being moved to, and from, within the Center-South? There is no question that the "new" coffee regions of central-western São Paulo and the Zona da Mata of Minas Gerais were strong net importers of bondspeople, particularly in the 1870s.[59] It has been suggested, however, that there was a significant transfer of slaves to these areas from the "old" coffee regions—particularly from the "upper," or western, part of the Paraíba valley in Rio de Janeiro, where Vassouras (studied by Stanley Stein) is located.[60] The data from the Campinas market (from the manuscripts of the tax on slave sales) are not very useful on this point, since they rarely included information about the county of origin.[61] Data about changes in the slave population and the volume of slave sales within the various subregions of Rio de Janeiro, however, speak directly to the question.

Between 1840 and 1850, the slave population over the age of ten increased in both plantation and nonplantation counties of Rio de Janeiro. Between 1850 and 1881 it rose only in the plantation counties, albeit at a considerably lower rate than before, with a slightly upward inflection in velocity between 1872 and 1881. The increase was definitely larger in the middle part of the Paraíba valley and in the District (Comarca) of Campos than in the older plantation region, the upper part of the valley. In this latter area, the slave population above the age of ten remained stagnant from 1850 to 1872, then increased somewhat until 1881. In absolute contrast, the nonplantation counties saw a population decline of almost 50 percent during the same period.[62]

Data about the number of slave sales in Rio province, available at the county level for many years after 1860, point to similar conclusions. The slave market was more robust in the 1870s than in the 1860s in all three of the plantation subregions, including the upper part of the valley (and even in Vassouras). In the nonplantation counties, in contrast, it was substantially less active in the 1870s than in the previous decade.[63] A further confirmation of these results comes from the official registry of entries and exits of slaves (by means of sale, inheritance, the migration of owners, and so on) in the various counties, which indicates that all plantation subregions (including the upper Paraíba valley and Vassouras) had a net gain of bondspeople between 1872 and 1881, while the nonplantation areas showed a large net loss. In sum, although the middle Paraíba valley (from the counties of Paraíba do Sul to Cantagalo) was certainly more vigorous than the other plantation regions of Rio in the 1870s, none of these areas was a net loser of slaves, either in the internal trade nor in the sum of both forms of migration (by sale or with owners). Indeed, all of them were characterized by robust slave markets with significant levels of slave imports.[64]

Part of the older bibliography concerning slavery, perceiving that planters in the Paraíba valley found themselves in a much more vulnerable position than that of their counterparts in central-western São Paulo when abolition came in the 1880s, postulated a difference in "mentality" between the two groups, or, alternatively, a paralyzing indebtedness to coffee factors among the former.[65] How else to explain why the Paraíba valley planters did not take significant steps in the 1860s and 1870s to adopt free labor or transfer their assets to other activities or areas that were more lucrative? More recent research, however, has provided a different answer to this question, implicitly or explicitly emphasizing that planters' confidence in the political future of slavery remained firm through the 1870s. As we have seen, my evidence for the correlation in that decade between the coffee-to-slave price ratio (the real value of the product of slave labor) and the stock of coffee planted, and then between the latter variable and the number of slaves purchased (fig. 14.6), certainly suggested planter profitability in the present, based on optimism about the future of slavery.[66] Confirming evidence came from Pedro Carvalho de Mello's direct calculations of profit margins.[67] Mello estimated the rates of return on capital invested in slaves in the Rio coffee region during the 1870s and found them equal to or above the current rates in the capital market. Joseph Sweigart overturned the myth that planters were hopelessly indebted to coffee factors and thus unable to avoid a slow slide into bankruptcy. In addition, he developed a new capital deflator based on the prices of Brazil's imports.[68] Although he did not apply it to calculate real slave capital values in the Rio area (in effect, to produce a series indicating the value of bondspeople in terms of the necessary equipment and "luxury" goods that planters imported to support their economic and social selves), this can easily be done. The result shows that real slave capital values in Rio were increasing during most of the 1870s and were at a historic high (for the period after 1850) during much of the last half of that decade.[69] That is, Rio coffee planters were realizing not only an adequate rate of return in the 1870s (see the coffee-to-slave price ratio in fig. 14.6, keeping in mind that it substantially underestimates the value of the product of slave labor to the producer in that decade) but also capital gains on their investments in bondspeople.

The data presented above concerning the growth of the slave population and the robustness of slave markets in the plantation areas of Rio during the 1870s are consistent with these other results. All of these findings, of course, imply that planters were operating as they would in "normal times." Mello's estimates of profitability, in fact, are valid only if planters were projecting capitalized income streams over the subsequent average lifetime of young bondspeople (which, for a twenty-year-old, was around twenty-eight or twenty-nine years);[70] in other words, planters as a group, as late as 1880, were not yet overly worried that slavery might end before their recently purchased slaves died.

Other studies have pointed to a similar "normality" in strategies of accumulation and in agricultural practices during the 1870s. Vilma Almada, in her work on the relatively new coffee economy of southern Espírito Santo, found that 27 percent of people married in the main parish of the county of Cachoeiro de Itapemirim between 1873 and 1880 were from Rio de Janeiro Province and that 96 percent of these were from Vassouras and three neighboring localities in the upper Paraíba valley.[71] Her findings take on an added significance in the light of subsequent work by Alida Metcalf, Carlos Bacellar, and Sheila Faria on planter (and small-landholder) strategies of intergenerational accumulation in the Center-South between 1750 and 1850.[72] Essential to these strategies was the migration of sons and married daughters to more productive land, made possible by the parental advance of part of their inheritance. It seems likely that Almada's results document a continuation of these practices, although her migrant stream must have included more than the children of property owners. Furthermore, it seems safe to assume that planters in the upper part of the Paraíba valley were not sending offspring with assets only to Espírito Santo. The population data just presented for the older part of the valley, however, make it clear that planters had not increased this practice to the point of bringing about a decline in the slave population of their home subregion. Whatever human capital migrating scions may have taken with them, it was made up for by their parents in subsequent slave purchases.

Finally, I have called attention to the use of agricultural strategies in the upper Paraíba valley (less intensive care of coffee bushes than in central-western São Paulo) that, though increasingly predatory, were rational from the individual planter's point of view.[73] They made it possible for proprietors to continue realizing a profit on investments already made in equipment and buildings, despite the declining productivity of land and of older coffee bushes. Neither the low rate of out-migration of planter sons and daughters nor the continued purchase of bondspeople nor the application of (even more) predatory agricultural practices, of course, made any sense unless planters were firmly convinced that their slave property would retain its value and liquidity for the foreseeable future, guaranteeing the possibility of making a quick transfer of assets if and when that became desirable.

In this section I have once again emphasized the transfer of bondspeople to the plantations. Within Rio province, I noted the large exports of slaves from the noncoffee counties. Within Minas Gerais, notable areas of decline were the Alto Paranaíba, the Paracatu, and the Metalúrgica-Mantiqueira regions, none of them centers of export agriculture, which had a net percentage loss of bondspeople during the 1872–81 period that was about equal to that of some of the major exporting provinces of the Northeast.[74] It must be stressed, however, that the Center-South, like the Northeast, had a slave sector oriented toward producing for the domestic market, which had probably gained in competitiveness because of the dramatic post-1850 rise in the price of foodstuffs, discussed above. Roberto Martins and Amilcar Martins Filho were the first to call attention to this phenomenon when they showed that slave labor in the Paraíba valley was almost entirely specialized in coffee production in the early 1870s, quite unlike central-western São Paulo, where many bondspeople produced foodstuffs for the internal market. In addition, they demonstrated that the Sul de Minas, a largely nonplantation region that mostly produced for the internal market, showed a net import of bondspeople during the 1870s.[75] Mattos de Castro then documented in detail the existence of a commercial slave sector in a nonplantation country of Rio that was producing food for the urban market.[76] Probably those who were able to prosper in this sector after 1850 were not petty capitalists but people blessed with a certain amount of assets and at least a middling number of slaves.[77]

As in the Northeast, the internal trade seems especially to have affected the urban slave community. In the Corte (the Court, or city of Rio and environs), the number of bondspeople had risen steadily until mid-century. From then on, it fell rapidly — by 57 percent between 1849 and 1872 and (with respect to the population above age fifteen) by 79 percent between that year and 1887.[78] The provincial capitals of São Paulo and Niterói saw similar large declines in the population over age fifteen, 76 percent and 56 percent, respectively, in the latter interval.[79] Although part of this decrease can be attributed to high manumission rates in the cities — particularly in the 1880s — undoubtedly much of it was due to strong net out-migration by means of the internal slave trade.

After 1850 the Corte received a large number of poor immigrants from Portugal, many of whom occupied the jobs vacated by slaves sold into the interior, as Luiz Felipe de Alencastro has shown.[80] On the face of it, then, Claudia Goldin's explanation of the decline of urban slave populations in the United States between 1820 and 1860 would also seem valid for Brazil, or at least for Rio, and Alencastro suggests as much.[81] In Goldin's view, there was a greater "elasticity of demand" for bondspeople in the city than on the plantation, where very few free workers were willing to submit themselves to the agricultural gang labor associated with slavery. Thus, beyond a certain point, owners or employers of slaves in urban areas would not continue to bid up slave prices or hire rates but would instead turn to free labor. Sidney Chalhoub, however, has contested the application of Goldin's interpretation to Rio, preferring instead Richard Wade's explanation for the decline of urban slavery yet insisting on "historicizing" it.[82] For Wade, owners and employers (in the southern United States) faced special difficulties in applying the discipline necessary to control urban slave populations; it was for this reason that they would not sustain slave prices or hire rates beyond a certain level but would turn to free labor. Chalhoub recognizes that Wade's argument patently does not hold for the Corte prior to mid-century. He argues, however, that the city of Rio after 1850, and particularly from the 1870s on, with its large number of free blacks and mulattoes and with slaves (encouraged by forced labor's declining legitimacy during the period) increasingly determined to test the dominion of their masters, may have presented special difficulties for owners and employers that even Wade did not consider. Indeed, Chalhoub makes a convincing case that the capital's "black city," which permitted slaves to move about incognito, increased bondspersons' chances of successfully running away, emboldened them to confront their masters, and thereby constituted an abiding headache for the political and social elite of the period.

Nonetheless, the two explanations are not mutually exclusive, as Chalhoub recognizes. Slaveowners probably would have been more willing to meet slave indiscipline with harsh countermeasures rather than with sale if they had not found ready replacements for them among free Portuguese men. At the same time, the market for hired ("rented") slave wet nurses seems to have remained strong—which points to the limits of both the Wade-Chalhoub and the Goldin arguments while also illustrating how such models must be tested on a sector-to-sector basis within the labor force. Slave wet nurses could be forcibly separated from their suckling children (which virtually condemned the latter to death) and then submitted to strict surveillance. Both precautions were probably deemed necessary by slaveowners or renters in order to guarantee an adequate supply of milk and insure its quality. (Strong emotions in a nursing mother, such as anger or sexual desire, were traditionally believed to spoil the milk and harm the child.)[83] In this case urban owners or renters had both the will and the power to impose an extreme form of discipline, belying Wade's general reasoning and even Chalhoub's historically specific argument about the peculiarities of urban slavery in post-1850 Rio. Yet it is also a case where the demand for labor was extremely inelastic—few of the Portuguese immigrants were female, and few free women would submit themselves to the conditions that hirers of wet nurses wished to impose, except out of dire necessity. Female slaves in domestic service, as a group, may have experienced essentially the same seigneurial will and ability to impose discipline, along with free women's distaste for replacing them. Perhaps it was partly for this reason that urban slaveowners after 1850 held on to more women than they did men. The sex ratio in the Corte (the number of males for every 100 females) declined from 146 to 107 between 1849 and 1872 and then (with respect to the population over the age of fifteen) from 109 to 97 between 1872 and 1887.

Yet another key factor in explaining this decline would seem to be planters' preference for male rather than female workers. Among slaves entering the port of Rio de Janeiro through the interregional trade, 67 percent in 1852 and 62 percent in 1879 were male.[84] The Campinas market in the 1860s and 1870s presents similar figures. Part of this predominance of men in the trade may reflect factors linked to supply; as has been observed with respect to the American domestic trade, a head tax on slave exports (the usual practice in the North and the Northeast) would tend to lead owners and merchants to prefer selling higher-priced bondspeople—in this case, males instead of females— since their rate of profit, after the tax, would then be greater.[85] Nonetheless, my impression, based on research in Campinas, is that demand factors were more important, yet at the same time highly variable. I suspect that young planters setting up new properties (which required intensive heavy labor to clear land) strongly tended to prefer males but later turned to a more balanced policy of purchase, in part out of a strategy of control; that is, they were

eventually pushed to this change by slave disgruntlement, as well as by transformations in labor requirements.[86] Yet the brisk expansion of coffee production after 1850 seems to have guaranteed the continued overall predominance
of males in the slave market. In comparative terms, the market demand for
bondspeople in the Center-South was more like that in sugar-producing Louisiana, where males were also favored rather than females, than like that in the
slave-importing American cotton states, where men and women were purchased in about equal numbers.[87]

In addition to being skewed toward men, the bonded labor market in the
Center-South was also strongly oriented toward adolescents and young adults.
Among slaves entering the port of Rio de Janeiro in 1852, 64 percent were
between the ages of ten and twenty-nine.[88] For several years in the 1860s and
1870s, 75 percent of bondspeople sold in the Campinas market were between
these ages.[89] These figures are close to Tadman's estimates regarding the presence of slaves in the same age group (71.9 percent) among persons transferred
in the interregional slave trade of the American South (excluding the Louisiana sugar area) from about 1830 to 1850.[90] The age and sex profiles here
reviewed, together with the large number of people sold, raise broader questions about the impact of the domestic trade on the slave community, to which
I now turn.

"His Parents Were Sold": The Internal Trade, Slave Experience, and Master-Slave Relations

The data presented above suggesting that interregional market transactions in people occurred roughly in the same proportions in Brazil and in the
United States, but also indicating that Brazilian bondspeople faced especially
unstable conditions in the 1870s, were largely interpreted through the prism
of Tadman's very persuasive analysis of the American documentation. I now
attempt to appraise the Brazilian material within its own context.

As previously noted, a full comparative appreciation of the Brazilian data
means focusing not only on people moved between regions by sale but also on
many of the persons uprooted by the intraregional commerce over distances
often rivaling those typical of the interregional trade in the American South. In
many areas, the combined impact of both these market transfers must have
been calamitous. Few people in small urban and rural holdings—which included at least a large minority of slaves in Brazil—would not have experienced separation from close relatives and friends at some point in their lives.
Many would have experienced such separation more than once.

Estimates of proportional net migration for the period 1872–81 from the six "provinces" that most lost slaves in that period (Ceará, Rio Grande do Norte, Paraíba, and Piaui in the Northeast, Rio Grande do Sul in the far South, and the Corte — deemed a province here because of the size of its population) give some idea of the vulnerability of bondspeople in these types of holdings.[91] The net loss (the balance of individuals actually transferred) from the original slave population under age forty during this nine-year period varied from 17 percent in Piaui to 31 percent in the Corte and 34 percent in Ceará. Overall, the net loss to this age group in these areas was 24 percent, or almost one person in four. Among adolescent males and young men, these percentages were considerably higher. It must be stressed again that the great majority of these migrants were transferred by sale.

Of course, the impact of the internal trade on slaves' family and community ties was, on the whole, smaller in the 1850s and 1860s. Yet for bondspeople themselves, the most relevant point of reference may have been the period before 1850. In her reflections on the slave family in the province of Rio during the first half of the nineteenth century, Hebe Mattos [de Castro] has called attention to the fact that, although the African trade created a severe imbalance in the ratio of men to women, it also guaranteed a certain shelter for family formation.[92] Since new Africans predominated in the slave market, and since owners' disciplinary strategies centered on making a sharp distinction between the treatment given these people (mostly the stick) and that given long-time resident Africans and creoles (the stick, but preferably the carrot), families created by the latter groups were less threatened by sale than they were in the United States — or, one may add, than they would be in Brazil after 1850, when an endogenous labor market replaced an exogenous one. In sum, if Mattos is correct, the abolition of the African trade in 1850 abruptly ended a period of relative stability for slave families and communities in properties whose owners were hard put to compete in the new internal labor market. Cast into a new era of great uncertainty, these slaves would then have seen their situation worsen even more in the 1870s. Bondspeople caught in this whirlwind, with personal or family memories of what they had lost, must have felt the change deeply.

Indeed, recent studies based on trial records from Rio de Janeiro Province and from the cities of Curitiba, Salvador, and Rio provide us with a glimpse of how slaves experienced these wrenching times. They recount harrowing tales in which the slaves' fear of being sold, being returned to bondage after living in freedom as runaways, or having loved ones torn from them by sale leaps from the pages. Four of these stories involve mothers who killed their children in order to avoid separation or reenslavement — similar to the case in the United States that inspired Toni Morrison's novel *Beloved*.[93]

These vivid reconstructions of individual cases help put the recent work on the Brazilian slave family into proper perspective. Most of this research, including my own book on the subject, examines the family in the plantation regions of the Center-South.[94] Indeed, the focus has been on medium and large holdings in these areas (those with about ten or more bondspeople), where researchers have found surprisingly high marriage rates and levels of family stability over time, given the earlier historiography on the question. To be sure, the greater vulnerability of slaves in the small holdings, even in the plantation areas, has not been denied. I considered an annotation about an eight-year-old boy—"his parents were sold"—on a Campinas matrícula list with two slaves to be paradigmatic for such properties.[95] Nonetheless, holdings with fewer than ten slaves contained only a small minority of the total number of bondspeople in the plantation counties of the Center-South. Thus there is a danger that readers of these recent studies might conclude that the relative stability of the medium and large holdings in this especially prosperous region was the norm for the majority of bondspeople in Brazil.

For this reason, the data for the six major geographical areas that most lost slaves in the 1870s offer a useful complement to the bibliography on the slave family. At the same time, the stories recovered from trial records by the authors just cited suggest that, although family ties in small holdings were extremely vulnerable, they were just as strongly valued as they were among bondspeople in medium and large properties. In other words, although a grim social reality is revealed by this evidence, there is no reason to revive the older Brazilian bibliography on the slave family, which (like its counterpart in the United States) drew a picture of extreme anomie, or social pathology, among bondspeople—including the psychological inability to form close affective relationships—supposedly resulting from the destruction of family ties.[96]

One final observation about the implications of the internal slave trade for the families of bondspeople is in order. The discovery that the sugar micro-regions of the Northeast were not major sellers of slaves in the internal trade— indeed, they seem to have been net buyers—suggests that the families on larger properties in this context may have borne some resemblance to those of plantation slaves in the Center-South. Lower sex ratios on the northeastern properties may mean that male slaves actually had better chances of finding a mate. Less prosperous economic conditions for northeastern planters, however, may mean that slave families were more unstable than they were on the plantations of Campinas—yet perhaps comparable in this respect to families on the similarly less well-endowed fazendas of the upper part of the Paraíba valley, where detailed work like that undertaken for Campinas has yet to be done.

I have referred to Mattos's important contribution to understanding slave family formation before 1850. As I indicated, however, her analysis of the family is embedded within a broader study of slaves' struggles for survival and planters' strategies for dominion. Her conclusions with respect to these topics also contribute to understanding the implications of the sudden shift at mid-century from an exogenous to an endogenous labor market.[97] In Rio during the first half of the nineteenth century, Mattos argues, ladino (partially assimilated) Africans and creoles tried to improve their condition by forming families in slavery, personal links to free people as friends and clients, and (if possible) reciprocal ties of dependency or "paternalism" with their owners. The latter, in turn, attempted to make a clear distinction between their treatment of these groups, on one hand, and newly arrived Africans, on the other, encouraging the former in their attempts to establish families and ties of dependency and also offering to them (especially to those of longer residence who had proved their "loyalty") more access to better jobs, garden plots, and manumission.

Mattos's analysis receives support from studies of manumission, which have consistently found that creoles had much better chances of obtaining freedom than did Africans.[98] It is also in agreement with data from the 1872 matrícula in Campinas regarding the distribution of occupations among plantation slaves of different origins.[99] In Campinas, creoles over the age of forty had a much better chance of holding skilled and domestic occupations. Africans, however (in 1872, all over the age of forty), were virtually excluded from these jobs, compared to creoles. Among the latter (controlling for age group), slaves from the Center-South — indeed, Campinas-born slaves, in the case of women — were given preference, whereas bondspeople from other regions were discriminated against. The Campinas data suggest that a disciplinary strategy established during the period of the African trade — one that distinguished between locally born people and "foreigners" of different degrees in an attempt to divide and conquer the workforce — continued into the second half of the century, at least on the plantations. Now, however, the new young slaves in this context were largely creole or (to a declining extent) ladino Africans, precisely the groups that before mid-century were used to being given preferential treatment. (The change for ladino Africans may have been especially great, for the Campinas data suggest that Africans in the 1870s had become almost universally discriminated against.)

In sum, people who found themselves in properties that were suddenly vulnerable after 1850 were confronted with the risk that their owners might renege on an implicit paternalist agreement. The very real possibility that their families could be dismembered by sale was only one aspect of a general shattering of former "rules" and expectations. Those in this situation who were thrown on the market and ended up on a plantation found their worst fears confirmed; suddenly, they were being treated, in effect, like "new Africans."

Yet even creoles who had been born on the plantations may have been confronted with a serious reduction in their life chances. Before 1850, their relatively small number, especially in the Center-South, and the fact that they were preferred by their owners in the distribution of favored jobs and manumissions probably meant that they had a realistic chance of at least some social mobility, even if they ended their lives in slavery. After 1850, however, creoles from elsewhere, treated now as Africans, may not have entered the plantations in sufficient numbers to guarantee to the resident group the same level of "privilege" as before.

What was the effect of this reduction of creoles' expectations? Hebe Mattos, using trial records from Rio Province, demonstrates that uprooted bondspeople were more prone to violence against masters and overseers, a finding that confirms slaveholder lore as it has been examined in central-western São Paulo by Célia de Azevedo.[100] Nonetheless, slave unrest after 1850 was clearly not confined to this group. Helena Machado, in particular, has called attention to the presence of long-resident bondspeople as well as newcomers in Paulista slave uprisings of the 1870s and 1880s, suggesting that such movements may have responded to increasing labor demands that cut across differences in slave origins.[101] In addition, yet another catalyst of slave rebelliousness after 1850 should probably be stressed: the fact that the peculiar institution was increasingly under siege. Although the frustration of creoles' expectations after mid-century probably helped form the culture from which slave unrest arose, it is also likely that many bondspeople sought to take advantage of the changing context and seize the day. In doing so, they joined other social actors on the front line of the struggle over slavery: the battle to shore up or tear down the "peculiar market."

The Politics of a Peculiar Market

I have delineated three characteristics of Brazil's post-1850 domestic commerce in slaves which distinguish it from its North American counterpart: its conjunction of two significantly autonomous slave markets, its considerable growth over time, despite the similarity in the average relative size of the American and Brazilian interregional trades, and its sudden, radical restructuring of slaveowners' disciplinary strategies (which had previously favored creoles over new Africans) and thereby of creoles' expectations.

Yet there is another characteristic of this internal trade that makes the case of Brazil unique: its development in an environment that was increasingly hostile toward slavery. As we have seen, bondspeople's productive lifetimes made them relatively long-term investments in "normal times." In a period of increasing challenges to forced labor—from external pressures to internal political and popular movements, including slave unrest—this aspect of wealth in people turned the peculiar market into a weathervane for expectations about the future of slavery and, indeed, a focus of action by those who wished to undermine or defend the institution.[102]

What was increasingly at stake in Brazil, particularly after the outbreak of the American Civil War in 1861, is encapsulated by the nationwide collapse of Brazil's preeminent capital exchange—the slave market—between 1881 and 1883. In the Center-South, slave prices and sales fell dramatically during these years (see figs. 14.2 and 14.3). Pedro Carvalho de Mello has demonstrated the revolution in market expectations behind these changes in an econometric study based on interest rates in the capital market and on the ratio of slave prices to hire rates (the projected long-term capitalized value and the short-term evaluation, respectively, of slave labor).[103] In 1881, he estimates, the Rio slave market still projected a lifetime of about twenty-nine years for an investment in a young adult male slave—about equal to such a man's further life expectancy. In 1883 this figure had fallen to six years and now projected the political death of slavery rather than the biological end of the chattel worker. Mello's estimates are not statistical artifacts; beginning in late 1882, banks authorized to give long-term mortgage loans to planters became increasingly cautious in assigning value to slave collateral and by 1884 had stopped doing so entirely.[104]

The crash of the slave market is a watershed in the history of Brazilian slavery. Yet it should not be interpreted as a divider between a time when the peculiar institution's future was unclouded and another when its abolition was proximate and inevitable. To be sure, the collapse came after a period of remarkable optimism about slavery's future. As we have seen, from 1872 to 1881 the demand for bondspeople in the Center-South reached its highest level in all the post-1850 period. Furthermore, despite signs of increasing elite anxiety about slave violence, investors still viewed the political death of slavery as beyond the horizon of their human capital's lifespan. The reason for this, however, is to be found in the 1871 "Rio Branco" law, which freed children thenceforth born of slave mothers, and in the subsequent political context.

The 1871 law put an end to a period of uncertainty regarding the future of forced labor that had expressed itself in the slave market by a slippage in the average price of young adult women relative to that of their male counterparts, as investors reduced their estimates of the capitalized value of women's future offspring. Judging from data from Campinas and Vassouras, this decline in the female-male price ratio began in the early 1860s, following the outbreak of the American Civil War, not after the airing of proposals in Brazil later in the decade to free slave children at birth.[105] Thus it is possible that such proposals arose partly in response to these market changes and aimed at forestalling a more serious erosion of expectations about slavery's future. To be sure, by the time the 1871 bill came to a vote, deputies from the coffee provinces in the lower house of Parliament were strongly against it, possibly because increased slave agitation in anticipation of the measure had now made change seem more dangerous than inertia.[106] Deputies from the northeastern sugar provinces were strongly for the bill, however, which would have guaranteed its approval even if other provinces had not voted favorably.

In any case, once the law was in place it became the point of reference for defenders of slavery everywhere. For one thing, last-minute changes in its text made it possible to argue that it did not actually free the wombs of slave women in an "arbitrary" act of government against property but only gave liberty to their children, while guaranteeing masters' subsequent remuneration in labor services or in government bonds.[107] (The name by which the measure is know in history texts — the "Free Womb Law" — was not consensual or even dominant at the time, and it may have come into common usage only in the 1880s or after the end of slavery.) Thus, as late as June 1888, one month after abolition, a prominent defender of slavery could argue that the 1871 law gave state recognition to the legitimacy of property in human beings and thus strong support to former slaveowners' demands for indemnification.[108]

In addition, the Conservative Party, under whose aegis the 1871 bill was passed, made it clear that it considered this the definitive measure concerning slavery. It was only when the 1878 elections brought the Liberals to power in Parliament, and with them a small group of vociferous abolitionists from the Northeast, that the state's implicit pact with slaveowners was broken.[109] In 1880, expectations regarding the future of the chattel market and forced labor were constantly challenged by three forces: (1) Spain's abolition of slavery in Cuba in January and its creation there of a transitional labor regime (the *patronato*), scheduled to end in 1888, (2) well-publicized proposals of gradual abolition by Joaquim Nabuco and Martinho Prado, dissident scions of planter families from Pernambuco and western São Paulo who both advocated putting an end to slave transactions, either immediately (Nabuco) or in 1886, and (3) by a vigorous abolitionist campaign in the Rio press, whose readership extended to the plantation "big houses" in the coffee provinces.[110]

These developments strengthened existing fears that the Northeast would soon sell most of its slaves to the Center-South and then vote for abolition in Parliament. As a result, the provincial legislatures of Rio de Janeiro, Minas

Gerais, and São Paulo approved prohibitive taxes on the interprovincial slave trade in December 1880 and January 1881.[111] Ironically, the very success of the internal trade in supplying the Center-South with slaves within the context of a declining slave population caused slaveowner-dominated legislatures to suppress it when the political weather turned threatening. The new taxes, combined with a dramatic fall in international coffee prices from 1880 on, probably were among the initial causes of the subsequent sharp decline in slave transactions and prices in the Center-South. Soon, however, it became clear that the crash, far from being conjunctural, was that of the "peculiar market" itself.

Yet this watershed crisis was not the end of the story, for the collapse of the market was followed by a vigorous attempt to revive it. The 1885 "Sexagenarian Law" — so called because it liberated slaves aged sixty to sixty-four conditionally and gave immediate freedom to the more elderly — included a table that assigned higher-than-current market values to bondspeople by age group and sex and provided for the depreciation of those values to zero over the following thirteen years at especially gentle initial rates. While ostensibly meant to set the price of slaves whose freedom might thenceforth be adjudicated,[112] the table, which went into effect in 1887, also implied the state's recognition of the legitimacy of those values and thus its commitment to slaveowner indemnification should forced labor be outlawed before 1900. As abolitionists intimated at the time, this could have had the effect of shoring up actual slave market values and pushing the expected political death of forced labor further into the future.[113] That this did not happen (according to P. Mello's data, the slave market in 1887 predicted abolition in only one year) was the result of a continued political struggle, one that included agitation by radical abolitionists and bondspeople themselves, as well as a last-minute defection from the cause of slavery on the part of certain elites in western São Paulo and Pernambuco.[114] The latter groups were in a strong position to attract free labor and low-interest loans in a postabolition environment — especially if government funds were not distributed indiscriminately to ex-slaveowners as indemnification for lost chattel.

If all institutions are constantly "imagined" — that is, owe their continued existence or their demise to socially defined expectations — modern slavery was peculiarly so. Expectations about the future of this institution had a direct impact on a highly visible capital market, which in turn, particularly when crisis threatened, could provoke counterimagining and corresponding action by diverse interested parties: not only slaveowners and dealers but also politicians, abolitionists, and bondspeople. It is not surprising, therefore, that the peculiar market in post-1850 Brazil was on the front line of the politics of slavery. And it is only fitting to close an essay on that market by reflecting on the political efficacy of the enslaved, the "commodities" traded, in themselves helping define "chattel futures."

Slaves were remarkably attuned to "big politics" abroad and in Brazil.[115] In the 1860s, with forced labor threatened and then destroyed in the hemisphere's major slave power, it is possible that bondspeople responded with increased pressure at the micro level, thus contributing to the uncertainty that provoked the slippage in women's prices and, thereby, to the creation of the context from which the 1871 bill emerged. Contrariwise, in the years of virtually unquestioned state backing of forced labor after 1871, even the high incidence of slave violence and flight in São Paulo could not break masters' optimism regarding the future of their investments. Yet the altered context of 1879–81 may have radically changed this situation. Significantly, the new abolitionist voices in Parliament were first raised to thwart a proposal by delegates from central-western São Paulo of draconian legislation to curb slave violence.[116] Surely, such highly visible confrontations would have led both the quarters and the big house to reevaluate the significance of already vigorous slave protest and reimagine the future of the institution that still bound them together.

This reappraisal may well have contributed to the crash of the Brazilian slave exchange beginning in 1881. Whatever the case, major slave conspiracies in Rio and São Paulo between 1881 and 1883 — precisely during the period of plummeting expectations about slavery's future — were probably both a cause and an effect of the continuing crisis. Maria Helena Machado, in a study of police and judicial archives that permitted her to overcome the "conspiracy of silence" of São Paulo authorities regarding slave unrest, has shown that a plan for rebellion in the Paraíba valley in March 1881 involving plantation slaves on both sides of the border between Rio and São Paulo severely exercised the imaginations of the local free population and of provincial police officials. In October and November 1882, several slave revolts in central-western São Paulo — possibly coordinated — erupted or were disarmed before they occurred; these were followed in 1883, and again in 1885, by new conspiracies. One of the uprisings of 1882 was sparked by rumors in the quarters that slavery had been abolished but that masters refused to apply the law.[117] Under the circumstances, this would not have been an inaccurate understanding of the slave market's signals, which bypassed official censorship and summarized social expectations in a simplified and thus highly readable form.

In subsequent years, the sum of continued slave imaginings at the micro level surely helped defeat the elite's efforts to shore up confidence in the future of chattel labor. The greatly increased flight of slaves from plantations in São

Paulo from late 1887 to abolition in May 1888 is a case in point.[118] Nonetheless, a banal 1886 episode in Rio Province is perhaps even more suggestive, first, because it occurred when the Rio slave markets were still holding relatively steady, predicting the political death of slavery five years in the future, and second, because it confirms that slaves read the market and were determined to be their own "brokers."[119] In June 1886, an owner in Vassouras, wishing to manumit twelve slaves conditionally, approached a judge for permission: a necessary step, since these bondspeople figured as collateral in a loan contract. Shortly thereafter, however, he withdrew his request. The slaves — most faced with the proffered condition of another five or six years of labor, but one with obligations for only two years — had refused the offer.[120]

Notes

1. Of course, complete autonomy was never realized, either in the United States or in Brazil. See Laird Bergad, *Slavery and the Demographic and Economic History of Minas Gerais, Brazil, 1720–1888* (Cambridge: Cambridge University Press, 1999), 167–73. For a still-useful overview of the Brazilian internal trade, see Robert Conrad, *The Destruction of Brazilian Slavery, 1850–1888* (Berkeley: University of California Press, 1972), ch. 4.

2. See slave prices between about 1820 and 1850 from Salvador, the Recôncavo (near Salvador), Caitité (in the interior of Bahia), Vassouras (in Rio Province), Rio de Janeiro city and rural hinterland, Minas Gerais, and Goiás, respectively, in Maria José de Souza Andrade, *A Mão de Obra Escrava em Salvador, 1811–1860* (São Paulo/Brasília: Editora Corrupio/CNPq, 1988), 169; Bert Barickman, *A Bahian Counterpoint: Sugar, Tobacco, Cassava, and Slavery in the Recôncavo, 1780–1860* (Stanford: Stanford University Press, 1998), 139; Erivaldo Fagundes Neves, *Uma Comunidade Sertaneja: Da Sesmaria ao Minifúndio; Um Estudo de História Regional/Local* (Salvador: Editora da Universidade Federal da Bahia; Feira de Santana: Editora da Universidade Estadual de Feira de Santana, 1998), 260; Stanley J. Stein, *Vassouras: A Brazilian Coffee County, 1850–1900,* 2nd. ed. (Princeton: Princeton University Press), 229; Pedro Carvalho de Mello, "The Economics of Labor in Brazilian Coffee Plantations, 1850–1888" (Ph.D. diss., Department of Economics, University of Chicago, 1977), 52, 56; Bergad, *Slavery,* 268–69; Eurípedes Funes, "Goiás, 1800–1850: Um Período de Transição da Mineração à Agropecuária" (master's thesis, Department of History, Universidade Federal Fluminense, 1983), 117. The movement of slave prices during this period shows little relation to fluctuations in sugar or coffee prices, although the trend of all three was to increase. See Barickman, *Bahian Counterpoint,* 80; Mello, "Economics of Labor," 35.

3. Ulrich B. Phillips, *American Negro Slavery,* foreword by Eugene D. Genovese (1918; reprint, Baton Rouge: Louisiana State University Press, 1966), 371.

4. Robert W. Slenes, "The Demography and Economics of Brazilian Slavery: 1850–1888" (Ph.D. diss., Department of History, Stanford University, 1976), 155–57.

5. My assumption is that underregistration of sales did not vary enormously over time.

6. Since I used the Rio and Santos port data for slaves entering from the North and the Northeast (27.6 percent higher than the estimate obtained by my global census survival method: Slenes, "Demography and Economics," 616–17), I here increase the census survival estimates for migration from the South and the West by the same percentage.

7. Intercensal-survival methods assume uniform national mortality; thus, within a closed national population, differences from one census to another (in this case, the 1872 and 1887 slave registries) between projected and actual regional populations may be interpreted as the net results of internal migration. I used "global" regional populations (after adjusting them for the effects of manumission), because data on ages did not permit analysis by age cohorts (Slenes, "Demography and Economics," 611–18).

8. Primary sources frequently mention an overland trade from Bahia. Yet the Campinas market in the 1870s — which should have attracted this trade because of its high slave prices — does not suggest that it was very large. Slenes, "Demography and Economics," 633–38. This trade may have been more significant in the 1850s and 1860s, however; see Erivaldo Fagundes Neves, "Sampauleiros Traficantes: Comércio de Escravos do Alto Sertão da Bahia para o Oeste Cafeeiro Paulista," *Afro-Asia* 24 (2000): 97–128.

9. The estimate for 1850–1863 is from the average annual port data in fig. 14.3 for 1852–1862, expressed as a percentage of that for 1874–1881 (49.5 percent using only Rio port information, 48.1 percent using combined Rio and Santos data). The estimate for 1863–1872 is based on the fact (see fig. 14.6) that slave sales in the plantation counties of Rio Province — a good proxy for slave imports through Rio port — appear to grow at a steady rate over this period.

10. Subtotals of 65,000 (5000/year) for 1850–1863 and 67,500 (7,500/year) for 1863–1872 were added to the 90,000 for 1872–1881.

11. Michael Tadman, *Speculators and Slaves: Masters, Traders, and Slaves in the Old South,* rev. ed. (Madison: University of Wisconsin Press, 1996), 241, 242. I take Tadman's estimates of the annual transfer of individuals from exporting to importing regions in the 1820s and 1850s and convert them to a percentage of the average population affected in each case by migration (the average of the total populations present at the beginning and end of the decade in question). The average of the two results is 1.31 percent per year. I follow the same procedure for the Brazilian case, calculating the slave population of the exporting regions in 1850, 1863, and 1881 from the population in 1872 (668,439), assuming a 1.5 percent annual decline from natural causes, manumission, and runaways over the whole period (see Slenes, "Demography and Economics," 363–70) and adding or subtracting the total number of out-migrants during each period to the respective estimated population. (I did this using two models, the first assuming that all migration occurred before the onset of other causes of attrition, the second assuming that it occurred after the impact of other causes; the final population figures for 1850, 1863, and 1881 were the averages of the estimates produced in each case by the two models.) The weighted average of annual out-migration for the three subperiods in Brazil (0.52 percent, 1.00 percent, and 1.71 percent, respectively) was 1.00 percent. (I used the number of years in each period as the weight.)

12. I use the table's upper limits for the "residual category" and thus for total transfers. Using the lower limit of this category and the assumption that 75 percent of slaves not

included in the port police statistics migrated via sale, I calculate that the number sold is 94 percent of total gross migration, probably a more reasonable estimate.

13. Tadman, *Speculators and Slaves,* 246–47.

14. Robert William Fogel and Stanley L. Engerman, *Time on the Cross,* 2 vols. (Boston: Little, Brown, 1974), 1:46–52. A subsequent estimate of migration via sale suggested that this figure could be as high as 60 percent: Vernon Carstenson and S. E. Goodman, "Trouble on the Auction Block: Interregional Slave Sales and the Reliability of a Linear Equation," *Journal of Interdisciplinary History* 8 (1977): 315–18. In 1989, Fogel reported both estimates without choosing between them: Robert William Fogel, *Without Consent or Contract: The Rise and Fall of American Slavery* (New York: W. W. Norton, 1989), 67. Compare Gerald Friedman and Ralph A. Galantine, "Regional Markets for Slaves and the Interregional Slave Trade," in *Without Consent or Contract: The Rise and Fall of American Slavery; Evidence and Methods,* ed. Robert W. Fogel, Ralph A. Galantine, and Richard L. Manning (New York: W. W. Norton, 1992), 195–96.

15. Calculations for the American South were made as follows: $.693 \times 1.26$ percent = 0.87 percent/year (1820s); $.610 \times 1.36$ percent = 0.83 percent/year (1850s); the average for both periods = 0.85 percent/year. For Brazil: the annual percentage transfers for each of the subperiods given in note 11, multiplied by .86, yields, respectively, 0.47 percent, 0.86 percent, and 1.47 percent/year, or a weighted average of 0.87 percent/year.

16. Respectively (see estimates at note 15), 0.47 percent/0.85 percent = 0.55; 1.47 percent/0.85 percent = 1.73.

17. Strictly speaking, I work with "regions" composed of several provinces, whereas Tadman works with states; however, probably all provinces in my slave-exporting regions were also net losers of bondspeople when considered individually. Slenes, "Demography and Economics," 616–17 ff.

18. For instance, the various microregions of Minas Gerais that lost slaves in the "1873–1880 period" according to Martins Filho and Martins (I take this as equivalent to 1872–1881) suffered a rate of decline through migration (with owners or by sale) of 2.18 percent per year, compared to the 1.73 percent per year I estimated for slave-exporting regions in the interregional trade (calculated from data in Amilcar Martins Filho and Roberto Borges Martins, "Slavery in a Non-Export Economy: Nineteenth-Century Minas Gerais Revisited," *Hispanic American Historical Review* 63:3 [August 1983]: 537–68, tables on 553–54; I correct an error in the second table, which identifies the Jequitinhonha-Mucuri-Doce microregion as an exporter).

19. Peter L. Eisenberg, *The Sugar Industry in Pernambuco: Modernization Without Change, 1840–1910* (Berkeley: University of California Press, 1974), ch. 3; David Denslow, "Sugar Production in Northeastern Brazil and Cuba, 1858–1908" (Ph.D. diss., Yale University, 1974).

20. The slave export figures were undercounted, especially along land routes through the interior. I use the data, however, as an index of the relative volume of exports over time.

21. This was probably the case in Bahia even in the very early 1850s, before data about slave exports became available (1853), since one suspects that the sale of bondspeople from the province must have risen sharply in that period from levels in earlier years.

22. Herbert S. Klein, "The Internal Slave Trade in Nineteenth-Century Brazil," in *The*

Middle Passage: Comparative Studies in the Atlantic Slave Trade (Princeton: Princeton University Press, 1978), 95–120 (revised version of "The Internal Slave Trade in Nineteenth-Century Brazil: A Study of Slave Importations into Rio de Janeiro in 1852," *Hispanic American Historical Review* 51:4 [November 1971]: 567–85).

23. Slenes, "Demography and Economics," 207; indeed, the majority of the sugar areas of Bahia were slight net gainers of bondspeople.

24. Josué Modesto dos Passos Subrinho, "Tráfico Inter e Intra-provincial de Escravos no Nordeste Açucareiro: Sergipe (18⁵⁰/₁₈₈₇)," *Anais do 190 Encontro Nacional de Economia* (Curitiba: ANPEC, 1991), 4:343–62; and Passos Subrinho, *Reordenamento do Trabalho: Trabalho Escravo e Trabalho Livre no Nordeste Açucareiro; Sergipe 18⁵⁰/₁₉₃₀* (Aracaju, Sergipe: Funcaju, 2000), ch. 3.

25. Bert Barickman, "Persistence and Decline: Slave Labour and Sugar Production in the Bahian Recôncavo, 1850–1888," *Journal of Latin American Studies* 28 (1996), 581–633.

26. Eisenberg, *Sugar Industry,* ch. 8.

27. For the 1872 matrícula, see Directoria Geral de Estatística, *Relatorio e Trabalhos Estatísticos apresentados . . . em 30 de abril de 1875* (Rio de Janeiro, 1875), table for Pernambuco, n.p.; for the 1887 matrícula, see the table from *Diário de Pernambuco,* November 24, 1887, reprinted in *O Diário de Pernambuco e a História Social do Nordeste,* 2 vols., ed. José Antonio Gonsalves de Mello, n.p. (Recife: Diário de Pernambuco, 1975). My results are "preliminary" because I have not yet been able to identify the location of a few counties in 1887.

28. Izabel Andrade Marson, "O Império da 'Conciliação': Política e Método em Joaquim Nabuco—a Tessitura da Revolução e da Escravidão" (Livre Docência [postdoctoral] thesis, Department of History, Universidade Estadual de Campinas, 1999), ch. 4.

29. For a case in Bahia, see Rebecca Scott, "Defining the Boundaries of Freedom in the World of Cane: Cuba, Brazil, and Louisiana After Emancipation," *American Historical Review* 99:1 (February 1994): 70–102, at 93.

30. Slenes, "Demography and Economics," 621.

31. The cotton boom probably increased the employment of slaves in cotton production. In any case, it must have stimulated an ancillary slave sector (in domestic service, production of foodstuffs, and so on) that would have been hard-hit when the boom ended.

32. Passos Subrinho, "Tráfico," 343–63. Data about relative provincial slave prices (Slenes, "Demography and Economics," 653) also support the argument.

33. These percentages describe data from the second semester of 1865 and 1866 and from fiscal year 1878–79 (Slenes, "Demography and Economics," 192–93). Alagoas is included here as a sugar province (sugar was more important in the 1870s), whereas it was defined as a cotton province in ibid. (as it was in the 1860s).

34. Slenes, "Demography and Economics," 633–41.

35. Berenice Corsetti, "Estudo da Charqueada Escravista Gaúcha no Século XIX" (master's thesis, Department of History, Universidade Federal Fluminense, 1983).

36. Significantly, the Pernambuco and Bahia curves are consistent with Milet's observations (Marson, "Império da 'Conciliação,'" 256, 291–94) that the profits of planters and mill owners were squeezed from 1872 to 1876 but improved in subsequent years with modifications in the exchange rate.

37. Robert W. Slenes, "Grandeza ou Decadência? O Mercado de Escravos e a Economia Cafeeira da Província do Rio de Janeiro, 1850–1888," in *Brasil: História Econômica e Demográfica*, ed. Iraci del Nero da Costa, (São Paulo: Instituto de Pesquisas Eonômicas, Universidade de São Paulo, 1986), 103–56.

38. Stuart B. Schwartz, "Patterns of Slaveholding in the Americas: New Evidence from Brazil," *American Historical Review* 87:1 (February 1982): 55–86; Francisco Vidal Luna and Herbert S. Klein, "Slaves and Masters in Early Nineteenth-Century Brazil: São Paulo," *Journal of Interdisciplinary History* 21:4 (Spring 1991): 549–73; Barickman, *Bahian Counterpoint*, 144–45; José Flávio Motta, *Corpos Escravos, Vontades Livres: Posse de Cativos e Família Escrava em Bananal (1801–1829)* (São Paulo: Annablume, 1999), 141–76.

39. In 1856 the British Consul at Salvador noted that small slaveowners could not resist "the great demand [for slaves] from Rio" (Barickman, *Bahian Counterpoint*, 138).

40. Neves, "Sampauleiros," 111; Andrade, *Mão de Obra*, 312. Caitité's prices (males aged fifteen to twenty-nine) as a percentage of Salvador's prices (healthy young Brazilian males ["*moços*"], with occupations) for the years when data are available for both markets are as follows: 1850–1856: 86.4 percent; 1857–1861: 75.3 percent (1850–1861: 81.8 percent); 1862–1869: 97.8 percent; 1874–1879: 99.5 percent.

41. Campinas sales tax records rarely indicate slaves' county of origin; thus their occasional mention of Rio de Contas and Caitité, in Bahia's gold-mining region, seems significant.

42. Barickman, *Bahian Counterpoint*, 138. Significantly, the difference between slave prices in Salvador and in Caitité was the greatest in the years 1857–1861, the period of the drought, according to Neves.

43. Robert Edgar Conrad, "O Tráfico Interno de Escravos," in *Tumbeiros: O Tráfico de Escravos para o Brasil* (São Paulo: Editora Brasiliense, 1985), 187–207. See the eyewitness account reproduced in Robert Edgar Conrad, ed., *Children of God's Fire: A Documentary History of Black Slavery in Brazil* (Princeton: Princeton University Press, 1983), 354–55.

44. Klein, "Internal Slave Trade," 108.

45. Evaldo Cabral de Melo, "O Norte, o Sul e a Proibição do Tráfico Interprovincial de Escravos," in *O Norte Agrário e o Império, 1871–1889* (Rio de Janeiro: Editora Nova Fronteira, 1984), 30.

46. See, e.g., Stein, *Vassouras*, 49, for Rio City and Vassouras.

47. See, e.g., Barickman, *Bahian Counterpoint*, ch. 6.

48. Diana Soares de Galliza, *O Declínio da Escravidão na Paraíba, 1850–1888* (João Pessoa: Editora Universitária [Universidade Federal da Paraíba], 1979).

49. Dora Isabel Paiva da Costa, "Posse de Escravos e Produção no Agreste Paraibano: Um Estudo sobre Bananeiras, 1830–1888" (master's thesis, Department of History, Universidade Estadual de Campinas, 1992), ch. 5.

50. Barickman, *Bahian Counterpoint*, ch. 8.

51. In 1875 (Stein, *Vassouras*, p. 293), the milréis was worth 55 American cents. See the discussion of slave transportation costs in Slenes, "Demography and Economics," 176.

52. Slenes, "Demography and Economics," 175, n. 64.

53. See Raimundo Girão, *A Abolição no Ceará* (Fortaleza: Editora A. Batista Fontenele,

1956), 69, and Galliza, *Declínio da Escravidão*, 121, on exporters in Fortaleza and Paraíba.

54. Slenes, "Demography and Economics," 603–4.

55. Bahia (Province), Relatório [do Tesouro da Província], April 2, 1880 (Salvador, Bahia, 1880), annexed to: Bahia (Province), Relatório [do Presidente da Província], May 1, 1880 (Salvador, Bahia, 1880), 17.

56. Slenes, "Demography and Economics," 136.

57. Klein, "Internal Slave Trade," 113, cites data from the 1872 census on origin to suggest that interregional imports to the Center-South were negligible. Bondspeople born outside the province, however, were severely undercounted in that census.

58. Slenes, "Demography and Economics," 136. The absolute number of noncampineiro Center-South slaves sold per year grew during the period.

59. On São Paulo, see Slenes, "Demography and Economics," chs. 3–4 and Appendix A. On the impact of the internal trade on the various regions of Minas, see Roberto Borges Martins, "Growing in Silence: The Slave Economy of Nineteenth-Century Minas Gerais, Brazil" (Ph. D. diss., Department of Economics, Vanderbilt University, 1980), 113–54, 208–28 (n.b. table, 217); Martins Filho and Martins, "Slavery in a Non-Export Economy," 553–55; Robert W. Slenes, "Comments on 'Slavery in a Nonexport Economy' (I)," *Hispanic American Historical Review* 63:3 (August 1983): 569–581, especially 576–80.

60. Klein, "Internal Slave Trade," 113–14, cites the "rapid decline of slaves in the adult work-force" in Vassouras to argue that Paraíba valley counties "were the chief suppliers for the Western Paulista plantations." This change, however, can be explained by the aging of young Africans bought in large numbers in the 1840s, within a context of purchases of new slaves that were barely enough to keep the population stationary. Slenes, "Grandeza ou Decadência."

61. Still, they do indicate that Rio de Janeiro (capital and province) provided far more slaves to Campinas than did Minas Gerais but considerably fewer than São Paulo (Slenes, "Demography and Economics," 627).

62. Slenes, "Grandeza ou Decadência," 112.

63. The difference may be seen in fig. 14.6; slave sales in the plantation counties increased much more than those in the province as a whole from the early 1860s to the 1870s.

64. Slenes, "Grandeza ou Decadência," 115–23.

65. For the first view, see Octávio Ianni, "Capitalismo e Escravidão," in *Raças e Classes Sociais no Brasil* (Rio de Janeiro: Civilização Brasileira, 1966), 75–86; Eugene D. Genovese, *The World the Slaveholders Made: Two Essays in Interpretation* (New York: Pantheon Books, 1969), 84–89; Robert Brent Toplin, *The Abolition of Slavery in Brazil* (New York: Atheneum, 1972), 11–17; Florestan Fernandes, *A Revolução Burguesa no Brasil: Ensaio de Interpretação Sociológica* (Rio de Janeiro: Zahar, 1975), 107, 120–21. For the second view, see Maria Sylvia de Carvalho Franco, *Homens Livres na Ordem Escravocrata* (São Paulo: Instituto de Estudos Brasileiros 1969), 176. Stein, *Vassouras*, chs. 9–10, does not explicitly embrace the "two mentalities" argument, but the impression he conveys of Vassouras planters' impotence in solving their problems seems to have been influenced by it. See Slenes, "Grandeza ou Decadência," for a review of this literature.

66. Slenes, "Demography and Economics," 137, 201; Slenes, "Grandeza ou Decadência," 119.

67. Mello, "Economics of Labor," ch. 4; Mello, "Rates of Return on Slave Capital in Brazilian Coffee Plantations, 1871–1881," in *Without Consent or Contract: The Rise and Fall of American Slavery. Markets and Production; Technical Papers*, vol. 1, ed. Robert William Fogel and Stanley L. Engerman (New York: W. W. Norton, 1992), 63–79.

68. Joseph Earle Sweigart, "Financing and Marketing Brazilian Export Agriculture: The Coffee Factors of Rio de Janeiro, 1850–1888" (Ph. D. diss., Department of History, University of Texas at Austin, 1980), ch. 4 and 233–49.

69. I applied Sweigart's capital deflator to the Vassouras slave prices in fig. 14.2.

70. Mello, "Economics of Labor," 123, table 31; Slenes, "Demography and Economics," ch. 8.

71. Vilma Paraíso Ferreira de Almada, *Escravismo e Transição: O Espírito Santo (1850–1888)* (Rio de Janeiro: Ed. Graal, 1984), 73–74.

72. Alida C. Metcalf, *Family and Frontier in Colonial Brazil: Santana de Parnaíba, 1580–1822* (Berkeley: University of California Press, 1992), chs. 4–5; Carlos de Almeida Prado Bacellar, *Os Senhores da Terra: Família e Sistema Sucessório entre os Senhores de Engenho do Oeste Paulista, 1765–1855* (Campinas: Centro de Memória—Unicamp, 1997), especially ch. 6; Sheila Siqueira de Castro Faria, *A Colônia em Movimento: Fortuna e Família no Cotidiano Colonial* (Rio de Janeiro: Ed. Nova Fronteira, 1998), chs. 2–4.

73. Slenes, "Grandeza ou Decadência," 139–40.

74. Martins Filho and Martins, "Slavery in a Nonexport Economy," table on 554; Slenes, "Comments," 578–79. See also note 18. Net exports from the Metalúrgica-Mantiqueira, the major mining region of Minas, were also very high in absolute terms, given the substantial slave population of the area.

75. Martins Filho and Martins, "Slavery in a Non-Export Economy," 547, 554.

76. Hebe Maria Mattos de Castro, *Ao Sul da História* (São Paulo: Editora Brasiliense, 1987).

77. Ibid. For the career of one such individual, see Robert W. Slenes, "Senhores e Subalternos no Oeste Paulista," in *História da Vida Privada no Brasil*, vol. 2, *Império: A Corte e a Modernidade Nacional*, ed. Luíz Felipe de Alencastro (São Paulo: Companhia das Letras, 1997), 233–90.

78. I use the criterion of age fifteen and above for 1872–87 because after 1871 children born of slave mothers no longer appear in the slave population data.

79. *Correio Mercantil* (Rio), January 7, 1851, 3–4, and sources used in Slenes, "Demography and Economics," for tables B-3, B-7. For 1887, I assumed that the population aged sixty-five or older equaled that aged sixty to sixty-four.

80. Luíz-Felipe de Alencastro, "Prolétaires et esclaves: Immigrés portugais et captifs africains à Rio de Janeiro—1850–1872," *Cahiers du CRIAR* (Publications de l'Université de Rouen) 4 (1984).

81. Claudia Goldin, *Urban Slavery in the American South, 1820–1860: A Quantitative History* (Chicago: University of Chicago Press, 1976).

82. Sidney Chalhoub, *Visões da Liberdade: Uma História das Ultimas Décadas da Escravidão na Corte* (São Paulo: Companhia das Letras, 1990), 185–86, 189–91;

Richard Wade, *Slavery in the Cities: The South, 1820–1860* (London: Oxford University Press, 1964).

83. On slave wet nurses in Rio, see Charles Expilly, *Le Brésil tel qu'il Est* (Paris: Jung-Treutel, 1862), 185–86, particularly Expilly's attempt to ensure the good humor of his hired wet nurse and her isolation from male slaves. On traditional beliefs about the effects of strong emotions on mothers' milk, see Jean-Louis Flandrin, *Families in Former Times* (Cambridge: Cambridge University Press, 1976), 206.

84. The data are from Klein, "Internal Slave Trade," and Slenes, "Demography and Economics," 658, respectively.

85. Herman Freudenberger and Jonathan B. Pritchett, "The Domestic United States Slave Trade: New Evidence," *Journal of Interdisciplinary History* 31:3 (Winter 1991): 447–77.

86. I follow one such case over time in Robert W. Slenes, *Na Senzala, uma Flor: Esperanças e Recordações na Formação da Família Escrava — Brasil Sudeste, Século XIX* (Rio de Janeiro: Editora Nova Fronteira, 1999), 111–12.

87. Tadman, *Speculators and Slaves*, 23.

88. Klein, "Internal Slave Trade," 102.

89. Slenes, "Demography and Economics," 620.

90. Tadman, *Speculators and Slaves*, 26.

91. Slenes, "Demography and Economics," 621, revised; I used the global intercensal-survival method and data on the ages of slaves traded in the Campinas market.

92. Hebe Maria Mattos [de Castro], *Das Cores do Silêncio: Os Significados da Liberdade no Sudeste Escravista — Brasil, Século XIX*, 2nd ed. (Rio de Janeiro: Ed. Nova Fronteira, 1998 [orig. ed. 1995, under the surname "Mattos de Castro"]), ch. 7.

93. Eduardo Spiller Pena, *O Jogo da Face: A Astúcia Escrava frente à Lei e aos Senhores na Curitiba Provincial* (Curitiba: Aos Quatro Ventos, 1990), 203–9; Mattos [de Castro], *Das Cores do Silêncio*, 111–15, recounting two stories; Isabel Cristina Ferreira dos Reis, *Histórias da Vida Familiar e Afetiva de Escravos na Bahia do Século XIX* (Salvador: Centro de Estudos Baianos, 2001), ch. 3. See also the many dramatic episodes recounted by Chalhoub, *Visões da Liberdade*.

94. In addition to a large periodical literature, samples of which can be found in the special issues of *Estudos Economicos* (São Paulo: IPE-USP) 17:2 (May–August 1987) and *População e Família* (São Paulo: CEDHAL) 1:1 (January–June 1998), see Metcalf, *Family and Frontier*, ch. 6; Manolo Florentino and José Roberto Góes, *A Paz das Senzalas: Famílias Escravas e Tráfico Atlântico. Rio de Janeiro, c. 1790–c. 1850* (Rio de Janeiro: Civilização Brasileira, 1997); Mattos [de Castro], *Das Cores do Silêncio*, ch. 7; Faria, *Colônia em Movimento*, ch. 5; Motta, *Corpos Escravos*; Slenes, *Na Senzala, uma Flor*.

95. Slenes, *Na Senzala, uma Flor*, 107–8. For the presence of children in the market, see Rômulo Garcia de Andrade, "Havia um Mercado de Famílias Escravas? (A Propósito de uma Hipótese Recente na Historiografia da Escravidão)," *Locus: Revista de História* (Universidade Federal de Juíz de Fora, Minas Gerais) 4:1 (1998), 93–104.

96. I review this bibliography in *Na Senzala, uma Flor*, ch. 1, and, more briefly, in "Black Homes, White Homilies: Perceptions of the Slave Family and of Slave Women in Nineteenth-Century Brazil," in *More Than Chattel: Black Women and Slavery in the*

Americas, ed. David Barry Gaspar and Darlene Clark Hine, 126–46 (Bloomington: Indiana University Press, 1996).

97. Mattos [de Castro], *Das Cores do Silêncio,* ch. 7.

98. See Peter Eisenberg, "Ficando Livre: As Alforrias em Campinas no Século XIX," in *Homens Esquecidos: Escravos e Trabalhadores Livres no Brasil—Séculos XVIII e XIX* (Campinas: Editora da Unicamp, 1989), 255–314 (originally published in *Estudos Econômicos* 17:2 [May–August 1987]: 175–216), and the bibliography cited therein; Douglas Cole Libby and Clotilde Andrade Paiva, "Manumission Practices in a Late Eighteenth-Century Brazilian Slave Parish: São José d'El Rey in 1795," *Slavery and Abolition* 21:1 (April 2000): 96–127.

99. Slenes, "Demography and Economics," 534–37; Slenes, "Senhores e Subalternos," 272–73.

100. Mattos [de Castro], *Das Cores do Silêncio,* chs. 8–9; Célia Maria Marinho de Azevedo, *Onda Negra, Medo Branco: O Negro no Imaginário das Elites—Século XIX* (Rio de Janeiro: Editora Paz e Terra, 1987), ch. 2.

101. Maria Helena Pereira Toledo Machado, *Crime e Escravidão* (São Paulo: Brasiliense, 1987), 48–49.

102. In American historiography, Gavin Wright has particularly emphasized the engagement of the slave capital market with the political arena. Wright, *The Political Economy of the Cotton South: Households, Markets, and Wealth in the Nineteenth Century* (New York: Norton, 1978), 147.

103. Pedro Carvalho de Mello, "Expectations of Abolition and Sanguinity of Coffee Planters in Brazil, 1871–1881," in *Without Consent or Contract: The Rise and Fall of American Slavery. Conditions of Slave Life and the Transition to Freedom; Technical Papers,* vol. 2, ed. Robert William Fogel and Stanley L. Engerman, 629–46, esp. 638, 644 (New York: Norton, 1992).

104. Slenes, "Demography and Economics," 239–40.

105. Ibid., 266–67, for Campinas; Slenes and P. Carvalho de Mello, "Male and Female Slave Prices and the 1871 Free Birth Law in Campinas, Vassouras, and Salvador." Bergad, *Slavery,* 269, finds that in Minas Gerais this change began in the late 1860s; my data, however, probably provide more sensitive measures, since they portray a smaller, younger age group (fourteen to twenty-two in Vassouras) than Bergad's cohort, aged fifteen to forty.

106. See the discussion of planter letters to Parliament and the press in José Murilo de Carvalho, "A Política da Abolição: O Rei contra os Barões," in *Teatro de Sombras: A Política Imperial* (Rio de Janeiro: Edições Vértice/IUPERJ, 1988), 69–70.

107. A master could keep these children under his tutelage until they reached age twenty-one or give up all rights in them at age eight in exchange for government bonds.

108. Speech of Baron Cotegipe, Senate, June 19, 1888, *Anais do Senado,* vol. 2 (1888), 107–12, in *O Parlamento e a Evolução Nacional, 1871–1889* (3d ser.), ed. Fábio Vieira Bruno (Brasilia: Senado Federal, 1979), 6:515.

109. The abolitionist Joaquim Nabuco was the first to argue that the 1871 law "anesthetized" slaveowners for many years. See Nabuco, *Um Estadista do Império,* 5th ed. (Rio de Janeiro: Topbooks, 1997), 2:848–50. His insight, however, did not lead historians to study the slave market as a political arena.

110. Nabuco's and Martinho Prado's plans were published in the newspapers *O Aboli-cionista,* January 1 and February 1, 1880, and *A Província de São Paulo,* April 24, 1880, respectively. Nabuco's was subsequently presented to Parliament on August 24 but not debated. On the abolitionist movement in 1880, see Conrad, *Destruction,* ch. 10; Toplin, *Abolition,* ch. 3; Rebecca Bergstresser, "The Movement for the Abolition of Slavery in Rio de Janeiro, Brazil, 1880–1889" (Ph.D. diss., Department of History, Stanford University, 1973).

111. Conrad, *Destruction,* 170–74; Melo, "O Norte." See, however, C. Azevedo, *Onda Negra,* ch. 2, who stresses the fear of violence on the part of uprooted slaves as a motive for São Paulo legislators (probably, indeed, more important before 1879).

112. Joseli Maria Nunes Mendonça, *Entre a Mão e os Anéis: A Lei dos Sexagenários e os Caminhos da Abolição no Brasil* (Campinas: Editora da Unicamp/Centro de Pesquisa em História Social da Cultura, 1999), ch. 3.

113. Conrad, *Destruction,* 226; Speech of Joaquim Nabuco, July 3, 1885, Anais da Câmara de Deputados, vol. 2 (1885), 150–61, in *O Parlamento e a Evolução Nacional, 1871–1889* (3d ser.), ed. Fábio Vieira Bruno (Brasilia: Senado Federal, 1979), 1:335–36.

114. On the first question, see especially Maria Helena Pereira Toledo Machado, *O Plano e o Pânico: Os Movimentos Sociais na Década da Abolição* (Rio de Janeiro: Editora UFRJ/EDUSP, 1994), chs. 4–5. On the second, see Conrad, *Destruction,* ch. 16; Marson, "O Império da 'Conciliação,'" ch. 2.

115. See the two works by Flávio dos Santos Gomes: *Histórias de Quilombolas: Mocambos e Comunidades de Senzalas no Rio de Janeiro — Século XIX* (Rio de Janeiro: Arquivo Nacional, 1995); "A Hidra e os Pântanos: Quilombos e Mocambos no Brasil: Séculos XVI a XIX" (doctoral thesis, Department of History, Universidade Estadual de Campinas, 1997). See also Dale Graden, "'An Act Even of Public Security': Slave Resistance, Social Tensions, and the End of the International Slave Trade to Brazil, 1835–1856," *Hispanic American Historical Review* 76:2 (May 1996): 249–82.

116. Toplin, *Abolition,* 60–61.

117. Machado, *Plano e o Pânico,* chs. 2, 3, 5. I suspect that research like Machado's for other provinces will reveal similar slave and popular movements throughout Brazil in the 1880s, thereby radically revising the image of abolition as a peaceful process.

118. Ibid., 241, n. 134. Some historians place the onset of mass flight from the plantations in 1885; however, this is an interpretive error based on inflated population estimates for that year. See Slenes, "Demography and Economics," 75–76.

119. Mello, "Expectations of Abolition," 644.

120. "Requerimento para Liberdade," 1886, M. S. de Souza Pinto, petitioner. Archive of Juizo de ãrfãos, Cartório do Primeiro Ofício (now housed in Centro de Documentação Histórica, Universidade Severino Sombra), Vassouras.

Contributors

EDWARD E. BAPTIST is assistant professor of history at Cornell University.

MANUEL BARCIA PAZ is a final-year Ph.D. student at the University of Essex.

HILARY McD. BECKLES is professor of social and economic history at the University of the West Indies, Cave Hill campus, Barbados, where he is also the principal and pro–vice chancellor.

STEVEN DEYLE is assistant professor of history at University of California, Davis.

SEYMOUR DRESCHER is University Professor of History and professor of sociology at University of Pittsburgh.

RICHARD GRAHAM is F. H. Nalle Professor of History emeritus at University of Texas, Austin.

LACY K. FORD is professor of history at University of South Carolina.

WALTER JOHNSON is associate professor of history and American studies at New York University.

DAINA RAMEY BERRY is assistant professor of history at Michigan State University.

ADAM ROTHMAN is assistant professor of history at Georgetown University.

Robert W. Slenes is professor of history at the Universidade Estadual de Campinas in Campinas, São Paulo, Brazil

Michael Tadman is senior lecturer in history at the University of Liverpool.

Phillip Troutman is assistant professor of writing at George Washington University.

Index

Abbeville District (South Carolina) Presentment, 133

Abolition Acts (British, *1806–7*), 238

abolitionism, in Brazil, 306, 311, 323n77, 359; landowners' support for, 302; in Parliament, 358, 360

abolitionism, in Britain and British Empire, 49n13, 235, 250; colonial census counts and, 266; frontier colonies in West Indies and, 271; incremental strategy of, 1, 244, 245–46, 248; jurisdictional boundaries and, 23; localized slave trade and, 257; in Parliament, 24, 236, 238

abolitionism, in United States, 4, 5, 16, 76, 96–97, 170; on agricultural profitability, 129; appeal to northern women, 100–101; Boston as seat of, 219; congressional regulation of slave trade and, 101–5; domestic slave trade and, 99–100; escaped slaves and, 213; former slave traders as abolitionists, 91; Garrisonian wing of, 101, 110; imagery of sexual coercion and, 190;

slave resistance and, 7; social/economic changes in America and, 97–98; on subregional differences in South, 121

abroad (interplantation) marriages, 22, 64, 131, 206

Act to Prevent the Importation of Slaves (British, *1806*), 264

Adams, John Quincy, 104

Adderley, Roseanne, 216

Africa, 84, 214, 249, 318n16; African traditions, 11; Dutch in, 292; geographic literacy in cultures of, 222; Portuguese explorers in, 168

African American culture, 146, 173–74, 206–7, 214, 222–23

"Africanization," fear of, 249

age, of slaves: in Brazil, 352, 359, 362n11; in British West Indies, 269; in Cuba, 241; in United States, 15, 56, 57, 59, 78, 123–24

Alabama, 42, 80, 91; black belt of, 156; interstate slave trade and, 118, *119*, 120, 121, 156; slave trade banned in, 134